D0190308

SALAMANDERS

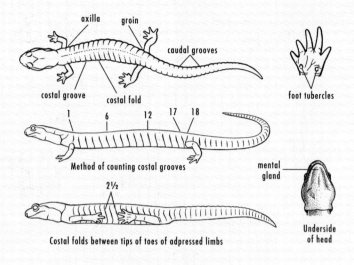

axilla

groin

caudal grooves

costal groove

costal fold

foot tubercles

1 6 12 17 18

Method of counting costal grooves

mental gland

2½

Costal folds between tips of toes of adpressed limbs

Underside of head

FROGS AND TOADS

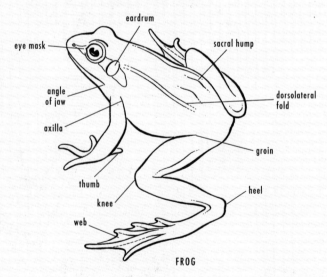

eardrum

eye mask

sacral hump

angle of jaw

dorsolateral fold

axilla

groin

thumb

knee

heel

web

FROG

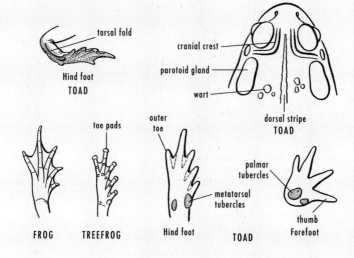

tarsal fold

Hind foot
TOAD

cranial crest

parotoid gland

wart

dorsal stripe
TOAD

toe pads

FROG **TREEFROG**

outer toe

palmar tubercles

metatarsal tubercles

Hind foot

thumb
Forefoot

TOAD

TURTLES

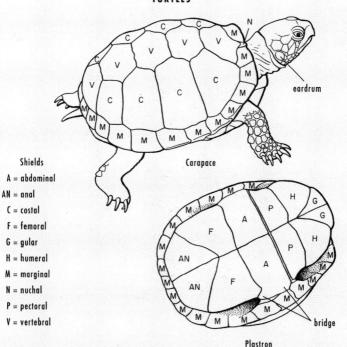

N

eardrum

Carapace

Shields

A = abdominal
AN = anal
C = costal
F = femoral
G = gular
H = humeral
M = marginal
N = nuchal
P = pectoral
V = vertebral

bridge

Plastron

A FIELD GUIDE TO

WESTERN REPTILES
AND AMPHIBIANS

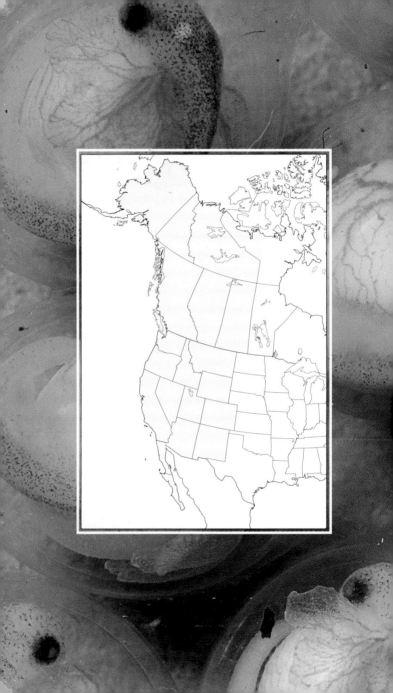

A FIELD GUIDE TO

WESTERN REPTILES AND AMPHIBIANS

THIRD EDITION

Text and Illustrations by
ROBERT C. STEBBINS

Professor Emeritus of Zoology
and Curator Emeritus of Herpetology,
Museum of Vertebrate Zoology,
University of California, Berkeley

SPONSORED BY
THE NATIONAL WILDLIFE FEDERATION
AND THE ROGER TORY PETERSON INSTITUTE

For information about permission to reproduce selections from
this book, write to Permissions, Houghton Mifflin Company,
215 Park Avenue, New York, New York 10003.

Visit our Web site: www.houghtonmifflinbooks.com.

PETERSON FIELD GUIDES and PETERSON FIELD GUIDE SERIES
are registered trademarks of Houghton Mifflin Company.

Library of Congress Cataloging-in-Publication Data

Stebbins, Robert C. (Robert Cyril).
A field guide to western reptiles and amphibians/Robert C. Stebbins.—3rd. ed.
p. cm. — (Peterson field guide series)
Includes bibliographical references (p. 514).
ISBN 0-395-98272-3
1. Reptiles—North America—Identification. 2. Amphibians—North America—
Identification. 3. Reptiles—West (U.S.)—Identification. 4. Amphibians—West
(U.S.)—Identification. I. Title. II. Series
QL651 .S783 2003
597.9'0978—dc21   2002027561

Book design by Anne Chalmers
Typeface: Linotype-Hell Fairfield; Futura Condensed (Adobe)

Photographs by William Leonard

Printed in Singapore

TWP 10 9 8 7 6 5 4 3 2 1

To the late

Raymond B. Cowles,

mentor and friend

Contents

LIST OF PLATES

Acknowledgments

It is with deep gratitude that I acknowledge the contribution of the many people who have helped in the preparation of this Field Guide, now entering its third edition and fourth decade. Many assisted me with previous editions, and their long commitment is especially appreciated. Some have told me they "grew up" with the guide, and now it's "payback time." What better reward could an author receive? Others, not mentioned, helped immensely at a time when this book was first taking form, and their assistance to a struggling author will not be forgotten. Some were dear friends and icons in the field of herpetology, and some, sadly, are no longer with us.

The present edition came close to not happening because of my age! Could I still illustrate? Would my eyes handle the detail and my hand still be steady enough? Other demands and desires beckoned. How could I get the live animals necessary to have all the plates in color, and update the maps after several decades of explosive growth in information on distribution? The following people saved the day for me. I could never have succeeded without them.

Persons who provided subjects for the new illustrations and/or help with species accounts and/or distributions (with the names of those who made especially important contributions in italics) were *Steve Abbors,* Liana Aker, Stevan Arnold, Sean Barry, Kent Beaman, Chris Bell, Roberto Bello, Kevin Bonine, *David Bradford,* George Bradley, Charles Brown, Herb Brown, Wendy Brown, Dan Buckholz, Kurt Buhlmann, R. Bruce Bury, *R. Wayne Campbell,* B. Carr, Bruce Christman, J. Clark, Nathan Cohen, Joseph T. Collins, Paul Stephen Corn, Jack Cryon, C. Cuciti, *Scott Eckert,* Ed Ely, Stephen Emerick, Edward Ervin, Todd Esque, B. G. Fedorko, C. R. Feldman, *Gary Fellers, Darrel R. Frost,* Kier Garcia, Lisa Gonick, *Lee Grismer,* D. F. Haines, John Hall, *Robert*

Hansen, Tyrone Hayes, Cynthia J. Hitchcock, Karin Hoff, Peter Holm, Richard Hoyer, Craig Ivanyi, Larry Jones, Robert Jones, Thomas Jones, *Mark Jorgensen,* Steve Kozlowski, Dominic Lannutti, A. K. Lappin, George Lardie, *Richard Lardie,* Dale Larsen, Megan Leonard, *William Leonard,* Peter Lewendal, K. Lohman, C. Malcolm, Mark Malfatti, *William Mautz, Sean McKeown,* L. McMahon, Jay Meyers, Jeff Motychak, *Daniel Mulcahy,* Allan Muth, Erin Muths, Richard Nauman, *Charles Painter, Ted Papenfuss,* J. Parham; Christopher Pearl, Trevor B. Persons, Marcia Radke, Damon Salceris, *Brad Schaffer,* Blaine Schubert, *Cecil Schwalbe,* Robert Seib, Joshua Shatsky, Wade C. Sherbrook, Eric Simandle, Tony Snell, Nancy L. Staub, Glenn R. Stewart, *Alan St. John, Robert M. Storm,* Jim Stuart, Luke Thirkhill, Barry Tomberlin, P. Ustach, R. S. Wagner, *R. Wayne Van Devender,* Vance Vredenburg, *David Wake,* Matt Whiles, Andrew Wilds; Peter Wilson.

A set of distribution maps, updated by the author, based on literature search, personal field observations, correspondence, and other sources was sent out for review. Persons who contributed information on distribution and/or participated in review were as follows:

CANADA

ALBERTA: Anthony Russell; **BRITISH COLUMBIA:** R. Wayne Campbell, Brent Matsuda, Kristiina Ovaska; **NORTHWEST TERRITORIES:** Brian Slough; **SASKATCHEWAN:** Andrew B. Didiuk, Keith Roney.

WESTERN UNITED STATES

ALASKA: Brian Slough;. **ARIZONA:** David Hall, Hans Koenig, Philip Rosen, Cecil Schwalbe, Brian Sullivan; **CALIFORNIA:** Kent Beaman, Kristin Berry, Robert Fisher, Robert Hansen, Javier Rodriguez, Bradley Shaffer, Sam Sweet, Jens Vindum, David Wake. **MONTANA:** Dennis Flath, Paul Hendricks, Bryce Maxell, Kirwin Werner; **NEVADA:** David Bradford, Alex Heindl, Ron Marlow. **NORTHWEST:** David Darda, William Leonard, Kelly McAllister; **OREGON:** Joseph Beatty, Matt Hunter, *Richard Nauman,* Deanna Olson; **UTAH:** Joseph Mendelson III, Daniel Mulcahy, Kirk Setser, Paul Ustach; **WYOMING:** Gary Beauvais, Jason Bennett, Douglas Keinath; **BAJA CALIFORNIA:** Lee Grismer.

Special thanks go to my son John Stebbins for undertaking the demanding task of preparing all the maps in color and for innovative suggestions on map format; to Lee Grismer for outstanding help with Baja California distributions; Charles Cole and Darrel Frost for reviewing the text on whiptail lizards; Scott Eckert for checking the accounts of sea turtles; David Wake for extensive assistance on salamanders; Richard Sargent for his skillful photographic reproduction of the art of the species identification plates; William Leonard for providing colored photographs of living amphibians and reptiles; Lisa White, Houghton Mifflin's field guide editor, and her assistant Elizabeth Kluckhohn, who provided much-appreciated guidance throughout the long period of the book's development; Joyce Bautista, Raul Eduardo Diaz Jr., Shannon Murray, and Erin Woodworth for extensive secretarial and research assistance without which this project would not have been completed. A U.C. Berkeley research grant provided financial assistance covering most clerical aspects of this revision.

The legacy of America's great naturalist, Roger Tory Peterson, is preserved through the programs and work of the Roger Tory Peterson Institute of Natural History. The RTPI mission is to create passion for and knowledge of the natural world in the hearts and minds of children by inspiring and guiding the study of nature in our schools and communities. You can become a part of this worthy effort by joining RTPI. Just call RTPI's membership department at 1-800-758-6841, fax 716-665-3794, or e-mail (webmaster@rtpi.org) for a free one-year membership with the purchase of this Field Guide.

A FIELD GUIDE TO

WESTERN REPTILES
AND AMPHIBIANS

INTRODUCTION

Many people are discovering the pleasures of observing amphibians and reptiles, and biologists are turning increasingly to these animals as subjects for scientific research. Such growing interest has greatly expanded the information available on the habits, distribution, and taxonomic relationships of our western herpetofauna since this Field Guide was first published in 1966 and revised in 1985. The present book attempts to bring things up to date. Allowances must be made, however, for the lag time between the author's efforts and publication, along with some probable oversights. This new edition includes 49 species of salamanders (compared to 31 in the second edition), 47 species of frogs and toads (44 in the second), 17 species of turtles (16), 88 species of lizards (76), 1 mole lizard (amphisbaenid) (1), and 78 species of snakes (76)—a total of 280 species, 36 more than in my 1985 edition. The increase in total count results chiefly from the discovery of new species of Slender Salamanders (*Batrachoseps*) and recent molecular studies that have raised some subspecies to full species status.

The primary function of the book is identification. To this end, I have included information on methods of capture, for—in contrast to birds—a reptile or amphibian often must be in hand to be identified. Captivity should be only temporary, however, and after examination the animal should be released where it was found. An attitude of "leave it alone, watch, and study" should be developed. The undisturbed animal in its natural setting can provide much valuable information. Some collecting may be necessary for scientific studies and can be arranged by state and federal permits. Federal and state wildlife agencies' regulations should therefore be consulted before collecting anywhere in the area covered by this guide.

When traveling through natural terrain, stop occasionally to explore the roadsides. Armed with an easily improvised lizard noose, (see p. 16), a jar for temporarily holding captives, and the information supplied in this book, you may find much of interest. The desert, which may appear forbidding at first, will seem a far more hospitable place after you meet some of its inhabitants. Discovery of a Long-tailed Brush Lizard, hiding camouflaged on the branch of a creosote bush, will leave a pleasant memory. The desert will never look the same again.

AREA COVERED

This book covers western North America, including Baja California, from a line formed by the eastern boundaries of New Mexico, Colorado, Wyoming, Montana, and Saskatchewan north to the Beaufort Sea. The area is referred to in the text as "the West" or "our area." The remaining portion of North America is referred to as "the East."

HOW TO USE THIS BOOK

To identify reptiles and amphibians, often scales must be examined, costal grooves counted, and details of pattern studied (see front endpapers for amphibians and rear endpapers for reptiles). Fortunately, nearly all species can be caught easily, and nearly all western forms are harmless. Only the rattlesnakes, Western Coral Snake, and Gila Monster are dangerous, and they are easily recognized. A few harmless species may bite hard enough to break the skin, but such injury can usually be avoided with proper handling (see pp. 15, 271).

When making identifications, you should have no difficulty in finding the appropriate major sections of this book. Turtles, snakes, and frogs are all easily recognized as to group. Salamanders, although resembling lizards in form, lack claws and scales and have soft, moist skin. Our only snakelike lizards (two) have movable eyelids, which all snakes lack. If you're familiar with reptiles and amphibians, go directly to the proper plates; if you're inexperienced, consult the keys (pp. 25–34). When you make an identification, check the appropriate distribution map at the back of the book to see if the species is expected in the area. If it's not, you've probably made a mistake. Most reptiles and amphibians do not have great mobility, so natural vagrants are rare. However, escaped or released captives of many species are now being found in increasing numbers.

Once you've checked range and illustration, turn to the species accounts for verification. The accounts give a more detailed description as well as information on behavior, habitat, and similar species; important characteristics are highlighted in italics. The **IDENTIFICATION** section in each account mentions key features of color and structure of adult animals and is sometimes followed by a brief section describing the young when they differ notably from adults. As much as possible, familiar terminology has been used. However, a few technical terms are unavoidable. A brief time spent learning them will speed use of the book. Anatomical terms are explained in the figures on the pages mentioned above, in front and rear endpapers, and in the text; other terms are in the glossary at the back of the book.

Although most of the characteristics mentioned in the descriptions can be seen easily, it has been necessary to refer to a few internal ones — tooth arrangements in salamanders, gill rakers in larvae, and cranial-boss structure in spadefoot toads. If you must look at teeth, with the exception of the Pacific Giant (and its relatives) and Arboreal Salamanders the mouths of our salamanders can be opened without danger of being bitten. See p. 26 for how to do so. To study the teeth of preserved specimens, you usually have to sever the jaw on one side to free it enough to expose the teeth, unless the specimen has been preserved with mouth open.

ILLUSTRATIONS: With rare exceptions I have painted from living animals. The area designation of the animal illustrated is usually indicated in parentheses on the legend page opposite the plate. The live animal is a far cry from the often contorted specimen in the museum jar. A toad's eyes may be jewel-like, and the geometry of reptilian scales is a harmony of line and shape. Life colors of some species rival the brilliance of brightly colored birds. Each species has its characteristic facial "expression."

I have tried to record what I have seen in the living animals. Many illustrations are generalizations based not only on the subject in hand but upon long personal acquaintanceship with the species. In some cases, however, my artistic sense has prevailed, and I have illustrated a particularly colorful individual. My bias in such instances will be remedied by the species description. To attempt to render a scientifically accurate drawing is time-consuming. This is especially true in illustrating reptiles with scales too large to suggest. It becomes necessary to draw them all, faithfully recording size, number, shape, and arrangement to obtain a satisfactory result.

To show details in structure, young animals and some smaller species have been enlarged relative to the other illustrations. The treefrogs, ground snakes, and black-headed snakes are examples. Refer to size on the legend pages opposite the plates.

SIZE: Range in adult size is given in inches and centimeters at the beginning of each description and applies to each species throughout its geographic range. Measurements are of snout-to-vent (SV) length in salamanders, frogs, and lizards, shell length (SL) in turtles, and total length (TL) in snakes.

COLOR: Colors may vary with locality, age, sex, and color phase. In some species color may change within a few minutes. A dark frog or lizard may become pale while being handled. The brief color descriptions presented here will often be lacking, and one can expect to find individuals that fit neither description nor illustration. In such instances, special attention must be given to structure and geographic range. Counts of middorsal blotches or crossbands in snakes do not include those on the tail, unless so indicated.

YOUNG: Proportions usually differ from those of adults. Head, limbs, and eyes may be relatively larger. Young turtles usually have a more rounded shell with a median ridge, and a relatively long tail. At hatching, many young turtles, including hatchlings of some large marine turtles, are only an inch or so in length. The colors of young animals may also differ. In identifying young, rely heavily on structural characteristics—scale counts and arrangement, costal-groove counts, and other traits that do not change with age. Amphibian larvae are described on pp. 434–461.

SEX DIFFERENCES: The species accounts give details pertaining to species. General remarks are set forth here.

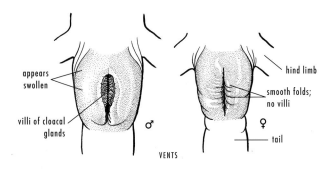

Fig. 1. *Sexual characteristics of salamanders*

1. *Salamanders.* Breeding males usually have a swollen vent, the lining of which is roughened by tubercles (villi) of the cloacal glands (Fig. 1). In contrast, the vent of females is not enlarged (Rough-skinned Newt excepted) and lacks tubercles; the lips and

walls are usually smooth or pleated. Hold the salamander in a damp cloth or paper towel and spread the vent with forceps. View with hand lens or dissecting microscope. In addition to vent differences, males generally have a longer tail and, in the aquatic stage, broader tail fins.

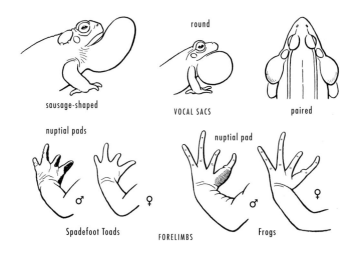

sausage-shaped

round

VOCAL SACS

paired

nuptial pads

nuptial pad

♂   ♀

Spadefoot Toads   FORELIMBS   Frogs

♂   ♀

Fig. 2. Sexual characteristics of frogs

2. *Frogs and Toads.* Males usually have a voice and a well-developed vocal sac or sacs, one on each side of the throat (Fig. 2); voice in females is weak or absent. When the vocal sac is deflated, the skin of the throat is often dark and loose. When breeding, males develop nuptial pads (often dark colored) of minutely roughened (sandpaperlike) skin on one or more of the inner fingers (Fig. 2). In frogs the base of the innermost finger (or "thumb") may become enlarged (Fig. 2). The forelimbs often become stout and muscular, and webbing of the hind feet increases. Males are generally smaller than females. Amplexus may be pectoral or pelvic, the male embracing the female from behind. In pectoral amplexus the male holds the female about her chest; in pelvic amplexus he holds her about her waist.

3. *Turtles.* Males typically have a concave plastron and longer tail than females. When the tail is extended full length the vent lies at or beyond the shell margin. Females have a flat or convex plastron, and the vent is situated inside the shell margin.

4. *Lizards.* In breeding males, the base of the tail usually appears swollen. The enlargement results from the hemipenes (copulatory organs), which are embedded there. These organs can often be everted in most species by gentle squeezing with thumb and forefinger, applying pressure toward the vent opening from a point at or just behind the swollen tail base. If the organs are not readily everted, do not continue pressure. In an individual in which eversion does not occur, hold the lizard by the sides of its head and *gently probe* the rear edge and sides of the vent with a toothpick, straightened paper clip, or bobby pin, thrusting the probe backward. If the animal is an adult male in breeding condition, the probe should pass into the opening of the inverted hemipenis. If the probe does not easily penetrate, stop procedure.

5. *Snakes.* Males usually have longer tails than females and a broader tail base. Their hemipenes can seldom be everted by finger pressure, thus the probing technique will have to be used.

VOICE: With the exception of the Tailed Frog—an apparently mute species—males of most of our western frogs and toads have well-developed voices, which can be helpful in identification. The calls described in the accounts are the mating or "advertisement" calls; other vocalizations are usually not included. Pitch, cadence, and duration of calls are usually given, but these characteristics may vary with locality, size or age of the individual, and temperature. In particular, individuals from the extremes of the range of some of the more widely ranging species may differ in vocal characteristics or may have different dialects. Young adults, as a consequence of their small size, may have higher-pitched voices than older adults. A cold frog may produce slower and lower-pitched calls than a warm one. In hybrid areas, unusual combinations may occur. When an unfamiliar call is heard, locate the frog by triangulation (see p. 18). Attempt to imitate the animal and write a description of both its voice and the method you used to imitate it. Try whistles, vocal sounds, tongue clicks, or combinations thereof. Some calls can best be imitated mechanically. I have stimulated the Northern Cricket Frog to call by striking pebbles together, one held in each hand and struck with a sliding motion. A Western Chorus Frog may respond to your stroking the teeth of a pocket comb. Knowledge of animal sounds can greatly increase enjoyment of the outdoors, but many of us have become accustomed to ignoring sounds in our noisy civilized environment. An awareness of animal sounds usually must be cultivated.

Knowledge of amphibian voices makes it possible to determine the species present in mixed choruses, and, during the height of the breeding season, their vocalizations can be used to help locate the boundaries of ranges. I observed the western border of the range of the Western Chorus Frog one spring as I traveled at night from Wyoming into Utah. The sounds of this frog, which I had heard for several hundred miles throughout southern Wyoming, suddenly stopped at the western base of the Central Plateau at the edge of the Great Basin. For help in recognizing the voices of our frogs and toads, listen to *Frog and Toad Calls of the Pacific Coast* and *Frog and Toad Calls of the Rocky Mountains*, by Carlos Davidson, Library of Natural Sounds, Cornell Laboratory of Ornithology (copyright 1995 and 1996, respectively). These outstanding publications contain recordings of all the species included in this Field Guide except for the Tailed and Tarahumara Frogs, which appear to be voiceless. (The Tarahumara Frog may produce grunts but otherwise is not, at present, known to vocalize.) They also include descriptions of the voices, time of breeding, and locations where recordings were made.

TIME OF ACTIVITY AND BREEDING: Many amphibians and reptiles have limited periods of yearly activity. Calling and other activity often reaches its peak during the breeding season. Some amphibians may gather in large numbers then, but are seldom seen at other times. The duration of the breeding period is included when information is available and reliable. Clutch size, given as a range in number of eggs laid during a single laying period, is based on counts of eggs actually laid and/or the presence of mature eggs (ova) in the oviducts or ovaries. Numbers in parentheses, following egg counts, are average or more common counts. For most reptiles the minimum size is a single egg, but published ranges may not go that low. Abdominal eggs have also been used in estimating the duration of the egg-laying period. In species that lay two or more clutches per season, total egg counts for the season are sometimes given. Unfortunately, information on clutch size, total egg complement per season per female, and other aspects of reproduction is often fragmentary. Statements in the accounts are general and apply to the species over its entire range. Information on egg-laying and birth dates in captives have seldom been used. In a wide-ranging form, activity usually begins sooner and lasts longer in the south and in the lowlands than in the north and at higher elevations. However, local climatic effects and, with amphibians, fluctuations in pond and stream water levels, may influence the timing of breeding activity.

Prolonged retreat from the surface may occur in winter (hibernation), summer (estivation), or both. The former is an escape from cold; the latter an escape from heat and dryness. Hibernation occurs in many species even in some lowlands and southern desert areas. Only the smallest species there escape its grip during brief warm spells. It is universal and prolonged at high elevation and in the far north. Even the cold-tolerant salamanders of the humid coastal district may disappear for short periods during cold snaps. The depth of torpor in hibernating amphibians and reptiles is usually not as great as in mammals, however, and most can be easily aroused by warming. Estivation occurs in most species in the arid and semiarid warm areas and in most of our northwestern salamanders. In dry summers, the soil and duff of even the shady forests may dry out. Exceptions are certain frogs and toads that breed during the period of summer rains.

Conditions of temperature and rainfall are usually the best guide for successful field observation. Select warm days in spring and fall for reptiles and cool (but not freezing) wet weather for salamanders. Go to the mountains in summer, when spring reaches the highest elevations, or to the lowlands of the southwest during the period of summer rainfall for reptiles and frogs. Weather, however, is not the entire story. Some seasonal activity patterns appear to be inborn and partly independent of climatic and seasonal effects. Possibly in response to internal timing mechanisms, some species disappear from the surface when conditions of temperature and humidity seem favorable. Use the information in the accounts as a guide.

Knowledge of the pattern of daily activity is also important. Most species are diurnal (active during the day), and, unless otherwise noted, diurnality may be assumed. In many species, activity is greatest in midmorning and in mid- or late afternoon. Many amphibians, the geckos, and some snakes are nocturnal. Some species change their daily pattern with the season, being diurnal when days are short and cool and nocturnal during warm summer months. Crepuscular species prowl at twilight.

HABITS: Manner of locomotion, defense postures, and other aspects of behavior may aid identification. The defense pose of the salamander Ensatina (p. 174) and the tail-coiling habit of the Ringnecked Snake (p. 345) are as useful in identifying these animals as their color. Habits and behavior that may be helpful in identification are included in the species accounts.

FOOD: Amphibians will eat almost any creature that moves, is not distasteful, and can be swallowed; therefore food items have not been listed. Reptiles, on the other hand, are usually more particular in their tastes, so their food habits are described in some detail. I have emphasized foods eaten in nature and have tried to avoid listing items taken in captivity. Information on diet may be of interest to persons who keep reptiles and amphibians for enjoyment and study.

SUBSPECIES: The characteristics of many species differ in various parts of their ranges. Color may change with the prevailing color of the soil, scale counts and arrangements and proportions may differ with latitude and/or elevation, and less easily detected but important changes may occur in physiology and behavior. Many such variants have been described as subspecies, and the variable species of which they are a part is referred to as *polytypic*. However, professional herpetologists differ in their opinions as to the magnitude and nature of differences justifying application of subspecies names. Many people using this book may have little interest in subspecies. Nevertheless, some geographic variants are well marked and in certain respects display greater differences than exist among some species. Subspecies of the salamander Ensatina (illustrated on Plates 6 and 7) are an example. It would be unfortunate to disregard such distinct forms.

The subspecies concept is now increasingly challenged because of a lack, in many cases, of concordance between molecular and morphological findings. Many morphological features (in the broad sense of the term) such as color, structure, proportions, size, and behavior reflect adaptations to environmental conditions: colors and structure of local environments, temperature, humidity, availability of shelter and food, competition, and predation risks that vary from place to place and may be subject to quite rapid evolutionary changes. Molecular information, on the other hand, focuses on the genetics of relationships — on genealogy — resulting from the accumulation of genetic changes, sometimes over vast stretches of time, less subject to the more immediate effects of variable environmental factors. One of its contributions has been the discovery of "cryptic" species — populations that closely resemble one another, or even appear to be identical, that are actually full species. The problem is compounded further by the often fragmentary information, sometimes both molecular and morphological, upon which the taxon is based. I have, therefore, been rather ruthless in my handling of subspecies and perhaps have not always been fair because of my own bias or lack of information. Sometimes the molecular information, when available, has, in my judgment, been inadequate, as has the morphological, so whether or not the two are in accord cannot be determined. In such cases I have opted to be noncommittal by avoiding subspecies recognition altogether. This position should not be construed as an abandonment of support for efforts to carefully work out morphological responses to the environment. This is an equally important part of the evolutionary story. I have, therefore, been selective in recognizing subspecies, ignoring certain ones pending intensive study of total species variation, and others because the differences described are not easily detected. In some cases species color and patterning is sufficiently uniform such that subtle subspecies variation may be of little interest to the average field observer. I have also been influenced by the need for space in the "Remarks" section of the species accounts, where I have added important information on conservation, taxonomy, distribution, natural history, and other matters.

A word of caution: the printed word sometimes carries more weight in shaping thought than is desirable. The scientific enterprise is constantly in a state of flux, and science advances by a continual reevaluation of currently accepted "truths." The nomenclature, or classification scheme, presented in this book should be viewed in this light. No two authors would have made precisely the same taxonomic decisions. This applies with special force to subspecies. Subspecies, along with higher categories in the hierarchy of classification, are, of course, a construction of the human mind and sometimes may only crudely represent the real world of animal and plant evolutionary relationships in nature. Unfortunately, the subspecies category has all too frequently been applied in the absence of adequate information and with considerable subjectivity.

DISTRIBUTION MAPS: The range of each species is shown in color on the 204 maps at the back of the book. One or more species is included on each map. Specific and subspecific names on the maps can be distinguished by type size: species names are larger and are followed by the scientific name; scientific names of subspecies are given in the text. Question marks on the maps signify doubt about the accuracy of range boundaries or about whether the species occurs in the area—the situation that applies usually can be determined by referring to the text. Parts of ranges, shown in pale blue, are where extinctions or marked declines have occurred often in recent decades and usually as a result of mounting human environmental pressures.

Subspecies distributions usually fit together like pieces of a jigsaw puzzle. At points of contact, characteristics of one subspecies may change gradually or sometimes abruptly into those of another, and individual characteristics may change at different rates. Such zones of change are known as areas of "intergradation," and often reflect gradients in selective forces in the environment. Intergradation zones are shown in gray.

In reality, no intergradation zone has such abrupt boundaries as shown on the maps. Map boundaries only approximate the limits of character change. Furthermore, since different characteristics may change at different rates throughout the zone of change, drawing boundaries can become quite arbitrary, yet they do serve a purpose. For example, I have shown an extensive zone of intergradation between the Yellow-eyed and Monterey Ensatinas (see Map 12), based primarily on two characteristics—ventral coloration and hue. In the intergrade zone the uniformly orange venter and yellowish orange tone of the dark dorsal coloration of the Yellow-eyed Ensatina give way to the whitish venter and a more pinkish color of the dorsum of the Monterey Ensatina (see Pl. 7). This change occurs over a large area of some 150 miles. The yellow eye patch, on the other hand, is abruptly lost, with sometimes only hints of its presence close to the northern juncture of the two taxa. Few areas of intergradation have been studied in sufficient detail to make precise representation possible on all maps.

Hybrid zones, usually the result of secondary contacts, after the divergent taxa have approached or reached species levels of differentiation, are identified in the text and shown on the maps. They are usually narrower than intergradation zones, and changes in characteristics are more erratic (see Map 12). Molecular studies are an aid in distinguishing between primary (intergradation) zones and secondary (often hybrid) zones of contact.

Ranges of species and sometimes subspecies may overlap—the taxa coexist, are sympatric (see Glossary). How such overlaps are shown on maps as follows:

(1) *Simple "two taxa" (species or subspecies) overlaps:* Each taxon involved is identified by a colored box that contains two colors, the upper one representing its range outside the area of overlap and the lower one that is shared with its overlap partner. (Examples—see Maps 1, 85, 91, and 167.)

(2) *Complex overlaps (see Slender Salamanders, p. 182 and Map 24):* Numbered black patches on Map 24 indicate two taxa coexist at each site. However, a given taxon may share range with more than one other taxon. A colored box in the legend identifies one of the taxa. To determine the other (or others), check the flagged number(s) on the map as follows: The California Slender Salamander (orange box) coexists with the Hell Hollow Slender Salamander (deep purple box) in the Sierra at 1. It also coexists at 2 with the Gabilan Slender Salamander (lavender box)—in two places. The orange box is thus followed by numbers 1 and 2. The Santa Lucia Mountains Slender Salamander (dark blue box) coexists with the Gabilan Slender Salamander. Its box is followed by number 12. The Black-bellied Slender Salamander (yellow box) coexists with many other species (numbers 3 to 9) as follows: at 3 with the Gabilan Slender Salamander; 4 and 5 with the San Simeon and Lesser Slender Salamanders (ranges shown in black); 6 with the Tehachapi Slender Salamander in the Tehachapi Mountains (shown in black), but yet not found farther north

(pink box); 8 with the Channel Islands Slender Salamander (on Santa Cruz Island); 7 with the San Gabriel Mountains Slender Salamander (green box) and 9 at many localities in the range of the common Garden Slender Salamander. The Enlarged View shows two other overlap areas—between the Gregarius and Sequoia Slender Salamanders at 10 (blue and purple boxes) and Kern Canyon and Relictual Slender Salamanders at 11 (pink and red boxes).

Not all overlap areas mentioned in the text are shown on the maps because of the lack of precise information on the extent and configuration of overlap zones.

Ranges are never as continuous as shown. In the West, with its varied topography and climate, spotty or "disjunct" distributions are often the rule. Agriculture and other human impacts have also eliminated large segments of the ranges of some species. In many parts of Canada, particularly in the far north, information is spotty because the harsh climate and travel conditions make it difficult to conduct field studies. Supplement map information with knowledge of habitat. Fringe-toed lizards, for example, are not usually found on rocky hillsides without sand, nor Chuckwallas on sand dunes. Many miles of uninhabited territory may separate populations of such species.

Isolated populations are represented on the maps by patches or dots of appropriate color. Many of these isolated populations are also mentioned in the accounts. Often in mainland areas, they are remnants of populations that formerly lived over a much larger area. Examples are salamanders and frogs on mountaintops in the desert. Some isolates, however, are the result of introductions, such as the Bullfrog west of the Rocky Mountains.

If a reptile or amphibian is found outside of its known range, one of the following explanations may apply: (1) A new locality of occurrence may have been discovered. Many areas in the West remain little explored. (2) Even distinctive new native species still turn up: the Inyo Mountains Salamander was found in 1973 in the Inyo Mountains of California, and the Barefoot Gecko in Baja California in 1974. Many new species of slender salamanders (*Batrachoseps*) have been described since my 1985 edition, and more seem surely yet to come. Other species probably await discovery. (3) An unusual individual may have been found—a hybrid or oddly marked specimen that does not fit the brief descriptions in this book. Such individuals are especially likely to occur in areas of intergradation or where two species have come into contact and hybridized. Consult the species accounts for remarks concerning areas of hybridization. (4) A waif may have been found—an individual transported out of its normal range by natural or human means. Tiger Salamanders appear in cotton fields in the desert in Arizona, some perhaps having metamorphosed from escaped larvae used as fish bait. Increasing commercial and private traffic in amphibians and reptiles is a growing source of such introductions. I have included in the species accounts both those introduced species that appear to have established breeding colonies and ones that may not have, the latter indicated with a question mark. This information is incomplete. I have made no thorough survey. I learned recently an established colony of Yellow-crested Jackson's Chameleons (*Chamaeleo jacksonii*), a live-bearing species, at Morro Bay, San Luis Obispo County, California.

Maps showing the distribution of natural vegetation (pp. 464–67) are included to help explain the boundaries of the species and subspecies ranges and to aid in the search for new localities. Because of the small size of the maps, the distribution of vegetation can only be roughly indicated. The Sonoran Desert, for example, shown as occupying most of Baja California (p. 467), actually consists of an extensive patchwork of different plant communities. Vegetation belts reflect conditions of climate and terrain that greatly influence distribution, but there is seldom a close relationship between the distribution of amphibians and reptiles and that of particular plant species. However, the ranges of the Chuckwalla and Desert Iguana stop at the northern limit of the creosote bush plant community in southern Nevada. In some of the accounts I list plant species with which the species may be associated, although they are not all necessarily found at a given locality. With the construction of new roads and increasing numbers of people entering remote areas, much new information on distribution will be forthcoming. Keep the maps up to date by adding localities from the literature and personal study. *Use them as a life list by checking off species as you encounter them.*

I have tried to make the range maps as accurate as possible. Given the vast numbers of specimens in collections and the rate of growth in new distributional information, deficiencies will certainly be found. This should serve as a stimulus for users of the book to improve range information by noting changes on maps. As noted in the acknowledgments, many knowledgeable people have helped update the maps; however, I am obviously responsible for the final product.

USE OF NAMES: I have tried to follow common names set forth in official lists and in use in other field guides, to minimize confusion and multiplicity of names. With the appearance in 2000 of *Scientific and Standard English Names of Amphibians and Reptiles of North America North of Mexico,* published by the Society for the Study of Amphibians and Reptiles (see bibliography, Brian I. Crother, chair), I have reviewed all names used in this Field Guide and have followed, for the most part, the committee's recommendations. In most cases where I have not, it is because I wished to adhere to common names that have become widely used as a result of many decades of use in the eastern and western Peterson Field Guides and recommendations of earlier common name committees. I have also not followed all recommendations concerning scientific names. Where I have changed an established common name, or deviated from a name set forth in the standard herpetological lists, I usually have placed the previous name in parentheses. In cases where, in the past, a subspecies common name has been the same as the species name, I have changed one or the other (usually the subspecies name) to avoid such confusing duplication. When the previous species name (common or scientific) contained the name of a person, I have tried to retain this honorary patronym by applying it to the subspecies (if any exists) that bears the patronymic scientific name. In one case, Henshaw's Night Lizard, I have used the patronymic name as the species name and the species name as a subspecies name, following the *Scientific and Standard English Names* list.

I have returned to the possessive in common names (Woodhouse Toad, for example, is now Woodhouse's Toad), having failed to find much support for my earlier position.

With the emergence of the molecular approach to taxonomy, many changes in nomenclature are being recommended. Many species, long recognized on morphological grounds, are now being subdivided into one or more new species. In some cases I have followed these new arrangements, but with others I await a period of peer review. I do not feel that a field guide is the place for quick acceptance of every new taxonomic change. This trend toward an increase in the number of species based on molecular studies and the need for time for peer review has influenced my decision about the number of species recognized in some of the accounts of genera and families.

METRIC SYSTEM: Metric equivalents follow measurements in inches, feet, and miles throughout the book. Elevation measurements sometimes have been rounded off to the nearest 1 o meters.

2

MAKING CAPTURES

Many reptiles and amphibians can simply be picked up. No special methods are needed to capture them. However, it is dangerous to handle venomous species—the Gila Monster, Western Coral Snake, and rattlesnakes. Sooner or later, as when playing with a loaded gun, disaster may strike. Other species can be taken in hand but should be handled with care to avoid injuring or overheating them. Hold large individuals just behind the head to avoid being bitten. Those that have taken refuge under logs, rocks, and boards may be sluggish or momentarily light-struck. Active ones abroad on the surface can sometimes be overtaken before they escape into a burrow or other retreat. A fast snake may be pinioned lightly underfoot while a neck hold is secured, but be very careful not to apply too much pressure. Gloves will help reduce wear and tear but must not be counted on as protection against venomous species. Success in making captures is greatly increased if a few standard techniques are used.

MAKING AND USING A SNAKE STICK: The traditional forked stick is unsatisfactory for catching snakes. Instead, attach an angle iron (2 × 2 inches, $^5/_8$ inch wide) to the end of a broom handle or a 3-foot-plus length of 1-inch doweling, placing the surface of the iron flush with the end of the dowel. With a file, bevel the free edge of the angle iron so that it will slip easily beneath a snake when the animal is on a hard surface such as pavement. The snake stick can thus be used either as a hook to pull a snake from brush or rocks or to pin it down while a neck hold is secured. It can also be used to lift a snake, without touching it, to place it in a container. Although the bite of even our largest nonvenomous species will usually only superficially lacerate the skin, there is a risk of infection and sometimes a toxic reaction; therefore, it is best to avoid being bitten. Use gloves to capture large snakes, or maneuver the snake stick to the head region so that you can grasp the animal just behind the head. Thumb and index finger should be against the rear of the jaws; if there is slack the snake may turn and bite.

NOOSING: When they are warm, most lizards and some snakes are too fast to catch by hand. A slip noose of thread, fishing line, or copper wire can be used to snare them. Use number 50 thread for lizards up to about 4 or 5 inches (10–12 cm) long from snout to vent, and number 8 thread or fishing line for larger species. The noose should be tied to the notched end of a slender stick or through the last rung of a telescopic fishing rod to prevent its pulling off. The shank should be short, usually no more than 6 inches (15 cm) long when the noose is open. If excessively long it may become tangled in vegetation or be blown about, making it hard to control. A wire noose (see below) avoids this difficulty and can be bent to thrust into small openings. Make a small loop of $^1/_4$-inch (6 mm) diameter at the end of a thread. Tie the loop with a square knot so it will not close. Pass the shank through the loop and attach it to the pole. Should the noose tend to close when in use, open it to the desired diameter and use saliva to moisten both loop and shank where they come into contact, or apply a small pinch of wax.

To make a copper wire noose, cut a 10- or 12-inch (25–30 cm) length from an electric light cord. Or use "zipcord," available in most hardware stores. Remove the insulation and separate out a single strand of wire. Twist the ends of the remaining strands in opposite directions so that they will not separate. Coil the bundle to make it easy to carry. Since copper wire nooses must be replaced frequently, you'll need a reserve supply. Twist a small loop of $^1/_8$- to $^1/_4$-inch (3–6 mm) diameter at the end of the strand. Pass the shank through and orient the loop so the shank moves freely; compress the sides of the loop slightly to make it somewhat elongate; then curve the loop to conform to the lizard's neck. When attaching the noose, take several turns around the end of the pole and twist the free end of the wire along the shank to strengthen its base. It is here that most breakage occurs. After noosing a lizard, reduce the diameter of the noose to $^1/_2$ inch (12 mm) or less and carefully untwist all kinks. Pass the shank between thumb and index finger to straighten it. Re-form the noose to the desired diameter and reshape the "neck" curve in the loop.

When noosing a lizard, avoid quick movements. When the noose is within 5 or 6 inches (12–15 cm) of the head, move it slowly or pause for a moment, allowing the animal to become accustomed to the presence of a strange object nearby, then move the remaining distance gradually. When the noose has passed over the lizard's head and has reached the neck region, jerk upward and slightly backward. Remove the animal quickly, before it has a chance to wriggle free. Wary species can sometimes be noosed by creating a diversion. Gently shake a handkerchief at arm's length to one side or wriggle your fingers to attract attention away from the noose.

Although noosing may appear cruel, it rarely does harm. Only a heavy-bodied lizard or snake with a slender neck may be injured if it thrashes violently when suspended. Support part of the weight of such animals by resting their hindquarters on the ground.

The noose pole can be extended by drilling a hole into the free end of the snake stick. Depth of the hole may be around an inch. I usually carry a fiberglass fishing pole segment without rungs, about 4 feet long, with a base diameter of $^3/_8$ inch. My snake stick is around 3 feet in length. Thus I can quickly increase the length of my noose pole to around 7 feet. The two collecting tools are easy to carry in one hand.

NIGHT DRIVING: Certain snakes, geckos, toads, and salamanders can be found on highways at night. Reptiles may be attracted to the warmth of the pavement and amphibians to roadside ditches. Night driving to observe animals on roadways must be done with great care. With constant vigilance for approaching cars, it is safe on little-traveled roads. Drive slowly (15 to 20 miles per hour) on roads that pass through suitable habitat and watch both pavement and shoulders. An ideal road is dark colored, little traveled, and without curbs or broad, bare shoulders. Roads with bordering wild-plant growth are especially favorable. It is easy to overlook small species. On dark pavement the yellow spots of a Tiger Salamander may resemble pale-colored pebbles, a blind snake can be mistaken for a twig, and a toad for a rock. Check all suspicious-looking objects, even if it means stopping for fan belts, banana peels, and other artifacts.

Success in night collecting depends in large part on weather conditions, particularly temperature, and not just the weather at the time but that of several days or a week before. Avoid cool evenings when looking for reptiles. Air temperatures below 60° to 65°F (15–18°C) are usually too low. If the pavement remains warm, however, you may find some individuals. Bright moonlight and windy conditions seem to depress activity. Warmth is less important to amphibians. Some salamanders may be abroad at a few degrees above freezing.

Wet weather is the time to find amphibians. After rains in arid portions of the Southwest, the response of frogs and toads, long ensconced below dry sunbaked earth, may be dramatic. Within an hour an area powder-dry for many months may reverberate with their cries, and the ground may swarm with hopping forms. Watch for thunderstorms. In open terrain where there are good roads and broad vistas, one can sometimes spot a storm and drive to it in time to arrive just after dark or shortly after a rain.

TRIANGULATION: Locating a small calling animal hidden in a large expanse of rough terrain would appear to be almost impossible. However, it can usually be accomplished easily by means of triangulation. The technique is particularly helpful for finding creatures whose voices are ventriloquial and thus give a deceptive impression of location. Triangulation is best done by two people. When, for example, a calling frog has been singled out of a chorus and its approximate position determined, move 15 to 30 feet (5–10 m) apart and listen quietly. After a few moments of listening, each person, without discussion with the other, should decide on the location of the sound. Then, at a signal, each should point with arm extended and sight on a distant object beyond the expected location of the sound that will serve as a reference point. Finally, both should walk directly toward their reference points and seek the animal where their pathways cross. If you are alone, you can listen at one position for a time, decide on a direction, then move to one side and listen again. Triangulation is often easier to do at night than in the daytime if flashlights or headlamps with distinct beams are used; the point where the beams intersect can be determined precisely. The lights should not be turned on, however, until direction has been determined. Sudden illumination may alarm wary species, and they may not call again for some time. First trials may not bring success, and it may be necessary to withdraw and repeat the procedure several times.

EYESHINES: Fortunately for the nighttime observer, many animals' eyes reflect light. One of the pleasures in the field is to walk quietly through wild country at night in search of eyeshines, pausing occasionally to illuminate the surroundings with a headlamp or flashlight. Dewdrops and the eyes of spiders glint silver and green, those of moths and toads yellow or red; a murky stream becomes a cascade of light. To obtain an eyeshine, the light source must be held near your eyes. Hold a flashlight at the side of your head or with the base resting on your forehead; a headlamp works well and frees the hands. The eyeshine method works best on toads, frogs, and turtles. Eyeshines of snakes and salamanders are too faint to be seen well, and our lizards are chiefly active in the daytime.

TRACKING: Seek areas of fine, loose soil, sand, or mud—sandy flats, dunes, dusty roads, trails, fresh mud of washes, or the banks of ponds and streams. Go out when the sun is low and highlights and shadows are strong. Start early, before there is a maze of tracks, or later in the day after a wind has erased old tracks and new ones are appearing. Follow a fresh track. Direction of travel can be determined by toe marks and ridges formed by the backward pressure of toes, feet, or coils of a snake. Tracking demands paying attention to details and using clues. From meager evidence an interesting story may unfold. I once tracked a lizard across the barren rippled surface of a sand dune. The track indicated that at first the animal had moved slowly. Marks of all four feet showed, the stride was short, the tail dragged. Then there appeared the tracks of a roadrunner, a lizard-eating bird. The lizard's stride suddenly lengthened and marks of only two feet could be seen; the tail mark disappeared. The lizard was running now, on its hind legs with tail lifted. An occasional small dent indicated that at high speed it occasionally touched down with its front feet to maintain balance. Just over the crest of the dune the track suddenly stopped. To one side was a faint V-shaped mark in the sand. The roadrunner track continued at full clip over the hill, then slowed and wandered. The bird seemed confused. I grabbed at the V-shaped mark and something wriggled beneath it. In my hand I held a beautiful fringe-toed lizard.

ONTAINERS FOR SPECIMENS: Cloth bags are standard for transporting reptiles. Use flour sacks, inexpensive pillowcases, or bags made for the purpose. Useful sizes are 24 × 10 inches (60 × 25 cm) and 40 × 20 inches (100 × 50 cm). They may be made from unbleached muslin. Sew with French seams and hem the top. Attach a drawstring 2 to 4 inches (5–10 cm) below the hem by sewing a 12-inch (30 cm) length of heavy twine, at its midpoint, to the side of the bag. The bags are long and the top can be wound around your belt to prevent the bag from working loose. The length also enables you to double back the top when you tie it closed—some snakes have a remarkable ability to work their way out of sacks. Inspect the sacks occasionally for holes or loose threads that might snarl specimens. Even small holes may cause trouble, because they may be enlarged by the probing efforts of captives. Do not carry a venomous species in a sack next to your body.

Quart or gallon glass or plastic jars with screw caps are usually better than bags for carrying amphibians. However, plastic bags with ziplike closures are suitable for small amphibians and reptiles. Place damp moss, leaves, or moist paper towels in the bottom of the container to provide moisture. Avoid dirt and rocks. With lidded containers, punch a few holes in the lid for air, poking the holes outward so that sharp edges will not damage specimens, and file the edges to avoid personal injury when handling (or make the holes with an electric drill). When perforating lids, make only four or five ⅛-inch (3 mm) openings. Numerous holes may result in excessive drying of specimens. A knapsack or canvas shoulder bag is convenient for carrying sacks and other collecting gear.

3

FIELD STUDY AND PROTECTION

FIELD STUDY: There is much to be learned about the distribution, habits, and behavior of western reptiles and amphibians. The many question marks on the range maps should be a challenge to fill in the gaps in our knowledge of distribution. We have not found the eggs or young of some species, and much is not known about time of breeding, courtship behavior, predators, and other matters.

A field notebook is essential. Herewith are directions for note-taking established at the University of California Museum of Vertebrate Zoology. Write notes in nonfading waterproof black ink to make a permanent record. Higgins Eternal Ink has proved to be long-lasting but tends to clog pens. Black deluxe Uni-ball pens work well. Use a hardback (7 1/4 × 10 inch–18 × 25 cm) loose-leaf notebook. Enter your name in the upper-left-hand corner (Fig. 3) and head each page with the species name, entering below your observations by locality, date, and time of day. Group together pages pertaining to each species. In addition to the species account, keep a journal. Describe the route traveled and general features of terrain, vegetation, and weather. When you find an animal, watch it for a time from a distance if possible. Field glasses will help. Describe the ground surface (sand, hardpan, rock), vegetation (grassland, chaparral, or forest, listing species of plants if possible), temperature, and moisture conditions. Note other animals present. Try to interpret what you see.

If you can visit the locality frequently, you can carry out an extended study of the species that live there. Individuals of a species can be marked, measured, sexed, and released at points of capture. Map the area, using as reference points rock outcrops, trees, and other natural features, or numbered stakes set out in a grid. Ascertain movements of individuals, their interrelationships, activity patterns, and growth rate.

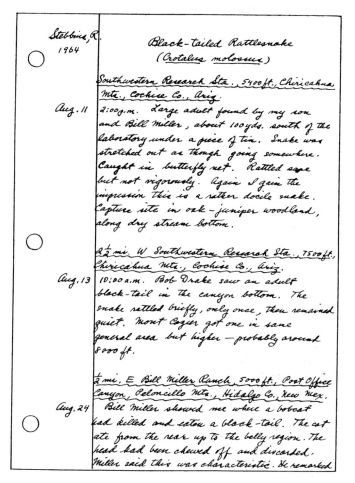

Fig. 3. Sample page from a field notebook

Always use care when studying individuals so as not to reduce their chances of survival. Devise various methods of distinctively marking individuals. With species that have differing colors and patterns, photographs in color arranged rather like a fingerprint system have been successful in making possible individual recognition once growth changes have stabilized. Consult an experienced professional herpetologist before embarking on such studies. Give each identified animal a number in the field notebook, and record the date and place of captures, its sex, and size (snout-vent length). Plot the locations of captures on the map of the study area. Such field studies are recommended rather than the amassing of large numbers of hapless captives. The animals remain little disturbed in their natural setting. Since they are recognizable as individuals and under study, they appeal in much the same way as one's pets, yet do not demand care. Information obtained is more likely to be reliable than that procured under artificial conditions, and there is always the excitement of the hunt and the anticipation of meeting an old friend.

PROTECTION: Reptiles and amphibians are important to us in many ways. They play a part in the balance of nature; they are a storehouse of unexplored scientific information that can benefit us; they have contributed enormously to the advance of vertebrate physiology and embryology; and they enhance the outdoor experiences of a growing number of people who gain pleasure from observing them. Yet at a time of growing awareness of their value, their numbers are declining. The greatest destructive force is habitat disturbance and loss. Most species of wild animals are adapted to a specific and complex set of conditions that must be met if they are to survive. Growth of the human population brings great and rapid changes. Marshes are drained, streams are placed in concrete troughs, canyons are dammed and inundated, ground is cleared for subdivisions and highways, agriculture spreads into marginal lands and, spurred on by water developments, reaches out even into deserts, the stronghold of reptiles. Air, water, and soil are contaminated. Although a few species may temporarily benefit from some of these changes, most do not, and the list of creatures rendered extinct in historic times can be expected to grow. The trend is toward a domesticated world, reduced in organic variety and crowded with people and their possessions. Interest in wildlife preservation and the well-being of humanity cannot be separated from concern for efforts to limit human population growth and prevent careless exploitation of remaining natural areas.

Many of the species covered in this book have thus suffered declines in their populations, and among our frogs, some populations are on the brink of extinction or have disappeared. The Las Vegas Valley Leopard Frog was last seen in 1942 and is considered extinct, and the last known Tarahumara Frog in the United States was found dead in 1983. Efforts are underway to reestablish the latter from populations in Mexico. It is, therefore, very important to follow state and federal regulations designed to protect species. Since such legislation varies geographically and is modified often, I have not attempted to include it in this guide. Be sure to consult state and federal statutes before collecting.

Areas on the maps of ranges shaded in pale blue show approximate limits of known areas of significant species decline, most of which appear to have occurred in the last 30 years or so. Happily, good things are happening. A worldwide network has formed to understand the causes and find ways to stem the tide of frog declines. This is translating into some remarkable local civic actions. See p. 209 for the Amargosa Toad recovery from the brink of extinction. Efforts at restoration of some losses are underway, but since specific causes of decline are usually complex and, when identified, often cannot be adequately mitigated, success is usually highly uncertain. Unfortunately, my information on declines is fragmentary and surely underestimates what is happening. It is not within the scope of this guide to undertake a comprehensive survey, but the hope is that others may contribute to the study of this disturbing trend. The previous remarks point to the big problem of human population growth and the disconnection, physically and emotionally, of many people from nature that characterizes industrial civilization, trends that threaten ourselves and natural living systems worldwide. The overriding theme in public education in the United States and around the world now must become nature-oriented to instill in human hearts respect and concern for each other and the Earth with all its physical and biological grandeur.

Throughout this book I have given particular attention to methods of capture, because it is often necessary to have an animal in hand for identification. This information can be misused. Some populations of reptiles and amphibians have been severely damaged by overcollecting and disruption of habitat. Commercial traffic in reptiles and amphibians has sometimes been damaging as a result of overcollecting and damage to habitats, and increases the probability of the establishment of exotics, to the detriment of native species. Amateur trading of live specimens has a similar effect. This practice and the development of private collections should, in general, be discouraged. Establishment of study collections is better left to educational and scientific institutions. The number of animals kept as pets should be small. In obtaining specimens, treat the habitat with special care. So far as possible, put back rocks, logs, and other objects turned over in the search, to minimize disturbance to the microenvironment and in consideration of the people who will follow. Moss-covered talus, long stabilized, is particularly vulnerable to disruption as are crevice habitats as a result of rock flaking. Some populations are so small that they should not be disturbed at all. Many of the isolated populations represented on the maps by dots are examples.

Captive breeding of reptiles and amphibians for the market and for conservation goals is helping to reduce collecting pressures on wild populations. This program should receive strong public support.

4

IDENTIFICATION KEYS

The four keys in this chapter are designed to help you locate the plates illustrating the species. All major groups of reptiles and amphibians are included except the turtles—they are easily recognized as there are few western species (see Plates 20–23). Baja California "endemics" (see pp. 419–432) are also excluded. They can readily be identified by consulting Plates 53 to 56. To aid recognition, species have been grouped by means of easily observed characteristics, sometimes without regard for taxonomic relationships. For example, the kingsnakes, Long-nosed Snake, and Sonoran Coral Snake are grouped because they are banded; the Brown Vine Snake, hook-nosed, leaf-nosed, and Western Hog-nosed Snakes because they have modified snouts. Those interested in taxonomic relationships will find such information in the text.

At each step in a key a choice must be made between two alternatives. To illustrate: in the salamander key below, decide first whether or not the animal has a nasolabial groove (furrow between the nostril and edge of lip), alternatives 1A and 1B. Examine also its teeth and skin. If 1A is selected, go to alternatives 3A and 3B, where again a choice must be made. If 1B is chosen, go to 2A or 2B, thence to the plates.

Drawings illustrating key characteristics accompany each key. Numbers in parentheses in the keys refer to the numbered parts of each drawing; the right-hand column leads to the next step in the key or else to the identification plate(s). Consult also the illustrations on the endpapers of the book for types and locations of scales and other structural characteristics.

SALAMANDERS

Salamanders are lizardlike but lack scales and claws and have a moist, soft skin. See Fig. 4 for numbers in parentheses.

1 A.   Nasolabial groove present (1); clusters of teeth at back of roof of mouth (2); skin always smooth [Lungless Salamanders]   **see 3**

1 B.   Nasolabial groove and tooth clusters absent; skin smooth or rough   **see 2**

2 A.   Teeth in roof of mouth in 2 diverging lengthwise rows* (3); skin rough, except in breeding males [Newts]   **Pl. 4**

2 B.   Teeth in roof of mouth in transverse row (4); skin smooth [Mole, Giant, and Olympic Salamanders]   **Pls. 1–3**

*Care must be taken not to damage the salamander's mouth. Carefully insert a fingernail between its jaws at tip of snout, then gently apply force on lower jaw until animal yields to pressure.

3 A.   Tail constricted at base [Ensatina]   **Pls. 6, 7**

3 B.   Tail not constricted at base   **see 4**

4 A.   Four toes on both front and hind feet (5); often wormlike [Slender Salamanders]   **Pls. 9–11**

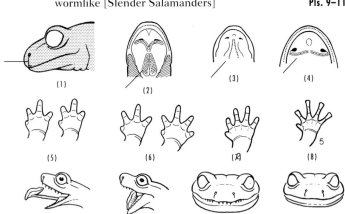

Fig. 4. Characteristics of salamanders

4B. Four toes on front feet, 5 on hind feet (6); never
   wormlike   **see 5**

5A. Toes short and webbed (7); tongue unattached
   in front, edges free all around (9) [Web-toed
   Salamanders]   **Pl. 11**

5B. Toes relatively longer than in 5A, with little or
   no web (6); tongue attached in front (10)   **see 6**

6A. Adult males often with noticeably protruding
   upper jaw teeth—felt by stroking tip of salamander's snout from below while holding its
   mouth closed (11); toes often with squarish tips
   (8); usually no distinct stripe on back [Climbing
   Salamanders]   **Pl. 8**

6B. Teeth rarely protrude sufficiently to be detected
   by stroking (12); toe tips round (6); back stripe
   usually present [Woodland Salamanders]   **Pl. 5**

FROGS AND TOADS

See Fig. 5 for numbers in parentheses.

1A. Eyes without lids; sharp black claw on each of 3
   inner toes of hind feet [African Clawed Frog]   **Pl. 19**

1B. Eyes with lids; no claws on toes   **see 2**

2A. Fifth outer toe of hind foot broader than other
   toes (1) [Tailed Frog]   **Pl. 15**

2B. Fifth toe not broadened (2)   **see 3**

3A. Fold of skin across head behind eyes (8)   **see 4**

3B. No skin fold on head. If skin is stretched, fold
   many not be evident. Move skin about in head
   region   **see 6**

4A. Small brown or gray toad, adult body length under 1 1/2 in.; small black eyes [Great Plains Narrow-mouthed Toad]   **Pl. 15**

4B. Adults larger than in 4A, eyes not small and
   black   **see 5**

5A. Eardrum conspicuous, partly transparent; many
   tubercles on underside of toes (4); back blotched
   [Barking Frog]   **Pl. 19**

5B.   Eardrum not transparent; toes without conspicuous tubercles; back has large spots with definite borders [Northern Casque-headed Frog]   **Pl. 15**

6A.   Parotoid glands present (9) [True Toads]   **Pls. 12–14**
6B.   Parotoid glands absent   **see 7**

7A.   Single sharp-edged black "spade" on underside of hind foot (5); eye with vertical pupil—except when pupil is greatly dilated (11) [Spadefoot Toads]   **Pl. 12**
7B.   No sharp-edged black "spade" on hind foot; rounded pale or brownish tubercle(s) sometimes present on hind foot; pupil not vertical (12)   **see 8**

8A.   Extra joint at tips of toes (6) (move tip of toe to detect); toe pads often present (3); no dorsolateral folds [Treefrogs and Allies]   **Pl. 15**
8B.   No extra joint at tip of toes (7); no toe pads; dorsolateral folds often present (10) [True Frogs]   **Pls. 16–19**

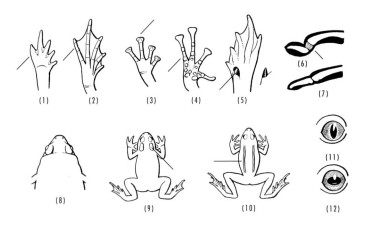

Fig. 5. Characteristics of frogs and toads

LIZARDS

All have scales and (with the exception of the snakelike legless lizards) clawed toes; movable eyelids distinguish the latter from the snakes. See Fig. 6 for numbers in parentheses.

1 A. Eye with a fixed transparent covering; no movable eyelids   **see 2**
1 B. Movable eyelids present   **see 3**

2 A. Tips of toes very broad, with pair of large flat scales or transverse plates (1) [Leaf-toed, San Lucan, House, and Mediterranean Geckos]   **Pls. 24, 55**
2 B. Toe tips not broadened [Night Lizards]   **Pl. 35**

3 A. Large, pale yellow catlike eyes with vertical pupil [Banded, Texas, and Barefoot Geckos]   **Pl. 24**
3 B. Eyes not unusually large and pupil round or not easily seen (eyes dark)   **see 4**

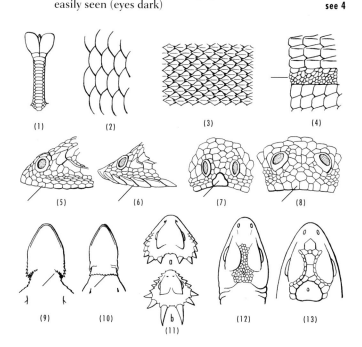

(1)   (2)   (3)   (4)

(5)   (6)   (7)   (8)

(9)   (10)   (11)   (12)   (13)

Fig. 6. Characteristics of lizards

4A. Snakelike, legless, but tiny eyes with movable lids (watch closely to see lizard blink) [Legless Lizards] **Pls. 40, 55**

4B. Limbs present **see 5**

5A. Scales cycloid, very smooth and shiny all over body (2) [Skinks] **Pl. 36**

5B. Scales not cycloid all over body **see 6**

6A. Horns at back of head (11a, 11b); usually 1 or 2 rows of enlarged sharp-pointed fringe scales at sides of body [Horned Lizards] **Pls. 33–34**

6B. No horns or fringe scales **see 7**

7A. A fold on side of body, separating large squarish scales on back and belly (4) [Alligator Lizards] **Pls. 41, 53**

7B. No fold on side of body separating squarish back and belly scales **see 8**

8A. 4th and 5th toes about same length; tail stout, much shorter than body, often sausage-shaped [Gila Monster] **Pl. 25**

8B. 4th toe much longer than 5th; tail as long as or longer than body, not swollen **see 9**

9A. Great difference between back and belly scales —those on back fine and granular, those on belly many times larger and arranged in straight transverse and lengthwise rows (see Plate 39 Common Spotted Whiptail) [Whiptails] **Pls. 37–40, 53**

9B. Back and belly scales not greatly different in size —those on belly usually overlap like shingles **see 10**

10A. A single enlarged row of scales down middle of back, extended as spines on neck in Spiny-tailed Iguana [Desert and Spiny-tailed Iguanas] **Pls. 25, 55**

10B. No enlarged row of scales down middle of back **see 11**

11A. Rostral absent (8) [Chuckwalla] **Pl. 25**

11B. Rostral present (7) **see 12**

12A. All scales on back keeled and pointed (3);an in complete gular fold (9) [Spiny Lizards] **Pls. 30, 31, 54**

12B. Some or all scales on back granular, if keeled often not pointed; complete gular fold (10) **see 13**

13A. Upper labials separated by diagonal furrows (6);
usually with distinct black crossbars or spots on
underside of tail [Zebra-tailed, Earless, and
Fringe-toed Lizards]   **Pls. 28, 29**
13B. Upper labials separated by vertical furrows (5);
underside of tail without black crossbars   **see 14**

14A. Scales on top of head between and behind eyes
small (12) [Leopard and Collared Lizards]   **Pls. 26, 27, 53**
14B. Scales on top of head between and behind eyes
variously enlarged (13) [Side-blotched, Tree,
Brush, and Rock Lizards]   **Pls. 32, 54, 55**

SNAKES

All are legless and lack eyelids; our legless lizards have movable
eyelids and small ventral scales. See Fig. 7 for numbers in parentheses.

1A. Cycloid scales completely encircling body (1);
no large ventral (belly) scales; eyes are pigmented spots under head scales [Blind Snakes]   **Pl. 42**

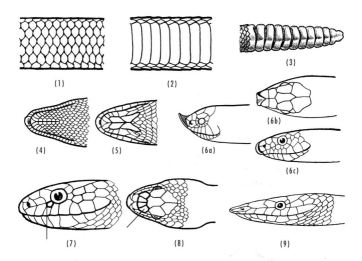

Fig. 7. Characteristics of snakes

1 B. Belly scales (2) more than twice as broad as those on back and sides; eyes well developed see 2

2 A. Tail with rattle (3) or horny segment at tip (recently born young) [Rattlesnakes] Pls. 51, 52, 56
2 B. Tail without rattle or horny segment at tip see 3

3 A. Only small scales on underside of lower jaw between labials (4) [Boas] Pl. 42
3 B. Large scales on underside of lower jaw between labials (5) see 4

4 A. Rostral modified—much enlarged, turned up, and pointed (6A), or flat and attached patchlike to tip of snout (6B, 6C) [Hognose, Hook-nosed, Patch-nosed, and Leaf-nosed Snakes] Pl. 47
4 B. Rostral normal, not greatly enlarged or shaped as in 4A see 5

5 A. Dorsal (back) scales smooth see 9
5 B. Some or all dorsal scales keeled see 6

6 A. Scales weakly keeled along middle of back only, becoming smooth on sides [Rat Snakes] Pls. 45, 56
6 B. All dorsal scales keeled see 7

7 A. Usually 4 prefrontals (8) [Gopher Snake] Pl. 46
7 B. Two prefrontals (6B) see 8

8 A. Anal single; no scale pits [Garter and Lined Snakes] Pls. 48–50
8 B. Anal divided; scale pits present; in our area found only in e. Colorado and se. New Mexico. [Water Snakes] Pl. 48

9 A. Plain green above (gray in preservative), and plain white or pale yellow below see 10
9 B. Not colored as in 9A see 11

10 A. Lower preocular wedged between upper labials (7) [Racer] Pl. 43
10 B. Lower preocular·not wedged between upper labials [Smooth Green Snake] Pl. 46

11A. Lower preocular wedged between upper labials (7)* [Racer and Whipsnakes] **Pls. 43, 56**

11B. Lower preocular not wedged between upper labials **see 12**

> *Shovel-nosed Snakes may occasionally have a divided upper labial below the preocular area, the lower portion of which might be mistaken for a wedged lower preocular. The countersunk lower jaw (see glossary) of these snakes alone, however, sets them apart from Racers and Whipsnakes.

12A. Extremely slender, vinelike; head and snout very long (9) [Brown Vine Snake] **Pl. 47**

12B. Not vinelike; head not extremely long **see 13**

13A. All ventral scales marked with regular narrow black crossbands,* a band at base of each scale; tail with sharp spinelike point [Sharp-tailed Snake] **Pl. 46**

13B. Ventrals not uniformly marked with black crossbands; markings, when present, more widely spaced, confined to sides, or in less regular arrangement; tail without sharp point **see 14**

> *Ring-necked Snakes occasionally have such markings but they usually have a neck band and lack the sharp spinelike tail tip.

14A. Plain-colored, without pattern on dorsum (back). Uniformly colored head cap, often darker than body and sometimes set off from body color by whitish, yellow, or orange collar [Ring-necked and Black-headed Snakes] **Pl. 46**

14B. Body with dorsal pattern of spots, blotches, crossbands, or stripes **see 15**

15A. Belly pale and plain-colored or with dusky bars, scattered dots, or fine speckling, usually confined to sides **see 16**

15B. Belly marked with bold crossbands or bars, or sometimes plain black with pale spots
[Coral, Long-nosed, and Kingsnakes] **Pl. 44**
[Ground, Shovel-nosed, and Sand Snakes] **Pl. 45**

16A. Dorsal scales in 17 or fewer rows at midbody **see 17**

16B. Dorsal scales in more than 17 rows **see 8**

17A. Dorsal pattern of spots; vertical pupils [Night Snake]   **Pl. 46**

17B. Dorsal surface plain or with pattern of cross-bands or a broad lengthwise stripe; pupils round or not visible [Ground, Shovel-nosed, and Sand Snakes]   **Pl. 45**

18A. Head much broader than neck, usually with lyre-shaped marking; pupils vertical [Lyre Snake]   **Pl. 46**

18B. Head only slightly broader than neck, no lyre-shaped marking; pupils not distinctly vertical [Glossy Snake]   **Pl. 46**

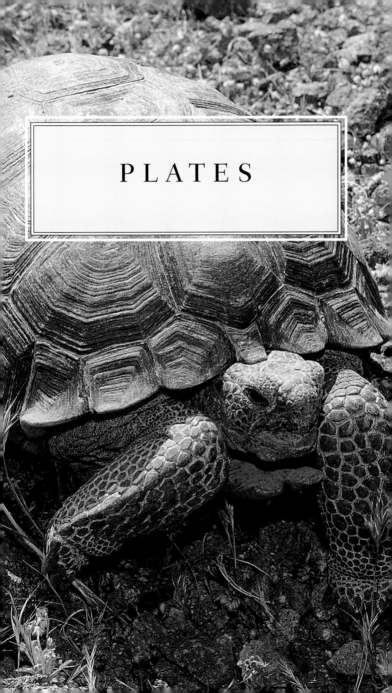

PLATES

PLATE 1

MOLE SALAMANDERS (*Ambystoma*)

Costal grooves distinct. Teeth in roof of mouth in transverse row (Fig. 4, No. 4, p. 26).

CALIFORNIA TIGER SALAMANDER *A. californiense* **P. 153, MAPS 5, 6**
Yellow or cream spots on black ground color. Found only in Calif. (Contra Costa Co.) (3–5 in. SV)

TIGER SALAMANDER *A. tigrinum* **P. 152, MAP 7**
Pattern varies, but over much of its range spotted and/or barred with black, on a gray or greenish ground color; or spotted and barred with yellowish or cream on a black background. (3–6½ in. SV)

Color variants
A. NW Enid, Garfield Co., Okla. Large blotches of yellow on dark ground color
B. Vicinity of Kanab, Utah. Similar individuals found at Hurricane, Wash Co., Utah.
C. Near Cedar Breaks Nat'l Monument (el. 10,335 ft., 3,150 m) Similar individuals found in high country of s. Utah and n. Ariz.
D. Near Gothic, Gunnison Co., Colo.
E. Birder's Corner, Grant Co., Wash.

NORTHWESTERN SALAMANDER *A. gracile* **P. 155, MAP 2**
Conspicuous parotoid glands and glandular ridge on tail. (Humboldt Co., Calif.) (3–5⅕ in. SV)

PLATE 1

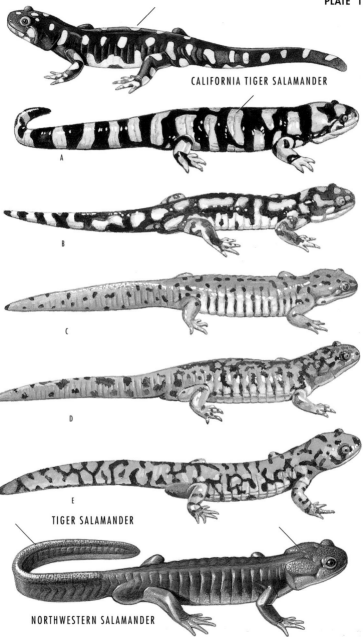

CALIFORNIA TIGER SALAMANDER

A

B

C

D

E

TIGER SALAMANDER

NORTHWESTERN SALAMANDER

PLATE 2

MOLE SALAMANDERS (*Ambystoma*) (Continued)

LONG-TOED SALAMANDER A. *macrodactylum*   **P. 156, MAP 3**
Long slender toes; dorsal stripe or series of blotches. (1 ⅗–3 ½ in. SV)
Southern A. m. *sigillatum*   **P. 157**
Yellow dorsal stripe variously broken into series of blotches. (Amador Co., Calif.)
Santa Cruz A. m. *croceum*   **P. 157**
Yellow-orange blotches on back; ground color black. Greatly restricted range in Santa Cruz and Monterey Cos., Calif.
Western A. m. *macrodactylum*   **P. 157**
Greenish to yellowish dorsal stripe; sides may seem whitewashed. (Benton Co., Ore.)
Eastern A. m. *krausei*   **P. 157**
Well-defined yellow stripe originating on head. (Latah Co., Idaho)

TORRENT SALAMANDERS (*Rhyacotriton*)

Large eyes; tail flattened side-to-side; male with large squarish vent lobes. (1 ⅔–2 ½ in. SV)   **MAP 4**

SOUTHERN R. *variegatus*   **P. 163**
Mottled above; many dark blotches on yellowish green venter. (Trinity Co., Calif.)

OLYMPIC R. *olympicus*   **P. 162**
Mostly plain brown above; yellow-orange below, with scant blotching. (Mason Co., Wash.)

CASCADE R. *cascadae*   **P. 163**
Dorsal dark blotching forms a relatively straight line along sides.

PLATE 2

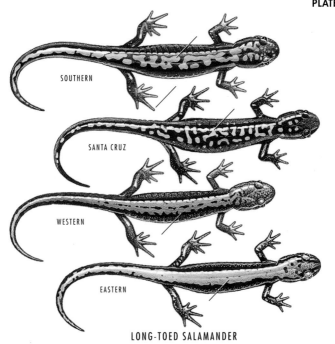

SOUTHERN

SANTA CRUZ

WESTERN

EASTERN

LONG-TOED SALAMANDER

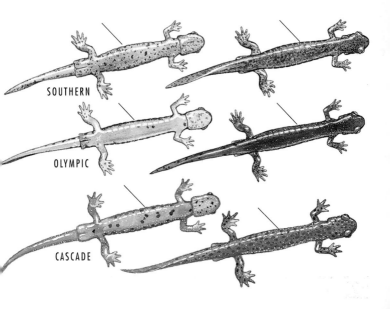

SOUTHERN

OLYMPIC

CASCADE

PLATE 3

GIANT SALAMANDERS *(Dicamptodon)*

Skin smooth; teeth in roof of mouth in transverse row (Fig. 4, No. 4, p. 26). Costal grooves usually distinct.

CALIFORNIA GIANT SALAMANDER *D. ensatus*　　　　**P. 158, MAP 1**

Usually tan to reddish brown above with rather coarse marbled pattern. To around 6 in. (15.2 cm). (Santa Cruz Co., Calif.) (2½–6⅘ in. SV)

PACIFIC GIANT SALAMANDER *D. tenebrosus*　　　　**P. 159, MAP 1**

Tends to be darker and with less coarse mottling than above. (Thurston Co., Wash.)

IDAHO GIANT SALAMANDER *D. aterrimus*　　　　**P. 159, MAP 1**

Darkest and most intricately blotched of the Giant Salamanders. (Latah Co., Idaho)

COPE'S GIANT SALAMANDER *D. copei*　　　　**P. 160, MAP 1**

Transformed individual (Grays Harbor Co., Wash.) Larva. Head shape rectangular from above; gills filamentous (Mason Co., Wash.) (2½–4¾ in. SV) Larva of coexisting Pacific Giant Salamander has wedge-shaped head and bushy gills. (Thurston Co., Wash.)

PLATE 3

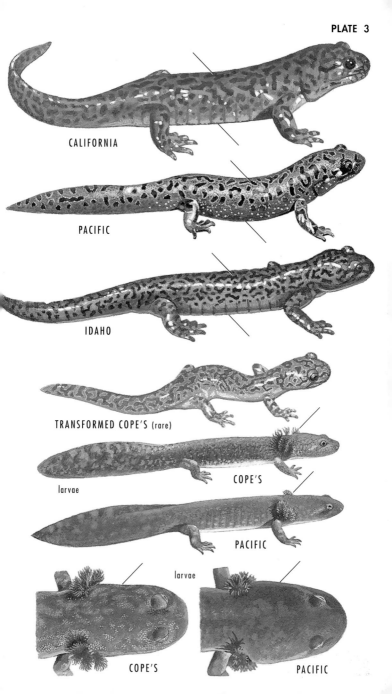

CALIFORNIA

PACIFIC

IDAHO

TRANSFORMED COPE'S (rare)

larvae

COPE'S

PACIFIC

larvae

COPE'S

PACIFIC

PLATE 4

PACIFIC NEWTS *(Taricha)*

Skin rough in terrestrial stage, smooth in breeding male. Teeth in roof of mouth in diverging lengthwise rows (Fig. 4, No. 3, p. 26). Costal grooves indistinct.

CALIFORNIA NEWT *T. torosa*   **P. 166, MAP 11**
Lower eyelids and subocular areas pale; eyes usually reach outline of head, viewed from above (Fig. 24, p. 165). Teeth usually in Y-shaped pattern. (Contra Costa Co., Calif.) (2¾–3½ in. SV)

Coast Range Newt *T. t. torosa*   **P. 167, MAP 11**
Upper eyelids not notably pale colored; ventral coloration usually yellowish orange; iris generally deeper yellow than Sierra Newt. Above rough-skinned terrestrial stage; below smooth-skinned aquatic male (both from Contra Costa Co., Calif.)

Sierra Newt *T. t. sierrae*   **P. 167, MAP 11**
Upper eyelids often quite pale, more contrasting than Coast Range Newt; ventral color orange to burnt orange; iris silvery to pale yellow. Smooth-skinned aquatic male. (Tuolumne Co., Calif.)

ROUGH-SKINNED NEWT *T. granulosa*   **P. 165, MAP 8**
Lower eyelids and subocular areas dark; eyes usually fail to reach outline of head, viewed from above. Teeth usually in V-shaped pattern. Often curls tip of tail in defense pose. See Fig. 24, p. 165. Aquatic male above, female below (Thurston Co., Wash.) (White speckling is caused by highlights on moist skin tubercles.) (2¼–3½ in. SV)

RED-BELLIED NEWT *T. rivularis*   **P. 167, MAP 10**
Eyes dark brown. (Sonoma Co., Calif.) (2¾–3½ in. SV)

PLATE 4

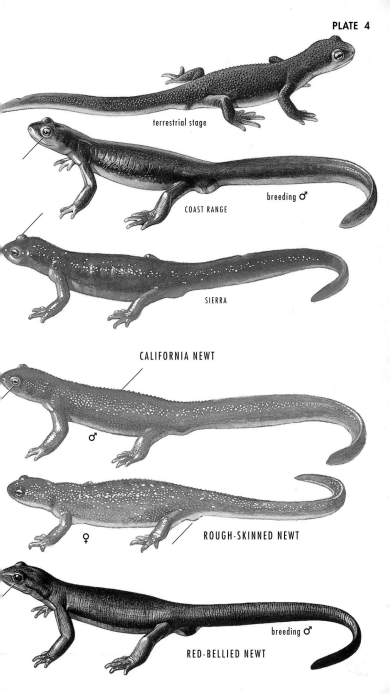

terrestrial stage

breeding ♂

COAST RANGE

SIERRA

CALIFORNIA NEWT

♂

♀

ROUGH-SKINNED NEWT

breeding ♂

RED-BELLIED NEWT

PLATE 5

WOODLAND SALAMANDERS *(Plethodon)*

Slim-bodied, short-legged; often with dorsal stripe. Nasolabial grooves (Fig. 4, No. 1, p. 26).

DUNN'S SALAMANDER *P. dunni*　　　　　　　　　　**P. 169, MAP 14**
Mottled tan to greenish yellow stripe does not reach tip of tail. Usually 15 costal grooves. (Benton Co., Ore.) (2–3 in. SV)

WESTERN RED-BACKED SALAMANDER *P. vehiculum*　　　**P. 170, MAP 13**
Tan, reddish brown, orange, or yellow stripe, even-edged and extending to tip of tail; belly mottled (Fig. 8a). Usually 16 costal grooves. (Red phase, Benton Co., Ore.) (1½–2½ in. SV)

COEUR D'ALENE SALAMANDER *P. idahoensis*　　　　**P. 172, MAP 18**
Dark coloring generally more intense than in Van Dyke's Salamander. (Kootenai Co., Idaho) (1¾–2⅗ in. SV)

VAN DYKE'S SALAMANDER *P. vandykei*　　　　　　**P. 170, MAP 18**
Stripe with even or scalloped edges; large pale throat patch (Fig. 8b). Usually 14 costal grooves. (1¾–2½ in. SV)

LARCH MOUNTAIN SALAMANDER *P. larselli*　　　　**P. 172, MAP 16**
Belly red to reddish orange or salmon pink. Usually 15 costal grooves. (Multnomah Co., Ore.) (1½–2⅛ in. SV)

JEMEZ MOUNTAINS SALAMANDER *P. neomexicanus*　　**P. 173, MAP 17**
Fifth toe absent or reduced. Usually 19 costal grooves. Known only from Jemez Mts. (Sandoval Co., N.M.) (1⅞–2⅝ in. SV)

DEL NORTE SALAMANDER *P. elongatus*　　　　　　**P. 173, MAP 15**
Toes short and partly webbed. Usually 18 costal grooves. (2⅜–3 in. SV)

Striped Del Norte Salamander *P. e. elongatus*　　**P. 174, MAP 15**
6½–7½ costal folds between toes of adpressed limbs. Brown or black above, with or without brown stripe.

Siskiyou Mountains Salamander *P. e. stormi*　　**P.174, MAP 15**
4–5½ costal folds between toes of adpressed limbs. Brown above, heavily speckled with small light flecks. (Jackson Co., Ore.)

Fig. 8a (left). Venters of Western Red-backed Salamander
Fig. 8b (right). Van Dyke's Salamander.

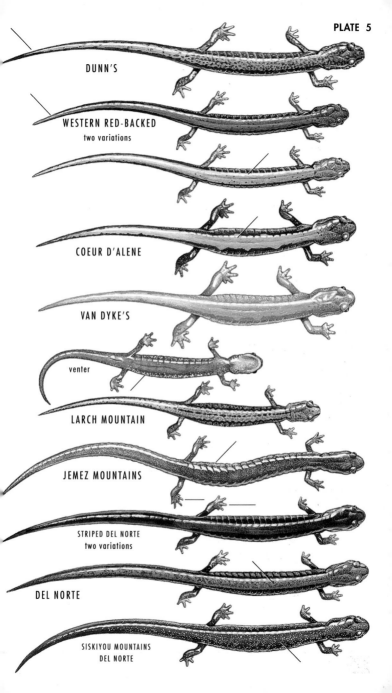

PLATE 5

DUNN'S

WESTERN RED-BACKED
two variations

COEUR D'ALENE

VAN DYKE'S

venter

LARCH MOUNTAIN

JEMEZ MOUNTAINS

STRIPED DEL NORTE
two variations

DEL NORTE

SISKIYOU MOUNTAINS
DEL NORTE

PLATE 6

ENSATINA *(Ensatina eschscholtzii)*

Tail constricted at base; nasolabial grooves (Fig. 4, No. 1, p. 26). See page 174. (1 ½–3 ⅕ in. SV)

BLOTCHED SUBSPECIES

Sierra Nevada *E. e. platensis*　　　　　　　　**P. 177, MAP 12**
Orange spots on brownish ground color. (Kern Co., Calif.)

Yellow-blotched *E. e. croceater*　　　　　　　　**P. 177, MAP 12**
Greenish yellow to cream-colored blotches on blackish ground color. Young have greenish yellow blotches. (Kern Co., Calif.)

Intergrade (between Yellow-blotched and Large-blotched Ensatinas)　　**P. 177**
Like Yellow-blotched, but markings less irregular in outline. Blotch color changes from greenish to yellow-cream with age. (San Bernardino Co., Calif.)

Large-blotched *E. e. klauberi*　　　　　　　　**P. 177, MAP 12**
Orange or cream bars, bands, and blotches on blackish ground color. Young has bright orange marks. (San Diego, Calif.)

Hybrid (between Monterey and Large-blotched Ensatinas)　　　　**P. 177**
(Lower Pine Valley, San Diego Co., Calif.)

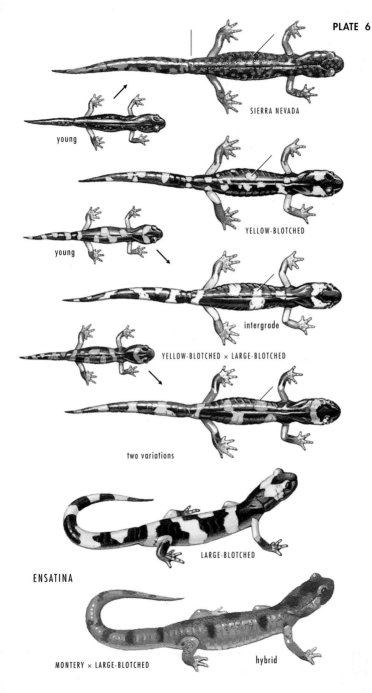

PLATE 6

SIERRA NEVADA

young

YELLOW-BLOTCHED

young

intergrade

YELLOW-BLOTCHED × LARGE-BLOTCHED

two variations

LARGE-BLOTCHED

ENSATINA

MONTERY × LARGE-BLOTCHED

hybrid

PLATE 7

ENSATINA (*Ensatina eschscholtzii*)

Tail constricted at base; nasolabial grooves (Fig. 4, No. 1, p. 26). (1 ½–3 ⅕ in. SV)

BLOTCHED AND PLAIN-COLORED SUBSPECIES

Intergrade (between Oregon and Sierra Nevada Ensatina)   P. 176
Diffuse orange spots on brownish ground color. Young black with yellow limb bases. (Shasta Co., Calif.)

Painted *E. e. picta*   P. 176, MAP 12
Mottled pattern of black and pale yellow or orange spots, especially on tail. (Del Norte Co., Calif.) (1 ½–2 ¼ in. SV)

Oregon *E. e. oregonensis*   P. 176, MAP 12
Usually plain brown above; belly pale with minute black specks. (King Co., Wash.) Young dark-blotched. (Multnomah Co., Ore.) (Regarded as morphotype rather than subspecies.)

Yellow-eyed *E. e. xanthoptica*   P. 176, MAP 12
Belly orange; conspicuous yellow eye patch. (Contra Costa Co., Calif.)

Monterey *E. e. eschscholtzii*   P. 175, MAP 12
Belly whitish; eyes black.

PLATE 7

intergrade

OREGON × SIERRA NEVADA

young

PAINTED

young

OREGON

YELLOW-EYED

MONTEREY

ENSATINA

PLATE 8

CLIMBING SALAMANDERS *(Aneides)*

Triangular head; males have projecting upper-jaw teeth (Fig. 4, No. 11, p. 26).

ARBOREAL SALAMANDER *A. lugubris* **P. 181, MAP 22**

Adults usually brown with yellow spots; squarish toe tips. Young mottled; limb bases, tail, and shoulders yellowish or rust. (Contra Costa Co., Calif.) (2 1/4–4 in. SV)

BLACK SALAMANDER *A. flavipunctatus* **P. 178, MAP 21**

Slim-bodied; short toes and limbs; belly black, sometimes with ash gray markings. Dorsal coloration varies: solid black, black with white or cream spots, or suffused with ash gray to greenish. (2–3 3/4 in. SV)

Young. Mendocino Co., Calif.
A. San Mateo Co., Calif.
B. Lake Co., Calif.
C. Mendocino Co., Calif.

WANDERING SALAMANDER *A. vagrans* **P. 180, MAP 20**

Clouded above with mottled pattern of gray, gold, or reddish; squarish toe tips. Young with patches of brassy, copper, or pinkish on snout, shoulders, limb bases, and tail. (1 4/5–3 in. SV)

SACRAMENTO MOUNTAINS SALAMANDER *A. hardii* **P. 178, MAP 23**

Limbs short; toe tips rounded; belly pale. Confined to Sacramento, White, and Capitan Mts. of s. N.M. (1 3/4–2 1/2 in. SV)

PLATE 8

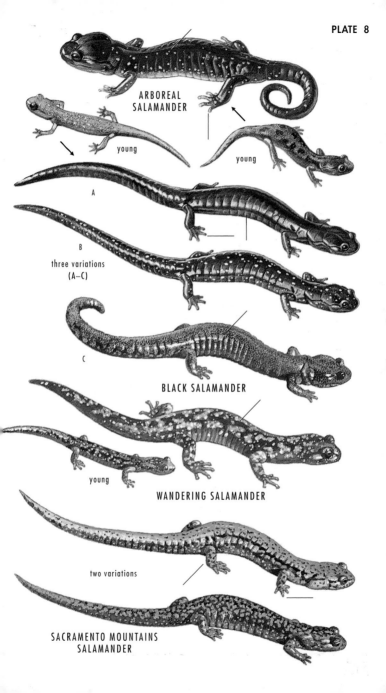

ARBOREAL
SALAMANDER

young

young

A

B

three variations
(A–C)

C

BLACK SALAMANDER

young

WANDERING SALAMANDER

two variations

SACRAMENTO MOUNTAINS
SALAMANDER

PLATE 9

SLENDER SALAMANDERS (*Batrachoseps*)

(See also Pls. 10 and 11.)
Slender body; short limbs; 4 toes on front and hind feet.

OREGON *B. wrighti*   P. 183, MAPS 19, 24
Large white spots on black belly. (Lane Co., Ore.) (1 ⅓–2 ⅖ in. SV)

INYO MOUNTAINS *B. campi*   P. 184, MAPS 19, 24
Tail short. Brown above with gray blotches, or entirely suffused with gray. (Inyo Co., Calif.) (1 ⅓–2 ⅖ in. SV)

KERN PLATEAU *B. robustus*   P. 184, MAPS 19, 24
Dark spots above. Kern Plateau, s. Sierra Nevada, Calif., related to Inyo Mountains Slender Salamander. (Kern Co., Calif.) (1 ¾–2 ¼ in. SV)

TEHACHAPI *B. stebbinsi*   P. 185, MAP 24
Head broader, limbs longer, and feet larger than in other species except Inyo Mountains and Kern Plateau Slender Salamanders. No gray blotches or suffusion as in Inyo Mountains Slender Salamander. (Caliente Creek, Kern Co., Calif.) (2–2 ⅖ in. SV)

SAN GABRIEL MTS. *B. gabriele*   P. 189, MAP 24
Coppery colored dorsal stripe or remnants over shoulders and on tail, or black with dorsal frosting. (L.A. Co., Calif.) (1 ½–2 in. SV)

PLATE 9

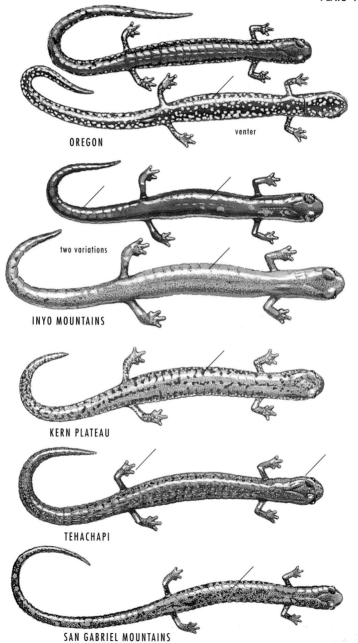

OREGON

venter

INYO MOUNTAINS

two variations

KERN PLATEAU

TEHACHAPI

SAN GABRIEL MOUNTAINS

PLATE 10

SLENDER SALAMANDERS *(Batrachoseps)*

(See also Pls. 9 and 11.)
Slender body; short limbs; 4 toes on front and hind feet.

CHANNEL ISLANDS *B. pacificus*   **P. 187, MAP 24**
Robust and relatively long-legged; brown to pinkish brown above; belly whitish or slate colored (Middle Anacapa Is., Ventura Co., Calif.) (1 ⅔–2 ¾ in. SV)

GARDEN SLENDER SALAMANDER *B. major*   **P. 188, MAP 24**
Garden Slender Salamander *B. m. major*   **P. 188, MAP 24**
Pale above, often with rust tinges, especially on tail. Light below, with small specks or a broken network of blackish melanophores. (L.A. Co., Calif.) (1 ¼–2 ¼ in. SV)
Desert Slender Salamander *B. m. aridus*   **P. 189, MAP 24**
Adults have extensive suffusion of silvery gray over upper surfaces. Broad-headed, long-legged. (Guadalupe Canyon, Riverside Co., Calif.) (1 ¼–2 in. SV)

KERN CANYON *B. simatus*   **P. 185, MAP 24**
Limbs and tail relatively long, but head narrow; head and body somewhat flattened. (Kern Canyon, Kern Co., Calif.) (1 ⅝–2 ⅕ in. SV)

RELICTUAL SLENDER SALAMANDER *B. relictus*   **P. 193, MAP 24**
Relatively small, short-bodied, and dark-colored. Molecular information needed for identification. (1 ⅜–1 ⅞ in. SV)

SANTA LUCIA MOUNTAINS *B. luciae*   **P. 190, MAP 24**
Moderately robust and short-bodied; a broad reddish or brassy dorsal stripe that may be obscure. (Ponderosa Campground, Monterey Co., Calif.) (1 ¼–1 ⅘ in. SV)

GABILAN MOUNTAINS *B. gavilanensis*   **P. 190, MAP 24**
Moderately elongate; above dull gray or with dorsal stripe of ocher or tan that may be gray centrally. (Fort Hunter Liggett, Monterey Co., Calif.) (1 ½–2 ¾ in. SV)

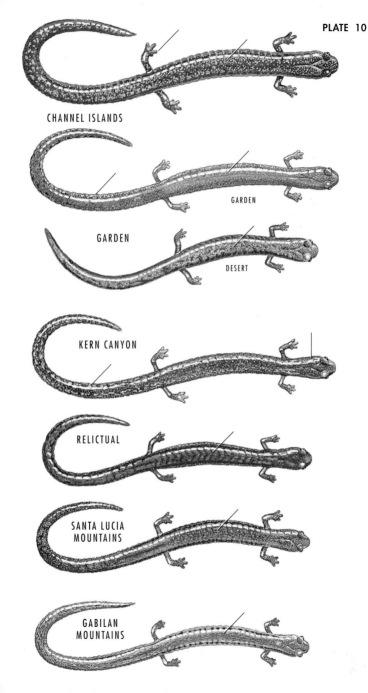

PLATE 10

CHANNEL ISLANDS

GARDEN

GARDEN

DESERT

KERN CANYON

RELICTUAL

SANTA LUCIA
MOUNTAINS

GABILAN
MOUNTAINS

PLATE 11

SLENDER SALAMANDERS (*Batrachoseps*)

(See also Pls. 9 and 10.)
Slender body; short limbs; 4 toes on front and hind feet.

BLACK-BELLIED *B. nigriventris*   **P. 186, MAP 24**
Narrow head, short limbs, long tail. Usually a dorsal stripe. (Kern Co., Calif.) (1 ¼–1 ⅞ in. SV)

CALIFORNIA *B. attenuatus*   **P. 194, MAP 24**
No suitable field characteristics separate this species from the Black-bellied Salamander, but it is biochemically distinct. Narrow head, small limbs. Usually a dorsal stripe. (Contra Costa Co., Calif.) (1 ¼–1 ⅞ in. SV)

GREGARIUS *B. gregarius*   **P. 187, MAP 24**
Small and very slim; short limbs; often streaky coloration above, especially dorsolaterally and on tail. (Three Rivers, Tulare Co.) (1 ⅕–1 ⅘ in. SV)

WEB-TOED SALAMANDERS (*Hydromantes*)

Toes short and webbed; tongue on stalk (Fig. 4, Nos. 7 and 9, p. 26).

LIMESTONE SALAMANDER *H. brunus*   **P. 197, MAP 9**
Adult plain brown above. Young apple green to pale yellow. (Merced Co., Calif.) (2–3 in. SV)

MOUNT LYELL SALAMANDER *H. platycephalus*   **P. 195, MAP 9**
Adult has granite-matching pattern. Young greenish. (Tuolumne Co., Calif.) (1 ¾–2 ¾ in. SV)

SHASTA SALAMANDER *H. shastae*   **P. 196, MAP 9**
Adult gray-green to reddish, mottled; tail yellow to yellow-orange. Young resembles adult. (Shasta Co., Calif.) (1 ¾–2 ½ in. SV)

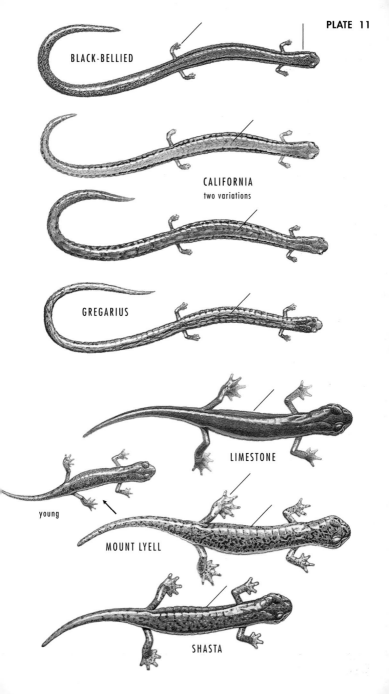

PLATE 11

BLACK-BELLIED

CALIFORNIA
two variations

GREGARIUS

LIMESTONE

young

MOUNT LYELL

SHASTA

PLATE 12

SPADEFOOT TOADS (*Spea* and *Scaphiopus*)

Single black "spade" on hind foot; contracted pupils vertical.

WESTERN SPADEFOOT *Spea hammondii*   **P. 203, MAP 27**
No boss between eyes. (San Joaquin Co., Calif.) (1 ½–2 ½ in. SV)

GREAT BASIN SPADEFOOT *Spea intermontana*   **P. 204, MAP 25**
Boss between eyes tends to be glandular. (Benton Co., Wash.)
(1 ½–2 ½ in. SV)

PLAINS SPADEFOOT *Spea bombifrons*   **P. 205, MAP 26**
Bony boss between eyes. (Phillips Co., Colo.) (1 ¼–2 ½ in. SV)

COUCH'S SPADEFOOT *Scaphiopus couchii*   **P. 202, MAP 28**
No boss; eyes widely separated; sickle-shaped spade (Fig. 9).
(Cochise Co., Ariz.) (2 ¼–3 ⅗ in. SV)

MEXICAN SPADEFOOT *Spea multiplicata*   **P. 206, MAP 27**
No boss; wedge-shaped spade. (Cochise Co., Ariz.) (1 ½–2 ½ in.
SV)

COUCH'S
sickle-shaped

OTHER SPECIES
wedge-shaped

Fig. 9. "Spades" of spadefoot toads

TRUE TOADS (*Bufo*)

(See also Pls. 13 and 14.)
Stocky build; parotoid glands; warts.

SONORAN GREEN TOAD *B. retiformis*   **P. 217, MAP 39**
Large, divergent parotoids. Large, oval, greenish to yellowish
spots above, set off by black network. (Pima Co., Ariz.) (1 ⅛–2 ⅘
in. SV)

GREEN TOAD *B. debilis*   **P. 217, MAP 39**
Resembles Sonoran Green Toad, but usually smaller and with
less complete black network. (Socorro Co., N.M.) (1 ⅛–2 in. SV)

PLATE 12

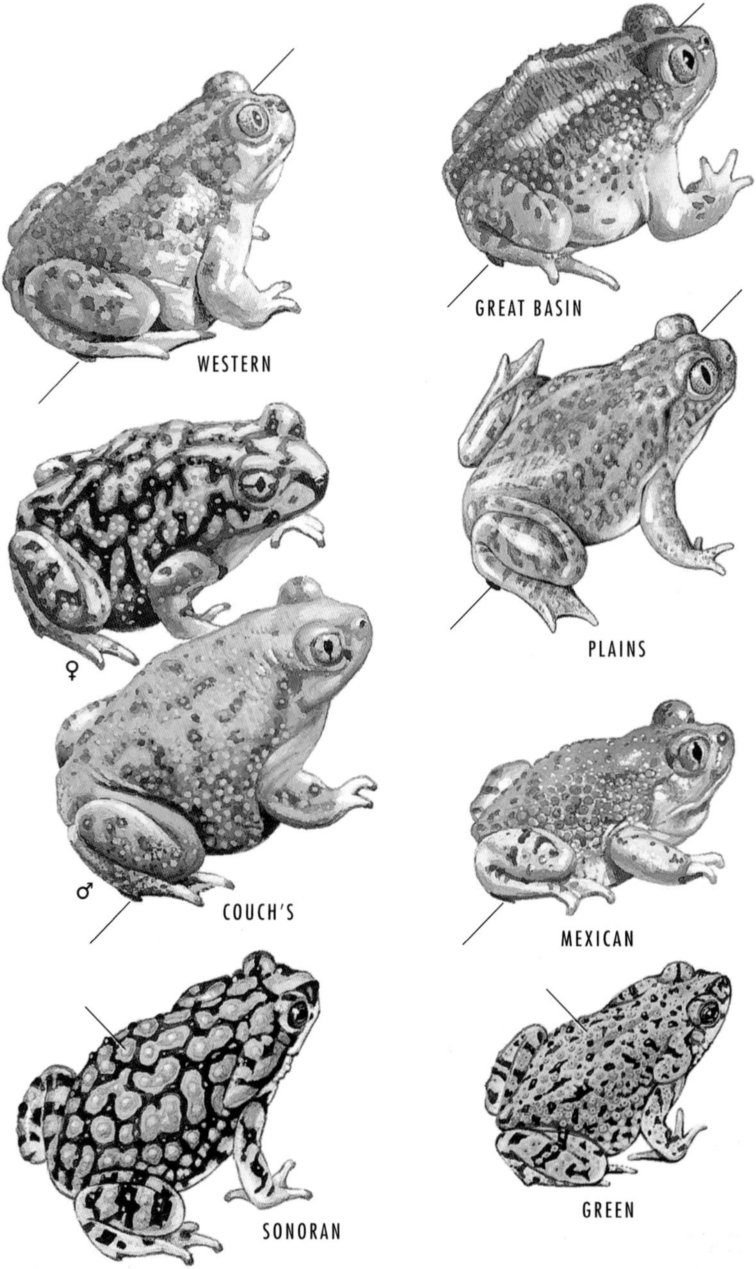

WESTERN

GREAT BASIN

PLAINS

♀

COUCH'S

MEXICAN

SONORAN

GREEN

PLATE 13

TRUE TOADS (*Bufo*)

(See also Pls. 12 and 14.)
Stocky build; parotoid glands; warts.

WESTERN TOAD *B. boreas* P. 208, MAP 32
Whitish dorsal stripe; weak cranial crests. (Contra Costa Co., Calif.) (2–5 in. SV)

AMARGOSA TOAD *B. nelsoni* P. 209, MAP 32
Whitish dorsal stripe, but shorter legs and longer snout than above. (2–3 in. SV)

BLACK TOAD *B. exsul* P. 210, MAP 32
Nearly solid black with whitish flecks and lines. Small size. (1 ¾–3 in. SV)

RED-SPOTTED TOAD *B. punctatus* P. 214, MAP 41
Small round parotoids. (Clarke Co., Nev.) (1 ½–3 in. SV)

TEXAS TOAD *B. speciosus* P. 215, MAP 38
No stripe. Cranial crests weak or absent. (Chaves Co., N.M.) (2–3 ½ in. SV)

GREAT PLAINS TOAD *B. cognatus* P. 215, MAP 37
Blotches on back often in pairs; prominent cranial crests. (Pima Co., Ariz.) (1 ⅘–4 ½ in. SV)

YOSEMITE TOAD *B. canorus* P. 210, MAP 33
Large, flat parotoids. Female with black blotches, absent or reduced in male. Found only in Sierra Nevada of Calif. (1 ¾–2 ¾ in. SV)

PLATE 13

WESTERN

AMARGOSA

BLACK

RED-SPOTTED

TEXAS

♂

♀

GREAT PLAINS

YOSEMITE

PLATE 14

TRUE TOADS *(Bufo)*

(See also Pls. 12 and 13.)
Stocky build; parotoid glands; warts.

WOODHOUSE'S TOAD *B. woodhousii*   **P. 211, MAP 35**
Pale dorsal stripe. Prominent cranial crests. (Benton Co., Wash.)
(1 ¾–5 in. SV)

CANADIAN TOAD *B. hemiophrys*   **P. 216, MAP 36**
Boss on top of head. (Alta., Canada) (1 ½–3 in. SV)

ARROYO TOAD *B. californicus*   **P. 212, MAP 34**
Dorsum flecked and spotted; skin tuberculate. (Ventura Co.,
Calif.) (1 ⅘–3 ⅖ in. SV)

ARIZONA TOAD *B. microscaphus*   **P. 213, MAP 34**
Dark spotting weak or absent. Skin tends to be smoother than the
above. (Yavapai Co., Ariz.)

SONORAN DESERT TOAD *B. alvarius*   **P. 207, MAP 40**
Skin relatively smooth; large warts on hind legs. To 6 in. (Pima
Co., Ariz.) (4–7 ½ in. SV)

PLATE 14

WOODHOUSE'S

CANADIAN

ARROYO

ARIZONA

SONORAN DESERT

PLATE 15

GREAT PLAINS NARROW-MOUTHED TOAD, TREEFROGS, AND TAILED FROG

(First two species life-size, the rest nearly life size.)

GREAT PLAINS NARROW-MOUTHED TOAD   **P. 243, MAP 31**
Gastrophryne olivacea
Fold of skin at back of head; narrow, pointed head. (Santa Cruz Co., Ariz.) (⅘–1 ⅝ in. SV)

NORTHERN CRICKET FROG *Acris crepitans*   **P. 218, MAP 45**
White bar on side of face; dark stripe on rear of thigh. (⅝–1 ½ in. SV).

WESTERN CHORUS FROG *Pseudacris triseriata*   **P. 219, MAP 42**
Back striped or occasionally somewhat spotted; stripe through eye, but no toe pads. (¾–1 ⅗ in. SV)

PACIFIC TREEFROG *Hyla regilla*   **P. 222, MAP 44**
Stripe through eye. Toe pads; webbing moderately developed (Fig. 10). (Contra Costa Co., Calif.) (¾–2 in. SV)

MOUNTAIN TREEFROG *Hyla eximia*   **P. 224, MAP 46**
Resembles Pacific Treefrog, but stripe extends well back along side of body. Webbing poorly developed (Fig 10). (Cochise Co., Ariz.) (¾–2¼ in. SV)

CANYON TREEFROG *Hyla arenicolor*   **P. 221, MAP 47**
No eye stripe. Toe pads prominent; webbing well developed (Fig. 10). Voice a hoarse trill. (Washington Co., Utah) (1¼–2¼ in. SV)

CALIFORNIA TREEFROG *Hyla cadaverina*   **P. 221, MAP 47**
Resembles Canyon Treefrog, but voice a quacking sound. (1–2 in. SV)

NORTHERN CASQUE-HEADED FROG *Pternohyla fodiens*   **P. 220, MAP 43**
Fold of skin at back of head; 1 metatarsal tubercle (see endpapers). (Pima Co., Ariz.) (1½–2½ in. SV)

TAILED FROG *Ascaphus truei*   **P. 199, MAP 29**
Outer hind toe broadest; tail-like copulatory organ in male. (Shoshone Co., Idaho) (1–2 in. SV)

CANYON   PACIFIC   MOUNTAIN

Variation in webbing

Fig. 10. Hind feet of treefrogs

PLATE 15

GREAT PLAINS
NARROW-MOUTHED
TOAD

NORTHERN CRICKET
FROG

WESTERN
CHORUS
FROG

two variations

PACIFIC TREEFROG

MOUNTAIN TREEFROG

CANYON TREEFROG

two
variations

CALIFORNIA TREEFROG

two variations

NORTHERN CASQUE-HEADED FROG

TAILED FROG

PLATE 16

TRUE FROGS (*Rana*)

(See also Pls. 17, 18, and 19.)
Most have dorsolateral folds and long hind limbs (Fig. 5, No. 10, p. 28).

RED-LEGGED FROG *R. aurora*   **P. 225, MAP 50**
Light jaw stripe usually ends in front of shoulder (Fig. 11). Usually with coarse, black, yellow, and/or red mottling in groin; red on underside of hind limbs. Well-developed dorsolateral folds. (Duckwater, Nye Co., Nev.) (1 ¾–5 ¼ in. SV)

CASCADES FROG *R. cascadae*   **P. 230, MAP 53**
Ink-black spots on back, often with light centers. (Grays Harbor Co., Wash.) (1 ¾–3 in. SV)

COLUMBIA SPOTTED FROG *R. luteiventris*   **P. 229, MAP 52**
Light jaw stripe usually reaches shoulder. Adults usually orange or yellow on underside of hind limbs and often on lower belly. Eyes upturned (Fig. 11). (Pend Oreille Co., Wash.) (To around 4 in. SV)

OREGON SPOTTED FROG *R. pretiosa*   **P. 228, MAP 52**
Reddish or salmon on sides and venter. Eyes upturned (Fig. 11). (Klickitat Co., Wash.) (1 ¾–4 in. SV)

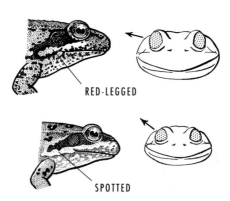

RED-LEGGED

SPOTTED

Fig. 11. Characteristics of frogs

PLATE 16

RED-LEGGED

CASCADES

COLUMBIA SPOTTED

OREGON SPOTTED

PLATE 17

TRUE FROGS *(Rana)*

(See also Pls. 16, 18, and 19.)
Most have dorsolateral folds and long hind limbs. Leopard frogs
have round or oval spots on back.

NORTHERN LEOPARD FROG *R. pipiens*   **P. 234, MAP 56**
Well-defined oval or round dark spots with pale borders. Dorsolateral folds continuous and not angled toward midline of body.
Brown phase (Coconino Co., Ariz.); Green phase (Colo.). (2–4⅜
in. SV)

CHIRICAHUA LEOPARD FROG *R. chiricahuensis*   **P. 236, MAP 61**
Spots on back usually small and numerous. Dorsolateral folds
broken toward rear and often angled toward midline.(New Tank,
Coconino Co., Ariz.) (2–5⅖ in. SV)

PLAINS LEOPARD FROG *R. blairi*   **P. 237, MAP 58**
Spots on back have very narrow pale borders (if any).Usually a
well-defined pale spot in center of eardrum. Dorsolateral folds
usually interrupted toward rear. (Douglas Co., Kans.) (2–4⅜ in.
SV)

LOWLAND LEOPARD FROG *R. yavapaiensis*   **P. 239, MAP 59**
Similar to Chiricahua Leopard Frog, but has dark network on
rear of thighs. (Maricopa Co., Ariz.) (1⅘–3⅖ in. SV)

RIO GRANDE LEOPARD FROG *R. berlandieri*   **P. 240, MAP 57**
Eyes large. Dorsolateral folds interrupted toward rear and angled
toward midline. (Nueces R., Dimmit Co., Tex.) (2¼–4½ in. SV)

RELICT LEOPARD FROG *R. onca*   **P. 238, MAP 61**
Similar to Northern Leopard Frog but smaller and with shorter
legs. (Hand-reared) (1¾–3½ in. SV)

PLATE 17

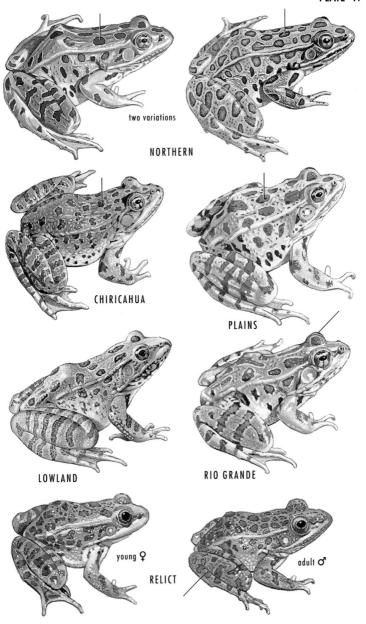

two variations

NORTHERN

CHIRICAHUA

PLAINS

LOWLAND

RIO GRANDE

young ♀

adult ♂

RELICT

PLATE 18

TRUE FROGS (*Rana*)

(See also Pls. 16, 17, and 19.)
Most have dorsolateral folds and long hind limbs (Fig. 5, No. 10, p. 28).

MOUNTAIN YELLOW-LEGGED FROG *R. muscosa*   **P. 233, MAP 54**
Vague dorsolateral folds. Dusky toe tips; yellow or orange on belly and underside of hind legs. (Fresno Co., Calif.) (1 ⅗–3 ½ in. SV)
A. Kings Canyon Nat'l Park, Fresno Co., Calif.
B. El Dorado Co., Calif. Hand-reared from eggs.
C. Near Peregoy Meadow, Yosemite Nat'l Park, Calif.

FOOTHILL YELLOW-LEGGED FROG *R. boylii*   **P. 231, MAP 51**
Pale triangle on snout. Dorsolateral folds vague. Underside of hind limbs yellow. Reared from tadpole. (Sonoma Co., Calif.) (1 ½–3 ⅕ in. SV)

TARAHUMARA FROG *R. tarahumarae*   **P. 234, MAP 55**
No mask or light-colored jaw stripe; often dusky below, including throat. (Pima Co., Ariz.) (2 ½–4 ½ in. SV)

WOOD FROG *R. sylvatica*   **P. 227, MAP 48**
Conspicuous dark mask contrasts with whitish jaw stripe; dorsal stripe may be present or absent. Light phase. (1 ¼–3 ¼ in. SV)

PLATE 18

A

venter

three variations
(A–C)

MOUNTAIN
YELLOW-LEGGED FROG

B

C

FOOTHILL
YELLOW-LEGGED FROG

venter

TARAHUMARA FROG

WOOD FROG

PLATE 19

TRUE FROGS (*Rana*)

(See also Pls. 16, 17, and 18.)
Most have dorsolateral folds and long hind limbs (Fig. 5, No. 10, p. 28).

BULLFROG *R. catesbeiana*   **P. 240, MAP 49**
Fold around conspicuous eardrum; no dorsolateral folds. (3½–8 in. SV)

GREEN FROG *R clamitans*   **P. 242, MAP 51**
Prominent dorsolateral folds that do not reach groin; often with broad light green upper-jaw stripe. (Whatcom Co., Wash.) (2⅛–4⅕ in. SV)

LEPTODACTYLID FROGS

BARKING FROG *Eleutherodactylus augusti*   **P. 201, MAP 30**
Fold of skin at back of head; semitransparent eardrum. Young with broad body band. (Chaves Co., N.M.) (2–3¾ in. SV)

CLAWED FROGS (*Xenopus*)

AFRICAN CLAWED FROG *X. laevis*   **P. 244, MAP 60**
No eyelids or dorsolateral folds; claws on hind toes. Introduced. (San Diego, Calif.) (2–5⅝ in. SV)

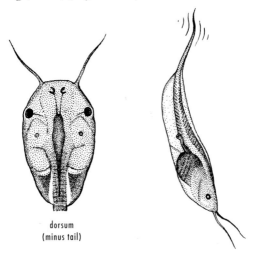

dorsum
(minus tail)

Fig. 12. Tadpole of African Clawed Frog. A good indicator of the presence of this nonnative pest species. (See p. 244.)

PLATE 19

BULLFROG

GREEN FROG

adult

venter

young

BARKING FROG

AFRICAN CLAWED FROG

PLATE 20

TURTLES

YELLOW MUD *Kinosternon flavescens*   **P. 247, MAP 67**
Like Sonora Mud Turtle but head not mottled (Fig. 13) and 9th marginal shield usually higher than wide. (Alfalfa Co., Okla.) (3¼–6⅝ in. SL)

SONORA MUD *Kinosternon sonoriense*   **P. 248, MAP 66**
Nipplelike projections on throat; head mottled (Fig. 13). Ninth marginal shield not higher than wide. (Pima Co., Ariz.) (3⅛–6½ in. SL)

WESTERN POND *Clemmys marmorata*   **P. 249, MAP 64**
Dark flecks and lines radiating from center of shields. (Alameda Co., Calif.) (3½–8½ in. SL)

PAINTED *Chrysemys picta*   **P. 251, MAP 68**
Front edge of shields bordered with yellow, orange or reddish; rear of carapace smooth-edged. (Spokane Co., Wash.) (2½–10 in. SL)

YELLOW

pale throat
dark dorsum

SONORA

mottled

Fig. 13. Head pattern in mud turtles

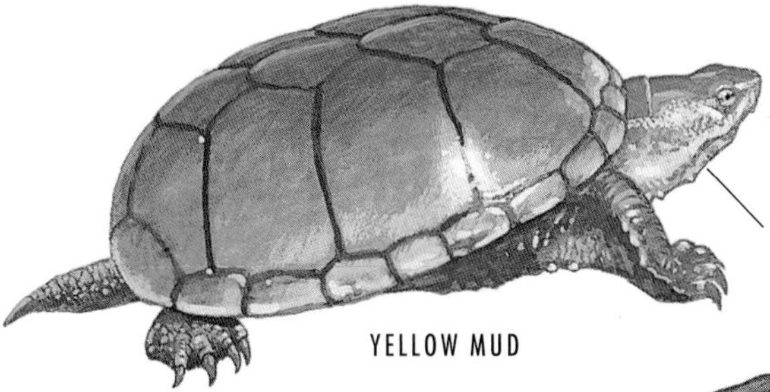

PLATE 20

YELLOW MUD

SONORA MUD

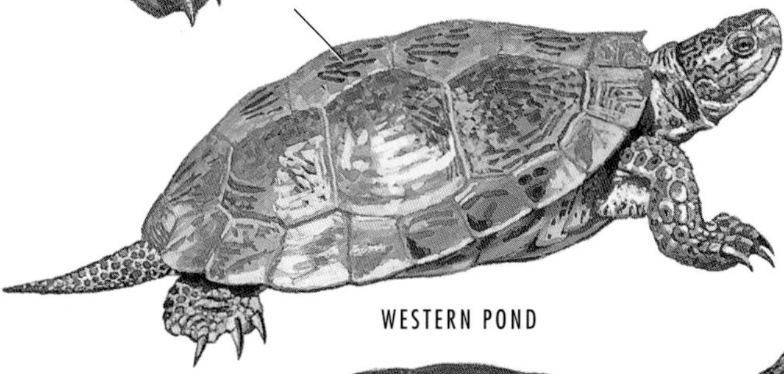

WESTERN POND

PAINTED

PLATE 21

TURTLES

BIG BEND SLIDER *Trachemys gaigeae*   **P. 253, MAP 69**
Large oval black-bordered spot of yellow, orange, or red on each side of head. (Sierra Co., N.M.) (5–11 in. SL)

POND SLIDER *Trachemys scripta*   **P. 252, MAP 69**
Vertical streaking on costal shields. (Alfalfa Co., Okla.) Red-eared subspecies usually has broad stripe of red or yellow on side of head. (3½–14½ in. SL)

RIO GRANDE COOTER *Pseudemys gorzugi*   **P. 254, MAP 70**
Second costal shield usually with yellowish C-shaped marking. Contour map like markings on carapace. (Eddy Co., N.M.) (3⅕–11½ in. SL)

PLATE 21

BIG BEND SLIDER

POND SLIDER

RIO GRANDE COOTER

PLATE 22

TURTLES

WESTERN BOX *Terrapene ornata*   **P. 254, MAP 65**
Shell with light and dark striping; plastron hinged in front. (Cochise Co., Ariz.) (4–5¾ in. SL)

SNAPPING TURTLE *Chelydra serpentina*   **P. 246, MAP 62**
Small narrow plastron. Long tail with sawtoothed crest. (Okla.) (8–18½ in. SL)

SPINY SOFTSHELL *Trionyx spiniferus*   **P. 261, MAP 71**
Flexible, pancakelike shell. Pointed snout; whitish ridge on each side of septum between nostrils. (Garfield Co., Okla.) (5–21 in. SL)

DESERT TORTOISE *Gopherus agassizii*   **P. 255, MAP 63**
High-domed shell with prominent growth lines; elephant-like limbs. (Kern Co., Calif.) (8–15 in. SL)

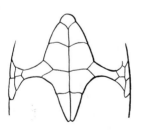

SNAPPING

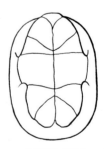

TYPICAL FORM

Fig. 14. Plastrons of turtles

PLATE 22

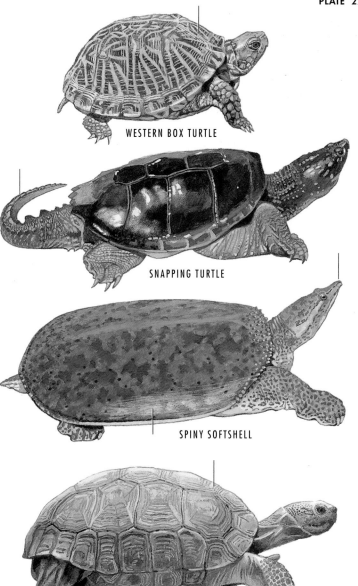

WESTERN BOX TURTLE

SNAPPING TURTLE

SPINY SOFTSHELL

DESERT TORTOISE

PLATE 23

SEA TURTLES

Forelimbs modified as flippers; marine.

HAWKSBILL *Eretmochelys imbricata* **P. 259**
Hawkbill-like mandibles. Strongly overlapping, shinglelike shields. (18–36 in. SL)

OLIVE RIDLEY *Lepidochelys olivacea* **P. 259**
Two pairs of prefrontals. Five–9 costal shields on each side of carapace; bridge with 4 shields. (20–29 in. SL)

GREEN TURTLE *Chelonia mydas* **P. 257**
One pair of prefrontals. Four costal shields on each side of carapace. (30–60 in. SL)

LOGGERHEAD *Caretta caretta* **P. 258**
Shell high in front; 5 or more costal shields on each side of carapace, but bridge with 3 shields. (8–36 in. SL in our area; to 84 in. SL elsewhere)

LEATHERBACK *Dermochelys coriacea* **P. 260**
Carapace with lengthwise toothed ridges. Close-up of head showing serrated upper jaw. (48–96 in. SL)

PLATE 23

HAWKSBILL

OLIVE RIDLEY

GREEN TURTLE

LOGGERHEAD

LEATHERBACK

PLATE 24

GECKOS

Pupils vertical (when contracted); scales mostly granular above.

BAREFOOT *Coleonyx switaki*   **P. 265, MAP 75**
Eyes with lids. No toe pads. Small sooty spines on upper sides.
Dark form (with regenerating tail) from region of dark rocks. (n.
Baja Calif.) (2–3⅓ in. SV)

WESTERN BANDED *Coleonyx variegatus*   **P. 264, MAP 74**
Similar to Barefoot Gecko, but lacks spines on back; usually has
7 or more preanal pores which meet at ventral midline (see rear
endpapers). (Upper individual is from Pisgah Crater area, San
Bernardino Co., and lower one is from San Diego Co., Calif.)
(2–3 in. SV)

LEAF-TOED *Phyllodactylus xanti*   **P. 266, MAP 73**
Immovable eyelids; pair of large leaflike pads at tip of each toe.
(Riverside Co., Calif.) (1⅗–2½ in. SV)

MEDITERRANEAN HOUSE *Hemidactylus turcicus*   **P. 266, MAP 75**
Immovable eyelids; back with tubercles. Toe pads present, but
different in structure from those of Leaf-toed Gecko. Introduced.
(Chandler, Maricopa Co., Ariz.) (1¾–2⅜ in. SV)

PLATE 24

two variations

dark phase

BAREFOOT

two variations

WESTERN BANDED

dark phase

LEAF-TOED

MEDITERRANEAN HOUSE

PLATE 25

DESERT IGUANA, COMMON CHUCKWALLA, AND GILA MONSTER

DESERT IGUANA *Dipsosaurus dorsalis*   **P. 268, MAP 79**
Row of slightly enlarged scales down middle of back. (Kern Co., Calif.) (4–5¾ in. SV)

COMMON CHUCKWALLA *Sauromalus obesus*   **P. 269, MAP 78**
Loose folds of skin on sides of neck and body; no rostral. Tail banded with black and yellow in young. (Darwin Falls, Inyo Co., Calif.) Adults: dark phase, Granite Mts., San Bernardino Co., Calif., and red-backed phase near Oatman, Mohave Co., Ariz. (5–9 in. SV)

GILA MONSTER *Heloderma suspectum*   **P. 338, MAP 125**
Venomous. Beadlike scales and contrasting pattern of orange or yellow and black. (9–14 in. SV)

PLATE 25

DESERT IGUANA

dark phase
(torso deflated)

young

COMMON CHUCKWALLA

red-backed phase
(torso inflated)

GILA MONSTER

PLATE 26

LEOPARD LIZARDS

BLUNT-NOSED *Gambelia sila*   **P. 275, MAP 84**
   Resembles Long-nosed Leopard Lizard, but throat usually spotted rather than streaked and snout blunt. Female shown in breeding color. (Pixley National Wildlife Refuge, Tulare Co., Calif.)
   (3–5 in. SV)

LONG-NOSED *Gambelia wislizenii*   **P. 274, MAP 84**
   Pattern of spots and pale crossbars; throat usually streaked with
   gray; long snout. Female shown in breeding color. (Kern Co.,
   Calif.) Below: Spotted form. (Professor Valley, Grand Co., Utah.)
   (3¼–5¾ in. SV)

COPE'S *Gambelia copeii*   **P. 276, MAP 84**
   Reduced spots anteriorly, especially on upper back and head. (To
   5 in. SV)

PLATE 26

♂

♀

BLUNT-NOSED

♀

two variations

LONG-NOSED

COPE'S

PLATE 27

COLLARED LIZARDS

All have distinctive collar markings. (Only adult males are shown.)

EASTERN *Crotaphytus collaris* **P. 271, MAP 85**
Most have some greenish color. Adult males from w. Colo. and e. Utah may be especially colorful—bright green with yellow head when in light phase (upper illustration—animal from Professor Valley, Grand Co., Utah; lower one from Aravaipa Canyon, Pinal Co., Ariz.). Tail round. (3–4⅗ in. SV)

GREAT BASIN *Crotaphytus bicinctores* **P. 272, MAP 85**
Above brown to grayish brown with numerous small whitish dots and dashes. Crossbars of alternating gray and orange or pink. Tail tends to be flattened side-to-side. (Pisgah Crater, San Bernardino Co., Calif.) (3⅖–4⅖ in. SV)

SONORAN *Crotaphytus nebrius* **P. 274, MAP 85**
Above yellowish to dull tan with numerous round whitish spots. (Estrella Mt. area, Maricopa Co., Ariz.) (To 4⅖ in. SV)

PLATE 27

two variations

EASTERN

GREAT BASIN

SONORAN

PLATE 28

EARLESS AND ZEBRA-TAILED LIZARDS

LESSER EARLESS *Holbrookia maculata*   **P. 278, MAP 80**
Ear openings absent. Underside of tail without markings. (Cochise Co., Ariz.) (1 ⅝–2 ½ in. SV)

GREATER EARLESS *Cophosaurus texanus*   **P. 279, MAP 81**
Ear openings absent. Underside of tail with black bars; belly markings behind midpoint of body. (Brewster Co., Tex.) (1 ⅞–3 ½ in. SV)

ZEBRA-TAILED *Callisaurus draconoides*   **P. 279, MAP 82**
Ear openings present. Underside of tail with black bars; belly marking at midpoint of body. (Kern Co., Calif.) (2 ½–4 in. SV)

PLATE 28

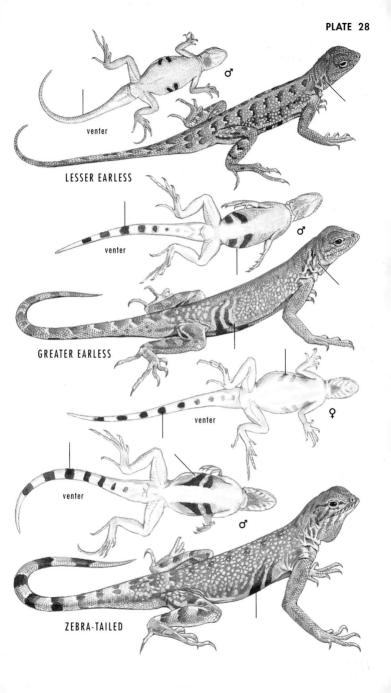

venter

LESSER EARLESS

venter

GREATER EARLESS

venter

venter

ZEBRA-TAILED

PLATE 29

FRINGE-TOED LIZARDS (*Uma*)

Prominent fringe scales on hind toes.

MOJAVE *U. scoparia*   P. 282, MAP 83
Crescents on throat; black spots on sides of belly. (Pisgah area, San Bernardino Co., Calif.) (2 ¾–4 ½ in. SV)

COACHELLA VALLEY *U. inornata*   P. 282, MAP 83
Streaks on throat; belly marking absent or reduced to small black dot(s) on each side. (2 ¾–4 ⅞ in. SV)

COLORADO DESERT *U. notata*   P. 281, MAP 83
Streaks on throat; prominent black spots on sides of belly. (Algodones Dunes, Imperial Co., Calif.) (2 ¾–4 ⅘ in. SV)

PLATE 29

venter
♂

MOJAVE

venter
♀

COACHELLA VALLEY

venter
♂

COLORADO DESERT

PLATE 30

SPINY LIZARDS (*Sceloporus*)

Dorsal scales keeled and pointed; gular fold incomplete (Fig. 6, No. 9, p. 29).

SLEVIN'S BUNCHGRASS LIZARD S. *slevini*   **P. 283, MAP 94**
Rows of scales on sides, parallel rows on back. Males have blue belly patches. (Cochise Co., Ariz.) (1 ¾–2 ¾ in. SV)

SAGEBRUSH LIZARD S. *graciosus*   **P. 293, MAP 92**
Scales relatively small; scales on back of thighs mostly granular; axilla often rust-colored. Males have blue throat and belly patches. (Contra Costa Co., Calif.) (1 ⅞–3 ½ in. SV)

√**WESTERN FENCE LIZARD** S. *occidentalis*   **P. 288, MAP 90**
Scales coarser than in Sagebrush Lizard; scales on back of thighs mostly keeled. Males have blue on throat and sides of belly. (Contra Costa Co., Calif.) (2 ¼–3 ½ in. SV)

STRIPED PLATEAU LIZARD S. *virgatus*   **P. 292, MAP 93**
Striped pattern; no blue patches on belly. Small blue spot on each side of throat in male—absent or reduced in female. Mountains. (1 ¾–2 ⅘ in. SV)

MOUNTAIN SPINY LIZARD S. *jarrovii*   **P. 284, MAP 95**
Black lace-stocking pattern; black collar edged with white. (Cochise Co., Ariz.) (1 ⅘–4 ⅓ in. SV)

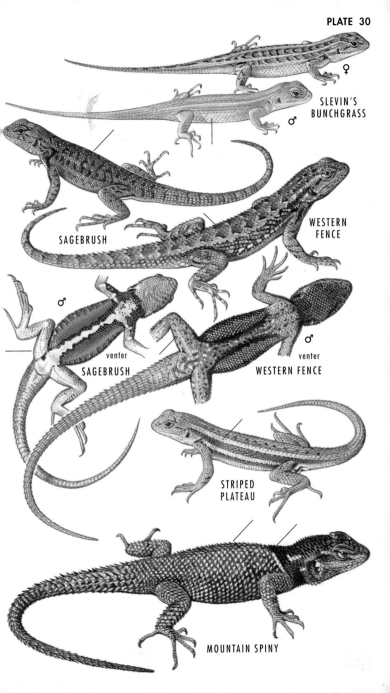

PLATE 30

♀

SLEVIN'S
BUNCHGRASS

♂

SAGEBRUSH

WESTERN
FENCE

♂

venter
SAGEBRUSH

venter
WESTERN FENCE

STRIPED
PLATEAU

MOUNTAIN SPINY

PLATE 31

SPINY LIZARDS (*Sceloporus*)

Dorsal scales keeled and pointed; gular fold incomplete (Fig. 6, No. 9, p. 29).

CREVICE *S. poinsettii* **P. 285, MAP 88**
Conspicuous collar marking and banded tail. A rock-dweller. (N.M.) (3–5²⁄₅ in.SV)

GRANITE *S. orcutti* **P. 287, MAP 89**
Dark coloration; males with blue belly and throat, purple stripe on back in light phase; black wedge on shoulder inconspicuous. (n. Baja Calif., Mex.) (3¼–4⅝ in. SV)

CLARK'S *S. clarkii* **P. 287, MAP 87**
Black wedge on shoulder and black bars on forelimbs. Males with blue belly patches and throat. (Pima Co., Ariz.) (2⅞–5³⁄₅ in. SV)

DESERT *S. magister* **P. 285, MAP 86**
Paler than Granite Spiny Lizard; scales more pointed; conspicuous black wedge on shoulder. Males with blue belly patches and throat; sometimes a purple area on back. (Pima Co., Ariz.) Below, a variant from cape region of Baja Calif. (3¼–5³⁄₅ in. SV)

DESERT SPINY
[Baja California variant]

PLATE 31

CREVICE

GRANITE

CLARK'S

DESERT

PLATE 32

SIDE-BLOTCHED, TREE, AND ROCK LIZARDS

(All adult males.)
Complete gular fold (Fig. 6, No. 10, p. 29); large scales on top of head between eyes (Fig. 6, No. 13).

COMMON SIDE-BLOTCHED *Uta stansburiana*　　　　　**P. 295, MAP 98**
Dark blotch on side near forelimb. (Upper individual, Corral Hollow, San Joaquin Co.; lower one, vicinity of Cottonwood Spring, Joshua Tree Nat'l Park, Riverside Co., Calif.) (1½–2½ in. SV)

BLACK-TAILED BRUSH *Urosaurus nigricaudus*　　　　**P. 297, MAP 99**
Resembles Ornate Tree Lizard. Dorsal scales gradually enlarge toward midline. (San Diego Co., Calif.) (See also Pl. 55) (1½–2 in. SV)

ORNATE TREE *Urosaurus ornatus*　　　　　　　　**P. 296, MAP 96**
Large scales on back interrupted along midline by small scales (Fig. 15). (Cochise Co., Ariz.) (1½–2¼ in. SV)

LONG-TAILED BRUSH *Urosaurus graciosus*　　　　　**P. 295, MAP 97**
Uninterrupted broad band of large scales down middle of back. (Fig. 15); long tail. (Riverside Co., Calif.) (1⅞–2⅗ in. SV)

BANDED ROCK *Petrosaurus mearnsi*　　　　　　**P. 298, MAP 100**
Single black collar; banded tail. A rock-dweller. (Riverside Co., Calif.) (2⅗–4⅕ in. SV)

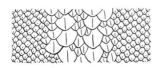

TREE　　　　　　　　　LONG-TAILED BRUSH

Fig. 15. Back scales in Tree and Long-tailed Brush Lizard

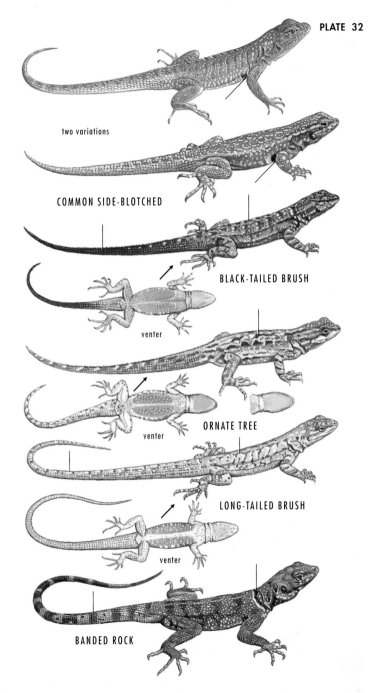

PLATE 32

two variations

COMMON SIDE-BLOTCHED

BLACK-TAILED BRUSH

venter

ORNATE TREE

venter

LONG-TAILED BRUSH

venter

BANDED ROCK

PLATE 33

HORNED LIZARDS (*Phrynosoma*)

(See also Pl. 34.)
Horns at back of head. Body flattened; tail short.

TEXAS *P. cornutum*   **P. 299, MAP 106**
Stripes radiate from eye. (Cochise Co., Ariz.) (2½–5 in. SV)

COAST *P. coronatum*   **P. 300, MAP 102**
Conspicuous lateral fringe scales; prominent pointed scales on throat (Fig. 16). (Fresno Co., Calif.) (2½–4½ in. SV)

REGAL *P. solare*   **P. 305, MAP 105**
Four horns at back of head with bases in contact. (Pima Co., Ariz) (3–4⅝ in. SV)

FLAT-TAILED *P. mcallii*   **P. 304, MAP 107**
Dark middorsal line; flat tail. (Yuma Co., Ariz.) (2½–3⅖ in. SV)

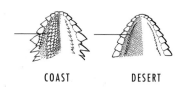

COAST   DESERT

Fig. 16. Throat scales of horned lizards

PLATE 33

TEXAS

COAST

REGAL

FLAT-TAILED

PLATE 34

HORNED LIZARDS (*Phrynosoma*)

(See also Pl. 33.)
Horns at back of head. Body flattened; tail short.

GREATER SHORT-HORNED *P. hernandesi*   **P. 302, MAP 101**
Horns short; deep notch at back of head. (Coconino Co., Ariz.)
(1 ¾–4⅞ in. SV)

PIGMY SHORT-HORNED *P. douglasii*   **P. 303, MAP 101**
Horns mere nubbins at back of head; no deep notch separating
horns at back of head. Small size. (Grasshopper Flat, Siskiyou
Co., Calif.) (1 ¼–2 ½ in. SV)

ROUND-TAILED *P. modestum*   **P. 304, MAP 104**
Slender rounded tail; no fringe scales on side of body. (Cochise
Co., Ariz.) (1 ½–2⅘ in. SV)

DESERT *P. platyrhinos*   **P. 301, MAP 103**
Lateral fringe scales and scales on throat small (Fig. 16). (Upper
individual—Kern Co., Calif.; lower one Deep Springs Valley,
Inyo Co., Calif.) (2⅝–3¾ in. SV)

PLATE 34

GREATER SHORT-HORNED

PIGMY SHORT-HORNED

rock-mimicking pose

ROUND-TAILED

two variations

DESERT

PLATE 35

NIGHT LIZARDS (*Xantusia*)

Lidless eyes; vertical pupils; scales granular above, squarish below.

ISLAND *X. riversiana*   P. 309, MAP 76
Large size. Striped or coarse reticulate pattern. Two rows of supraoculars. Found only on islands off s. Calif. (San Clemente I.) (2 ½–4 ⅕ in. SV)

DESERT *X. vigilis*   P. 307, MAP 76
1 row of well-developed supraoculars. Olive, gray, or dark brown above, speckled with black. (1 ½–2 ¾ in. SV)
Yucca Night Lizard *X. v. vigilis*   P. 308, MAP 76
Small dark body spots; flattened head and body. (San Bernardino Co., Calif.)
Arizona Night Lizard *X. v. arizonae*   P. 308, MAP 76
Coarse dark body spots; postorbital stripe on side of head and neck. (Yavapai Co., Ariz.)

HENSHAW'S *X. henshawi*   P. 306, MAP 77
Large dark spots; head and body flat. A rock-dweller. (San Diego Co., Calif.) (2–2 ¾ in. SV)
Granite Night Lizard *X. h. henshawi*   P. 306, MAP 77
Black speckling on ventral surfaces. Dorsal pattern of large dark spots. Dark to light color change. (San Diego Co., Calif.)
Sandstone Night Lizard *X. h. gracilis*   P. 306, MAP 77
Ventral speckling reduced. Dorsal pattern of small, quite uniform round spots. Little color change. (Truckhaven Rocks, Anza-Borrego Desert State Park, San Diego Co., Calif.)

PLATE 35

two variations

ISLAND

YUCCA

ARIZONA

DESERT

light phase

GRANITE

dark phase

SANDSTONE

HENSHAW'S

PLATE 36

SKINKS (*Eumeces*)

Smooth cycloid scales (Fig. 6, No. 2, p. 29).

GREAT PLAINS *E. obsoletus*   P. 310, MAP 109
Network of heavy spotting of black or dark brown; scale rows on sides diagonal to longitudinal rows on back. Young black, with white spots on labials. (Kans.) (3½–5⅔ in. SV)

GILBERT'S *E. gilberti*   P. 314, MAP 108
Adults plain olive or brown, with varied amounts of dark spotting (Fig. 17). Young with blue or red tail; dark side stripe stops at base of tail. (2½–4½ in. SV)

WESTERN *E. skiltonianus*   P. 312, MAP 110
Adults striped (Fig. 17). Young with blue tail; dark side stripe extends well out on tail. (Young, San Luis Obispo Co., Calif; adult, Contra Costa Co., Calif.) (2⅛–3⅔ in. SV)

MOUNTAIN *E. callicephalus*   P. 312, MAP 112
Pale Y-shaped marking on head. (Santa Cruz Co., Ariz.) (2–2⅘ in. SV)

MANY-LINED *E. multivirgatus*   P. 311, MAP 111
Short limbs; many dark and light lines on body (Fig. 17). Some individuals dark-colored, without striping. (Adams Co., Colo.) (2¼–3 in. SV)

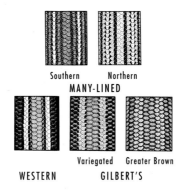

Southern   Northern
MANY-LINED

WESTERN   Variegated   Greater Brown
GILBERT'S

Fig. 17. Dorsal pattern of skinks

PLATE 36

GREAT PLAINS

GILBERT'S

WESTERN

MOUNTAIN

MANY-LINED

adult

young

young

adult

young

adult

PLATE 37

WHIPTAILS (*Cnemidophorus*)

(See also Pls. 38, 39, 40, and 53.)
Scales granular above, large and squarish below.

WESTERN WHIPTAIL *C. tigris*   P. 326, MAP 115
Back spotted with black or dusky; pale stripes usually present.
Postantebrachials not enlarged as in Fig. 18. (2⅜–5 in. SV)

California Whiptail *C. t. mundus*   P. 327, MAP 115
Usually 8 stripes, but lateral ones often have irregular borders
and are sometimes indistinct. (Alameda Co., Calif.)

Marbled Whiptail *C. t. marmoratus*   P. 327, MAP 115
Marbled pattern on back. (Dona Ana Co., N.M.)

DESERT GRASSLAND WHIPTAIL *C. uniparens*   P. 321, MAP 117
Tail greenish olive to bluish green. Dark fields (Fig. 18) unspotted. (Yavapai Co., Ariz.) (2⅘–3⅖ in. SV)

SIX-LINED RACERUNNER *C. sexlineatus*   P. 322, MAP 114
Foreparts greenish in adults. Dark fields unspotted. (2⅛–3⅗ in.
SV)

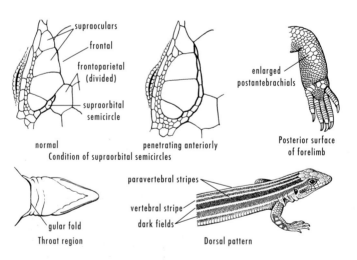

Fig. 18. Characteristics of whiptail lizards

PLATE 37

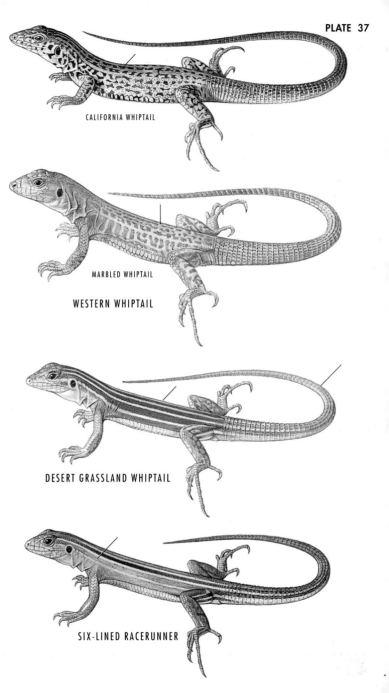

CALIFORNIA WHIPTAIL

MARBLED WHIPTAIL

WESTERN WHIPTAIL

DESERT GRASSLAND WHIPTAIL

SIX-LINED RACERUNNER

PLATE 38

WHIPTAILS (*Cnemidophorus*)

(See also Pls. 37, 39, 40, and 53.)
Scales granular above, large and squarish below.

LITTLE STRIPED *C. inornatus*   **P. 320, MAP 118**
No spots in dark fields; tail bluish, especially toward tip. Bluish white to blue below. (Luna Co., N.M.) (2–3⅖ in. SV)

PLATEAU STRIPED *C. velox*   **P. 321, MAP 120**
Tail light blue. Whitish below, with tinge of bluish green. (Socorro Co., N.M.) (2½–3⅜ in. SV)

NEW MEXICO *C. neomexicanus*   **P. 319, MAP 122**
Wavy middorsal (vertebral) stripe; supraorbital semicircles penetrate far forward (Fig. 18, opp. Pl. 37). Tail greenish or greenish blue toward tip. (Luna Co., N.M.) (2⅜–3⅜ in. SV)

COMMON CHECKERED *C. tesselatus*   **P. 328, MAP 113**
Back with conspicuous black bars and spots; scales in front of gular fold abruptly and conspicuously enlarged. (Sierra Co., N.M.) (2½–4³⁄₁₆ in. SV)

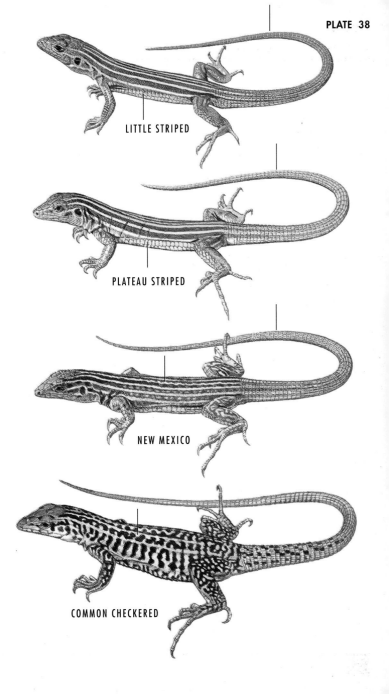

PLATE 38

LITTLE STRIPED

PLATEAU STRIPED

NEW MEXICO

COMMON CHECKERED

PLATE 39

WHIPTAILS (*Cnemidophorus*)

(See also Pls. 37, 38, 40, and 53.)
Scales granular above, large and squarish below.

COMMON SPOTTED *C. gularis*   **P. 325, MAP 121**
Whitish to yellow-brown spots in greenish to dark brown dark fields. Throat salmon-pink, and chest and belly purplish or bluish, often darkened with black in breeding male. (Tarrant Co., Tex.) (2¼–4⅕ in. SV)

CHIHUAHUAN SPOTTED *C. exsanguis*   **P. 323, MAP 116**
Cream to pale yellow spots in dark fields; some individuals have bright yellow spots on rump. Enlarged postantebrachials (Fig. 18, opp. Pl. 37). (Dona Ana Co., N.M.) (2½–4 in. SV)

SONORAN SPOTTED *C. sonorae*   **P. 324, MAP 120**
Pale stripes lack light spots. Usually 3 preanals. (Santa Cruz Co., Ariz.) (2½–3½ in. SV)

GILA SPOTTED *C. flagellicaudus*   **P. 325, MAP 119**
Light spots on back in both dark fields and on pale stripes. Usually 2 preanals. (Catron Co., N.M.) (2½–3¾ in. SV)

PLATE 39

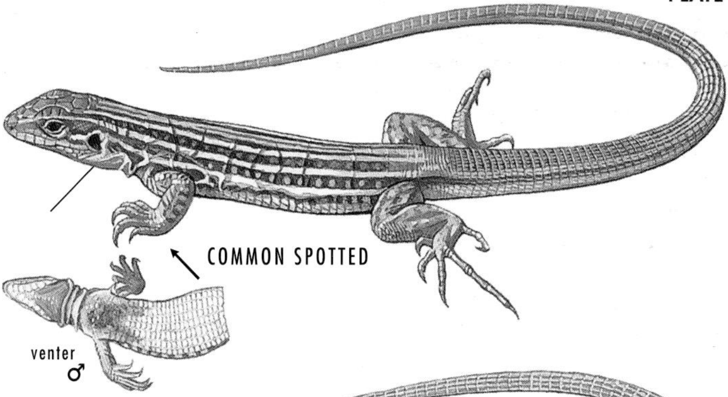

COMMON SPOTTED

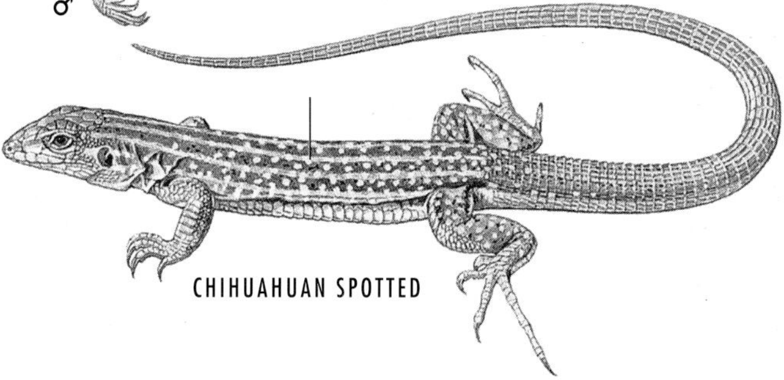

venter ♂

CHIHUAHUAN SPOTTED

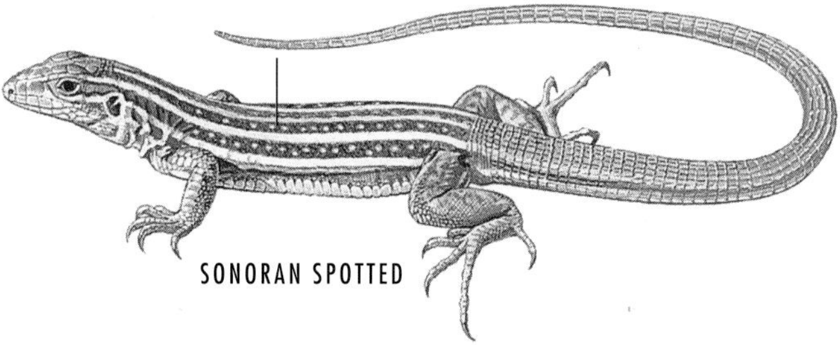

SONORAN SPOTTED

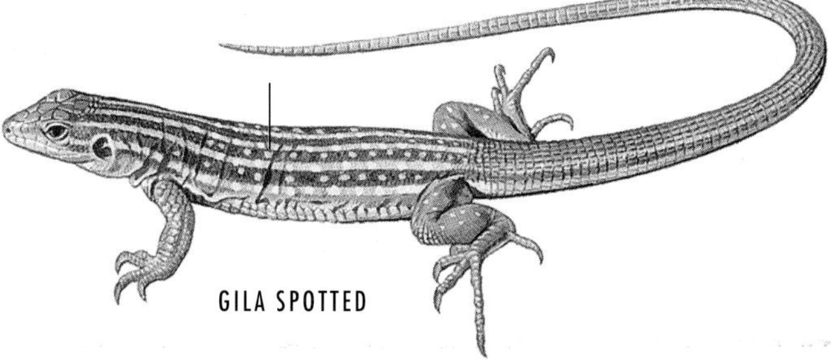

GILA SPOTTED

PLATE 40

WHIPTAILS (*Cnemidophorus*)

(See also Pls. 37, 38, 39, and 53.)
Scales granular above, large and squarish below.

CANYON SPOTTED *C. burti*   **P. 318, MAP 123**
Reddish color on head and neck, sometimes over entire back.
(3½–5½ in. SV)
Red-backed Whiptail *C. b. xanthonotus*   **P. 319, MAP 123**
Reddish color on back stops abruptly on sides. (Pima Co., Ariz.)
Giant Spotted Whiptail *C. b. stictogrammus*   **P. 319, MAP 123**
Adults with large spots; striping faint or absent.

ORANGE-THROATED *C. hyperythrus*   **P. 317, MAP 116**
Frontoparietal single (divided in other species, as shown in Fig.
18, opp. Pl. 37). Throat and sometimes chest and remaining underparts orange in breeding male. (2–2¾ in. SV)

LEGLESS LIZARDS (*Anniella*)

CALIFORNIA *A. pulchra*   **P. 336, MAP 127**
Legless. Eyelids movable. Skin appears polished (unless shed-
ding). Black form in coastal areas. (4⅜–7 in. SV)

PLATE 40

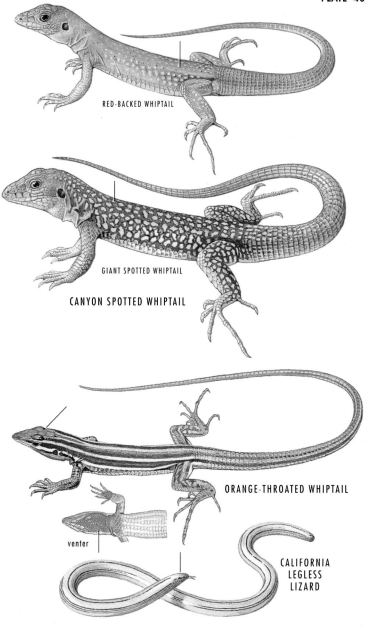

RED-BACKED WHIPTAIL

GIANT SPOTTED WHIPTAIL

CANYON SPOTTED WHIPTAIL

ORANGE-THROATED WHIPTAIL

venter

CALIFORNIA
LEGLESS
LIZARD

PLATE 41

ALLIGATOR LIZARDS (*Elgaria*)

Conspicuous fold on side of body; short limbs.

MADREAN (ARIZONA) *E. kingii*   **P. 334, MAP 124**

Black and white spots on upper jaw; prominent crossbands on body and tail. Young banded. (Ariz.) (3–5⅕ in. SV)

PANAMINT *E. panamintina*   **P. 334, MAP 124**

Paler than Madrean Alligator Lizard; lacks jaw markings. Young with contrasting dark and light crossbands. (Inyo Co., Calif.) (3⅝–6 in. SV)

SOUTHERN *E. multicarinata*   **P. 331, MAP 124**

Dusky lengthwise stripes or dashed lines down middle of scale rows on belly; crossbands usually distinct. Young with broad dorsal stripe. (2⅞–7 in. SV)

NORTHERN *E. coerulea*   **P. 332, MAP 126**

Dusky stripes between scale rows on belly; crossbands indistinct, often irregular. Young striped, as in Southern Alligator Lizard. (2¾–5⅜ in. SV)

PLATE 41

MADREAN

adult

PANAMINT

young

young

SOUTHERN

adult

NORTHERN

PLATE 42

BLIND SNAKES AND BOAS

Smooth scales.

WESTERN BLIND SNAKE *Leptotyphlops humilis*   **P. 340, MAP 128**
Vestigial eyes; body covered with cycloid scales; 1 scale between oculars (Fig. 19). (San Diego Co., Calif.) (7–16 in. TL)

TEXAS BLIND SNAKE *Leptotyphlops dulcis*   **P. 341, MAP 130**
Similar to Western Blind Snake, but usually 3 scales between oculars (Fig. 19). (5–11 ½ in. TL)

RUBBER BOA *Charina bottae*   **P.342, MAP 132**
Vertical pupils; large plates on top of head; plain olive to brown above. (Contra Costa Co., Calif.) Young pinkish, dull orange to tan above (Tuolumne Co., Calif.) (14–33 in. TL)

ROSY BOA *Charina trivirgata*   **P. 343, MAP 131**
Vertical pupils; broad lengthwise stripes or variegated pattern; small scales on top of head. (Above, San Diego Co., Calif.; below, vicinity of La Paz, Baja Calif.) (17–44 in. TL)

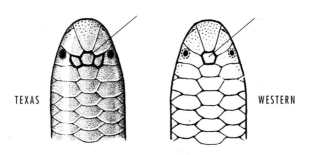

Fig. 19. Head scales of blind snakes

PLATE 42

WESTERN BLIND SNAKE

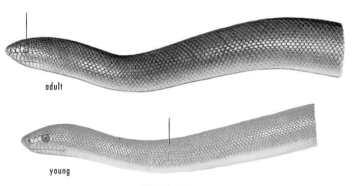

adult

young

RUBBER BOA

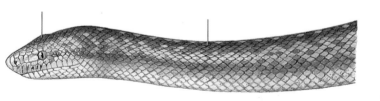

two variations

ROSY BOA

PLATE 43

RACER, COACHWHIP, AND WHIPSNAKES

RACER *Coluber constrictor*　　　　　　　　　　**P. 351, MAP 141**
Plain olive or brown above. Young blotched. (Contra Costa Co., Calif.) (20–75 in. TL)

CALIFORNIA WHIPSNAKE *Masticophis lateralis*　　　**P. 353, MAP 137**
Single cream, yellow, or orange stripe on each side; underside of tail pink. (30–60 in. TL)
　Chaparral Whipsnake *M. l. lateralis*　　　　　**P. 354, MAP 137**
　Stripes cream or yellow, 2 half-scale rows wide. (Ventura Co., Calif.)
　Alameda Whipsnake *M. l. euryxanthus*　　　　**P. 354, MAP 137**
　Stripes and anterior ventral surface orange; stripes 1 and 2 half-scale rows wide. (Contra Costa Co., Calif.)

SONORAN WHIPSNAKE *Masticophis bilineatus*　　　**P. 355, MAP 140**
Two or 3 light-colored stripes on each side; yellow on underside of tail. (Cochise Co., Ariz.) (24–67 in. TL)

STRIPED WHIPSNAKE *Masticophis taeniatus*　　　**P. 354, MAP 139**
Cream or white stripe on side bisected by continuous or dashed black line. (Inyo Co., Calif.) (30–72 in. TL)

COACHWHIP *Masticophis flagellum*　　　　　　**P. 352, MAP 138**
Lacks well-defined lengthwise stripes. (36–102 in. TL)
　Red Racer *M. f. piceus*　　　　　　　　　　**P. 352, MAP 138**
　Reddish or pinkish above often grading to tan toward tail; wide black, dark brown, or pink crossbands on neck, often more or less united and sometimes faint. (e. San Bernardino Co., Calif.)
　San Joaquin Coachwhip *M. f. ruddocki*　　　**P. 353, MAP 138**
　Light yellow, olive brown, or reddish above with a few or no neckbands. (Santa Cruz Co., Calif.)

PLATE 43

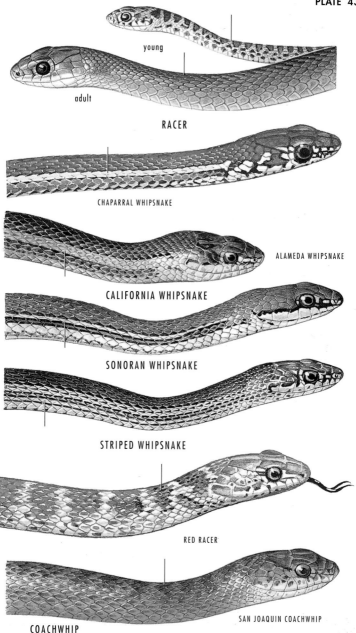

young

adult

RACER

CHAPARRAL WHIPSNAKE

ALAMEDA WHIPSNAKE

CALIFORNIA WHIPSNAKE

SONORAN WHIPSNAKE

STRIPED WHIPSNAKE

RED RACER

COACHWHIP

SAN JOAQUIN COACHWHIP

PLATE 44

CORAL AND LONG-NOSED SNAKES

Smooth scales.

SONORAN CORAL SNAKE *Micruroides euryxanthus*   **P. 405, MAP 181**
Venomous. Red bands bordered by yellow or white (not by black, as in Kingsnakes). (Santa Cruz Co., Ariz.) (11–24½ in. TL)

LONG-NOSED SNAKE *Rhinocheilus lecontei*   **P. 370, MAP 155**
White spots on sides in black bands. (San Joaquin Co., Calif.) (20–60 in. TL)

KINGSNAKES (*Lampropeltis*)

Smooth scales; usually a banded pattern.

SONORAN MOUNTAIN KINGSNAKE *L. pyromelana*   **P. 367, MAP 154**
Red bands bordered by black; white rings usually not widened below. Snout whitish or flecked with white. (Ariz.) (18–42 in. TL)

CALIFORNIA MOUNTAIN KINGSNAKE *L. zonata*   **P. 366, MAP 151**
Red bands and white rings as in Sonoran Mountain Kingsnake. Snout usually black, with or without red markings. (Santa Cruz Co., Calif.) (20–48¼ in. TL)

MILK SNAKE *L. triangulum*   **P. 368, MAP 152**
White bands widen below. (14–54 in. TL)

COMMON KINGSNAKE *L. getula*   **P. 364, MAP 153**
Broad dark and light banding, or flecked with white or cream on a dark background (Fig. 20). (Contra Costa Co., Calif.) (30–85 in. TL)

GRAY-BANDED KINGSNAKE *L. alterna*   **P. 369, MAP 151**
Widely spaced crossbands of black on a gray background are often narrowly to widely split with orange or reddish. (Eddy Co., N.M.) (20–57 in. TL)

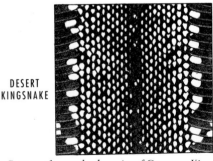

DESERT
KINGSNAKE

Fig. 20. Pattern of spotted subspecies of Common Kingsnake

PLATE 44

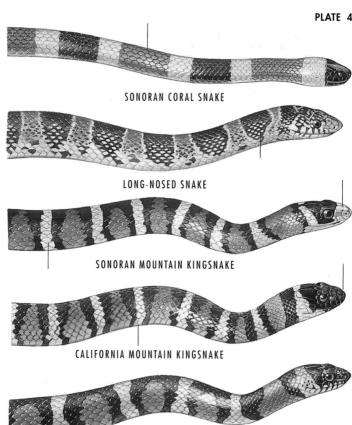

SONORAN CORAL SNAKE

LONG-NOSED SNAKE

SONORAN MOUNTAIN KINGSNAKE

CALIFORNIA MOUNTAIN KINGSNAKE

MILK SNAKE

COMMON KINGSNAKE

GRAY-BANDED KINGSNAKE

PLATE 45

SHOVEL-NOSED AND GROUND SNAKES

Dorsal scales smooth; anal divided.

WESTERN SHOVEL-NOSED SNAKE *Chionactis occipitalis*   **P. 393, MAP 172**
Snout flat or only slightly convex; usually 21 or more black body bands. Red saddles may or may not be present. (10–17 in. TL)

SONORAN SHOVEL-NOSED SNAKE *Chionactis palarostris*   **P. 394, MAP 171**
Snout convex; usually fewer than 21 black body bands. (10–17 in. TL)

VARIABLE SANDSNAKE *Chilomeniscus cinctus*   **P. 395, MAP 173**
Rostral separates internasals. Some individuals (upper illustration) completely lack dark saddles (San Bartolo, Baja Calif.) Bandless form especially common in cape region of Baja Calif. (7–11 in. TL)

WESTERN GROUND SNAKE *Sonora semiannulata*   **P. 391, MAP 170**
Dark blotch at base of scales; back with stripe, dark crossbands, or plain. (8–18 in. TL)

RAT SNAKES (*Elaphe*)

Dorsal scales weakly keeled, in 25 or more rows; anal divided.

CORN SNAKE *E. guttata*   **P. 358, MAP 148**
Spear point between eyes. (Travis Co., Tex.) (18–72 in. TL)

TRANS-PECOS RAT SNAKE *Bogertophis subocularis*   **P. 360, MAP 150**
H-shaped markings on back; large eyes. (Young individual, Brewster Co., Tex.) (34–66 in. TL)

GREEN RAT SNAKE *Senticolis triaspis*   **P. 359, MAP 149**
Plain green or olive above. (Cochise Co., Ariz.) (24–50 in. TL)

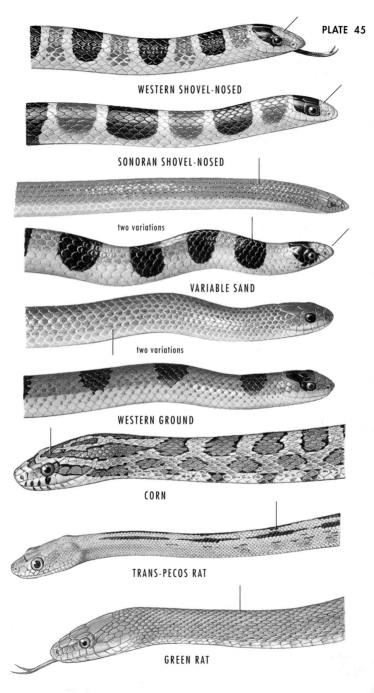

PLATE 45

WESTERN SHOVEL-NOSED

SONORAN SHOVEL-NOSED

two variations

VARIABLE SAND

two variations

WESTERN GROUND

CORN

TRANS-PECOS RAT

GREEN RAT

PLATE 46

GOPHER, GLOSSY, LYRE, NIGHT, AND SMOOTH GREEN SNAKES

GOPHER SNAKE *Pituophis catenifer*   **P. 361, MAP 146**
Usually 4 prefrontals; dorsal scales keeled. (Contra Costa Co., Calif.) (30–110 in. TL)

GLOSSY SNAKE *Arizona elegans*   **P. 362, MAP 147**
Faded coloration; scales smooth and glossy. (San Joaquin Co., Calif.) (26–70 in. TL)

WESTERN LYRE SNAKE *Trimorphodon biscutatus*   **P. 403, MAP 182**
Head broad and triangular, with a lyre-shaped marking (sometimes obscure or absent). Pupils vertical. (18–47¾ in. TL)

NIGHT SNAKE *Hypsiglena torquata*   **P. 403, MAP 180**
Usually has large dark blotches on neck and spotted pattern on back. Pupils vertical. (Contra Costa Co., Cailf.) (12–26 in. TL)

SMOOTH GREEN SNAKE *Opheodrys vernalis*   **P. 350, MAP 142**
Plain green above; dorsal scales smooth. (11–32 in. TL)

RING-NECKED, BLACK-HEADED, AND SHARP-TAILED SNAKES

RING-NECKED SNAKE *Diadophis punctatus*   **P. 345, MAP 133**
Entire belly yellow to orange-red; orange or reddish neck band, occasionally absent. (8–34 in. TL)

CALIFORNIA BLACK-HEADED SNAKE *Tantilla planiceps*   **P. 399, MAP 177**
Blackish head; white neckband; belly orange or reddish along midline. See Fig. 28 (p. 398) for distinguishing our five species of these similar small snakes. (5–15½ in. TL)

SHARP-TAILED SNAKE *Contia tenuis*   **P. 346, MAP 134**
Belly marked with regular black crossbars on pale gray ground color; tail ends in small sharp spine. (Contra Costa Co., Calif.) (12–18 in. TL)

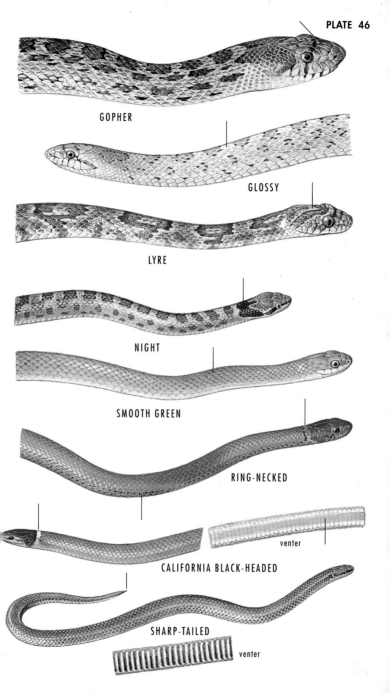

PLATE 46

GOPHER

GLOSSY

LYRE

NIGHT

SMOOTH GREEN

RING-NECKED

CALIFORNIA BLACK-HEADED

venter

SHARP-TAILED

venter

PLATE 47

HOG-NOSED, LEAF-NOSED, PATCH-NOSED, HOOK-NOSED, AND VINE SNAKES

All have modified rostrals.

WESTERN HOG-NOSED SNAKE *Heterodon nasicus* **P. 347, MAP 129**
Rostral keeled above and turned upward. (Cochise Co., Ariz.) (15–36 in. TL)

SADDLED LEAF-NOSED SNAKE *Phyllorhynchus browni* **P. 349, MAP 135**
Rostral and pupils as in Spotted Leaf-nosed Snake, but pattern of large dark brown saddles. (Pima Co., Ariz.) (12–20 in. TL)

SPOTTED LEAF-NOSED SNAKE *Phyllorhynchus decurtatus* **P. 349, MAP 136**
Rostral patchlike, not completely separating internasals; spotted pattern; vertical pupils. (Maricopa Co., Ariz.) (12–20 in. TL)

MOUNTAIN PATCH-NOSED SNAKE *Salvadora grahamiae* **P. 357, MAP 145**
Rostral patchlike, not completely separating internasals; broad, pale dorsal stripe bordered on each side by dark stripe (Fig. 21).(22–47 in. TL)

WESTERN PATCH-NOSED SNAKE *Salvadora hexalepis* **P. 356, MAP 143**
Similar to Mountain Patch-nosed Snake, but dorsal stripe bordered on each side by several dark stripes (Fig. 21). (20–46 in. TL)

CHIHUAHUAN HOOK-NOSED SNAKE *Gyalopion canum* **P. 396, MAP 174**
Rostral upturned but flat or convex above, completely separating internasals; brown crossbands. (Hudspeth Co., Tex.) (7–15 in. TL)

THORNSCRUB HOOK-NOSED SNAKE *Gyalopion quadrangulare* **P. 396, MAP 175**
Rostral as in Chihuahuan Hook-nosed Snake; pattern of black saddles setting off pale squarish areas on back. (Sinaloa, Mex.) (6–12 in. TL)

BROWN VINE SNAKE *Oxybelis aeneus* **P. 402, MAP 144**
Extremely slender, vinelike; snout greatly elongated. (36–60 in. TL)

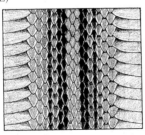
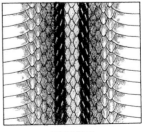

WESTERN MOUNTAIN

Fig. 21. Patterns of patch-nosed snakes

PLATE 47

WESTERN HOG-NOSED

venter

SADDLED LEAF-NOSED

SPOTTED LEAF-NOSED

MOUNTAIN PATCH-NOSED

CHIHUAHUAN HOOK-NOSED

THORNSCRUB HOOK-NOSED

BROWN VINE

PLATE 48

WATER SNAKES (*Nerodia*)

Keeled scales with apical pits (see rear endpapers); anal divided.

PLAIN-BELLIED *N. erythrogaster*   **P. 371, MAP 156**
Belly plain yellow, often tinged with orange and faintly spotted.
(w. Tex.) (30–62 in. TL)

COMMON *N. sipedon*   **P. 372, MAP 157**
Crossbands on front part of body; black or reddish half moons on
belly. (Kans.) (22–53 in. TL)

GARTER SNAKES (*Thamnophis*)

(See also Pls. 49 and 50).
Keeled scales with no apical pits (see rear endpapers); anal single.

NARROW-HEADED *T. rufipunctatus*   **P. 374, MAP 163**
Eyes set high on head. Olive or brown above, with spotted pattern. (Catron Co., N.M.) (18–44 in. TL)

COMMON *T. sirtalis*   **P. 375, MAP 162**
Eyes relatively large. Usually 7 upper labials. Belly often bluish.
(18–55 in. TL)
San Francisco Garter Snake *T. s. tetrataenia*   **P. 377, MAP 162**
Red on side usually forms continuous stripe; belly greenish blue.
(San Mateo Co., Calif.)
California Red-sided Garter Snake *T. s. infernalis*   **P. 377, MAP 162**
Red spots on sides; lateral stripe distinct. (San Francisco Bay
area)
Red-spotted Garter Snake *T. s. concinnus*   **P. 376, MAP 162**
Well-defined broad dorsal stripe; above black with red or orange-
red blotches on sides; top and sides of head usually reddish or or-
ange. (Clark Co.,Wash.)
Puget Sound Garter Snake *T. s. pickeringii*   **P. 376, MAP 162**
Dark-colored including top of head; narrow dorsal stripe.
(Thurston Co., Wash.)
Valley Garter Snake *T. s. fitchi*   **P. 376, MAP 162**
Ground color slaty, black, or brownish; well-defined usually
broad dorsal stripe; top of head dark. (Klickitat Co., Wash.)

PLATE 48

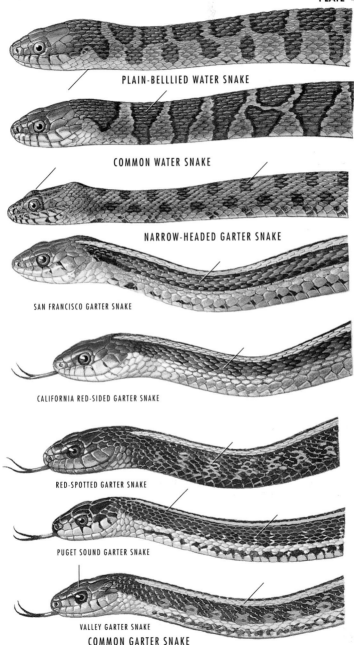

PLAIN-BELLLIED WATER SNAKE

COMMON WATER SNAKE

NARROW-HEADED GARTER SNAKE

SAN FRANCISCO GARTER SNAKE

CALIFORNIA RED-SIDED GARTER SNAKE

RED-SPOTTED GARTER SNAKE

PUGET SOUND GARTER SNAKE

VALLEY GARTER SNAKE

COMMON GARTER SNAKE

PLATE 49

GARTER SNAKES (*Thamnophis*)

(See also Pls. 48 and 50.)
Keeled scales with no apical pits; anal single.

WESTERN TERRESTRIAL *T. elegans*   **P. 378, MAP 166**
Usually 8 upper labials. Belly color varies but seldom bluish; great variation in dorsal pattern (Fig. 26, p. 380). (18–43 in. TL)
Wandering Garter Snake *T. e. vagrans*   **P. 379, MAP 166**
Dark spots on body usually small and well separated but sometimes absent or variously enlarged; venter with black markings or sometimes black except ends of belly scales. (Lincoln Co., Wash.)
Mountain Garter Snake *T. e. elegans*   **P. 379, MAP 166**
Distinct vertebral and lateral stripes separated by uniform dark color (often velvety black) (Douglas Co., Ore.)
Coast Garter Snake *T. e. terrestris*   **P. 379, MAP 166**
Red flecks usually present on belly and sides, including lateral stripe. (Contra Costa Co., Calif.)

AQUATIC *T. atratus*   **P. 384, MAP 167**
Upper labials usually 8, 7th longer than 6th. Internasals elongate and pointed in front. (18–40 in. TL)
Santa Cruz Aquatic Garter Snake *T. a. atratus*   **P. 384, MAP 167**
Throat whitish to lemon yellow. Iris nearly black. (Santa Cruz Co., Calif.)
Oregon Aquatic Garter Snake *T. a. hydrophilus*   **P. 384, MAP 167**
Color between stripes gray or olive gray with 2 alternating rows of dark spots, brown with spots less distinct, or nearly black. Below light-colored and usually unmarked. (Josephine Co., Ore.)

SIERRA *T. couchii*   **P. 381, MAP 167**
Usually 8 upper labials, 6th longer than 7th. Internasals tend to be longer than wide and pointed in front. Blotched above; dorsal stripe indistict or absent. (Tuolumne Co., Calif.) (18–38 in. TL)

GIANT *T. gigas*   **P. 382, MAP 167**
Upper labials 8, 6th shorter than 7th. Above brown or olive with 2 alternating rows of well-separated small dark spots between stripes. Reaches large size. (Natomas Basin, Sacramento Co., Calif.) (37–65 in. TL)

TWO-STRIPED *T. hammondii*   **P. 385, MAP 167**
Middorsal stripe absent or with only a trace on neck. No red spots on sides. (Ventura Co., Calif.) (24–40 in. TL)

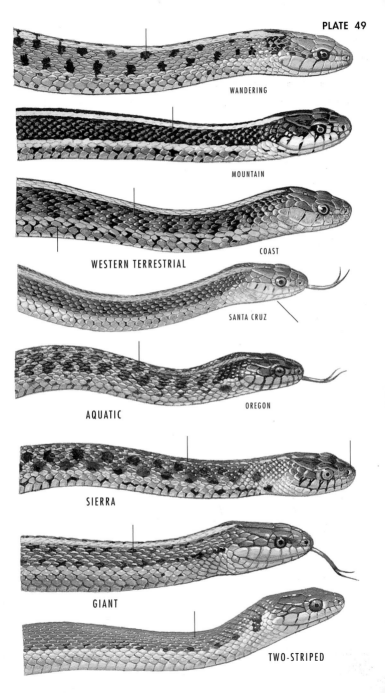

PLATE 49

WANDERING

MOUNTAIN

COAST

WESTERN TERRESTRIAL

SANTA CRUZ

OREGON

AQUATIC

SIERRA

GIANT

TWO-STRIPED

PLATE 50

GARTER SNAKES (*Thamnophis*)

(See also Pls. 48 and 49.)
Keeled scales with no apical pits; anal single.

MEXICAN GARTER SNAKE *T. eques*   P. 388, MAP 160
Paired black blotches on head; side stripe on 3rd and 4th scale rows at front of body. Eight or 9 upper labials. (Mexico) (18–49 in. TL)

BLACK-NECKED GARTER SNAKE *T. cyrtopsis*   P. 387, MAP 161
Paired black blotches on head; side stripe on 2nd and 3rd scale rows. (Pima Co., Ariz.) (16–46 in. TL)

CHECKERED GARTER SNAKE *T. marcianus*   P. 389, MAP 159
Checkered pattern; side stripe usually confined to 3rd scale row. (Santa Cruz Co., Ariz.) (12¾ in.–42¼ in.TL)

PLAINS GARTER SNAKE *T. radix*   P. 390, MAP 165
Side stripe on 3rd and 4th scale rows at front of body. Usually fewer than 8 upper labials. (Boulder Co., Colo.) (14¼–42¼ in. TL)

NORTHWESTERN GARTER SNAKE *T. ordinoides*   P. 386, MAP 169
Belly often flecked or suffused with red; usually 7 upper and 8 or 9 lower labials. (Benton Co., Ore.) (Bottom illustration Thurston Co., Wash.) (13–38 in. TL)

WESTERN RIBBON SNAKE *T. proximus*   P. 390, MAP 164
Pale, unmarked upper labials; usually contrast with dark head color. (18–48½ in. TL)

LINED AND RED-BELLIED SNAKES

LINED SNAKE *Tropidoclonion lineatum*   P. 391, MAP 168
Five or 6 upper labials; usually 2 rows of black spots on belly. (Bernalillo Co., N.M.) (7½–22½ in. TL)

RED-BELLIED SNAKE *Storeria occipitomaculata*   P. 373, MAP 158
Blackish head; dorsal stripe; dorsal scales in 15 rows. In our area, found in Black Hills of ne. Wyo. (Clare Co., Mich.) See p. 373 for color notes on subspecies in our area. (8–16 in. TL)

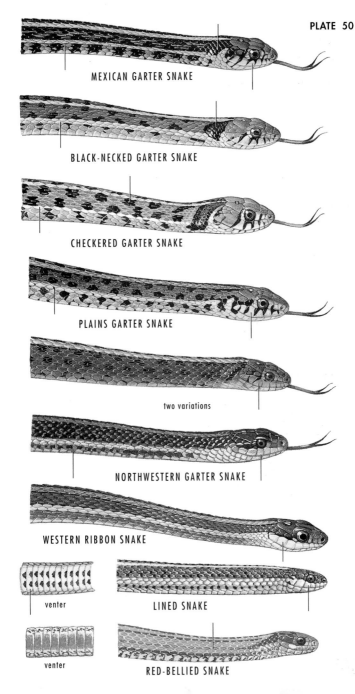

PLATE 50

MEXICAN GARTER SNAKE

BLACK-NECKED GARTER SNAKE

CHECKERED GARTER SNAKE

PLAINS GARTER SNAKE

two variations

NORTHWESTERN GARTER SNAKE

WESTERN RIBBON SNAKE

venter

LINED SNAKE

venter

RED-BELLIED SNAKE

PLATE 51

RATTLESNAKES *(Crotalus)*

Venomous. Horny "button" or rattle on tail; keeled scales.

WESTERN RATTLESNAKE *C. viridis* **P. 414, MAP 189**
Our only rattler with usually more than 2 internasals touching rostral (Fig. 22). (Contra Costa Co., Calif.) Size and shape of dorsal blotches vary. See Fig. 23 (below). (15–65 in. TL)

MOJAVE RATTLESNAKE *C. scutulatus* **P. 416, MAP 194**
Light scales of dorsal pattern usually unmarked; large scales on snout and between supraoculars (Fig. 22). (Santa Cruz Co., Ariz.) (24–51 in. TL)

WESTERN DIAMOND-BACKED RATTLESNAKE *C. atrox* **P. 409, MAP 190**
Markings often indefinite and peppered with small dark spots; conspicuous black-and-white bands on tail. (Pima Co., Ariz.) (30–90 in. TL)

RED DIAMOND RATTLESNAKE *C. ruber* **P. 410, MAP 192**
Often reddish or tan; tail as in Western Diamond-backed. First pair of lower labials usually divided transversely. (Riverside Co., Calif.) (30–65 in. TL)

SPECKLED RATTLESNAKE *C. mitchellii* **P. 412, MAP 193**
Back often with salt-and-pepper speckling. Supraoculars pitted or creased (Panamint subspecies, Fig. 22), or prenasals separated from rostral by small scales (Southwestern subspecies, Fig. 22). (Riverside Co., Calif.) (23–52 in. TL)

SIDEWINDER *C. cerastes* **P. 412, MAP 191**
Supraoculars hornlike. Crawls sideways. (Pima Co., Ariz.) (17–33 in. TL)

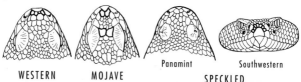

WESTERN   MOJAVE   Panamint   Southwestern

SPECKLED

Fig. 22. Head scales of rattlesnakes

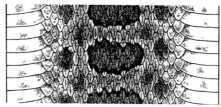

Fig. 23. Pattern of subspecies of Western Rattlesnake

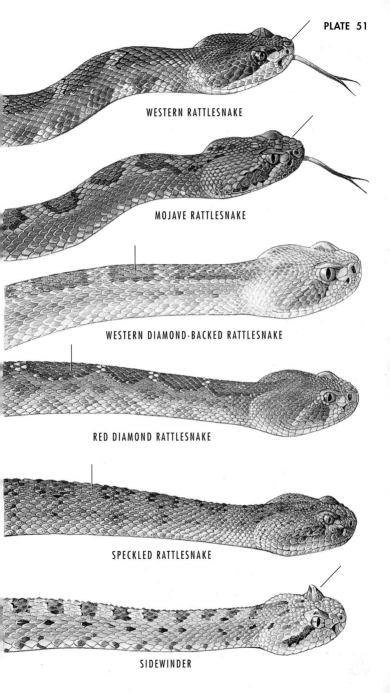

PLATE 51

WESTERN RATTLESNAKE

MOJAVE RATTLESNAKE

WESTERN DIAMOND-BACKED RATTLESNAKE

RED DIAMOND RATTLESNAKE

SPECKLED RATTLESNAKE

SIDEWINDER

PLATE 52

RATTLESNAKES *(Crotalus)*

Venomous. Horny "button" or rattle on tail; keeled scales.

TIGER RATTLESNAKE *C. tigris*   **P. 414, MAP 186**
Pattern of crossbands, often faint. Small head and relatively large rattle. (Pima Co., Ariz.) (18–36 in. TL)

ROCK RATTLESNAKE *C. lepidus*   **P. 411, MAP 187**
Pattern of distinct, widely spaced crossbands. (15–33 in. TL)

BLACK-TAILED RATTLESNAKE *C. molossus*   **P. 413, MAP 185**
Tail, and often snout, black; light-colored scales interrupt dark markings on back. (Cochise Co., Ariz.) (28–54 in. TL)

RIDGE-NOSED RATTLESNAKE *C. willardi*   **P. 418, MAP 188**
Ridge contours snout. Whitish crossbars on back edged with dusky. (15–25½ in. TL)

TWIN-SPOTTED RATTLESNAKE *C. pricei*   **P. 417, MAP 184**
Two rows of brown spots on back. (12–27 in. TL)

MASSASAUGA *Sistrurus catenatus*   **P. 408, MAP 183**
Large plates on top of head; head markings extend onto neck. (Young individual, se. Colo.) (16–40½ in. TL)

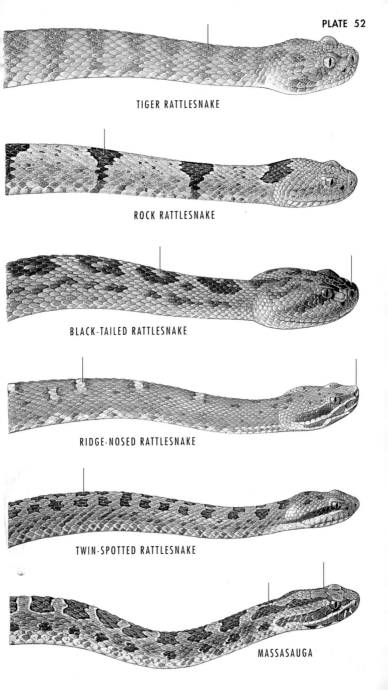

PLATE 52

TIGER RATTLESNAKE

ROCK RATTLESNAKE

BLACK-TAILED RATTLESNAKE

RIDGE-NOSED RATTLESNAKE

TWIN-SPOTTED RATTLESNAKE

MASSASAUGA

PLATE 53

BAJA CALIFORNIA "ENDEMICS"

GRISMER'S COLLARED LIZARD *Crotaphytus grismeri*   **P. 422, MAP 200**
Greenish color within light bar that separates black collars; tail
strongly flattened side-to-side with, especially in males, a bold
dorsal white stripe; males dark brown above with pattern of white
spots without transversely oriented light-colored bars. (Sierra de
los Cucapás, Baja Calif.) (To 3 9/10 in. SV)

CENTRAL PENINSULAR ALLIGATOR LIZARD *Elgaria velazquezi* **P. 427, MAP 198**
Numerous pale crossbands on body and anterior portion of tail;
postorbital dark stripe weak or absent; strongly keeled dorsal
scales. (To around 3 3/5 in. SV)

SAN LUCAN ALLIGATOR LIZARD *Elgaria paucicarinata*   **P. 424, MAP 198**
Lacks numerous pale dorsal crossbands; usually a distinct dark
postocular stripe; weakly keeled dorsal scales. (3–5 in. SV)

BAJA CALIFORNIA WHIPTAIL *Cnemidophorus labialis*   **P. 425, MAP 199**
Dark fields on sides usually reddish brown to tan; 6–8 pale
stripes. Middorsal stripe often forked at front, but single and usually squiggly toward rear. (Colonet) (2–2 1/3 in. SV)

PLATE 53

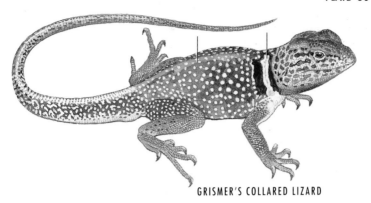

GRISMER'S COLLARED LIZARD

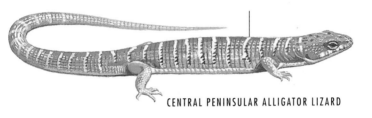

CENTRAL PENINSULAR ALLIGATOR LIZARD

SAN LUCAN ALLIGATOR LIZARD

BAJA CALIFORNIA WHIPTAIL

PLATE 54

BAJA CALIFORNIA "ENDEMICS"

SAN LUCAN ROCK LIZARD *Petrosaurus thalassinus*　　**P. 424, MAP 197**
　　Flattened body; collar marking and crossbands on body. (San Bar-
　　tolo) (3½–7 in. SV)

HUNSAKER'S SPINY LIZARD *Sceloporus hunsakeri*　　**P. 423, MAP 199**
　　Dark coloration. Males with blue to blue-green belly and throat,
　　and purple stripe evident on back in light phase. (San Bartolo)
　　(2½–3½ in. SV)

CAPE SPINY LIZARD *Sceloporus licki*　　**P. 422, MAP 199**
　　Light stripe on upper side fades toward tail. Throat pale with di-
　　agonal gray streaks, the 2 at center usually parallel. (San Bartolo)
　　(2½–3⅛ in. SV)

PLATE 54

SAN LUCAN ROCK LIZARD

♂

♀

HUNSAKER'S SPINY LIZARD

venter

♂

CAPE SPINY LIZARD

venter

PLATE 55

BAJA CALIFORNIA "ENDEMICS"

BAJA CALIFORNIA SPINY-TAILED IGUANA　　　　　　　**P. 421, MAP 196**
Ctenosaura hemilopha
　　　Spiny tail. To over 1 o in. (25.4 cm). (San Bartolo) (8–1 o in. SV)

BLACK-TAILED BRUSH LIZARD *Urosaurus nigricaudus*　　**P. 424, MAP 99**
　　　Sooty to blackish tail; broad area of enlarged keeled scales down
　　　center of back. (San Bartolo) (See also Pl. 32) (1 ½–2 in. SV)

BAJA CALIFORNIA BRUSH LIZARD *Urosaurus lahtelai*　　**P. 423, MAP 198**
　　　Tail not darkened; strip of enlarged keeled scales down center of
　　　back; 1 frontal. (Catavina) (1 ½–2 ⅛ in. SV)

SAN LUCAN GECKO *Phyllodactylus unctus*　　　　　　**P. 420, MAP 195**
　　　Eyes without movable lids. A pair of leaflike scales at tip of each
　　　toe. Granular scales with intermixture of large tubercles. (Buena
　　　Vista) (1 ½–2 ⅛ in. SV)

BAJA CALIFORNIA LEGLESS LIZARD *Anniella geronimensis*　**P. 428, MAP 200**
　　　Snakelike, with glossy, smooth scales, but eyelids movable. Black
　　　and whitish lines on sides. (Colonia Guerrero) (4–6 in. SV)

MOLE LIZARD *Bipes biporus*　　　　　　　　　　**P. 428, MAP 200**
　　　Molelike clawed forelimbs; no hind limbs. (La Paz) (7–9 ½ in. SV)

PLATE 55

BAJA CALIFORNIA
SPINY-TAILED IGUANA

BLACK-TAILED
BRUSH LIZARD

venter

♂

BAJA CALIFORNIA BRUSH LIZARD

SAN LUCAN GECKO

BAJA CALIFORNIA LEGLESS LIZARD

MOLE LIZARD

PLATE 56

BAJA CALIFORNIA "ENDEMICS"

CAPE WHIPSNAKE *Masticophis aurigulus*   **P. 429, MAP 202**
Note series of dark dashes below light side stripe. Scales smooth (30–62 in. TL).

BAJA CALIFORNIA RAT SNAKE *Bogertophis rosaliae*   **P. 429, MAP 202**
Uniformly olive, yellowish, or reddish brown above, often with no dark markings. Scales smooth, in 33 or 34 rows. (34–60 in. TL)

CAPE GARTER SNAKE *Thamnophis validus*   **P. 430, MAP 203**
Eyes large, dark, set high on head. Scales keeled. Some individuals with stripes. (San Jose del Cabo) (23–38 in. TL)

BAJA CALIFORNIA NIGHT SNAKE *Eridiphas slevini*   **P. 430, MAP 204**
Pupils vertical. Parietal scale touches lower preocular. Scales smooth. (Vicinity of Mulege) (12–22½ in. TL)

BAJA CALIFORNIA RATTLESNAKE *Crotalus enyo*   **P. 431, MAP 201**
Blotches on back often with black or dusky spot attached to lower border of blotch on each side, especially from midbody toward rear. No strongly contrasting light and dark rings on tail. (Guerrero Negro) (20–35½ in. TL)

YELLOW-BELLIED SEA SNAKE *Pelamis platurus*   **P. 406**
Completely aquatic (marine). Eyes and nostrils set high on head. (20–45 in. TL)

PLATE 56

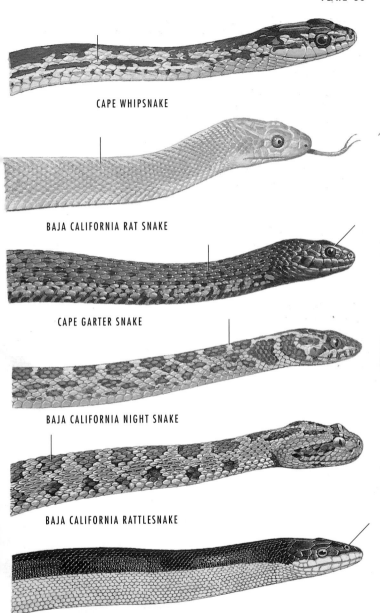

CAPE WHIPSNAKE

BAJA CALIFORNIA RAT SNAKE

CAPE GARTER SNAKE

BAJA CALIFORNIA NIGHT SNAKE

BAJA CALIFORNIA RATTLESNAKE

YELLOW-BELLIED SEA SNAKE

SPECIES
ACCOUNTS

SALAMANDERS

MOLE SALAMANDERS: FAMILY AMBYSTOMATIDAE

Mole salamanders are confined to the New World. They range from se. Alaska and s. Labrador to the U.S. Gulf Coast and southern part of the Mexican Plateau. Some 33 species, 12 in the East, 4 in the West, and the remainder in Mexico, are all here treated as members of the genus *Ambystoma*. Transformed Mole Salamanders are often stocky in body form, have rounded, rather blunt snouts, broad heads, and relatively small protuberant eyes. Costal grooves are usually prominent, and the tail is somewhat flattened from side to side, serving as an important swimming organ. Teeth in the roof of the mouth form a continuous or medially broken transverse row (see Fig. 4, No. 4, p. 26). Males tend to have longer tails than females and a bulbous vent. Many species, as adults, are conspicuously marked with spots, bars, stripes, or reticulations of black on a yellow, orange, whitish, olivaceous, or dusky ground color. Some, however, are less conspicuously patterned and some are nearly plain-colored.

Some species are neotenic (capable of breeding as larvae) and others, such as many Mexican species, including the axolotl (*A. mexicanum*), are paedomorphic — have larval characteristics but do not transform. Transformed adult Mole Salamanders are most likely to be found during overland migrations to and from breeding sites at ponds, lakes, and streams, or when breeding. Migrations often occur at night, during or after rains. Most breed with the onset of spring rains, but in our area in places with mild winter temperatures, breeding often coincides with early winter rains. In colder areas, breeding may start early, soon after ice melts from lakes and ponds, but at high elevations and in the north it may be delayed until summer. The rest of the year, except occasionally during rains, ambystomatid salamanders stay inside rotten logs and animal burrows, or in other moist places underground.

Larvae may be found all year. At high elevations and in the north, where temperatures are low and the growing season short, they may not transform until their second or third season.

To find ambystomatids, go out at night, during or shortly after the first hard rain at the start of the breeding season, and drive slowly or walk through favorable habitats. Carry a lantern or some other light that will illuminate a large area. Seine the water of breeding ponds with a dip net, or look under objects in moist places on land.

TIGER SALAMANDER *Ambystoma tigrinum*   Pl. 1, Map 7

IDENTIFICATION: 3–6 1/2 in. (7.6–16.5 cm). A large stocky salamander with *small protuberant eyes;* a broad, rounded snout; and *tubercles on the underside of front and hind feet* (one on each side of rear undersurface). No parotoid glands. Color varies greatly depending upon age and locality. In our area, markings range from dorsal spots, stripes, reticulations, and large bars of black or dusky on a yellowish, orange-yellow, cream, dull greenish, or grayish ground color. However, coloration may be mostly plain olive or yellowish in north-central part of the range with scant to vague dark markings (see Pl. 1 A-E for examples of some color variation).

Frequents quiet water of ponds, reservoirs, lakes, temporary rain pools, streams, and stock ponds from deserts, arid sagebrush plains, and grassland to mountain meadows and forests. Found in subtropical environments in se. U.S. and Mexico. Adults found under objects near water or crawling at night to and from breeding sites. Migrations generally occur during or shortly after rains, in cold areas soon after ice begins to melt from ponds. Adults spend much time underground, in self-made burrows or the burrows of prairie dogs, ground squirrels, gophers, badgers, and other burrowing animals. Time of breeding varies greatly over species' extensive range, depending on elevation, latitude, and local conditions of temperature and rainfall. Breeds chiefly in spring to fall in the Plains and in parts of the Rocky Mts., spring and summer in the arid Southwest during periods of rainfall, fall through spring, and some populations in summer, during mild winters in N.M., late winter and early spring in Columbian Basin, Wash. In cold areas larvae may overwinter, transforming the following year or in some areas requiring two or three years for transformation. Where cold or other stressful conditions occur on land, some larvae may be neotenic. Neotenics may reach a total length of 7–15 in. (17.8–38.1 cm). Four adult morphs occur—

typical and cannibalistic metamorphosed adults and typical- and cannibalistic-gilled adults. Cannibal morphs have a wide U-shaped mouth, slitlike eyes, enlarged teeth in the roof of the mouth, and include members of their own species in their diet.
SIMILAR SPECIES: (1) Northwestern Salamander (p. 155) has parotoid glands, a glandular ridge on tail, and lacks foot tubercles. (2) Light-spotted Black Salamanders (p. 178) have a more rounded tail and projecting upper-jaw teeth, felt by stroking tip of snout.
RANGE: E. to w. coasts of N. America; s. Canada to Puebla, Mex. Absent from most of Great Basin, most of Pacific Coast, Mojave and Colorado Deserts, Appalachian region, and s. Fla. Old records along Columbia R. in Klickitat Co., Wash. and Wasco Co., Ore. need verification. Near sea level to around 12,000 ft. (3,660 m) in Rocky Mts.
SUBSPECIES: In light of increasing information on variation in this species, I abandon recognition of subspecies at this time.
REMARKS: Molecular studies suggest a species break at approximately the 95th meridian, dividing the present taxon into eastern and western species. Expanding irrigation in arid lands and perhaps the use of larvae as fish bait have resulted in introductions of this species outside its natural range and in mixing of natural populations. Larvae have been found in many reservoirs in Calif., along the Colorado R., in the vicinity of Las Vegas and near Beatty, Nev., and elsewhere in the Southwest. An isolated population in Moon Reservoir, Harney Co., Ore. is presumed to have been introduced. The origin of the population at Grass Lake, Siskiyou Co. in n. Calif. is uncertain (note question mark). The animals' distinctive color pattern, remote location, and ephemeral nature of the aquatic habitat resulting in erratic breeding behavior, thus long delaying its discovery, suggest it may be natural. It is unknown whether the populations at Worden, Klamath Co., Ore. and near Boise and Caldwell in sw. Idaho are natural or introduced. Origin of populations in Ariz. south of Salt and Gila Rs. is uncertain, although those in San Rafael Valley, including sites in the Huachuca (Parker and Scotia Canyons) and Patagonia Mts., may be natural.

CALIFORNIA TIGER SALAMANDER Pl. 1, Map 6
Ambystoma californiense
IDENTIFICATION: 3–5 in. (7.6–12.7 cm). In general body form closely resembles Tiger Salamander but head profile tends to be flatter. Tubercles on underside of feet. Black above, with large pale yellow to white spots and bars often scarce or absent along middle of back. Individuals from south coastal Calif. may have few spots and a prominent, sometimes irregular, cream band on lower sides. Usually 12 costal grooves.

Frequents grassland, oak savanna, and edges of mixed woodland and lower elevation coniferous forest. Usually breeds in tem-

California Tiger Salamander. It may spend 9 or more months in rodent burrows. It emerges during wet weather, Dec. to March, to breed.

porary ponds that form during winter and may dry out in summer, but also breeds in slower parts of streams and in some permanent waters, primarily in grassland and woodland areas. Some pools may be quite alkaline. Spends much time underground in burrows of California ground squirrels, gophers, and other animals. Juveniles also take refuge in such burrows and in soil crevices in summer. Emerges with autumn rains, often by early Nov. Most breeding occurs from Dec. through March. Larvae metamorphose usually in late spring or early summer, but the process may extend to late July. **SIMILAR SPECIES:** (1) Tiger Salamander has a less flattened head. (2) Santa Barbara Tiger Salamanders, which some herpetologists consider a distinct species, seem to have a greater frequency of bars and reticulations rather than small round spots on dorsum and more often a complete yellow or white lateral band on flanks. (3) Light-spotted Black Salamanders have more elongate bodies. **RANGE:** Highly fragmented. Coastal Calif. from vicinity of Santa Rosa, Sonoma Co., south to Lompoc area, Santa Barbara Co.; cen. Great Valley and adjacent foothills—in the Sierra from s. Sacramento Co. to nw. Tulare Co. and in the inner Coast Range to the Temblor Range. Apparently isolated populations at Sacramento and Gray Lodge (1965 report), Wildlife Refuges, respectively, in Glenn and Butte Cos., and at Dunnigan, Yolo Co. Whether they are viable is unknown.

REMARKS: Introduced Tiger Salamanders (*Ambystoma tigrinum*) have been found within the range of the California Tiger Salamander. Introduction with extensive hybridization has occurred in some areas such as Monterey and San Benito Cos., where virtually all known populations are now hybrids and the pure native species appears absent (Map 6—area circled with blue line). It is now illegal to sell Tiger Salamanders as fish bait in Calif.

The California Tiger Salamander has sustained extensive habitat losses and fragmentation of populations as agriculture, housing, and other developments have destroyed vernal pools (particularly long-lasting ones) where they breed most effectively. Introduction of fish (including mosquito fish) and bullfrogs into breeding sites, road kills, declines of burrowing rodents, especially destruction of ground squirrels whose burrows provide moist underground retreats, and drainage of wetlands are among other factors. Extensive control of California ground squirrels and pocket gophers is considered a serious threat to this species.

This species is estimated to have disappeared from about 55 percent of its historic range. The widespread spotty nature of losses has made it impossible to show, in blue color, on a small map, the seriousness of decline. Populations in w. Santa Barbara Co., isolated from the rest (see Map 5) and with a severely limited and fragmented distribution, may prove to be members of a separate species. They are currently seriously threatened by expanding vineyard and row crop agriculture.

NORTHWESTERN SALAMANDER
Ambystoma gracile

Pl. 1, Map 2

IDENTIFICATION: 3–5 ¹/₅ in. (7.6–13.2 cm). Brown, gray, or black above with a broad head and relatively small eyes, *parotoid* glands, and a *glandular thickening along upper border of the tail*. Glandular areas are pitted with openings of poison glands and the skin there is rougher than elsewhere. No tubercles on underside of feet. In northern part of range, dorsum may be flecked with cream or yellow.

Inhabits open grassland, woodland, or forest by day under rocks, boards, and logs near water. Look under driftwood on streambanks after storms, when water is receding. Spawns in ponds, lakes, and slower parts of streams Jan.–Aug., later in the

Northwestern Salamander larva. Found in ponds, lakes, and quieter parts of streams. Roughened skin on either side of the base of the dorsal fin marks the location of batteries of the poison glands that are distinctive for this species.

season in the north and at high elevations. In the Willamette Valley and Puget Sound lowlands breeding occurs in Feb. and March. In cold areas larvae may overwinter and some may be neotenic. When molested, adults close their eyes, assume a butting pose, elevate the tail, and secrete sticky white poison from glands on the head, back, and tail. This secretion may cause skin irritation in some people. **SIMILAR SPECIES:** See Tiger Salamander (p. 152). **RANGE:** Humid coast from Chichagof (at Pelican) and May (Mary) Islands se. Alaska, chiefly west of crest of Cascade Mts. to mouth of Gualala R., Calif. Sea level to around 10,200 ft. (3,110 m).

REMARKS: Neotenics are quite common in permanently ponded wetlands in Puget Sound lowlands of w. Wash. and elsewhere, increasing in frequency with elevation.

LONG-TOED SALAMANDER   Pl. 2, Map 3
Ambystoma macrodactylum

IDENTIFICATION: 1 3/5–3 1/2 in. (4.1–8.9 cm). Dusky or black above usually with a *dorsal stripe* of tan, yellow, or olive green. Stripe often with irregular borders and in some subspecies more or less broken into a series of spots. Usually a sprinkling of fine white or pale bluish flecks on the sides. Belly dark brown or sooty. Foot tubercles as in Tiger Salamander (p. 152), but sometimes weakly developed.

Frequents a great variety of habitats, from semiarid sagebrush and cheatgrass plains east of Cascade Mts. to alpine meadows and barren rocky shores of high mountain lakes. Found in piles of rotten wood, under bark, rotting logs, rocks, and other objects near quiet water of ponds, lakes, or streams. Ephemeral waters may be frequented. When in water, adults seem to prefer shallows near shore.

Time of breeding varies with elevation and latitude: in general, at lower elevations and to the south it occurs in fall, winter, and early spring, and at higher elevations and to the north in spring and early summer, the salamanders sometimes entering ponds not yet completely free of ice. In some lowland areas, except for cold spells, adults may remain active all winter. In cold areas larvae may overwinter, transforming the following summer or fall, or may require even longer periods for transformation. **SIMILAR SPECIES:** Striped woodland salamanders have nasolabial grooves (Fig. 4, No. 1, p. 26), a different tooth pattern, and no foot tubercles. **RANGE:** Se. Alaska (Sokolof Is. in the Vank Is. group, Alexander Archipelago), and Taku and Stikine (Telegraph Creek area) watersheds of se. Alaska and nw. B.C. south to Garner Meadows and Spicer Reservoir in Sierra Nevada of e. Tuolumne Co., Calif., east to Rocky Mts., south to cen. Idaho and w. Mont. Isolated populations near Aptos, Santa Cruz Co., Calif. Near sea level to about 10,000 ft. (3,000 m) in Calif. Sierra Nevada.

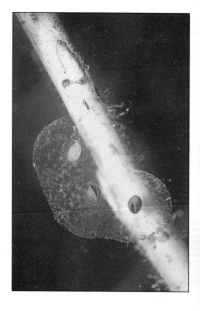

Long-toed Salamander eggs. In many amphibians, the gelatinous capsules surrounding the eggs are transparent, allowing direct viewing of embryonic development. Thurston Co., Wash.

SUBSPECIES: WESTERN LONG-TOED SALAMANDER, *A. m. macrodactylum* (Pl. 2). Gray above, with a greenish to yellowish dorsal stripe that has indefinite edges; stripe diffuse on head. Sides heavily sprinkled with small white flecks, sometimes appearing whitewashed. CENTRAL LONG-TOED SALAMANDER, *A. m. columbianum*. Dorsal stripe bright yellow to tan, usually unbroken on body, even-edged or irregularly indented, its width exceeding distance between nostrils. Stripe broken into spots on head. Cannibal morph larvae have been reported. SOUTHERN LONG-TOED SALAMANDER, *A. m. sigillatum* (Pl. 2). Dorsal stripe bright yellow, with irregular borders and often broken into smooth-edged spots; its greatest width less than distance between nostrils. Small, distinct yellow spots on head. SANTA CRUZ LONG-TOED SALAMANDER, *A. m. croceum* (Pl. 2). Similar to Southern Long-toed Salamander, but stripe broken up into many orange-yellow to orange spots and bars on a black ground color. Valencia Lagoon near Aptos, Ellicott Pond area near Watsonville (a state wildlife reserve), Santa Cruz Co., and north of Elkhorn Slough, Monterey Co., Calif. EASTERN LONG-TOED SALAMANDER, *A. m. krausei* (Pl. 2). Dorsal stripe narrow, its edges nearly parallel; stripe yellow and unbroken, continuing onto snout and widest behind eyes. A large patch of stripe color on each eyelid.

REMARKS: The introduction of fish to fish-free lakes in the Calif. Sierra Nevada has adversely affected this species.

GIANT SALAMANDERS: FAMILY DICAMPTODONTIDAE

In the previous edition of this book, two species were recognized, the Pacific Giant Salamander (*Dicamptodon ensatus*) and Cope's Salamander (*D. copei*), a neotenic larval form that rarely transforms. Biochemical studies now recommend that three species within the former taxon (*D. ensatus*) be recognized.

Large robust salamanders, the adult terrestrial forms of which can deliver a painful bite. Handle with care. Neoteny is common in many local populations and predominates in Cope's Salamander. Four species, confined to the Pacific Northwest.

CALIFORNIA GIANT SALAMANDER Pl. 3, Map 1
Dicamptodon ensatus

IDENTIFICATION: 2 1/2–6 4/5 in. (6.3–17.3 cm). A large heavy-bodied salamander with massive head, stout limbs, and a *usually coarse-grained marbled coloration. Color above tan to light reddish brown* with usually a well-defined irregular network and spots of coppery tan to dark brown. Below whitish (southern counties) or dull yellowish usually unmarked except for dark flecks and blotches on throat and underside of legs. Marbling on chin notable in southern part of range. Skin smooth. No tubercles on undersides of feet. Tail flattened from side to side, especially toward tip.

Frequents damp forests in or near clear, cold streams and seepages. Found under logs, bark, rocks, and other objects near streams, or crawling exposed in damp woods, even in daytime. Occasionally climbs; recorded in trees and shrubs to a height of 8 ft. (2.4 m). In spring, adults may be found near springs in headwaters of streams, where they lay their eggs. Breeding occurs in both spring and fall. Larvae frequent clear cold streams, creeks, and lakes, and can be found by carefully turning over stones in shallow water or searching the bottom and plant debris, especially along downstream borders of shallow pools. Larvae hatch in winter, but may not transform until second or third summer. **VOICE:** May emit a startling, low-pitched rattling sound when molested. **SIMILAR SPECIES:** (1) Mole salamanders (*Ambystoma* species, p. 151) lack distinctive marbled pattern of Pacific Giant Salamanders, have smaller eyes, and tubercles on undersides of feet. See species accounts of (2) Pacific, (3) Idaho, and (4) Cope's Giant Salamanders. **RANGE:** Coast Range from just north of s. boundary of Mendocino Co. (vicinity of Point Arena) to s. Santa Cruz Co.; inland north of San Francisco Bay to vicinity of Middletown, Lake Co. and w. Glenn Co. Absent from e. Bay area. Sight record for Little Sur R., Monterey Co. requires confirmation. Near sea level to around 3,000 ft. (915 m).

REMARKS: Species hybridizes with its close relative the Pacific Giant Salamander in a narrow zone along the coast, approx. 6 mi. (10 km) north of Gualala, Mendocino Co. What happens inland is not yet determined.

PACIFIC GIANT SALAMANDER
Dicamptodon tenebrosus

Pl. 3, Map 1

IDENTIFICATION: Similar to California Giant Salamander but head perhaps averages smaller, limbs somewhat shorter, and fewer teeth in upper jaw. *Ground color, both dorsally and ventrally, is usually darker. Marbling tends to be somewhat finer-grained,* and dark marbling and flecking usually does not extend onto underside of throat and limbs. Some individuals may be nearly patternless. Coloration highly variable.

Occurs especially in and about permanent and semipermanent streams in forested areas, but also associated with rivers, mountain lakes, and ponds. Look for terrestrial individuals under rocks, logs, and bark in moist coniferous forests. Most females appear to lay their eggs during early to mid-May and then guard them. **SIMILAR SPECIES:** (1) California Giant Salamander has a larger head, longer limbs, and more upper-jaw teeth. (2) Idaho Giant Salamander is generally darker and perhaps has a flatter head. (3) See also Cope's Salamander. **RANGE:** Extreme sw. B.C. from Chilliwack Valley through w. Wash. (except Olympic Peninsula), w. Ore. and nw. Calif. to coastal Mendocino Co. (vicinity of Gualala R.). East of Cascade crest at Sears Creek nw. Wenatchee Lake, Chelan Co., and n. side Kachess Lake, Kittitas Co., Wash. and at Oak Spring near Maupin, Wasco Co., Ore. Coastally to Willapa Hills area (to north of Willapa R.), and Long I., Wash. In Calif., ranges inland to vicinity of Shasta Reservoir, Shasta Co., and McCloud, Siskiyou Co. Overlaps range of Cope's Giant Salamander in sw. Wash. and nw. Ore. Near sea level to 7,086 ft. (2,160 m) but mostly below 3,149 ft. (960 m).
REMARKS: Species is threatened by logging where streamside banks are not protected to retain shade, fallen timber, and natural rock accumulations in streams. Stream siltation due to logging markedly reduces population densities.

IDAHO GIANT SALAMANDER
Dicamptodon aterrimus

Pl. 3, Map 1

IDENTIFICATION: *Darkest of Giant Salamanders with fine-grained dark dorsal marbling and/or spotting.* May have a dark brown middorsal region lacking a pattern. Some may have a greatly reduced or no dorsal pattern. Head flattened, especially toward front.

Inhabits stream and streamside habitats in moist forests. A terrestrial female found near the base of a waterfall in Idaho in Sept. laid 185 unpigmented eggs in an aquarium. The eggs were attached singly by short pedicels. **SIMILAR SPECIES:** See Pacific Giant Salamander. **RANGE:** Rocky Mts. of extreme w. Montana and Idaho, where it is found in headwater streams from Salmon R. to the Coeur d'Alene drainage.

COPE'S GIANT SALAMANDER
Dicamptodon copei

IDENTIFICATION: 2 1/2–4 3/4 in. (6.3–12 cm). A "larval" species that rarely transforms. Larval form resembles larva of Pacific Giant Salamander (p. 159). Since ranges of both species (PG and CG) broadly overlap in sw. Wash. and nw. Ore., the following comparisons of gilled adults will aid identification. *Head shape* (from above)—PG wedge-shaped, CG rectangular; *limbs*—PG longer, CG shorter; *tail fin*—PG high, CG low; *ventral color*—PG light, CG darker (at sizes greater than 2 in. [5.1 cm]); *gills*—PG bushy, CG filamentous; *light-colored dorsal markings*—PG longitudinal streaking, CG granular clumped; *body*—PG heavier build, CG slender; *tail*—PG more mottled with dark tip, CG less so; *eye stripe*—PG more conspicuous, CG less so; *toe tips*—PG more keratinized, CG less keratinized; *size*—PG smallest female gilled adult larger than CG largest gilled female adult. Some measurements are: 4 3/4 in. (12 cm) SV vs. 2 4/5–4 1/5 in. (7.1–10.6 cm SV). A transformed individual found near Spirit Lake, Wash. before the eruption of Mt. St. Helens was sooty with no pattern above and dark gray below, with faint mottling on lower sides. Others displayed marbled pattern (see Pl. 3). The scarce transformed stage has also been found in the Olympic Peninsula, Willapa Hills area, and Cascade Mts., Wash.

Found in cold rocky streams, seepages, and sometimes in mountain lakes and ponds, usually in moist coniferous forests. Coexists with larval Pacific Giant Salamanders over an extensive area (see Map 1) and long considered a variant of that species. Questioned area lies between the Chehalis and Willapa Rs. where sympatry is presumed. Cope's Giant Salamander apparently lays

Cope's Giant Salamander. This species rarely transforms to the terrestrial stage. It coexists with the Pacific Giant Salamander in southwestern Washington and northwestern Oregon. Skamania Co., Wash.

its eggs throughout spring, summer, and fall; females guard their eggs. **SIMILAR SPECIES:** Toes of adpressed limbs of other Giant Salamander larvae usually meet or overlap as many as 4 costal folds. **RANGE:** Olympic Peninsula, Wash., south through the s. Cascades and Willapa Hills to streams that drain into the Columbia R. gorge in nw. Ore. Near sea level to around 4,500 ft. (1,370 m).

TORRENT OR SEEP SALAMANDERS: FAMILY RHYACOTRITONIDAE

Previous editions of this Guide treated these small salamanders as a single species in the family Dicamptodontidae. Their small size (1 2/3–2 1/2 in. [4.2–6.3 cm]) and large eyes are distinctive among our aquatic and semiaquatic salamanders. Diameter of eye opening roughly equals the distance between the front corner of the eye and the tip of the snout. In other salamanders except the Slender Salamanders (*Batrachoseps* species, p. 182), eye diameter is only 1/2–1/3 this distance. Head small, body long, limbs and tail short. Plain brown above or olive mottled with dusky. Orange or yellow below. 14–15 costal grooves. Males have prominent squarish vent lobes (see Pl. 2).

Torrent Salamanders inhabit cold streams, springs, and seepages in the coniferous belt of the humid coast and portions of the Cascade Mts. Old-growth forests appear to be optimal habitat. When on land, usually found under stones within the splash zone of streams and in moss-covered talus where water trickles among the rocks. Torrents may be entered chiefly for refuge. Boulder clusters in steep-gradient streams appear to be especially attractive habitat. Streams frequented are cold, often around 6 to 10° C, and usually well shaded, the banks often grown to moss and ferns. Adults have greatly reduced lungs, probably related to buoyancy problems and to the cold oxygen-rich waters occupied. The mating season appears to be prolonged in all four species — occurring almost any time of year. However, most breeding seems to occur in spring and early summer with a lesser peak in fall and winter, depending on locality. Larvae are of stream type, have very short gills and adult proportions, and live in clear shallow water, in the muck of seepages, and in accumulations of dead leaves in creeks. Growth to maturity is slow in these cold-water animals. Three to five years may be required for metamorphosis.

Four species, confined to Pacific Northwest. Closely similar in morphology, their recognition has been based primarily on molecular information.

REMARKS: Clear-cutting of old-growth forests near drainages is severely damaging to Torrent Salamanders.

Olympic Torrent Salamander larva. Adapted to live in cold flowing water. Lungs are greatly reduced thus decreasing buoyancy and improving swimming control in turbulent waters. Skin and gill respiration compensates in oxygen-rich waters.

OLYMPIC TORRENT SALAMANDER   Pl. 2, Map 4
Rhyacotriton olympicus

IDENTIFICATION: Largest of Torrent Salamander species. Dark brown, greenish, or gray above with little or no dark spotting and yellowish to yellowish orange below; *the dark dorsal coloration stops abruptly on the sides where it forms a distinct wavy margin.* Below has scant to moderate, and usually distinct, spotting of dark brown. Some are unspotted or have only dusky mottling of the throat. **SIMILAR SPECIES:** All other Torrent Salamanders lack this species' abrupt wavy margin between the dorsal and ventral coloration. **RANGE:** Olympic Peninsula in Clallam, Grays Harbor, Jefferson, and Mason Cos., Wash. Range to the south probably does not extend beyond the Chehalis R. valley.

COLUMBIA TORRENT SALAMANDER   not shown, Map 4
Rhyacotriton kezeri

IDENTIFICATION: Above uniformly colored brown, greenish, or gray; generally lacking in dorsal spotting and blotching, the *darker dorsal coloration forming a quite straight, often relatively indistinct, line of demarcation between it and the paler ventral color.* Ventral surfaces may be yellow or orange, unspotted, or weakly spotted with dusky. **SIMILAR SPECIES:** (1) Columbia Olympic Salamander near contact with Southern Torrent Salamander may be difficult to distinguish from the latter. A combination of the following characteristics in the Columbia species may aid identification—absence of dorsal spotting and of small speckles in throat and chest regions beyond the contact zone, lighter upper-limb bases, and perhaps less dark pigmentation of soles of feet. (2) See also Cascade Torrent Salamander. **RANGE:** Coast Ranges from near Chehalis R., Grays Harbor Co., Wash., south to zone of contact with Southern Torrent Salamander along Little Nestucca R. and Grande Ronde Valley in Polk, Tillamook, and Yamhill Cos., Ore. Sea level to 3,937 ft. (1,200 m).

OUTHERN TORRENT SALAMANDER
hyacotriton variegatus

IDENTIFICATION: Above brownish to olive or pale olive ground color largely obscured by numerous spots, blotches, and reticulation of black to blackish brown, but amount of spotting can vary considerably within populations. *Dark markings on sides grade into similar markings on venter.* Below generally greenish yellow commonly heavily flecked and spotted with dark blotches of variable size. Northern populations may have reduced, finer grained, and less reticulate dark spotting, and more orange in ventral coloration. **SIMILAR SPECIES:** (1) Olympic Torrent Salamander has abrupt wavy demarcation on sides between dorsal and ventral coloration. (2) Columbia Torrent Salamander lacks dorsal spotting found in Southern Torrent Salamander. (3) Cascade Torrent Salamander's spots are usually denser than Southern Torrent Salamander's, and heavy spotting on its sides usually makes the line of demarcation between dorsal and ventral color more distinct than in either the Southern or Columbia Salamanders. **RANGE:** From near Point Arena in s. Mendocino Co., Calif., north through Coast Ranges to Little Nestucca R. and Grande Ronde Valley in Polk, Tillamook, and Yamhill Cos., Ore. Populations on w. slope Cascade Mts. near Steamboat, Douglas Co., Ore. and in upper drainage of McCloud R. (1 mi. south of McCloud), Siskiyou Co., Calif. Near sea level to 4,560 ft. (1,390 m), perhaps to over 5,000 ft. (1,500 m).

REMARKS: This species and other Torrent Salamanders are susceptible to local extinction because of the small size and isolation of populations. Perhaps 50–90 percent of suitable habitat in Calif. has been radically altered or eliminated. Rapid, large-scale harvesting of old-growth forests and lack of protection of small springs and seeps are primarily responsible.

:ASCADE TORRENT SALAMANDER
hyacotriton cascadae

IDENTIFICATION: Above usually heavily blotched and spotted, *especially along sides where blotching forms a relatively straight line of demarcation between the dorsal and ventral color,* however, some populations and individuals may be unspotted. Spots may be defined and well spaced in some populations. Below yellow to yellowish orange. Ventral markings highly variable. Spotting may occur as distinct black blotches along the midline (Wahkeena Falls,

Multnomah Co., Ore.) as tiny grayish flecks concentrated in throat area, but also sometimes elsewhere; some populations have a dark band across the venter, posterior to the cloaca. Almost every population seems to differ from every other one, and the range of variation seems to encompass that of all species of the Coast Ranges. **SIMILAR SPECIES:** See Southern Torrent Salamander. **RANGE:** W. slope of Cascade Mts. from just north of Mt. St. Helens, Skamania Co., Wash. south to ne. Lane Co., Ore.

NEWTS: FAMILY SALAMANDRIDAE

In North America this family is represented by the Pacific and Eastern Newts, with 3 species in each genus. Pacific Newts are found from Alaska to s. Calif, Eastern Newts chiefly east of the Great Plains from se. Canada to ne. Mexico. The family is also represented in Europe, North Africa, and Asia, where they are the dominant salamanders. About 60 species.

Pacific Newts are plain brown or black above and yellow, orange, or red below. Terrestrial and rough-skinned much of the year, they still must enter ponds and streams to breed. Breeding males develop a smooth skin and flattened tail. Eastern Newts are more aquatic and change directly from the larval stage into water-dwelling adults or into rough-skinned, roundtailed red efts that live on land for awhile and then return to water.

PACIFIC NEWTS: GENUS *Taricha*

Readily distinguished from all other western salamanders by distinctive tooth pattern (Fig. 4, No. 3, p. 26), lack of costal grooves, and rough skin (except in breeding males). The latter have a smooth skin, flattened tail, swollen vent, and dark patches of roughened skin (nuptial pads) on undersides of feet (Fig. 24).

Newts are familiar salamanders on the Pacific Coast. Less disturbed by light than other salamander species, they are often seen crawling over land in the daytime or moving about fully exposed on pond, lake, and stream bottoms. Their potent skin secretion repels most predators.

The poisonous properties of newts are not confined to skin secretions but are widespread throughout the body and can cause death in most vertebrates, including man, if newt tissue is eaten in sufficient quantity. A person died after ingesting a Rough-skinned Newt on a dare. Newts can be handled without danger, but wash your hands after doing so. When a newt is slapped on the back or seized, it assumes a characteristic swaybacked defense pose with eyes closed, head and tail bent upward, limbs extended, and toes flexed. This brings the bright color of the ventral surface into view, probably as a warning to potential predators.

During or after rains in fall, winter, and spring (except during cold weather), newts are often seen moving in large numbers to aquatic breeding sites. Larvae transform at end of first or second summer. Terrestrial newts summer under bark, inside decayed logs, in rock crevices, and in burrows of other animals.

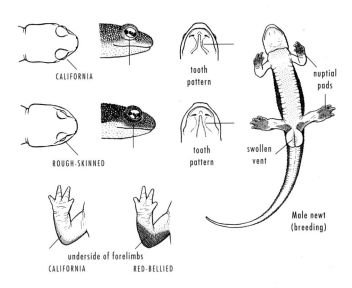

CALIFORNIA

tooth pattern

nuptial pads

ROUGH-SKINNED

tooth pattern

swollen vent

underside of forelimbs
CALIFORNIA   RED-BELLIED

Male newt (breeding)

Fig. 24. Characteristics of newts

ROUGH-SKINNED NEWT *Taricha granulosa* Pl. 4, Map 8

IDENTIFICATION: 2 1/4–3 1/2 in. (5.7–8.9 cm). Note *dark lower eyelids and subocular areas*. Black to dark brown above, sometimes yellowish brown or tan. Yellow to reddish orange below. Dark color of the back stops abruptly on the sides or blends into the belly color. *Eyes relatively small, usually not extending to outline of head when viewed from above.* Iris yellow or silvery. Teeth in roof of mouth usually in V-shaped arrangement. **BREEDING MALE:** Brown to olive above, with a broad dusky patch on each side, smooth skin, bulbous vent, flattened tail, and dark skin on underside of feet. **FEMALE:** Distinctive *cone-shaped vent* most evident when breeding.

Individuals at Gravina Is., Alaska, have dark blotches on ventral surfaces. At Crater Lake, Ore. and vicinity, some are nearly all black

Mating Rough-skinned Newts. The male mounts piggy-back and strokes the snout of the female with chin glands that increase her receptivity. He then dismounts and deposits a sperm capsule that she picks up with her vent.

below. Some in the Siskiyou Mts., Calif., have dark blotches on both dorsal and ventral surfaces, and some at Fay Lake, Linn Co., Ore., and 13 Lakes, Del Norte Co., Calif. have dorsal blotches.

Frequents grassland, woodland, and forest. Time of breeding varies, in general earlier at lower elevations and latitudes. Considering the entire species range, it occurs somewhere almost any time of year. Breeds chiefly from late Dec. to July in ponds, lakes, reservoirs, or slowly flowing streams. When on land it may be found crawling in the open or under rocks, logs, bark, and in rotten wood. Differs from other western newts in usually laying its eggs singly and, in some parts of its range, in curling the tip of its tail into a coil when in the extreme defense pose (see p. 164). Our most aquatic and poisonous newt. **SIMILAR SPECIES:** (1) The California Newt (below) usually has light-colored lower eyelids, larger eyes, and teeth in a Y-shaped arrangement. When in defense pose the tail is held straight rather than being curled at tip. However, in some areas some individuals defy identification even by experts. (2) Red-bellied Newt (p. 167) has dark eyes. **RANGE:** Humid coast from se. Alaska to s. Santa Cruz Co., Calif., chiefly west of crest of Cascade Mts.; south in foothills of Sierra Nevada to Magalia, Butte Co., Calif. Populations near Moscow, Latah Co., Idaho and Saunders Co., Mont. probably have been introduced. Sea level to around 9,200 ft. (2,800 m).

CALIFORNIA NEWT *Taricha torosa*   **Pl. 4, Map 11**
IDENTIFICATION: 2 3/4–3 1/2 in. (7–8.9 cm). Similar to Rough-skinned Newt, but usually with less contrast between dorsal and ventral color on the sides. Light-colored lower eyelids and subocular areas (Fig. 24, p. 165); larger eyes, the corneal surfaces usually ex-

tending to or beyond outline of head when viewed from above; teeth in roof of mouth usually in a Y-shape. **BREEDING MALE:** Smooth skin, bulbous vent, flattened tail, dark skin on undersides of feet.

Habitat similar to Rough-skinned Newt's but generally less humid. Breeds in ponds, reservoirs, and slowly flowing streams. In Sierra Nevada and mountains of s. Calif. it enters larger rivers and streams where it may frequent fast water. Goes to water during the first fall rains, breeding Dec. to May, with a peak from Feb. to April. In the Sierra, migrations start in Jan. or Feb. and breeding lasts until early May. Adults sometimes cannibalize eggs and larvae. **SIMILAR SPECIES:** (1) Red-bellied Newt (below) has dark eyes. (2) See also Rough-skinned Newt (above). **RANGE:** Coast Ranges of Calif. from Mendocino to San Diego Cos. and w. slope of s. Cascades at Squaw Creek, Shasta Co., Calif. south through w. slope of Sierra Nevada to Breckenridge Mt. and Mill Creek, Kern Co. Fragmented s. Calif. range includes the Santa Monica, San Gabriel, and Santa Ana Mts. Southernmost area on map represents high-risk populations that still persist in the upper San Diego R. watersheds, San Diego Co. Near sea level to 7,800 ft. (2,377 m).

SUBSPECIES: COAST RANGE NEWT, *T. t. torosa.* Above yellowish brown to dark brown; below pale yellow to orange; eyelids and snout less commonly so extensively light-colored and iris generally deeper yellow than in Sierra Newt; tail fins of breeding male well developed. Coexists with the Rough-skinned Newt from Santa Cruz to Mendocino Cos., Calif. SIERRA NEWT, *T. t. sierrae.* Above generally reddish brown to near chocolate brown; below burnt orange (sometimes yellowish in breeding individuals); upper eyelids and tip of snout generally lighter than rest of head; iris silvery to pale yellow; tail fins of breeding male less developed.

REMARKS: California Newts in s. Calif. have suffered marked population declines due to human activity. Some of these declines appear to be due to the introduction of exotic predators—green sunfish, mosquito fish, and crayfish.

RED-BELLIED NEWT *Taricha rivularis*   Pl. 4, Map 10

IDENTIFICATION: 2 3/4–3 1/2 in. (7–8.9 cm). Dark-eyed. Eyes larger, head narrower, and snout longer than in other western species. Brown to nearly black above, tomato red below. Dark color conspicuous on underside of limbs. Prominent dark band across vent, especially broad in males. Less sex difference in skin texture than in other species.

A stream- or river-dwelling newt of coastal woodlands, entering water as early as the first week in Feb. and breeding from late Feb. to May in flowing water of rocky rivers and creeks. **SIMILAR SPECIES:** (1) California and (2) Rough-skinned Newts (p. 165) have bright eye color and less dark color on undersides of limbs (Fig. 24, p. 165). **RANGE:** Coastal region of Calif. from Salmon Creek near Bodega, Sonoma Co., and Lower Lake and Kelsey Creek, Lake Co., north to Honeydew, Humboldt Co. Coexists with Rough-skinned Newt but generally breeds in flowing water. Occasionally hybridizes with Rough-skinned Newt.

LUNGLESS SALAMANDERS:
FAMILY PLETHODONTIDAE

The largest family of salamanders, with over 350 described species. Confined to the New World—s. Canada to n. Bolivia and e. Brazil—except for the web-toes (*Hydromantes*), represented by 7 species in Europe and 3 in Calif. Most species are terrestrial, including all of ours. They are found by day in moist places under rocks, bark, logs, in rotten wood and animal burrows, and emerge at night under conditions of suitable moisture. However, in e. N. America many species live in and near streams. Most terrestrial forms avoid immersion, but some may seek temporary refuge in water when threatened. They live and lay eggs in moist places on land, and in many species females brood their eggs (our Slender Salamanders apparently excepted). Terrestrial species lack free-living larvae; the young hatch fully formed.

All plethodontids are lungless. They breathe through their thin, moist skin, which is smooth and slippery. All have a nasolabial groove (Fig. 4, No. 1, p. 26)—a hairline furrow that extends from each nostril to the edge of the upper lip and sometimes out onto a lobe (or palp). The grooves function to transport waterborne chemicals from the substrate to the nose and are considered important in social interactions. Most have well-defined costal grooves and folds, sometimes useful in distinguishing species. When counting grooves, include the groove at the rear of the front limb (in the axilla), even if not well developed, and both parts of a pair of grooves that may join in the groin (see front endpapers). Costal groove counts between tips of the toes, or overlap of toes, of adpressed limbs may be important in identifying some plethodontid species (see front end papers for method of counting). The procedure applies only to adults, or near adults. Young have relatively longer legs in relation to body length. Tooth pattern is distinctive (Fig. 4, No. 2, p. 26). The family name means "many teeth."

In N. America mating occurs in fall, winter, and spring, the time depending on the species and locality. Breeding males typically have a well-developed mental (or hedonic) gland (see p. 511) and often projecting upper-jaw teeth (see key, p. 26) that they may use to scratch the skin surface of the female, which allows secretion (an aphrodesiac?) from the gland to enter her bloodstream, thereby increasing her receptivity to courtship. Eggs are usually deposited in spring and summer (some Slender Salamanders, *Batrachoseps*, lay their eggs in winter).

WOODLAND SALAMANDERS: GENUS *Plethodon*

Slim-bodied and short-legged, our species usually have a dorsal stripe of reddish, tan, or yellow. Around 40 species live in the U.S. and Canada; 7 or 8 (?) in the Pacific Northwest, 1 in northern N.M., the rest in the East.

There are 4 toes on the front and 5 on the hind feet, the edges of the tongue are free except in front, the tail is round or oval with no constriction at the base, and upper-jaw teeth extend to the corner of the mouth. Males typically have a broader head, a more pointed lower jaw, and a longer tail than females. Costal-groove counts are useful in distinguishing species (see above).

Usually frequent damp woods, by day under bark, logs, moss and in moist leaf litter, rotten wood, rock outcrops, and talus. Active on the surface at night, usually during or shortly after rains. Eggs are laid in moist concealed places on land.

DUNN'S SALAMANDER *Plethodon dunni*   Pl. 5, Map 14
IDENTIFICATION: 2–3 in. (5.1–7.6 cm). *Dorsal stripe tan, yellow, or greenish yellow, brightening on tail but not reaching its tip.* Stripe flecked with dusky, the flecks sometimes nearly concealing it. Occasional melanistic individuals, dark-colored and unstriped (Mary's Peak Salamander — see Remarks), coexist at some localities with striped individuals. Sides dark brown or black, spotted with yellowish or tan and speckled with white. Upper surface of base of limbs yellow, flecked with dusky, like the dorsal stripe. Slaty below, with small spots of yellowish or orange. Tail slightly flattened from side to side. Fifteen costal grooves (rarely 16). 2½–4 costal folds between tips of toes of adpressed limbs. **Young:** Usually brighter and more even-edged dorsal stripe than adults that may extend to tip of tail. **Male:** Small lobe on each side of rear edge of vent and a large mental gland.

Lives in moss-covered rock rubble of talus slopes or seepages and under rocks and logs on shady streambanks, preferring wetter locations than other western plethodons except Van Dyke's Salamander (p. 170). Sometimes found beneath stones in water trickles. Presumably lays its eggs mainly in spring and early summer in underground retreats. **SIMILAR SPECIES:** Western Red-backed Salamander (p. 170) usually has 16 costal grooves, a network of light and dark markings on the belly (Fig. 8, Pl. 5, p. 44), and the stripe color extends to tip of tail. In yellow-striped individuals the stripe lacks the greenish yellow tone of Dunn's Salamander. **RANGE:** From e. bank of North R., Grays Harbor Co. (Willapa Hills area), Wash., west of Cascade crest, to the Smith R. area, Del Norte Co., Calif. Sea level to around 3,200 ft. (1,000 m).

REMARKS: Mary's Peak Salamander (*P. gordoni*) — unstriped when adult and sympatric with striped individuals in Benton, Lincoln, and Lane Cos., Ore. — is regarded in this guide as an unstriped morph of Dunn's Salamander.

WESTERN RED-BACKED SALAMANDER   Pl. 5, Map 13
Plethodon vehiculum

IDENTIFICATION: 1 1/2–2 1/2 in. (3.8–6.3 cm). Dorsal stripe usually well defined — tan, reddish brown, orange, yellow, or dusky edged with black. *Stripe with even edges, extending to tip of tail.* Tan or reddish brown colors are most common, but sometimes all stripe colors are present at the same locality. Sides of body dusky, sprinkled with white. Occasionally all dark color is subdued and the stripe color suffuses the entire body. Such plain-colored individuals may be orange or pale yellow. Occasionally melanistic (dark) individuals are found, especially in coastal areas. Blue-gray below, with varying amounts of yellowish, orange, or whitish flecking, which sometimes reduces the dark ventral color to a network or to scattered spots and blotches (Fig. 8, Pl. 5, p. 44). *Usually 16 costal grooves,* occasionally 14 to 18. 2 1/2–5 1/2 costal folds between toes of adpressed limbs. **Male:** Squarish snout, protruding premaxillary teeth, and small vent flaps.

Found under rocks, logs, bark, boards, and inside rotting logs in damp locations in humid forests, but in areas occupied by Dunn's Salamander, which shares its range in Ore., it tends to occupy somewhat drier locations. In Wash., in the n. Puget Trough and Cascade foothills, in the absence of Dunn's Salamander, the Redbacked Salamander may be associated with rocky seeps, springs, and small streams. In Ore. mates chiefly from Nov. through early March. Eggs laid in spring or early summer and brooded by the female. **SIMILAR SPECIES:** See (1) Dunn's Salamander (p. 169) and (2) Larch Mountain Salamander (p. 172). **RANGE:** Chiefly west of Cascade crest from sw. B.C., including Vancouver I., to vicinity of Powers, Coos Co., and Rogue R., Curry Co., Ore. Near sea level to about 4,100 ft. (1,250 m).

VAN DYKE'S SALAMANDER   Pl. 5, Map 18
Plethodon vandykei

IDENTIFICATION: 1 3/4–2 1/2 in. (4.4–6.3 cm). Dorsal stripe yellowish, tan, or reddish, usually with even edges, bordered with black or dark brown. *Throat pale yellow* (Fig. 8, Pl. 5, p. 44), contrasting in

Van Dyke's Salamander attending her egg clutch. It is thought that her skin secretions may help protect the eggs from mold and other pathogens.

some individuals with belly color. Stripe color on upper surfaces of base of limbs. Large adults may be nearly plain dull yellow, tan, dark-colored, or pinkish rose (especially in Willapa Hills), and darker color of the sides and belly may be faint or absent. Fourteen costal grooves, rarely 15. One half to 3 costal folds between toes of adpressed limbs. Parotoid glands often evident in large adults. **Young:** Similar in color to adult Coeur d'Alene Salamander. Conspicuous yellow dorsal stripe, dark sides and belly, and *large yellow throat patch*. **Male:** Nasolabial groove ends in a tubercle on upper lip. A short rounded free flap on each side of rear of vent. Vent flaps less developed in females.

Populations are often fragmented, separated by glacial and alluvial deposits. Perhaps the most "aquatic" *Plethodon*, attracted particularly to seepages and splash zones of waterfalls and cascades in rocky habitats along streams in coniferous forests, it also occurs in woodland and more open areas that have rocky, sufficiently moist sites. Search under logs, bark, rocks and in moist cave entrances and talus. Most egg-laying occurs in spring, with hatching occurring in late summer or fall. Eggs are guarded. **SIMILAR SPECIES:** (1) Coeur d'Alene Salamander is darker, has more contrast between dorsal stripe and dark color on sides. (2) Dunn's and (3) Western Red-backed Salamanders (p. 170) lack the pale throat. (4) Larch Mountain Salamander is reddish below. (5) Lack of constriction at base of tail distinguishes unstriped individuals from plain-colored Ensatinas (p. 174). **RANGE:** W. Wash. on Olympic Peninsula, in Willapa Hills and nearby Long I., and in s. Cascades. Near sea level to around 5,000 ft. (1,550 m). Sometimes sympatric with Dunn's and Western Red-backed Salamanders. Coexists with the former southeast of South Bend, Pacific Co.

COEUR D'ALENE SALAMANDER
Plethodon idahoensis

Pl. 5, Map 18

IDENTIFICATION: 1 3/4–2 3/5 in. (4.4–6.6 cm). Similar to Van Dyke's Salamander but generally darker. Dorsal stripe narrower and usually with scalloped borders, contrasting sharply with dark color of upper sides. Limb bases dark or with only a small area of dorsal stripe color at their bases. Sooty below. Yellow throat conspicuous. **YOUNG:** Resemble adults in patterning. **MALE:** As in Van Dyke's Salamander.

Habitat similar to that of Van Dyke's Salamander. Mating occurs from late summer through spring. Eggs presumably laid chiefly in spring. **SIMILAR SPECIES:** See (2) to (4) in account of Van Dyke's Salamander. **RANGE:** N. Idaho, extreme nw. Mont. and se. B.C. Some localities are: Idaho — s. shore of Wolf Bay, Coeur d'Alene Lake, Kootenai Co.; south of Emida, Benewah Co.; and Lochsa R. east of Lowell, Idaho Co. Mont. — Big Hoodoo Mt., Lincoln Co., and Cascade Creek south of Paradise, Mineral Co. B.C. — western slopes of the Purcell Mts. along Kootenay Lake. 1,601–5,000 ft. (488–1,524 m).
REMARKS: A close relative of Van Dyke's Salamander.

LARCH MOUNTAIN SALAMANDER
Plethodon larselli

Pl. 5, Map 16

IDENTIFICATION: 1 1/2–2 1/8 in. (3.8–5.4 cm). Dorsal stripe reddish, tan, or yellowish, tending to become obscure on head. Stripe edged with black or dark brown, often speckled or heavily mottled with small dark flecks that may be concentrated along midline. Sides black or dark brown sprinkled with white. *Red to reddish orange, salmon pink, to gray with pink hues below,* brightest on tail, lightly and irregularly speckled with black. Underside of feet usually reddish. Throat cream or dull yellow. Toes partly webbed as in Van Dyke's Salamander and *only 1 segment in 5th toe.* Usually 15 costal grooves. **MALE:** Apparently lacks mental gland and has weakly developed vent lobes. **YOUNG:** Dorsal stripe well defined. Less reddish below, with more dark color than adult.

Inhabits gravelly talus slopes (rocks about 3/8 to 2 1/2 in. wide seem to be favored) in forested areas often of mixed Douglas-fir and hardwoods but also in open nonforested areas and in some places not notably rocky. In wooded areas canopy may be dense but ground cover sparse. Talus often has relatively large amounts of decaying plant material where there is considerable moss and humus. Found in rotten wood and under rocks and bark. Breeds in spring and fall. **SIMILAR SPECIES:** Differs from all other woodland salamanders in having reddish color on belly and underside of feet and tail. (1) Dorsal stripe heavily mottled with small dark flecks, darker than in Van Dyke's Salamander (p. 170), which typically has 2 segments (not 1) in the 5th toe. (2) Edges of dorsal stripe more irregular and belly pattern less variegated than in Western Red-backed Salamander (p. 170). **RANGE:** N. Cascades in Ore. to s. and cen. Cascades in Wash. from s.-cen. Hood R. Co., Ore. north to at least Snoqualmie Pass — Kachess Lake area, Wash. Many localities along Columbia R. Gorge between Troutdale and Hood R., Ore. and Archer Falls, Skamania Co., and vicinity of Lyle, Klickitat Co., Wash. Distribution fragmented. To around 3,900 ft. (1,200 m).

REMARKS: A relict species, highly vulnerable to removal of gravel for road fills, clear-cutting of timber, and overcollecting.

EMEZ MOUNTAINS SALAMANDER Pl. 5, Map 17
Plethodon neomexicanus

IDENTIFICATION: 1 7/8–2 5/8 in. (4.7–6.7 cm). Our slimmest plethodon, approaching the Slender Salamanders in proportions. Usually 18–19 costal grooves. Legs short, in adults 6–8 1/2 costal folds between tips of toes of adpressed limbs. 5th toe absent, or with only 1 segment. Brown above, with fine brassy-colored stippling. Sooty to pale gray below, lighter on throat and tail. **YOUNG:** A faint gray or brassy dorsal stripe. Molecular data suggests it is most closely related to the Larch Mountain Salamander.

Found in moss-covered rockslides, especially on north-facing slopes and under bark and beneath logs in and near mixed forests of fir, spruce, aspen, and maple. This subterranean salamander spends little time on the surface except during the period of summer rains — June–Aug. Mating occurs in July and Aug. Eggs laid between mid-Aug. and spring. May be locally abundant. **SIMILAR SPECIES:** (1) Del Norte Salamander (below) has 2 segments in the 5th toe and usually 18 costal grooves. (2) Larch Mountain Salamander has a reddish venter and usually 15 costal grooves. **RANGE:** Jemez Mts., Sandoval, and Los Alamos Cos., N.M. 7,185–9,186 ft. (2,190–2,800 m).

DEL NORTE SALAMANDER Pl. 5, Map 15
Plethodon elongatus

IDENTIFICATION: 2 3/8–3 in. (6–7.6 cm). Long-bodied, dark brown or black above with 18–20 costal grooves and short limbs. *Toes short and slightly webbed.* An even-edged dorsal stripe of brown, reddish brown, or olive tan, often lacking in specimens from outer coastal areas, where adults are dark brown or solid black. Interiorly, in the Siskiyou Mountains, species is also unstriped chocolate to purplish brown with pale speckling above. Sides sprinkled with fine white flecks in all color phases. Belly black, slaty, or lavender, usually flecked with light gray. Pale orange-yellow flecks on underside of head. **Young:** Sooty to nearly black above, or with a reddish brown or tan dorsal stripe that usually fades with age. **Male:** Mental gland present, absent in female.

Frequents stabilized talus associated with rock outcrops, road fills, and rock rubble of old riverbeds in older, shaded, often closed-canopy forests of mixed hardwoods and conifers. Especially attracted to older forest sites. Also found under bark, logs, and other objects on the forest floor, usually in rocky areas. North-facing slopes seem to be favored. Generally found in drier locations than Dunn's Salamander. Mating appears to occur from fall to spring. Females remain with eggs in well-hidden nest sites until fall, when eggs hatch. **SIMILAR SPECIES:** Dark-colored Dunn's Salamander (p. 169) has 15 (rarely 16) costal grooves, less webbing between toes, and 2½–4 costal folds between toes of ad-pressed limbs. **RANGE:** Humid coastal forest from near Port Orford, Curry Co., and Powers, Coos Co., Ore. to near Orick, Humboldt Co., Calif. and inland to near Salyer, Trinity Co., and Seiad Valley, Siskiyou Co., Calif. Coexists with Dunn's Salamander at some localities in s. Ore. Sea level to around 5,905 ft. (1,800 m).
SUBSPECIES: STRIPED DEL NORTE SALAMANDER, *P. e. elongatus* (Pl. 5). Usually 6½–8 costal folds between adpressed limbs. Usually 18 costal grooves. Brown or black above, unstriped or with a brown stripe (inland areas). SISKIYOU MOUNTAINS SALAMANDER, *P. e. stormi* (Pl. 5). Usually 4–5½ costal folds between adpressed limbs. Usually 17 costal grooves. Chocolate or light purplish brown above, profusely speckled with whitish or yellowish. No dorsal stripe. Occurs chiefly in Applegate R. and Thompson Creek drainages in Ore., Seiad Creek drainage in Ore. and Calif., and Horse Creek drainage in Calif. Considered a full species by many herpetologists.
REMARKS: Species is already adversely affected by loss of forest canopy. Some contact points between the two subspecies are the western water-shed boundary of Thompson Creek, Scott/Salmon R. boundary at North Fork Camp, headwaters of Grider Creek, thence to Klamath R.

ENSATINAS: GENUS *Ensatina*

One species in the genus. Most closely related to *Plethodon*. Pacific coastal areas from sw. B.C. to n. Baja Calif.

ENSATINA *Ensatina eschscholtzii*   Pls. 6 and 7, Map 12
IDENTIFICATION: 1½–3⅕ in. (3.8–8.1 cm). A smooth-skinned sala-mander with 12–13 costal grooves and "swollen" tail constricted at its base. Defense posture is characteristic: when tapped on the back an Ensatina may stand stiff-legged and swaybacked with its

tail arched. Color varies greatly (see plates and subspecies accounts), but nearly all have yellow or orange limb bases. **Male:** Enlarged upper lip. Tail slimmer and longer than in female.

In deciduous and evergreen forests under rotting logs, bark, and rocks. To the south, frequents forests and well-shaded canyons as well as oak woodland and mixed grassland and chaparral. Permanent water may or may not be present. In the north it lives in forest clearings and wooded areas. During cold or dry weather, Ensatinas retreat to the interior of rotten logs and wood rat nests, or enter rotted-out root channels and the burrows of gophers and meadow mice. Breeds chiefly in spring and fall. At higher elevations and to the north, activity may extend into early summer and occur during summer rains in the mountains. Females brood eggs underground or under bark of or within rotting logs in summer. **SIMILAR SPECIES:** See Van Dyke's Salamander (p. 170). **RANGE:** Sw. B.C. (including northernmost coastal localities at S. Bentinck Arm and Kitlope R.) to extreme nw. Baja Calif., chiefly west of Cascade-Sierran crest. Locality (dot) east of crest in Wash. is at Cle Elum Ridge, Kittitas Co. Isolated population of Large-blotched Ensatina occurs near La Tasajera (7,644 ft., 2,330 m) in San Pedro Martir Mts., Baja Calif. Some insular occurrences at Tatoosh and Ozette Is., Clallam Co., Wash. and Castle and Whale Rocks areas of Crescent City, Del Norte Co., Calif. Recently found in Clayoquot R. area on west coast of Vancouver I., B.C. Apparently absent in Great Valley of Calif. lowlands. Sea level to around 11,000 ft (3,350 m).

SUBSPECIES: MONTEREY ENSATINA, *E. e. eschscholtzii* (Pl. 7). Reddish or pinkish brown above; plain whitish below. Eyes dark brown to nearly

Juvenile Ensatina. Note the bright orange upper leg segments. All Ensatinas have such markings. They may be orange, yellow, or cream-colored. They appear to contribute to the camouflage of the animals when on forest floor backgrounds.

black. Ranges from near Atascadero, San Luis Obispo Co., Calif. south to extreme nw. Baja Calif., and inland in s. Calif. to Kitching Peak above Cabazon and to Sawmill Canyon, headwaters of San Gorgonio R. above Banning, where it hybridizes with intergrades between the Yellow-blotched and Large-blotched Ensatina (p. 177). Widespread in the San Gabriel and San Bernardino Mts., ranging in elevation to over 6,000 ft. (1,968 m). In upland areas in this region the dark color of the dorsum is often blotchy and may extend farther down on the sides than in lowlands. YELLOW-EYED ENSATINA, *E. e. xanthoptica* (Pl. 7). Orange-brown to dark brown (Santa Cruz Mts.) above; orange below. Conspicuous yellow patch in eye. Ranges from s. side Russian R. near Healdsburg, Sonoma Co. to Pacheco Pass, Merced Co. and Hecker Pass near Watsonville, Santa Cruz Co. Hybridizes with Sierra Nevada Ensatina in Sierran foothills. Arrow on Map 12 shows presumed historic dispersal route across Central Valley of Calif. OREGON ENSATINA, *E. e. oregonensis* (Pl. 7). This taxon does not qualify as a subspecies—use term "morphotype" (see glossary, p. 511). Usually light brown above, often with small light-colored gaps in ground color giving a salt-and-pepper coloration; whitish to pale yellow or yellowish orange below with very fine black speckling. PAINTED ENSATINA, *E. e. picta* (Pl. 7). Small form—averages about ⅔ size of Ensatinas to south. Brown above, blotched with black, yellow, or orange or sometimes plain-colored. Tail usually mottled with black and yellow, including sometimes on otherwise plain-colored individuals. Young Oregon Ensatinas are often similarly blotched. In the intergrade zone with the Sierra Nevada Ensatina the common coarsely mottled style of coloration of the Painted Ensatina changes, in a narrow zone, to a uniformly dark coloration then, over the remaining distance, in a gradient of increasing spot size, to the large orange blotches of the Sierra Nevada Ensatina. However, most populations in the intergrade zone con-

Adult Yellow-eyed Salamander, an Ensatina subspecies that may be a California Newt mimic. Newts are so poisonous that they have few predators. The color match is remarkably close, including the yellow eye-patch of the newt.

tain some plain-colored individuals and some lack spotting. SIERRA NEVADA ENSATINA, *E. e. platensis* (Pl. 6). Gray, brown, to dark brown (nearly black) above, usually with prominent orange spots. YELLOW-BLOTCHED ENSATINA, *E. e. croceater* (Pl. 6). Blackish above with large greenish yellow, yellow, or cream blotches. Tehachapi Mts., Mt. Pinos, vicinity of Fort Tejon, and the Frazier–Alamo Mt. area, Calif. This subspecies has been found about 4 1/2 mi. (7.3 km) (air line) from the Monterey Ensatina, the latter at Dripping Springs around 3,281 ft. (1,000 m) and the former near McDonald Peak around 6,233 ft. (1,900 m), Ventura Co. LARGE-BLOTCHED ENSATINA, *E. e. klauberi* (Pl. 6). Blackish above, with large orange or pale salmon blotches. In San Bernardino Mts., intergrades with the Yellow-Blotched Ensatina have cream-colored or yellowish orange blotches in adults, greenish yellow in young. Similar colors are also found in the San Jacinto Mts. to the south. Coexists with the Monterey Ensatina at some localities in the Peninsular Ranges and hybridizes with it on Mt. Palomar and elsewhere in s. Calif.(see hybrid, Pl. 6). Arrow on Map 12 shows presumed dispersal route, or former connection, between blotched forms in Transverse Mt. system in s. Calif. At present no blotched Ensatinas have been found in this area although what appear to be reliable sightings have been reported from Coldbrook Campground below Crystal Lake and in the vicinity of Bouquet Reservoir in the San Gabriel Mts. A sight record for a blotched Ensatina in Perry Aiken Canyon on the east side of the White Mts., Mono Co., Calif., requires confirmation.

REMARKS: Black dots indicate areas of apparent incipient species level breaks based on current molecular studies. Until the taxonomic situation stabilizes, I continue my previous taxonomy except for eliminating the Oregon Ensatina's range in Calif. The large area of intergradation so created is an expedient awaiting further studies in the area.

Bark on the ground alongside logs and around the base of "exfoliating" snags often provides especially favorable retreats for these salamanders. Forest managers should take this into account in maintaining suitable habitat for Ensatinas as well as other creatures attracted to coarse woody debris on the forest floor. Where removal for fire protection is considered essential, a clean sweep seems unnecessary. Scattered pockets of forest litter should be left as refuges for animals requiring such cover.

CLIMBING SALAMANDERS: GENUS *Aneides*

Four western species. Most, but not all, climb; the Black Salamander spends most of its time on the ground. A fifth climbing species, the rock-dwelling Green Salamander (*Aneides aeneus*), occurs in the Appalachian Mts. of e. U.S.

Distinct costal grooves. Prominent jaw muscles (especially well developed in males) give the head a triangular shape. In adult males, front teeth in upper jaw are enlarged and penetrate upper lip. To feel them, stroke tip of snout while holding animal's mouth closed. Males have oval or heart-shaped mental gland and broader head than females. Adaptations for climbing are the well-developed limbs; long, often somewhat truncate (squared-off) toes; and rounded, somewhat prehensile tail. One species, the Black Salamander, however, is mainly terrestrial. Eggs develop during summer and are brooded by the female.

SACRAMENTO MOUNTAINS SALAMANDER Pl. 8, Map 23
Aneides hardii

IDENTIFICATION: 1 ¾–2 ½ in. (4.4–6.3 cm). A slim-bodied, short-legged climbing salamander, 14 or 15 costal grooves. 2–4 ½ costal folds between tips of toes of adpressed limbs. Toe tips somewhat rounded. Light to dark brown above, with varying amounts of greenish gray to bronze mottling. Below brown, gray to cream-colored with throat blotched with whitish or cream, or sometimes uniformly light-colored. Some may have dorsum covered with fine-grained mottling of spots and reticulations of tan separated by dark brown interspaces. Others may have a broad dorsal stripe of yellowish (see Pl. 8). **Young:** Throat flesh-colored, light gray, or whitish. Dorsal stripe brown or bronze.

Found during period of summer rains under bark and inside rotting logs, in old rockslides, and beneath logs, bark, and boards in mixed coniferous forests of Douglas-fir, white fir, and spruce. Usually most abundant on north- and east-facing slopes. Ranges to above timberline in alpine tundra. Emerges late June and July. Brooding females can be found in hollows in decaying logs in summer. **RANGE:** Isolated in Sacramento, White, and Capitan Mts. of s. N.M. Some localities are Cloudcroft, Agua Chiquite, Wofford Lookout, southwest of Monjeau Lookout (Sacramento Mts.); Sierra Blanca Peak area (White Mts.) north of Summit Spring, and southeast of Koprian Springs (Capitan Mts.). From around 7,800 to 11,700 ft. (2,377–3,600 m).

BLACK SALAMANDER *Aneides flavipunctatus* Pl. 8, Map 21

IDENTIFICATION: 2–3 ¾ in. (5.1–9.5 cm). Dorsal coloration of adults varies greatly depending upon locality—uniformly black, or black with very small white flecks (extreme southern part of range); black with large white spots (interior Coast Range from Alder Springs, Glenn Co., and Lucerne, Lake Co., Calif. south); black with pale yellow or whitish spots (outer Coast Range from Sonoma Co. to middle Mendocino Co.); black frosted with gray, olive, or green but few or no light spots (redwood country of Mendocino and Humboldt Cos.); and black with many small white spots (Klamath Mts. east to near Mt. Shasta). *Black or slaty below.* In males, projecting upper-jaw teeth (felt by stroking salamander's snout when mouth is closed) and triangular head will distinguish it as a climbing salamander. 14–16 costal grooves. Limbs short, 3–5 costal folds between adpressed limbs. *Toe tips rounded.* **Young:** Black above, often suffused with olive or green — brilliant green (in light phase) in redwood country of the Northwest coast. Limb bases yellow. **Male:** Heart-shaped mental gland. Small gray glands on belly.

Frequents mixed deciduous woodland, coniferous forests, and coastal grasslands. Chiefly ground-dwelling. Found under rocks along streams, in talus of road cuts, under logs, bark, boards, and other objects, and occasionally beneath bark and in cracks in logs. Some populations are more tolerant of wet soil than other climbing salamanders, often occurring under rocks in seepages but rarely completely immersed. Females brood eggs in summer. **SIMILAR SPECIES:** (1) Tiger Salamander (p. 152) has a flattened tail and widely set small eyes. (2) Arboreal Salamander (p. 181) and (3) Clouded Salamander (below) have fewer than 2 costal folds between adpressed limbs, and squarish toe tips. (4) Arboreal Salamander has a whitish belly, and (5) Clouded Salamander a brown or gray belly. **RANGE:** Coastal areas from sw. Ore. to cen. Santa Cruz Co. and w. Santa Clara Co., Calif. Interiorly, in n. part of range, to near s. base of Mt. Shasta, Calif. Headwaters of Applegate R., Jackson Co., Ore. Record from Feather R., Butte Co., Calif., requires confirmation. Near sea level to over 5,500 ft. (1,700 m), but generally seems to prefer lower elevations.

Eggs of the Black Salamander. Laid in grapelike clusters suspended, often by intertwined gelatinous strands, from the roof of cavities in the soil and under rocks. Amphibian eggs laid in very dark locations are usually unpigmented.

WANDERING SALAMANDER *Aneides vagrans* Pl. 8, Map 20

IDENTIFICATION: 1 ⁴/₅–3 in. (4.6–7.6 cm). Slim, long-legged, and agile; an excellent climber. Tips of toes of adpressed limbs separated by usually no more than 1 ½ costal folds and sometimes overlapping by as much as 1 ½ folds. Usually 16 costal grooves. Toes slightly broadened with squarish tips. *Brown above, clouded with ash, greenish gray, pale gold, or reddish;* dusky or tan below. In dark phase may be nearly plain dark brown above. In light phase, pale gray color may predominate and brown color may be reduced to a network. **Young:** Hatchlings have a pinkish, copper, or brassy dorsal stripe that, with growth, soon becomes reduced to patches on the snout, shoulders, and tail. Stripe color on upper surface of base of limbs. **Male:** Heart-shaped mental gland, absent in female.

Occurs in forests of Douglas-fir, cedar, alder, and redwood, often at borders of clearings. Found under bark of standing or fallen dead trees, in rotten logs, under loose bark on the ground, under rocks, and in crevices in cliffs. Seems to prefer logs with a firm interior and bark separated ¼ in. (6 mm) or so from the heartwood. Search piles of leaf litter on top of sawed stumps, especially Douglas-fir. In summer, colonies sometimes occur deep inside large decayed logs. Eggs laid in spring and early summer. A female and occasionally both sexes have been found together at nest sites. **SIMILAR SPECIES:** See (1) Arboreal Salamander (p. 181) and (2) Black Salamander (p. 178). **RANGE:** Coastal Calif. from nw. Sonoma Co. (vicinity of Stewart's Point) to Smith R. near Crescent City, Del Norte Co. Vancouver I., B.C. where it may have been introduced. Near sea level to around 5,400 ft. (1,650 m).

REMARKS: A new taxon resulting from splitting the former "Clouded Salamander" into two species. Unfortunately, present knowledge of morphological variation is inadequate for reliably distinguishing the two. Geographic location must therefore suffice for identification.

Populations on Vancouver I. and vicinity probably introduced from Calif. with shipments of Tan Oak bark used for tanning during the latter half of the 19th century.

CLOUDED SALAMANDER *Aneides ferreus* not shown

IDENTIFICATION: Similar to Wandering Salamander in structure and proportions. Appears to average less clouding of dorsum, but detailed color and pattern variation not adequately studied. In area of contact between the two species in Del Norte Co., Calif., the Wandering Salamander seems, on average, to have a more striking dorsal pattern of contrasting gray and black whereas the Clouded Salamander has a more diffuse mix of brown and gold. Dorsum often brown with extensive pale speckling and flecking, which may extend to limbs and tail. Speckling on tail may be so

Clouded Salamander eggs showing the large yolk supply characteristic of amphibians that have direct development (emerge fully formed). Benton Co., Ore.

abundant as to coalesce into a nearly solid dorsal stripe. **Young:** Similar to Wandering Salamander.

Clouded Salamander appears to more commonly shelter under rocks or on rocky slopes than the Wandering Salamander, which seems more often to seek openings under bark and beneath downed logs. **SIMILAR SPECIES:** See (1) Arboreal Salamander (below) and (2) Black Salamander (p. 178). **RANGE:** From Smith R., including areas adjacent to, and on s. side of, South Fork of Smith R., Del Norte Co., Calif., north through w. Ore. including coastal area and Cascades Mts. to vicinity of Columbia R. Sea level to around 5,400 ft. (1,650 m).

REMARKS: In zone of contact with Wandering Salamander in Calif. some hybridization has occurred. An area of sympatry occurs along Rock Creek tributary of South Fork of the Smith R., Del Norte Co., Calif.

ARBOREAL SALAMANDER *Aneides lugubris*   **Pl. 8, Map 22**
IDENTIFICATION: 2 1/4–4 in. (5.7–10.1 cm). Plain brown above, usually spotted with yellow. Spotting conspicuous in the Gabilan Range in San Benito and Monterey Cos., and on South Farallon I. off San Francisco Bay; weak or absent in Sierra Nevada. *Whitish below, unmarked.* Enlarged jaw muscles give head a triangular shape. Toes have slightly enlarged, squarish tips. *Adpressed limbs overlap, or separated by as much as 1 costal fold.* Usually 15 costal grooves. Prehensile tail, usually coiled when salamander is at rest. **Young:** Dark above, clouded with light gray or brassy color and a rust or brassy mark on snout, on each side above forelimbs, on upper surface of bases of limbs, and along upper surface of tail. **Male:** Chunky, broad head with powerful jaw muscles. Heart-shaped mental gland, absent in female.

Occurs chiefly in oak woodland but ranges into forests of pine and black oak, especially in Sierra Nevada. Found both on the ground and in trees. In summer during dry weather it enters damp caves and mine shafts; large numbers may aggregate in tree hollows. Found under logs, boards, and rocks and under bark of standing or fallen dead trees. Examine tree trunks, rock surfaces, and crevices of rock walls at night with a flashlight. (A slender wire with a "shepherd's hook" can remove salamanders from cracks.) Sometimes squeaks when first caught. Large adults can bite severely but usually not prone to do so. Eggs are brooded in hollows in trees, logs, and the ground in summer. **SIMILAR SPECIES:** (1) Clouded Salamander (p. 180) usually has 16 costal grooves, mottled dorsal coloration, and dark belly finely speckled with white. See also (2) Black Salamander (p. 178) and (3) Limestone Salamander (p. 197). **RANGE:** Coastal mountains and valleys of Calif. from Humboldt Co. to nw. Baja Calif. (to vicinity of Santo Tomás). Foothills of Sierra Nevada, from El Dorado Co. to Madera Co., Calif. S. Farallon, Año Nuevo, and Catalina Is. off coast of Calif., and Los Coronados Is. off coast of Baja Calif. Sea level to around 5,000 ft. (1,520 m).

REMARKS: Large oaks with cavities, used as nesting sites and summer retreats, are important to survival of Arboreal Salamanders. A 5-million-year-old fossil of this species is known from the Calif. Sierran foothills.

Slender Salamanders: Genus *Batrachoseps*

Confined to the Pacific Coast. All but 1 of the currently recognized 20 species occur in Calif. with only 2 of the Calif. species ranging slightly beyond the state's boundaries (see Map 24). The remaining species is confined to Oregon. More attenuate forms are sometimes called "worm salamanders" because many have a slim form, and all have conspicuous costal and caudal grooves that give a segmented appearance; most have small limbs. All Slender Salamanders have 4 toes on both front and hind feet; all other western salamanders typically have 4 toes on front and 5 toes on hind feet. Many have a dorsal stripe of reddish, tan, or buff. Considerable variation in proportions, from extremely slender species with minute limbs to robust forms with much longer ones (see Pls. 9, 10, 11). The three most "generalized" species, with traits presumed to reflect ancestral stock, the Oregon, Kern Plateau, and Inyo Mountains Slender Salamanders, are of the latter type and sufficiently different in other respects to warrant recognition as members of subgenus *Plethopsis,* estimated to be an ancient group for on the order of 10 million years or more. Remaining species are contained in subgenus *Batrachoseps.* Proportions and color differences are so subtle among some species as to defy certain identification. Rely heavily on locality information.

Young Slender Salamanders of all species have relatively long limbs, a large head, and short tail. Males have a blunt snout, and premaxillary teeth perforate the upper lip (San Simeon Slender Salamander may be an exception). A mental gland (see glossary, p. 511) may be evident toward tip of underside of lower jaw.

Found in a variety of habitats—desert spring areas, grassland, chaparral, woodland, and forests. Look in damp locations under logs, bark, and rocks, in leaf litter and termite galleries, and in crevices of rocks, logs, and stumps. When first exposed, especially the more elongate species may remain motionless, sometimes coiled like a watch spring. Occasionally when first picked up, they may slip away and bounce randomly over the ground. Tail may break when seized, but is usually soon regenerated.

OREGON SLENDER SALAMANDER Pl. 9, Map 19
Batrachoseps wrighti

IDENTIFICATION: 1 1/3–2 2/5 in. (3.4–6.1 cm). Long-legged with black belly *marked with large white blotches*. 16 or 17 costal grooves, counting one each in axilla and groin. 4 1/2–7 1/2 costal folds between adpressed limbs. Dark brown above, often with reddish or yellowish brown or occasionally gold or greenish gold (especially along Columbia R. Gorge) stripe. In some, back color contrasts with brick red tail.

Frequents moist woods of Douglas-fir, maple, hemlock, and red cedar. Found under boards, rocks, and wood, or bark and wood chips at bases of stumps, under bark and moss of logs, and inside logs in crevices or termite burrows. Generally scarce, occurring in scattered and often widely separated colonies, but sometimes locally common. Becomes active on the surface in April or May. Retreats from the surface with onset of summer. Probably lays eggs underground or in rotting logs in spring or early summer. **SIMILAR SPECIES:** Differs from all other Slender Salamanders in having conspicuous white blotches on belly. **RANGE:** N. base of Mt. Hood, along Columbia R. from Starvation Falls, Hood R. Co., to near Crown Point, Multnomah Co.; south on w. slope of Cascade Mts. to northeast of Westfir and just south of Waldo Lake area, Lane Co., Ore. Also near mouths of Moose and Trout Creeks, tributaries of Quartzville Creek, Middle Santiam R., Linn Co.; and 2 mi. (3.2 km) south of McKenzie Bridge, Lane Co. E. slopes of Cascade Mts. in Hood River and Wasco Cos. Near sea level to around 4,700 ft. (1,430 m).

REMARKS: Mature and old-growth forests essential in maintaining high density populations of this species. The Oregon, Kern Plateau, and Inyo

Mountains Slender Salamanders (below) are considered closest to the ancestral stock that gave rise to the genus *Batrachoseps.*

INYO MOUNTAINS SALAMANDER   Pl. 9, Map 19
Batrachoseps campi

IDENTIFICATION: 1 ⅓–2 ⅖ in. (3.4–6.1 cm). Stockiest of Slender Salamanders, with nearly the proportions of a Web-toed Salamander. *Tail short,* averaging only about ¾ of the SV length. 16–18 costal grooves. Two to 5 costal folds between adpressed limbs. Brown above with gray blotches, which may be very sparse to numerous depending on the locality. Populations on the east side and toward the north in Inyo Mts. may have a continuous pale gray tinge (often with a faint greenish cast) on the back. Some may have a gray dorsolateral stripe on each side. **Young:** Dark, usually without an extensive gray tinge.

Found in isolated spring and stream areas chiefly below the piñon-juniper belt. Willows and wild rose grow along the watercourses. Found under stones and in crevices in damp places near water. Surrounding slopes arid, grown to sagebrush, buckwheat, rabbitbrush, and cactus. **SIMILAR SPECIES:** (1) Differs from other Slender Salamanders in having gray lichenlike blotches or suffusion on a dark brown ground color. (2) Web-toed Salamanders (*Hydromantes* species, p. 195) have 5 toes on hind feet. **RANGE:** Inyo Mts., Inyo Co., Calif. From around 1,800–8,600 ft. (550–2,620 m).
REMARKS: Disturbance of springs and seeps through capping, piping, and domestic animal access are threats to this species.

KERN PLATEAU SALAMANDER   Pl. 9, Map 19
Batrachoseps robustus

IDENTIFICATION: 1 ¾–2 ¼ in. (4.4–5.7 cm.) Large and robust; proportions somewhat similar to Inyo Mountains Salamander. Head broad, limbs, feet, and toes relatively large. Tail quite short and stout. Four to 7 costal folds between toes of adpressed limbs. 16–17 costal grooves. Above with a mottling of rusty, bronze, and gray, often with a broad dorsal band and scattering of dark irregular flecks and spots. Below gray to black. Throat heavily mottled with white. Individuals from driest portion of range have lightest coloration of grayish or silver. Those from areas of red fir and Jeffrey pine forests tend to have colors that harmonize with the darker environment of reds and browns of decaying logs and bark rubble.

Frequents habitats mainly of Jeffrey pine and red fir in northern and eastern humid parts of its range and of lodgepole and/or piñon pine, rabbitbrush, big sagebrush, black oak, and canyon oak in drier areas. Found under rocks, bark fragments, logs, and within and under wet logs, especially in spring and seep areas near outflow streams. Lower-elevation populations probably restricted to activity in late winter and spring and those at higher elevations perhaps May or June to perhaps Oct. Eggs probably laid under cover in vicinity of seepages and springs. **RANGE:** Se. Sierra Nevada on Kern Plateau, Sierran e. slope (Olancha Peak to Ninemile Canyon), and in Scodie Mts., Kern Co. 5,298–9,199 ft. (1,615–2,804 m.)—Portuguese Canyon, Inyo Co., Sierran e. slope and Sherman Pass, Kern Plateau, respectively.

TEHACHAPI SLENDER SALAMANDER Pl. 9, Map 24
Batrachoseps stebbinsi
IDENTIFICATION: 2–2⅖ in. (5.1–6.1 cm). Broad-headed and long-limbed, with broad toes and feet. Toes seem more fully webbed than in other Slender Salamanders, with only 1 segment of each toe free of the web. 18–19 costal grooves; 6–7 costal folds between toes of adpressed limbs. Tail relatively short, slightly less than body length. Above light to dark brown, reddish, or with light beige patches. Dorsal stripe, when present, often diffuse with uneven borders. Few or no light specks along central part of belly.

Occurs chiefly in moist canyons and ravines in oak or mixed pine-oak woodland. Found under rocks often in or near talus slopes and beneath rotting logs, especially in areas of considerable leaf litter. **SIMILAR SPECIES:** Black-bellied Slender Salamander (below), with which it coexists at several localities in Tehachapi Mts., is slimmer, has a narrower head, shorter legs, and smaller feet. **RANGE:** Scattered localities in Caliente Creek drainage, Paiute Mts., at s. end Sierra Nevada, Kern Co., Calif. Populations scattered through Tehachapi Mts. to Fort Tejon, Kern Co. From around 2,000–4,600 ft. (610–1,400 m)

KERN CANYON SLENDER SALAMANDER Pl. 10, Map 24
Batrachoseps simatus
IDENTIFICATION: 1⅝–2⅕ in. (4.1–5.6 cm). Narrow-headed, with relatively long limbs and long body and tail (to about 1½ times SV length). *Head and body somewhat flattened*, suggestig crevice-dwelling habits. 20–21 costal grooves. Seven to 9 costal folds between toes of adpressed limbs. Vague dorsal stripe may be present. Sides and undersurfaces dark, speckled with small light flecks.

Occurs in isolated colonies along stream courses and on ridges and hillsides. North-facing slopes and shaded narrow tributary canyons seem to be favored. Found in talus slopes and under logs and other surface objects, especially after rains. Frequents streamside vegetation of willows and cottonwoods, and slopes grown to interior live oak, canyon oak, and pine. Found laying eggs in mid-June at Squirrel Meadow, 6,300 ft. (1,920 m) on Breckenridge Mt., Kern Co. **SIMILAR SPECIES:** See Relictual (p. 193), Gregarius (p. 187), and Kings Canyon Slender Salamanders (p. 192). **RANGE:** Kern R. drainage in s. Sierra, Calif., from Cottonwood Creek beyond canyon mouth (around 980 ft.–330 m) Kern Co. to above Fairview and beyond, to just s. of Johnsondale Bridge (around 3,800 ft.–1,158 m), Tulare Co.; Breckenridge Mt., Kern Co. (6,300 ft.–1,920 m).

REMARKS: Animals from Breckenridge Mt., Cottonwood Creek, and Fairview are somewhat different from those in lower Kern River Canyon and are therefore only tentatively included in this species.

BLACK-BELLIED SLENDER SALAMANDER   Pl. 11, Map 24
Batrachoseps nigriventris

IDENTIFICATION: 1 1/4–1 7/8 in. (3.2–4.7 cm). Head narrow, little wider than neck. Shares with the Gregarius and California Slender Salamanders the shortest limbs among all Slender Salamanders. Tail to around 2 times SV length, but may be about body length on Santa Cruz I. 9–15 *costal folds* between toes of adpressed limbs. 18–21 costal grooves. Usually has dorsal stripe of tan, brown, reddish, or beige. Dark below, with a sprinkling of fine white specks, *usually over all ventral surfaces.*

Chiefly an oak-woodland salamander, but also ranges into mixed oak-pine forests, streamside habitats, and treeless grassland. Found under rocks and logs, under bark, and in termite channels in damp locations. Often occurs in scattered colonies. In s. Calif. eggs are laid in winter and hatch in winter and early spring. **SIMILAR SPECIES:** (1) Relictual Slender Salamander has a broader head, longer limbs, and shorter tail. (2) Garden Slender Salamander has a broader head, longer limbs, and usually paler coloration. (3) Gabilan Mountains Slender Salamander is biochemically distinct, but aside from much larger size and somewhat broader head appears to be indistinguishable in appearance in areas where it coexists with the Black-bellied Slender Salamander. **RANGE:** S. coastal mts., chiefly south of Calif. State Hwy. 198 and San Simeon, in extreme s. Monterey Co., through Transverse Mt. Ranges to Cajon Pass, San Bernardino Co., thence south into the n. uplands of the Peninsular Ranges and coastally (black area 9 on Map 24) to various places in Los Angeles and Orange Cos., where it coexists with Garden Slender Salamander, including the Baldwin Hills–Palos Verdes region, Monterey Park, Baldwin Park, La Puente, Chino, and San Joaquin Hills, and along the coast to Aliso Creek, Orange Co. to Tenaja Canyon in sw. Riverside Co. at the southern limit of its currently known distribution. Also coexists with Tehachapi Slender Salamander at Fort Tejon and in w.

and cen. Tehachapi Mts., and with Pacific Slender Salamander on Santa Cruz I. off Santa Barbara. Sea level to around 8,202 ft. (2,500 m) on Mt. Pinos.

GREGARIUS SLENDER SALAMANDER
Batrachoseps gregarius

Pl. 11, Map 24

IDENTIFICATION: 1 ⅕–1 ⅘ in. (3–4.6 cm). Rather small, short-bodied, and very slim with short limbs. 8–11 costal folds between toes of adpressed limbs. 17–19 costal grooves. Head relatively narrow, only slightly wider than neck. Fore and hind feet relatively small and narrow. Dorsal stripe of brown, sometimes obscured by dark pigment. Beige to rust longitudinal *streaky patches* often present, particularly in dorsolateral areas and on tail. **Male:** Mental hedonic gland evident in most adult individuals.

Frequents a variety of habitats from upland mixed coniferous and oak forests through woodlands to open grasslands at low elevations. **SIMILAR SPECIES:** Appears to be distinguishable from all other Slender Salamanders, whose ranges are closely associated (see Map 24), by presence of mental hedonic gland in males. However, this structure varies in conspicuousness depending on reproductive condition, and studies as yet have not been comprehensive enough to fully validate this observation. Furthermore, morphological differences among these species, especially little studied color differences, are usually inadequate for field recognition. Rely primarily on geographic location and species accounts. **RANGE:** S. boundary of Yosemite Nat'l Park, south nearly to Kern R. on w. slope of Sierra to w. Greenhorn Mts. Low elevation records occur along eastern edge of the Central Valley, as along White R. drainage in Kern and Tulare Cos. From around 984–5,905 ft. (300–1,800 m) at Dinkey Creek drainage, Fresno Co. Coexists with Sequoia Slender Salamander along S. Fork of Kaweah R. **REMARKS:** Populations west of the main Sierran range, in n. Kern and s. Tulare Cos. live in areas of intense summer heat and drought. Individuals very slender with relatively longer bodies, shorter limbs, and smaller feet than those in the north that live in canopy forests in areas of high rainfall and mild temperatures. Proportions of the southern populations may reflect greater fossorial habits relating to aridity and heat. They lay their eggs in the fall, at the beginning of the rainy season, whereas more northerly upland populations lay in the spring.

CHANNEL ISLANDS SLENDER SALAMANDER
Batrachoseps pacificus

Pl. 10, Map 24

IDENTIFICATION: 1 ⅔–2 ¾ in. (4.2–7 cm). Typically robust and relatively long-legged with brown to pinkish brown dorsum. Often with a broad dorsal stripe that usually has indefinite borders.

Stripe may be composed of numerous light-colored flecks. Throat and underside of tail are pale, often suffused with yellowish tan. *Belly whitish or slate-colored, frequently without enough dark pigment to form a continuous network,* under magnification seen to be sprinkled with black and white flecks. White speckling along midline of underside of tail often present. 18–20 costal grooves. *6–8 costal folds between toes of adpressed limbs.* Tail to about 1 ¼ of SV length. **Young:** Often with brown or reddish brown dorsal stripe; belly dusky.

Quite widespread in insular habitats of coastal scrub, grass, and oak woodland, they also occur under beach driftwood. **RANGE:** San Miguel, Santa Rosa, Santa Cruz, and Anacapa Is. off coast of Santa Barbara, Calif.

REMARKS: Black-bellied Salamander coexists with this species on Santa Cruz I.

GARDEN SLENDER SALAMANDER   Pl. 10, Map 24
Batrachoseps major

See subspecies accounts below for morphological and ecological differences that separate two taxa. Differences are sufficiently great to make a general species account inadequate.

SUBSPECIES: GARDEN SLENDER SALAMANDER, *B. m. major* 1 ¼–2 ⅓ in. (3.2–5.9 cm): A rather robust habitus. Body elongate, with relatively short limbs, long tail, and rather narrow head. Usually pale above — brownish, light tan, pink, or grayish, frequently with rust on tail, snout, and shoulders, but some populations are dark in uplands of Peninsular Ranges, Calif. and in San Pedro Martir Mts. and on Todos Santos I., Baja Calif. Individuals from near El Rosario, Baja Calif. are very pale. Stripe often has diffuse borders or is obscure. Belly light gray with a weak network or speckling of melanophores. White speckling along midline of underside of tail often lacking. 17–21 costal grooves. *9–12 costal folds between adpressed limbs.* Tail to about 2 times SV length.

Inhabits oak woodland, open chaparral, and grassland of washes, canyon bottoms, and lower mountain slopes, often where soil is sandy or gravelly. On the Los Angeles coastal plain it formerly was most common on alluvial deposits at mouths of canyons. Found under rocks, bark, and logs in oak woods and elsewhere and formerly quite common in gardens beneath stones, boards, and potted plants. Individuals may share old earthworm burrows. Egg-laying in the s. Calif. lowlands occurs in fall and winter. Breeding habits elsewhere appear to be unknown. **SIMILAR SPECIES:** Black-bellied Slender Salamander is slimmer, generally darker, including a darker belly. **RANGE:** S. Calif. from San Fernando Valley (Panorama City) and s. foothills of Santa Monica, San Gabriel, and San Bernardino Mts. to vicinity of El Rosario and w. slope of San Pedro Martir Mts. in n. Baja Calif. Catalina I. off s. coast of Calif. and Los Coronados and Todos Santos I. off nw. coast Baja Calif. Enters s. Calif desert through San Gorgonio Pass, occurring s. of Cabazon, in Snow Creek Canyon and Palm Springs. Perhaps introduced at Hanford, Tulare Co., Calif. Sea level to around 7,644 ft. (2,330 m). Black-bellied Salamander coexists with Common Garden Slender Salamander at scattered localities in Los Angeles and Orange Cos., Calif. **REMARKS:** Once common in coastal lowlands of s. Calif., this subspecies has suffered decline and extinctions due to habitat loss primarily from modern methods of subdivision development, which eliminated or severely disturbed native topsoil. Gardens of older homes tend to retain their native subterranean fauna.

DESERT SLENDER SALAMANDER, *B. m. aridus.* 1 1/4–2 in. (3.2–5.1 cm). Relatively long-legged and broad-headed. Tail short. 16–19 costal grooves (usually 18). 3 1/2–6 1/2 costal folds between adpressed limbs. *Dorsal surfaces suffused with silvery to brassy flecks,* giving adults a pale gray, whitish, or pinkish coloration. Underside of tail flesh-colored, contrasting with the dark belly. **Young:** Black to dark brown above, often with little or no frosty to brassy tinge.

Found in canyons on e. slope of Santa Rosa Mts. in s. Calif. California fan palms, willows, mesquite, and sugar bush grow in canyons, but surrounding slopes are arid and contain creosote bush, juniper, manzanita, buckwheat, and cactus. In Hidden Palm Canyon salamanders occur beneath limestone slabs and talus in the canyon bottom and in rock crevices and holes in moist soil on canyon walls. **RANGE:** Isolated in Hidden Palm Canyon, at around 2,800 ft. (850 m), a tributary of Deep Canyon southwest of Palm Desert and in nearby Guadalupe Canyon, Riverside Co., Calif. The Hidden Palm Canyon site is a state ecological reserve, entered only by permit.

SAN GABRIEL MOUNTAINS SLENDER SALAMANDER
Batrachoseps gabrieli   **Pl. 9, Map 24**

IDENTIFICATION: 1 1/2–2 in. (3.8–5.1 cm). Of moderate size, roughly intermediate in proportions of limb length and head width among members of the genus. Head flattened. 4–7 1/2 costal folds between toes of adpressed limbs. 18–19 costal grooves. Above with bright coppery to orange-colored dorsal stripe or diffuse remnants over shoulders and above pelvic region, becoming patches on tail. An adult from Kimbark Canyon (see Range) had no coppery or orange coloration. Ground color above black with profuse whitish flecking and speckling, giving a frosted appearance.

Talus slopes in areas of oak, big cone spruce, pine, incense cedar, California laurel, and maple. Individuals found in Feb. and March with surface temperatures close to freezing. **SIMILAR SPECIES:** Black-bellied Salamander has a much narrower head, shorter limbs, smaller fore and hind feet, and a generally longer, less tapered tail. **RANGE:** Upper drainage of San Gabriel R. at pine flats, east-southeast of Crystal Lake, and Rockbound and Alpine (about 2 mi. air line south of pine flats site) Canyons; Mt. Baldy area, Los Angeles Co. and Kimbark and Waterman Canyons, western end of San Bernardino Mts., San Bernardino Co., Calif. 1,200–5,085 ft. (366–1,550 m). Coexists with Black-bellied Salamander at Rockbound and Kimbark Canyons; has been found less than 2 miles (3.2 km) from a Garden Salamander site at Devore in Cajon Pass Canyon, San Bernardino Co.

GABILAN MOUNTAINS SLENDER SALAMANDER
Batrachoseps gavilanensis   Pl. 10, Map 24

IDENTIFICATION: 1 ½–2 ⅗ in. (3.8–6.6 cm). Moderately elongate, with limbs of intermediate length, *separated by 9–12 ½ costal folds between toes of adpressed limbs. 9–21 costal grooves.* Tail to around 1 ½ times SV length. Above dull gray or with distinct dorsal stripe that may be gray centrally but grading to ocher, tan, or coppery-tan laterally. Stripe obscure in dark individuals.

Found chiefly in oak-woodland, gray pine, chaparral, and grass-land habitats of the Gabilan and s. Diablo Ranges and on e. slope of Santa Lucia Mts. in deeply shaded, moist redwood, and mixed evergreen forests. **SIMILAR SPECIES:** (1) Santa Lucia Slender Salamander is darker above and below, stouter, shorter bodied, and has longer legs. (2) California Slender Salamander is somewhat smaller (where sympatric) and has a narrower head. (3) See also Black-bellied Slender Salamander (p. 186). **RANGE:** Vicinity of Soquel (Rodeo Gulch area) and San Benito R., Santa Cruz Co., south throughout the Gabilan and s. Diablo Ranges to Polonia Pass area in n. San Luis Obispo Co. Extends across Salinas Valley to e. slope Sierra de Salinas and Santa Lucia Mts. of the coast. Coexists with California Slender Salamander in a narrow strip from Aptos-Soquel area of Santa Cruz Co. to e. San Benito Co., and with Black-bellied Salamander on Mustang Ridge and Peachtree Valley, Monterey Co., and Coalinga Mineral Springs, Fresno Co., of the s. Diablo Range. Near sea level to around 5,000 ft. (1,524 m).

SANTA LUCIA MOUNTAINS SLENDER SALAMANDER
Batrachoseps luciae   Pl. 10, Map 24

IDENTIFICATION: 1 ¼–1 ⅘ in (3.2–4.6 cm). Moderately robust and short-bodied, with limbs of moderate length, *separated by 7–10 costal folds between toes of adpressed limbs. 18–19 costal grooves.* Tail to around 1 ¾ times SV length. Broad reddish or brassy dorsal stripe that may be obscure in darker individuals.

Frequents moist habitats in redwoods and mixed evergreen forests, generally in wetter locations than Gabilan Mountains

Slender Salamander. Inland it occurs mainly on wooded north-facing slopes with tanbark oak and maples. Search especially under objects in deep leaf litter of moist canyons. **SIMILAR SPECIES:** Distinguished from (1) Gabilan, (2) California, and (3) Black-bellied Slender Salamanders by its more robust form and shorter distance between limbs and (4) from Lesser Slender Salamander by its larger size and relatively shorter limbs and (5) from San Simeon Slender Salamander by having fewer maxillary teeth and presence of enlarged premaxillary teeth in adult males. **RANGE:** Chiefly w. slope Santa Lucia Mts. from the Monterey area south to near n. San Luis Obispo Co. line, Calif., where its range overlaps that of Black-bellied Salamander. Near sea level to higher elevations (range not known).

LESSER SLENDER SALAMANDER   not shown, Map 24
Batrachoseps minor

IDENTIFICATION: 1–2 3/10 in. (2.5–5.8 cm). Small and robust, relatively long legs and short body. 5–8 costal folds between toes of adpressed limbs. 17–18 costal grooves. Tail long and slender. Above dark blackish brown; dorsal stripe may or may not be present and may be tan with pink to apricot highlights especially prominent on the tail. **SIMILAR SPECIES:** This species has the smallest mature body size yet recorded among members of this genus. Differs from Black-bellied Slender Salamander with which it is sympatric in being somewhat more robust, with larger limbs and feet and broader head. The species has been found in habitats with trees such as tanbark oak, coast live oak, blue oak, sycamore, and laurel. **RANGE:** Known only from s. Santa Lucia Range of n.-cen. San Luis Obispo Co., Calif. Occurs immediately north of Black Mt., thence south and east into drainages of Paso Robles and Santa Rita Creeks. Generally found above 1,300 ft. (around 400 m).

REMARKS: Once common, in recent years this species has been difficult to find.

SAN SIMEON SLENDER SALAMANDER   not shown, Map 24
Batrachoseps incognitus

IDENTIFICATION: 1 1/2–1 9/10 in. (3.8–4.8 cm). Relatively elongate and somewhat robust, with limbs of moderate length. Head rather broad. 7 1/2–9 1/2 costal folds between adpressed limbs. 18–20 costal grooves. Tail long and slender. Above blackish brown with or without a dorsal stripe. **SIMILAR SPECIES:** San Simeon Slender Salamander coexists with Black-bellied Slender Salamander at several locations. It is generally larger, more robust, and has relatively longer limbs, larger feet, and a broader head. Found in closed-canopy forest dominated by yellow pine but near the coast under a canopy of laurel and sycamore. Also found farther inland in open oak woodland. **RANGE:** Santa Lucia Mts. in extreme sw. Monterey and n. San Luis Obispo Cos., Calif. In the north it ranges to the Monterey–San Luis Obispo Co. line and to the south into n. San Luis Obispo Co., where it occurs on Pine Mt. and Rocky Butte. Found in sympatry with Black-bellied Slender Salamander along San Simeon Creek Rd. Near sea level to about 3,280 ft. (1,000 m) (Pine Mt. and Rocky Butte).

KINGS RIVER SLENDER SALAMANDER   **not shown, Map 24**
Batrachoseps regius
IDENTIFICATION: 1 ¼–1 ⅜ in. (3.2–3.5 cm). Relatively short-bodied, with limbs of moderate length, 6½–10 costal folds between toes of adpressed limbs. 18–19 costal grooves. Fore and hind feet moderate size. Blackish above with little pattern. Dorsal stripe of brown or tan may be present, but it is often obscure.

Locality where this species was first found is a well-shaded, north-facing slope in an area of mixed chaparral with buckeye, laurel, canyon and blue oak, and ponderosa and lowland pine. Found under rocks in areas of talus at the roadside. **SIMILAR SPECIES:** (1) Gregarius Slender Salamander has narrower head, shorter limbs, smaller feet, and fewer maxillary teeth. (2) Relictual Slender Salamander has longer limbs and fewer maxillary teeth. (3) Sequoia Slender Salamander has a less robust form, shorter and narrower head, and somewhat more maxillary teeth, and (4) Hell Hollow Slender Salamander has fewer maxillary teeth. (5) Kern Canyon Slender Salamander has a more flattened head and body. **RANGE:** Known from lower drainage of Kings R. system, elevation about 1,099 ft. (335 m), in area of the type locality, and at 8,104 ft. (2,470 m) at Summit Meadow, Kings Canyon Nat'l Park, Fresno Co.

SEQUOIA SLENDER SALAMANDER   **not shown, Map 24**
Batrachoseps kawia
IDENTIFICATION: 1 ¼–1 ⅞ in. (3.2–4.7 cm). Rather small and short-bodied, with a relatively broad head and distinct neck. Limbs of moderate length. 7½–10½ costal folds between toes of adpressed limbs. 18–20 costal grooves. Generally dark-colored with a usually dark brown, beige, or rust-colored dorsal stripe that may be obscure. Fine, punctuate whitish speckling may be present on both dorsal and ventral surfaces.

Usually found in habitats with scattered trees, however the type locality is a protected mesic site in a generally dry area shaded with blue and interior live oaks, sycamore, white alder, California buckeye, Fremont cottonwood, and western redbud. At higher elevations it occurs in mixed coniferous forest. **SIMILAR SPECIES:** (1) Gregarius Slender Salamander has a narrower head, shorter limbs, smaller fore and hind feet, fewer maxillary teeth, and males have a mental gland. (2) Relictual Slender Salamander has shorter limbs (at least in geographically neighboring sites) and far fewer maxillary teeth. (3) Kings River and Hell Hollow Slender Salamanders have a less slender form and fewer maxillary teeth. **RANGE:** Known only from drainage of Kaweah R. system, Tulare Co., Calif. From around 1,640 ft. (500 m) to 7,218 ft. (2,200 m). **REMARKS:** Gregarius Slender Salamander coexists with this species at its type locality and both species occur throughout Kaweah drainage. Relictual Slender Salamander, a close relative, also occurs over a similar wide range in elevation, but not found to coexist with Sequoia Slender Salamander. At present its nearest locality is about 25 mi. (40 km) south in the Tule R. drainage.

RELICTUAL SLENDER SALAMANDER Pl. 10, Map 24
Batrachoseps relictus

IDENTIFICATION: 1 3/8–1 7/8 in. (3.5–4.7 cm). Relatively small, dark-colored, and short-bodied, with moderately long limbs. Usually 16–20 costal grooves. 7–9 1/2 costal folds between toes of adpressed limbs (3 1/2–7 at type locality, lower Kern R. Canyon). Dorsal stripe reddish, yellowish, or dark brown but often obscure in large individuals. Molecular information usually required for certain identification.

The common high-elevation Slender Salamander of s. Sierra Nevada. In lower Kern Canyon, where species has not been found in recent years, habitat consists of rocky terrain with scanty tree cover mainly of live oaks, scattered pines and buckeyes, and a few sycamores in creek bottoms. At higher elevations the animals occur in forested areas of pine, fir, incense cedar, sometimes with considerable numbers of deciduous oaks. **SIMILAR SPECIES:** (1) Gregarius Slender Salamander has small fore and hind feet and males have a mental hedonic gland. (2) Kern Canyon Slender Salamander has a longer trunk (20–21 costal grooves), is larger, and has a dark venter speckled with small light-flecks. (3) Sequoia Slender Salamander has more teeth and larger limbs. (4) Kings River Slender Salamander has longer limbs and more maxillary teeth and (5) Hell Hollow Slender Salamander has longer limbs and broader head. **RANGE:** Lower Kern R. Canyon, Kern Co., to highlands drained by the Tule and Kern Rs. in cen. Tulare Co., Calif. (in vicinity of Quaking Aspen Meadow). Also known from a site on w. margin of the Kern Plateau, east of Kern R. It coexists in parts of its range with the Kern Canyon Slender Salamander. Range, 2,395–8,202 ft. (730–2,500 m).

REMARKS: Species may now be extinct at the type locality at 2,395 ft. (730 m) in lower Kern R. Canyon. Localities in the lower Kern Canyon occurred as low as about 1,640 ft. (500 m). Elsewhere the species has been found to be an upland form.

HELL HOLLOW SLENDER SALAMANDER
Batrachoseps diabolicus   not shown, Map 24

IDENTIFICATION: 1 ¼–1 ⅞ in. (3.2–4.7 cm). Small and slim with relatively broad head and only slightly narrower neck. Limbs moderately long. Fore and hind feet large for the slender members of the genus. 18–20 costal grooves. Dorsal stripe brown, sometimes obscured with dark pigment.

Frequents Sierran western foothills in brushy margins of chaparral and open woodland of oaks, pines, and buckeye, generally in areas subject to long periods of hot dry weather. **SIMILAR SPECIES:** Distinguished from geographically neighboring species as follows: (1) California Slender Salamander (with which it coexists) has shorter limbs with narrower fore and hind feet and a less robust body. (2) Gregarius Slender Salamander has shorter limbs, smaller fore and hind feet, and adult males have hedonic mental glands. **RANGE:** Foothills of w. slope Sierra Nevada from lower American R. drainages to Merced R. (Sweetwater Creek, Mariposa Co.), around 1,640 ft. (500 m). Known to coexist with California Slender Salamander on n. slopes of American R. at Hwy. 49 in vicinity of Auburn, around 656 ft. (200 m.).

CALIFORNIA SLENDER SALAMANDER   Pl. 11, Map 24
Batrachoseps attenuatus

IDENTIFICATION: 1 ¼–1 ⅞ in. (3.2–4.7 cm). Head narrow, body and tail long (overall length to over 1 ½–2 times SV length). Limbs very short. *Belly black or dusky, the dark color usually arranged in a fine unbroken network.* Underside of tail often lighter than belly and tinged with yellow. Ventral surfaces, including midline of tail, finely speckled with white. Dorsal stripe often present—brick red, brown, tan, buff, or yellow, the frequency of colors varying with locality. Red to reddish brown predominates in redwood belt in the Northwest. Individuals with a variety of stripe colors can be found near San Francisco Bay. Remaining dorsal ground color is sooty to black. 18–21 costal grooves. 10–12 costal folds between adpressed limbs. **Male:** Lower jaw more pointed and snout broader and more squared-off than in female. Premaxillary teeth project slightly beyond edge of closed mouth.

Frequents grassland (that usually has scattered trees), chaparral, woodland, forest, and yards and vacant lots in some suburban areas. Found under logs, boards, bark, in damp leaf litter and rotting logs from first fall rains to beginning of dry period in late spring or summer. Eggs are laid in late fall and winter, often in communal nests, and young emerge in winter and spring. **SIMILAR SPECIES:** Shares with Relictual, Black-bellied, and Gregarius Slender Salamanders distinction of being among the slimmest, shortest legged, and with the narrowest feet with inconspicuous toes of the Slender Salamander complex. (1) Gabilan Mountain Slender Salamander is somewhat more robust, less attenuate, has longer limbs and larger feet with more conspicuous toes. However, in area of overlap in sw. Santa Cruz Co. the two species are difficult to distinguish. (2) See also Hell Hollow Slender Salamander (p. 194). **RANGE:** Coastal area from extreme sw. Ore. (near mouth of Rogue R.) to near San Benito R. in n. San Benito Co., Calif., and in Sierran foothills from Big Chico Creek to Calaveras Co. Scattered populations in cen. and n. portions of Great Valley of Calif., including Sutter Buttes. Isolated populations at Clipkapudi and Little Cow Creeks, Shasta Co., Calif. Sea level to about 4,000 ft. (1,220 m).

WEB-TOED SALAMANDERS: GENUS *Hydromantes*

Webbed toes, a mushroomlike tongue with free edges (unattached at front), and a flattened body are distinctive. Tongue very long; can be extended over ⅓ the length of the body (excluding tail) to capture prey. Males have projecting upper-jaw teeth and an oval mental gland.

Web-toes are excellent climbers, moving with ease over smooth rock surfaces. When on a steep slope the California species use the tail as an aid in locomotion, curling the tip forward and placing it against the ground as the hind foot on the downhill side is lifted. When climbing directly upslope the tail is swung from side to side. Such regular use of the tail as an aid in climbing distinguishes them from other salamanders in our area and their European relatives.

These salamanders live in rocky habitats, hiding by day under stones and in crevices and caves. They frequent cliff faces, vertical walls of caverns, and level ground. Ten species, 3 in Calif., the rest in Mediterranean Europe.

MOUNT LYELL SALAMANDER　　　　　　　　　　Pl. 11, Map 9
Hydromantes platycephalus
IDENTIFICATION: 1 ¾–2 ¾ in. (4.4–7 cm). Easily recognized by its flattened head and body, *granite-matching coloration,* blunt webbed

toes, and short tail. Dusky below, flecked with white. Usually ½–1½ costal folds between adpressed limbs. Thirteen costal grooves. **Young:** Black ground color above overlain with a greenish tinge (under magnification seen to consist of pale gold flecks). **Male:** Enlarged premaxillary teeth; mental gland present; wider head than female. During courtship the enlarged teeth are used to scratch the female's skin in order to introduce mental gland secretion.

Found chiefly among granite exposures of Sierra Nevada of Calif. Typical habitat includes rock fissures, seepages from streams or melting snow, shade, and low-growing plants. Look under rocks near cliffs, cave openings, melting snowbanks, and in spray zone of waterfalls. Rocks (including glacial erratics) resting on broad areas of exposed glaciated rock surfaces in vicinity of melting snowbanks often attract these salamanders. Seems to favor north-facing slopes. Active from late spring to fall depending upon elevation and local moisture conditions. **SIMILAR SPECIES:** (1) Adult Shasta Salamander (below) often tan to reddish above, without or with less definite granitelike markings; usually has white blotches on chest, and toes of adpressed limbs overlap by ½–1½ costal folds. (2) Limestone Salamander (p. 197) uniformly brown above, whitish or yellowish below. Young pale green or yellowish. **RANGE:** Sierra Nevada from Sierra Buttes, Sierra Co. to Franklin Pass area, Tulare Co., Twin Lakes, Silliman Gap, Sequoia Nat'l Park, and Mt. Williamson, Calif. Low-elevation records are from upper edge of talus slope on s. side of Yosemite Valley (Staircase Falls, base of Cathedral Rocks, and base of Bridal Veil Falls). Occurs east of Sierran crest near outflow streams around base of Sierran escarpment; streams flowing into Owens Valley from near Independence to Bishop and Mammoth Lakes area. 4,000–12,000 ft. (1,220–3,660 m).

REMARKS: Skin secretion of these salamanders appears to be potent. A person who got some of it in his eyes was temporarily blinded.

SHASTA SALAMANDER *Hydromantes shastae*   **Pl. 11, Map 9**
IDENTIFICATION: 1¾–2½ in. (4.4–6.3 cm). Primarily a cave dweller, less specialized for crevice dwelling than Mount Lyell Salamander (above). Body not so flat, toes less webbed, and limbs longer. Adpressed limbs overlap by ½–1½ costal folds. 13 costal grooves. *Gray-green, beige, tan, or reddish above, usually with yellow on tail.* White blotches on chest and abdomen.

Found in moist limestone fissures and caves, and in wet weather under rocks or other objects in the open, in mixed forests of Douglas-fir, foothill pine, and black and canyon oak. Although mostly associated with limestone outcrops or nearby slopes, one

Shasta Salamander. A cave and crevice dweller in limestone country near Lake Shasta, Calif. Eggs have been found in recesses in limestone caves. Young hatch fully formed.

population is known from a volcanic rock outcrop. Enters moist caves or crevices in summer, where it lays and broods its eggs. **SIMILAR SPECIES:** See (1) Mount Lyell Salamander (p. 195) and (2) Limestone Salamander (below). **RANGE:** Known only from limestone country, although not strictly confined to limestone, in n. Calif. south of Mt. Shasta in vicinity of Shasta Reservoir. Some localities are Backbone Ridge, Mammoth Butte, Hirz Mt., Potter and Low Pass Creeks, McCloud R., Brock Mt., Samwell Cave, and near Ingot. 1,000–3,000 ft. (300–910 m).

LIMESTONE SALAMANDER
Hydromantes brunus

Pl. 11, Map 9

IDENTIFICATION: 2–3 in. (5.1–7.6 cm). *Uniformly brown above and pale below.* Underside of tail yellowish. Eyes larger, and limbs, toes, and tail longer than Mount Lyell Salamander's (p. 195). Toe tips of adpressed limbs overlap by around 1½ costal folds. Thirteen costal grooves. **Young:** Pale yellowish green above, changing with age through pale yellow and beige to brown.

Frequents limestone in gray pine, oak, California buckeye, and chaparral belt of lower Merced Canyon, Calif., living in crevices of cliffs and ledges and in talus, especially where rocks are overgrown with moss. Active during period of fall, winter, and early spring rains, except during cold spells. Often coils body when molested. **SIMILAR SPECIES:** (1) See Mount Lyell Salamander (p. 195). (2) Shasta Salamander (p. 196) usually tan or reddish above, with dusky belly. (3) Arboreal Salamander (p. 181) has triangular head, tongue attached in front, and unwebbed toes with broadened, squarish tips. **RANGE:** Near Briceburg, Mariposa Co., Calif., at confluence of Bear Creek and Merced R., along tributaries of Bear

Creek, on N. Fork of Merced R., and at Hell Hollow. Around 980–2,600 ft. (300–800 m). Briceburg locality is a state ecological reserve.

REMARKS: Suitable habitat for this species occurs farther up Merced R. toward Yosemite Nat'l Park, especially along north-facing slope. Possible contact or overlap with Mount Lyell Salamander may occur.

Because of the special requirements of this rare salamander (its association with often moss-covered, long-stabilized limestone talus, steep slopes that face northwest to east, and frequent presence in oak/buckeye woodland with thick understory), any proposed road or trail construction, or damming of drainages that would raise water levels that might inundate or destabilize talus, must be carefully reviewed before considering implementation. The Hell Hollow site is of special concern because it appears to have the largest existing population.

FROGS AND TOADS

TAILED FROGS: FAMILY ASCAPHIDAE

The Tailed Frog is named for its tail-like copulatory organ. Fertilization is internal by copulation, a method of breeding unique among frogs. It inhabits cold streams, where its tadpole lives in torrents or quiet water and clings to rocks with its large suckerlike mouth. Two to 4 years may be required for larvae to transform, and breeding may not occur until frogs are 7–8 years. old. Amplexus is pelvic.

TAILED FROG *Ascaphus truei* Pl. 15, Map 29

IDENTIFICATION: 1–2 in. (2.5–5.1 cm). Olive, brown, gray, or reddish above, usually with pale yellow or greenish triangle on snout and dark eye stripe. Colors match rock colors in and near streams. Flat-bodied and toadlike. Skin rather rough. Eye with a vertical pupil. *Outermost hind toe broadest.* **Male:** Tail-like copulatory organ with vent opening at tip. Palmar and forearm tubercles (see front endpaper) darken in fall and small, horny, black pads develop on each side of chest. No "tail" or pads in female.

Frequents clear, cold, rocky streams in humid forests of Douglas-fir, pine, spruce, hemlock, redwood, maple, and alder. Grassland, chaparral, or shrub growth may be interspersed. Trees sometimes absent. The frog quickly reestablished itself on treeless terrain created by eruption of Mt. St. Helens in Wash. In dry weather, found on moist stream banks or under stones on bottom of streams. A rocky streambed is important in providing hiding places for larvae and sites of attachment for eggs and cover for adults. Larvae often found foraging on organic films on rocks. Look for eyeshine near water's edge at night. Usually stays close to water but may venture into damp woods after rains. Adults abroad from April to Oct., but time varies with locality. Males may

Tailed Frog. The "tail" is actually a copulatory organ that ensures effective transfer of sperm in the fast-flowing waters commonly occupied. This is the only frog known to have such an organ.

clasp females any time of year, but most breeding appears to occur in early fall (late Aug. and Sept.). Eggs usually laid in June and July, hatching in Aug. and Sept. (n. Idaho and se. Wash.). Eggs unpigmented; laid in globular clusters of rosary-like strings under stones. **VOICE:** Apparently none. **SIMILAR SPECIES:** (1) Foothill Yellow-legged Frog (p. 231) has a horizontal pupil; 5th toe is not enlarged. (2) Pacific Treefrog (p. 222) has toe pads. **RANGE:** Chiefly west of crest of Cascades Mts., from sw. B.C. to near Anchor Bay, Mendocino Co., Calif. Rocky Mts. of extreme se. B.C., Idaho, and Mont.; extreme se. Wash. and ne. Ore. in Blue and Wallowa Mts. Unverified reports from Ochoco Mts., Ore. Ranges east in n. Calif. to vicinity of Big Bend, Shasta Co. Many isolated populations, including one at Kitimat near coast and several in Crowfoot Mts. (Shuswap Lake area), B.C. Near sea level to at least 8,390 ft. (2,557 m).

REMARKS: Coastal and inland populations have been proposed as separate species.

LEPTODACTYLID FROGS: FAMILY LEPTODACTYLIDAE

A large family of New World frogs (over 900 species), well represented in the American tropics—in s. U.S., Mexico, Central America, S. America, and Caribbean Is. Land-dwelling, aquatic, and arboreal. Most lay eggs in water, and tadpoles develop in the usual fashion, but some lay eggs in foamlike masses in pockets in the ground; rains wash tadpoles into nearby pools. Others, such as members of the genus *Eleutherodactylus,* are completely terrestrial, lay eggs on land, and guard them; young emerge fully formed. A Puerto Rican species, the Golden Coqui Frog (*E. coqui*), is ovoviviparous.

Proportions froglike or toadlike. Underside of toes usually has prominent tubercles at joints, teeth are present in upper jaw, and eardrums generally are smooth and semitransparent. Some species have a circular fold of skin on belly.

Six species in U.S., 1 introduced.

BARKING FROG *Eleutherodactylus augusti*   Pl. 19, Map 30

IDENTIFICATION: 2–3¾ in. (5.1–9.5 cm). Toadlike, but toes slender and unwebbed, with tips slightly expanded and prominent tubercules beneath joints. Walks in stilted fashion with hindquarters and heels well off the ground. *Fold of skin across back of head and circular fold on belly. Eardrum smooth and semitransparent.* Greenish to light brown above, marked with dark blotches that often have light borders. Conspicuous dark brown eyes. **Young:** Light-colored band across back that rapidly fades with age. **Male:** Much smaller than female.

Secretive, terrestrial, often rock-dwelling species frequently found in limestone areas. Hides by day under rocks and in mines, wells, caves, fissures, and rodent burrows. Ranges from creosote bush flats, treeless, dry, yucca-covered hills, or brushy woodland into open pine forests. In Tex., found in juniper–live oak woodland; in Sonora in large, low, dense clumps of cactus. Breeds with onset of summer rainy season. Eggs large-yolked and unpigmented; laid Feb.–June in caves, fissures, or under rocks during periods of rainfall. Young hatch fully formed (no aquatic larval stage). **VOICE:** Resembles bark of a small dog—a series of rapid yapping notes at intervals of 1½–3 seconds, but more of a guttural *whurr* at close range. May also sound like croak of a raven. **SIMILAR SPECIES:** Northern Casque-headed Frog, although having fold of skin at back of head, lacks transparent eardrums and numerous tubercles on underside of feet. **RANGE:** Extreme s. Ariz. (Santa Rita, Pajarito, and Huachuca Mts.), se. N.M. (lower Pecos R. drainage), and cen. Tex. (escarpment of Edwards Plateau) south to Isthmus of Tehuantepec. An old report for Parker Canyon, Sierra Anchas, Gila Co., Ariz., requires confimation. Limestone outcrops in the area. Distribution spotty. Near sea level to 8,900 ft. (2,710 m) in Mexico.

SPADEFOOT TOADS AND RELATIVES:
FAMILY PELOBATIDAE

Our species, members of genera *Spea* and *Scaphiopus*, are found only in the New World. In general appearance they look a lot alike. Five species occur in our area. They are distinguished from True Toads (genus *Bufo*) by their catlike eyes, the single black, sharp-edged "spade" on each hind foot, teeth in upper jaw, and rather smooth skin; parotoid glands are absent or indistinct. Pupils vertical in bright light, round at night. Males may have dusky throat and dark nuptial pads on innermost front toes. Amplexus is pelvic. True toads typically have horizontally oval pupils, 2 rounded brown tubercles on each foot, no teeth, warty skin, large parotoid glands, and amplexus is pectoral.

Spadefoots breed in pools that form after heavy rains or in slow streams, springs, reservoirs, or irrigation ditches. Voices of males are audible for a great distance and are important in bringing the sexes together for breeding in arid country where the number, location, and suitability of breeding sites is uncertain. A parched region may reverberate with their cries soon after rain begins. They are "explosive" breeders, responding quickly to heavy rainfall, often of thunderstorms. Breeding aggregations are usually brief: males scramble to compete for females, the larger males often more successful. Development is rapid—egg to transformation may occur in 8–16 days.

Dry periods are spent in self-made burrows or those of gophers, squirrels, or kangaroo rats. Spadefoots are active chiefly at night during spring and summer rains. When burrowing they back into the ground by pushing aside dirt with their spades while rotating the body, the hind feet moving alternately in a circular fashion. Since Spadefoots often spawn in temporary pools that form in shallow natural depressions, they suffer from the cratering effects of cattle hoofs that isolate water pockets where tadpoles may become trapped as the pool shrinks. In the New World, Spadefoots range from Canada to Mexico and from coast to coast. 11 species, 5 in our area. Other members of the family occur in Europe, sw. Africa, Asia, and E. Indies.

COUCH'S SPADEFOOT *Scaphiopus couchii*   **Pl. 12, Map 28**
IDENTIFICATION: 2 1/4–3 3/5 in. (5.7–9.1 cm). A large greenish, greenish yellow, or brownish yellow spadefoot with an irregular network, blotches, or flecks of black, brown, or dark green. Whitish below. Eyes widely separated—width of eyelids about the same as or less than the distance between them. *No boss or fontanelle between eyes, and no pug-dog profile. Spade* on hind foot black, *sickle-shaped* (Fig. 9, Pl. 12, p. 58). **Young:** Often heavily dark-blotched. **Male:** Often more greenish than female. Dark dorsal markings usually subdued or absent. Throat pale.

Frequents shortgrass prairie, mesquite savanna, creosote bush desert, thorn forest, and tropical deciduous forest (w. Mexico), and other areas of low rainfall. Sneezing and discharge from eyes and nostrils have been reported from handling this species. **VOICE:** Plaintive nasal cry or groan, declining in pitch, like the anxious bleat of a lamb, lasting ½–1 ¼ seconds. In our area breeds chiefly from May–Sept. during periods of rainfall. Vocal sac round. **SIMILAR SPECIES:** Other Spadefoots have wedge-shaped spade, eyes set closer together, and a pug-dog profile. Plains Spadefoot (p. 205) and Great Basin Spadefoot (p. 204) have cranial boss between the eyes. **RANGE:** From sw. Okla., n.-cen. N.M., and s.-cen. Ariz., to tip of Baja Calif., Nayarit, s. San Luis Potosí, and cen. Veracruz, Mex.; se. Calif. to cen. Tex. Isolated populations at Petrified Forest Nat'l Park, Ariz., and southeast of La Junta, Otero Co., Colo. Scattered populations in Calif. between Amos and Ogilby on e. side of Algodones Dunes; Purgatory and Buzzard's Peak Washes, Imperial Co.; and 15 mi. (24 km) north of Vidal Junction, San Bernardino Co. Near sea level to around 5,905 ft. (1,800 m).

WESTERN SPADEFOOT *Spea hammondii* Pl. 12, Map 27

IDENTIFICATION: 1 ½–2 ½ in. (3.8–6.3 cm). *No cranial boss between eyes.* Dusky green or gray above, often with 4 irregular, light-colored stripes on the back; the central pair sometimes set off a dark, hourglass-shaped area. Skin tubercles tipped with orange or reddish. Eye usually pale gold. Whitish to light gray below, without markings. Wedge-shaped, glossy black spade on each hind foot. Distance between eyes usually less than width of eyelid.

Primarily a species of the lowlands, frequenting washes, floodplains of rivers, alluvial fans, playas, and alkali flats, but also ranges into foothills and mountains. Prefers areas of open vegetation and short grasses, where soil is sandy or gravelly. Found in valley and foothill grasslands, open chaparral, and pine-oak woodlands. Breeds Jan.–May in quiet streams and temporary pools. When handled, this toad may smell like roasted peanuts. Its skin secretion may cause sneezing. **VOICE:** Hoarse, snorelike; lasting about ½–1 second. May call from a floating position. A distant chorus suggests the sound of someone cutting wood with a handsaw. **SIMILAR SPECIES:** (1) Plains Spadefoot (p. 205) and (2) Great Basin Spadefoot (p. 204) have a boss between the eyes. (3) Mexican Spadefoot (p. 206) has a more elongate spade, is brownish above, and has a copper-colored iris. (4) Couch's Spadefoot (p. 202) has an elongate, sickle-shaped spade and widely spaced eyes. **RANGE:** Great Valley, bordering foothills, and Coast Ranges south of Monterey Bay, Calif., into nw. Baja Calif. (to Mesa de San Carlos). To over 4,000 ft. (1,219 m) but mostly below 3,000 ft. (910 m). Now apparently extinct throughout much of lowland s. Calif. but still persists in coastal Orange, w. Riverside, and inland San Diego Cos. Extensive losses in n. Calif. but still present near Black Butte Reservoir, Glenn Co.

REMARKS: From Santa Clara R. valley, Los Angeles, and Ventura Cos. southward, an estimated 80 percent of habitat has been lost, and severe damage has occurred in the Central Valley. Loss of vernal pools and perhaps mosquito abatement are among factors.

GREAT BASIN SPADEFOOT   Pl. 12, Map 25
Spea intermontana

IDENTIFICATION: 1 ½–2 ½ in. (3.8–6.3 cm). Resembles Western Spadefoot (p. 203) in structure and color. Ash gray streaks usually set off a well-defined hourglass marking of gray or olive on the back. Ground color above is gray, olive, or brown. Dark brown spot usually present on each upper eyelid. Spade on hind foot wedge-shaped. *Glandular boss between eyes* may help protect head when spadefoot pushes its way to the surface after a period of burial underground.

Found in Great Basin and outlying areas in sagebrush flats, semidesert shrublands, and piñon-juniper woodland to high elevations in the spruce-fir belt (Cedar Breaks, Utah). Inhabits agricultural areas of Columbian Basin of e. Wash. and elsewhere. Breeds April–July in permanent and temporary water, often (but not necessarily) after spring and summer rains. In Great Basin breeding seems usually to occur in response to winter-spring rainfall. May emit a peanutlike odor when handled. **VOICE:** A low-pitched hoarse snore, *wa-wa-wa;* a series of short rapid calls, each lasting about ⅕–1 second, repeated over and over. Rounded, slightly bilobed vocal sac. **SIMILAR SPECIES:** (1) Western (p. 203) and

Great Basin Spadefoot. Spadefoot toads live in arid and semiarid environments of uncertain rainfall. They depend on burrowing abilities to survive. Grant Co., Wash.

The digging spade of the Great Basin Spadefoot. The spade is horny, sharp-edged, and located on the inside of the hind foot.

(2) Couch's Spadefoot (p. 202) lacks the boss between the eyes. (3) In the Plains Spadefoot (below), the boss is hard and supported by thickened bone. Differences in interorbital boss area among Spadefoots are subtle and cannot be determined adequately without dissection. **RANGE:** From extreme s. B.C. (north to 70 Mile House), south through Great Basin to extreme nw. Ariz., and from eastern base of Cascade-Sierran mountain system to Rockies. In Wyo. it ranges east to near Alcova, Natrona Co. To around 9,200 ft. (2,800 m). Hybridizes with the Southern Spadefoot in eastern Utah.

PLAINS SPADEFOOT *Spea bombifrons* Pl. 12, Map 26

IDENTIFICATION: 1 ¼–2 ½ in. (3.2–6.3 cm). A spadefoot with *prominent boss* (often supported by thickened bone) between eyes and a pug-dog profile. Usually has 4 light stripes of irregular outline, the middle pair often setting off an hourglass shape in middle of back. Above generally dusky, purplish brown, dark brown, grayish, or greenish, flecked with orange to yellow-tipped tubercles; white below. A single glossy, black, wedge-shaped spade on each hind foot. Width of eyelids usually greater than distance between them.

Inhabits plains, hills, and river bottoms in mixed-grass prairie, sagebrush habitats, desert grassland, and farmland chiefly east of the Rocky Mts., in regions of low rainfall. Prefers loose, sandy, or gravelly soil suitable for burrowing. Usually breeds in flooded areas and temporary pools. In southern part of its range it breeds during period of summer rains in N.M., in Colo. from May to Aug., in Okla. mid-March to mid-July, and in the north (Alberta) as early as the latter part of May and into summer, and May to Aug. in Manitoba. Tadpoles often cannibalistic. VOICE: Snorelike rasping sound lasting ½–¾ second. Pulse rate faster than the Mexican Spadefoot, call shorter and more rapidly trilled. Fast mating calls are heard in southwestern portion of species range. These calls may last only a half second or less, are rapidly repeated, and sound like the quack of a duck. SIMILAR SPECIES: (1) Western Spadefoot (p. 203), (2) Mexican Spadefoot (below) (except some hybrids with the Plains Spadefoot), and (3) Couch's Spadefoot (p. 202) have no boss between the eyes. Couch's Spadefoot has a sickle-shaped spade, widely spaced eyes, the width of the eyelid equal to or slightly less than the interorbital distance; it also tends to be greenish yellow above with dorsal mottling. (4) In the Great Basin Spadefoot (p. 204) the boss tends to be more glandular (fleshy), and the spade is longer and narrower. (5) The Great Plains Toad (p. 215) has 2 brown tubercles on each hind foot. RANGE: E. and s. outwash plains of Rocky Mts. from s. Alberta, Saskatchewan, and Manitoba to N.M., southwest to nw. Tex., east across Mo. along Missouri River valley and to e. Okla. Skirts Rockies to south and enters e. Ariz. and Chihuahua, Mex. Isolated populations in s. Tex. and extreme ne. Mexico. An old record from Dauphin, Manitoba. To about 8,000 ft. (2,440 m). Frequently hybridizes with Mexican Spadefoot in southern part of its range.

MEXICAN SPADEFOOT *Spea multiplicata*   Pl. 12, Map 27

IDENTIFICATION: 1 ½–2 ½ in. (3.8–6.3 cm). Above uniformly brown or dark gray with scattered dark spots or blotches and red-tipped large and numerous dorsal tubercules. Iris often copper colored. Lacks cranial boss (hybrids with Plains Spadefoot may be exceptions). Distance between eyes unusually less than width of eyelid. Spade on hind foot wedge-shaped.

Frequents desert grassland, shortgrass plains, creosote bush and sagebrush desert, mixed grassland and chaparral, piñon-juniper and pine-oak woodlands, and open pine forests. Soil often sandy or gravelly. Breeds during period of summer rains. When handled, may emit a peanutlike odor and cause tearing and nasal discharge if skin secretion comes close to or in contact with one's face. VOICE: Similar to other Spadefoot calls but when given at same temperature, tends to be longer, slower trill, lasting about ¾–1 ½ seconds. A metallic vibrating snore. The sound has been compared to running a fingernail along stiff teeth of a comb. SIMILAR SPECIES: See Western Spadefoot (p. 203). RANGE: Sw. Utah and s. Colo. to Guerrero and Oaxaca, Mex.; w. Ariz. to w. Okla. and w. Tex. Near sea level to around 9,000 ft. (2,743 m).

Worldwide, but absent from extremely cold or dry areas and remote oceanic islands. Over 400 species. The only true toad in Australia, the Marine Toad, *Bufo marinus*, has been introduced. Many toads can live under adverse conditions. They range from below sea level in Death Valley, Calif., to above 16,000 ft. (4,880 m) in the Andes of S. America and from the tropics nearly to the Arctic Circle. Fourteen species are found in the West.

Our species (genus *Bufo*), containing more than half the family's species, are chunky, short-legged, and warty. Parotoid glands distinguish them from all our other tail-less amphibians (see Spadefoot Toads, p. 201). The parotoids and warts secrete a sticky white poison, which in some species can paralyze or kill dogs and other predators. Many animals, however, eat toads with no ill effect. Skin secretion may irritate eyes or mouth, and if swallowed in quantity can cause illness. However, ordinary handling appears to pose no danger, and handling toads does not cause warts.

Western U.S. species differ in color, size, shape of the parotoid glands, prominence and arrangement of cranial crests, wartiness, and appearance of foot tubercles. Color may change from light to dark in response to temperature.

Breeding usually occurs in spring and summer, often after rains. Adult males of most species have a dark throat; exceptions are the Western, Black, Yosemite, Arroyo, Arizona, and Sonoran Desert Toads. All male toads develop dark roughened nuptial pads on thumb and inner fingers that help them cling to the slippery female body during amplexus, which is pectoral in True Toads.

SONORAN DESERT TOAD (COLORADO RIVER TOAD)
Bufo alvarius   **Pl. 14, Map 40**

IDENTIFICATION: 4–7½ in. (10.1–19 cm). Our largest western toad. Dark brown, olive, or gray above, with smooth skin; long, kidney-shaped parotoids; and prominent cranial crests. *Several large warts on hind legs stand out conspicuously against smooth skin.* Enlarged whitish wart near angle of jaw. Cream below. **Young:** Light-colored warts, set in dark spots. **Male:** Throat pale, as in female.

Ranges from arid mesquite-creosote bush lowlands and grasslands into the oak-sycamore-walnut plant community in mountain canyons, and montane pine-oak-juniper associations. Enters tropical thorn forest in Mexico. Often found near permanent water of springs, reservoirs, canals, and streams, but also frequents temporary pools and reported several miles from water. Widespread throughout desert. Nocturnal. Activity stimulated by rainfall, but not dependent on rainfall for breeding. Breeds May–Sept. Most active May–July. Like most toads, it assumes a butting pose when molested, with its parotoid glands directed toward the intruder. A dog may be temporarily paralyzed (or, rarely, killed) if it mouths one of these toads. The skin secretion also has hallucinogenic properties. **VOICE:** Low-pitched, resembling a ferry-boat whistle. Hoots last ½ to about 1 second. Vocal sac absent or vestigial. **SIMILAR SPECIES:** (1) Woodhouse's Toad has pale median dorsal stripe. (2) Great Plains Toad has paired blotches on dorsum. (3) Arizona Toad has oval-shaped parotoid glands and lacks enlarged warts on hindlimbs. (4) Spadefoot Toads lack parotoid glands. **RANGE:** From the Bill Williams R. and lower Colorado R. drainages across cen. and s. Ariz. to extreme sw. N.M., south to nw. Sinaloa; extreme se. Calif., where it is now apparently extinct. Sight record for mouth of Seventy-five Mile Canyon below Hance Creek, Grand Canyon. Reported from Tiburon I., Gulf of Calif., Mex. Sea level to 5,784 ft. (1,763 m). Several presumed hybrids resulting from matings with Woodhouse's Toad have been found in cen. Ariz.

WESTERN TOAD *Bufo boreas* Pl. 13, Map 32

IDENTIFICATION: 2–5 in. (5.1–12.7 cm). *The white or cream-colored dorsal stripe and lack of cranial crests will usually identify this toad.* Parotoid glands are oval, well separated, and slightly larger than upper eyelids viewed from above. Well-developed tarsal fold. Dusky, yellowish, tan, gray, or greenish above, with warts set in dark blotches and often tinged with rust. **Young:** When recently transformed, around ¼ in. (6 mm). Dorsal stripe weak or absent.

Western Toad. The most widely distributed endemic amphibian in our area. Formerly common and familiar to many, this appealing creature is now declining in many parts of its range. (See Map 32.)

Larger young have prominent spotting, with undersides of feet yellow. **Male:** Usually less blotched and with smoother skin than female. Throat pale, as in female.

Frequents great variety of habitats: desert streams and springs, grassland, woodland, montane forests, and mountain meadows. In and near ponds, lakes, reservoirs, rivers, and streams. Active at night in warm, low-lying areas; diurnal at high elevations and in the north. Buries itself in loose soil or seeks shelter in burrows of gophers, ground squirrels, and other animals. Tends to walk rather than hop. Active Jan.–Oct., breeding late Jan.–July, depending on latitude (April–June in Alberta), elevation, and local conditions. **VOICE:** Mellow high-pitched *chirruping* or *plinking* sound, suggesting peeping of a chick. A chorus may sound like a distant flock of geese. No vocal sac. **SIMILAR SPECIES:** (1) Woodhouse's Toad (p. 211) has conspicuous cranial crests or a cranial boss, and male has a dark throat. (2) Black Toad (p. 210) heavily mottled above and below with black. (3) See also Yosemite Toad (p. 210). **RANGE:** S. Alaska (Tasnuna R. area and Montague I.) and Liard Basin se. Yukon south to n. Baja Calif. to Bahia de Los Angeles; Rocky Mts. to Pacific Coast. Absent from most of arid Southwest, but some isolated populations at Owens Valley, Darwin Falls, Grapevine Canyon near Owens Peak, and Calif. City (where apparently introduced), Kern Co., and Afton Canyon and Newberry Mts., San Bernardino Co., Calif. In N.M. it occurred in San Juan Mts., Rio Arriba Co. Hybridizes with Red-spotted Toad (p. 214) at Darwin Falls, and occasionally with Canadian Toad (p. 216) in cen. Alberta. However, Red-spotted Toad at Darwin Falls may no longer be present. Sea level to over 11,800 ft. (3,600 m). **SUBSPECIES:** BOREAL TOAD, *B. b. boreas.* Considerable dark blotching both above and below. Sometimes almost all dark above, and individuals from e. side of Hot Creek Range, Nye Co., Nev., are dark-bellied. CALIFORNIA TOAD, *B. b. halophilus.* Generally less dark blotching than in Boreal Toad. Head wider, eyes larger (less distance between upper eyelids), and feet smaller. **REMARKS:** Species has seen a substantial range reduction in s. Rocky Mt. region and Pacific Northwest the past two or three decades. Populations in the s. Medicine Bow Mts. of Wyo. are considered severely imperiled, and toad may now be extinct in n. N.M.

MARGOSA TOAD *Bufo nelsoni* Pl. 13, Map 32

IDENTIFICATION: 2–4⅖ in. (5.1–11.2 cm). Resembles Western Toad but head narrower, snout long, and limbs short—elbow and knee do not touch when placed along sides with body held straight. Well-defined whitish dorsal stripe. Spotted and blotched above with black and cream, beige, or tan.

Usually found near water. Diurnal in spring, becoming nocturnal in summer. Breeds March–early April. **VOICE:** Resembles Western Toad's. **SIMILAR SPECIES:** (1) Western Toad (p. 208) tends to have a broader head, blunter snout, longer limbs, larger feet with more webbing, and rougher skin. (2) Black Toad (below) much darker in color. **RANGE:** Amargosa R. valley (Oasis Valley) in vicinity of and at Beatty, Nye Co., Nev. Formerly at nearby Springdale and Indian Springs: apparently no longer present.

REMARKS: This toad was on the edge of extinction. Fortunately, efforts are underway to save it. Protection against crayfish and mosquito fish introductions and habitat management will be crucial to recovery. *Nature Conservancy* (May/June 2000) reports that surveys six years ago turned up 30 adult toads. Lately counts have reached well over 2,000. A conservancy reserve and citizen efforts in and around Beatty, Nev., have been key to recovery.

BLACK TOAD *Bufo exsul* Pl. 13, Map 32

IDENTIFICATION: 1 ¾–3 in. (4.4–7.6 cm). *A small, dark-colored* relative of the Western Toad (p. 208). Often nearly solid black above, with scattered whitish flecks and lines. Narrow white or cream middorsal stripe. White or cream below, heavily spotted and blotched with black. Skin relatively smooth. **Young:** Olive-colored above. Foot tubercles yellow-orange, becoming whitish or cream in older individuals. **Male:** Throat pale, unmarked or lightly spotted, like female's.

Found only in marshes of grass, sedge, dwarf bulrush, and watercress formed by water flow from springs in Deep Springs Valley. Surrounding areas are dry. Highly aquatic, but seen on dry soil over 40 ft. (12 m) from nearest water. Blends with surroundings when on damp soil along canal banks, among bushes, and in dark-colored watercourses, but conspicuous on pale, dried-out soil. Diurnal, but in warmer weather active at night. Active late March–mid-Sept. Breeds chiefly from mid-March–May, perhaps as late as June. **VOICE:** Resembles Western Toad's, but higher pitched. **RANGE:** Deep Springs Corral and Buckhorn Springs at around 5,000 ft. (1,520 m) and Antelope Springs 5,600 ft. (1,710 m), Deep Springs Valley, between the Inyo and White Mts., Inyo Co., Calif. Because of decline in native grazers, it is thought that controlled grazing by cattle at Buckhorn Springs benefits this species by removing vegetation that would choke the habitat and by supplying droppings that attract insects that these toads eat.

YOSEMITE TOAD *Bufo canorus* Pl. 13, Map 33

IDENTIFICATION: 1 ¾–2 ¾ in. (4.4–7 cm). The toad of the high Calif. Sierra Nevada, close relative of Western Toad. Differs in having smoother skin; *large, flat parotoids less than the width of a gland apart*; and closely set eyes—distance between them less than width of upper eyelid (as viewed from above). Sexes differ greatly in color. **Female and Young:** Many blotches on a pale background, parotoids usually tan-colored, dorsal stripe usually narrow or absent. **Male:** Pale yellow-green or dark olive above, with dark blotches virtually absent or reduced to small scattered flecks. Throat pale like female's.

Frequents high mountain meadows and forest borders, emerging soon after the snow melts. Active April–Oct., breeding in shallow pools and lake margins or in quiet water of streams, May–July and perhaps Aug. Chiefly diurnal and usually active only in sunlit areas. On cool days may not be active until afternoon. Seeks shelter in burrows of pocket gophers, meadow mice, Belding's ground squirrels, marmots, and in clumps of grass, sedges, or willows near water. **VOICE:** Mellow, sustained musical trill of 10–20 or more notes, usually uttered rapidly and at frequent intervals. Calls may last 4–5 seconds. **SIMILAR SPECIES:** Immature Yosemite Toads are colored like the Western Toad (p. 208), but parotoids of the latter are farther apart (separated by about twice the width of a gland). Western Toad is present at high elevations in s. Sierra Nevada south of Kaiser Pass, Fresno Co., where habitat resembles that occupied by the Yosemite Toad farther north. **RANGE:** High Sierra of Calif. from vicinity of Grass Lake, Eldorado Co., to south of Kaiser Pass and Evolution Lake, Fresno Co. From 4,800–12,000 ft. (1,460–3,630 m), mostly above 9,000 ft. (2,740 m). Hybridizes with Western Toad in Blue Lakes region and elsewhere in northern part of its range.

REMARKS: Appears to have disappeared from more than 50 percent of historic sites. In addition, reproduction in remaining populations appear to be below replacement levels.

WOODHOUSE'S TOAD *Bufo woodhousii* Pl. 14, Map 35

IDENTIFICATION: 1¾–5 in. (4.4–12.7 cm). *The whitish dorsal stripe, prominent cranial crests, and elongate, divergent parotoids* are important rocognition characteristics. Boss sometimes present between cranial crests. Gray, yellowish brown, olive, greenish, or blackish above, usually with dark blotches. Yellow and black network on rear of thighs. Cream to beige below, with or without dark flecks. **Young:** Dorsal stripe may be weak or absent. **Male:** Throat sooty, setting off pale yellow border of lower jaw.

Frequents a great variety of habitats—grassland, sagebrush flats, woods, desert streams, valleys, floodplains, farms, even city backyards. It seems to prefer sandy areas, breeding in quiet water of streams, marshes, lakes, freshwater pools, and irrigation ditches, usually during or soon after rains. Breeds Feb.–July, sometimes as late as early Sept. **VOICE:** Has been compared to a snore, an infant's cry, and bawling of a calf—a nasal *w-a-a-a-ah*. An explosive, wheezy sound lasting 1–3 seconds, sometimes suddenly dropping in pitch at the end. Vocal sac round. **SIMILAR SPECIES:** (1) Arizona Toad (p. 213) lacks dorsal stripe, has weak cranial crests (if any), more rounded parotoids, and males have pale throats. (2) Canadian Toad (p. 216) has narrow, parallel-sided boss, is heavily spotted below, and has a softer, more musical call. (3) See also Western Toad (p. 208) and Red-spotted Toad (p. 214). **RANGE:** N. Mont. to Durango; Atlantic Coast to se. Wash., w. Utah, and se. Calif. Big Sandy R. near Wikieup, Mohave Co., Ariz. (see dot on map). Near sea level to around 8,500 ft. (2,590 m.). E. U.S. subspecies *B. w. fowleri* has been proposed as a full species based primarily on reinterpretation of the zone of mixing of the two taxa, *fowleri* and *woodhousii*, as a hybrid rather than an intergrade zone. Hybridizes with the Arizona Toad (p. 213), Texas Toad (p. 215), Red-spotted Toad (p. 214), and apparently with the Western Toad (p. 208) in Ash Meadows area west of Spring Mts., s. Nev.

ARROYO TOAD *Bufo californicus*   Pl. 14, Map 34
IDENTIFICATION: 1 ⁴⁄₅–3 ²⁄₅ in. (4.6–8.6 cm). Rather uniformly warty and stocky, usually with light-colored stripe across head, including eyelids. Warts with brown-tipped tubercles. Parotoid glands oval-shaped and widely separated, pale toward front. Above usually greenish gray, olive, or dull brown. *Usually a light area on each sacral hump and in middle of back.* Dorsal stripe rarely present. Buff to whitish below, often unspotted. Cranial crests weak or absent. Inner metatarsal tubercle, small, dull, and rounded. **Young:** Pale above, often with dark spots; yellowish-tipped tubercles on back. Underside of feet yellow to yellow-orange. **Male:** Throat pale, like female's.

A toad of sandy riverbanks, washes, and arroyos. Breeds in and near streams; does not depend directly on rainfall. Frequents riparian areas grown to mulefat, willows, cottonwoods, and/or sycamores or coast live oaks. Has perhaps the most specialized habitat requirements of any of our anuran species, except its close relative, the Arizona Toad—shallow, exposed streamside, quiet water stretches, or overflow pools with silt-free sandy or gravelly bottoms especially favored for breeding. Nearby sandy terraces, dampened in places by capillary action, and with some scattered vegetation providing surface sheltering and burrowing sites for both young and adults. Adults chiefly nocturnal except during breeding season. Hops high and fast more often than walks. Breeds March–July. **VOICE:** Melodious rapid trill, usually lasting 8–10 seconds; often rising in pitch at first and usually ending abruptly. Vocal sac round. **SIMILAR SPECIES:** See (1) Woodhouse's Toad (p. 211) and (2) Texas Toad (p. 215). **RANGE:** S. Calif., chiefly west of desert in coastal mts. and valleys from Hunter Liggett Military Reservation, Monterey Co., to San Quintin–San Simon area in nw. Baja Calif. Desert populations along lower Whitewater R., Riverside Co., and Mojave R., San Bernardino Co., Calif. Near sea level to around 3,000 ft. (900 m).

ARIZONA TOAD *Bufo microscaphus* Pl. 14, Map 34

IDENTIFICATION: Similar to Arroyo Toad but dorsum usually less dark-spotted and relatively smooth. Warts low and with few or no tubercles. General color above often gray but hightly variable at some localities. At Grotto Campground in Zion Nat'l Park, Washington Co., Utah, for example, the following adult dorsal colors were noted: gray, beige, pale dull yellow, rust, brown, and pink. A juvenile was nearly red, brighter than any adult. Front of parotoids, central portion of upper eyelids, and especially central portion of upper back and sacral hump areas often paler than surrounding ground color. **Young:** Above light olive or salmon. Warts often reddish brown. **Male:** Throat pale, like female's.

Frequents riparian areas from lowlands (Fort Mohave area, Ariz.) to high in the uplands of Ariz. Central Plateau. Habitat similar to Arroyo Toad's but ranges in upland areas into pine-oak woodland. Breeds Feb.–July with height of breeding season in June in sw. Utah, but at higher elevations breeding may occur until July and perhaps Aug. **VOICE:** Similar to that of Arroyo Toad. Vocal sac round. **SIMILAR SPECIES:** Differs from Arroyo Toad (p. 212) in having fewer warts on dorsum, less development of tubercles, less dorsal spotting, and apparently greater overall variation in dorsal coloration. **RANGE:** Highly fragmented. Sw. Utah and se. Nev. to near Fort Mohave, Mohave Co., Ariz.; Mogollon Rim of sw. N.M. and cen. Ariz. Associated with drainages of Virgin R. in Utah and Meadow Valley Wash in Nev. (now occupied by apparent hybrids with Woodhouse's Toad), Gila and San Fransico Rs. in N.M., and tributaries of Gila in Ariz. (Verde, Agua Fria, Hassayampa, etc.); along the Santa Maria and Big Sandy Rs., tributaries of Bill Williams R. in w. Ariz. From around 600 to 6,000 ft (190–1,829 m). Hybridizes with Woodhouse's Toad along Virgin R. and in cen. Ariz.

REMARKS: Arizona Toad now absent in riparian habitats greatly altered by construction of impoundments. The quieter waters so formed favor breeding of Woodhouse's Toad with which it hybridizes. Now considered extinct in the Las Vegas area and has lost its distinctiveness through hybridization with Woodhouse's Toad at the lower Meadow Valley Wash area and in lower Virgin R. drainage. Arroyo Toad (p. 212) also extirpated due to habitat loss in large areas of s. Calif. and threatened by water surges from dams, placer mining, exotic predators, and off-road vehicle and foot traffic on sandy banks and within shallow nursery areas of streams. Estimated to have disappeared from around 75 percent of its known historic range.

RED-SPOTTED TOAD *Bufo punctatus*   Pl. 13, Map 41

IDENTIFICATION: 1 ½–3 in. (3.8–7.6 cm). Small with a *flattened head and body and round parotoids*, each about same size as toad's eye. Snout pointed. Cranial crests weak or absent. Light gray, olive, or reddish brown above, with reddish or orange warts. Whitish to buff below, with or without spotting. **Young:** Numerous red- or orange-tipped warts. Dark-spotted below. Underside of feet yellow. **Male:** Throat dusky.

A toad of desert streams and oases, open grassland and scrubland, oak woodland, rocky canyons, and arroyos. Sometimes found on floodplains of rivers; more often on or among rocks, where it shelters in crevices. Climbs rocks with ease. Breeds March–Sept. during or after rains in springs, rain pools, reservoirs, and temporary pools of intermittent streams. May breed in spring independent of rainfall. Chiefly nocturnal, but may be diurnal when breeding. **VOICE:** A prolonged, clear musical trill, less rapid and clearer than the Green Toad's (p. 217), lasting 4–10 seconds. Pitch high, often nearly constant but occasionally dropping toward the end. Vocal sac round. **SIMILAR SPECIES:** Young Woodhouse's Toads (p. 211), which may have reddish-tipped warts, usually have elongate parotoids and a middorsal stripe. **RANGE:** S. Nev. and sw. Kans. to Hidalgo and tip of Baja Calif., Mex.; cen. Tex. to se. Calif. From below sea level (Death Valley, Calif.) to around 7,200 ft. (2,200 m). Has hybridized with Western Toad at

A Red-spotted Toad vocalizing. Its voice is a prolonged melodious trill often heard in spring and summer in rocky canyons and arroyos of the arid Southwest. Clark Co., Nev.

Darwin Canyon, Inyo Co., and at Rawson Canyon near Skinner Reservoir, Riverside Co., Calif.; with Woodhouse's Toad in the Grand Canyon region, Ariz., and apparently near Grand Junction, Mesa Co., Colo.

GREAT PLAINS TOAD *Bufo cognatus* Pl. 13, Map 37

IDENTIFICATION: 1 ⅘–4 ½ in. (4.6–11.4 cm). Large with well-defined, *pale-bordered dark blotches, in symmetrical pairs on its back.* Cranial crests diverge widely toward rear and are more or less united on the snout to form a boss. Inner tubercle on each hind foot usually sharp-edged. Generally light brown, olive, or gray above, with dusky, olive, or green blotches. Sometimes a narrow middorsal stripe. Whitish below, usually unspotted. **Young:** Numerous small brick-red tubercles. Crests form a V. **Male:** Dark loose skin of deflated vocal sac often partly concealed by pale skin flap.

Inhabits prairies or deserts, often breeding after heavy rains in summer in shallow temporary pools or quiet water of streams, marshes, irrigation ditches, and flooded fields, where it may gather in large numbers. Primarily a grassland species but frequents creosote bush desert, mesquite woodland, and sagebrush plains in the West. Mostly nocturnal. A proficient burrower. Breeds Feb.–Sept., in spring and summer in the far north (Alberta). **VOICE:** Harsh explosive clatter resembling a jackhammer, lasting 5–50 or more seconds, almost deafening when large numbers are heard at close range. When inflated, vocal sac sausage-shaped, ⅓ size of body. **SIMILAR SPECIES:** (1) Texas Toad (below) may have pairs of spots on its back, but they are smaller and less well defined. Cranial crests and boss on snout less prominent. Voice a series of short trills rather than a prolonged clatter. (2) See also Plains Spadefoot (p. 205). **RANGE:** Great Plains, extreme s. Canada to San Luis Potosí, Mex.; w. Tex. to extreme se. Calif. and s. Nev. Spotty distribution in desert part of range. Near sea level to around 8,000 ft. (2,440 m). Hybridizes with Texas Toad and apparently rarely with Red-spotted, Woodhouse's, and Canadian Toads.

TEXAS TOAD *Bufo speciosus* Pl. 13, Map 38

IDENTIFICATION: 2–3 ½ in. (5.1–8.9 cm). Close relative of the Great Plains Toad (above). Rather *plain-colored, uniformly warty with no dorsal stripe. Cranial crests weak or absent.* Tubercles on hind foot usually blackish and sharp-edged, the inner one sickle-shaped. Parotoid glands oval and widely separated. Greenish gray to brown above, sometimes with dark blotches on back arranged in symmetrical pairs. White to cream below, unmarked or with dark spots. **Young:** Gray-brown above, blotched with green and flecked with black. Warts tipped with red. **Male:** Olive-colored skin of deflated vocal sac covered by pale skin fold.

Nocturnal, burrowing species of mesquite savanna, prairie, and farmland. Breeds after rains, April–Sept., in quiet water of rain pools, reservoirs, and cattle tanks. **VOICE:** Continuous series of explosive, shrill trills like a riveting gun, usually all on one pitch, each lasting about ½–1½ seconds, often given at intervals of about 1 second. After minutes of calling, may be a distinct drop in pitch followed by return to original pitch. Vocal sac sausage-shaped. **SIMILAR SPECIES:** (1) Arizona Toad (p. 213) has light-colored band across the head and light-colored patch at front end of each parotoid gland and on each sacral hump. Hind foot tubercles brown, not sharp-edged. (2) See also Great Plains Toad (p. 215). **RANGE:** Extreme sw. Kans., s. N.M., and Tex. into ne. Mex. Near sea level to around 4,200 ft. (1,300 m). Hybridizes with Woodhouse's Toad (p. 211) and Great Plains Toad (p. 215).

CANADIAN TOAD *Bufo hemiophrys* Pl. 14, Map 36

IDENTIFICATION: 1½–3 in. (3.8–7.6 cm). Generally brownish, greenish, to light gray above, with reddish tubercles located in dark spots. Spots usually lack light-colored borders. Individuals may be rust red to reddish brown, some may be tinged greenish. Whitish stripe on back. *Parallel-sided boss on head;* boss may be slightly convex or flat, sometimes with furrow down the middle. Whitish below, spotted with dusky and becoming yellowish on sides. **Young:** Cranial crests appear with age and eventually unite to form a boss. **Male:** Throat dark-colored.

A prairie and aspen parklands toad, usually found in or near water. Frequents lakes, ponds, streams, marshes, potholes, and roadside ditches, where it usually breeds in shallows. May swim well out from shore when frightened. Chiefly diurnal during breeding season, retiring to sandy or loamy areas to bury itself at night. May be active on warm nights. Overwintering may occur at communal sites. Active from late March–Sept.; breeds May–July, depending on locality. **VOICE:** A clear trill lasting about 1⅓–5 seconds. Similar to call of Woodhouse's Toad. Call usually ends abruptly. Vocal sac round. **SIMILAR SPECIES:** See Woodhouse's Toad (p. 211). **RANGE:** Fort Smith area, NW Terr., Canada to ne. S.D.; cen. Alta. to nw. Minn. A report for Sawmill Bay, s. side Great Bear Lake, NW Terr., is considered dubious. Isolated populations in se. Wyo. (the Wyoming Toad) formerly along Big and Little Laramie Rs. to about 15 mi. (24 km) north and 15 mi. (24 km) west of Laramie, Albany Co. From around 1,000–7,000 ft. (300–2,130 m). Interbreeds with American Toad (*B. americanus*) outside our area in eastern part of its range. Coexists with Western Toad in cen. Alta. (north of Edmonton).

REMARKS: Wyoming Toad considered to be on brink of extinction. Now apparently only one free-ranging population at a small lake in Laramie Valley. Efforts are underway to reestablish toad through captive breeding. Victim of a variety of human disturbances. Populations in Alta., Canada, have also undergone significant declines since 1986. The Wyoming Toad is considered a full species, *Bufo baxteri,* by some herpetologists.

GREEN TOAD *Bufo debilis*   Pl. 12, Map 39

IDENTIFICATION: 1 ⅛–2 in. (2.8–5.1 cm). A small, flat, *green or yellow-green* toad with small black spots and bars on its back. Black markings may be more or less united to form a network. Large, elongate, widely separated parotoids. Cranial crests weak or absent. White below. **Male:** Throat dark; yellow or cream in female.

A species of arid and semiarid plains, valleys, and foothills — treeless or with scattered shrubs and trees and grass around the pools usually sought as spawning sites. Frequents grasslands, mesquite savanna, and creosote bush flats. Ordinarily not found on steep slopes or in barren rocky areas. A secretive, burrowing, nocturnal toad, generally abroad for only a brief period during and after rains. Breeds April–Aug. in temporary streams and pools that form during summer rainy season; occasionally in irrigation ditches and reservoirs. When trilling, Green Toads often hide under clumps of grass or other growth near water and are difficult to see. However, they may also call from exposed locations on muddy banks near water or from floating positions. Use triangulation to find them (see p. 18). **VOICE:** A wheezy buzz lasting about 2–10 seconds and ending abruptly; usually given at intervals of 5 seconds or more. Vocal sac round. **SIMILAR SPECIES:** See Sonoran Green Toad (below). **RANGE:** Se. Colo. and sw. Kans. to Zacatecas; se. Ariz. to e. Tex. To above 6,000 ft. (1,830 m), but mostly to around 4,000 ft. (1,220 m).

SUBSPECIES: WESTERN GREEN TOAD, *B. d. insidior,* occurs in our area.

SONORAN GREEN TOAD *Bufo retiformis*   Pl. 12, Map 39

IDENTIFICATION: 1 ⅛–2 ⅘ (2.8–7.1 cm). Similar to Green Toad (Pl. 12) but *vividly marked above with network of black* or brownish that sets off oval areas of greenish yellow ground color. These oval areas about twice the size of those on Green Toad of similar size. **Male:** Throat dark.

A secretive nocturnal species of creosote bush flats, upland saguaro–palo verde association, and mesquite grassland. Breeds July–Aug. in rainwater sumps and wash bottoms bordered by fresh grass and scattered shrubs. Males begin to call at nightfall after summer rains, usually from among grass, often close to the water's edge, but occasionally from more distant sites. **VOICE:** A combined high-pitched buzz and whistle, a wheezy call usually lasting 1–4 seconds, gradually lowering in pitch or remaining constant and ending abruptly. May be highly ventriloquial, sounding as if 20 ft. (6 m) away when within 5 ft. (1.5 m). Voice resembles the Great Plains Narrow-mouthed Toad's. Vocal sac round. **SIMILAR SPECIES:** Green Toad (p. 217) has a more broken black network dorsally, often represented by scattered spots and bars that enclose areas of light ground color that are usually only half the size of those of the Sonoran Green Toad. **RANGE:** S.-cen. Ariz. south to w.-cen. Sonora. In s. Ariz. from Santa Rosa Wash, Pinal Co., and Organ Pipe Cactus Nat'l Monument to near the San Xavier Mission, Pima Co. From about 500–2,400 ft. (150–730 m). Hybrids between this species and Red-spotted Toad found near Quijotoa, Pima Co., Ariz.

TREEFROGS AND THEIR ALLIES: FAMILY HYLIDAE

A large family (around 800 species) of usually slim-waisted, long-legged frogs, mostly of small size. Many hylids are arboreal and have well-developed toe pads set off from the rest of the toe by a small, extra segment (Fig. 5, No. 6, p. 28). Found on all continents except Antarctica, these frogs are most abundant and varied in the New World tropics. Treefrogs (*Pternohyla* and *Hyla*), a Cricket Frog (*Acris*), and a Chorus Frog (*Pseudacris*) occur in our area. Amplexus is pectoral.

NORTHERN CRICKET FROG *Acris crepitans*   Pl. 15, Map 45

IDENTIFICATION: ⅝–1½ in. (1.6–3.8 cm). A small, slim-waisted frog with webbed hind toes and triangular mark on head (occasionally absent). No obvious toe pads. Above gray, light brown, green, reddish, or mix of reddish and green, usually with middorsal stripe of similar color. Gray form is common in western and northern parts of range. Dark markings on back and dark bands on legs. *White bar or blotches* usually extend from eye to base of foreleg. *Dark stripe on rear of thigh.* **Male:** Throat dusky, often suffused with yellow. More spotting below than in female.

Ranges widely over e. and cen. U.S., entering shortgrass plains of e. Colo. and N.M. along streams and rivers. Basks on sunny banks of shallow pools. Often found in groups; individuals scatter when frightened, leaping high and fast or skittering over water's surface. Active all year except in cold weather in the north and at high elevations. Breeds Feb.–Aug. **VOICE:** A metallic *gick, gick, gick* —resembling sound you can make by striking two stones together; about 1–3 calls per second, the rate gradually increasing and sometimes decreasing toward the end. Vocal sac round. **SIMILAR SPECIES:** Young frogs (*Rana* species, p. 224) may be mistaken for a Cricket Frog. Look for thigh stripe, triangular mark on the head, and white facial blotches or bar of Cricket Frog. **RANGE:** Mich. to ne. Mex.; Long I., N.Y. to e. Colo. and se. N.M. Near sea level to around 4,000 ft. (1,220 m).

SUBSPECIES: BLANCHARD'S CRICKET FROG, *A. c. blanchardi*, occurs in our area.

REMARKS: This species has declined in the northern and northwestern margins of its range. May now be extinct in Colo.

WESTERN CHORUS FROG   Pl. 15, Map 42
Pseudacris triseriata

IDENTIFICATION: ¾–1 ⅗ in. (1.9–4.1 cm). A small, slim frog *without toe pads* and little webbing. Proportions stockier, tibia shortened in western and northwestern part of range. Dorsal coloration highly variable gray, brown, reddish, olive, or green. Several different color types may occur at same locality. Dark stripe from snout through eye region to groin, contrasting with white stripe on the upper jaw. Usually 3 dark stripes on back, sometimes broken or replaced by spots, especially in northern and western populations. Often a triangular spot on head. Whitish, yellowish, or pale olive below; unmarked or with a few dark spots on throat and chest. **Male:** Throat greenish yellow to dark olive, with lengthwise folds of loose skin.

A frog of grassy pools, lakes, and marshes of prairies and mountains. Frequents grassland, woodland, and forest. Usually breeds Nov.–July (April–June in Alta.) in shallow, temporary pools in the open, but also uses deep, more permanent water in dense woods. Breeds earliest in the south. Has adapted well to human habitation, occurring on farms and in cities except in areas of heavy pesticide use. **VOICE:** Vibrant *prreep, prreep,* each call with rising inflection, and lasting ½–2 seconds; some 18–20 calls a minute, 30–90 at higher temperatures. To imitate the call, stroke small teeth of a pocket comb. Choruses occur night and day during height of breeding season; calling may continue to Aug. Vocal sac round and slightly flattened. **SIMILAR SPECIES:** (1) Pacific Treefrog (p. 222) and (2) Mountain Treefrog (p. 224) have toe pads. In Pacific Treefrog, eye stripe stops at shoulder. **RANGE:** Great Bear Lake in nw. Canada to Gulf of Mexico; N.J. to cen. Ariz. and e. border Great Basin. In Yukon, ranges as far n. as La Biche R. drainage. Reported from Carp Lake, B.C. Population at Lordsburg, Hidalgo Co., N.M., needs confirmation. It may be extinct. Near sea level to above 12,000 ft. (3,670 m) in Uinta Mts., Utah.

REMARKS: A proposed taxonomic change recognizes our western form as a separate species, the Boreal Chorus Frog (*P. maculata*). Populations displaying voice and morphological differences from one another reported to overlap in a broad central portion of range (Colo., Nev., Kans.), suggesting species level differences.

NORTHERN CASQUE-HEADED FROG   Pl. 15, Map 43
(LOWLAND BURROWING TREEFROG)
Pternohyla fodiens

IDENTIFICATION: 1 ½–2 ½ in. (3.8–6.3 cm). A *casque-headed* frog— upper surface of head is very hard and skin firmly attached. Prominent ridge between eye and nostril, and *fold of skin at back of head*. Toe pads small but distinct. *Single large whitish tubercle on each hind foot.* Brown or pale yellow above, with large dark brown spots edged with black. Plain white below. **Male:** Dark patch each side of throat.

A terrestrial, burrowing, nocturnal frog of open grassy terrain and tropical scrub forests. Occurs in mesquite grassland in extreme s. Ariz., where it breeds June–Sept. during period of summer rains. After first hard rain in July, choruses quickly form around temporary pools that often form in washes. **VOICE:** A loud, low-pitched *wonk, wonk, wonk* or *quack-quack-quack;* 2–3 calls per second, each lasting ⅕–½ second and given on one pitch. Resembles somewhat call of Pacific Treefrog, but is lower-pitched, hoarser, shorter, faster, and with no rising inflection. Large vocal sac looks slightly bilobed from the front. **SIMILAR SPECIES:** See Barking Frog (p. 201). **RANGE:** San Simon Valley between Sells and Ajo, Ariz., north to near Hickiwan, Pima Co., Ariz., south in w. Mex. from Sonora to Michoacan. Near sea level to about 4,900 ft. (1,490 m). Ariz. localities associated mainly with washes that flow south toward Mex.— San Simon Wash, and its two largest tributaries, Hickiwan and Sells Washes. Also found near Gu Komelick, Pinal Co., on Santa Rosa Wash floodplain, which extends north from Quijotoa Mts.

TREEFROGS: GENUS *Hyla*

Found on all continents except Antarctica and Australia, but in Africa only north of the Sahara. Most diverse and abundant in the American tropics. Probably well over 400 species; 12 in the U.S. —most in the Southeast, 4 in the West.

Typically, these frogs have a rather large head, a rounded snout, large eyes, a slim waist, and prominent toe pads. Most are jumpers and climbers and can cling to twigs or climb a vertical surface with their adhesive toe pads. The genus includes both tree-dwelling and ground-dwelling species. Most can rapidly change color.

CANYON TREEFROG *Hyla arenicolor*   Pl. 15, map 47

IDENTIFICATION: 1 ¼–2 ¼ in. (3.2–5.7 cm). Brown, cream, or olive-gray above, *usually no eye stripe;* blotched or spotted with dark brown or olive, but sometimes with little or no pattern (sw. Utah). Cream below, grading to orange-yellow to yellow on groin, rear of thighs, and hind legs. Large toe pads. Webbing of hind foot moderately well developed (Fig. 10, Pl. 15, p. 64). Skin rather rough. **Male:** Throat dusky.

A small, well-camouflaged frog that, during the day, often huddles in niches on sides of boulders or streambanks, often within easy jumping distance of water. However, individuals in N.M. have been found associated with high mountain talus slopes far removed from nearest permanent water (Animas Mts., Hidalgo Co.). Favors intermittent or permanent streams with quiet pools that have a hard, rocky bottom. Frequents arroyos in semiarid grassland, streams bordered by cottonwoods and sycamores, including those in piñon-juniper and pine-oak woodlands, and tropical scrub forests (Mex.). Chiefly ground-dwelling but occasionally climbs trees. Breeds March–July, perhaps through Aug., often in rock-bound pools in canyon bottoms. **VOICE:** Explosive series of single-pitched whirring sounds that resemble a rivet gun. Calls last ½–3 seconds. Vocal sac looks weakly bilobed from above. **SIMILAR SPECIES:** See California Treefrog (below). **RANGE:** W. Colo. and s. Utah to n. Oaxaca; w. Tex. to Colorado R. in nw. Ariz. Isolated populations in Mogollon Highlands of Ariz., on the Canadian and upper Pecos Rs., in the Big Florida Mts. and Cookes Peak area, N.M., and in the Davis and Chisos Mts. in w. Tex. Old record (1886) for Mesa de Maya, Las Animas Co., Colo., recently confirmed. A report for Bent Canyon, Purgatoire R., Las Animas Co., Colo., requires confirmation. From near sea level to around 9,800 ft. (2,990 m).

REMARKS: Vulnerable to overcollecting due to its habit of crouching exposed on rock surfaces along streams.

CALIFORNIA TREEFROG *Hyla cadaverina*   Pl. 15, Map 47

IDENTIFICATION: 1–2 in. (2.5–5.1 cm). Typically *gray or brown above with dark blotches; usually no eye stripe.* Blends well with background—frogs on granite tend to be dark-blotched, those on sandstone usually plain. Whitish below with yellow on underside of hind legs, in groin, and on lower abdomen. Toes with well-developed webbing and conspicuous pads. **Male:** Throat dusky.

Found near canyon streams and washes with rocks, quiet pools, and shade. Ranges from desert and coastal stream courses to pine belt in mountains. Sometimes occurs along stretches of rather rapidly flowing water. Breeds Feb.–early Oct. **VOICE:** A ducklike quack—short, low-pitched, ending abruptly and given repeat-

California Treefrog, a master at background matching, which sequesters itself among rocks along streams, here shown for clarity on a contrasting background. Frogs in granitic areas match granite, those found on sandstone match sandstone.

edly; lacks whirring quality of Canyon Treefrog's. Calls usually last ⅕–½ second, have little or no inflection, and seldom have two parts. Usually heard day and night at peak of breeding season. Vocal sac round. **SIMILAR SPECIES:** (1) Canyon Treefrog (p. 221) tends to be more brown than pale gray, and has reduced webbing on hind foot and larger toe pads and eardrums; voice is quite different. (2) See also Pacific Treefrog (below). **RANGE:** Distribution spotty. Mountains of s. Calif., including western fringe of desert along streams and at oases (desert slope of Peninsular Ranges, Forty-nine Palms, Indian Cove), south into n. Baja Calif. to somewhat s. of Cataviña (Las Palmas). Isolated populations in Sierra de Juarez and San Pedro Martir. From near sea level to around 7,500 ft. (2,290 m).

REMARKS: Vulnerable to overcollecting along stream courses. Although range overlaps that of Pacific Treefrog in s. Calif. and n. Baja Calif., the two species are seldom found together at the same locality. This species and the Pacific Treefrog are considered by some herpetologists members of genus *Pseudacris* (thus aligned with the chorus frogs). (See p. 219.)

PACIFIC TREEFROG *Hyla regilla* Pl. 15, Map 44

IDENTIFICATION: ¾–2 in. (1.9–5.1 cm). A small frog with toe pads and *black or dark brown eye stripe*. The stripe almost always present but difficult to see in dark individuals. Dorsal coloration highly variable—green, tan, reddish, gray, cream, brown, or black, but usually green or shades of brown. May change from dark to light phase in a few minutes, but basic hue does not change. With darkening, a green frog becomes dark green and a brown one dark brown. Often triangular or Y-shaped dark spot on head. Dark spots on back and legs vary in distinctness depending on color phase. Cream below, yellowish on hindquarters. **Male:** Throat dusky, wrinkled.

Frequents a variety of habitats from sea level high into mountains—grassland, chaparral, woodland, forest, desert oases, and farmland. Breeds Nov.–July in both permanently and seasonally ponded wetlands, in marshes, lakes, ponds, roadside ditches, reservoirs, and slow streams. Chiefly a ground-dweller, found among low plant growth near water. **VOICE:** Most commonly heard frog on Pacific Coast. Calls often uttered in sequence, about 1 per second; a loud, two-parted *kreck-ek* or *ribbit*, the last part with rising inflection. Call resembles California Treefrog's but is longer, higher-pitched, inflected, more musical, and more often has two parts. Other sounds identified—territorial, close-range mate attraction, fall "awakening" calls, etc. Vocal sac round. **SIMILAR SPECIES:** (1) California Treefrog (p. 221) usually has no eye stripe, has larger toe pads and more fully webbed hind toes, and is rarely green. (2) In Mountain Treefrog (p. 224), eye stripe extends well beyond the shoulder. Webbing is reduced (Fig. 10). (3) See Tailed Frog (p. 199). **RANGE:** From Mt. Scriven and McBride areas, B.C., to tip of Baja Calif., Pacific Coast east to w. Mont., and e. Nev. Only native frog considered indigenous to islands off coast of s. Calif. Introduced at Ketchikan, Alaska. Desert populations in s. Calif. at California City and Soda Springs, probably also introduced. Pushwalla Palms population appears to be native. In Baja Calif. range continuous only in Cape and northwestern region. In intervening area only some of the isolated localities could be shown. Sea level to around 11,600 ft. (3,540 m).

Pacific Treefrog. A small frog with a big voice, widely distributed from southern British Columbia to the tip of Baja California. Hollywood movie producers often use its voice for nocturnal background sounds, sometimes regardless of location.

IDENTIFICATION: ¾–2 in. (1.9–5.1 cm). Resembles Pacific Treefrog (p. 222). Green to brownish above, with *dark eye stripe that extends beyond shoulder,* sometimes to groin; toward rear the stripe may break up into spots. Note thin white line separating dark stripe from back color. Spotting on head and upper back usually scarce or absent. May have a spot on each upper eyelid and dark lengthwise bars or spots on lower back; some completely lack such markings. Toe pads distinct but small. Webbing reduced. **Male:** Throat dusky.

Frequents meadows in oak-pine or pine-fir forests in the U.S., generally above 5,000 ft. (1,520 m). In Mex. in mesquite grassland, scrub, and pine-oak forests. Found both on the ground and in shrubs and trees, usually near grassy shallow pools and along slower parts of streams. Breeds June–Aug., during and after rains. **VOICE:** A series of short, low-pitched notes, sometimes distinct and separate or given as a trill. Individual notes are brief, metallic *quacks* or *clacks,* each lasting about ½ second or less, uttered around 40 to over 150 times per minute depending on temperature and individual variation. Lacks two-parted quality of Pacific Treefrog's voice. Vocal sac round. **SIMILAR SPECIES:** See Pacific Treefrog (p. 222). **RANGE:** Mountains of cen. Ariz. and w. N.M., south in Sierra Madre Occidental to Guerrero, Mex. Isolated population in Huachuca Mts., Cochise Co., Ariz. From around 3,000–9,500 ft. (910–2,900 m).

TRUE FROGS: FAMILY RANIDAE

Typically slim-waisted, long-legged, smooth-skinned jumpers with webbed hind feet, often with a pair of dorsolateral folds (glandular ridges) that extend from behind eyes to lower back (see Fig. 5, p. 28). Any western tail-less amphibian with distinct dorsolateral folds is a True Frog. Family is best represented in Africa, but species are found on all continents except Antarctica. Australia has only one "native" species—a recent (in geological terms) arrival from New Guinea. More than 700 species. Only the large, widespread genus *Rana* (with some 270 species) occurs in the New World. Twenty-five species in N. America north of Mexico; 15 in the East, 16 in our area. A dozen or so more live in New World tropics. Two of our species, Bullfrog and Green Frog, have been introduced. Two native species, the Northern Leopard Frog and Wood Frog, range across N. America. Some of our western frogs are difficult to identify—rely heavily on the range maps.

In males during the breeding season, forelimbs and thumb bases become enlarged and webbing increases; a dark nuptial pad appears on each thumb. Amplexus is pectoral. Vocal sac paired or single, sometimes inconspicuous. When paired a sac inflates on each side above forelimbs.

RED-LEGGED FROG *Rana aurora* Pl. 16, Map 50

IDENTIFICATION: 1¾–5¼ in. (4.4–13.3 cm). Red on lower abdomen and underside of hind legs, often overlying yellow ground color. Usually has *dark mask bordered by whitish jaw stripe* (Fig. 11, Pl. 16, p. 66). Back often has many small black flecks and larger, irregular dark blotches with indistinct outlines on brown, gray, olive, or reddish ground color. In some the flecks join to form a more or less continuous network of black lines. Dark bands on legs. *Usually with coarse black (or gray), red, and yellow mottling in groin.* Often greenish wash in light-colored areas of groin. Relatively long legs; heel of adpressed hind limb extends to or beyond nostril. Eyes turned outward, well covered by lids as viewed from above. Prominent dorsolateral folds. **Young:** May have yellow instead of red on underside of legs and in groin. **Male:** Enlarged forelimbs, thumb base, and webbing.

Chiefly a pond frog that inhabits humid forests, woodlands, grasslands, and streamsides, especially where cattails, bulrushes, or other plants provide dense riparian cover. Most common in lowlands and foothills. Frequents marshes, streams, lakes, reservoirs, ponds, and other, usually permanent, sources of water. Generally found in or near water, but disperses after rains and may appear in damp woods and meadows far from water. Overland movements of over two miles recorded in Santa Cruz Mts., Calif. Breeding period short, often lasting only 1–2 weeks; late Nov. to usually Jan.–April, depending on locality. When not breeding, may be found in a variety of upland habitats. **VOICE:** Stuttering, sometimes accelerating, series of guttural notes (4–7) on one pitch—*uh-uh-uh-uh-uh-rowr*; the last note, sometimes omitted, resembles a growl or groan, *waaaa*, and appears not to be given in northern part of species range. Calls last 1–3 seconds but are weak and easily missed. Occasionally only 2–4 chuckles given. When frogs are in chorus a continual low clucking may be heard. Calls of Northern Red-legged Frog (p. 226) are typically given underwater. When Red-legged Frogs call, throat enlarges at center and sides. Vocal sacs absent north of Smith River, Del Norte Co., Calif., whereas populations south of San Francisco Bay have small paired subgular sacs. Intermediate conditions found in intervening area. **SIMILAR SPECIES:** (1) In Oregon Spotted Frog (p. 228), groin usually unmottled, or less conspicuously so, and eyes slightly upturned and less completely covered by the lids (Fig. 11, p. 66). Ventral color usually orange-red rather than deep red, and appears painted on rather than beneath the skin surface. (2) Cascades Frog (p. 230), a mountain species, usually has distinct black spots on back; yellowish color on lower abdomen and underside of legs; yellowish, lightly mottled groin; and generally rougher skin. (3) See also Foothill Yellow-legged Frog (p. 231).

RANGE: Chiefly west of Cascade-Sierran crest from sw. B.C. (Sullivan Bay) to nw. Baja Calif. (Arroyo Santo Domingo). Coastal Calif. and Sierran foothills, but only scant dubious records for Great Valley at Lodi, Gadwall, and Buena Vista Lake. Reported absent from lowlands of Sacramento Valley in mid-1920s and continues so. Former desert outposts were Mojave R., Whitewater Canyon, and San Felipe Creek in s. Calif. In Nye Co., Nev., introduced at Millett and elsewhere in Big Smoky Valley and at Duckwater. An old record (1919) from Santa Cruz I. (near Pelican Bay), Calif., where introduced. From near sea level to about 8,000 ft. (2,440 m).

SUBSPECIES: NORTHERN RED-LEGGED FROG, *R. a. aurora*. Dorsal spots often lack light centers. To 3 in. (7.6 cm). This taxon may be more closely related to Cascades Frog than California Red-Legged Frog. CALIFORNIA RED-LEGGED FROG, *R. a. draytonii*. Dorsal spots more numerous, usually with light centers. Skin rougher, limbs shorter, and eyes smaller than in Northern Red-legged Frog. To 5¼ in. (13.3 cm).

REMARKS: Overlap zone between above two taxa (Map 50) lies between Point Arena and Elk, Mendocino Co. Some studies support elevating the California form to full species status.

Sierran and s. Calif. populations seriously depleted. Species estimated to have disappeared from around 75 percent of former range throughout state. However, it still exists at a few localities in n. and cen. Sierra—French Creek, Butte Co., to Weber Creek near Pollock Pines, El Dorado Co., and Swamp Lake Reserve in Yosemite Nat'l Park. Also persists at a reserve in the

California Red-legged Frog. Mark Twain's famed "notorious jumping frog of Calaveras Co." Now listed as a threatened subspecies.

Santa Rosa Mts. in s. Calif. Introduction of Bullfrog and nonnative fishes, pesticides and other pollutants, loss of habitat to developments, all may be factors involved in decline. Heavily marketed in cen. Calif. and elsewhere as a source of frog legs in the late 1800s and early 1900s.

WOOD FROG *Rana sylvatica* Pl. 18, Map 48

IDENTIFICATION: 1 ¼–3 ¼ in. (3.2–8.2 cm). *A black or dark brown mask* ends abruptly just behind the eardrum and is bordered below by *white jaw stripe.* Brown, pink, gray, or greenish above, often with 2 broad, light-colored stripes down back, separated by a dark stripe. Dark middorsal stripe sometimes bisected by whitish line. Dark spot on each side of chest, near base of foreleg. Prominent dorsolateral folds. Individuals in northwestern part of range short-limbed and toadlike in proportions. The white-striped form, rare in the East, occurs with increasing frequency to the northwest. **Male:** Swollen and darkened thumb base.

In the East this species is truly a wood frog, inhabiting damp shady woods and forests near clear streams and leafy pools. Favors shade, but when breeding may move out of forests. In Northwest, in colder parts of range, it is chiefly diurnal and less of a forest dweller. There it may be found in open grassy areas bordered by thickets of willow and aspen, and in tundra ponds. Spruce or other trees often present nearby. Coloration blends well with fallen leaves and mottled light and shade of forest floor. Breeds Jan.–July, usually starting soon after ice begins to melt from ponds — in southern part of range (s. Appalachians and Ozarks) in Jan. and Feb., at the coldest time of year, and in far Northwest from April–June. Breeding lasts 1–2 weeks, after which frogs usually disperse. **VOICE:** Resembles Northern Leopard Frog's (p. 234), including the sound made by rubbing an inflated balloon, but shorter, higher-pitched, and weaker. A series of rather high grating notes lasting 1 second or less, like clucking of a small domestic duck. Paired vocal sacs, one over each forelimb. **SIMILAR SPECIES:** (1) Oregon and Columbia Spotted Frogs (pp. 228–29) have a less distinct mask, no stripes except on jaw, and are red, orange, or yellow below. (2) Red-legged Frog (p. 225) has a less well defined mask and reddish color on underside of hind legs. **RANGE:** North of Brooks Range, Alaska, to Labrador, southward in e. U.S. to s. Appalachian Mts. Distribution follows closely the distribution of spruce over much of its range. Ranges farther north than any other N. American amphibian. In our area isolated populations in se. Alta. (Cypress Hills), n. Colo. (near Rand, Jackson Co., northwest of Grand Lake, Grand Co., and Chambers Lake, Larimer Co.), and adjacent s. Wyo. (Medicine Bow Mts.), and in n. Wyo. (Bighorn Mts.). Sea level to about 10,000 ft. (3,050 m).

IDENTIFICATION: 1 ¾–4 in. (4.4–10.1 cm). Brown, dull olive green, or reddish above, with varying numbers of usually black spots often having rather indistinct borders and generally light centers. Mask present, sometimes faint. Light-colored *jaw stripe* (Fig. 11, Pl. 16, p. 66). Reddish or salmon on sides and venter. In contrast to Red-legged Frog, color appears to be more superficial, almost painted on. Groin unmottled or faintly so. Throat, and sometimes entire ventral surface, spotted and mottled with dusky. Legs relatively short, heel of adpressed hind limb seldom reaching nostril. *Eyes turned slightly upward.* Dorsolateral folds usually present. **Young:** Reddish ventral color faint or absent. **Male:** Swollen and darkened thumb base.

Highly aquatic species found near cool, usually permanent, water—streams, rivers, marshes, springs, pools, and small lakes, but may move considerable distance from water after breeding. Chiefly a pond or quiet-water frog that frequents mixed coniferous and subalpine forests, and marshlands. Rather sluggish. Breeds from Jan. to early July, beginning as early as winter thaw will permit. At Dempsey Creek, Thurston Co., Wash., found in early Feb. in breeding condition beneath pond ice. **VOICE:** A series of faint, rapid, low-pitched clicks or tapping notes, increasing in intensity, some 4–50 clicks or tapping notes (often 7–12) per call. Calls last 1–10 seconds, given above or occasionally underwater. Imitate by clicking your tongue against the roof of your mouth. When held in your fingers, in position of amplexus, males may produce a stuttering sound lasting 1–2 seconds per call. Imitate with a tongue flutter. Apparently lacks vocal sacs. **SIMILAR SPECIES:** Distinguished from (1) Cascades Frog (p. 230) and (2) Red-legged Frog (p. 225) by lack of usual mottling on sides, shorter legs, greater webbing, and rougher skin. (3) See also Wood Frog (p. 227). **RANGE:** Fragmented distribution from extreme sw. B.C. (general area from Aldergrove to Agassiz, where rare) south through w. Wash and Ore. to ne. Calif. Now apparently extinct in Puget Sound Lowlands, Wash., except for several localities along Black R. drainage, and depleted or extinct throughout Willamette Valley, Ore. Last seen at Surrey, B.C., in 1981. Now occurs primarily in Cascade Mts. of Ore. Near sea level to around 5,000 ft. (1,524 m).

REMARKS: Spotted Frog is losing ground to the Bullfrog in some areas. Bullfrog appears to have been a factor in its decline in B.C., and in w. Ore. and Wash., where the Spotted Frog now appears to be nearly extinct. Introduction of nonnative fish and degradation of wetlands also probably contributed to decline. Also appears to be on verge of extinction in Calif., having disappeared from an estimated 99 percent of its limited former range.

Rana luteiventris

Identification: To around 4 in. (10.1 cm). Similar to Oregon Spotted Frog, including *slightly upturned eyes and dark spotting on dorsum*. In parts of range the venter is known to be *orange or salmon*, sometimes reddish, these colors brightest especially on the hind limbs and rear of belly. Dorsum may be grayish or light or dark brown. Color and other possible differences between it and Oregon Spotted Frog have yet to be carefully studied over the entire range of the two species, therefore geographic location must be relied upon to aid identification.

Extensive range encompasses more diverse habitats than those of Oregon Spotted Frog. In arid and semiarid southern part of range, in se. Ore., Nev., and Utah, distribution is greatly fragmented and some isolated populations at mountaintop refugia and desert springs may be approaching species levels of differentiation. In far north it hibernates in pond bottoms beneath pond ice. Breeds in late Feb.–July. Breeding in Utah has been reported for mid-March and in Wyo. in May and June. **VOICE:** Series of rapid (5–50) hollow sounds, like tapping a hollow log, often accelerating, then decelerating, and lowering slightly in pitch toward the end. Similar to Oregon Spotted Frog's. **SIMILAR SPECIES:** (1) Red-legged Frog (p. 225) and (2) Cascades Frog (p. 230). **RANGE:** Alaskan Panhandle (including Sergrief I.) and Bennett Lake area, sw. Yukon south through B.C. and extreme sw. Alta., through n. and e. Wash., e. Oregon, Idaho, w. Mont., and nw. Wyo. to nw. Utah and n. and cen. Nev. Some isolated populations are Bighorn Mts., Wyo.; Deer Creek near Ibapah, Toole Co., Utah; Humboldt

The swollen "thumb" of a male Columbia Spotted Frog, used for clasping the female during breeding. This structure is common among frogs.

drainage and headwaters of Reese R., Nev. Near sea level to around 10,000 ft. (3,048 m).

REMARKS: Not known to overlap range with Oregon Spotted Frog (p. 228). However, the two taxa occasionally hybridize at points of contact.

CASCADES FROG *Rana cascadae*   Pl. 16, Map 53

IDENTIFICATION: 1 ¾–3 in. (4.4–7.6 cm). Brown, tan, olive green, or olive brown above, *inky black spots on back (usually sharply defined)*, and dark spotting on legs. Black flecks between spots scarce or absent. *Yellow, orange-yellow, or yellowish tan on lower abdomen and underside of hind legs.* Groin usually bright yellow with dark mottling; lower sides yellowish or cream. Dorsolateral folds present. **Male:** Swollen and darkened thumb base.

A mountain frog, usually found near water. Frequents small streams, potholes in meadows, ponds, and lakes usually in open coniferous forests. Found in water or among grass, ferns, and other low herbaceous growth nearby. Ranges to near timberline. Rather sluggish, often allowing close approach. When frightened it usually attempts to escape by swimming rather than seeking refuge on the bottom. May swim to opposite bank or return to same bank downstream. Diurnal. Breeds March–mid-Aug., often soon after pond ice begins to melt. **VOICE:** Low-pitched grating, clucking sound, resembling the Red-legged Frog's, commonly 4–5 notes per second. A series of rapid clucks or double clucks, each often lasting about ½ second. Number of clucks in a series in Cascades of Jefferson Co., Ore. varied from 4–39 and were given at a rate of 6.7 notes per second (water temp. 12° C). Shorter calls were usually given by stationary males. *Ow* or *mew* calls sometimes given, particularly at end of a series of clucks.

Cascades Frog. A mountain species that ranges above timber line. Inky black spots on the dorsum are characteristic. Pierce Co., Wash.

May call from above or underwater. Typically lacks vocal sacs. **SIMILAR SPECIES:** (1) Range overlaps slightly with Columbia Spotted Frog (p. 229), which has a more conspicuous light-colored upper-jaw stripe, no mask, and nostrils set closer together and higher on the snout; eyes turned upward. (2) See also Red-legged Frog (p. 225). **RANGE:** Cascades Mts. from n. Wash. south to Feather R. in n. Butte Co., Calif., where range is highly fragmented with populations in the tributaries of the Salmon, Scott, and Trinity Rs. of coastal drainage and McCloud, Pit, Mill, Big Butte Creeks, and others, with drainage into Sacramento R. Coexists with Red-legged Frog at intermediate elevations in w. Ore. and Wash. and prior to its decline, coexisted with Mountain Yellow-Legged Frog (also now in serious decline) at many localities. From around 755–9,000 ft. (230–2,740 m).

REMARKS: Estimated to have disappeared from about 50 percent of former range in Calif. Most losses in Sacramento R. drainage. Airborne chemical pollution is suspect.

FOOTHILL YELLOW-LEGGED FROG   Pl. 18, Map 51
Rana boylii

IDENTIFICATION: 1 ½–3 ⅓ in. (3.8–8.1 cm). Gray, brown, reddish, or olive above; sometimes plain-colored but more often spotted and mottled with dusky. Colors usually harmonize with prevailing color of rocks and soil. Truly *yellow-legged;* yellow extends from underside of hind legs onto lower abdomen. *Snout with triangular, usually buff-colored patch* from its tip to a line connecting the eyelids. No mask. Throat and chest often dark-spotted. Skin, including eardrums, granular. Indistinct dorsolateral folds. **Young:** Yellow on hind legs faint or absent. **Male:** Swollen and darkened thumb base.

Tadpole of Foothill Yellow-legged Frog. The mouth of this camouflaged tadpole is supplied with large numbers of labial teeth used to scrape algae and other organic substances off surrounding rock and other surfaces. (See Fig. 39, p. 459.)

Foothill Yellow-legged Frog. This stream-dwelling frog usually matches the general background of its habitat. Linn Co., Ore.

Stream or river frog of woodland, chaparral, and forest. Usually found near water, especially near riffles with rocks and sunny banks. When frightened it dives to the bottom and takes refuge among stones, silt, or vegetation. Breeds mid-March–early June, after high water of streams subsides. **VOICE:** Seldom heard. A guttural, grating sound on one pitch or sometimes with rising inflection, a single croak lasting ½–¾ second. Four or five croaks may be given in rapid series followed by a rattling sound, the entire sequence lasting about 2½ seconds. Piglike oinks or grunts and a quiet slow *quack* may also be heard. May vocalize underwater. Throat swells when calling, especially in front of forelimbs. **SIMILAR SPECIES:** (1) Red-legged Frog (p. 225) has red on underside of hind legs, usually a dark mask, well-defined dorsolateral folds, and smooth eardrums. (2) Mountain Yellow-legged Frog (p. 233) has smoother skin, generally heavier spotting and mottling dorsally, usually lacks snout patch, and often has dark toe tips. (3) See also Tarahumara Frog (p. 234) and Tailed Frog (p. 199). **RANGE:** From Mehama on the Santiam R., Marion Co., Ore., west of crest of Cascades Mts., south in coastal mts. of Calif. to San Gabriel R., Los Angeles Co.; Sierra Nevada foothills to about 6,000 ft. (1,830 m) (near McKessick Peak, Plumas Co.), and in Trinity Co. at Snow Mt. to 6,365 ft. (1,940 m); San Pedro Martir, lower end of La Grulla Meadow, 6,700 ft. (2,040 m), Baja Calif. (found in 1965 but not reported since). Isolated populations in Elizabeth Lake Canyon and San Gabriel R. drainage (near Camp Rincon), Los Angeles Co.; Sutter Buttes, Butte Co., Calif. Camp Rincon population now considered extinct. A single record 5 mi. (8 km) north of Lodi, San Joaquin Co., Calif., was perhaps a stray from Sierran foothills. Formerly coexisted with Mountain Yellow-legged Frog (below) along N. Fork of San Gabriel R. Now apparently extinct from s. border of Monterey Co. throughout s. Calif. No records since 1970–71, despite intensive search. Near sea level to around 6,700 ft. (2,040 m).

REMARKS: Has disappeared from an estimated 55 percent of its range in Ore., 45 percent of its overall former range in Calif., and 66 percent of its range in the Calif. Sierra where the few scattered sites south of I-80 may not be viable. High water conditions, spring of 1969 in s. Calif., may have been a factor in southland decline. Silts and poorly timed water release from reservoirs and introduction of Bullfrog and exotic fishes may have also taken their toll.

MOUNTAIN YELLOW-LEGGED FROG   Pl. 18, Map 54
Rana muscosa

IDENTIFICATION: 1 3/5–3 1/2 in. (4.1–8.9 cm). The only True Frog of the Sierran highlands in Calif. Olivaceous, yellowish, or reddish brown above, with black or brown spots or lichenlike markings. *Toe tips usually dusky.* No mask. Underside of hind legs and sometimes entire belly yellow or orange, usually more opaque than in Foothill Yellow-legged Frog. Yellow often extends forward to level of forelimbs. Dorsolateral folds present but frequently indistinct. When handled these frogs smell like garlic. **Male:** Swollen, darkened thumb base.

A frog of sunny riverbanks, meadow streams, isolated pools, and lake borders in the high Sierra Nevada and rocky stream courses in the mountains of s. Calif. Seems to prefer sloping banks with rocks or vegetation to water's edge. Often found within 2 or 3 jumps of water. Chiefly diurnal. At high altitudes, breeds May–Aug., beginning as soon as lakes and streams are free of snow and ice. At lower elevations and in s. Calif., breeds March–Aug., when high water in streams subsides. Sierran tadpoles often overwinter and at higher elevations in Sierra are thought not to transform until end of third or perhaps even fourth summer. **VOICE:** A short rasping call, sounding strained, often followed by a loud *woof.* Apparently lacks vocal sacs. Appears to call primarily underwater. **SIMILAR SPECIES:** See (1) Foothill Yellow-legged Frog (p. 231) and (2) Tarahumara Frog (p. 234). **RANGE:** Sierra Nevada, Calif., from around 3,525 ft. (Pinkard Creek area, Butte Co.) to over 12,000 ft. (1,370–3,660 m), where it ranges from north of Feather R., Butte Co. and vicinity of Thompson Peak (Lowe Flat), Plumas Co. to Taylor Meadow, Tulare Co. Ranges east of Sierra crest in Lake Tahoe area at Mt. Rose in Carson Range and, historically, occurred at Edgewood Creek, Douglas Co., Nev. Still exists on s. side of Mono Lake about 15 mi. southeast of Lee Vining, Mono Co., Calif. In s. Calif. in San Gabriel

Mts., from Pacoima R. area, east into San Bernardino Mts., thence south in San Jacinto Mts. to Mt. Palomar, from around 984–7,500 ft. (370–2,290 m).

REMARKS: Populations have deteriorated nearly everywhere in Sierra except in n. Sequoia and Kings Canyon Nat'l Parks. Mt. Rose area populations now considered extinct. On brink of extinction in s. Calif. where formerly abundant and widespread, having lost about 99 percent of historic range. Some impacts are introduction of bullfrogs and trout, and airborne pollution. In s. Calif. problems include toxins and silt from recreational placer mining, off-road vehicles, and public dumping in stream channels. Scouring floodwaters in 1968–69 followed by drought may also have played a role.

TARAHUMARA FROG *Rana tarahumarae*   Pl. 18, Map 55

IDENTIFICATION: 2½–4½ in. (6.3–11.4 cm). Rust, olive, or dark brown above, and dark spots often with light centers. Prominent dark banding on hind legs. Whitish to cream below, *often clouded with dusky. No mask or jaw stripe.* Dorsolateral folds and eardrums indistinct; eardrum frequently granular. **Male:** Swollen and darkened thumb base.

A species of the Sierra Madre Occidental, barely entering U.S. in mountains of extreme s. Ariz. Ranges from oak woodland into pine forest along rocky, gravelly stream courses. A "plunge pool" frog, usually within a jump or two of water, on banks of pools, under stones, in niches in cliffs, or sitting in riffles. While apparently preferring moving water, they gather at quiet pools and springs in dry weather. In Ariz., breeds July–Aug. during period of summer rains. **VOICE:** Apparently unreported except for an occasional series of grunts, given by both sexes. **SIMILAR SPECIES:** Foothill and Mountain Yellow-legged Frogs (above) are smaller and usually have a spotted throat. **RANGE:** In Ariz. in the Pajarito, Tumacacori, and Santa Rita Mts. (Alamo Spring and Sycamore, Tinaja, Big Casa Blanca, Adobe, and Gardener Canyons); south in Sierra Madre Occidental to e. and n. Sonora, w. Chihuahua, and n. Sinaloa. 1,500–over 6,100 ft. (460–1,860 m).

REMARKS: Last known Tarahumara Frog in U.S. was found dead in 1983. Efforts are underway to reestablish the frog using stock from Mexico. However, the causes of its demise in the first place have not been determined, although chemical pollution is suspect.

NORTHERN LEOPARD FROG *Rana pipiens*   Pl. 17, Map 56

IDENTIFICATION: 2–4⅜ in. (5.1–11.1 cm). A slim green or brownish frog with well-defined, *pale-bordered, oval or round dark spots* on its back. White to cream below. White stripe on upper jaw. Well-defined, pale dorsolateral folds usually *continuous and not angled* *inward toward rear.* **Young:** Spotting may be reduced or absent. **Male:** Swollen, darkened thumb base and loose skin between jaw and shoulder during breeding season.

Found in a variety of habitats—grassland, brushland, woodland, and forest, ranging high into mountains. The most cold-adapted of all leopard frogs. Frequents springs, slowly flowing streams, marshes, bogs, ponds, canals, and reservoirs, usually permanent water with grass, cattails or other aquatic vegetation. May forage far from water in damp meadows. When frightened on land it often seeks water in a series of zigzag jumps. Breeds mid-Mar–June. **VOICE:** A low "motorboat" or snorelike rattling sound, that tends to accelerate toward the end. Vocalization may be interspersed with grunting and chuckling sounds, and lasts about 1–5 seconds. Choruses are a medley of moaning, grunting, and chuckling sounds; some of these are suggested by rubbing a well-inflated rubber balloon. Paired vocal sacs expand over forelimbs. May squawk when jumping into the water and "scream" when caught. **SIMILAR SPECIES:** (1) Plains Leopard Frog (p. 237) is paler, with spots less set off by pale borders; usually has well-defined light eardrum spot. Dorsolateral folds not continuous (broken at rear), and folds curve slightly inward toward rear. (2) Chiricahua Leopard Frog (p. 236) has "salt-and-pepper" pattern of small tubercles on back of thighs, and stockier proportions. (3) Lowland Leopard Frog (p. 239) is stockier and paler. (4) Relict Leopard Frog (p. 238) is smaller, with shorter legs; spotting on head often reduced; underside of hind limbs yellow to yellow-orange. **RANGE:** Great Slave Lake and s. shore Hudson Bay, Canada, south to n. Va., Neb., N.M., and cen. Ariz.; ne. Atlantic coast to se. B.C. (formerly Kootenay and Columbia R. valleys) and perhaps at north end Lake Osoyoos where possibly introduced; e. Wash., Ore., and Calif. Introduced on Vancouver I. (Parksville area), B.C. and in Calif. at Red Bluff, near Mineral, at Yettem, Malibu Creek, Santa Ana R. (Prado Basin), and other localities. Source and status of introductions not clear. Historically, presumed native populations existed in ne. Calif. and Owens Valley where severe reductions, but perhaps not total extinction, has occurred. Disjunct colonies occur in e. Colo. and s. N.M. along Rio Grande south of Caballo Reservoir, Socorro Co. Old records from east of Cascades, Ore., along Columbia, Malheur, and Snake Rs. Range in the West now greatly fragmented and lacking confirmation in recent years. From near sea level to around 11,000 ft. (3,350 m).
REMARKS: Distribution of this frog in Nev. and elsewhere in arid parts of West is spotty. Frogs at Mescalero in Sacramento Mts., Otero Co., and disjunct populations in the Rio Grande valley, N.M., have been reported

as this species. In our area the Northern Leopard Frog coexists and occasionally hybridizes with Plains Leopard Frog (*Rana blairi*, p. 237) in se. Colo. (Big Sandy Creek area). It also hybridizes with the Chiricahua Leopard Frog (below) in areas of cen. Ariz. where ranges overlap. Severe declines have occurred in this species in many parts of its range. For example, it has disappeared from East Kootenays and Okanagan Valley, B.C., suffered a marked decline since 1978 in Alta., roughly north of lat. 51 and in Nev. over the past 70 years (See Map 56). The survival status of many scattered populations in Calif. is unknown. Drought, loss of habitat, and a variety of other human disturbances appear to be largely responsible.

CHIRICAHUA LEOPARD FROG
Pl. 17, Map 61
Rana chiricahuensis

IDENTIFICATION: 2–5⅖ in. (5.1–13.7 cm). Similar to Northern Leopard Frog (p. 234) but stockier, with more rounded head, shorter limbs, and slightly upturned eyes. *Dorsolateral folds usually broken into short segments toward rear and angled inward.* Skin rougher, with more tubercles; dorsal spots usually smaller and more numerous than in other Leopard Frogs. Ground color above greenish or brown. Upper lip stripe diffuse or absent in front of eye. Face usually green. *Rear of thigh speckled with "salt-and-pepper" markings—small light dots, each with a tubercle,* scattered over a dark ground color. Dull whitish or yellowish below, usually with gray mottling on throat and sometimes on chest. Yellow in groin and on lower abdomen. Many separate populations in restricted aquatic sites, differing in color and pattern. **Male:** Swollen and darkened thumb base.

Highly aquatic, found chiefly in oak and mixed oak and pine woodlands and pine forests where it frequents rocky streams with deep rockbound pools. Also ranges into areas of chaparral, grassland, and even desert, and, in addition, to streams; is also attracted to river overflow pools, oxbows, permanent springs, ponds, and earthen stock tanks. In upland areas breeds late May–Aug. and in lower, warmer localities from mid-March to June and sporadically through the fall. May breed throughout year at Alamo Warm Springs, Socorro Co., N.M. **VOICE:** Long and snorelike; a single note lasting 1–2 seconds, sometimes dropping in pitch slightly at the end, and repeated intermittently. Pulses that make up the call are given more rapidly (usually over 30 per second) than in our other Leopard Frogs, with possible exception of Northern Leopard Frog. Sometimes calls from underwater. **SIMILAR SPECIES:** See (1) Northern Leopard Frog (p. 234). (2) Plains Leopard Frog (p. 237). (3) Lowland Leopard Frog (p. 239). **RANGE:** Mountain regions of cen. and se. Ariz., sw. N.M., and Sierra Madre Occidental to s. Durango in Mexico. Gap in range in s.

Gila R. basin in N.M. See descriptions of Northern, Plains, and Lowland Leopard Frogs for interactions of the Chiricahua Leopard Frog with those species. From around 3,500–8,530 ft. (1,070–2,600 m).

REMARKS: Has undergone severe declines throughout much of range in Ariz. and N.M.

PLAINS LEOPARD FROG *Rana blairi* Pl. 17, Map 58

IDENTIFICATION: 2–4⅜ in. (5.1–11.1 cm). Generally pale-colored. Light buffy brown to dull green above with brown to olive green dorsal spots that lack or have very narrow pale borders. Dark spot present on snout. Whitish stripe on upper lip. *Usually well-defined pale spot in center of eardrum.* White below, sometimes with some fine dark stippling or mottling on throat. Some yellow may be on groin, on lower abdomen, and at base of thighs. *Dorsolateral folds usually not continuous* (segmented on lower back) and angled inward toward rear. **Young:** Whitish upper-lip stripe often well defined. **Male:** Deflated vocal sacs (below jaw angle) tend to have lengthwise folds (skin usually less folded in Northern Leopard Frog, p. 234).

Found chiefly on cen. and s. Great Plains, in prairie and desert grassland, but also enters oak and oak-pine woodland and farmland. Frequents prairie ponds, streams, and playas where water at times is muddy and shallow. Often breeds in temporary waters. More drought-resistant than Northern Leopard Frog. Breeds Feb.–Oct. Tends to breed later than Northern Leopard Frog where ranges overlap or approach one another. **VOICE:** Usually 2–4 guttural, chucklelike notes, *tuck, tuck, tuck,* each call usually lasting less than 1 second—shorter and slower-pulsed than Northern Leopard Frog's. Voice also described as a series of short, fast kissing sounds. Grunt and grind notes may also be given. **SIMILAR SPECIES:** (1) Chiricahua Leopard Frog (p. 236) has smaller and more numerous spots, "salt-and-pepper" markings on back of thighs, green on face, lacks whitish eardrum spot, and has upturned eyes. (2) Rio Grande Leopard Frog (p. 240) has large eyes and faint upper-lip stripe, fading or absent in front of eye. (3) Lowland Leopard Frog (p. 239) usually lacks whitish eardrum spot. See also (4) Northern Leopard Frog (p. 234). **RANGE:** Se. and cen. S.D. and w. Iowa to e. and s. N.M. and cen. Tex.; se. Colo. to cen. Ind. and cen. Okla. Extends west in N.M. along the Rio Bonito, Rio Hondo, and upper Rio Penasco to around 7,000 ft. (2,130 m) near Sierra Blanca, Lincoln Co.; along the Pecos R. to near Carlsbad, Eddy Co. and in the Rio Grande, including Ash Canyon near Truth or Consequences, Sierra Co. Isolated on w. side Chiricahua Mts. (Turkey Creek, etc.) and adjoining Sulphur

Springs Valley, Cochise Co., se. Ariz. From around 350–8,500 ft. (110–2,590 m). In N.M. hybridizes with Northern Leopard Frog along Cimarron R. near Springer, along Mora R. just downstream from confluence with Wolf Creek, and along Rio Grande just north of Elephant Butte Reservoir.

REMARKS: Coexists with Chiricahua Leopard Frog (p. 236) at Turkey Creek, Cochise Co., Ariz. and at Cuchillo Negro Warm Springs, Sierra Co., N.M.; elsewhere, range overlaps with Rio Grande Leopard Frog (p. 240) in se. N.M. Hybridizes with the latter in cen. Tex.

RELICT LEOPARD FROG *Rana onca*   Pl. 17, Map 61

IDENTIFICATION: 1¾–3½ in. (4.4–8.9 cm). Resembles Northern Leopard Frog (Pl. 17) but usually smaller, with shorter legs (heel of leg extended alongside body usually does not reach tip of snout). *Dorsolateral folds often end well before groin.* Brown, gray, or greenish above, with greenish brown or *brown spots often reduced or obscure on front of body usually with no spots on nose.* Whitish below, sometimes with gray or brown mottling, especially on throat. Undersides of hind limbs yellow or yellow-orange. **Male:** Swollen, darkened thumb base and usually less spotting than in female.

Frequents lowland streamsides and springs in areas surrounded by desert. Usually found in or near water. Probably breeds March–May. **VOICE:** Resembles Northern Leopard Frog's but not as long or loud. During courtship, grunts, clicks, and trills reported. Long grunts heard when frogs call from underwater. **SIMILAR SPECIES:** See (1) Northern Leopard Frog (p. 234) and (2) Lowland Leopard Frog (p. 239). **RANGE:** Formerly Vegas Valley, Clark Co., Nev., and Virgin R. valley, Washington Co. of extreme sw. Utah and nw. Ariz. Along Virgin R. and its lower Muddy R. tributary in Clark Co., Nev., to Colorado R., thence to Black Canyon area below Boulder Dam. From 1,200–2,500 ft. (370–760 m).

REMARKS: The Vegas Valley Leopard Frog, originally described as a distinct species, *Rana fisheri*, now considered extinct, is here treated as a subspecies of the Relict Leopard Frog. It occurred in an artesian spring area northwest of Las Vegas and at Tule and Indian Springs, Clark Co., Nev. It suffered from loss of habitat to human developments, including manipulation of water sources and perhaps also from the introduction of the bullfrog, game fishes, and crayfish. At present the Relict Leopard Frog survives at only two (perhaps three) remaining areas over its extensive former range in the desert. This Virgin River subspecies may experience the same fate as the Vegas Valley Frog unless prompt steps are taken to protect it. Last individuals reported from Utah found in 1950 at Berry Springs, Washington Co.

Rana yavapaiensis

IDENTIFICATION: 1⅘–3⅖ in. (4.6–8.6 cm). Similar to Chiricahua Leopard Frog (Pl. 17), but biochemically distinct. Tan, gray-brown, or light gray-green to green above; yellow below. Usually no spots on head anterior to eyes. Dorsolateral folds, tuberculate skin, and usually vague upper-lip stripe as in Chiricahua Leopard Frog. Chin mottled in older individuals. *Dark network on rear of thighs.* Yellow groin color often extends onto rear of belly and underside of legs. **Male:** Swollen and darkened thumb base.

Frequents desert, grassland, oak and oak-pine woodland, entering permanent pools of foothill streams, often overgrown with cottonwoods and willows, overflow ponds and side channels of major rivers, permanent springs, and, in drier areas, more or less permanent stock tanks. Usually stays close to water. Breeds Jan.–April, sometimes in fall. **VOICE:** Similar to Plains Leopard Frog (p. 237). Pulse number almost as low but repetition rate faster, 10–16 pulses per second rather than 4–7. Calls may last 3–8 seconds, the first note held longer than 6–15 accelerating notes that follow. Call is a series of faint high-pitched chuckling notes and short guttural grunting sounds suggestive of rubbing an inflated rubber balloon. **SIMILAR SPECIES:** (1) Chiricahua Leopard Frog (p. 236) has more prominent vocal sacs and dark thighs with a scattering of light dots rather than a dark network. (2) Plains Leopard Frog usually has spots on nose. See also (3) Northern Leopard Frog (p. 234), and (4) Rio Grande Leopard Frog (p. 240). **RANGE:** Cen. and se. Ariz. below around 4,800 ft. (1,460 m) south of Mogollon Rim; sw. N.M. (Gila R. near Red Rock and Rio San Francisco); probably n. Sonora and nw. Chihuahua, Mexico. Historically, also along lower Colorado R. and major tributaries from near St. George, Utah, and Grand Canyon to near mouth of Colorado R. in Mexico. Also present in s. Calif. in Imperial Valley and drainage of San Felipe Creek. Either extinct or seriously depleted throughout these areas. Survival prospects for isolated populations in Imperial Co., Calif., appear grim. Range of this frog overlaps that of Chiricahua Leopard Frog on Rio San Francisco and in cen. and s. Ariz.; the two frogs hybridize at California Gulch and in Casa Blanca Canyon, Santa Rita Mts., Ariz. Near sea level to around 5,577 ft. (1,700 m) (Yavapai Co., Ariz.).
REMARKS: Lowland Leopard Frog hybridizes with Chiricahua Leopard Frog in areas where ranges overlap in Ariz. (p. 236). Reservoir construction, agricultural practices, and introduction of predatory fishes, crayfish, and Bullfrogs are associated with significant decline of this species in desert Southwest.

Rana berlandieri

IDENTIFICATION: 2¼–4½ in. (5.7–11.4 cm). Resembles Northern Leopard Frog but generally much paler above, varying from grayish brown, brownish olive, to green or even blue-green (Rio Grande Valley); dorsal spots lighter and less clearly edged with light color. Usually has bold, dark thigh reticulations. *Dorsolateral folds segmented in front of groin and deflected inward. Eyes large.* Wide, light-colored jaw stripe fades or is absent in front of eye. Often dusky below, especially on chest and throat where dark pigment is mottled. Groin and underside of hind limbs often yellow. **Male:** Swollen and darkened thumb base; paired external vocal sacs.

Frequents grassland and woodland, where it enters streams, rivers and their side pools, springs, pools along arroyos, and stock tanks. Over much of range it appears to dwell chiefly in streams. Waters may be permanent or temporary. In more arid parts of its range, as in our area, it breeds opportunistically after rainfall at almost any time of year. **VOICE:** Short, guttural trill or rattle lasting ½–1 second, given singly or in rapidly repeated sequences of often 2–3 trills. Grunts and grind notes may also be given. **SIMILAR SPECIES:** (1) Lowland Leopard Frog is less likely to have greenish coloration and conspicuous dark reticulated thigh pattern. (2) See also Plains Leopard Frog (p. 237). **RANGE:** Extreme se. N.M. (Pecos R. drainage), cen. and w. Tex., south into Mexico. Established through introductions along the lower Colorado R. from Mex. border north to Yuma and east along Gila R. to near Buckeye, Maricopa Co., Ariz. Has entered Imperial Co., Calif. Coexists with Plains Leopard Frog at Delaware Creek southeast of Guadalupe Mts. near N.M.-Tex. border and in n.-cen. Tex. where some hybridization occurs. Near sea level to around 5,000 ft. (1,520 m).

REMARKS: A close relative of this species, Forrer's Grass Frog (*Rana forreri*), has been reported from La Presa region in Sierra de la Giganta of Baja Calif. Sur.

BULLFROG (AMERICAN BULLFROG)   **Pl. 19, Map 49**
Rana catesbeiana

IDENTIFICATION: 3½–8 in. (8.9–20.3 cm). Our largest True Frog. Olive, green, or brown above, often grading to light green on head; sometimes light green only on upper jaw. Legs banded and blotched with dusky, and usually some spotting on back. Whitish mottled or spotted with gray or brown below; often a yellowish tinge, especially on chin and hindquarters. *A fold of skin extends from eye around eardrum and down toward base of forearm. No*

Bullfrog tadpole. Often confused with that of the Red-legged Frog. The latter, however, has a pinkish iridescence on its belly, lacking in the Bullfrog.

dorsolateral folds. Eardrums conspicuous. **Young:** Often with numerous small spots on dorsum. Skin fold from rear of eye around eardrum. **Male:** Yellow throat. Eardrum larger than eye (about same size as eye in female). Swollen and darkened thumb base.

Highly aquatic, usually remaining in or near permanent water, its activities largely independent of rainfall. However, lengthy excursions away from water occur. Frequents prairie, woodland, chaparral, forests, desert oases, and farmland. Enters marshes, ponds, lakes, reservoirs, and streams—usually quiet water with thick growth of cattails or other aquatic vegetation. Wary by day but readily found at night by its eyeshine. Often easily caught when dazzled by light. When first seized may "play possum," hanging limp and motionless; be alert for sudden recovery! In the East, where this frog is native, it breeds Feb.–Aug. (earliest in the South); in the West it breeds Feb.–July. Tadpoles often overwinter. **VOICE:** Deep-pitched bellow suggesting *jug-o-rum* or *br-wum.* When frightened, especially young frogs, may give a squawk, chirp, or catlike meow when they leap into the water. When distressed, Bullfrogs may emit an open-mouth scream! Vocal sac single and internal. **SIMILAR SPECIES:** Green Frog (p. 242) has dorsolateral folds. **RANGE:** Native range Atlantic Coast to e. Colo. and e. N.M.; s. Canada to ne. Mex. Near sea level to around 9,000 ft. (2,740 m) at Hot Springs Creek, Gunnison Co., Colo., and Kelly Warm Springs; above 6,500 ft. (2,000 m) near Grand Teton Nat'l Park, Wyo., where introduced. These high elevation introductions are made possible by warm spring waters.
REMARKS: Bullfrog is not native west of Rockies (see Map 49), but has been successfully introduced at many localities in the West. It has even become widespread on Catalina I. off the s. Calif. coast. In some areas has ad-

versely affected populations of native frogs. Also introduced in Hawaiian Is., Mex., Cuba, Jamaica, S. America, Asia, and Europe.

GREEN FROG *Rana clamitans*   **Pl. 19, Map 51**

IDENTIFICATION: 1 ¼–4 ⅕ in. (3.2–10.6 cm). Above, green, brown, or bronze with a plain or dark-spotted back and often with green or bronze on sides of head (especially in southern part of range). Broad light green upper-jaw stripe. White below with irregular dusky lines or blotches. *Prominent dorsolateral folds* that do not reach groin. Eardrum conspicuous. **Young:** Usually profusely dark-spotted above. **Male:** Eardrum twice as large as eye (eye-sized in female). Throat usually yellow or yellow-orange, and thumb base swollen and darkened.

A "shoreline" frog usually found in or near water of marshes, ponds, lakes, streams, and springs. Introduced in the West. Breeds in spring and summer. In the East, where it is native, breeds March–Sept. Tadpoles may overwinter. **VOICE:** An explosive *bung* or *c'tung,* a low-pitched note resembling the sound made by plucking the lowest string of a banjo, often repeated several times in succession. Calls sometimes two-parted. When startled this frog emits a high-pitched squawk as it leaps. Vocal sacs paired and internal; throat forms a flattened pouch when inflated. **SIMILAR SPECIES:** See Bullfrog (p. 240). **RANGE:** In the West, introduced in lower Fraser Valley and at Victoria, Vancouver I., and at Duncan, Coombs, and on Texada I., B.C.; at Toad Lake, Whatcom Co., Lake Washington, King Co., and Lake Gillette, Stevens Co., Wash., and along lower Weber R., Ogden, Utah. Reportedly introduced at Glacier Nat'l Park, Mont. Native from Maritime Provinces to n.-cen. Fla., west to Minn. and e. Tex.

NARROW-MOUTHED TOADS: FAMILY MICROHYLIDAE

Large, diverse family of toad- and froglike amphibians, with representatives in the Americas, Africa, Madagascar, Asia, and Indo-Australian archipelago. Around 330 species. Habitat and habits vary: some burrow, others are terrestrial, still others are arboreal. Arboreal species often have adhesive toe pads. Some microhylids lay their eggs on land and the young hatch fully formed.

Two closely related genera, *Gastrophryne* (Narrow-mouthed Toads) and *Hypopachus* (Sheep Frogs), are primarily tropical, with most species in Central America. They are the only genera that reach the U.S. Only 1 species, the Western Narrow-mouthed Toad (*Gastrophryne olivacea*), occurs in our area. Another species, the Eastern Narrow-mouthed Toad (*G. carolinensis*), occurs in se.

U.S., and the Sheep Frog (*H. variolosus*) reaches extreme s. Tex. In the New World these toads are small, stout amphibians with a small, pointed head; tiny eyes; a fold of skin across the back of the head; short legs; and a smooth, tough skin, which probably helps protect them against ants, upon which they feed.

GREAT PLAINS NARROW-MOUTHED TOAD
Gastrophryne olivacea   **Pl. 15, Map 31**

IDENTIFICATION: ⅘–1 ⅝ in. (2–4.1 cm). A tiny brown or gray, smooth, thick-skinned, toadlike amphibian with a *small, pointed head and broad waist.* Hind legs short and stout. Fingers and toes lack webbing. Fold of skin often present across back of head. **Young:** A dark, leaf-shaped pattern may cover up to half the width of the back. Color becomes paler and leaf pattern disappears with growth. **Male:** Dark or yellowish throat. Small tubercles on lower jaw and chest. Glands on venter, the secretion of which aids the male in sticking to the back of the female during amplexus.

A secretive toad, hiding by day in damp burrows, crevices, and under rocks, bark, and boards, in the vicinity of streams, springs, flooded roadside ditches, and rain pools. Look under bark and in interior of rotten termite-infested stumps and under flat rocks near or covering ant nests. This toad is an anteater. In Ariz. it ranges from mesquite grassland in San Simon Valley, Pima Co., to oak woodland in the Pajarito and Patagonia Mts. In N.M. found in desert scrub of mesquite and creosote bush. Narrow-mouths are difficult to find because of their small size and habit of calling from sites hidden in grass. They are chiefly nocturnal. Use triangulation (see p. 18). Breeds from mid-March–Sept., especially during period of summer rains. Breeding stimulated by rainfall. **VOICE:** Short *whit* followed by a nasal high-frequency buzz usually lasting 1–2, occasionally to 4 seconds and declining in pitch. At a distance a chorus sounds like a band of sheep; nearby like a swarm of bees. Short calls, a low-pitched nasal buzz, lasting a half second, have been reported as probably territorial in nature. Vocal sac round, about the size of a pea. **RANGE:** In the West occurs in s. Ariz. from vicinity of Patagonia, Santa Cruz Co., and just south of San Xavier Mission and near Robles, Pima Co., west to Organ Pipe Cactus Nat'l Monument and Rio Sonoyta, Sonora, Mex.; ranges north to 24 mi. (38 km) south of Casa Grande; Peña Blanca Springs area and Sycamore Canyon, Pajarito Mts. In N.M. in vicinity of Hermanas, Luna Co. Ranges south, mostly west of crest of Sierra Madre Occidental, to n. Nayarit, Mex. East of Continental Divide it occurs from se. Neb. to s. Coahuila and from Chihuahua to e. Tex. Near sea level to around 5,000 ft. (1,525 m).

REMARKS: These toads have been found in varying numbers (up to 9) in tarantula burrows where they receive shelter and perhaps protection by the tarantula against certain predators such as small snakes. The toads, in turn, may protect the tarantula and its eggs and young against attacks from marauding ants.

TONGUELESS FROGS: FAMILY PIPIDAE

Somewhat flattened, rather smooth-skinned, and tongueless; almost completely aquatic. Head is small and eyes generally lack movable lids. Fingers slender, hind feet large and fully webbed. Adults of some species may reach 10 in. (25.4 cm).

These frogs (some 30 species) occur in sub-Saharan Africa, in Panama and n. S. America. The African Clawed Frog, *Xenopus laevis*, has become established in the West a result of released aquarium and laboratory animals.

Family includes Surinam Toad (*Pipa pipa*) and other aquatic species in which the young develop in capped pits in soft skin on the mother's back and emerge as tiny froglets.

AFRICAN CLAWED FROG *Xenopus laevis*   **Pl. 19, Map 60**
IDENTIFICATION: 2–5⅝ in. (5.1–14.3 cm). Head and body flattened; head small, snout blunt, and skin smooth, except where ridges of lateral line system give it a "stitched" appearance. Eyes small, without lids, and turned upward. No tongue. Fingers slender, unwebbed. Hind feet large, fully webbed, and with *sharp black claws on inner toes.* Olive, ocher, to brown above, with dark spots, blotches, or mottling. Whitish below, with or without dark spots. **MALE:** Averages ¾ size of female, lacks protruding cloacal claspers, and has small dark tubercles on fingers and forelimbs during breeding season.

Highly aquatic; seldom leaves the water. In native habitat in Africa it frequents veldt ponds, lakes, marshes, and reservoirs in arid and semiarid regions. Tadpole is translucent, has soft mouth parts, a tentacle on each side of the mouth, and a slender tail that ends in a filament (see Fig. 12, Pl. 19, p. 72). The tadpole hangs suspended with its head downward and tail filament vibrating as it filters protozoa, bacteria, and other small food particles from the water. In a small space it may virtually sterilize the water. Adults feed on aquatic invertebrates and vertebrates including smaller amphibians and fish. The latter include larvae and recently transformed western toads, arroyo chubs, mosquito fish, unarmored threespined sticklebacks, and tidewater gobies. The last two are federally endangered species! They also cannibalize their larvae and recently transformed froglets. In Calif. breeds

Jan.–Nov. and produces multiple clutches. A peak in male calling occurs in April and May. Amplexus is pelvic. **VOICE:** Lacks vocal sacs but gives a two-parted trill, rising and falling, lasting about ½–¾ second, sometimes uttered over 100 times a minute. Calls are given underwater. **RANGE:** Established in s. Calif. Some localities are as follows: Santa Barbara Co. (Goleta Slough), San Diego Co. (lower Sweetwater R. drainage, w. Mt. Helix area, and Tijuana R.), Orange Co. (many localities in western part), Riverside Co. (Arroyo Seco Creek and Vail Lake), Los Angeles Co. (throughout Santa Clara R. and tributaries), San Bernardino Co. (Prado Basin, Chino Hills State Park), Kern Co. (Edwards AFB). Recently reported in extreme nw. Baja Calif. Introduced into golf course ponds in the Tucson area, Ariz.

REMARKS: Brought to U.S. in 1940s for human pregnancy tests and later, in increasing numbers, was used for experimental studies and kept as an aquarium pet. Widely established in slow streams and ponds in s. Calif. where it threatens certain native amphibians and fish. The importation and/or possession of this species is now prohibited in our area by the states of Calif., Ariz., and Nev. Introduced (prior to the ban) in the 1960s in ponds on the U.C. Davis campus, where it persisted until eradicated in the late 1970s.

TURTLES

SNAPPING TURTLES: FAMILY CHELYDRIDAE

Large freshwater turtles with long tails, powerful hooked jaws, and small plastrons, less than half the width of the carapace. Two species: the large Alligator Snapping Turtle of the se. U.S., and the Snapping Turtle.

SNAPPING TURTLE *Chelydra serpentina* Pl. 22, Map 62

IDENTIFICATION: 8–18½ in. (20.3–47 cm). Seems too large for its shell. Chunky head with powerful hooked jaws, *long tail with saw-toothed crest, and small, narrow plastron.* Tail usually longer than half the length of carapace. Carapace black, brown, olive, or horn-colored. **Young:** 3 prominent, lengthwise sawtoothed ridges on the carapace, becoming less prominent with age. Tail as long as or longer than shell. Generally dusky. Carapace margin and plastron with white spots.

Inhabits marshes, ponds, lakes, rivers, and slow streams, especially where aquatic plants are abundant. Usually found in or near water. Well camouflaged when resting on the bottom among plants, its concealment sometimes enhanced by the growth of algae on its shell. Individuals sometimes bask in shallow water or float at the water's surface. Often ill-tempered and prone to bite. Take care. A bite from a large individual can be severe. Emerges from hibernation March–May and may be active in parts of its range until Nov. Clutch of 8–60 (up to over 100) eggs, laid May–Oct., but mostly in June and July. Eats crayfish, snails, insects, fish, frogs, salamanders, reptiles, birds (including waterfowl eggs and young), mammals, and aquatic plants. Often scavenges. **SIMILAR SPECIES:** The small plastron (Fig. 14, Pl. 22, p. 78) and serrated tail crest distinguishes this turtle from all other western species. **RANGE:** S. Canada to Ecuador; e. base of Rocky Mts. to

Atlantic Coast. Introduced at a number of localities in the West (not all listed). In Calif. at Andree Clark Bird Refuge in Santa Barbara, and elsewhere; in Ore. at Coos Bay and near Roseburg; in Wash. at Lake Washington, King Co., and near Yelm, Thurston Co.; in Nev. west of Fallon; in Utah at St. George; in Ariz. at Phoenix; along the lower Colorado R. and in the Battle R. area, Alta., Canada. Whether populations are established in all these areas is unknown. Sea level to around 6,726 ft. (2,050 m).

SUBSPECIES: COMMON SNAPPING TURTLE, *C. s. serpentina,* occurs in our area.

MUSK AND MUD TURTLES: FAMILY KINOSTERNIDAE

In the U.S. represented by 2 genera, musk turtles (*Sternotherus*) and mud turtles (*Kinosternon*). 22 species in family. Other members occur in Central and S. America. These turtles give off a musky odor when handled, hence sometimes called "stinkpots" or "stinking-jims." Odor glands are located on each side of body where skin meets bridge that connects plastron with carapace. Note barbels (nipplelike projections) on chin and neck, the short tail (prehensile in males), and number of marginal shields, including the nuchal (these turtles usually have 23; most others have 25).

Two species of mud turtles (*Kinosternon*) occur in our area.

YELLOW MUD TURTLE   Fig. 13, Pl. 20, Map 67
Kinosternon flavescens

IDENTIFICATION: 3 1/4–6 5/8 in. (8.2–16.8 cm). *Head and neck brown, gray, or olive above, contrasting with plain yellow or cream below.* Nipplelike barbels present on throat. Carapace elongate and high, flat or slightly concave on top, sometimes with single keel down the middle and without flaring edges; olive or brown, occasionally with black borders along seams between the scutes. *Supraorbital ridge above each eye. 9th and 10th marginal shields,* counting from front of shell, *usually distinctly higher than 8th.* Bridge with distinct lengthwise groove. Tail short, without sawtoothed edge above and ending in a nail. Musky odor when handled. **Young:** Carapace nearly round, with weak middorsal ridge. Shell edge yellow in hatchlings, with a dark speck at rear border of each marginal scute. 9th and 10th marginals not enlarged. **Male:** Two patches of horny scales on inner surface of each hind leg. Tail with horny, hooked tip. Horny scale patches are used to catch female's tail or rear margin of her shell as an aid to mating.

Highly aquatic, of semiarid grasslands and open woodland, frequenting both permanent and intermittent waters. Primarily a pond turtle; found in ponds, marshes, lakes, streams, rivers, canals, and reservoirs. Seems to prefer mud or sandy bottoms. Often only its snout is seen when it rises to the surface for air. Clutch of 1–10 (5–6) eggs, laid May–June. Eats insects, centipedes, millipedes, spiders, crustaceans, worms, mollusks, amphibians, fishes, carrion, and aquatic plants. **SIMILAR SPECIES:** Distinguished from all western turtles except Sonora Mud Turtle (below) by its single gular shield and 5 pairs of plastral shields. Sonora Mud Turtle lacks supraorbital ridges, usually has 3 lengthwise keels on carapace, the 9th marginal shield is not enlarged, and head and neck are more heavily mottled (Fig. 13, Pl. 20, p. 74). **RANGE:** Neb. and Ill. to Durango and Veracruz (Mex.); e.-cen. Tex. to s. Ariz. In Ariz., occurs in Swisshelm Mt. area, Cochise Co., west to a few miles east of Sells, Pima Co., and Tempe-Mesa area, Maricopa Co. Near sea level to around 5,200 ft. (1,600 m).

SUBSPECIES: PLAINS YELLOW MUD TURTLE, *K. f. flavescens.* 1st vertebral scute usually overlaps 2nd marginal scute; gular scute is no more than 43 percent of length of anterior lobe of plastron. ARIZONA YELLOW MUD TURTLE, *K. f. arizonense.* 1st vertebral scute fails to overlap 2nd marginal scute; gular scute longer than the above. Molecular information suggests that these taxa have perhaps reached the species level of differentiation.

REMARKS: Because of similarity between the Yellow and Sonora Mud Turtles, uncertainty exists as to distribution of the 2 species in western part of their ranges.

SONORA MUD TURTLE
Kinosternon sonoriense
Pl. 20, Map 66

IDENTIFICATION: 3⅛–6½ in. (7.9–16.5 cm). Resembles Yellow Mud Turtle (p. 247), but lacks supraorbital ridges. Carapace has 3 lengthwise keels (except in very old individuals); 9th marginal shield not enlarged; bridge of plastron lacks lengthwise groove. *Head and neck heavily mottled with contrasting light and dark markings.* **Male:** As in Yellow Mud Turtle.

Chiefly a stream-dweller; frequents springs, creeks, ponds, and water holes of intermittent streams. Sometimes common in stock ponds. Inhabits woodlands of oaks and piñon-juniper, or forests of ponderosa pine and Douglas-fir. Also occasionally inhabits foothill grasslands and desert. Less often found in lowlands than Yellow Mud Turtle. Usually stays in or near water. Clutch of 1–11 eggs, laid May–Sept. sometimes three or four times a year (Ariz.). Eats insects, crustaceans, snails, fish, frogs, tadpoles, and some plant materials. **SIMILAR SPECIES:** See Yellow Mud Turtle (p. 247). **RANGE:** Cen. Ariz. to Durango; w. Tex. to se. Calif. In Ariz., in cen.

and se. Gila R. drainage (to slightly over 5,000 ft. [1,520 m]), at Quitobaquito Spring, Pima Co., near Laguna Dam, Yuma Co., and in Big Sandy–Burro R. drainages. Habitat along lower Gila R. destroyed by dam construction. In N.M., in Animas and Peloncillo Mts. and headwaters of Gila R. east to Taylor Creek, Catron Co., at 6,700 ft. (2,040 m). Old records for Palo Verde and Yuma Indian Reservation, Imperial Co., Calif., along Lower Colorado R. Formerly from near sea level to around 6,700 ft. (2,040 m).

REMARKS: Isolated populations at Quitobaquito Springs (Organ Pipe Cactus Nat'l. Monument) and neighboring Rio Sonoyta (Mex.) require special protection. Species now apparently extinct along Colo. R. and in decline elsewhere in Ariz. and Mex.

BOX AND WATER OR POND TURTLES: FAMILY EMYDIDAE

The most diverse family of turtles (around 100 species), with representatives nearly worldwide; absent from high latitudes and Australian continent, Madagascar, and Africa south of Sahara. Many species are aquatic and have webbed toes, but box turtles are mainly terrestrial. Well represented in e. N. America; 5 species in the West.

WESTERN POND TURTLE
Clemmys marmorata

Pl. 20, Map 64

IDENTIFICATION: 3½–8½ in. (8.9–21.6 cm). Carapace low; olive, brown, or blackish, occasionally without pattern but usually with a *network of spots, lines, or dashes of brown or black that often radiate from growth centers of shields.* Large old males from San

Western Pond Turtle. The native turtle of our Pacific Coastal states and northwestern Baja California. This two-year-old may not breed until 8 to 10 years old. Trinity Co., Calif.

Joaquin Valley, Calif. may be marked with large areas of beige and pinkish beige. Plastron with 6 pairs of shields—yellowish, blotched with blackish or dark brown, occasionally unmarked. Limbs with prominent scales, flecked and lined with black. Head usually with spots or network of black. Crushing surface of upper jaw usually smooth or rippled. **Young:** Tail nearly as long as shell. Carapace uniformly brown or olive above with yellow markings at edge of marginals; shields with numerous small tubercles. Plastron yellowish, with large irregular central black figure. Head, limbs, and tail marked with dusky and pale yellow. **Male:** Throat lighter, often white to light yellow without flecking, and shell usually flatter and less heavily marked than in female.

A thoroughly aquatic turtle of ponds, lakes, marshes, rivers, streams, and irrigation ditches that typically have a rocky or muddy bottom and grown to watercress, cattails, water lilies, or other aquatic vegetation. Found in woodland, grassland, and open forest. May be seen basking on logs, cattail mats, and mudbanks. May enter brackish to full-strength seawater. Found Feb.–mid-Nov. in the north; all year in the south. Clutch of 3–14 eggs, laid April–Aug.; the time varying with locality. Eats aquatic plants, insects, worms, fish, amphibian eggs and larvae, crayfish, cladocera, and carrion. **SIMILAR SPECIES:** (1) Painted Turtle (p. 251) has yellow lines on head and limbs. (2) See Pond Slider (p. 252). **RANGE:** Formerly w. Wash. where now probably extinct, or nearly so, south to nw. Baja Calif., chiefly west of Cascade-Sierran crest. Outlying areas are Mojave R. (Camp Cody and Afton Canyon), Calif., and Truckee, Carson, and East Walker Rs., Nev.; Susanville, Lassen Co., Calif.; Drews Creek, Lake Co., Canyon Creek area, Grant Co., and along the Deschutes R. at Bend, Deschutes Co., Ore., where introduced. Formerly lower Fraser Valley (Burnaby Lake), east of Vancouver, B.C., where perhaps introduced, but now appears to be extinct. Sea level to around 6,696 ft. (2,041 m) but mostly below 4,980 ft. (1,371 m). **SUBSPECIES:** NORTHWESTERN POND TURTLE, *C. m. marmorata.* Pair of triangular inguinal plates (in groin region). Neck markings dull. SOUTHWESTERN POND TURTLE, *C. m. pallida.* Inguinal plates usually small or absent. Neck markings contrast with light ground color. Individuals south of Transverse Ranges in s. California tend to be lighter in coloration—yellowish brown to light brown. **REMARKS:** Species is estimated to be in decline throughout 75–80 percent of its range. In s. San Joaquin Valley, where species now borders on extinction, population was estimated at over 3⅓ million prior to heavy exploitation of turtles for food and other disturbances. Afton Canyon population near terminus of Mojave R. needs special protection. It may be a distinct taxon. Its habitat should be kept fenced to exclude cattle and off-road vehicles. A recent proposal aligns this species with genus *Emys* that will also include Blanding's Turtle of ne. U.S.

PAINTED TURTLE *Chrysemys picta* Pl. 20, Map 68

IDENTIFICATION: 2½–10 in. (6.3–25.4 cm). Carapace low, smooth, unkeeled; generally black, brown, or olive, *with olive, yellowish, or red borders along front edge of shields.* Shell sometimes has open network of lines, and red or yellow middorsal stripe (e. U.S.). Yellow lines on head and limbs. In our area plastron is usually marked with red and with large, dark central figure that has branches extending along furrows between scutes. Crushing surface of upper jaw often with ridge or row of tubercles parallel to jaw margin. Rear of carapace with smooth border. **Young:** Plastron red or orange, the central dark figure well developed; carapace may have indistinct vertebral stripe and weak dorsal keel. **Male:** Much smaller than female. Very long nails on front feet.

Aquatic; frequents ponds, marshes, small lakes, ditches, and streams where water is quiet or sluggish and bottom sandy or muddy, grown to aquatic plants. Often seen sunning on mudbanks, logs, or rocks near water, sometimes in groups of a dozen or more. May not emerge from hibernation until March or April in north but as early as Feb. in south (N.M.). A cold-tolerant species over much of its range. Clutches of 1–25 eggs, laid May–Aug.; 1–2 clutches in north, 2–4 in south. Eats aquatic plants, insects, spiders, earthworms, mollusks, crayfish, fish, and amphibian adults and larvae. Sometimes scavenges. **SIMILAR SPECIES:** See (1) Western Pond Turtle (p. 249) and (2) Pond Slider (p. 252). **RANGE:** S. Canada to Gulf of Mex. and n. Chihuahua (Rio Santa Maria); Atlantic Coast to Pacific Northwest. Isolated popu-

Painted Turtle. This colorful, widely distributed turtle is a favorite of the pet trade. It has been introduced in a number of localities in the West. Kalama R., Cowlitz Co., Ore.

lations in San Juan R. drainage of sw. Colo. and nw. N.M., perhaps
including upper Zuni R. drainage, tributary to Little Colorado R.,
McKinley Co.; also in Rio Grande and Pecos Rs., N.M. Unverified
report from Labyrinth Canyon, Kane Co., Utah. In upper Little
Colorado R. watershed near St. Johns and Lyman Reservoir,
Apache Co., Ariz. Transplanted to many localities outside its natu-
ral range. Evidently introduced and apparently established at
Kaiser Meadow area, Siskiyou Co., and in vicinity of Goleta at Lake
Los Carneros, Santa Barbara Co., Calif. Introduced at Phoenix and
Tucson, Ariz., and Snake R. area near Ontario, Malheur Co., Ore.
May have been introduced in Puget Sound area, Wash., on Van-
couver I. and some small neighboring islands, at Vanderhoof, B.C.;
and in Alta., Canada, at Hines Creek, Edmonton, Banff NP, and
Cypress Hills. Sea level to around 8,500 ft. (2,590 m).

SUBSPECIES: The WESTERN PAINTED TURTLE, *C. p. bellii,* occurs in
our area.

POND SLIDER *Trachemys scripta*   Pl. 21, Map 69

IDENTIFICATION: 3½–14½ in. (8.9–36.8 cm). Carapace usually has
lengthwise wrinkles and streaks and bars of yellow on olive or
dusky background. Yellow markings sometimes more or less hidden by black pigment; some individuals almost completely black.
Streaking on 2nd and 3rd costal shields tends to parallel long axis
of shields. Head and limbs striped with yellow. *Usually broad red,
yellow, or occasionally orange stripe, or blotch behind eye.* Underside of carapace and plastron yellow with dusky blotches, or "eyespots," usually in symmetrical arrangement. Lower jaw appears
rounded when viewed from front. Rear of carapace with sawtoothed margin. **Young:** Carapace green, streaked with yellow. Usually red or yellow stripe behind eye. Plastron with many dark eyelike spots. **Male:** More often dark-colored than female. Usually
long nails on front feet.

Thoroughly aquatic; seldom ventures far on land except when
moving overland between habitats. Often seen basking singly or
in groups on logs or other objects in the water. Prefers quiet water
with abundant aquatic vegetation. One to 3 clutches of 2–25
eggs, laid April–July. Young widely sold as pets, leading to
widespread opportunities for introduction of released or escaped
individuals. Eats aquatic plants, crayfish, snails, tadpoles, fish,
and insects, which are especially preferred by young Sliders. **SIMI-
LAR SPECIES:** (1) Carapace of Painted Turtle (p. 251) usually marked
with red and lacks lengthwise wrinkles and sawtoothed rear margin; Painted Turtle lacks red earstripe behind eye. (2) Rio Grande
Cooter (p. 254) usually has maze of light and dark lines on the
2nd and 3rd costal shields, a C-shaped marking on 2nd costal

scute rather than vertical streaking, and lower jaw that looks flattened when viewed from the front. (3) Big Bend Slider has isolated yellow or orange black-bordered spot on side of head and branched dark central figure on plastron rather than paired dark, often eyespot-like, blotches. (4) Western Pond Turtle (p. 249) has spotted head and limbs. **RANGE:** N. Illinois and cen. Kans. to Gulf Coast and n. Mex.; Atlantic Coast to N.M. Widely introduced in w. U.S. and elsewhere including Europe (and Guam!) primarily as a result of the pet trade; status of many introductions unknown. Red-eared Slider, most favored as a pet, has been the subject of most introductions. Some localities of introduction in our area are extreme sw. mainland and s. tip of Vancouver I., B.C., Puget Sound lowlands (old records), Wash.; Columbia R. Gorge.; San Pablo Reservoir, Contra Costa Co., Andree Clark Bird Refuge, Goleta, Santa Barbara, and Montecito in Santa Barbara Co., Long Beach, San Diego R. and associated reservoirs, Sacramento–San Joaquin drainage area, Calif. Phoenix (Papago Park) and along the Gila R. southwest of Buckeye, Ariz.; Rio Grande drainage (probably introduced), N.M.; Baja Calif. from San Ignacio south to the cape. Sea level to around 4,921 ft. (1,500 m).
SUBSPECIES: RED-EARED SLIDER, *T. s. elegans.* Usually has broad reddish stripe (occasionally yellowish) behind eye. Plastron with eyelike spots. BAJA CALIFORNIA SLIDER, *T. s. nebulosa.* Head with yellow markings. Plastron usually lacks eyespots. Adult males often very black. Considered a full species, *T. nebulosa,* by some researchers.
REMARKS: Red-eared Slider is apparently established in the Rio Grande drainage, N.M.

BIG BEND SLIDER *Trachemys gaigeae*   **Pl. 21, Map 69**
IDENTIFICATION: 5–11 in. (12.7–27.9 cm). *A large black-bordered ovoid spot of yellow, orange, or red on each side of head* with a smaller similar spot between it and eye. Carapace brownish or olive with many dull orange curved lines, some forming ocelli. Rear margin of carapace serrated. Plastron olive, pale orange, or yellowish with a branched dark median marking. Eyelike spots on underside of marginals. Patterning may become obscure with age but pale head spots usually remain. **Young:** Pattern lighter, more contrasting, often with light-contoured spots and blotches. **Male:** Nails on forefeet do not enlarge.

Frequents permanent or near-permanent waters of ponds, lakes, sloughs, canals, tanks, and rivers, often at sites of considerable vegetation. Active from April–Oct., in warmer weather Feb.–Nov. Six to 11 oviducal eggs were found in a sample of 4 females. Presumably omnivorous. **SIMILAR SPECIES:** (1) Pond Slider has wide orange, red, or yellow stripe or blotch rather than large black-bordered spot of similar color on each side of head; carapace lacks curved lines and ocelli. (2) Rio Grande Cooter has C-shaped marking on 2nd costal scute. (3) Painted Turtle lacks large headspot and serrations on posterior margin of carapace. **RANGE:** Rio Grande drainage in s.-cen. N.M., Tex., and Mex., and Rio Conchos, a Rio Grande tributary in Chihuahua, Mex. In N.M. found between 4,199 and 4,626 ft. (1,280–1,410 m).

RIO GRANDE COOTER *Pseudemys gorzugi*   Pl. 21, Map 70

IDENTIFICATION: 3⅕–11½ in. (8.1–29.2 cm). Carapace ornately marked with complicated pattern resembling a contour map of swirls of yellow, dusky, and black lines and scattering of large blackish spots and blotches. *2nd costal scute usually bears conspicuous yellowish C-shaped marking.* Yellowish green stripes on head and neck. Usually a yellow or yellowish green large blotch on each side of head. Feet and tail striped with yellowish, red, and black. Plastron largely without pattern except for dark color along seams. Carapace has serrated rear margin. **Young:** Plastron may be marked with thin gray lines along seams. **Male:** Long claws on forefeet. Old adults may become melanistic.

Primarily a river turtle, especially attracted to quieter water of deeper pools. Substratum may be mud, sand, and/or rocks. Eats algae, probably other plants, and presumably fish and a variety of invertebrates. **SIMILAR SPECIES:** (1) Shell of Painted Turtle has smooth rear margin and plastron is ornately marked. (2) Pond Slider has patch of red on each side of head and smooth rear margin to carapace. **RANGE:** From extreme se. N.M. throughout w. and s. Tex. along Pecos and Rio Grande drainages and adjacent Coahuila and Nuevo León to n. Tamaulipas, Mex. In N.M. found in Pecos R. drainage where it ranges north to Brantley Reservoir. Range includes Black and Delaware Rivers. Report from Bitter Lakes area, Chavez Co., requires verification. From sea level to 3,609 ft. (1,100 m).

WESTERN BOX TURTLE (ORNATE BOX TURTLE)
Terrapene ornata   Pl. 22, Map 65

IDENTIFICATION: 4–5¾ in. (10.1–14.6 cm). Land turtle that can completely enclose itself in its shell, however it does not shun water. *Front of plastron hinged and can be drawn up tightly against carapace.* Shell high, rounded, and typically marked with radiating lines or series of dots of black or dark brown on yellow or horn-colored background. Similar markings may be found on plastron. Occasional individuals have plain yellow or horn-colored shell. **Young:** Carapace with yellowish middorsal stripe and spots; plastron cream or yellowish with large dark central blotch. **Male:** First nail on each hind foot turns inward, which aids male in clinging to shell of female during copulation. Iris red (yellowish or reddish brown in female) and head sometimes greenish.

Primarily a prairie turtle. Over much of range inhabits treeless plains and gently rolling country grown to grass or scattered low bushes, but also occurs in open woodlands. Seeks sites where soil is sandy or otherwise suitable for burrowing. Both self-constructed burrows or those made by kangaroo rats may be used. May also be found under boards, rocks, and other objects. Box Turtles are omnivorous, eating a great variety of animal and plant foods—insects (beetles, grasshoppers, crickets, caterpillars) and other invertebrates, including earthworms and crayfish; reptiles, eggs, carrion; berries, melons, cactus fruits and pads, tender shoots, and leaves. In some areas tortoise "sign" consists of disturbed piles of cow dung into which they have dug in search of beetles and other insects. Active March–Nov. Breeds both spring and autumn. Clutch of 2–8 eggs, laid May–Aug. Activity stimulated by rainfall. **RANGE:** Sw. S.D., s. Mich., and Ind. south to Gulf Coast and extreme n. Mex.; e. Tex. across s. N.M. to se. Ariz. (to as far west as e. base of Baboquivari Mts.) and Sonora. Near sea level to around 7,546 ft. (2,300 m).
SUBSPECIES: DESERT BOX TURTLE, *T. o. luteola*. Pale radiating lines on shell more numerous than in Ornate Box Turtle, 11–14 on 2nd costal shield. Markings become less distinct with advancing age and eventually are lost; shells of most old individuals are uniform straw color or pale greenish brown. ORNATE BOX TURTLE, *T. o. ornata*. Fewer pale radiating lines (5–10) on 2nd costal shield than in Desert Box Turtle. Usually no obvious fading of shell with advancing age.

LAND TORTOISES: FAMILY TESTUDINIDAE

Land-dwelling chelonians with domed shell and elephant-like limbs, ranging into some of the most arid parts of the world. About 40 species. Majority are herbivorous, feeding on leaves, soft stems, and fruits, but some occasionally eat animal matter. Occur on all continents except Australia and Antarctica. Includes giant tortoises of Galapagos Is. and islands in Indian Ocean. Only the gopher tortoises (genus *Gopherus*) occur in N. America. In addition to our species, the Desert Tortoise (below), gopher tortoises include its close relative the Texas Tortoise of s. Tex. and ne. Mexico, the Gopher Tortoise of se. U.S., and the large Bolson Tortoise of n.-cen. Mexico.

DESERT TORTOISE *Gopherus agassizii*   Pl. 22, Map 63
IDENTIFICATION: 8–15 in. (20.3–38.1 cm). A high-domed shell, usually with prominent growth lines on shields of both carapace and

plastron. Carapace brown, gray, or horn-colored, usually without definite pattern. Plastron yellowish or brownish, without a hinge. Forelimbs covered with large conical scales; when drawn in, limbs block openings of shell. Limbs stocky. Tail short. **Young:** Flexible shell. Nails longer and sharper than in adult. Carapace dull yellow to light brown; shields usually with dark borders. **Male:** Gular shields longer than in female, and lump (chin gland) on each side of lower jaw larger.

Completely terrestrial desert or semidesert species, requiring firm, but not hard, ground for construction of burrows (in banks of washes or compacted sand) or uses shelters among rocks and exposed, eroded caliche layers in walls of washes.; adequate ground moisture for survival of eggs and young; and herbs, grass, cacti, and other plants for food. Frequents desert oases, riverbanks, washes, dunes, and rocky slopes. In U.S. it ranges from creosote bush flats and hillsides up into areas of blackbrush and juniper woodland. Populations in Ariz. tend to scattered and associated with palo verde–saguaro cactus communities. In Mex. occurs mostly in upland areas of thornscrub to the lower edges of evergreen oak and juniper woodland. Tortoise tracks consist of parallel rows of rounded dents, direction of travel indicated by sand heaped up at rear of each mark. Burrows, often found at base of bushes, have half moon–shaped openings. Burrows of adults often 3–9 ft. (1–2.8 m) in length, but refuges up to 30 ft. in length are known from colder northeastern part of range. Clutch of 1–12 (often 4–6) eggs, laid May–July, even as late as Aug. in Sonoran Desert, with 2 or rarely 3 clutches in favorable years in Mojave Desert. Nests often constructed at opening of, or just inside, tortoise burrows. **RANGE:** S. Nev. and extreme sw. Utah

Desert Tortoise. The native tortoise of the Mojave and Sonoran Deserts with an ancestry extending back to the Pleistocene era. This "indicator" of desert health is now approaching extinction in many parts of the California Desert.

(Beaver Dam slope and Dixie Valley) to n. Sinaloa (Mex.); se. Ariz. (Rincon Mts., Pima Co.) west to Mojave Desert and e. side of Salton Basin, Calif.; with exception of Boyd Deep Canyon Research Center area, appears to be absent from Coachella Valley, Calif., although habitat seems suitable. Occurrences in extreme se. Ariz. and sw. N.M. may not represent established populations. Recent remains found at Lehman Caves in Great Basin Nat'l Park, Nev. Near sea level to around 5,241 ft. (1,600 m).

REMARKS: Desert Tortoise is considered an "indicator" species with respect to the health of our natural desert ecosystems. Regrettably, its widespread decline, particularly over the last 5–6 decades, tells us that all is not well in the desert. Impacts are many—including urban and military expansion, on and off-road vehicle use, road developments, mining, overgrazing, weed intrusion, increase in ravens attracted to expanding garbage sources, road kills, irresponsible shooters, and spread of disease. Map 63 shows some areas of major losses. Reserves and management plans are being established for tortoise protection, but the long-term outcome of these efforts remains to be determined.

SEA TURTLES: FAMILIES CHELONIIDAE AND DERMOCHELYIDAE

Large marine turtles that range from tropical to temperate seas. Low, streamlined shell and powerful flippers. In our area the cold Alaskan current usually keeps most of them south of Oregon, but occasional individuals range far north. Six species in family Cheloniidae, including 4 in our area, and 1 species in family Dermochelyidae.

SEA TURTLES: FAMILY CHELONIIDAE

GREEN TURTLE *Chelonia mydas*   **Pl. 23**

IDENTIFICATION: 30–60+ in. (76–152+ cm); usually 120–200 lbs., but some reach over 600 lbs. Carapace smooth, with *4 costal shields on each side,* the 1st not touching the nuchal; carapace greenish to olive, or brown, gray, or black sometimes mottled with reddish radiating lines and flecks on shields in younger animals. *Single pair of large scales (prefrontals) between upper eyelids.* Plastron without pattern, usually pale yellow or whitish sometimes with gray. Head plates olive, edged with yellowish. **Young:** Carapace scutes appear to overlap slightly and flippers relatively larger than adult's. Generally brown to blackish, shell and flippers edged with cream. Pale below. **Male:** Longer, narrower carapace than female's.

Very long prehensile tail, tipped with a horny nail. Enlarged curved claw on front flipper. Off Baja Calif., locally known as the Black Sea Turtle.

A thoroughly aquatic turtle of lagoons and bays that seldom comes on land. Basks and sleeps on remote rocky or sandy shores and lays eggs on gently sloping sandy beaches, usually of islands, at habitually used communal nesting sites. May be seen near mangroves, beds of eelgrass, or seaweed, where it comes to graze. Also eats some invertebrates, including jellyfish and sponges. When migrating, may occur far out at sea. Clutches average 100–120 eggs, laid 1–8 times per season. Commercially valuable; flesh is highly esteemed. Common name of this turtle comes from the color of its fat. **SIMILAR SPECIES:** See (1) Loggerhead (below) and (2) Hawksbill (p. 259). **RANGE:** Worldwide in warm seas. On Pacific Coast, common as far north as San Quintin Bay, Baja Calif; ranges south to Peru. Occasionally in San Diego Bay and elsewhere along coast of s. Calif. Records for w. coast Vancouver I., south of Tofino and Dundars Is.; Ucluelet Inlet, B.C., and Eliza Harbor, Admiralty I., and Prince William Sound, Alaska. A small population resides Nov.–April in warm-water effluent channel of San Diego Gas & Electric power plant in San Diego Bay.
REMARKS: This species is in serious trouble. It has undergone an estimated 90 percent population decline over the past 50 years.

LOGGERHEAD *Caretta caretta*   Pl. 23

IDENTIFICATION: Along our shores, mostly around 8–36 in. (20.3–91 cm). Our population consists of young individuals that migrate across the Pacific Ocean from their birthing shores in Japan. Elsewhere adults may be 300–400 lbs.; some to over 900 lbs. Shell high in front. *Five or more costal shields on each side,* not overlapping, the 1st touching the nuchal. Broad head with 2 pairs of prefrontals. Carapace usually reddish or orange-brown, shields often edged with yellow. Head shields yellowish brown to olive-brown, grading to yellowish at their edges. Cream below, more or less clouded with dusky. **Young:** Carapace yellowish buff, brown, or grayish black, with 3 lengthwise ridges and tendency toward slight overlapping of shields.

A wide-ranging turtle of the open ocean. Enters bays, lagoons, estuaries, salt marshes, and river mouths to forage and breed. Nests on gently sloping sandy beaches, singly or in groups. Average clutch of 120 eggs, laid 1–8 times a season. Eats crabs, mollusks, sponges, jellyfish, fish, eelgrass, and seaweed. **SIMILAR SPECIES:** (1) Green Turtle (p. 257) has 4 costal shields and 1 pair of prefrontals. (2) Hawksbill (p. 259) has 4 costal shields and hawklike mandibles. (3) See also Olive Ridley (p. 259). **RANGE:** Temperate parts of Pacific, Indian, and Atlantic Oceans and Mediterranean Sea. Pacific Coast from s. Calif. (near Santa Cruz I.) and upper end of Gulf of California to Chile. Sporadically farther north. Reported at mouth of Columbia R. (Fort Canby State Park, Ilwaco, Wash.).

OLIVE RIDLEY *Lepidochelys olivacea* Pl. 23

IDENTIFICATION: 20–29 in. (51–74 cm); 80–100+ lbs. A relatively small sea turtle with uniformly olive-brown to grayish green carapace that looks nearly round from above and rather flat-topped from the side. Skin somewhat grayer than shell. *Usually 6–8 (occasionally 5–9) costal shields on each side,* the 1st pair in contact with nuchal. Head large, with *2 pairs of prefrontals* (see rear endpapers). *Four enlarged inframarginals* (scales below marginals) *on each side on bridge,* each usually perforated by a pore. Plastron light greenish yellow or creamy white. **Young:** Nearly uniform grayish black, except for lighter shade on ventral keels, which are strong and sharp from humeral to anal shields. Carapace with lengthwise keels. **Male:** Carapace slightly longer and tail much longer and thicker than female's. Strongly developed curved claw on each forelimb.

Frequents protected and relatively shallow water of bays and lagoons, but also ranges well out to sea. Nests on beaches, on the Pacific Coast from the tip of Baja Calif. to Panama, and n. Peru; elsewhere widely throughout warmer coasts of the world. Most numerous sea turtle. Clutch of around 30–170 eggs. Eats seaweed, mollusks, crustaceans, jellyfish, sea urchins, and fish. **SIMILAR SPECIES:** The 2 pairs of prefrontals and high costal-shield count will distinguish this turtle from other marine turtles. **RANGE:** Chiefly warmer parts of Pacific and Indian Oceans. In Atlantic off w. coast of Africa and n. and e. coast of S. America; sporadically in Caribbean Sea to Puerto Rico and n. coast of Cuba. Off w. coast Calif. and Baja Calif., and Gulf of Calif. south to Chile. Records for Cordova area of Alaska and La Jolla, Monterey Bay, strandings on beaches of Mendocino and Humboldt Cos. (Table Bluff area), Calif.

HAWKSBILL *Eretmochelys imbricata* Pl. 23

IDENTIFICATION: 18–36 in. (46–91 cm); 30–280 lbs., most under 250 lbs. Carapace heart-shaped, with central keel and sawtoothed rear margin; note *strongly overlapping, shinglelike shields* that are dark brown with a yellow radiating or marbled pattern. *Four costal shields on each side,* the 1st not touching nuchal. Four inframarginals at outer edge of bridge. *Two pairs of prefrontals* (between eyelids). *Hawklike mandibles.* **Young:** Midkeel on carapace and carapace shields black or dark brown. Plastron with 2 lengthwise ridges and some dark blotching, especially toward the front. Lighter brown color on shell edges and ridges, and on neck and flippers. **Male:** Tail longer and thicker than in female; curved nail on each front flipper.

Pugnacious turtle that defends itself spiritedly with its sharp, hawklike beak. Lays clutches of 50–200+ eggs Aug.–Nov. Eats mollusks, sponges, coelenterates (including corals), sea urchins, crustaceans, fish, seaweed, and mangroves. A source of "tortoise shell" and human food. **SIMILAR SPECIES:** See (1) Loggerhead (p. 258). (2) Green Turtle lacks hawklike mandibles. **RANGE:** Warmer parts of the Pacific, Indian, and Atlantic Oceans; S. Calif. to Peru; Gulf of California.

LEATHERBACKS: FAMILY DERMOCHELYIDAE

LEATHERBACK *Dermochelys coriacea*   **Pl. 23**
IDENTIFICATION: 48–96 in. (122–244 cm); 600–1,600 lbs., possibly reaching a ton. The largest living turtle. *Carapace and plastron with smooth leathery skin (no horny shields) and prominent tuberculate lengthwise ridges.* Carapace dark brown, slaty, or black, unmarked or blotched with whitish or pale yellow, in profile often having a toothed outline from the tubercles on the median (central) ridge. **Young:** Hatchlings covered with small scales. Tail rudderlike, with a thin, high dorsal keel. Scales and keeling soon shed. Dark-colored above, with pale-edged flippers and light-colored ridges on shell.

A wide-ranging species that may be seen far out to sea. Females ascend sandy beaches of tropical and subtropical shores to lay their eggs, in clutches of 50–170 (averages 80 in Atlantic and Caribbean and 65 in e. Pacific). Eats jellyfish, sometimes gathering in schools to feed on them. Floating plastic bags and probably balloons (that resemble jellyfish) are also consumed, with likely detrimental effects. A Leatherback was found recently with 6 1/2 ft. of nylon fishing net protruding from her mouth, the remainder lodged in her digestive tract. Nests in e. Pacific Oct.–Feb.; w. Pacific March–Aug.; sporadically Oct.–Dec. Individual females nest only every 2–3 years. **RANGE:** Worldwide, chiefly in temperate to cool seas. Individuals may circumnavigate entire oceans in 1 year. On Pacific Coast recorded north to vicinity of Cordova, Alaska. Reported off w. coast Vancouver I.; Denman I.; s. Queen Charlotte Is. (off Skidegate and Lyell I.).
SUBSPECIES: PACIFIC LEATHERBACK, *D. c. schlegelii,* occurs in our area.
REMARKS: Increasing impact of modern longline, drift, and set gill-net fishing is of growing concern to fisheries managers and sea turtle conservationists. This species is undergoing rapid decline.

SOFTSHELL TURTLES:
FAMILY TRIONYCHIDAE

"Pancake" turtles, named for their round, flat, *flexible shell. Neck is long and nostrils open at end of a proboscis-like snout.* Feet broadly webbed and paddlelike. Thoroughly aquatic, but venture onto land to bask and nest. Softshells actively seek prey (insects, crayfish, worms) or ambush it as they lie with shell buried in mud or sand. When in shallows the long neck and snout can be extended to the surface from time to time for air while, in between, the turtle remains concealed. Handle with care—they are quick and can inflict a painful bite.

Twenty-five species; 3 in N. America and U.S., 2 in our area and others in Indo-Australian archipelago, s. Asia, E. Indies, and Africa.

SPINY SOFTSHELL *Trionyx spiniferus*   Pl. 22, Map 71

IDENTIFICATION: 5–21 in. (12.7–53.3 cm). Extremely flat with *flexible, pancakelike shell covered with leathery* skin rather than horny shields. Front edge of shell often covered with tubercles or "warts" (occasionally smooth in Texas Softshell subspecies). Limbs flat and toes broadly webbed. Flexible proboscis (snout). *Note whitish ridge in each nostril,* on either side of median septum. Lips fleshy, concealing sharp-edged jaws. Olive-brown, brown, or grayish above, variously flecked with dark brown or black, sometimes with dark eyelike spots on shell. Carapace with yellowish or cream-colored border. Cream or yellowish below, unmarked. Markings tend to fade with age. **Young:** Carapace border conspicuous. Shell often spotted with black, sometimes profusely so. Prominent dark markings on head and limbs. **Male:** Averages smaller than female and has a more contrasting pattern, retaining juvenile markings. Carapace with sandpaper-like texture. Tail thick and fleshy, extending beyond edge of shell. **Female:** Tends to become blotched and mottled with age. Carapace smoother than in male and with well-developed warts along front edge.

In the West, primarily a river turtle attracted to quiet water with bottom of mud, sand, or gravel. Also enters ponds, canals, and irrigation ditches, but generally avoids temporary water. Agile both in water and on land. Can retract head out of sight beneath shell, among folds of neck skin. Active April–Sept. in the north, all year in the south. One, perhaps 2, clutches of 3–39 eggs, laid May–Aug. on sandy banks. Eats earthworms, snails, crayfish, insects, fish, frogs, tadpoles, reptiles, and occasionally aquatic plants. Sometimes scavenges. **SIMILAR SPECIES:** Smooth Softshell (p. 262) has fewer contrasting marks on limbs, usually lacks tuber-

cles on carapace, and has no ridge on each side of septum between the nostrils. **RANGE:** Widespread throughout Mississippi R. basin and se. U.S. In West, in w. tributaries of Mississippi R.; Rio Grande and Pecos R., N.M.; Gila and lower Colorado Rs. Sea level to around 5,200 ft. (1,580 m). Probably introduced into Colorado R. system via Gila R. drainage from N.M. and Ariz. around 1900. Has extended its range through Imperial Valley, Calif., to Salton Sea. Introduced in Lower Otay Reservoir and San Diego R.: also found in San Pablo Reservoir, Contra Costa Co.; San Gabriel R., Los Angeles Co., Calif.; and Rio Colorado, Baja Calif. Coexists with Smooth Softshell in Canadian R. drainage in N.M.
SUBSPECIES: WESTERN SPINY SOFTSHELL, *T. s. hartwegi*. Retains juvenile pattern of small ocelli, or solid black dots, on carapace. Only 1 dark marginal line separates pale border of carapace from dorsal ground color; pale border not conspicuously widened toward rear. Bold pattern of dark and light markings on head and limbs. TEXAS SPINY SOFTSHELL, *T. s. emoryi*. Juvenile pattern of white dots confined to rear third of carapace. Pale border conspicuously widened, 4–5 times wider at rear than at sides. Pattern on head and limbs reduced.

SMOOTH SOFTSHELL *Trionyx muticus*   not shown

IDENTIFICATION: 3⅕–14½ in. (8.1–36.8 cm). Resembles Spiny Softshell (see Pl. 22) but *nostrils round, with no median ridges;* front end of carapace smooth. Juvenile pattern of large dusky spots (sometimes eyelike) or small dark dots and bars persists in males. Pale, usually unbroken stripe behind eye; side of head otherwise unpatterned. Usually lacks contrasting marks on dorsal surfaces of limbs. **Young:** Carapace brown or olive-gray, marked with dots and dashes only a little darker than ground color. **Male:** Tends to be colored like young. **Female:** Mottled with various shades of gray, brown, or olive.

Chiefly a river turtle, apparently more restricted to running water than Spiny Softshell. Frequents large rivers and streams but also lakes and impoundments, the latter principally in southern part of range. One to 3 clutches of 3–33 eggs, laid May–July on small islands or gently sloping muddy or sandy shores. Eats invertebrates, frogs, and fish. **SIMILAR SPECIES:** See Spiny Softshell (p. 261). **RANGE:** Chiefly Mississippi R. drainage from extreme w. Pa., s. Minn., and S.D. to Gulf Coast; from w. end of Fla. Panhandle to cen. Tex. In our area, known only from above Conchas Dam and downstream from Ute Resevoir on Canadian R. in ne. N.M. Sea level to around 4,500 ft. (1,370 m).
SUBSPECIES: MIDLAND SMOOTH SOFTSHELL *T. m. muticus* occurs in our area.

LIZARDS

GECKOS: FAMILIES GECKKONIDAE AND EUBLEPHARIDAE

A large group of tropical, subtropical, and arid temperate-zone lizards (around 1,000 species), found on all continents except Antarctica and widespread on oceanic islands. Most species are nocturnal and therefore limited in distribution by nighttime temperatures. Geckos communicate by chirping and squeaking; the name "gecko" is based on the sound made by an oriental species. Most geckos are excellent climbers. Many species crawl with ease on walls and ceilings and are often found in houses and public buildings in the tropics.

Geckkonids (represented in our area by 2 native and 3 introduced species) have soft skin with fine granular scales, large eyes with vertical pupils and immovable eyelids, a fragile tail easily lost but readily regenerated, and toes with broad flat tips and well-developed claws. Undersides of toes are covered with broad plates that bear numerous villi (microscopic hairlike structures with spatula-shaped tips). The villi, which cling to surfaces by friction, and the sharp claws, which anchor in surface irregularities, give these lizards their remarkable climbing ability.

The eublepharids, to which our 3 species of Banded Geckos (*Coleonyx*) belong, differ from other geckos in having movable eyelids and slender toes that lack villi.

Fifteen species occur in U.S. and Baja Calif., 7 are native, the rest are introduced. Eight species found in our area. Our 3 introduced species are the Mediterranean and Common House Geckos and Stump-toed Gecko. Most introductions have occurred in Fla. and other Gulf Coast states. Some geckos are parthenogenetic, like some of our whiptail lizards, but all our species are bisexual.

WESTERN BANDED GECKO
Coleonyx variegatus

IDENTIFICATION: 2–3 in. (5.1–7.6 cm). *Soft, pliable skin, vertical pupils, and movable eyelids* distinguish this lizard from all others except its close relatives, the Texas Banded and Barefoot Geckos. Scalation finely granular, *toes slender,* and tail constricted at base. Brown bands on both body and tail, on a pink to pale yellow background. Bands tend to break up with age or in certain localities into a blotched or mottled pattern. Plain whitish below. May squeak when caught. **Young:** Brown bands above usually well defined and unbroken. **Male:** Prominent spur on each side of base of tail. Spurs weak or absent in female. Usually 6–10 preanal pores, uninterrupted at midline. Corresponding scales in female usually enlarged and sometimes pitted but lack pores.

Appears delicate, but can live in extremely dry parts of the desert due to nocturnal and subterranean habits. Ranges from creosote bush flats and sagebrush desert to piñon-juniper belt, and from catclaw-cedar-grama grass plant community in eastern part of range to chaparral areas in West. Often associated with rocks, and may seek shelter under them or in crevices. In some parts of range it occurs on barren dunes. To find these lizards, drive slowly along blacktop roads and watch for small, pale, twiglike forms. In the daytime turn over rocks, boards, and other objects, especially in spring before ground surfaces heat up. One to 3 clutches, usually of 2 eggs, laid May–Sept. Eats insects such as beetles, grasshoppers, insect larvae, termites, and solpugids and spiders. **VOICE:** May squeak when disturbed. **SIMILAR SPECIES:** See Texas Banded Gecko (p. 265) and Barefoot Gecko (p. 265). **RANGE:** S. Nev. to tip of Baja Calif. and s. Sinaloa; coastal s. Calif. to sw. N.M. Ranges from desert across s. Sierra Nevada via Kern R. Canyon to Granite Station area and Caliente Creek drainage, Kern Co., on e. side San Joaquin Valley, Calif. Dot in n. Ariz. is at Antelope Point, Lake Powell, Coconino Co., Ariz. On islands in Gulf and Cedros I. off w. coast of Baja Calif. Below sea level in desert sinks to around 5,000 ft. (1,520 m).

SUBSPECIES: DESERT BANDED GECKO, *C. v. variegatus.* Usually 7 or fewer preanal pores in males. Dark body bands same width as, or narrower than, interspaces between them; bands with light centers, or replaced by spots. Light collar mark indistinct or absent. Head spotted. **TUCSON BANDED GECKO,** *C. v. bogerti.* Pattern similar to Desert Banded Gecko, but usually 8 or more preanal pores in males. **SAN DIEGO BANDED GECKO,** *C. v. abbotti.* Dark body bands uniform in color, same width as or narrower than interspaces. Distinct narrow, light-colored collar mark. Head unspotted in adults. **UTAH BANDED GECKO,** *C. v. utahensis.* Dark body bands in adult wider than interspaces;

edges of bands highly irregular, often merged with dark spots in interspaces. SAN LUCAN BANDED GECKO, *C. v. peninsularis*. Differs from other subspecies in having even-edged, dark dorsal bands wider than interspaces, reduced head spotting, and prominent lines on snout.

TEXAS BANDED GECKO *Coleonyx brevis*   not shown, Map 74

IDENTIFICATION: 1 ¾–2 ½ in. (4.4–6.3 cm). Closely resembles Western Banded Gecko (p. 264), but less dark spotting in the broad irregularly margined dark bands that, in adults, may encroach extensively on pale interspaces. Preanal pores 3–6, seldom more than 4, interrupted by one or more small scales at midline. Dark body bands wider than interspaces, often fading with age and often replaced by dark spotting. **Young:** Dorsal light and dark crossbands distinct and even-edged. **Male:** As in Western Banded Gecko (p. 264).

Frequents desert grassland, creosote bush scrub, and open arid brushland and woodland. Like its western relative is often associated with rocks. May be found in crevices and under rocks, on arid flats, hillsides, and in canyons. Nocturnal; found on roadways at night. One to 3 clutches of 1–4 (usually 2) eggs, laid April–June. Eats insects, spiders, centipedes, millipedes, and isopods. **SIMILAR SPECIES:** In Western Banded Gecko (p. 264) adults are usually more distinctly banded and males usually have 7 or more preanal pores in a continuous row. **RANGE:** S. N.M. to s.-cen. Tex., south to ne. Durango and s. Coahuila, Mex. In limestone areas of se. Eddy Co., N.M., but scarce or absent now in Rio Grande Valley, N.M. Near sea level to around 5,000 ft. (1,520 m).

BAREFOOT GECKO (SWITAK'S BANDED GECKO) *Coleonyx switaki*   Pl. 24, Map 75

IDENTIFICATION: 2–3 ⅓ in. (5.1–8.4 cm). Resembles Western Banded Gecko but has *small sooty tubercles on scales on upper sides, back of neck, and upper base of tail.* Pale beige, yellowish, yellowish olive, reddish brown to brown above, with numerous round to oval brown and often somewhat larger light spots; the light spots sometimes more or less unite to form pale crossbands. Individuals from areas with dark rocks may have dark ground color and contrasting light spots. Tail usually with conspicuous light and dark crossbands. **Young:** Pale crossbands on body and tail. **Male:** As in Western Banded Gecko (p. 264).

Frequents flatlands to arid hillsides, arroyos, and canyons, usually with many large boulders and massive rock outcrops, in thornscrub desert. Nocturnal habits and use of deep crevices make this gecko difficult to find. Squeaks when disturbed and walks with tail elevated, curled, and waving. **SIMILAR SPECIES:** Western Banded Gecko (p. 264) has broader lamellae on underside of toes and lacks tubercles on back. **RANGE:** S. Calif. from near Borrego Springs and Yaqui Pass, San Diego Co., southward along e. fringe of Peninsular Ranges into Baja Calif., to near Bahia de Los Angeles, San Ignacio, and Santa Rosalia. On San Marcos I., Gulf of Calif. Reported as far north as Palms to Pines Highway area, Riverside Co., Calif. Near sea level to around 2,297 ft. (700 m).

LEAF-TOED GECKO *Phyllodactylus xanti*   Pl. 24, Map 73

IDENTIFICATION: 1 ⅗–2 ½ in. (4.1–6.3 cm). Typical gecko with *enlarged leaflike toe pads* and large *eyes that have immovable eyelids*. Pupils vertical. Two large flat scales at tip of each toe, with claw between them. Scales on dorsal surfaces of body mostly granular, but *interspersed with enlarged keeled tubercles*. Pinkish, brown, or gray above, marked with dark brown spots. Pale below.

A rock-dweller, inhabiting areas of desert scrub, thornscrub, and broken chaparral. Often found in canyons with massive boulders. Likely to occur near streams and springs, but also frequents areas with no permanent water. Excellent climber that seldom ventures far from rocks, hence seldom found on roadways at night. Often squeaks when caught. Tail readily lost. Several clutches of 1–2 eggs, laid May–July. Eats insects and spiders. **SIMILAR SPECIES:** See (1) Henshaw's Night Lizard (Pl. 35, text p. 306) and (2) San Lucan Gecko (below). **RANGE:** Lower desert slopes of mountains of s. Calif., from north of Palm Springs to tip of Baja Calif. On islands in Gulf of Calif. and off w. coast Baja Calif. Sea level to around 2,000 ft. (610 m).

SUBSPECIES: CAPE LEAF-TOED GECKO, *P. x. xanti.* Usually smaller than Peninsular Leaf-toed Gecko; has tubercles on thighs. PENINSULAR LEAF-TOED GECKO, *P. x. nocticolus.* Usually larger than above subspecies; no thigh tubercles. Other subspecies occur on islands in Gulf of Calif. and on Magdalena and Santa Margarita Is. off w. coast Baja Calif.

REMARKS: Coexists with its relative the San Lucan Gecko (below) in the cape region of Baja Calif. (see Maps 195 and 73). Recently (1997) reported at Cottonwood Springs, Joshua Tree Nat'l Park — a single individual on the wall of a restroom at night. Observation requires confirmation. Might it have been the introduced Mediterranean House Gecko?

SAN LUCAN GECKO *Phyllodactylus unctus*   Pl. 55

Endemic to Cape region of Baja Calif. (see p. 420).

MEDITERRANEAN HOUSE GECKO   Pl. 24, Map 75
Hemidactylus turcicus

IDENTIFICATION: 1 ¾–2 ⅜ in. (4.4–6 cm). Eyes large, without lids, pupils vertical. *Broad toe pads of lobed transverse plates. Prominent, often keeled, knobby tubercles on dorsal surfaces.* Undergoes marked color change: In pale phase, ground color light pink to very pale yellow or whitish; dorsum (upper body) spotted and blotched with brown or gray. In dark phase, ground color darkens to gray or brownish and blotches become less evident. Markings often form banded pattern on tail. **Young:** Tail often more banded than in adult. **Female:** When gravid, whitish eggs can be seen through translucent skin of abdomen.

Chiefly nocturnal. A nonnative species. In U.S. and elsewhere where introduced it is usually an "urbanized" gecko that lives in or near human dwellings. Feeds on insects attracted by lights and may be seen on walls, ceilings, and window screens, stalking or awaiting prey. Also found in rock crevices, cracks in tree trunks, and occasionally under palm fronds and other objects on the ground. One to 3 clutches a year of 1–2 hard-shelled eggs, laid April–Aug. Communal nesting occurs. **VOICE:** Advertisement call of male a series of clicks in succession. Utters mouselike squeak when fighting or threatened. **SIMILAR SPECIES:** (1) Leaf-toed Gecko (p. 266) has 2 large flat scales at tip of each toe. (2) Banded Geckos (p. 264) and (3) Barefoot Gecko (p. 265) have movable eyelids and no toe pads. **RANGE:** In Calif. reported from near Blythe, Cathedral City, Desert Hot Springs, Palm Desert, Palm Springs, Riverside Co.; Earp, San Bernardino Co.; Ocotillo and El Centro, Imperial Co.; and San Diego, San Diego Co. In Ariz. in Tucson, Phoenix, Eloy, Casa Grande, and Yuma. Also reported from Las Cruces, N.M. and Las Vegas, Nev. Elsewhere in U.S. found in Tex., Okla., La., Ark., Miss., Ala., Ga., Fla., S.C., and Blacksburg, Va. Found also in Mex. (Ensenada, Baja Calif. and elsewhere), Cuba, Puerto Rico, Panama, Chile, and Canary Is. Native to w. India, Somalia, the Middle East, and Mediterranean basin.

REMARKS: Exotic species that spread rapidly aided perhaps in part by inadvertent transport of its communal egg clutches by humans (in nursery stock, bromeliads, etc.).

COMMON HOUSE GECKO
Hemidactylus frenatus

not shown, Map 195

Nonnative, close relative of Mediterranean House Gecko established at La Paz, Baja Calif. (see p. 420).

STUMP-TOED GECKO *Gehyra mutilata*

not shown, Map 195

Also nonnative, found at La Paz, Baja Calif. (see 420).

IGUANIAN LIZARDS

In 1989 the family Iguanidae, a large diverse group of mostly New World lizards, containing around 600 species, was reevaluated taxonomically. Eight families were recognized. Three occur in our area: the (1) Iguanidae—spiny-tailed iguanas and chuckwallas, (2) Crotaphytidae—collared and leopard lizards, and (3) Phryno-somatidae—all our remaining species. The number of families in this group is controversial.

DESERT IGUANA, CHUCKWALLA, SPINY-TAILED IGUANAS, AND RELATIVES: FAMILY IGUANIDAE

A mostly New World group of large herbivorous lizards ranging from sw. U.S. to s-cen. S. America. Outliers on Figi and Tonga I. groups, sw. Pacific Ocean. Includes Marine and Land Iguanas of the Galapagos Is. Thirty-five species, most native to tropical and subtropical environments. Three species in our area live in arid and semiarid environments.

DESERT IGUANA *Dipsosaurus dorsalis*   Pl. 25, Map 79
IDENTIFICATION: 4–5¾ in. (10.1–14.6 cm). Large, pale, round-bodied lizard with long tail and rather small, rounded head. Scales small, granular on sides, smooth and overlapping on belly. *Row of slightly enlarged, keeled scales down middle of back.* Pale gray above, with barring or network of brown or reddish brown on sides; variously spotted and blotched with light gray. Dark rings around tail. Pale below, with reddish, pinkish to buff areas on sides of belly in both sexes during breeding season.

Typical habitat in northern part of range consists of creosote bush desert with hummocks of loose sand and patches of firm ground with scattered rocks. In the south it frequents subtropical scrub.

Desert Iguana. Our most heat-tolerant lizard—mean of normal activity range 107°F and maximum voluntary tolerance 115°F. Humans 98.6°F; with fever, a few degrees or so above. Clark Co., Nev.

Most common in sandy habitats but also occurs along rocky streambeds, on *bajadas*, silty floodplains, and on clay soils. May be seen basking on rocks or sand hummocks, near a burrow in which it may take refuge. Tolerant of high temperatures, remaining out on hot, sunny days when most other lizards seek shelter. Chiefly herbivorous; climbs among branches of creosote bush and other plants to obtain fresh leaves, buds, and flowers. Also eats insects, carrion, and its own fecal pellets. Breeds April–July. Clutch of 3–8 eggs, laid June–Aug. **RANGE:** S. Nev. to tip of Baja Calif. and nw. Sinaloa. Desert side of mountains in s. Calif. to cen. Ariz. On islands off Gulf Coast, and on Magdalena and Santa Margarita Is. off the Pacific coast of Baja Calif. Below sea level in desert sinks to around 5,000 ft. (1,520 m). Range in U.S. coincides closely with that of creosote bush, a staple food.

OMMON CHUCKWALLA *Sauromalus obesus* Pl. 25, Map 78
IDENTIFICATION: 5–9 in. (12.7–22.8 cm). A large, flat, often dark-bodied lizard with *loose folds of skin on neck and sides*. Often seen sprawled on a rock in the sun. Skin on back covered with small granular scales. Tail with blunt tip and broad base. *Rostral scale absent.* **Young:** Crossbands on body and tail. Bands on tail conspicuous—black on olive-gray or yellowish background. **Male:** Head, chest, and limbs usually black, sometimes spotted and flecked with pale gray. Back black, red, or light gray, depending on age and locality. Tail usually cream-colored or pale yellow. Tail orange (!) in adult males from South Mt. south of Phoenix, Ariz. Individuals from s. Mojave and Colorado Deserts in Calif. and from sw. to cen. Ariz. north of Gila and Salt Rs., may have torso suffused with red.

Common Chuckwalla. Cross-bands on body and tail and the distended torso indicate that this individual is probably a gravid female. Chuckwallas often bask near their rock crevice retreats. Clark Co., Nev.

Upper Colorado R. and Virgin R. drainage males and those from cen. Sonora and Baja Calif. Sur commonly have transverse dark body bands. Bands particularly distinct in Virgin R. drainage. **Female:** Tends to retain juvenile crossbands. Adults of both sexes usually banded in sw. Utah.

A rock-dwelling, herbivorous lizard widely distributed in the desert. The creosote bush occurs throughout most of range. At some localities, at least in the past, nearly every lava flow, rocky hillside, and outcrop in its range had Chuckwallas. Rocks provide shelter and basking sites. To find this lizard, drive on desert roads in late morning and afternoon to spot basking individuals among the rocks. Approach on foot and take note of the crevice the lizard enters, or listen for the sandpaper-like sound made as it slides into a crack. Look for droppings (elongate, cylindrical pellets containing plant fibers), which mark basking sites and favored retreats. Shine a flashlight into the crevice to see the "chuck" in its retreat. When disturbed, Chuckwallas gulp air, distend their body, and wedge themselves tightly in place. Clutch of 5–16 (6–7) eggs, laid June to perhaps Aug. Females may skip a year or two in egg-laying. Eats a variety of desert annuals, some perennials, and occasionally insects. **RANGE:** Throughout Calif. desert, s. Nev (perhaps to as far north as Railroad Valley, Nye Co.), and Virgin and Colorado R. drainages in s. Utah to Henry Mts., thence south through Baja Calif. to La Paz and w. and s.-cen. Ariz. to Guaymas, Sonora, Mex. On Tiburon I. and some other islands along the Gulf coast of Baja Calif. Chuckwallas currently recognized as other species occur on other islands in the Gulf.

BAJA CALIFORNIA SPINY-TAILED IGUANA
Ctenosaura hemilopha   **Pl. 55, Map 196**
Endemic to Baja Calif.

COLLARED AND LEOPARD LIZARDS: FAMILY CROTAPHYTIDAE

A small family of 12 species, confined to N. America and ranging from e. Mo. to Calif. and e. Ore. and from Colo. and s. Idaho into Mex., including most of Baja Calif. Two genera, *Crotaphytus,* the Collared Lizards and *Gambelia,* the Leopard Lizards. These are robust, pugnacious lizards with well-developed limbs and mostly granular scalation, widely distributed in arid and semiarid environments. In contrast to members of the large family Phrynosomatidae (see p. 277), they usually seek refuge beneath rocks and other surface objects or in burrows, whereas many phrynosomatids often bury in loose soil, sand, or duff.

EASTERN COLLARED LIZARD
(COMMON COLLARED LIZARD)
Crotaphytus collaris

IDENTIFICATION: 3–4⅗ in. (7.6–11.6 cm). Robust lizard with relatively large, broad head; short snout; and long, *rounded tail*. Scales mostly smooth, granular. *Two dark collars:* the first (anterior) one is of equal width throughout or narrows at sides and *does not encircle throat;* the second (posterior) one often reaches the forelimbs in males, less often in females. Numerous light spots and often a series of dark crossbands on body. Ground color above varies — may be greenish, bluish, olive, brown, or yellowish depending on locality, sex, age, and color phase. Markings tend to fade with age, the collar least. Throat spotted. *Mouth and throat lining usually black. Some greenish reflections usually present on upper surfaces over most of range.* Often some yellowish color on head, especially well developed in e. Utah, w. Colo., and nw. N.M. where in males entire head may be yellow, contrasting with a vivid green body. Dorsal surface of tail usually spotted and crossbanded. Belly whitish or cream. **Young:** Broad dark crossbands or transverse rows of dark spots on body and tail. Sometimes with red or orange markings like breeding female's (see below). **Male:** Broader head than female. Usually considerable greenish color on dorsal surfaces, including sides and limbs. Throat dark-spotted — green, bluish, and in eastern part of range, orange or yellow. Enlarged postanal scales. **Female:** Lacks or has slight tinge of green above. Throat unmarked or lightly spotted with brown or gray. In breeding season, develops spots and bars of red or orange on sides of neck and body, which fade after eggs are laid.

A rock-dweller; frequents canyons, rocky gullies, limestone ledges, mountain slopes, and boulder-strewn alluvial fans, usually where vegetation is sparse. Occupies desert shrublands, sagebrush, piñon-juniper woodlands, and forested or grassland riparian areas. Essentials appear to be boulders for basking and lookouts, open areas for running, and adequate warmth. Collared lizards jump nimbly from rock to rock and seize other lizards and insects with a rush, often running with forelimbs lifted off the ground and tail raised. Most are easily caught in the morning when they bask at the top of boulders. To avoid being bitten, handle these lizards by the sides of the head. Do not cage them with smaller animals (potential prey). One to 2 clutches of 1–14 eggs, laid April–July. Eats insects (grasshoppers, lepidopterans, beetles, hymenopterans), spiders, lizards, and occasionally berries, leaves, and flowers. **SIMILAR SPECIES:** (1) Great Basin Collared Lizard (p. 272) lacks greenish color and dark mouth lining, and has large dark patches on flank and groin. See also (2) Long-nosed Leopard

Lizard (p. 274), (3) Crevice Spiny Lizard (p. 285), and (4) Banded Rock Lizard (p. 298). **RANGE:** Se. Utah, sw. and se. Colo., east to Mo., south through cen. Tex., N.M., and Ariz. to ne. Sonora to Zacatecas and San Luis Potosí. Around 300–9,800 ft. (90–3,000 m).

GREAT BASIN COLLARED LIZARD Pl. 27, Map 85
Crotaphytus bicinctores

IDENTIFICATION: 3⅖–4⅖ in. (8.6–11.2 cm). *Ground color above brown to grayish brown with numerous small whitish dots and dashes.* Anterior and posterior black collar markings present, the latter often without dorsal gap. Throat-lining pale. **Male:** *Usually well-developed broad alternating crossbands of gray and orange or pink.* Anterior black collar complete ventrally. Throat slate gray to bluish with black central patch. Black inguinal patches. *Tail somewhat flattened side-to-side* and with well-developed pale dorsal stripe. **Female:** Generally duller than male, grayish brown above, lacks tail stripe, and tail more rounded than in male. Dark pigment on throat and inguinal areas lacking. Breeding female develops orange or reddish bars on sides.

Inhabitant of Great Basin, Mojave, and Sonoran Deserts, where it is attracted to rocky hilly terrain with generally scant vegetation. However, the species has been found in rolling gravelly hills with only occasional rocks. Eats insects (beetles, grasshoppers, hymenopterans, lepidopterans), spiders, lizards, and some plant materials. In Tule Valley, Millard Co., Utah, egg-laying occurred in June. Clutch size from 3–7 eggs. **SIMILAR SPECIES:** (1) See Baja California (p. 273) and (2) Grismer's Collared Lizards (p. 422). **RANGE:** Se. Ore. and sw. Idaho (mainly along Snake R.

Great Basin Collared Lizard. Like other collared lizards this species frequents rocky habitats. Rocks provide shelter, basking sites, and lookouts for sighting prey. Harney Co., Ore.

drainage) south throughout Great Basin and some adjoining upland areas to extreme se. Calif. and w. Ariz. Ne. Calif. to w. and cen. Utah. Throughout Calif. desert to nw. Ariz. Localities beyond desert in s. Calif. are N. Fork of Lytle Creek and San Antonio Canyon, headwaters of E. Fork of San Gabriel R.; San Antonio Wash near where N. Fork of San Antonio R. enters main wash. In this area, near San Gorgonio Pass, closely approaches northern limits of range of Baja California Collared Lizard. The two species appear to be separated by the Pass. Old record for Kernville in s. Sierra Nevada. In Ariz., hybridizes with Eastern Collared Lizard in Cerbat Mts., Mohave Co., and west of Cameron, Coconino Co., near Little Colorado R. where it penetrates upland range of Eastern Collared Lizard. In sw. Ariz. its southern distributional limit is largely defined by Gila R. However, it occurs south of the river near Sentinel on the Sentinel Plain, Maricopa Co. Dots on map in se. Idaho may represent relict populations northeast of Atomic City, Butte Co., and Montpelier, Bear Lake Co. Near sea level to around 7,500 ft. (2,290 m).

BAJA CALIFORNIA COLLARED LIZARD   not shown, Map 85
Crotaphytus vestigium

IDENTIFICATION: To 5 in. (12.7 cm). Ground color of dorsum brown or grayish, *patterned with well-spaced slender crossbars of whitish or aligned whitish spots and intervening areas dotted and dashed with whitish.* Fore and aft black collar markings (posterior collar rarely absent), the front collar complete ventrally in males. *Collars with wide dorsal gaps, posterior collar especially so. Tail flattened side-to-side* and with pale dorsal stripe. Throat lining pale. **Male:** Tail stripe well defined. Gular area dark blue-gray with central dark patch. Black inguinal patches present. In Baja Calif. ventrolateral coloration olive green north of Bahía de San Luis Gonzaga and golden orange from Bahía de Los Angeles southward. **Female:** Color generally duller than male's. Above usually gray or greenish gray. Tail stripe absent or faint. No dark throat or inguinal markings. Vivid orange or reddish bars on sides when breeding.

Frequents arid rocky habitats of desert hillsides, canyons, alluvial fans, and lava flows. Adult males in breeding color have been observed at San Ignacio, Baja Calif. Sur in early April. **SIMILAR SPECIES:** Distinguished from all other Collared Lizards in our area by presence of wide gap in posterior black collar (or absence of collar) and narrow crossbars on body. **RANGE:** Desert side of Peninsular Ranges of s. Calif. from n. slope San Jacinto Mts. southward through Baja Calif. to s. margin of volcanic Magdalena Plain near Misión San Javier. Near sea level to around 4,000 ft. (1,094 m).

Crotaphytus nebrius

IDENTIFICATION: To 4⅖ in. (11.2 cm). Above yellowish to dull tan with *conspicuous round whitish spots, large on dorsum and becoming much smaller on sides. Vague or no crossbars on body.* No defined dorsal stripe on tail; tail rounded. Fore and aft black collar markings present; posterior one sometimes uninterrupted dorsally. **Male:** Throat slate gray or dark brown, often with a yellow cast; no black central spot. Anterior collar complete ventrally. When breeding develops burnt orange ventrolateral abdominal coloration. Small dark inguinal patches present. **Female:** Color duller than in male, often browner. No complete anterior collar marking nor dark inguinal patches. Orange or reddish lateral bars when gravid.

Frequents mountain ranges in Sonoran Desert. In our area, in Ariz., some ranges occupied are Gila, Mohawk, Ajo, Pozo Redondo, Puerto Blanco, Sikort Chuapo, Estrella, Buckeye Hills, Quijotoa, Silverbell, and Tucson Mts. Habitats may be diverse but rocks almost always present. In southern part of range it may occur in rather dense arid-tropical thornscrub. Adults active from March–Sept. with juveniles abroad until Oct. or Nov. **SIMILAR SPECIES:** (1) Eastern Collared Lizard adult males lack ventrally complete anterior black collar and, when breeding, lack burnt orange ventrolateral abdominal coloration. (2) Great Basin and (3) Baja California Collared Lizard adult males have tail flattened side-to-side, dorsal stripe on tail, and pale throat lining. (4) Grismer's Collared Lizard has tail flattened side-to-side and lacks dark throat lining. **RANGE:** From s. side of lower Gila R., Ariz., to Guaymas, Sonora, Mex., and vicinity of Yuma, Ariz., east to just west of Tucson. In Sonora it ranges east to w. foothills of Sierra Madre Occidental near Bacadéhuachi.

GRISMER'S COLLARED LIZARD
Pl. 53, Map 85
Crotaphytus grismeri

Endemic to Baja Calif.

LONG-NOSED LEOPARD LIZARD
Pl. 26, Map 84
Gambelia wislizenii

IDENTIFICATION: 3¼–5¾ in. (8.2–14.6 cm). *A large lizard with many dark spots, rounded body, long round tail, and large head.* Dorsal body scalation granular. Capable of marked color change: in dark phase, spots are nearly hidden and light crossbars are conspicuous on both body and tail; in light phase the reverse is true. Ground color gray, pinkish, brown, or yellowish brown above. Throat streaked or spotted with gray. Scales on top of head small, including interparietal. **Young:** Markings, especially crossbars, usually more contrasting than in adults; upper back often rust-colored. Young of some populations have bright crimson spots. **Male:** Usually smaller than female. **Female:** During breeding season, reddish orange color appears on underside of tail, and as spots and bars on sides of neck and body. Reddish color disappears after breeding season.

Inhabits arid and semiarid plains grown to bunch grass, alkali bush, sagebrush, creosote bush, or other scattered low plants. Ground may be hardpan, gravel, or sand. Rocks, often used as basking sites, may or may not be present. Avoids dense grass and brush that can interfere with running. Often lies in wait for insect or lizard prey in shade of a bush, where its spotted pattern blends. Tap bushes with a stick to flush these lizards. They run with forelimbs raised when running fast. Will attempt to bite when caught. Do not cage with smaller animals. Clutch of 1–11 (5–6) eggs, laid March–July; a second clutch may be laid in the south. Eats insects (grasshoppers, crickets, beetles, termites, butterflies, caterpillars, bees, wasps), spiders, lizards, snakes, small rodents (pocket mice), and soft leaves, blossoms, and berries. **VOICE:** When sufficiently agitated, may hiss and sometimes squeal. **SIMILAR SPECIES:** (1) Collared lizards (*Crotaphytus* species, pp. 271–74) have collar markings; sides of tail flattened in Grismer's and Baja California Collared Lizards. (2) See Blunt-nosed Leopard Lizard (below). **RANGE:** Se. Ore. and s. Idaho, throughout the Great Basin, south to the Magdalena Plain near tip of Baja Calif., nw. Sonora, and extreme n. Zacatecas. On Tiburón I. in Gulf of Calif., desert base of mountains in s. Calif. east to extreme w. Colo., cen. and s. N.M. and w. Tex. Old records from Gavilan Peak area, Riverside, Calif., and Hat Rock, Umatilla Co., and The Dalles, Wasco Co., Ore. Latter locality is in doubt. Near sea level to around 6,000 ft. (1,830 m).

REMARKS: Scattered populations in upper Cuyama drainage (Cuyama Badlands, nw. Ventura Co.), Calif. have characteristics that indicate former interbreeding (hybridization or intergradation) between Long-nosed Leopard Lizard and Blunt-nosed Leopard Lizard (below). At present, however, there is no known contact between them; unknown whether interbreeding could now occur. In behavior, structure, and color these populations appear to favor the Long-nosed parental type (*G. wislizenii*). Parts of the hybrid zone in Ballinger Canyon have been degraded by off-road vehicle driving and agricultural developments. Hybrids now reported as eliminated from these areas.

LUNT-NOSED LEOPARD LIZARD

Pl. 26, Map 84

Gambelia sila

IDENTIFICATION: 3–5 in. (7.5–12.5 cm). Resembles Long-nosed Leopard Lizard (p. 274) in body proportions, but snout blunt. Grayish to yellowish above, with dark spots that tend to be arranged in rows on each side of dorsal midline. Pale crossbands on body usually distinct, except when in light phase or in older individuals. *Throat with pale gray to dusky spots,* sometimes merging to form network or lengthwise streaks. **Young:** Red or rust-colored spots on body; yellow on thighs and underside of tail. Sides often blotched with yellow in young females. **Male:** Larger head broader than in female. During breeding season males develop pink, salmon, or rust wash on throat, chest, and sometimes over most of body except on top and sides of head. **Female:** When breeding, reddish orange spots and blotches appear on head and sides and reddish orange on underside of thighs and tail. Reddish color fades after eggs are laid.

Frequents semiarid grasslands, alkali flats, and washes of San Joaquin Valley, Calif., and nearby valleys and foothills. Soil may be sandy, gravelly, loamy, or occasionally hardpan. Vegetation often includes clump grasses, annual grasses, saltbush, and, in some areas, Mormon tea. Frequently seek refuge in burrows of small mammals. One to perhaps 3 clutches of 1–6 eggs, laid June–July. Eats chiefly insects (crickets, cicadas, grasshoppers, bees, lepidoptera) and lizards. **SIMILAR SPECIES:** Long-nosed Leopard Lizard (p. 274) has a much longer snout, and more often has lengthwise stripes on throat. **RANGE:** San Joaquin Valley and surrounding foothills, originally from sw. San Joaquin Co. south to extreme Santa Barbara and Ventura Cos. In south, range extends from Carrizo Plains south over Temblor and Caliente Ranges into Middle Cuyama Valley, Calif. From about 100–2,400 ft. (30–730 m).
REMARKS: Eliminated over large portions (perhaps over 90 percent) of former range by agriculture, urbanization, livestock grazing, petroleum, mineral, and water developments, and off-road vehicle use. Encroachment continues. Protected in the Pixley Wildlife Refuge and at several other localities in San Joaquin Valley. (see also Remarks under Long-nosed Leopard Lizard).

COPE'S LEOPARD LIZARD   *Gambelia copeii*   **Pl. 26, Map 84**
IDENTIFICATION: To 5 in. (12.7 cm). A close relative of the Long-nosed Leopard Lizard. In northern part of range, dorsum is usually dark brown with paired large dark brown to black spots down middle of back. *Spotting weakens anteriorly and may disappear on upper back and head.* Spots unite to create dark crossbands on tail. Paired spots separated by cream-colored transverse bars. Spots give way to flecking on sides. To the south, ground color becomes paler, often becoming a golden tan (Vizcaino Desert), dorsal spots become fragmented, and lateral spots may be present or spotting may give way to fine pale speckling (especially in sandy areas). Subadults, however, may be colored more like northern individuals. **Female:** Usually smaller than male. Gravid individuals have red or orange coloration like that of female Long-nosed Leopard Lizard.

Inhabits chaparral, coastal sage scrub, and oak woodland in northern part of range and farther south more xeric habitats such as windblown sand deposits of Vizcaino Peninsula, where it is particularly common. Dry scrub habitats with creosote bush are frequented. May be found basking on rocks and road berms. Eats lizards and insects. Eggs probably laid April–July. **SIMILAR SPECIES:** (1) Blunt-nosed Leopard Lizard males during breeding season have pink to orange wash on throat and chest and sometimes over most of body. (2) Long-nosed Leopard Lizard tends toward paler coloration and usually has many small dark spots on head. **RANGE:** Extreme sw. Calif. (Cameron Corners, Campo, and Potrero Grade) southward in Baja Calif. to nw. part of cape region. On Cedros, Magdalena, and Santa Margarita Is. off west coast. Absent from San Felipe Desert region ne. Baja Calif., occupied by Long-nosed Leopard Lizard. Apparently absent from gulf coast area between Bahía San Francisquito and La Presa region, possibly excluded by the Sierra San Pedro and Sierra de La Giganta.

REMARKS: Variation in color and pattern of Long-nosed Leopard Lizard makes it difficult to distinguish from Cope's Leopard Lizard using color alone. However, both forms are reported to coexist, without evidence of integration, along a narrow zone within Paseo de San Martias in ne. Baja Calif. (see black dot on Map 84).

ZEBRA-TAILED, EARLESS, FRINGE-TOED, SPINY, TREE, SIDE-BLOTCHED, AND HORNED LIZARDS: FAMILY PHRYNOSOMATIDAE

A diverse New World group of around 125 species ranging from extreme sw. Canada and coast to coast, south to Panama. They vary in form from slim-bodied, long-legged runners (Zebra-tailed and Earless Lizards) to chunky, squat, short-legged Horned Lizards. Habitats vary from extreme desert environments to tropical forests. There are terrestrial, rock-dwelling, and arboreal species. These lizards have specialized kitchen-sink-trap-like nasal passages that trap fine particles when they are buried in fine soil, sand, or duff, or when on the surface in dusty environments.

ZEBRA-TAILED AND EARLESS LIZARDS: GENERA *Callisaurus*, *Cophosaurus* AND *Holbrookia*

Slim, long-legged, granular-scaled lizards found chiefly in arid and semiarid regions of cen. and sw. U.S., s. to cen. Mex. There are 4 species of Earless Lizards, 2 of which occur in our area. All lack external ear openings. The Zebra-tailed Lizard, a close relative widespread in the West, however, has well-developed external ear structure. All readily bury themselves in sandy or loose soil, entering headfirst and rapidly burying themselves with a shimmying motion. When fleeing, the Zebra-tailed Lizard curls its tail over its back as it runs, often waving it at the beginning and end of its dash, then lowering it and "melting" into the background as the bold black-and-white markings disappear. The tail markings, briefly displayed, are thought to attract the attention of predators that may become confused when the markings suddenly disappear. The Greater Earless Lizard may also engage in tail-curling behavior.

LESSER EARLESS LIZARD
Holbrookia maculata
Pl. 28, Map 80

IDENTIFICATION: 1⅝–2½ in. (4.1–6.3 cm). A small, ground-dwelling lizard with *no ear openings. Smooth, granular scales above.* Upper labials overlap and are separated by diagonal furrows. A fold of skin across the throat. Tail short; *no black bars on underside.* Ground color brown, tan, gray, or whitish above, usually closely matching soil color of habitat. Lizards at White Sands Nat'l Monument, N.M., are almost pure white. Back usually marked with scattered light spots and 4 lengthwise rows of dark blotches, each blotch pale-edged at rear. A pair of black marks on each side of belly. Light-bordered dark stripe on rear of thighs. **Male:** Enlarged postanal scales. Dark blotches on back often faint; usually light-edged when present. Belly markings more conspicuous than in female and set off by blue borders. **Female:** Often develops vivid orange or yellow patch on throat during breeding season.

Primarily a plains lizard, most common where there are exposed patches of sand or gravel. Frequents washes, sandy streambanks, sand dunes (White Sands, N.M.), shortgrass prairie, mesquite and piñon-juniper woodland, sagebrush flats, and farmland. Not particularly fast; can sometimes be caught by hand. One or 2 clutches of 1–12 (usually 4–6) eggs, laid April–Sept. Eats insects (beetles, ants, grasshoppers, lepidoptera), spiders, and small lizards. **SIMILAR SPECIES:** (1) Side-blotched Lizard (p. 295) has ear openings and usually has a dark spot behind the axilla ("armpit"); upper labials do not overlap. (2) Greater Earless and (3) Zebra-tailed Lizards (p. 279) have black bars on underside of tail, and Zebra-tailed Lizard has ear openings. **RANGE:** Great Plains and cen. Mex. plateau, from s. S.D. to Jalisco and Guanajuato, Mex.; across s. Continental Divide in U.S. to se. Utah and n. and cen. Ariz. West of Sierra Madre Occidental, it ranges through Sonoran Desert, thence on at least to s. Sinaloa. Sea level to about 7,000 ft. (2,130 m).

GREATER EARLESS LIZARD
Cophosaurus texanus

IDENTIFICATION: 1 ⅞–3 ½ in. (4.7–8.9 cm). Slim-legged, and long, flat tail with black crossbars on underside (bars missing if tail regenerated). Ground color above tends to blend with soil color of habitat and may be gray, brown, or reddish, with numerous small light flecks. *Each side of belly marked with 2 black or sooty crescents, which extend up onto sides. Black markings behind midpoint of body. No ear openings.* Light-bordered dark stripe on rear of thigh. Dorsal scales granular. Diagonal furrows between upper labials. Gular fold present. **Male:** Enlarged postanal scales. Black crescents bordered by blue or greenish on belly and by yellowish on flanks. **Female:** Dark crescent-shaped markings faint or absent. During breeding season some females develop pinkish to orange-pink wash, especially on flanks, and vivid pinkish to orange throat patch.

A lizard of middle elevations, avoiding extreme desert lowlands and higher mountains. Look for this lizard where cactus, mesquite, ocotillo, creosote bush, and palo verde grow. Seems to prefer sandy, gravelly soil of flats, washes, and intermittent stream bottoms where plants are sparse and there are open areas for running. Occasionally found on rocky hillsides. Sometimes runs with tail curled over body, but not as consistently as Zebra-tailed Lizard (below). Clutches of 2–9 eggs, laid March–Aug. Eats insects (grasshoppers, caterpillars, bees, wasps, etc.) and spiders. **SIMILAR SPECIES:** (1) Zebra-tailed Lizard (below) has ear openings, and black belly bars are located at midbody. (2) See also Lesser Earless Lizard (p. 278). **RANGE:** W. Ariz., N.M., and n. Tex. south to Zacatecas and s. Tamaulipas, Mex., cen. Tex. west to e. edge Mojave Desert at Bill Williams R. and in Cerbat Mts., Mohave Co., Ariz. Near sea level to around 6,890 ft. (2,100 m). **SUBSPECIES:** CHIHUAHUAN EARLESS LIZARD, *C. t. scitulus.* Usually 28 or more femoral pores. Numerous small orange, red, or yellow flecks on back, and series of large, prominent, paired dark spots down middle of back. Some males very colorful—pinkish on upper back and yellowish or greenish on lower back and groin. TEXAS EARLESS LIZARD, *C. t. texanus.* Usually 27 or fewer femoral pores. Usually no orange or yellow spots on back; dark middorsal spots, when present, not prominent.

ZEBRA-TAILED LIZARD
Callisaurus draconoides

IDENTIFICATION: 2 ½–4 in. (6.3–10.1 cm). Slim-bodied with a long, flat tail and extremely long, slender legs, well adapted for running at high speed. Fringe of pointed scales on rear of toes in lizards from Viscaino Desert, Baja Calif., but not reported elsewhere. *Ear openings present. Black crossbars on white undersurface of tail* (the "zebra" markings). Dorsal scales granular. Upper labials separated by diagonal furrows. Gular fold present. Gray network on back and dusky crossbars on upper surface of tail. Sides usually lemon yellow. Two or 3 black or gray bars (3 in Viscaino Desert, Baja Calif.) on each side of belly, extending slightly up the sides. *Black belly markings at or in front of midpoint of body.* Light-bordered dark stripe on rear of thigh. Throat dusky, often with pink or orange spot at center. **Male:** Enlarged postanal scales. Belly markings conspicuous and located in blue patches on each side of belly. **Female:** Belly markings faint or absent.

Frequents washes, desert "pavements" of small rocks, and hardpan, where plant growth is scant and there are open areas for running. Occasionally found in rocky arroyos (Baja Calif.) and on fine windblown sand, but usually not far from firm soil. When about to run, it curls and wags its tail; it runs at great speed, with the tail curled forward. Bold tail markings may divert attack of hawks or other predators to the tail, which can be regenerated. One to perhaps 5 clutches (more in southern part of range) of 2–15 (usually 1–8) eggs, laid June–Aug. Eats insects (grasshoppers, beetles, caterpillars, robberflies, etc.), spiders, other lizards, and occasionally plants. On a beach in Sonora, Mex., one was found to have eaten many beach hoppers (amphipods) and a young crab. Arboreal feeding on insects attracted to blossoms has also been recorded (near El Centro, Calif.). **SIMILAR SPECIES:** See (1) Greater Earless Lizard (p. 279), (2) Fringe-toed Lizards (below), and (3) Lesser Earless Lizard (p. 278). **RANGE:** Nw. Nev. from as far north as Black Rock Desert (near ghost town of Sulphur) south to s. Sinaloa and tip of Baja Calif.; extreme sw. N.M. to desert slope of mountains in s. Calif. and on coastal slope along Cajon and San Jacinto Washes (see dots on map). On islands in the Gulf of Calif. Below sea level in desert sinks to around 5,000 ft. (1,520 m).
SUBSPECIES: COMMON ZEBRA-TAILED LIZARD, *C. d. draconoides.* Usually only 2 dark bars on abdomen, most evident in male. No fringe of pointed scales on toes. VISCAINO ZEBRA-TAILED LIZARD, *C. d. crinitus.* Three dark bars on abdomen, most evident in male. Fringe of pointed scales along rear border of 2nd, 3rd, and 4th toes, probably an adaptation for running on sand. Toe fringe and spots on back and tail suggest those of Fringe-toed Lizards (below). Apparently more likely to bury itself in sand than Common Zebra-tailed Lizard. A sand-adapted lizard, found only in the Viscaino Desert of Baja Calif.

FRINGE-TOED LIZARDS: GENUS *Uma*

Adapted for life in fine windblown sand of dunes, hummocks, desert flats, and washes. Projecting scales form a fringe on sides of toes that aid traction, speed, and reduce sinkage into the sand; finely granular, velvetlike scalation aids rapid burial; lower jaw is countersunk, which helps prevent sand getting into the mouth when burying; overlapping eyelids and earflaps protect eyes and ears; and valvular nostrils and kitchen-sink-trap-like nasal passages (see p. 279) protect respiratory tract against inspiration of fine particles. When frightened, Fringe-toes often dart suddenly to opposite side of a sand hummock or bush, where they freeze, plunge into the sand, or disappear into a burrow. When running at high speed they run primarily on their hind legs (are bipedal). Tracks are distinctive, consisting of alternating large, round dents made by hind feet and occasional smaller ones made by front feet in maintaining balance. Usually so wary, you will probably need help of a companion to catch them. Walk abreast, 25 or 30 ft. (7–9 m) apart, keeping sand hummocks and bushes between; this will let you see hiding places as the lizards dash to the opposite side of hummocks. Fringe-toed lizards are highly vulnerable to off-road vehicle activity and establishment of windbreaks (salt cedar, etc.) that affect sand deposition. Four species; 3 in our area, confined to Sonoran and Mojave Deserts. Fourth species occurs in Chihuahuan Desert of n.-cen. Mex.

COLORADO DESERT FRINGE-TOED LIZARD
Uma notata   **Pl. 29, Map 83**
IDENTIFICATION: 2¾–4⅘ in. (7–12.2 cm). A flattened, sand-dwelling lizard with velvety skin and *fringed toes* that have projecting pointed scales. (See generic description for structural features related to life in fine windblown sand.) Well camouflaged—dorsal ground color and pattern of black flecks and eyespots (ocelli) harmonize with background. Ocelli tend to form broken lengthwise lines that extend over shoulders. White below, with dark *diagonal lines on throat,* black bars on underside of tail, and *conspicuous black spot or bar on each side of belly.* Sides of belly with a permanent orange or pinkish stripe; these colors more vivid during breeding season. In Sonoran populations, pinkish wash appears along sides, usually only during breeding season. **Young:** Orange or pink belly color faint or absent. **Male:** Enlarged postanal scales.

Restricted to fine, loose, windblown sand of dunes, flats, riverbanks, and washes in some of the most arid parts of the desert. Vegetation usually scant, consisting of creosote bush, burroweed, croton, mesquite, or other scrubby growth. Clutches of 1–5 (2) eggs, laid May–Aug. Eats chiefly insects, but occasionally other lizards and buds, leaves, and flowers. **SIMILAR SPECIES:** (1) Mojave Fringe-toed Lizard (p. 282) has black crescents on throat, and belly usually tinged with greenish yellow. (2) In Coachella

Valley Fringe-toed Lizard (below), black belly spots are absent or reduced to one or several small dots. (3) Zebra-tailed Lizard (p. 279) usually lacks fringed toes (the Viscaino Desert subspecies of Baja Calif. has weakly developed fringes), is slimmer, and less often found in areas of fine windblown sand. **RANGE:** Vicinity of Salton Sea and Imperial Sand Hills, Calif., south across Colorado R. delta, around head of Gulf of Calif. to Tepoca Bay, Sonora; extreme ne. Baja Calif. Below sea level to around 600 ft. (180 m).

COACHELLA VALLEY FRINGE-TOED LIZARD
Uma inornata   **Pl. 29, Map 83**

IDENTIFICATION: 2¾–4⅞ in. (7–12.4 cm). Similar to Colorado Desert Fringe-toed but paler. *Black spots on each side of belly (if present) are reduced to single small dot or cluster of dots;* streaks on throat are paler. Breeding coloration consists of pinkish wash on sides of belly in males and bright orange in gravid females.

Habits and habitat similar to those of Colorado Desert Fringe-toed (p. 281). Clutches of 2–4 eggs, laid April–Sept. Eats insects (beetles, ants, bees, grasshoppers, caterpillers, etc.), blossoms, leaves and seeds of desert dicoria (*Dicoria canescens*), a plant particularly important to species survival. **SIMILAR SPECIES:** (1) Mojave Fringe-toed Lizard (below) has black crescents on throat. Ocelli on its back do not form broken lines that extend over the shoulders; belly tinged with yellow-green during breeding season. (2) See also Colorado Desert Fringe-toed Lizard (p. 281). **RANGE:** Sand deposits of Coachella Valley, Riverside Co., Calif. Near sea level to around 1,600 ft. (490 m).

REMARKS: Has lost an estimated 75–90 percent of its habitat to human activities—housing and commercial development, agriculture, golf links, weed intrusion, sand compaction, control of drift sand, off-road vehicles, etc. Reserves have been established at Thousand Palms, Willow Hole, and Whitewater River. However, they collectively protect only a small portion of the lizard's original range. Few Fringe-toed Lizards now exist outside their boundaries, which represent only small remnants of original natural ecosystem of Coechella Valley.

MOJAVE FRINGE-TOED LIZARD
Uma scoparia   **Pl. 29, Map 83**

IDENTIFICATION: 2¾–4½ in. (7–11.4 cm). Resembles Colorado Desert Fringe-toed (p. 281) but ocelli on back do not form broken lengthwise lines that extend over shoulders and *dark throat markings are crescent-shaped.* Conspicuous black spot on each side of belly. Breeding coloration consists of a yellow-green ventral wash that becomes pink on sides of body.

Habits and habitat resemble those of Colorado Desert Fringe-toed. Clutches of 1–5 eggs, laid May–July. Eats insects, spiders, seeds, and flowers. **SIMILAR SPECIES:** See (1) Colorado Desert and (2) Coachella Valley Fringe-toed Lizards (pp. 281–82). **RANGE:** Sand deposits of Mojave Desert, Calif., north to s. end of Death Valley Nat'l Park. Enters Ariz. along Bouse Wash, south of Parker, Yuma Co. From about 300 to around 3,000 ft. (90–910 m).

SPINY LIZARDS: GENUS *Sceloporus*

Our "blue-bellies." Males of many species have a blue patch on each side of belly and on throat. As is common among iguanids, males have enlarged postanal scales and, when adult, a broad tail base where the inverted copulatory organs are sequestered, one on each side. Blue color reduced or absent in females. Spiny Lizards have keeled, pointed, overlapping scales on dorsal surfaces, which (along with incomplete gular fold) will distinguish them from utas (*Uta* and *Urosaurus*). Usually gray or brown above with a pattern of crescents or stripes, are round-bodied or sometimes somewhat flattened, and the tail is longer than body. Limbs moderate length. Adult males of some species may be beautifully colorful, especially when in the light phase and engaging in display.

Below sea level to above 13,500 ft. (4,110 m). New England in the east and n. Wash. in the west, south through U.S. and Mex. to northern Panama. Some 80 species. Habitats vary from semidesert, brushland, thornscrub, and tropical forests to sparse growth of timberline. Some are ground-dwellers; others climb on rocks, stumps, tree trunks, and sides of buildings with ease. Confirmed baskers, many are frequently seen on top of rocks, fence posts, stumps, or other objects in full sun. Some species are live-bearing.

SLEVIN'S BUNCHGRASS LIZARD   Pl. 30, Map 94
Sceloporus slevini

IDENTIFICATION: 1 3/5–2 3/4 in. (4.1–7 cm). Chiefly a mountain form distinguished from all our other Spiny Lizards by arrangement of femoral-pore rows, and scales on sides of the body. *Femoral rows are separated at midline by only 1 or 2 scales* rather than 3 or more, and the *lateral scale rows parallel the dorsal rows.* In other Spiny Lizards the lateral rows extend diagonally upward. Various shades of brown above, with white or orange stripe on each upper side and brown blotches on back; rear edge of each dorsal blotch black, edged with lighter color. Some individuals, both males and females, may lack blotches. Often a black blotch at base of each front leg. **Male:** Usually has orange stripe on each upper side and blue patches on belly. **Female:** Blue markings on belly reduced or absent.

Found in our area chiefly in isolated mountains, mostly above 6,000 ft. (1,830 m), where it occupies sunny patches of bunchgrass in open coniferous woods; also occurs as low as about 4,000 ft. (1,220 m), on grassy plains. Search for these lizards in late morning on warm, bright days. Walk softly through the grass. Individuals may be seen or heard scurrying into grass clumps or hiding places under rocks, logs, or pieces of bark. Trap them by hand in the grass tangles. Most active during period of summer rains. Clutch of 9–13 eggs, laid June–Aug. Perhaps sometimes ovoviviparous. Eats insects (hemipterans, ants, beetles, wasps, grasshoppers) and spiders. **SIMILAR SPECIES:** In Striped Plateau Lizard (p. 292), with which the Bunchgrass Lizard coexists in some areas, lateral scales are in diagonal (not lengthwise) rows; no blue markings on belly. **RANGE:** Huachuca, Santa Rita, Dragoon, Whetstone, and Chiricahua Mts., Ariz.; Animas Mts., N.M.; Sierra Madre Occidental and Sierra del Nido to n. Durango, Mex. To around 11,000 ft. (3,350 m). Found at lower elevations in Empire Valley, 4,300 ft. (1,310 m), Santa Cruz Co., Ariz.; upper Animas Valley, east of Cloverdale, 5,200 ft. (1,580 m), N.M.; and on grassy plains between desert and Sierra Madre, Chihuahua, Mex.

MOUNTAIN SPINY LIZARD   Pl. 30, Map 95
Sceloporus jarrovii

IDENTIFICATION: 1 4/5–4 1/5 in. (4.6–10.6 cm). Black-edged scales form a *meshlike (lace stocking) pattern above;* center of scales whitish with pinkish or bluish green sheen. Head with sooty markings or nearly all black in adult males. Broad black collar edged with whitish along rear; collar often connected with dark markings on head. *Supraocular scales small, sometimes in more than 1 row.* Usually over 40 scales between interparietal and rear of thighs. **Young:** Usually a blue patch on rear part of throat, on each side of belly behind the axilla, and in front of groin. **Male:** Sides of belly and throat patch blue. **Female:** Blue colors subdued, back often spotted and flecked with gray.

A mountain species, attracted to rocky canyons and hillsides. Frequents open oak woodland, thornscrub, and mixed oak and pine forests, mostly above 5,000 ft. (1,520 m). On lower mountain slopes, lives in more humid areas near streams, canyon pools, or damp sand. Occasionally climbs trees, but more often seen perched on boulders or climbing nimbly over rocks. When first emerging from retreats, they are nearly black and conspicuous on light-colored rocks. Live-bearing, 2–14 young, born May–June.

Eats insects (grasshoppers, beetles, caterpillars, ants, wasps) and spiders. **SIMILAR SPECIES:** Crevice Spiny Lizard (below) has larger scales (usually less than 40 between interparietal and rear of thighs) and a black collar band with conspicuous whitish anterior border. **RANGE:** Chiricahua, Dos Cabezas, Dragoon, Graham, Huachuca, Santa Rita, Quinlan, and Baboquivari Mts. in Ariz.; Peloncillo, Pyramid, San Luis, Animas, and Hatchet Mts. in N.M.; Sierra Madre Occidental and Oriental to Morelos and s.-cen. Veracruz. From around 4,500–11,600 ft. (1,370–3,550 m). **SUBSPECIES:** YARROW'S SPINY LIZARD, *S. j. jarrovii*, occurs in our area.

CREVICE SPINY LIZARD *Sceloporus poinsettii*   Pl. 31, Map 88

IDENTIFICATION: 3–5⅖ in. (7.6–13.7 cm). A large, flat-bodied, spiny rock-dweller. *Conspicuously banded tail and broad black collar* can be seen from a great distance. Collar bordered in front and back with whitish. Ground color yellowish, olive, or reddish above. Beige to pale orange below, grading to pinkish orange on underside of tail. *Scales large, keeled, and pointed;* usually less than 40 between interparietal and rear of thighs. Outer row of supraoculars about same size as inner row. **Young:** Crossbands on body and tail often more conspicuous than in adult. Sometimes a narrow dark stripe down middle of back. **Male:** Sides of belly and throat blue. Belly markings bordered with black toward midline. Crossbands on back usually indistinct or absent. **Female:** Blue color weak or absent; crossbands usually retained.

An often wary lizard that inhabits rocky canyons, gullies, hillsides, and outcrops of limestone, granite, or lava in mesquite grassland, creosote bush desert, and arid woodland. Usually retreats to opposite side of a rock or into a crevice when approached. Use mirror or flashlight to see animal in its retreat. Live-bearing, 7–16 young, born June–July. Eats insects (including grasshoppers, ants, beetles, termites, caterpillers), spiders, and buds, blossoms, and leaves. **SIMILAR SPECIES:** (1) Collared lizards (*Crotaphytus* species, pp. 272–74) have a double black collar; no dark crossbands on tail; and small, smooth scales. (2) See also Yarrow's Spiny Lizard (above). **RANGE:** S. N.M. from the San Mateo and Magdalena Mts. south to Zacatecas; sw. N.M. to cen. Tex. From around 1,000–8,400 ft. (300–2,560 m). **SUBSPECIES:** NORTHERN CREVICE SPINY LIZARD, *S. p. poinsettii*, occurs in our area.

DESERT SPINY LIZARD *Sceloporus magister*   Pl. 31, Map 86

IDENTIFICATION: 3¼–5⅗ in. (8.2–14.2 cm). Stocky, usually light-colored, with large, pointed scales and *black wedge-shaped mark on each side of neck.* Rear edge of neck markings whitish or pale yellow. Straw-colored, yellow, yellowish brown, or brown above, with crossbands or spots of dusky that usually fade with age. Sides often tinged with rust. Head sometimes orange. 5–7 pointed ear scales (auriculars). Supraorbital semicircles incomplete. **Young:** Usually many small blotches arranged in 4 lengthwise rows. Crossbands often conspicuous. **Male:** Dorsal markings vary (see Remarks section). Enlarged postanals and swollen tail base. Blue to bluish green patch on throat and on each side of belly. Belly patches edged with black and sometimes joined at midline. **Female:** Blue markings faint or absent. Head may be orange or reddish when breeding.

Inhabits arid and semiarid regions on plains and lower slopes of mountains. Found in Joshua tree, creosote bush, and shad-scale deserts, mesquite-yucca grassland, juniper and mesquite woodland, subtropical thornscrub, and along rivers grown to willows and cottonwoods. A good climber of rocks and trees, but also found on the ground. Seeks shelter in crevices, under logs and other objects on the ground, in woodrat nests, and in rodent burrows. Often bites when captured. Clutch of 4–19 eggs, laid May–Aug.; more than 1 clutch may be laid per season. Eats insects (including their larvae, ants, beetles, grasshoppers, termites, and caterpillars), spiders, centipedes, lizards, and occasionally buds, flowers, berries, and leaves. **SIMILAR SPECIES:** (1) Clark's Spiny Lizard (p. 287) is gray, greenish, or bluish above, has dark crossbands on wrists and forearms, and usually 3 ear scales (auriculars). (2) Granite Spiny Lizard (p. 287) is darker, lacks conspicuous neck markings, and has more rounded, less spiny scales. Western Fence Lizard lacks dark wedge on shoulder, has smaller, less protuberant spiny scales, and averages smaller size. **RANGE:** Nw. Nev. (as far north as 16 mi. north of Sulphur) and s. Utah, north to near Green River (town) to cape region of Baja Calif., nw. Sinaloa, and sw. Coahuila; inner Coast Ranges and desert of s. Calif. to N.M. and w. Tex. In Coast Ranges north to Panoche Hills. Near sea level to around 5,000 ft. (1,520 m).

REMARKS: Based on differences in dorsal color patterns of adult males, 8 subspecies have been recognized in previous editions of this Guide. There is now some question as to their geographic cohesiveness. However, I mention here some of the variation and general areas where it has been reported: (1) 2 parallel lengthwise rows of dorsal dark blotches (se. Ariz., s. N.M., w. Tex., and n.-cen. Mex.); (2) broad black to deep purple lengthwise dorsal stripe (sw. Ariz., nw. Mex.); (3) 6–7 dark dorsal crossbars (e.-cen. Calif. and adjacent Nev.); (4) 5–6 chevron-shaped dorsal bars, head yellowish orange (se. Utah, ne. Ariz.); (5) light tan or yellowish above, usually without distinct markings (n.-cen. and nw. Ariz., Nev. except w.-cen. part, Calif.); (6) extensive areas of black pigment on venter and contrasting dark and light pattern on throat and lower sides of head (cape region of Baja Calif.).

CLARK'S SPINY LIZARD *Sceloporus clarkii* **Pl. 31, Map 87**

IDENTIFICATION: $2\frac{7}{8}$–$5\frac{3}{5}$ in. (7.3–14.2 cm). A large, often wary lizard, usually only glimpsed as it scrambles to opposite side of a limb or tree trunk. *Gray, bluish green, or blue above, with dusky or black bands on wrists and forearms.* Black shoulder mark as in Desert Spiny Lizard. Irregularly crossbanded with dark and light markings, which may become faint or disappear, especially in old males. Projecting spine-tipped scales on body. Incomplete supraorbital semicircles. Usually 3 ear scales (auriculars). **Young:** Crossbands on body and tail. **Male:** Enlarged postanals and swollen tail base. Throat patch and sides of belly blue. **Female:** Blue markings usually weak or absent.

Inhabits chiefly lower mountain slopes in oak-pine woodland, tropical deciduous forest, and subtropical thornforest. Prefers more humid environments, generally at higher elevations than Desert Spiny Lizard. Chiefly a tree-dweller but also occurs on the ground among rocks. Often heard before seen. Two people are usually required to keep these lizards in sight because they tend to stay on opposite side of rocks and tree trunks. To noose them usually requires careful stalking while a companion diverts their attention. Clutch of 4–24 eggs, laid May–Nov.; sometimes more than 1 clutch may be laid each season. Eats insects (such as grasshoppers, beetles, ants, wasps, caterpillars), spiders, and occasionally leaves, buds, and flowers. **SIMILAR SPECIES:** (1) Yarrow's Spiny Lizard has complete neckband and a black lace-stocking body pattern. (2) Crevice Spiny Lizard has a broad black collar. Also see (3) Desert Spiny Lizard (p. 285). **RANGE:** Cen. Ariz. and sw. N.M. to n. Jalisco. In Ariz. ranges west to Kitt Peak, Ajo, and Puerto Blanco Mts., Pima Co., and north to Valentine, Mohave Co. On Tiburón and San Pedro Nolasco Is. in the Gulf of Calif. Sea level to around 6,000 ft. (1,830 m).

GRANITE SPINY LIZARD *Sceloporus orcutti* **Pl. 31, Map 89**

IDENTIFICATION: $3\frac{1}{4}$–$4\frac{5}{8}$ in. (8.2–11.7 cm). *A large, spiny, dark-colored rock-dweller.* Dark wedge-shaped mark on each side of neck and crossbands on body and tail often hidden by general dark coloration. *Scales with rounded rear margins, weakly keeled on body, strongly keeled and pointed on tail.* Incomplete supraorbital semicircles. **Young:** Head rusty. Crossbands and neck markings evident. **Male:** When in light phase, one of our most beautiful lizards. Dorsal scales marked with yellow-green and bluish, a broad purple stripe down middle of back, and blue or blue-green throat and belly patches; entire ventral surface sometimes vivid blue. **Female:** No gaudy blue and purple markings; crossbands more distinct than in male.

On coastal side of mountains in s. Calif., this lizard frequents granite outcrops in areas of oak and chaparral, ranging into the yellow pine belt below 5,500 ft. (1,680 m). On the desert side, found in rocky canyons and on rocky upper portions of alluvial fans where there is sufficient moisture for growth of chaparral, palms, or mesquite. In Baja Calif. it occurs in piñon-juniper woodland and subtropical thornforest. Excellent climber on rocks and vegetation. Conspicuous on light-colored rocks, but wariness makes up for lack of camouflage. Look for these lizards when they first emerge; once they warm up, they will seldom allow close approach. Clutch of 6–15 eggs, laid May–July. Eats insects, lizards, and occasionally buds and fleshy fruits. **SIMILAR SPECIES:** (1) Clark's Spiny Lizard (p. 287) has well-defined black neck patch, is paler, and has more pointed and prominently keeled scales. (2) See also Desert Spiny (p. 285) and (3) Hunsaker's Spiny Lizards (below). **RANGE:** Lower slopes of Peninsular Ranges of s. Calif. from n. side of San Gorgonio Pass south to just north of cape of Baja Calif. On coastal side of Peninsular Ranges north to Santa Ana R. Sea level to around 7,000 ft. (2,130 m).

HUNSAKER'S SPINY LIZARD
Sceloporus hunsakeri

Pl. 54, Maps 89, 199

Close relative of Granite Spiny Lizard, endemic to Baja Calif. (see p. 423).

WESTERN FENCE LIZARD
Sceloporus occidentalis

Pl. 30, Map 90

IDENTIFICATION: 2¼–3½ in. (5.7–8.9 cm). A black, gray, or brown lizard with blotched pattern. Longitudinally dark-striped individuals occasionally found in s. Calif. and Baja Calif. Sides of belly blue. Rear surfaces of limbs yellow or orange. Dorsal scales keeled and pointed, relatively smaller than in Desert, Clark's, and Granite Spiny Lizards. *35–57 scales between interparietal and rear of thighs.* Complete supraorbital semicircles. Scales on back of thigh mostly keeled. **Young:** Little or no blue on throat. Blue belly markings faint or absent. No yellow or orange on limbs in hatchlings. **Male:** Enlarged postanals, swollen tail base. Blue patch on throat, sometimes partly or completely divided (occasionally absent). Blue belly patches edged with black. When in light phase, dorsal scales become blue or greenish. **Female:** No blue or green above. Dark crescents or bars on back. Blue markings below usually less vivid or absent.

A male Western Fence Lizard. Note the pale blue markings characteristic of an adult in top breeding condition. Shasta Co., Calif.

One of the most common western lizards seen on fenceposts, rocks, logs, piles of lumber, and sides of buildings. Occupies a great variety of habitats—grassland, broken chaparral, sagebrush, woodland, open coniferous forest, and farmland—but absent from severe parts of the desert, although it may descend close to desert floor on mountain slopes. Occasionally climbs trees, but more often found on or near the ground. 1 to perhaps 3 clutches of 3–17 eggs, laid April–July. Eats insects and spiders. **SIMILAR SPECIES:** (1) Both sexes of Eastern Fence Lizard (p. 290) have small blue patch (often faint in female) on each side of throat; patches usually edged in front with black in male. Western Fence Lizard (where the two species approach one another or coexist—see below) has a large single or partly divided throat patch, usually weak or absent in female (see Fig. 25, p. 291). (2) Sagebrush Lizard (p. 293), with which Western Fence Lizard sometimes coexists, usually has rust on sides of neck and body, a black bar on each shoulder, usually lacks yellow color on rear of limbs, and has smaller dorsal scales. Blue throat patch of male flecked with white or pink. (3) Side-blotched Lizard (p. 295) has small, usually slightly or unpointed scales on back, usually black or dusky spot behind the axilla, and a complete gular fold. (4) See also Desert Spiny Lizard (p. 285). **RANGE:** Wash. to nw. Baja Calif.; Pacific Coast to w. Utah. Absent from desert except in mountains. Desert outposts are Ord, Providence, and New York Mts., Midhills region, and Kingston Range, San Bernardino Co., Calif., Channel Is. (Santa Cruz, Santa Rosa, and San Miguel) off s. Calif. coast, and Todos Santos and Cedros Is. off w. coast Baja Calif. Scattered localities in Puget Sound, including Port Townsend, Wash. Sea level to around 10,800 ft. (3,300 m). Overlaps range of Eastern Fence Lizard from Gunlock Reservior, Pine Valley Mts., to Zion Nat'l Park, Washington Co., Utah.

REMARKS: High Sierra Nevada populations distinctive. Adult males may reach 3 ¼ in. (8.2 cm) or more and usually have solid blue venters. They range from Tuolumne R. drainage to Sequoia Nat'l Park and occur mostly above 7,000 ft. (1,800 m) to around 11,000 ft. (3,353 m).

EASTERN FENCE LIZARD
Fig. 25, Map 91
Sceloporus undulatus

IDENTIFICATION: 1 ⅝–3 ⅗ in. (4.1–9.1 cm). Similar to Western Fence Lizard (Pl. 30). Coloration highly variable—grayish white, gray, brown, reddish, or nearly black above, with pattern of crossbars, crescents, or lengthwise stripes. Striped patterns prevalent in Great Plains area. *Blue on throat usually divided,* often into 2 widely separated patches, a characteristic that distinguishes this lizard from the Western Fence Lizard where their ranges come close together or overlap in sw. Utah (Maps 90 and 91). Maximum number of scales between median ends of femoral pore rows 11. **Male:** As in Western Fence Lizard, but usually has 2 widely separated blue patches on throat (Fig. 25, p. 291).

Lives in a great variety of habitats—forests, woodland, prairie, shrubby flatlands, sand dunes, rocky hillsides, and farmlands. Seeks shelter in bushes, trees, old buildings, woodpiles, rodent burrows, and under rocks, logs, or other objects on the ground. In forested parts of range it climbs trees, and when frightened keeps to opposite side of the trunk. Where trees are scarce this lizard is primarily a ground-dweller. Active throughout year in southern part of its range. Clutches of 4–17 eggs, laid March–Aug. As many as 4 layings may occur a season at some localities. Eats insects (grasshoppers, beetles, flies, ants, wasps, termites, and some larvae), spiders, ticks, millipedes, snails, and small lizards. **SIMILAR SPECIES:** (1) Sagebrush and (2) Dunes Lizards have 9 or more scales between median ends of femoral pore rows and granular scales on rear surfaces of thighs. Dunes Lizard (p. 294) lacks blue marking on throat or has only a scattering of flecks. (3) Slevin's Bunchgrass Lizard has scale rows on sides in longitudinal parallel rows. (4) Striped Plateau Lizard lacks belly markings and has notched femoral pore scales. See also Western Fence Lizard (p. 288). **RANGE:** Cen. S.D., s. Ill., and se. N.Y. to cen. Fla., Gulf Coast, and Zacatecas and San Luis Potosí, Mex.; sw. Utah and nw. Ariz. (including Hualapai Mts.) to Atlantic Coast. Virgin Mts., Clark Co., and Caliente, Lincoln Co., Nev. Sea level to around 10,000 ft. (3,048 m).

SUBSPECIES: NORTHERN PLATEAU LIZARD, *S. u. elongatus* (Fig. 25). Forty-five or more scales between interparietal and rear of thighs. Most other subspecies have lower scale counts (44 or fewer). Narrow crossbars

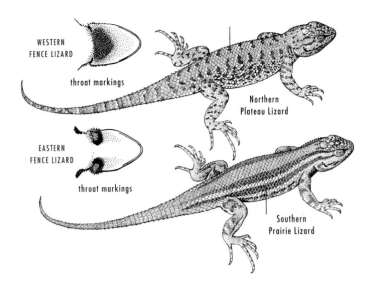

WESTERN
FENCE LIZARD

throat markings

Northern
Plateau Lizard

EASTERN
FENCE LIZARD

throat markings

Southern
Prairie Lizard

Fig. 25. Pattern variation in Eastern Fence Lizard

or wavy crosslines usually present on back in both sexes. Blue throat and belly patches. SOUTHERN PLATEAU LIZARD, *S. u. tristichus.* Light stripes usually present on back. Breeding male has intense blue patches on throat and sides of belly. Female often has pale blue patches on belly. Throat patches are separate or joined in male, separate in female. Forty-five or more scales between interparietal and rear of thighs. On Map 91 the small isolated patch of distribution in se. Ariz. represents the Santa Catalina Mts. An uplands subspecies. RED-LIPPED PLATEAU LIZARD (Orange-lipped Plateau Lizard), *S. u. erythrocheilus.* Light stripes on upper sides weakly developed, broken, or absent. Blue throat patches often connected at midline in both sexes. In breeding season lips, throat, and sometimes head turn red or orange, especially in males. A rock-dweller, usually found below 7,000 ft. (1,800 m), rarely above 9,000 ft. (2,770 m). Not known to overlap range of Northern Prairie Lizard. NORTHERN PRAIRIE LIZARD, *S. u. garmani.* Light stripes on upper sides distinct in both sexes. Blue belly patches, but no blue on throat in males. A prairie species. Isolated populations in sandhill country in e. N.M., surrounded by *S. u. consobrinus* in nonsandy areas and on rocky slopes. Isolated dot in e-cen. Colo. represents population in ne. Elbert Co. of uncertain taxonomic relationship. WHITE SANDS PRAIRIE LIZARD *S. u. cowlesi.* Pale gray to nearly white above, with an obscure dorsal pattern. Otherwise

closely resembles Southern Prairie Lizard. White Sands, N.M. SOUTH-
ERN PRAIRIE LIZARD, *S. u. consobrinus* (Fig. 25). Resembles Southern
Plateau Lizard, but females usually lack blue belly patches. MESCA-
LERO PRAIRIE LIZARD *S. u. tedbrowni*. Uniformly light colored, with
usually faint longitudinal stripes or almost without pattern. Mescalero
Dunes, Chaves Co., N.M. and perhaps other dunes southward to Monahans Dunes, Ward Co., Tex. Coexists with Dunes Sagebrush Lizard (*Sceloporus arenicolus*) from which it can be distinguished by being less wary,
somewhat smaller (under 2 ⅗ in. [6.6 cm] SV), less strictly associated with
dunes and having fewer scales between inner ends of femoral pore rows
(4–6 vs. more than 12). Closely related to Northern Prairie Lizard.

REMARKS: In our area, subspecies of this lizard form two groups: Plateau
and Prairie Lizards. The former tend to be larger, have blue ventral colors,
dark coloration above with disruptive pattern that conceals them among
shadows of rocks and trees. The latter usually not over 2 ⅘ in. (7.1 cm)
SV, usually pale, striped, lack dark crossbarred dorsal pattern, have reduced ventral colors in both sexes (Southern Prairie Lizard excepted), and
appear to be adapted for concealment and speed. Northern Prairie Lizard
and Red-lipped Plateau Lizard coexist in ne. N.M. (black area on Map 91)

STRIPED PLATEAU LIZARD　　　　　Pl. 30, Map 93
Sceloporus virgatus

IDENTIFICATION: 1 ¾–2 ⅘ in. (4.4–7.1 cm). A brownish lizard, usually
with distinct striped pattern. *2 unbroken light stripes on each side
(1 dorsolateral and 1 lateral), separated by broad, dark brown band.*
Each dorsolateral stripe bordered above by row of brown or brown
and white spots; rows of dark dorsal spots separated along dorsal
midline by a broad, pale gray area. Usually some dark flecking on
throat and chest. *Belly plain white or cream,* without blue markings. Small blue patch on each side of throat. **Young:** Stripes well
defined. Blue patches on throat faint or absent. **Male:** Enlarged
postanals; swollen tail base. Blue throat patches more prominent
than in female, and dorsal dark spots usually absent or reduced.
Each dorsolateral stripe may be bordered above by a brown stripe
and the dorsal spots may be vague or absent. **Female:** When breeding, blue throat patches surrounded or replaced by orange.

　　A mountain form, most abundant in mixed pine and oak woods,
but ranges upward into coniferous forest and downward in oak
woodland along streams. Found within a mile of Eastern Fence
Lizard, which occurs in lowlands, but is not known to overlap the
range of this species. Most abundant near rocky and sandy intermittent streams where there is shade and water or damp sand.
Chiefly a ground-dweller but readily climbs boulders, logs, and
trees. Clutch of 5–15 eggs, laid June–July. Eats insects, cen-

tipedes, and other arthropods. **SIMILAR SPECIES:** Differs from (1) Eastern Fence Lizard (p. 290) in lacking blue belly patches and usually having notches on the femoral-pore scales. (2) Slevin's Bunchgrass Lizard (p. 283) has scales on sides in longitudinal rows. **RANGE:** Mts. of extreme se. Ariz. and sw. N.M., south in Sierra Madre Occidental at least to s. Chihuahua. In U.S., in Chiricahua, Peloncillo, Guadalupe, and Animas Mts. From 4,900 to around 10,000 ft. (1,490–3,080 m).

SAGEBRUSH LIZARD *Sceloporus graciosus*   Pl. 30, Map 92

IDENTIFICATION: 1 7/8–3 1/2 in. (4.7–8.9 cm). Resembles Western Fence Lizard but averages smaller and more scales (42–68 rather than 35–51) between interparietal and rear of thighs. Gray or brown above, usually with blotches or transverse, usually irregular, bands on body and tail; a lateral and dorsolateral light stripe (vague in some populations) present on each side. Often a *black bar on shoulder. Usually rust in axilla and often on sides of neck and body.* Usually no yellow or orange on rear surfaces of limbs. Blue belly patches. *Scales on back of thigh mostly granular.* **Young:** Orange on neck, blue markings below subdued or absent. **Male:** Enlarged postanals; swollen tail base. Blue throat with white or pink flecks, but throat patch sometimes absent. Belly patches darker blue than throat, edged with black. In light phase, blue or blue-green flecks appear in dorsal scales. In some areas males may also develop bright orange breeding colors. **Female:** Little or no blue below, none above. When breeding, sometimes yellow below, and orange may become more vivid on neck and sides.

Sagebrush lizard over much of its range, but also occurs in manzanita and ceanothus brushland, piñon-juniper woodland, pine and fir forests, and along river bottoms in coastal redwood forests. West of Great Basin it lives chiefly in mountains, generally occurring at higher elevations than Western Fence Lizard, but often overlapping in range at intermediate altitudes. Requirements seem to be well-illuminated areas of open ground and scattered low bushes. Chiefly a ground-dweller, usually found near bushes, brush heaps, logs, or rocks. When frightened, retreats to rocks, thick brush, or occasionally climbs trees. In rocky habitats, appears more agile on rock outcrops than Western Fence Lizard. 1 or 2 clutches of 2–10 eggs, laid June–Aug. Eats insects (ants, termites, beetles, grasshoppers, hemipterans, flies, lepidopterans), spiders, mites, ticks, and scorpions. **SIMILAR SPECIES:** See Western Fence Lizard (p. 288). **RANGE:** Cen. and se. Wash., s. Idaho, and cen. and se. Mont. to nw. N.M., n. and ne. Ariz., and n. Baja Calif. (Sierra San Pedro Martir); w. Colo. to coast in n. Calif. and sw.

Ore., to eastern slope of Cascade Mts. farther north. Isolated populations in N.D. and in Calif. in mts. to south and at Sutter Buttes, Mt. Diablo, San Benito Mt., Telescope Peak (Panamint Mts.), and elsewhere. From 500 to around 10,500 ft. (150–3,200 m).

SUBSPECIES: NORTHERN SAGEBRUSH LIZARD, *S. g. graciosus.* 42–53 (avg. 48) dorsal scales between interparietal and rear of thighs. Usually distinct light and dark dorsolateral stripes on upper sides. WESTERN SAGEBRUSH LIZARD, *S. g. gracilis.* 50–68 (avg. 61) scales between interparietal and rear of thighs. Striping less distinct than in preceding subspecies. Blue throat and belly patches in male separated by whitish areas. Female whitish below. SOUTHERN SAGEBRUSH LIZARD, *S. g. vandenburgianus.* 48–66 (avg. 55) scales between interparietal and rear of thighs. Blue belly patches in male separated by narrow strip of dark or light color, or connected. Blue or black color on belly often joins blue throat patch. Ventral surface of both tail and thighs frequently blue. Female often dusky below.

DUNES SAGEBRUSH LIZARD
Sceloporus arenicolus

not shown, Map 92

IDENTIFICATION: 2–2¾ in. (5.1–7 cm). A small light brown (often yellowish brown) lizard *lacking dorsal pattern except for faint grayish brown dorsolateral stripe on each side extending from head to tail. No blue markings on throat or only a scattering of blue flecks.* Ventrolateral blue patches widely separated and reduced. When breeding, females develop a wash of yellow-orange from the throat, along the sides, to tail. Scale rows around midbody 41–52 (mean 48). Granular scales on rear of thighs. Scales separating femoral pore rows 9–13 (sometimes more). **Male:** Ventrolateral blue patches edged with deep blue. No or scant blue on throat.

Restricted to sandy habitats with scattered stands of dwarf shin oak, clumps of sand sagebrush, prairie yuccas, and other plants. Oak removal associated with significant decline in populations. Clutches of 3–6 eggs laid June–early Aug. Eats insects (ants and their pupae, beetles, grasshoppers, etc.) and spiders. **SIMILAR SPECIES:** (1) Eastern Fence Lizard has 7 or fewer scales between ends of femoral pore rows, pointed (rather than granular) scales on rear of thighs, and usually paired blue throat patches. (2) Sagebrush Lizard averages more scale rows at midbody (48–60) and has a more definite dorsal pattern. **RANGE:** In N.M. chiefly on Mescalero sands from vicinity of San Juan Mesa, Chaves Co., to s. Lea Co. and in Monahans Sandhills of adjacent Tex. from Andrews to Ward and Crane Cos. From around 2,700–4,593 ft. (822–1,400 m).

CAPE SPINY LIZARD *Sceloporus licki*

Pl. 54, Map 199

Endemic to Baja Calif. (see p. 422).

These share some similarities with Spiny Lizards (*Sceloporus*). They have somewhat similar proportions, and the Brush and Tree Lizards (*Urosaurus*) have enlarged, although weakly keeled, dorsal scales, and belly patches (usually blue) in males. They differ, however, in lacking enlarged strongly keeled scales of Spiny Lizards and have a fully developed gular fold.

COMMON SIDE-BLOTCHED LIZARD   Pl. 32, Map 98
(SIDE-BLOTCHED LIZARD)   *Uta stansburiana*

IDENTIFICATION: 1 ½–2 ½ in. (3.8–6.3 cm). A small, often brownish lizard with *bluish black blotch on each side of chest, behind forelimb*; side blotch occasionally faint or absent. Ground color above brown, gray, or yellowish to nearly black—blotched, speckled, or sometimes unpatterned. Populations with little or no dorsal pattern widespread in upper Colorado R. drainage of w. Colo., e. Utah, nw. N.M., and n. Ariz. Whitish to bluish gray below, sometimes with orange to reddish orange on throat and sides of belly. A gular fold. Scales on back small and smooth, without spines at end. Frontal divided. **Male:** Slightly enlarged postanals; swollen tail base. In light phase, speckled above with pale blue. No distinct blue belly patches. **Female:** Blotched with brown and whitish, occasionally striped. No blue speckling. Side blotch usually less well defined than in male.

One of the most abundant lizards in the arid and semiarid regions of the West. Habitat varies—sand, rock, hardpan, or loam with grass, shrubs, and scattered trees. Often found along sandy washes where there are scattered rocks and low-growing bushes. Chiefly a ground-dweller, active all year in south. Eggs laid March–Aug. In the north, 1–3 clutches of 1–5 eggs, and in the south 2–7 clutches, each of 1–8 eggs. Eats insects (grasshoppers, beetles, ants, termites, leaf-hoppers, insect larvae), scorpions, spiders, mites, ticks, and sowbugs. **SIMILAR SPECIES:** See (1) Lesser Earless Lizard (p. 278), (2) Western Fence Lizard (p. 288), and (3) Ornate Tree Lizard (p. 296). **RANGE:** Cen. Wash. to tip of Baja Calif., n. Sinaloa, and n. Zacatecas, Mex.; Pacific Coast to w. Colo. and w. Tex. On many islands off coasts of Baja Calif., and on Santa Cruz, Anacapa, San Clemente, and Catalina Is. off coast of s. Calif. Below sea level (desert sinks) to around 9,000 ft. (2,750 m).

LONG-TAILED BRUSH LIZARD   Pl. 32, Map 97
Urosaurus graciosus

IDENTIFICATION: 1 ⅞–2 ⅗ in. (4.7–6.6 cm). A well-camouflaged, shrub- or tree-dweller; often lies motionless, with its slim body aligned with a branch. *Tail long and slender—often twice as long as body.* Gray above, with dusky to black crossbars, but when captured may change color from dark gray to pale beige in less than 5 minutes. Pale lateral stripe usually extends from upper jaw along each side of neck and body. Broad band of enlarged scales down middle of back (Fig. 15, Pl. 32, p. 98). Well-developed gular fold. Frontal usually divided. **Male:** Pale blue or greenish patch flecked with white on each side of belly, lacking in female. Both sexes may have a reddish, orange, or lemon yellow throat.

A desert species. Frequents areas of loose sand and scattered bushes and trees, creosote bush, burro brush, big galleta, catclaw, mesquite, and palo verde. Creosote bushes with exposed roots seem to be especially favored, perhaps because of shelter afforded by root tangle. Being more heat-tolerant than its relative the Tree Lizard, it can live in sparser growth. At night and on windy days, may seek shelter in sand or burrows of other animals. At Palm Springs, Calif., lives in olive trees and Washington palms near houses. Since these lizards resemble bark and tend to remain motionless when approached, carefully examine branches of bushes and trees to find them. Search the lower bare branches of creosote bushes on the side facing early morning sun. Although this lizard is diurnal, after a hot day it may sleep aloft and can sometimes be found by searching tips of branches at night. 1 or perhaps 2 clutches of 2–10 eggs, laid May–Aug. Eats insects, spiders, and occasionally parts of plants. **SIMILAR SPECIES:** See (1) Ornate Tree Lizard (below) and (2) Black-tailed Brush Lizard (p. 297). **RANGE:** S. Nev. (north to Hiko, Lincoln Co.) to nw. Sonora and ne. Baja Calif.; desert slope of mts. of s. Calif. to cen. Ariz., Bahia San Luis Gonzaga, Baja Calif. Coexists with Tree Lizard near Wickenburg in Hassayampa R. drainage and along Verde R. near Tempe, Ariz. Near sea level to around 3,500 ft. (1,070 m).

ORNATE TREE LIZARD *Urosaurus ornatus* **Pl. 32, Map 96**
IDENTIFICATION: 1 ½–2 ¼ in. (3.8–5.7 cm). A slim, dark brown, black (when in dark phase), tan, sooty, or gray lizard with small scales and long slender tail. Often rusty area at base of tail. A gular fold. *Band of enlarged scales down middle of back, separated into 2 or more parallel rows by center strip of small scales* (Fig. 15, Pl. 32, p. 98). Above usually blotched or crossbarred with dusky. Fold of skin on each side of body. **Male:** *Vivid blue or blue-green belly patches,* sometimes united and occasionally connected with blue throat patch. Throat sometimes yellow, orange, greenish, or pale blue-green. **Female:** Throat whitish, orange, or yellow. No belly patches.

Climbing lizard that spends much of its time on rocks and occasionally trees; sometimes seen clinging head downward. Color often blends with background. Frequents mesquite, oak, pine, juniper, alder, cottonwood, and nonnative trees such as tamarisk and rough-bark eucalyptus, but also may occur in treeless areas. Appears to be especially attracted to river courses. Ranges from desert to lower edge of spruce-fir zone. When encountered on the ground, may run to a rock or tree and climb upward, keeping out of sight. One to 6 (higher counts in the south) clutches, each of between 2 and 16 eggs, laid March–Aug. Eats insects (including aphids, beetles, flies, ants, termites, grasshoppers) and spiders. **SIMILAR SPECIES:** (1) Differs from Spiny Lizards (*Sceloporus* species, pp. 283–94) in having complete gular fold and enlarged scales down middle of back. (2) Side-blotched Lizard (p. 295) is a ground-dweller, has dark blotch behind axilla, back scales of uniform size, and lacks blue belly patches. (3) Long-tailed Brush Lizard (p. 295) has broad band of enlarged scales down back, unbroken by small scales (see Fig. 15, Pl. 32, p. 98). (4) See also Black-tailed Brush Lizard (below). **RANGE:** Sw. Wyo. to Nayarit and n. Coahuila, Mex.; lower Colorado R. to cen. Tex. Along Colorado R. in Calif., ranges inland to Corn Spring area on ne. slope of Chuckwalla Mts. Tiburón I. in Gulf of Calif. Sea level to around 9,000 ft. (2,770 m).

BLACK-TAILED BRUSH LIZARD
Urosaurus nigricaudus

IDENTIFICATION: 1 ½–2 in. (3.8–5.1 cm). Gray, yellow-brown, brownish olive to black or sooty brown above, usually with *sooty to blackish tail*, especially in males; dark tail contrasts with paler body when lizard is in light phase. A row of gray or dusky to black blotches or crossbars on each side of back, sometimes separated by an irregular, pale gray or brownish stripe with scalloped borders down middle of back. Crossbars or spots edged or spotted with whitish. Tinges of rust or yellowish brown often present on neck, tail base, and upper sides. Whitish to yellowish gray below, sometimes spotted and mottled with dusky on underside of tail. *Broad area of enlarged keeled scales down center of back,* giving way at sides to small granular scales. Scales on tail keeled and pointed (mucronate — see rear endpapers). **Male:** *Cental pattern of throat orange or yellow.* Blue to blue-green belly patches, sometimes joining at midline. Enlarged postanal scales. **Female:** Throat yellow- orange, lemon yellow, to whitish. Lacks belly patches and enlarged postanal scales.

In dark phase these lizards are highly conspicuous when on light-colored rocks. In excited males, tail and crossbars on body darken, setting them off from bordering white spots and bars and enhancing overall contrast in pattern. Conspicuous black tail is thought to divert a predator's attention to an expendable part that can be regenerated. In dark-phase females scalloped middorsal stripe may remain pale, contrasting strongly with darkened sides. In both sexes in light phase, dark neck bars or blotches tend to remain conspicuous when rest of body pales.

Found in a variety of habitats from coastal plains to mountains. In Baja Calif. common in thornscrub. Especially abundant near streams and oases. In s. Calif. frequents rocky habitats grown to oak, sycamore, desert willow, and chaparral. Quick, agile species that climbs readily and frequents rocky areas, trees, and old buildings. Seldom found on level ground except when moving between elevated sites. Eats insects and other small arthropods. **SIMILAR SPECIES:** (1) In Spiny Lizards (*Sceloporus* species; pp. 283–94), gular fold is incomplete and scales down middle of back are not enlarged. (2) Side-blotched Lizard (p. 295) is more of a ground-dweller, has dark blotch behind forelimb, back scales of nearly uniform size, and lacks distinct blue belly patches. **RANGE:** From extreme sw. Calif. throughout Baja Calif. to tip of peninsula. In s. Calif. found from Borrego Palm Canyon on desert side of the mountains to Marron Valley, Cottonwood, Deerhorn Flat areas on coastal side.

BAJA CALIFORNIA BRUSH LIZARD   Pl. 55, Map 198
Urosaurus lahtelai.
Endemic to Baja Calif. (see p. 423).

BANDED ROCK LIZARD *Petrosaurus mearnsi*   Pl. 32, Map 100
IDENTIFICATION: 2⅗–4⅕ in. (6.6–10.6 cm). A flat-bodied lizard with *single narrow black collar and banded tail;* restricted to rocks. Scales on dorsal surfaces granular, except on tail and limbs, where keeled and pointed. Olive, brown, or gray above, with many small white or bluish spots. Wavy crossbars on back, sometimes faint. Ventral surfaces bluish or dusky. Whitish or pinkish spots on throat. **Male:** Throat pattern and bluish color more pronounced than in female. In light phase, blue spots on back, tail, and hind limbs. **Female:** When gravid, orange on throat and above eye.

Crawls over sides and undersurfaces of rocks with ease, limbs extended well out from its sides, body held low, and hindquarters swinging from side to side. Most abundant among massive rocks in shady, narrower parts of canyons, on desert slopes of mountains. Often wary. To catch rock lizards use a fine copper-wire noose opened to diameter of 1½–2 in. (3.8–5.1 cm). When you are within a foot or so, sweep the noose over the lizard's head with a single quick stroke. Clutch of 2–6 eggs, laid June–Aug. Eats insects (beetles, ants, bees, flies, caterpillars, etc.), spiders, blossoms, and buds. **SIMILAR SPECIES:** Collared lizards (*Crotaphytus* species, pp. 270–74) have 2 black collar marks; a nonspiny, unbanded tail; and a round body. **RANGE:** S. Calif from San Gorgonio Pass south through Peninsular Ranges and n. third of Baja Calif. where its range overlaps that of Short-nosed Rock Lizard (below). Near sea level to around 3,600 ft. (1,100 m).

SHORT-NOSED AND SAN LUCAN ROCK LIZARDS
Petrosaurus repens and *P. thalassinus*   **Pl. 54, Map 197**

Relatives of the Banded Rock Lizard, endemic to Baja Calif. (see pp. 425 and 424).

HORNED LIZARDS: GENUS *Phrynosoma*

These are the "horny toads." Most are armed with daggerlike head spines ("horns") and sharp projecting scales on dorsal surfaces of the body. The horns, the flattened oval form, and pointed fringe scales on sides of the body are distinctive. Males have enlarged postanal scales and, when breeding, a swollen tail base.

Horned Lizards are often difficult to find. Usually solitary, when approached they often crouch low and "sit tight." Their coloration and spiny skin often blend well with background. A person may nearly step on one before it moves. Ants and fine loose soil for burial seem to be essential for most species. When picked up, a Horned Lizard may inflate by gulping air and jab with its horns. Some species may even spurt blood from the eyes. The blood comes from a sinus associated with the eye and emerges from a pore in the eyelid region, often spurting several feet. It has a repellent effect on coyotes, foxes, and perhaps other predators.

Although favored as pets, Horned Lizards ordinarily do not live long in captivity, probably because of inadequate care. However, individuals are recorded as living 8 to over 10 years in captivity. Since most species feed heavily on ants, providing suitable nutrition may be part of the problem. Because of their popularity as pets, escaped or released individuals may be found far beyond natural ranges.

The 15 species as a group range from extreme sw. Canada to Guatemala and from w. Ark. to Pacific Coast. Eight species occur in our area.

TEXAS HORNED LIZARD   **Pl. 33, Map 106**
Phrynosoma cornutum

IDENTIFICATION: 2½–5 in. (6.3–12.7 cm). *Dark stripes radiate from eye region* on each side of face. Mostly brown, yellowish, tan, reddish, or gray above; ground color varies with prevailing soil color. Beige or whitish middorsal stripe. Sooty or dark brown blotches on back and tail and pair of large dark blotches on neck. Rear edge of each blotch whitish or yellow. Skin of gular fold yellow. In adults yellowish color may also be present on chest, sides, and dorsum. The 2 central horns are notably long and sharp. Row of enlarged scales on each side of throat, surrounded by small scales. Two rows of pointed fringe scales on each side of body. Eardrums distinct. Belly scales weakly keeled.

Inhabits arid and semiarid open country with sparse plant growth—bunchgrass, cactus, juniper, acacia, and mesquite. Ground may be of sand, loam, hardpan, or rock. Some loose soil is usually present in which these lizards bury themselves. They also seek shelter under shrubs, in burrows of other animals, or among rocks. Clutch of 14–37 eggs (perhaps to around 50), laid May–July. Eats chiefly ants but also takes beetles and grasshoppers. **SIMILAR SPECIES:** (1) Regal Horned Lizard (p. 305) has 4 large horns with bases that touch at back of head. (2) Coast Horned Lizard (below) has 2–3 rows of enlarged pointed scales on each side of throat. (3) Desert Horned Lizard (p. 301) has a single rather than double row of pointed fringe scales on each side of body. **RANGE:** Kans. to Durango, San Luis Potosí, Tamaulipas, and Tex. Gulf Coast. E. Okla. and e. Tex. to se. Ariz. to extreme se. Ariz. Isolated records for Dauphin I., Mobile Co., and Daphne, Baldwin Co., Ala. Sea level to around 6,000 ft. (1,830 m). In the West it often coexists with the Round-tailed Horned Lizard (p. 304).
REMARKS: Widely released outside its natural range. Appears to be absent from much of its former range in Tex. and Okla. Habitat loss, introduction of fire ants, followed by careless use of pesticides to control them, and illegal collecting may have contributed to the decline.

COAST HORNED LIZARD   Pl. 33, Map 102
Phrynosoma coronatum
IDENTIFICATION: 2½–4½ in. (6.3–11.4 cm). Two horns at back of head, longer than rest; bases separated, not touching. *Two rows of pointed fringe scales on each side of body. Two or 3 rows of enlarged pointed scales on each side of throat* (Fig. 16, Pl. 33, p. 100). General coloration yellowish, brown, reddish, or gray. Wavy dark blotches on back and pair of large dark blotches on neck. No dark stripes on face. Cream, beige, or yellow below, usually with spots of dusky.

Frequents variety of habitats—scrubland, grassland, coniferous forests, and broadleaf woodland. In Baja Calif. widely distributed in Sonoran Desert habitats, coastal sage in northwest, and arid tropical scrub in south. Common in lowlands along sandy washes where scattered low shrubs provide cover. Other requirements seem to be open areas for basking, patches of fine loose soil where it can bury, and ants and other insect prey. Clutch of 6–49 (24–29) eggs, laid April–July. Ants (harvester and other native species) usually predominate in diet. However, also eats termites, beetles, wasps, flies, and grasshoppers. **SIMILAR SPECIES:** Desert Horned Lizard (below) has a blunter snout, shorter horns and body spines, only 1 row of well-developed fringe scales on each side of body, and 1 row of enlarged scales on each side of throat. **RANGE:** Throughout most of Calif. west of desert and Cascade-Sierran highlands; absent from humid Northwest; though-out Baja Calif. except northeastern part, and on Cedros I. off w. coast. In s. Sierra ranges to Kennedy Meadows, Chimney Peak area, and upper Ninemile Canyon, e. of Sierran Crest. Old record as far n. as Kennett, Shasta Co.; site now under waters of Shasta Reservoir. Sea level to around 8,000 ft. (2,438 m).

REMARKS: California populations in lowland areas greatly reduced and even completely eliminated in many areas due to urbanization and agricultural expansion. Deep-disc plowing considered especially damaging. In some areas, spread of nonnative, less palatable Argentine ant is displacing native ant species upon which the lizard feeds.

DESERT HORNED LIZARD
Phrynosoma platyrhinos

Pl. 34, Map 103

IDENTIFICATION: 2⅝–3¾ in. (6.7–9.5 cm). Desert counterpart of Coast Horned Lizard. Snout very blunt. Horns and body spines relatively short. *One row of well-developed fringe scales on each side of body, and 1 row of slightly enlarged scales on each side of the throat* (Fig. 16, p. 100). General coloration resembles soil color of habitat—beige, brown, tan, reddish, gray, or black, the latter in

Desert Horned Lizard. This lizard comes in many colors depending upon the ground surface it occupies—black on dark lava flows, reddish, brown, gray and nearly white on soils of such colors. Owyhee Co., Idaho.

individuals found on black lava flows. Wavy dark blotches on back and pair of large dark blotches on neck.

A lizard of arid lands, found on sandy flats, alluvial fans, along washes, and at the edges of dunes. Although this lizard is sometimes found on hardpan or among rocks, patches of sand are generally present. Associated with creosote bush, saltbush, greasewood, cactus, and ocotillo in the desert, and with Basin sagebrush, saltbush, and greasewood in the Great Basin. To find these lizards, drive slowly along little-traveled roads in morning or late afternoon. Watch for them on pavement and on rocks or earth banks along roadside where they bask. Usually easily caught by hand. One to 2 clutches of 2–16 eggs, laid May–July, perhaps to Aug. Eats ants, other insects (lepidopteran larvae, beetles), spiders, and some plant materials (berries, etc.). **SIMILAR SPECIES:** (1) Short-horned Lizards have much shorter horns. (2) See also Coast Horned Lizard (p. 300). **RANGE:** Sw. Idaho and se. Ore. (vicinity of dry lake beds, Lake Co., and Harney Basin, Harney Co.) south to ne. Baja Calif. and nw. Sonora, Mex.; w. base of central plateau of Utah to e. base of Sierra Nevada and desert slope of mountains of s. Calif.; reported from San Jacinto R. Wash, Riverside Co., Calif., on coastal side of mountains (verification desired); Ouray-Jensen area, Uintah Co., Utah. Below sea level (in desert sinks) to around 6,500 ft. (1,980 m). Occasionally found in same habitat with the Flat-tailed Horned Lizard. Hybrids found near Ocotillo, south of Salton Sea, Calif., but, in general, the two species seldom appear to coexist.

GREATER SHORT-HORNED LIZARD   Pl. 34, Map 101
(MOUNTAIN SHORT-HORNED LIZARD)
Phrynosoma hernandesi

IDENTIFICATION: 1 ¾–4⅞ in. (4.4–12.4 cm). The *short, stubby horns and single row of fringe scales* on each side of the body will distinguish this horned lizard from our other species, except its close relative the Pigmy Short-horned Lizard (p. 303). Throat scales all small (none notably enlarged). Beige, gray, brown, reddish, or tan above, blotched with dark brown and often speckled with whitish; color pattern usually closely matches background. Pair of large dark brown blotches on back of neck. Rear of throat and chest usually buff or orange-yellow.

Ranges from semiarid plains high into the mountains. Frequents a variety of habitats — shortgrass prairie, sagebrush, and open piñon-juniper, pine-spruce, and spruce-fir forests. Ground may be stony, sandy, or firm, but usually some fine loose soil is present. Except for its close relative, the Pigmy Short-horned Lizard, it is more cold-tolerant than other horned lizards. Live-bearing; 5–48 young, born July–Sept. In Alta., Canada, 6–13 young recorded born late June to early Aug. Ants often predominate in diet. Also eats other insects (termites, grasshoppers, beetles, wasps, caterpillars, and hemipterans) and spiders and snails. **SIMILAR SPECIES:** (1) Pigmy Short-horned Lizard has horns reduced to nubbins and averages considerably smaller. (2) Greatly reduced horn length and deep median notch separating horns will distinguish this species from other horned lizards. **RANGE:** Extreme s. Canada to s. Durango; w. Ariz. and Cascade crest in Ore. and Wash. to w. Dakotas, e. Colo., and Tex. Panhandle. Isolated population at Wadsworth, Washoe Co., Nev. An old record from Upper Firehole Basin, Yellowstone Park, Wyo., needs verification. Chiefly a mountain-dweller in more arid and southern parts of range. From around 900–11,300 ft. (170–3,440 m). **REMARKS:** Population of small (dwarfed) individuals inhabits San Luis Valley, s. Colo.

PIGMY SHORT-HORNED LIZARD
Phrynosoma douglasii

Pl. 34, Map 101

IDENTIFICATION: 1 1/4–2 1/2 in. (3.2–6.3 cm). Similar in body form to Mountain Short-horned Lizard but averages considerably smaller. Generally less colorful. *Horns greatly reduced to small vertically projecting nubbins. Lacks median deep notch separating horns at back of head.* Like its close relative, has single row of fringe scales at side of body. Above whitish, pale gray, grayish, or reddish brown, tan, or nearly black with paired dark brown to black blotches edged with white or pale yellow. Dorsum with speckling of whitish. Coloration usually closely matches background.

The Pigmy Horned Lizard and its relative, the Greater Horned Lizard, range farther north than any of our other Horned Lizards. They are cold-adapted and live-bearing. Juvenile, Kittitas Co., Ore.

Frequents open plains of sagebrush and bunch grass, piñon-juniper woodlands, and open pine forests. Substratum may be rocky, sandy, or hardpan, but pockets of fine loose soil or sand are usually present where lizards seek refuge by shimmy burial. Search vicinity of ant nests. Live-bearing; 3–15 young born July–Sept. Eats ants and to lesser extent other insects and their larvae. **SIMILAR SPECIES:** (1) Desert Horned Lizard has much longer horns. (2) See Greater Short-horned Lizard (p. 302). **RANGE:** Extreme s.-cen. B.C. (1910 record from Osoyoos Lake area, Okanagan Valley) where now perhaps extinct and s. Okanagan Co., Wash. through Cascades and Columbian Plateau of Wash. and Ore. to ne. Calif. From around 1,000–6,000 ft. (300–1,830 m).

FLAT-TAILED HORNED LIZARD
Phrynosoma mcallii

Pl. 33, Map 107

IDENTIFICATION: 2½–3⅔ in. (6.3–8.6 cm). Pale gray, buff, rusty brown, beige, or whitish above with color that closely matches background. Only horned lizard with a *dark middorsal stripe. Tail* long, broad, and *very much flattened.* Long slender horns. Two rows of fringe scales on each side of body. White below; unmarked.

Habitat consists primarily of low-lying desert flats of hardpan or gravel with patches of fine windblown sand that lizards shimmy-bury into for protection. They also sit tight, depending on their camouflage, or seek escape in rodent burrows. Creosote bush, indigo brush, burro-weed, bur-sage, and big galleta may be present. Flat-tails occasionally found on blacktop roads, where, although conspicuous, can easily be mistaken for rocks. One or 2 clutches of 3–10 eggs, laid May–June. Eats ants (especially harvester ants) and other insects, but ants form bulk of diet. **RANGE:** Sandy flats and dunes of low desert in s. Calif. from Coachella Valley to head of Gulf of Calif.; extreme ne. Baja Calif. (south to somewhat south of Laguna Salada) to extreme sw. Ariz. and nw. Sonora, Mex. Below sea level (in Salton Sink) to around 820 ft. (250 m).

REMARKS: Threatened by a variety of human disturbances within its highly restricted range caused by agricultural, urban, and geothermal developments, extensive off-road vehicle use, sand and gravel mining, and other impacts.

ROUND-TAILED HORNED LIZARD
Phrynosoma modestum

Pl. 34, Map 104

IDENTIFICATION: 1½–2⅘ in. (3.8–7.1 cm). A small horned lizard with relatively short, spiky, well-separated horns of about equal length. *Tail slender and round,* broadening abruptly at base. *No fringe scales on sides of body.* Dark blotch on each side of neck, above groin, and on side of tail base. Tail barred. Center of back usually unspotted. Mostly ash white, gray, light brown, or reddish above, generally matching predominant soil color.

Lives chiefly on gravelly, pebbly, or rocky soils of plains, desert flats, washes, and hill slopes in arid and semiarid habitats. Larger rocks may or may not be present. Plants present may be cedar, ocotillo, oak, mesquite, creosote bush, sumac, piñon, juniper, and ponderosa pine. When disturbed, may "freeze," close its eyes, and assume a pose that resembles a small rock. Its back is humped and the dark side markings look like shadows. In hot weather most often abroad in early morning or on overcast days. Clutch of 6–19 eggs, laid May–July. Eats mainly ants but also termites, caterpillars, beetles, hemipterans, and probably other insects. **RANGE:** Northern N.M. to San Luis Potosí; n. and w.-cen. Tex. to se. Ariz.; Cimarron Co., Okla. From around 700–6,000 ft. (210–1,850 m). Isolated population sse. of Fowler, Otero Co., Colo. Often shares habitat with Texas Horned Lizard (p. 299).

REGAL HORNED LIZARD *Phrynosoma solare* Pl. 33, Map 105
IDENTIFICATION: 3–4⅝ in. (7.6–11.7 cm). Our largest horned lizard, easily identified by *4 large horns at rear of head. Horn bases in contact.* Large light-colored area on back—light gray, beige, or reddish, bordered on each side by a broad dusky band. Sometimes a pale middorsal stripe. Single row of fringe scales on each side of body.

Frequents rocky and gravelly habitats of arid and semiarid plains, hills, and lower slopes of mountains. Much of range is succulent plant habitat of upland desert. Plants present may include cactus (saguaro, etc.), mesquite, and creosote bush. Seldom found on sandy flats. Search the ground near scrubby plant growth along washes, both in rocky canyons and on plains. Usually not found in same habitat with other species of horned lizards. Clutch of 7–33 eggs, laid July–Aug. Eats chiefly ants. **RANGE:** Most of range is in Sonoran Desert; cen. Ariz. to n. Sinaloa, west to Harquahala and Plomosa Mts., Ariz. and east to extreme sw. N.M. (Guadalupe Canyon). On Tiburon I., Gulf of Calif. Sea level to around 4,800 ft. (1,460 m).

NIGHT LIZARDS: FAMILY XANTUSIIDAE

Small family of New World lizards with representatives from sw. U.S. to Panama; a single species in Cuba. Eighteen species. Five to 7 species (depending on taxonomic viewpoint) occur in genus *Xantusia,* which ranges from s. Calif., Nev., and Utah to tip of Baja Calif. and to Zacatecas, Mex. Three species in our area.

Small, secretive, terrestrial, live-bearing lizards with lidless eyes and vertical pupils. Skin soft and pliable, dorsal scales granular, ventral scales large and squarish. Gular fold and fold of skin low on each side of the body.

HENSHAW'S NIGHT LIZARD

Pl. 35, Map 77

Xantusia henshawi

IDENTIFICATION: 2–2¾ in. (5.1–7 cm). *A flat-bodied lizard with soft, pliable skin. Back marked with large dark brown or black spots on pale background.* Light color between spots becomes reduced to a network of whitish or pale yellow when lizard is in dark phase. Color change may occur rapidly. Scales smooth and granular above, large and squarish on belly; ventral scales in 14 lengthwise rows. Eyes with fixed transparent covering and vertical pupils. Head broad and flat, with large symmetrically arranged plates. **Male:** Whitish, oval-shaped patch along front (leading) edge of femoral-pore row.

Inhabits rocky canyons and hillsides in arid and semiarid regions, where it seems to prefer massive exfoliating granitic outcrops in shadier parts of canyons or near water. Usually avoids hot, south-facing slopes at lower elevations (see also Sandstone subspecies below). Plant communities may be chaparral, chaparral/coastal sage scrub, and creosote bush/chaparral. Secretive and crevice-dwelling, seldom venturing from its hiding place among rocks except at night. Live-bearing; 1–2 young per brood, born in the fall. Eats insects, spiders, ticks, scorpions, centipedes, and some plant materials. **SIMILAR SPECIES:** (1) Leaf-toed Gecko (p. 266), with which it coexists in some parts of range, has broad, flat toe tips. (2) Desert Night Lizard (p. 307) has much smaller spots and 12 lengthwise rows of ventral scales. **RANGE:** From s. side of San Gorgonio Pass in s. Calif., southward in Peninsular Ranges, including their desert and coastal slopes, into Sierra Juárez and Sierra San Pedro Martir (to Arroyo Encantada) of n. Baja Calif., Mex., Lake Perris area, Calif. Population near Pedriceña, e. Durango, Mex. From 400–7,600 ft. (120–2,320 m).

SUBSPECIES: GRANITE NIGHT LIZARD, *X. h. henshawi.* Dark-to-light daily color change pronounced, as decribed above. Black speckling on ventral surfaces. Dorsal pattern of large dark spots. Enlarged ear scales (auriculars). SANDSTONE NIGHT LIZARD, *X. h. gracilis.* Lacks marked light and dark color phases. Almost complete absence of black speckling on ventral surfaces. Dorsal pattern of small, quite uniform round spots. Absence of enlarged ear scales. Found in sandstones and siltstones of Truckhaven Rocks in Anza-Borrego Desert State Park, Calif., where it seeks refuge in fissures and beneath exfoliating slabs and in rodent burrows. In captivity, ate Leaf-toed Gecko eggs.

REMARKS: Sandstone Night Lizard recently proposed for full species rank.

IDENTIFICATION: 1½–2¾ in. (3.8–7 cm). A slim, velvet-skinned lizard; usually *olive, gray, or dark to light brown above, speckled or blotched with light brown or black.* Ground color occasionally yellowish or orange-buff (especially in ne. Utah). In some areas spots may tend to form a network (s. Sierra) or lengthwise rows (cen. Ariz.). Usually a beige stripe edged with black extends from eye to shoulder. Light stripe may be present on each side of upper body in animals from cen. and s. Baja Calif. No eyelids; *pupils vertical.* Single row of well-developed supraoculars. Dorsal scales smooth and granular, generally in 30–50 lengthwise rows at midbody; ventral ones large and squarish, in 12 lengthwise rows at midbelly. Head and body somewhat flattened in individuals that habitually seek shelter in rock crevices (s. Sierra and cen. Ariz.). **Male:** Large femoral pores give thigh a more angular contour in cross-section than female's.

Secretive lizard of arid and semiarid lands that lives chiefly beneath fallen branches of Joshua trees, dead clumps of various other species of yucca (Mojave yucca, Whipple yucca, etc.), nolina, agave, and cardons. Also found under rocks and in rock crevices, beneath cow chips, soil-matted dead brush and other debris, and beneath logs and under bark of foothill pines (inner Coast Ranges and s. Sierra Nevada, Calif.). Ranges into piñon-juniper belt in Panamint Mts., in basin sagebrush and blackbrush habitat in Owens Valley, and into chaparral-oak belt in cen. Ariz. Chiefly diurnal and crepuscular; may be nocturnal during warm summer months. Seldom found in the open away from cover. Because of its secretive habits, this lizard was at one time considered extremely rare, but is now known to be one of the most abundant lizards in U.S. Live-bearing; 1–3 young per brood, born Aug.–Oct. Eats insects (termites, etc.), spiders, and other arthropods. **SIMILAR SPECIES:** See Henshaw's Night Lizard (p. 306). **RANGE:** Mojave Desert and inner s. Coast Ranges of Calif., s. Nev. (Spring Valley, Pioche area, Lincoln Co., southward), s. Utah and cen. Ariz., south to sw. Sonora and throughout most of Baja Calif. Isolated populations in Durango and Zacatecas, Mex. Sea level to around 9,300 ft. (2,830 m, on Telescope Peak, Panamint Mts., Calif.).

In Calif. ranges north in inner Coast Ranges to Pinnacles Nat'l Monument and Panoche Hills, in s. Sierra into Greenhorn and Piute Mts. and to Brin Canyon upper Kern R. Canyon, Tulare Co. (around 3,800 ft. [1,158 m]), and along e. slope of Sierra to west of Bishop. East of Sierra it extends into Inyo and Panamint Mts. To the south, found on coastal side of mountains in upper Santa Clara R. drainage and headwaters of Big Tujunga and upper San Gabriel R. drainage in the San Gabriel Mts. In Utah, from the

Henry Mts. east to Natural Bridges Nat'l Monument south to San Juan R. In Ariz., on w. slope of Central Plateau (Weaver, McCloud, and Superstition Mts., Tonto Nat'l Monument, and Valentine), in Hualapai, Harquahala, Kofa, and Castle Dome Mts., and other scattered localities. Catalina I. animals may have been introduced from the Calif. mainland.

SUBSPECIES: YUCCA NIGHT LIZARD, *X. v. vigilis.* When present, spots on upper surfaces cover 2–3 adjacent dorsal scales. Some individuals may be unspotted. A narrow, usually inconspicuous light stripe behind eye extends onto neck. 17–23 (avg. 21) lamellae on 4th toe. ARIZONA NIGHT LIZARD, *X. v. arizonae.* Dorsal spots often cover 5 or more scales, and sometimes tend to form lengthwise rows. High dorsal scale row count (at midbody), 38–49 (avg. 43). 21–29 (avg. 26) lamellae on 4th toe. Head and body somewhat flattened. SIERRA NIGHT LIZARD, *X. v. sierrae.* Spots on upper surfaces tend to be interconnected, forming a dark network. Light eye stripe broad and conspicuous. High dorsal scale row count, 40–44 (avg. 42). 22–25 (avg. 23) lamellae on 4th toe. Head and body often somewhat flattened. A rock crevice-dweller. Known only from w. edge Greenhorn Mts. in vicinity of Granite Station, Kern Co. Habitat easily destroyed by rock-flaking in efforts to collect lizards. UTAH NIGHT LIZARD, *X. v. utahensis.* Orange-buff to yellowish above, with small dorsal spots. 23–25 (avg. 24) lamellae on 4th toe. BAJA CALIFORNIA NIGHT LIZARD, *X. v. wigginsi.* Dorsal pattern of numerous small spots usually not fused to form blotches or lines. Tail with dark spots restricted to tips of dorsal scales. Some individuals may be unspotted. SAN LUCAN NIGHT LIZARD *X. v. gilberti.* Upper surfaces with large dark spots widely separated from each other, tending to concentrate on upper sides. A light stripe often present on each side of upper body. Tail with dark spots on tips of dorsal scales. 15–18 (avg. 17) lamellae on 4th toe. Seventh upper

Arizona Night Lizard, a large-spotted subspecies of the Desert Night Lizard, a crevice dweller that lives along the Mogollon Rim of cen. Ariz. Yarapai Co., Ariz.

labial as high as or higher than 6th (not true in other subspecies). Eyes relatively small.

REMARKS: A proposal for taxonomic changes raises the subspecies *X. v. arizonae* to full species rank and describes a new large-blotched species, Bezi's Night Lizard (*X. bezyi*), from rocky habitat in the vicinity of Sunflower, Maricopa Co., Ariz. (see green triangle on Map 76).

SLAND NIGHT LIZARD *Xantusia riversiana* Pl. 35, Map 76

IDENTIFICATION: 2 ½–4 ⅕ in. (6.3–10.6 cm). A large night lizard found only on islands off coast of s. Calif. *Sixteen instead of 14 or 12 lengthwise rows of squarish scales at midbelly. Two rows of supraoculars* (1 row in other species). Soft granular scalation above. Folds of skin on neck and alongside body. Coloration highly variable. Back mottled with pale ash gray and beige, rust or yellowish brown, darkened in varying amounts with black. Some individuals uniformly colored above (San Nicolas I.) and some have pale gray or whitish stripe on each side of upper body, edged with brown or black; brown or rust-colored middorsal stripe edged with black may be present. Brown tones vary. Olive-brown individuals quite common on Santa Barbara I. but not on San Clemente and San Nicholas Is. where reddish brown color predominates. Pale gray below, sometimes with a bluish cast, suffused on belly, and often on tail, with yellow. Underside of feet may be yellowish. **Male:** Femoral pores slightly larger than in female.

Inhabits grassland, chaparral, and oak savanna, clumps of cactus and boxthorn, dry sandy or rocky streambeds, cliffs, and rocky beaches. Found in ground and rock crevices, under rocks, driftwood, and fallen branches. Occasionally seen exposed in daytime. Live-bearing; 2–9 (4–5) young, born in Sept. Eats insects, spiders, centipedes, scorpions, marine isopods, mullosks, and blossoms, seeds, stems, and leaves of plants. **RANGE:** San Clemente, Santa Barbara, and San Nicolas Is. off coast of s. Calif. Also known from Sutil Islet near Santa Barbara I.

REMARKS: Striped individuals occur on San Clemente and San Nicolas Is., and rarely on Santa Barbara I. Behavioral studies indicate species is active in the daytime, belying its common name.

;KINKS: FAMILY SCINCIDAE

A widely distributed family with representatives on every continent (except Antarctica) and on many oceanic islands. Abundant in Australia and Old World tropics. About 1,200 species. The Great Skinks (*Eumeces,* with about 46 species, 5 in our area) occur in N. Africa, Asia, and from s. Canada to Costa Rica and Bermuda.

Skinks are usually alert, agile, slim-bodied lizards with *shiny, cycloid scales*, reinforced with bone. Scales of dorsal and ventral surfaces are similar in size, but those on top of the head are enlarged, symmetrically arranged, and of varied shape. Limbs are small, in some burrowing species variously reduced or absent. Tongue is forked and frequently protruded. Some skinks have a window in the lower eyelid that allows them to see when eyes are closed. All our species have limbs and lack the eyelid window.

These lizards often occur in habitats where some moisture is nearby—damp soil or a spring or stream. As a group, skinks seem to be more dependent on moisture than most lizards, yet some live in deserts.

It is almost impossible to noose skinks because of their wariness, slick scales, and often small head and thick neck. Look for them under stones, boards, logs, and other objects and catch them by hand. Don't grab the tail; it is easily shed.

Skinks lay eggs or are live-bearing. With perhaps one exception our species lay eggs.

GREAT PLAINS SKINK *Eumeces obsoletus* Pl. 36, Map 109
IDENTIFICATION: 3½–5⅗ in. (8.9–14.2 cm). Our largest skink. Unique among skinks in our area in having *oblique instead of horizontal scale rows on sides of body*. Light gray, olive-brown, or tan above, *usually profusely spotted with black or dark brown*, the spots uniting here and there to form scattered lengthwise lines. Spotting typically consists of dark margins on dorsal scales that can vary, producing individuals with a nearly uniform dorsal pattern more common toward the south, and ones with a broad middorsal stripe more common toward the north. Occasionally spotting is absent. Sides generally flecked with salmon. Ground color of tail and feet yellowish or pale orange. Pale yellow below, unmarked. **Young:** Black above, dark gray below. Tail iridescent blue. Gold or orange spots on top of head. Large white spots on each labial scale. With growth the black pigment fades and becomes limited to the rear edge or sides of scales. **Male:** Muscular enlargement of sides of head during breeding season.

Frequents both grassland and woodland from plains into mountains. In eastern and central part of range it is chiefly a prairie species, most abundant in open habitats with low vegetation. In the West it enters semiarid environments of canyons, mesas, and mountains, usually where there is grass and low shrubby growth. Rocky outcrops near thickets along permanent or intermittent streams are especially favored. Usually found on fine-grain loose soils, under rocks, logs, bark, and boards. Secretive, nervous; usually attempts to bite when caught. Nests beneath sunken rocks and tends its eggs. Clutch of 7–24 eggs, laid May–July. Eats insects (including grasshoppers, roaches, crickets, ants, caterpillars, and beetles), spiders, mollusks, and lizards. **SIMILAR SPECIES:** (1) Many-lined Skink is slimmer and scales on sides are in longitudinal rows. **RANGE:** S. Neb. to n. Tamaulipas and Durango; w. Mo. and e. Tex. to w.-cen. Ariz. (Hualapai Mts.). Near sea level to around 8,700 ft. (2,650 m).

ANY-LINED SKINK *Eumeces multivirgatus* Pl. 36, Map 111

IDENTIFICATION: 2¼–3 in. (5.7–7.6 cm). A slim, *short-limbed*, long-bodied skink with a very long tail. Proportions alone set it off from our other species. Dorsal coloration varies (Fig. 17, Pl. 36, p. 106): often many dark and light lengthwise stripes present, but some individuals may have weak or no stripes. When light stripes are present, one on each side is *confined to 3rd scale row* (counting from middle of back—see Fig. 17). Stripes vary in intensity and some dark ones may actually consist of rows of spots. **Young:** Darker stripes may be obscured by dark ground color or, as with adults, stripes may be absent. Tail blue, fading with age. **Male:** May develop bright orange or red lips during breeding season.

Lives in a variety of habitats, from sand hills and shortgrass prairie into mountains. Also occurs near houses and other buildings, in vacant lots, city dumps, and backyards. Local environments vary from creosote bush desert and dense streamside growth to juniper, pine-oak, and fir forests, and from arid to moist conditions. Soil may be loamy, sandy, or rocky. Most abundant where there is water or moist subsoil. Look under rocks, logs, boards, and dried cow chips. Clutch of 3–9 eggs, laid May–Aug. and tended by female. Eats mainly insects including ant larvae. **SIMILAR SPECIES:** (1) Mountain Skink (p. 312) has Y-shaped mark on head and neck. (2) Great Plains Skink has oblique instead of lengthwise scale rows on sides of body and is larger and less slender. **RANGE:** Southern S.D. to w. Tex. and perhaps Chihuahua, west through N.M. to se. Utah and cen. Ariz. Distribution spotty in southern part of range. From 3,000 to around 8,600 ft. (910–2,620 m).

SUBSPECIES: NORTHERN MANY-LINED SKINK, *E. m. multivirgatus.* Little variation in color pattern. Ground color of dorsum usually pale gray, with light stripes on upper body often only slightly lighter than ground color. Well-defined broad light middorsal stripe bordered by dark stripes that, on the body, have uninterrupted (not zigzag) margins: these dark dorsal stripes are located on adjacent parts of 1st and 2nd scale rows, counting from midline (Fig. 17, Pl. 36, p. 106). Plain-colored form rare. **Young:** Dorsum dark; light stripes consist of rows of minute spots; dorsolateral stripes brighter than middorsal stripe; tail bright blue (fades with age).

Sand hill and prairie habitats below 5,500 ft. (1,680 m). VARIABLE
SKINK, *E. m. epipleurotus*. Coloration highly variable; striped, intermediate, and plain-colored (unstriped) forms occur. Striped individuals usually
darker (typically olive-brown) than Northern Many-lined Skink and have
two dark-edged, prominent, white dorsolateral stripes. Additional dark
stripes may be present on sides but in most large adults all may be greatly
reduced. Dark stripes on body commonly form zigzag lines. Individuals
with pale ground color found in San Luis Valley, Colo., se. N.M., and w.
Tex. in areas of pale plains habitats. **Young:** Dorsum dark with 3 bold light
stripes; tail bright blue. Frequents chiefly rocky, partially wooded areas in
mountains, ranging into pine and spruce forests.
REMARKS: Morphological and geographic evidence shows that the two subspecies of the Many-lined Skink may qualify for full species recognition.
In Colo., ranges of the two taxa are separated by a distance of about 44
mi. (70 km) in valley of the Arkansas R. and so far there is no evidence for
intergradation (see Map 111).

MOUNTAIN SKINK *Eumeces callicephalus*   Pl. 36, Map 112

IDENTIFICATION: 2–2⅘ in. (5.1–7.1 cm). Olive or tan above, with pale
stripe on each upper side, extending from above the eye to the
trunk, where it is *confined to the 4th scale row* (counting from
dorsal midline). Below pale stripe is a broad, dark brown band extending from the eye to the groin. Sometimes a whitish or pale orange *Y-shaped mark on the head* with its base located on neck. Tail
bluish. **Young:** Blue tail and striping more vivid than in adult. Y-
shaped mark distinct.

    In the U.S. it frequents oak and pine habitats in rocky areas in
the mountains, but in Mex. ranges to near sea level. Lays and
broods its eggs, or gives birth to its young. Eats insects (such as
beetles, flies, and blattids), and spiders. **SIMILAR SPECIES:** In Many-
lined Skink (p. 311), light stripes are on the 3rd scale row from
dorsal midline (Fig. 17, p. 106). **RANGE:** Pajarito, Baboquivari,
Santa Rita, and Huachuca Mts., Ariz.; Guadalupe Mts.
(Guadalupe Canyon), N.M.; south in Mex., at low to moderate elevations west of Continental Divide to general area west of
Guadalajara. Near sea level to over 6,500 ft. (1,980 m).

WESTERN SKINK *Eumeces skiltonianus*   Pl. 36, Map 110

IDENTIFICATION: 2⅛–3⅔ in. (5.4–8.6 cm). Aside from fading with
age, color pattern of adults varies little. *Broad brown stripe down
back, edged with black and bordered on each side by conspicuous
whitish to beige dorsolateral stripe* that begins on nose and extends
over eye and back along side of body onto tail. Pale dorsolateral
stripes on joined halves of 2nd and 3rd scale rows (counting from
middle of back—see Fig. 17, Pl. 36, p. 106). A second pale stripe,

starting on upper jaw, occurs low on each side and is separated from the first by a broad dark brown or black band originating on side of head and usually extending well out onto tail. Tail dull blue or gray. In the breeding season reddish or orange color appears on side of head and chin and occasionally on sides, tip, and underside of tail. Usually 7 upper labials and 4 enlarged nuchals. **Young:** Striped pattern more vivid than in adult and tail bright blue. Dark lateral stripe *usually extends well out on side of tail.*

Frequents grassland, broken chaparral, piñon-juniper and juniper-sage woodland, and open pine-oak and pine forests. Seems to prefer rocky habitats near streams with abundant plant cover, but also found on dry hillsides far from water. In forested areas, search sunnier parts of clearings. Active in daytime but usually keeps out of sight. Clutch of 2–10 eggs, laid June–July and tended by female. Eats insects, spiders, and sowbugs. **SIMILAR SPECIES:** Striped, blue-tailed subspecies of Gilbert's Skink (Greater Brown and Northern Brown Skinks, p. 314) closely resemble Western Skink, but their dorsal scales within the light lines on the back are usually edged with brown or gray, and the blue tail color disappears in adults. Fortunately, where Western and Gilbert's Skinks coexist in s. Calif. they are easily distinguished (see Gilbert's Skink, p. 314). **RANGE:** Southern B.C. to tip of Baja Calif. and throughout most of Great Basin to extreme n. Ariz.; cen. Utah to Pacific Coast. Apparently absent from floor of San Joaquin Valley, cen. Sierra Nevada, and lowland deserts of Calif. In n. Baja Calif. occurs in northwestern part at least as far south as Colonia Guerro and in south in the cape and Comondú regions, Santa Agueda, and San Francisco de la Sierra. On Santa Catalina, Los Coronados, and Todos Santos Is. off coast of Calif.

Western Skink. Hatchlings have a bright blue tail that fades with age. If seized by a predator, the tail is cast and wriggles violently, attracting attention while the lizard may escape.

and Baja Calif. Populations in Calif. in upper Tule R. drainage where sympatric with Gilbert's Skink, Piute and Greenhorn Mts., and Kern Plateau in s. Sierra; Bodie Hills, White Mts., and e. slope Sierra west of Independence and Olancha. In Silver Peak Range and other montane localities, Nev., and reported on Mt. Logan, Ariz. Record at Comox on Vancouver I., B.C. Sea level to around 8,300 ft. (2,530 m). Coexists with Gilbert's Skink at some localities in Calif. and n. Baja Calif.

SUBSPECIES: SKILTON'S SKINK, *E. s. skiltonianus.* Pale dorsolateral stripe, usually including no more than half of 2nd scale row; at midbody, width of dorsolateral stripe less than half that of dark middorsal stripe. GREAT BASIN SKINK, *E. s. utahensis.* Dorsolateral stripe wider than in Skilton's Skink, including more than half of 2nd scale row, at midbody equal in width to half or more of dark dorsal stripe. In rocky areas in habitats of scrub oak, sagebrush, juniper, and grassland, from around 4,500–8,300 ft. (1,370–2,530 m). Red-tailed individuals (presumably of this subspecies) occur at Oak Grove on s. slope Pine Mt., Washington Co., Utah. SAN LUCAN SKINK, *E. s. lagunensis.* Differs from above subspecies in having interparietal enclosed by parietals. Dorsolateral stripes not bordered medially by coloration darker than adjacent ground color, and youthful dorsal pattern tends not to fade with growth, characteristics that tend to set this subspecies off from the others. Tail of adults deep purple; salmon to bright pink in juveniles. Regenerating tails of adults may be pink. Ranges in Baja Calif. from Pico Santa Monica area south through Sierra de la Giganta to Sierra de la Laguna in the cape region.

REMARKS: Full species status has been proposed for the San Lucan Skink.

GILBERT'S SKINK *Eumeces gilberti*   Pl. 36, Map 108

IDENTIFICATION: 2½–4½ in. (6.3–11.4 cm). Adults plain olive or brown above or have varied amounts of dark spotting, which may form an intricate pattern. Light and dark striping is more or less distinct in adults of some populations and varies with age and locality. Tail becomes brick red or orange with age in both sexes, and some individuals develop red on the head. At some localities is difficult to distinguish from Western Skink except when full-grown and striping has been lost. *Commonly 8 upper labials and often 2 or 3 enlarged nuchals.* Pair of whitish stripes on each side, enclosing broad black or dark brown stripe that narrows on tail and *usually stops abruptly near base of tail.* Broad olive stripe down middle of back. Tail blue in northern and eastern part of range, salmon or pink in south (see Subspecies). **Male:** Tends to lose striping sooner than female.

Lives in a variety of habitats—grassland, salt flats, high desert, open chaparral, piñon-juniper woodland, and open pine forest, often in rocky areas near intermittent or permanent streams and springs. Clutch of 3–9 eggs, laid in summer. Eats insects and spiders. **SIMILAR SPECIES:** In Western Skink (p. 312) the broad lateral stripe on each side is often uniformly brown (it is absent or variegated in Gilbert's Skink), blue or blue-gray tail color usually persists in adults, and young have blue tails. However, in areas where the two species are known to coexist (mountains of s. Calif.), young Gilbert's Skinks have pink or salmon tails, and dark lateral stripe stops near base of tail. Young Western Skinks have blue tails, and stripe extends well out on tail. **RANGE:** In Calif. found in foothills and middle elevations in Sierra Nevada from Yuba R. south; inner Coast Ranges opposite San Francisco Bay south into mountains of s. Calif. and to San Pedro Martir Mts., Baja Calif. Scattered localities in San Joaquin Valley, Calif. (subspecies relationships of some of these valley skinks uncertain, thus the valley floor is tentatively shown on Map 108 as an area of intergradation or a gap). Isolated populations in mountains of se. Calif., s. Nev., and w.-cen. Ariz., including Harquahala and Harcuvar Mts. Other isolated localities are Stoddard Ridge and along upper Mojave R. drainage, San Bernardino Co., Calif. From near sea level to around 7,300 ft. (2,220 m).

SUBSPECIES: GREATER BROWN SKINK, *E. g. gilberti*. Young with blue tail. Female averages smaller than male (not true of other subspecies). Usually 2 pairs of nuchals. For dorsal pattern, see Fig. 17, Pl. 36, p. 106. NORTHERN BROWN SKINK. *E. g. placerensis*. Young with blue tail. Retains striping longer than Greater Brown Skink. Usually 1 pair of nuchals. VARIEGATED SKINK, *E. g. cancellosus*. Young have pink tail tinged with blue above. Older young and adults have barring or latticework of dark markings above (Fig. 17, p. 106). WESTERN RED-TAILED SKINK, *E. g. rubricaudatus*. Young have pink tail (blue in Panamint Mts. and other desert mountains), with no bluish tinge (see above). Striping and barring lost earlier (especially in females) than in Variegated Skink. Many isolated populations. In Calif., at Covington Flat, Riverside Co., Deep Springs and Saline Valleys, Inyo Co., and in Panamint, Kingston, Clark, Stoddard, Granite, and Providence Mts., San Bernardino Co.; in Nev. in Sheep and Charleston Mts. and at Grapevine Peak, e. flank Yucca Mt., and Paiute Mesa; in Baja Calif. in San Pedro Martir Mts. and at San Antonio del Mar. Isolated populations in Arizona in piñon-juniper woodland and yellow-pine forest near Prescott, Bradshaw Mts.; and chaparral-oak woodland at Yarnell, Weaver Mts.; at Burro Creek in Santa Maria Mts.; in chaparral in Harquahala and Harcuvar Mts.; and in conifer woodland in Cerbat and Music Mts.

WALL LIZARDS: FAMILY LACERTIDAE

Large family of more than 200 species that resemble our whiptail lizards—found in Europe, Africa, and Asia.

COMMON WALL LIZARD   *Podarcis muralis*   **not shown**

IDENTIFICATION: 2–3 in. (5.1–7.6 cm). A slim, long-bodied lizard that moves with jerky gait *much like our whiptail lizards, which it closely resembles.* Dorsum brown to gray, sometimes tinged with green and marked with vertebral row of dark spots or longitudinal dark stripe. Sides often with network of dark color broken by many white spots. Tail brown, gray, or reddish often with light and dark markings on sides. Venter white to reddish or orange. *Belly scales rectangular, as in our whiptails, but aligned longitudinally in 6 instead of 8 rows.* Dorsum covered with small granular scales. **RANGE:** Introduced on Saanich Peninsula, s. tip Vancouver I., B.C. where it is known to be breeding. Established at two localities in Ohio. Native to Europe—cen. Spain to s. Belgium, Netherlands, east into nw. Asia Minor.

WHIPTAILS AND THEIR ALLIES: FAMILY TEIIDAE

A large New World family with about 117 species, distributed throughout the Americas and West Indies. S. America has greatest number and variety of species. There are about 40 species of whiptails (*Cnemidophorus*), 16 of which occur in the West.

Most larger teiids, including whiptails, are slim-bodied, long-tailed, alert, and active diurnal lizards. They move with a jerky gait, rapidly turning head from side to side, and frequently protrude slender forked tongue. Front feet may move gingerly, as though walking on a hot surface. At the other extreme are the smaller, more secretive burrowers with limbs and toes reduced, sometimes to mere stumps. They spend much time under stones, in leaf litter, or dense plant growth; none of these species occur in the U.S.

Whiptails have large, squarish belly scales (ventrals) in regular lengthwise and transverse rows (8 *lengthwise rows* in our species), and small scales on back, called dorsal granules. The number of granules (counted across back at midbody) is important in classifying whiptails; hence, although they are of little use in field identification, counts of these scales have been given for most species. Head plates are large and symmetrical, and snout is slender. Most species have divided frontoparietal. May be several throat folds. Hindmost fold, the gular, is sometimes referred to in the accounts as having mesoptychial scales (those scales just anterior to gular fold) notably abruptly enlarged or not. Supraorbital semicircles (Fig. 18, Pl. 37, p. 108) may extend forward only a short distance failing to reach the frontal, a condition referred to in the accounts as "normal," or they may penetrate far forward, separating supraoculars from frontal (Fig. 18). Scales on back of foreleg (postantebrachials) vary in size. The tail, covered with keeled scales, is long (2 or more times body length), slender, and whiplike, hence the common name. Some Whiptails are striped, others are striped and spotted, or spotted with marbled or checkered pattern. In many species, color pattern changes considerably with growth. In striped species and young of most species, narrow pale stripes alternate with broader darker areas, referred to as "dark fields" (Fig. 18, Pl. 37, p. 108).

Whiptails are among the most difficult lizards to capture. They sometimes allow close approach, but usually manage to stay just out of reach and may suddenly dash to cover. When relentlessly pursued they often seek shelter in rodent burrows. The broad neck, slender head, and great activity make them difficult to snare with a noose.

Difficult to identify because of subtle differences among some species in scale counts and coloration, and color variations that occur with sex, age, and geographic location. Characteristic color patterns in many instances are well developed only in large individuals, and females in particular may mature before "adult" pattern is fully attained. Rely on habitat differences and distribution to aid identification.

Of special interest because a number of species consist only of females. Such species, labeled "all-female" in the accounts, reproduce by parthenogenesis. They lay viable but unfertilized eggs, which hatch only into females that exist as clones. The mix of cloning, continuing hybridization, and parthenogenesis can make individuals within some taxa virtually impossible to identify in the field, even for professionals. Color pattern classes have been recognized in some species (see Common Checkered Whiptail, p. 328). They are geographic populations, each believed to be descendants of a single individual. In some areas within their ranges, some of these populations overlap. Differences in color pattern and scalation are often subtle, however, and thus are not described.

Whiptails eat insects, spiders, scorpions, centipedes, and other small animals including other lizards, some of which they evidently detect by odor and dig out of the ground. Termites are often a staple food.

REMARKS: Recent studies recommend a change in generic name to *Aspidoscelis*. However, the present generic name, *Cnemidophorus,* has such a long history, I await action of the International Commission on Zoological Nomenclature.

ORANGE-THROATED WHIPTAIL   Pl. 40, Map 116
Cnemidophorus hyperythrus

IDENTIFICATION: 2–2¾ in. (5.1–7 cm). A striped, unspotted whiptail with *orange throat. Frontoparietal single.* Top of head yellow-brown to olive-gray. Paravertebral stripes usually united, except in southern part of range. *Usually 6 or fewer light stripes.* Color of dark field between pale dorsolateral stripe and lowermost lateral stripe varies: may be gray, reddish brown, or dark brown to black. **Young:** Tail blue. **Male:** Throat, chest, and (far south in range) entire ventral surface (including underside of tail) may be orange, more distinctly so during breeding season.

Inhabits washes, streams, terraces, and other sandy areas often where there are rocks and patches of brush and rocky hillsides. Frequents coastal chaparral, thornscrub, and streamside growth. 1–2 clutches of 1–4 eggs, laid June–July in northern part of range. Eats insects (termites, beetles, etc.) and spiders. Records of feeding on a hatchling Zebra-tailed Lizard and Side-blotched Lizard. **SIMILAR SPECIES:** (1) Baja California Whiptail (Pl. 53; p. 428) always has at least 6 light dorsal stripes (usually 7 or 8); in areas where Orange-throated Whiptail shares its range, latter usually has fewer than 6 stripes. (2) Western Whiptail (p. 326) has only vague striping (if any), spotted pattern, and divided frontoparietal. **RANGE:** Santa Ana R., Orange Co., and near Colton, San Bernardino Co., Calif., west of crest of Peninsular Ranges, south to tip of Baja Calif. Sea level to perhaps around 2,000 ft. (610m). **REMARKS:** An estimated 75 percent of former range in U.S. detroyed by developments; remaining populations highly fragmented.

BAJA CALIFORNIA WHIPTAIL
Cnemidophorus labialis

Pl. 53, Map 199

Close relative of Orange-throated Whiptail endemic to Baja Calif. (see p. 428).

CANYON SPOTTED WHIPTAIL
Cnemidophorus burti

Pl. 40, Map 123

IDENTIFICATION: 3½–5½ in. (8.9–14 cm). A large, spotted whiptail with 6–7 light stripes; stripes faint or absent in *large* adult males. Vertebral (middorsal) stripe may be present or absent. More or less speckled with pale spots above. Often *reddish color on head and neck, sometimes over entire back.* Supraorbital semicircles normal (Fig. 18, Pl. 37, p. 108), extending toward snout, to or near front end of frontoparietal. Abruptly enlarged postantebrachials and scales on gular fold. 85–115 dorsal granules. **Young:** Striping distinct. Spots in dark fields. Orange or reddish tail.

Inhabits mountain canyons, arroyos, and mesas in arid and semiarid regions, entering lowland desert along stream courses. Found in dense shrubby vegetation, often among rocks near permanent and intermittent streams. Clutches of 1–10 eggs, laid in summer. Eats insects (ants, termites, caterpillars, beetles, insect larvae and pupae) and spiders. **SIMILAR SPECIES:** See Chihuahuan

Spotted Whiptail (p. 323), Sonoran Spotted Whiptail (p. 324), and Gila Spotted Whiptail (p. 325). **RANGE:** S. and se. Ariz., extreme sw. N.M., and Sonora, and n. Sinaloa, Mex.

SUBSPECIES: RED-BACKED WHIPTAIL, *C. b. xanthonotus* (Pl. 40). Back reddish brown to reddish orange; red color stops abruptly along upper sides. Sides and upper surfaces of neck, legs, and feet dark grayish green to bluish. Striping and spotting on back more or less obscured by reddish dorsal ground color, less so in young. Primarily montane, with fragmented distribution. Ranges north to Sierra Estrella, southwest of Phoenix, east to just northeast of Coyote Mts., Pima Co., and west to Agua Dulce Mts., west of Organ Pipe Cactus Nat'l Monument. Frequents desert-edge habitats of juniper, oak, cactus (organ pipe, etc.), desert scrub, and grassland. GIANT SPOTTED WHIPTAIL, *C. b. stictogrammus* (Pl. 40). Adults reach much larger size than Red-backed Whiptail. Reddish or rust color on upper surfaces less extensive — when present usually confined to head and neck. Young have bright orange to reddish tail. The only Whiptail in the West except the Texas Spotted Whiptail that has 100 or more dorsal granules. Some localities are Santa Catalina, Santa Rita, Baboquivari, and Pajarito Mts.; vicinity of Oracle (north end Santa Catalina Mts.), Pinal Co., and Mineral Hot Springs, Cochise Co., Ariz. Guadalupe Canyon in extreme sw. N.M.; Sonora. Near sea level to around 4,500 ft. (1,370 m).

NEW MEXICO WHIPTAIL (ALL-FEMALE)   Pl. 38, Map 122
Cnemidophorus neomexicanus

IDENTIFICATION: 2⅜–3⅜ in. (6–8.5 cm). A whiptail with 6–7 pale stripes, including *wavy middorsal stripe that forks on neck.* Supraorbital semicircles *penetrate deeply toward snout*, usually separating 3rd and often 2nd supraocular from the frontal. Small, diffuse light spots on sides between light stripes. Often pale greenish to bluish below. Tail grayish at base, grading to greenish or greenish blue toward tip. Postantebrachials not enlarged. 71–85 dorsal granules. **Young:** Ground color of body black, stripes yellow, well-defined whitish spots in dark fields on sides. Greenish to greenish blue tail.

Primarily lives in bottomlands of historically perpetually disturbed habitats caused by flooding. Frequents areas of loose sand or packed sandy soil amid low grass, saltbush, desert tea, and scattered yucca and mesquite. Inhabits mostly plains grassland, flood plain habitats of sandy river basins, and edges of desert playas. 1–2 clutches of 1–4 eggs, laid June–July. Eats insects (such as beetles, ants, lepidopterans, grasshoppers) and spiders. **SIMILAR SPECIES:** Distinguished from other striped whiptails by combination of forward extension of supraorbital semicircles, well-defined stripes with light spots in dark fields on sides, wavy middorsal stripe, and greenish tail. **RANGE:** Rio Grande valley from near

Chamita, north of Santa Fe through N.M. into extreme w. Tex. and probably n. Chihuahua. To the west in N.M. to lower Mimbres R. drainage and northwest of Lordsburg, Hidalgo Co. Probably introduced at Petrified Forest Nat'l Park, east of Holbrook, Ariz., and at Conchas Lake area on Canadian R., San Miguel Co., N.M. From around 3,300–6,200 ft. (1,010–1,890 m).

REMARKS: This species originated by hybridization between Western Whiptail (*C. tigris,* p. 326) and the Little Striped Whiptail (*C. inornatus,* below) and occasionally continues to hybridize with both species.

LITTLE STRIPED WHIPTAIL
Cnemidophorus inornatus

Pl. 38, Map 118

IDENTIFICATION: 2–3²⁄₅ in. (5.1–8.6 cm). 6–8 (usually 7) pale yellowish, gray, to whitish stripes in our area; middorsal stripe sometimes faint or absent. Dark field between stripes blackish, brown, or brownish green to gray, *without light spots;* dark field becomes lighter with age. *Tail blue to purplish blue toward tip.* Usually bluish white to blue below (brightest in males). A pale form with faint stripes occurs at White Sands, N.M. *Postantebrachials* (Fig. 18, Pl. 37, p. 108) *and scales in front of gular fold only slightly enlarged or not at all.* Supraorbital semicircles normal. 52–79 dorsal granules. Usually 3 enlarged, rounded scales in front of vent. **Young:** Less blue below than adult. **Male:** Chin and belly more bluish than in female. Both sexes have more vivid blue on underside of tail than on remaining underparts.

Chiefly a prairie grassland species, but ranges into grassy areas of shrubby desert, chaparral, the piñon-juniper zone, and, in northwestern part of range into open ponderosa pine forests. Frequents sandy or silty, sometimes gravelly ground of elevated plains or lowlands. Seldom found in rocky or very barren areas or in mesquite habitats occupied by Desert Grassland Whiptail (p. 321). Clutch of 1–3 eggs, laid May–July, perhaps Aug. Eats insects (beetles, termites, ants, insect larvae), spiders (including tarantulas), and centipedes. **SIMILAR SPECIES:** (1) Plateau Striped Whiptail (p. 321) is larger, has conspicuously enlarged scales on rear of forelimb and gular fold, and generally occurs at higher elevations. (2) Chihuahuan Spotted Whiptail (p. 323), (3) Sonoran Spotted Whiptail (p. 324), and (4) Gila Spotted Whiptail (p. 325) have enlarged postantebrachials and light spots in dark fields. (5) Six-lined Racerunner (p. 322) often has broad brownish stripe down middle of back and generally greenish foreparts. See also (6) Desert Grassland Whiptail (p. 321), which overlaps in range with Little Striped Whiptail in the grasslands of sw. N.M. and se. Ariz. **RANGE:** San Juan R. drainage southward throughout most of lowlands of N.M. and thence on to w. Tex., Zacatecas, and San

Luis Potosí. Scattered populations in nw. (to western end of Grand Canyon) and cen. Ariz. (Mazatzal Mts.) and in vicinity of Wilcox Playa and at Whitlock Valley, Cochise Co., in se. Ariz. Recently reported at Petrified Forest Nat'l Park, Navajo Co., and Chinle, Apache Co., Ariz. Populations at Fairbank, Cochise Co., now considered extinct. From around 1,000–5,500 ft. (300–1,680 m); occasionally to 7,000 ft. (2130 m).

REMARKS: Species in apparent decline in many areas, perhaps due to overgrazing and other human disturbances.

DESERT GRASSLAND WHIPTAIL (ALL-FEMALE)
Cnemidophorus uniparens   **Pl. 37, Map 117**

IDENTIFICATION: 2⅘–3⅖ in. (7.1–8.6 cm). A small whiptail with 6–7 dorsal stripes; dark fields black, dark brown, or reddish brown, without light spots. *Tail greenish olive to bluish green.* Postantebrachials and gular scales enlarged. Supraorbital semicircles normal. 59–78 dorsal granules. Usually 3 enlarged, rounded scales in front of vent. **Young:** Tail bright blue.

Chiefly a lowland species of desert and mesquite grassland, but follows drainages into mountains, where it occurs in evergreen woodland, as at Oak Creek, Ariz. Generally found on plains and gentle foothill slopes, occasionally in areas with scant cover of grasses and herbs, but more commonly where mesquite and yucca are present and often where mesquite is dense. Two to 3 clutches of 1–4 eggs, laid May–July. Eats termites and other insects. **SIMILAR SPECIES:** (1) Plateau Striped Whiptail (below) has blue tail, enlarged postantebrachials and gular scales, and more than 3 enlarged, angular (not rounded) scales in front of vent. Generally occurs at higher elevations than Desert Grassland Whiptail. (2) Little Striped Whiptail (p. 320) has blue tail; postantebrachials and gular scales only slightly enlarged, if at all, and usually 3 enlarged, rounded scales in front of vent. **RANGE:** Near Hualapai Mts. in nw. Ariz. to vicinity of El Paso, Tex., up Rio Grande Valley to La Joya and Rio Salado, Socorro Co., N.M., south into Chihuahua. Bernalillo Co. records probably a result of introductions. Isolated records from Mule Creek area, Grant Co., N.M. From about 3,500–5,000 ft. (1,070–1,520 m). Occasionally hybridizes with Little Striped Whiptail.

REMARKS: Range may be expanding in N.M. with overgrazing and desertification of grasslands and riparian areas. This species had a hybrid origin.

PLATEAU STRIPED WHIPTAIL (ALL-FEMALE)
Cnemidophorus velox   **Pl. 38, Map 120**

IDENTIFICATION: 2½–3⅜ (6.2–8.4 cm). Six to 7 dorsal stripes; when present, middorsal stripe less distinct than others. Few spots, if any, in black to blackish brown dark fields in either young or adults. *Tail light blue.* Whitish below, unmarked or with tinge of bluish, especially on chin. Postantebrachials enlarged. Scales bordering gular fold conspicuously enlarged and abruptly differentiated from adjacent granular scales. Supraorbital semicircles normal. 63–85 dorsal granules. *More than 3 enlarged, angular scales in front of vent.* **Young:** Bright blue tail.

Found chiefly in the mountains in piñon-juniper grassland, open chaparral, oak woodland, and lower edges of ponderosa pine and fir forests. At lower elevations, frequents broadleaf woodlands along permanent and semipermanent streams. Clutch of 3–5 eggs, laid June–July. Eats insects (grasshoppers, crickets, leafhoppers, caterpillars, ants) and spiders. **SIMILAR SPECIES:** (1) Chihuahuan Spotted Whiptail (p. 323), (2) Sonoran Spotted Whiptail (p. 324), and (3) Gila Spotted Whiptail (p. 325) lack blue tail color and have distinct light spots in dark fields. (4) Little Striped Whiptail (p. 320) usually averages fewer dorsal granules and has small (granular) postantebrachials and only slightly enlarged scales bordering gular fold. (5) Desert Grassland Whiptail (p. 321) usually has 3 enlarged, rounded scales in front of vent, and greenish on tail. **RANGE:** Colorado Plateau of cen. and n. Ariz. and n. N.M., s. Utah and w. Colo. In N.M. ranges east to upper Ute Creek area, Union Co. Introduced (perhaps in 1960s) and established at Cove Palisades State Park, Jefferson Co., Ore. Isolated record near Mule Creek, Grant Co., N.M. From around 3,937–8,000 ft. (1,200–2,440 m). **REMARKS:** A triploid species of uncertain and complicated hybrid origin. Occasionally hybridizes with Little Striped Whiptail.

SIX-LINED RACERUNNER
Pl. 37, Map 114
Cnemidophorus sexlineatus

IDENTIFICATION: 2⅛–3⅗ in. (5.4–9.1 cm). A small, unspotted whiptail with 6–8 light stripes (usually 7 in our subspecies). *Head and body greenish in the West.* Stripes usually fade from yellowish to white toward rear, or are sometimes pale gray or pale blue. A broad, brownish middorsal stripe, sometimes divided; when middorsal stripe is divided by dark middorsal line, a total of 8 pale stripes. Dark fields may be brown to blackish. Whitish or pale blue below. Tail brownish. Postantebrachials not or slightly enlarged. Scales bordering gular fold conspicuously enlarged and usually not grading gradually into smaller scales of fold. Supraorbital semicircles normal. 62–115 dorsal granules (62–91 in our subspecies). **Young:** Distinct stripes. Tail blue. **Male:** Throat and belly bluish to bluish green. Striping sometimes vague.

Frequents open grassland, often with scattered shrubs, and woodland edges, usually where soil is sandy or loamy, but also in

areas with gravel and hardpan. Found in both lowlands and hills, occurring on floodplains and banks of rivers, in clearings and dune areas, and near rock outcrops. One to 3 clutches of 1–6 eggs, laid May–Aug. Eats insects (grasshoppers, beetles, ants, leafhoppers, lepidopterans), spiders, and snails. **SIMILAR SPECIES:** (1) Little Striped Whiptail (p. 320) has blue tail and is bluish on head and sides of body. (2) Chihuahuan Spotted (below) and (3) Common Spotted Whiptails (p. 325) have light spots in dark fields and enlarged postantebrachials; Texas Spotted Whiptail lacks short, dark-bordered light stripe on side of tail. (4) Plateau Striped Whiptail (p. 321) has enlarged postantebrachials and bluish tail. (5) See also Common Checkered Whiptail (p. 328). **RANGE:** Southern S.D., se. Minn., and Md. south to s. Tex., the Gulf Coast, and Fla. Keys; e. Colo. and N.M. to the Atlantic Coast. Sea level to around 7,000 ft. (2,130 m). Hybridizes with Common Checkered at Higbee, Otero Co., Colo.
SUBSPECIES: PRAIRIE RACERUNNER, *C. s. viridis*, occurs in our area.

CHIHUAHUAN SPOTTED WHIPTAIL (ALL-FEMALE)
Cnemidophorus exsanguis   **Pl. 39, Map 116**

IDENTIFICATION: 2½–4 in. (6.3–10.1 cm). Striped whiptail with light spots in brown or reddish brown dark fields. Spots cream to pale yellow, *sometimes bright yellow on rump and across upper hind legs,* especially in older adults. Usually 6 light stripes, pale yellowish to gray on neck, grading to whitish or beige toward rear and invaded by light spots. Middorsal stripe variable, may be narrow and broken into series of spots, or indistinct or absent. Tail greenish, brownish, or tan. Whitish, cream, or bluish below, without pattern. Enlarged postantebrachials (4 or more times size of nearby scales) and enlarged scales (mesoptychials) along front edge of gular fold. Supraorbital semicircles normal. 65–86 dorsal granules. **Young:** Tail bluish or greenish. Light spots in dark fields present even in hatchlings (middorsally).

Chiefly an upland lizard, ranging from juniper grasslands into oak-piñon-juniper and ponderosa pine forests in mountains, where it occurs on rocky hillsides, along sandy washes, and in canyons often in disturbed habitats. Typical habitat is canyon bottom in oak and oak-pine belts. At some localities, ranges into desert habitat along drainages from mountains. Clutch of 1–6 eggs, laid June–Aug. Eats insects (grasshoppers, termites, beetles, and lepidopteran larvae), spiders, and scorpions. **SIMILAR SPECIES:** (1) Canyon Spotted Whiptail (p. 318) is larger, with more dorsal granules (over 95, where ranges overlap), and stripes tend to disappear with age. (2) New Mexico Whiptail (p. 319) has wavy vertebral (middorsal) stripe. (3) Plateau Striped Whiptail (p. 321), (4)

Desert Grassland Whiptail (p. 321), (5) Little Striped Whiptail (p. 320), and (6) Six-lined Racerunner (p. 322) lack pale spots on upper surfaces. See also (7) Common Checkered Whiptail (p. 328), (8) Sonoran Spotted Whiptail (below), (9) Gila Spotted Whiptail (p. 325), and Common Spotted Whiptail (p. 325). **RANGE:** N.-cen. N.M. to cen. Chihuahua; extreme se. Ariz. and e. Sonora to Trans-Pecos, Tex. From around 2,500–8,000 ft. (760–2,440 m).

REMARKS: Chihuahuan Spotted Whiptail originated through hybridization, according to one scenario, involving 3 species—Little Striped Whiptail and 2 Mexican species, *Cnemidophorus septemvittatus* and *C. costatus,* however, there is uncertainty as to its origin.

SONORAN SPOTTED WHIPTAIL (ALL-FEMALE)
Cnemidophorus sonorae   **Pl. 39, Map 120**

IDENTIFICATION: 2½–3½ in. (6.3–8.9 cm). Close relative of Chihuahuan Spotted and Gila Spotted Whiptails, with which this species was formerly confused. Six stripes; 5–8 dorsal granules between middorsal pair of stripes (paravertebrals). Sometimes a trace of middorsal stripe on neck and lower back. Dark fields blackish, brown, to reddish, with spots of white, pale tan, or dull yellowish. Some light spots overlapping (and more intense than) light stripes. Tail usually dull orange-tan, often grading to olive toward tip. Whitish to cream below, unmarked. 74–80 dorsal granules. 32–39 total femoral pores. Usually 3 preanals (enlarged scales in front of vent). **Young:** Hatchlings lack spots in dark fields.

Occurs primarily in upland habitats of oak woodland and oak grassland; also in streamside woodland, desert-grassland, desert scrub of palo verde and saguaro, and thornscrub. Clutch of 1–7 eggs. Eats insects (termites, beetles, grasshoppers) and spiders.

SIMILAR SPECIES: (1) Chihuahuan Spotted Whiptail (p. 323) is larger, and light stripes fade on neck. (2) Gila Spotted Whiptail (p. 325) has less mottling on upper surface of hind legs, olive-green tail often with bluish cast, and usually 2 preanals instead of 3. Four to 5 dorsal granules between middorsal pair of stripes. (3) Canyon Spotted Whiptail is much larger, loses its stripes with age, and has more than 95 dorsal granules. **RANGE:** Se. Ariz., to ne. Sonora; Santa Catalina Mts., Ariz. to basins of Rio Yaqui and Rio Sonora, Sonora, Mex., and from Baboquivari Mts., Ariz., east to Peloncillo and Animas Mts., Hidalgo Co., N.M. From around 700–7,000 ft. (210–2,130 m). Coexists with Gila Spotted and Chihuahuan Spotted Whiptails wherever edges of their ranges overlap. Hybridizes with Western Whiptail (*C. tigris,* p. 326) in s. Ariz.

REMARKS: The *Cnemidophorus sonorae/flagellicaudus* complex (p. 325), of hybrid origin, may contain 5 or more taxa, of which only 2 have been named.

GILA SPOTTED WHIPTAIL (ALL-FEMALE)

Cnemidophorus flagellicaudus **Pl. 39, Map 119**

IDENTIFICATION: 2½–3¾ in. (6.3–9.5 cm). Similar to Chihuahuan Spotted and Sonoran Spotted Whiptails, with which it was formerly confused. Six stripes, upper ones tending to become gold or greenish yellow on neck. Three to 6 dorsal granules between pair of middorsal stripes (paravertebrals). Traces of middorsal stripe rarely present. Dark fields coffee brown to blackish, sometimes rust. *Yellowish to golden or light beige spots on back, present in both dark fields and touching or located within pale stripes, especially paravertebral stripes.* Tail light olive-green, sometimes with bluish cast. Whitish to cream below, unmarked. 77–84 dorsal granules. 35–41 total femoral pores. *Usually 2 preanals,* enlarged scales anterior to vent (most whiptails have 3). **Young:** Hatchlings lack spots.

Frequents piñon-juniper and oak woodlands, chaparral, streamside growth, and upper edge of desert grassland. Clutch of 2–6 eggs laid June or July. **SIMILAR SPECIES:** (1) Chihuahuan Spotted Whiptail (p. 323) lacks bright greenish yellow or gold color in stripes on neck; tail olive-green, greenish brown, tan, or pinkish. May have bright yellow spots on rump. (2) See also Sonoran Spotted Whiptail (p. 324). **RANGE:** From Cerbat and Hualapai Mts., Mohave Co., to Gila R. basin on s. slope Central Plateau of Ariz. and uplands of extreme sw. N.M. Isolated populations in Catalina and Chiricahua Mts., Ariz. From 4,000–6,500 ft. (1,220–1,980 m).

REMARKS: See Remarks section, Sonoran Spotted Whiptail (p. 324).

COMMON SPOTTED WHIPTAIL
(TEXAS SPOTTED WHIPTAIL)

Pl. 39, Map 121

Cnemidophorus gularis

IDENTIFICATION: 2¼–4⅕ in. (5.7–10.6 cm). *A striped and spotted whiptail.* Ground color above often greenish. Seven to 8 light stripes; middorsal stripe broader and less distinct than others, often splitting in two to give a total count of 8. Whitish to yellow-brown spots, especially in greenish to dark brown dark fields on sides. Tail brown or reddish. Postantebrachials and scales on front edge of gular fold enlarged. Supraorbital semicircles normal. 76–96 dorsal granules, 10–21 (avg. 15) between middorsal pair of stripes (paravertebrals). **Young:** Striped, but spotting faint or absent. With growth, pair of wavy light lines down back tends to fuse into single broad light middorsal stripe of adults. Rump and tail reddish, fading with age. In our area, reddish cast to tail may persist even in some adults and can be seen at a considerable distance. **Male:** Throat and often underside of tail orange or pinkish salmon. Chest and belly purplish or bluish, often darkened with varying amounts of black. **Female:** Whitish to cream below, unmarked.

Frequents prairie grassland, rocky hillsides, washes, and river bottoms grown to mesquite, acacia, cactus, and shrubs. Soil is usually sandy or gravelly. More deliberate in movements than Six-lined Racerunner and generally less wary. One to 2 clutches (perhaps 3), each of 1–7 eggs; laid May–July, perhaps Aug. Eats insects (such as termites, grasshoppers, beetles, ants, lepidopterans) and spiders. **SIMILAR SPECIES:** (1) Six-lined Racerunner (p. 322) has short light stripe on each side of its tail, extending backward from each hind leg and bordered below by dark line; no spotting in the dark fields. (2) In areas where ranges overlap, Chihuahuan Spotted Whiptail (p. 323) has only 2–8 dorsal granules between paravertebral stripes and prefers more rugged upland habitats. Its young lack reddish tail and distinct middorsal stripe(s) of juvenile Texas Spotted Whiptail. (3) See also Common Checkered Whiptail (p. 328). **RANGE:** N. Tex. to n. Veracruz; e. Tex. to se. N.M. Co-exists on lower mountain slopes with Chihuahuan Spotted Whiptail. Sea level to perhaps around 4,000 ft. (1,220 m).

WESTERN WHIPTAIL (TIGER WHIPTAIL)
Cnemidophorus tigris   Pl. 37, Map 115

IDENTIFICATION: 2⅜–5 in. (6–12.7 cm). Back and sides with *spots, bars, or network of dusky or black markings on background of gray, brown, yellowish, or tan*. Light stripes may be present but often fade on lower back and base of tail. Ground color gray-brown, yellowish brown, yellowish, or olive. Tail becomes dark brown, dusky, or bluish toward tip. Usually cream-colored or yellowish below, with *scattered spots of blackish, especially on chest and throat*. In extreme darkening, the throat, chest, underside of front legs, and belly are black; orange or pink on throat may be reduced to a few tan flecks. Rust-colored patches often present on sides of belly. Scales in front of gular fold only slightly enlarged and grading gradually into small granules of fold. Postantebrachials not enlarged. Supraorbital semicircles extend far forward. 68–114 dorsal granules. **Young:** Spotted, marbled, or striped with black above; black fields alternating with narrow orange-yellow ones. Tail bright blue.

An active lizard of deserts and semiarid habitats, usually where plants are sparse and there are open areas for running. Ranges from deserts to montane pine forests where it prefers warmer, drier areas. Also found in woodland and streamside growth. Avoids dense grassland and thick growth of shrubs. Ground may be firm soil, sandy, or rocky. One to 2 (perhaps 3) clutches usually of 1–4 (rarely 8) eggs, laid April–Aug. Single clutches usually laid in cooler environments. Eats insects (including insect larvae, termites, grasshoppers, beetles), spiders, scorpions, and lizards. **SIMILAR SPECIES:** (1) Common Checkered (p. 328) and (2) Gray Checkered Whiptails have enlarged mesoptychial scales, strongly reticulated dorsal pattern, and mostly unmarked ventral surface. (3) Plateau Striped Whiptail has more distinct pale lengthwise stripes and pale unmarked venter. **RANGE:** N.-cen. and se. Ore. and s. Idaho, south through Great Basin and Calif. to Baja Calif. and s. Coahuila, east to w. Colo., N.M. and w. Tex. In Ore. in upper John Day Valley, in Alvord Basin and at Diamond Craters. Below sea level to around 7,000 ft. (2,130 m). A single record of hybridization with the Sonoran Spotted Whiptail (C. sonorae, p. 324) at Huerfano Butte, Pima Co., Ariz. More frequently hybridizes with C. neomexicanus and C. tesselatus.

SUBSPECIES: GREAT BASIN WHIPTAIL, C. t. tigris. Four light stripes on back that tend to become obscure with age, particularly in southern part of range. Usually vertical dark barring on sides. Hind limbs with black or dusky flecks or broken black network. Much variation in ventral color, from nearly plain unmarked throughout to heavily dark-spotted, particularly on chest. Both dorsal and ventral dark spotting tends to be reduced in southern part of range, but there is much variation. CALIFORNIA WHIPTAIL, C. t. mundus (Pl. 37). Typically 8 light stripes, but lateral stripes often have irregular borders and are sometimes indistinct. Dorsal dark markings often large and vivid. Usually no distinct dark barring on sides. Throat pale, usually with distinct black spots. Young are striped. COASTAL WHIPTAIL, C. t. stejnegeri. Resembles California Whiptail but stripes on sides usually less well defined. Perhaps a greater frequency of individuals with large dark spots on throat, but there is much variation. Young are spotted in San Diego area. SONORAN WHIPTAIL, C. t. punctilinealis. Typically with 4 distinct stripes on back and an additional less distinct one on each side. Striping vague or absent in some adults. Hind limbs, sides, and dark fields commonly with rounded light spots, giving overall spotted effect. Outstanding characteristic is strong tendency toward darkening of throat, chest, and underside of forelimbs. In large adults throat and chest may be uniformly black. PAINTED DESERT WHIPTAIL, C. t. septentrionalis. Striped as in Sonoran Whiptail, but stripes yellow. Dark stripes usually stop short of hind legs. Throat with small black spots. MARBLED WHIPTAIL, C. t. marmoratus (Pl. 37). Adult often has pronounced marbled pattern on dorsal surfaces but usually has alternating dark and light bars on sides and hint of dorsal striping. Some individuals have checkerboard pattern and some have pale spots in more or less lengthwise rows. Throat and chest pink or orange with some black spots. Throat sometimes plain white. Young spotted. REDDISH WHIPTAIL, C. t. rubidus. Brownish olive above, paler on sides, with narrow black crossbands. Rear bands may extend entirely across back, but others are broken into a series of black dorsal spots with corresponding bars on sides. Reddish or deep pinkish color on throat, about ears, and on underside of tail; sometimes extensive pinkish to reddish tinge on upper surfaces. Young have 4–6 light lengthwise lines with short, irregular black spots between them. GIANT WHIPTAIL, *C. t. maximus.* Gray or brownish above, fading to olive gray on sides, with 3 lengthwise dark chestnut bands on each side. Each band is twice as wide as the interspace between bands, and often so invaded by spots of ground color that it resembles a series of merged brown spots. Tail tawny olive, tinged and spotted with dark chestnut. Young have 5–6 bluish white lengthwise lines on a black ground color, more or less broken by spots of same color as lines. Tail and hind limbs suffused with bright pinkish color. To over 5 in. (12.7 cm). Other subspecies (or pattern classes) have been described for islands in Gulf of Calif. and off w. coast of Baja Calif.

REMARKS: Juncture shown between Marbled Whiptail and Western Whiptail is quite arbitrary. Actually, Western Whiptail is very restricted in se. Ariz. Population that does contact Marbled Whiptail extends north up Gila R. to north of Tucson, then south along San Pedro R. to near Benson, Cochise Co.

COMMON CHECKERED WHIPTAIL (ALL-FEMALE) (DIPLOID CHECKERED WHIPTAIL)
Cnemidophorus tesselatus   Pl. 38, Map 113

IDENTIFICATION: 2½–4³⁄₁₆ in. (6.3–10.6 cm). Resembles Western Whiptail (p. 326). Yellowish to cream above, usually with bold dark blotches in checkered pattern or lengthwise rows. At least 6 pale stripes. Single or paired middorsal stripe may bring number of stripes to 7 or 8, respectively; another pair of stripes on lower sides may bring total to 10 stripes. *Dark fields with light spots or bars that often merge with light stripes.* Whitish below, unmarked or with a few black spots on throat, chest, and belly. Tail brown to yellowish. Considerable variation can occur in patterning; thus, individuals from ne. N.M. tend to be distinctly striped whereas those from lower Rio Grande valley, N.M. are tesselated with dark and light markings. See also Triploid Checkered Whiptail (Colorado Checkered Whiptail, p. 329). *Scales in front of gular fold (mesoptychials) are abruptly and conspicuously enlarged. Postantebrachials not enlarged. 75–112 dorsal granules.* **Young:** Striped, with small pale spots in dark fields. Spotted or barred on sides.

Ranges from creosote bush plains to piñon-juniper zone in mountains. Also occurs along drainages grown to cottonwoods, willows, and tamarisk. Frequents flatlands, canyon slopes, bluffs, and gullies. Although soil conditions may vary from hardpan to sand, this lizard seems to prefer rocky habitats with scant vegetation and open areas for running. One (perhaps 2) clutch(es) of 1–8 eggs, laid June–July. Eats insects (termites, beetles, grasshoppers, lepidopterans), spiders, and centipedes. **SIMILAR SPECIES:** (1) In Chihuahuan Spotted Whiptail (p. 323) and (2) Common Spotted Whiptail (p. 325), postantebrachials are more enlarged. (3) Six-lined Racerunner (p. 322), (4) Little Striped Whiptail (p. 320), (5) Desert Grassland Whiptail (p. 321), and (6) Plateau Striped Whiptail (p. 321) typically are smaller and have striped pattern without light spots or other marks in dark fields. (7) See also Western (p. 326) and Gray Checkered (p. 330) Whiptails. **RANGE:** Se. Colo. to e. Chihuahua; w. Tex. to Rio Grande R. basin, N.M.. Tends to occur in isolated pockets, especially where bisexual whiptails are abundant. Six localized color-pattern classes have been described but not designated as subspecies (see Remarks below). From around 900–6,900 ft. (270–2,100 m).

REMARKS: Most pattern classes of Checkered Whiptail arose by hybridization between Western Whiptail (Marbled Whiptail subspecies) and a Mexican Whiptail, *C. septemvittatus.*

COLORADO CHECKERED WHIPTAIL (TRIPLOID CHECKERED WHIPTAIL) (ALL-FEMALE)
Cnemidophorus neotesselatus   not shown, Map 113

IDENTIFICATION: Similar to Diploid Checkered Whiptail. Paravertebral (see Fig. 18, p. 108) pale stripes are gray, *uninterrupted, straight, often fused with spots.* Vertebral stripe gray and, if present on neck, *relatively straight,* or stripe on neck followed with spots. Lateral stripe (lowest on body) gray, *relatively straight,* usually fused with some spots and/or bars. Upper dark field (see Fig. 18, opp. Pl. 37, p. 108) *with pale spots in a row* (some fused with stripes). Dorsal surface of thighs with many pale spots, *often fused into reticulum.* Scales anterior to gular fold (mesoptychials) conspicuously enlarged.

Frequents hillsides, arroyos, and canyons; juniper-grass association areas of rabbitbrush, prickly-pear cactus, and yuccas. Clutches of 1–4 (3) eggs laid June to late July. Nests defended during and immediately after egg-laying. Eats arthropods — insects (such as grasshoppers, termites, beetles including adults and larvae, caterpillars, leafhoppers, moths) and spiders. **SIMILAR SPECIES:** (1) In Colo., Diploid Checkered Whiptail has gray-tan to tan or gold paravertebral stripes irregular in outline, interrupted and/or fused with bars. Upper dark field with pale spots either longitudinally fused or transversely expanded into bars. (2) Western Whiptail lacks conspicuously enlarged scales anterior to gular fold. (3) Six-lined Racerunner lacks light spots or bars in dark fields. **RANGE:** Confined to se. Colo. Distribution spotty. Localities are associated with Arkansas R. drainage basin including the river's Purgatoire tributary. Range extends from foothills of Rockies, east to Pueblo area. To 6,900 ft. (2,105 m). Coexists with Diploid Whiptail near Higbee, Otero Co. Sometimes hybridizes with Six-lined Racerunner.

REMARKS: Formerly included in Common (Diploid) Checkered Whiptail species (p. 329). This triploid species originated through hybridization between a female Marbled Whiptail (*C. tigris marmoratus*) and a male Plateau Spotted Whiptail (*C. septemvittatus*), followed by hybridization of one of these hybrids with a male Six-lined Racerunner (*C. sexlineatus*). This species now appears to be extinct in the Pueblo area east of I-25, a historic area of research leading to the discovery of triploid parthenogenesis. Its loss in this area is ascribed to urban development and other man-made changes.

GRAY CHECKERED WHIPTAIL (ALL-FEMALE)
Cnemidophorus dixoni   **not shown, Map 113**

IDENTIFICATION: 2⅗–4⅓ in. (6.6–11 cm). Above grayish anteriorly often grading to orange-brown posteriorly, with dark squarish spots arranged in longitudinal rows and some irregular barring on sides; tail may be uniform in color with some vague longitudinal streaking or flecking. In many individuals orange-brown coloration may extend onto tail. Supraorbital semicircles usually do not completely separate 2nd supraocular from the frontal. 94–112 dorsal granules. *Mesoptychial scales* (those anterior to gular fold) *abruptly enlarged and not grading smoothly into anterior throat scales.* **Young:** Longitudinal yellow or cream light stripes on dark brown or black background. Well-defined light stripes on each side of body, and additional striping dorsolaterally and dorsally that fades toward tail. With growth and locality dark fields may be invaded with light spots, and spreading and fusion of segments of dark fields may disrupt light stripes.

In N.M., known only from Peloncillo Mts. area in Hidalgo Co., where found in creosote bush desert on sandy to gravelly soils. Other local plants are mesquite, allthorn, Mormon tea, cactus, desert-willow, and saltbush. Clutches of 2–8 eggs. Reproductive season may extend from May–July. Eats insects (termites, ants, beetles, and robberflies) and spiders. **SIMILAR SPECIES:** (1) Western Whiptail has granular mesoptychial scales (that grade smoothly into anterior throat scales) and is more darkly pigmented on chin, chest, and tail. (2) Checkered Whiptails (Diploid and Triploid) have more contrasting, coarser, reticulated dorsal pattern; unknown in Hidalgo Co. **RANGE:** Vicinity of Antelope Pass, Peloncillo Mts., Hidalgo Co., N.M., and sw. Chinati Mts., Presidio Co., Tex. In N.M., to 4,265–4,757 ft. (1,300–1,450 m).

REMARKS: Species is of hybrid origin. Parental species are Plateau Spotted Whiptail (*C. septemvittatus*) of Big Bend area of Tex. and Western Whiptail (*C. tigris,* subsp. *marmoratus*).

ALLIGATOR LIZARDS AND ALLIES: FAMILY ANGUIDAE

A small but widely distributed family (about 100 species) in the Americas, West Indies, Europe, North Africa, Asia, Sumatra, and Borneo. Only the Alligator Lizards (*Elgaria*) reach our area, ranging from sw. Canada to Jalisco, Mex. As here treated, 8 species, 7 of which occur in our area. They have short limbs, a slim body, long tail, and *distinctive fold* on each side of body, *formed in a strip of granular scales that separates large squarish scales* on back and belly. Since dorsal and ventral scales are reinforced with bone and form a firm exterior, the fold may enable the body to expand for breathing and accommodation of food, eggs, or developing young (some species are live-bearing). Lizards in this family tend to have a long body and short limbs (as in our species), or the limbs may be dwarfed, number of toes reduced, or limbs may be completely lacking, as in the "slow-worm" (*Anguis fragilis*) of Europe and snakelike glass lizards (*Ophisaurus*) of the Old and New Worlds.

Alligator lizards generally frequent moist environments in foothills and mountains, but may range into arid lowlands near springs and streams. Secretive, they generally seek cover among rocks or dense vegetation. Turn over logs, rocks, boards, and other objects in sunny glades that have abundant plant or rock cover. When caught they often attempt to bite and may writhe about, smearing their captor with feces. Males may extrude hemipenes. Avoid grabbing the tail—it is easily lost.

SOUTHERN ALLIGATOR LIZARD

Elgaria multicarinata   **Pl. 41, Map 124**

IDENTIFICATION: 2⅞–7 in. (7.3–17.8 cm). Dark lengthwise stripes or dashed lines on belly, *down middle of scale rows* or scales dusky with pale edges, but belly sometimes unmarked. *Dorsal scales in 14 rows at midbody.* Scales often strongly keeled on back, neck, and limbs. *Usually well-defined, regular dark crossbands* on back and tail; usually 9–13 bands (often 10–11) between back of head and rear of thighs. Black or dusky bars on sides, spotted with white. Mostly brown, gray, reddish, or yellowish above. *Eyes pale yellow.* Tail long; when not regenerated may be over twice the length of body. Tail somewhat prehensile, sometimes wrapped around branches in climbing. **Young:** Often broad dorsal stripe of tan, reddish, beige, or gray, brightening on tail. Sides barred as in adult. **Male:** Head broader (more triangular) than female's.

Frequents grassland, chaparral, oak woodland, and open pine forest. In drier parts of range most likely near streams or in moist canyon bottoms with abundant plant cover. Occasionally enters water to escape an enemy. Around houses, may live in old wood-piles and trash heaps. Partly nocturnal during warmer parts of year. One to 3 clutches, each of 5–20 eggs, laid May–July. Eats slugs, insects, centipedes, scorpions, and spiders, including the highly venomous black widow; also lizards and small mammals. May climb bushes and trees in search of insects and occasionally feeds on eggs and young of birds. **SIMILAR SPECIES:** (1) Northern Alligator Lizard (below) has lengthwise stripes between scale rows on belly, usually 16 dorsal scale rows, irregular markings on back, a shorter tail, and darker eyes. (2) See also Panamint Alligator Lizard (p. 334). **RANGE:** Chiefly west of Cascade-Sierran crest, from s. Wash. (Umtanum Creek Canyon, Kittitas Co.) to nw. Baja Calif. Islands off coast of s. Calif. (San Miguel, Santa Rosa, Santa Cruz, Anacapa, San Nicolas, and Catalina) and nw. Baja Calif. (San Martin). Isolated populations east of Sierra Nevada of Calif. at Grant Lake, Mono Co.; near Independence (Alabama Hills) and Walker Pass, Kern Co.; at Walker Creek near Olancha, Inyo Co.; and at Sierra La Asamblea, Baja Calif. Sur. In desert along Mojave R., Calif. Introduced at Las Vegas, and sight record at Boulder Beach Campground needs verification, Clark Co., Nev. Sea level to over 5,000 ft. (1,524 m).

SUBSPECIES: CALIFORNIA ALLIGATOR LIZARD, *E. m. multicarinata.* Red blotches on back. Top of head often mottled. One to 3 rows of scales on upper arm; scales weakly keeled in adult. SAN DIEGO ALLIGATOR LIZARD, *E. m. webbii.* Larger size and more prominent keeling than in other subspecies. Temporal scales keeled, upper ones strongly so. OREGON ALLIGATOR LIZARD, *E. m. scincicauda.* Dorsal scales less heavily keeled than in San Diego Alligator Lizard. Temporals smooth or only upper ones weakly keeled. Scales of lateral fold cinnamon. Head usually not mottled.

NORTHERN ALLIGATOR LIZARD   Pl. 41, Map 126
Elgaria coerulea

IDENTIFICATION: 2¾–5⅜ in. (7–13.6 cm). Dark *stripes on belly between scale rows;* sometimes absent. Dorsal scales *usually in 16 rows.* At midbody, crossbands seldom regular enough to count. Eyes completely dark or dark around pupils. Gray, olive, rust, greenish, or bluish above, usually heavily blotched or barred with dusky. Some individuals unpatterned; others have broad middorsal stripe. **Young:** Crossbanded or with broad (lengthwise) dorsal stripe of brassy, beige, or gray. **Male:** Head broader and more triangular than female's.

Chiefly inhabits woodland and forest, but also grassland and sagebrush habitats. Occurs under bark, inside rotten logs, and under rocks and other objects. Generally found in cooler, damper places than Southern Alligator Lizard. Live-bearing; 2–15 (4–5) young, born June–Sept. Eats insects and their larvae, ticks, spiders, centipedes, slugs, millipedes, snails, and worms. **SIMILAR SPECIES:** See Southern Alligator Lizard (p. 331). **RANGE:** Southern B.C. including Vancouver I., south through Wash., Ore., and n. Calif. from Cascade Mts. to coast. Ranges coastally in Calif. to n. Monterey Co. (Big Sur area) and interiorly throughout Sierra Nevada. Also occurs in Rocky Mts. of w. Mont. and n. Idaho. Isolated populations on Hart Mt. and in Warner Mts., Lake Co., Ore.; in the Breckenridge and Paiute Mts., Kern Co., Warner Mts., Modoc Co., Calif.; and Badger Mt., upper High Rock Canyon, Washoe Co., and Carson City Clear Creek and vicinity, Douglas Co., Nev. On islands in Puget Sound, Straits of Georgia, and Juan de Fuca; in San Francisco Bay and on Año Nuevo I. off Calif. coast. Sea level to around 10,500 ft. (3,200 m).

SUBSPECIES: SAN FRANCISCO ALLIGATOR LIZARD, *E. c. coerulea.* Usually large dark blotches or irregular crossbands on back. Scales of back and sides heavily keeled. Otherwise resembles Northwestern Alligator Lizard (below). SHASTA ALLIGATOR LIZARD, *E. c. shastensis.* Dorsal scales in 16 rows. Temporals smooth. In northern part of range, head may be slate gray and body yellowish green or tan. However, a variety of color morphs exists in range of this subspecies. Young crossbanded. NORTHWESTERN ALLIGATOR LIZARD, *E. c. principis.* Small—usually less than 4 in. (10.1 cm) long. Usually has broad stripe of tan, olive, golden brown or grayish down the back, with or without spots. Sides dusky, contrasting with back color. Dorsal scales weakly keeled, in 14 rows. Temporals (behind eye) weakly keeled. SIERRA ALLIGATOR LIZARD, *E. c. palmeri.* Markings extend across back, are confined to sides, or are absent. Dorsal scales in 16 rows. Temporals all keeled.

Northern Alligator Lizard. The dark eye is distinctive, separating this species from the Southern Alligator Lizard, which has a pale yellow eye. The two species share much of their ranges.

PANAMINT ALLIGATOR LIZARD
Elgaria panamintina

IDENTIFICATION: 3⅝–6 in. (9.2–15.2 cm). Light yellow or beige above, with *regular, broad brown crossbands; 7 or 8 bands between back of head (marked by ear openings) and front of thighs.* Similar bands on tail. Ventral markings in lengthwise stripes down center of scale rows or may be scattered. Eyes pale yellow. Dorsal scales in 14 rows, smooth or weakly keeled. Tail long—up to twice as long as body. **Young:** Dark crossbars contrast with pale ground color. **Male:** Head broader, more triangular than female's.

Ranges from creosote bush scrub desert and Joshua-tree zone into lower edge of the piñon-juniper belt. Found beneath thickets of willow and wild grape near water or in drier habitats grown to creosote bush and desert mint. Secretive; spends much of its time in rockslides and dense plant growth. Sometimes nocturnal. Look under rocks in damp gullies and along streams. Presumably lays eggs. An individual was found containing 12 developing eggs. Mating has been observed in May. Eats insects and other arthropods. **SIMILAR SPECIES:** (1) Madrean Alligator Lizard (below) has orange or pink eyes and 8–11 crossbands between back of head and front of thighs. (2) Southern Alligator Lizard (p. 331) has 9–13 crossbands; young often have a broad middorsal stripe on body and tail. **RANGE:** Desert Mts. of Inyo Co. and se. Mono Co., Calif. Some localities are Panamint Mts. (Surprise, Pleasant, and Wildrose Canyons and middle fork of Hanuapah Canyon), Nelson Mts. (Grapevine Canyon), Inyo Mts. (Long John, Daisy, and other canyons), and White Mts. (Marble, Silver Creek, and Cottonwood Canyons; Coldwater Creek). A sight record for Cosos Mts., Inyo Co. From around 2,500 to 7,513 ft. (760–2,290 m).

REMARKS: Species currently at risk from mining, feral and domestic livestock grazing, and off-road vehicle activity.

MADREAN ALLIGATOR LIZARD
Elgaria kingii

IDENTIFICATION: 3–5⅕ in. (7.6–13.2 cm). Belly with scattered dusky spots and bars; usually no lengthwise stripes. Pale gray, beige, or brown above, with distinct wavy crossbars, 8–11 between back of head (marked by ear openings) and front of thighs. Eyes orange or pink. *Conspicuous black and white spots on upper jaw.* Scales smooth or weakly keeled. Dorsal scales usually in 14 rows. **Young:** Contrasting dark crossbars on back and tail.

Chiefly a mountain form that frequents chaparral, oak woodland, and pine-fir forests in rocky places near permanent or temporary streams. May also occur in broadleaf stream-border habitats along major drainageways in desert and grassland. Also found

Madrean Alligator Lizard. Note the skin fold between the limbs. This flexible area of skin, positioned between the stiff bone-reinforced scales of the dorsum and venter, allows the body to expand with breathing.

in juniper grassland and on creosote bush flats. Found under logs, rocks, and in woodrat nests and leaf litter in and near dense plant growth. Sometimes abroad at dusk or after dark. Chiefly ground-dwelling but occasionally climbs. Clutch of 9–15 eggs, laid June–July. Eats insects (such as preying mantis, grasshoppers, caterpillars, and moths) and scorpions. **SIMILAR SPECIES:** See Panamint Alligator Lizard (p. 334). **RANGE:** S. edge Central Plateau of Ariz. southward in Sierra Madre Occidental to Jalisco. Huachuca, Santa Rita, Pajarito, and Chiricahua Mts., Ariz.; sw. N.M. east to Florida Mts., Luna Co. and near Las Cruces, Dona Ana Co. From 2,400 to around 9,000 ft. (730–2,770 m). **SUBSPECIES:** The ARIZONA ALLIGATOR LIZARD, *E. k. nobilis*, occurs in our area.

SAN LUCAN ALLIGATOR LIZARD   Pls. 53, Maps 124, 198
Elgaria paucicarinata

Relative of Madrean Alligator Lizard endemic to Baja Calif. (see p. 426).

Other Baja Calif. species are the Cedros Island (*E. cedrosensis*) and Central Peninsular (*E. velazquezi*) Alligator Lizards (p. 427, Map 198).

NORTH AMERICAN LEGLESS LIZARDS: FAMILY ANNIELLIDAE

Snakelike burrowing lizards, about the size of a lead pencil. Two species, confined to Calif. and Baja Calif. Covered with small, smooth, cycloid scales that makes it easy to move through sand or loose soil. Eyes small, with movable lids. Snout shovel-shaped;

lower jaw inset, forming a seal that keeps sand from getting in mouth when burrowing. No ear openings. Blunt tail aids in occasional backward movements in soil. Although limbless and snake-like, their movable eyelids distinguish them from all snakes. When picked up, may probe your hand with snout using surprising force.

Inhabits washes, beaches, and loamy sandy soil. Susceptible to drying and must live where they can reach damp soil. Live-bearing.

CALIFORNIA LEGLESS LIZARD
Anniella pulchra

Pl. 40, Map 127

IDENTIFICATION: 4⅜–7 in. (11.1–17.8 cm). Although eyes are small, lids can be seen. Watch an individual in good light to see it blink. Generally silver or beige above, yellow below. Black middorsal line runs length of body; other lines are present on sides where dorsal and ventral colors join. However, variants occur with middorsal stripe faint or absent and lateral striping reduced. Skin looks polished. Dark brown or black individuals with contrasting yellow underparts found in several areas along Calif. coast (see Subspecies below). **Young:** Cream or silver above, light gray or pale yellow below.

Needs loose soil for burrowing (sand, loam, or humus), moisture, warmth, and plant cover. Frequents sparse vegetation of beaches, chaparral, pine-oak woodland, and streamside growth of sycamores, cottonwoods, and oaks. Occasionally enters desert scrub. Bush lupine and mock heather often grow in dune habitats where conditions are suitable. Burrows in washes, dune sand of beaches, and loose soil near bases of slopes and near permanent or temporary streams. Forages in leaf litter by day. May emerge on surface at dusk or at night. Look in leaf litter under overhang of trees and bushes on sunny slopes and under rocks, driftwood, logs, and boards. To uncover buried individuals, drag a stick through soil exposed when objects are turned over. Sometimes enters twig base of woodrat nests. Live-bearing; 1–4 young born Sept.–Nov. Eats insects (termites, small lepidopterans, beetles, insect larvae, etc.) and spiders. **RANGE:** From south shore San Joaquin R. near Antioch, Contra Costa Co., Calif. south in Coast Ranges, Transverse Mts., and Peninsular Ranges into nw. Baja Calif. to as far south as just south of Colonia Guerrero. Scattered occurrences on floor of San Joaquin Valley, in s. Sierra, Walker Basin, Ninemile Canyon, and in Paiute, Scodie, and Tehachapi Mts. On e. and s. Los Coronados and Todos Santos Is., Baja Calif. Desert-edge localities at e. end of Walker Pass, Kern Co.; Morongo Valley, San Bernardino Co., in Little San Bernardino

Mts. at Whitewater, Riverside Co., Calif., and on e. slope Peninsular Ranges. Occurs in Antelope Valley (Lancaster area) in extreme w. Mojave Desert. Coexists with Baja California Legless Lizard (Pl. 55; p. 428) at mouth of Rio Santo Domingo near Colonia Guerrero and lives next to it at Arroyo Pabellon. Occurrence spotty. Eliminated by agriculture in many parts of San Joaquin Valley, Calif. Old records from Redwood Canyon, Marin Co., San Francisco, and Palo Alto, Calif. Sea level to around 5,100 ft. (1,550 m).

SUBSPECIES: SILVERY LEGLESS LIZARD, *A. p. pulchra.* Silvery, gray, or beige above, with dark middorsal line. Yellow below, with fine lengthwise lines between scale rows. Animals from Porterville area, Tulare Co., have dark blotches on underparts. BLACK LEGLESS LIZARD, *A. p. nigra.* Black or dark brown above. Yellow below, without lengthwise lines or lines very faint or confined to tail. Young resemble Silvery Legless Lizard but darken with age. Found in beach dunes of Monterey Peninsula and southern coast Monterey Bay. Dark individuals (chocolate-colored above) also occur in coastal dunes from Morro Bay south to Guadalupe at mouth of Santa Maria R. These populations, however, are not regarded as members of subspecies *nigra.*

REMARKS: Extensive damage to populations of this lizard caused by agriculture, introduced exotic vegetation (iceplant, etc., in dunes), housing development, sandmining, golf courses, off-road vehicles (especially in coastal dune areas), trampling, and other human activities.

AJA CALIFORNIA LEGLESS LIZARD Pl. 55
nniella geronimensis

Relative of California Legless Lizard, endemic to Baja Calif. (see p. 428).

ENOMOUS LIZARDS:
AMILY HELODERMATIDAE

The Gila Monster (*Heloderma suspectum*), of sw. U.S. and nw. Mexico, and Mexican Beaded Lizard (*H. horridum*) of Pacific Coast of Mexico and Guatemala, the only living members of the family, are the only known venomous lizards. Large, heavy body, massive head, sausage-shaped tail, and short limbs with strong, curved claws. Dorsal surfaces are covered with small, round, closely set scales and patterned with contrasting markings of pink, orange, or yellow and black, suggesting colorful beadwork. The tail, a fat-storage organ, becomes slim in starved individuals.

Lives in deserts, wooded areas, and sometimes around farms in arid lands, often near washes and intermittent streams for access to water or damp soil. In captivity they sometimes completely immerse themselves. Active by day as well as at dusk and occasionally at night, they crawl with an awkward, lumbering gait. Approach with care because they may lash out and bite quickly. Venom produced in glands on outside of lower jaw is expelled into the mouth along grooves in teeth and injected by chewing. Thought to be used primarily as defense against predators, it perhaps may be used in subduing some prey.

Although formidable in appearance, these lizards are not dangerous unless molested or handled and should not be killed.

GILA MONSTER *Heloderma suspectum* **Pl. 25, Map 125**

IDENTIFICATION: 9–14 in. (22.8–35.5 cm). A large, heavy-bodied lizard with short *swollen tail* and gaudy pattern of black and pink, salmon, orange, or yellow. *Dorsal surfaces with beadlike scales;* belly scales (ventrals) squarish. Loose folds of skin on neck. Well-developed gular fold. Unusual among lizards in having 4th toe nearly as long as 3rd toe. Dark forked tongue flicks out in snake-like fashion.

Inhabits chiefly shrubby, grassy, and succulent desert; occasionally enters oak woodland. Frequents lower slopes of mountains and nearby plains and beaches (Sonora). Found in canyon bottoms or arroyos with permanent or intermittent streams. Seeks shelter in self-made or mammal burrows, woodrat nests, dense thickets, and under rocks and in other natural cavities. Seems to prefer rocky areas grown to scattered bushes. Often abroad at dusk or after dark following warm rains in summer. Diurnal, especially in spring (occasionally in winter). Chiefly ground-dwelling but occasionally climbs, perhaps in search of bird eggs and nestlings. Color pattern may function as warning coloration and/or aid concealment, especially under conditions of dim light. On dark backgrounds the black markings blend and the light markings look like sticks and rocks, while on pale backgrounds the disruptive dark markings may delay recognition of the animal's shape. Clutch of 2–12 (5) eggs, laid July–Aug. Eats small mammals including nestlings; eggs and nestlings chiefly of ground-nesting birds (quail, mourning doves); eggs of reptiles (including Desert Tortoise's); lizards, insects, and carrion. Kills its prey chiefly by the crushing action of its powerful jaws. Caution: The bite of these lizards is tenacious and extremely painful. Fortunately, it is doubtful if any person has been killed by the bite alone, at least not for a century. **RANGE:** Extreme sw. Utah to n. Sinaloa; sw. N.M. to Colorado R. In Calif. in the Paiute, Clark, Kingston and perhaps New York Mts. (sight record), San Bernardino Co. Old records for Providence Mts., San Bernardino Co., vicinity of Desert Center, in Chuckwalla Mts., Riverside Co., and Imperial Dam area, Imperial Co. on the Colorado R. May occur as far east in N.M. as Kilbourne Holen-Aden Crater area. A sight record (1987) a few miles southeast of Rincon tends to support this observation. Sea level to around 6,397 ft. (1,950 m).

SUBSPECIES: RETICULATE GILA MONSTER, *H. s. suspectum.* Adults mottled and blotched with black and pink, with black predominating on back of most individuals; reticulate pattern with crossbands nearly or completely obscure. Dark tail bands mottled, and mottling in light interspaces. BANDED GILA MONSTER, *H. s. cinctum.* Adults retain juvenile pattern. Four black saddles or irregular double crossbands on body. Tail with 5 dark bands, little or not at all mottled; mottling slight or absent in interspaces. Melanistic individuals with reduced pale crossbanding occur on dark lava flows.

REMARKS: It is illegal to collect the Gila Monster without a permit.

SNAKES

BLIND SNAKES: FAMILY LEPTOTYPHLOPIDAE

Sometimes called "worm snakes" because of their resemblance to earthworms, they are usually under 1½ ft. (47 cm) in length; brown, gray, or pink above, lighter below. Body is slender and cylindrical; no neck constriction. Scales almost all uniform in size, cycloid, smooth, and shiny and appear moist. No enlarged ventrals. Our species have a spine at tip of the tail. Eyes are vestigial, appearing as dark spots beneath the oculars. Teeth are scarce and confined to the lower jaw. The slender form, uniform scalation, and degenerate eyes distinguish them from all our other snakes.

Blind snakes are crevice dwellers and burrowers. They live in loose soil—sand, loam, or humus—and emerge on the surface at night or on overcast days. In our species the track is distinctive: regular lateral undulations that show signs of skidding, and in the latter respect differ from tracks of ground snakes. Tail spine leaves a fine wavy line. Blind snakes are susceptible to drying and generally live where there is damp subsoil. They feed on ants; ant eggs, larvae, and pupae; and on termites. They find ant nests by following the scented trails of their prey. The solidly constructed skull; smooth, tough scales; and slender form permit them to enter ant nests and to resist attacks of their prey. Our species are egg-layers.

The genus *Leptotyphlops,* with over 80 species, ranges from sw. and s.-cen. U.S. to Argentina, the West Indies, tropical Africa, and sw. Asia.

WESTERN BLIND SNAKE   Pl. 42, Map 128
Leptotyphlops humilis
   IDENTIFICATION: 7–16 in. (18–41 cm). A slim snake with no neck constriction and *blunt head and tail.* Eyes vestigial, appearing as

dark spots under head scales. Tiny spine at tip of tail. Scales shiny and cycloid, not enlarged on belly. *Single scale between oculars* (Fig. 19, Pl. 42, p. 118). Purplish, brown to nearly black (Malibu Creek area, s. Calif.), or pink above with a silvery sheen. Somewhat lighter below—cream, pink, purplish, or light gray.

Ranges from desert to brush-covered mountain slopes where soil is suitable for burrowing. Often frequents rocky hillsides with patches of loose soil, and canyon bottoms or washes near permanent or intermittent streams. Found in beach sand above the high-tide mark. Burrows among roots of shrubs, beneath rocks, and enters ant nests in search of prey. Eats small insects such as ants and their larvae and pupae, termites, and occasionally beetle larvae. Occasionally crawls exposed on surface at night, and sometimes can be found by night driving. By day, search crevices and soil under objects on the ground including rock flakes that lie flat on the ground or against boulders, especially where soil is slightly damp. Clutch of 2–6 eggs, laid July–Aug. SIMILAR SPECIES: Texas Blind Snake (below) usually has 3 scales between oculars (Fig. 19, p. 118), and 2 labials rather than 1 between ocular and lower nasal. RANGE: S. Nev. and sw. Utah south to Colima and tip of Baja Calif.; w. Tex. to coast of s. Calif. Perhaps isolated in Cottonwood-Sedona area, Yavapai Co., Ariz. Below sea level in desert sinks to around 5,000 ft. (1,520 m).

TEXAS BLIND SNAKE
Leptotyphlops dulcis

Fig. 19, opp. Pl. 42, Map 128

IDENTIFICATION: 5–11 ½ in. (12.7–28 cm). Close relative of Western Blind Snake (p. 340). Brown, pink, to reddish brown above, often with silvery sheen. Pale gray or pink below. *Usually more than 1 scale between the oculars* (Fig. 19, Pl. 42, p. 118) and usually 2 labial scales between ocular and lower nasal.

Habits similar to Western Blind Snake's. Lives in prairies, canyon bottoms, and rocky or sandy deserts; ranges into juniper–live oak and piñon-juniper plant communities. Found in crevices, among roots of trees and shrubs, under stones and other objects, and on roadways at night. Favors fine loose soil suitable for burrowing. Most commonly seen after spring and summer rains. Diet similar to Western Blind Snake's. Clutch of 2–7 eggs, laid June–July. Females tend eggs and may share underground nesting sites. SIMILAR SPECIES: See Western Blind Snake (p. 340). RANGE: S. Kans. to n. Hidalgo, Mex.; cen. Tex. to se. Ariz. Unconfirmed sighting for south of Mesa de Maya, Los Animas Co., Colo. Near sea level to around 6,800 ft. (2,100 m).

BOAS AND PYTHONS: FAMILY BOIDAE

Family contains the world's largest snakes as well as many smaller forms. Around 70 species. Found throughout tropics and subtropics of both hemispheres and extending well into temperate w. N. America. Generally heavy-bodied with smooth, glossy scales and vertical pupils. Vestiges of hind limbs are present and usually show externally, in male snakes especially, as small spur on each side of vent. Temperature-sensitive pits on labial scales helps them find and capture warm-blooded prey. Prey is killed by constriction. Pythons and their relatives are found chiefly in Old World and are oviparous. Boas occur in both New and Old Worlds and are live-bearing. Two species of boas occur in the West, the only members of family native to U.S. They are thick-bodied snakes, seldom more than 3 ft. (1 m) long, with a small head, small eyes, a blunt tail, and small, smooth scales. Ventrals (see rear endpaper) are reduced in transverse length. When alarmed, may roll into a ball, concealing head among the coils.

RUBBER BOA *Charina bottae*   **Pl. 42, Map 132**

IDENTIFICATION: 14–33 in. (35–84 cm). Stout-bodied; looks and feels like rubber. Known as "two-headed snake" because *tail is blunt and somewhat resembles a head.* Skin smooth and shiny, thrown into folds when body is bent sharply. Tail short and blunt. Dorsal scales small and smooth. *Top of head covered with large symmetrical plates.* Pupil vertically oval. No enlarged chin shields. Dark to light brown, pinkish tan, to olive green above; yellow, orange-yellow to cream below, often with no pattern, with a few dusky flecks

Rubber Boa. Note the blunt-tipped elevated tail that has given rise to the name "Two-headed Snake." When disturbed this snake may bury its head among body coils and wave its projecting tail.

on lower sides, or sometimes with extensive dark mottling on belly. Ventrals with dark flecks or mottling of brown, orange, or black at some northern localities. **Young:** Pinkish to tan above, belly light yellow, pink to cream. **Male:** Anal spurs usually present; small or absent in female.

Frequents grassland, broken chaparral, woodland, and forest, in and beneath rotting logs, under rocks, and under bark of fallen and standing dead trees. Can be active at surface temperatures in mid-50s F. Good swimmer, burrower, and climber. Eats small mammals (especially mice, pocket gophers, and shrews), birds, salamanders (including Ensatina and their eggs), and lizards and snakes. When feeding on nestling mice, is reputed to fend off parental attacks with "strikes" of its blunt, elevated tail. Live-bearing; 2–8 young born Aug.–Nov. May live 40 to 50 years or longer in the field. **RANGE:** Southern B.C. (Quesnel area) to s. Utah (to Panguitch Lake), cen. Nev., and s. Calif.; Pacific Coast to n.-cen. Wyo. (Bighorn Mts.). In s. Calif. at Mt. Pinos, Mt. Abel, and Tehachapi, San Bernardino, and San Jacinto Mts. Sight record for Echo Park, Moffat Co., Colo. Distribution spotty in more arid parts of range. Near sea level to around 10,000 ft. (3,050 m).
REMARKS: Boas of small size have been found in San Bernardino and San Jacinto Mts., in Mt. Pinos region, and in Tehachapi Mts., Calif. "Dwarfs" also found on Breckenridge Mt.; may be elsewhere in s. Sierra (Green-horn and Paiute Mts.).

Full species rank suggested for San Bernardino and San Jacinto Mts. boas.

ROSY BOA (THREE-LINED BOA)   Pl. 42, Map 131
Charina trivirgata

IDENTIFICATION: 17–44 in. (43–112 cm). Heavy-bodied; head only a little wider than neck. Scales smooth and shiny. Eyes small, pupils vertical. *No chin shields or large head plates,* except on snout. Most common dorsal pattern is 3 longitudinal dark stripes, a middorsal, and 1 on each side, separated by pale interspaces. Depending on locality, color of stripes varies from nearly black, through brown, orange, rust, to reddish. Interspaces vary from steel blue, shades of gray, tan, yellowish, cream, to nearly white. Interspaces may be variously intruded with darker stripe color. Dorsal stripes may have even or irregular edges. In coastal Calif. and nw. Baja Calif. there is reduction, sometimes to near loss, of distinctiveness between dorsal and lateral stripes resulting from irregularity of dorsal stripe borders and flecking between stripes. The contrasting, often even-edged patterns are associated with more arid environments. **Young:** Generally lighter than adult and pattern more distinct. **Male:** Anal spurs usually well developed.

Inhabits rocky shrublands and desert. Attracted to oases and permanent or intermittent streams, but does not require permanent water. Chiefly nocturnal but may be active at dusk and (rarely) in the daytime. A good climber. Search blacktop roads in rocky canyons or along rocky buttes or lower mountain slopes. Eats small mammals, reptiles, amphibians, and birds. Live-bearing; 3–14 young, born Oct.–Nov. **RANGE:** Death Valley region (Hanaupah Canyon), Panamint Mts., Calif., to tip of Baja Calif., and Guaymas, Sonora; coastal s. Calif. to s.-cen. Ariz. In San Gabriel, San Bernardino, and Little San Bernardino Mts. and in Peninsular Ranges of s. Calif. Absent from Coachella Valley southward, in extreme low desert. Distribution spotty, especially in lower arid parts of range. For example, although the species is expected, there currently appear to be no records for the area between the Panamint and Providence Mts. region in the e. Mojave Desert, Calif. On Cedros, Natividad, and Santa Margarita Is. off w. coast Baja Calif., and on Cerralvo, San Marcos, Angel de la Guardia, and Tiburón Is. in the gulf. Sea level to around 6,790 ft. (2,070 m). Question area in w. Ariz., shown as a range gap, is apparently mostly an intergrade zone of spotty distribution.

SUBSPECIES: COASTAL ROSY BOA, *C. t. roseofusca* (Pl. 42). Stripes of pink, reddish brown, or dull brown, with irregular borders; on a brownish, olive gray, gray, or bluish gray ground color. Stripe color may be present on scattered scales between the stripes or, occasionally, over all dorsal surfaces. Below predominantly dark. DESERT ROSY BOA, *C. t. gracia.* Prominent stripes of rose, reddish brown, or tan; even-edged and contrasting with gray or beige ground color. Stripes more distinct than in Coastal Rosy Boa. Spotting of stripe color seldom present between the stripes. Brown flecking below. Isolated populations in Cerbat, Harquahala, Harcuvar, Kofa, Castle Dome, Gila and other mountains in w. and sw. Ariz. MEXICAN ROSY BOA, *C. t. trivirgata* (Pl. 42). Contrasting lengthwise even-edged stripes of chocolate brown to black on cream or yellow background. Creamy white below with only occasional black flecks. Mostly under 30 in. (76 cm). S. Ariz. (Organ Pipe Cactus Nat'l Monument) to Guaymas, Sonora; south half of Baja Calif. MID-BAJA BOA, *C. t. saslowi.* Stripes chestnut, edges even to evenly serrated. Spaces between light gray. Below smoke gray, extending to lateral stripes. Differs from other subspecies in means of ventral, ocular, and subocular scales (means, respectively, 226, 20.8, and 0.9). Young have unmarked ventrals but may become spotted, barred, or mottled with age.

REMARKS: Species name Rosy Boa is based on pinkish or salmon color of ventrals, found in nw. Baja Calif. populations. Since most widespread pattern feature is the triad of dark dorsal longitudinal stripes, perhaps use of the describer's common name (E. D. Cope, 1861), the Three-lined Boa, might be considered.

COLUBRIDS: FAMILY COLUBRIDAE

Members of this large family occur on all continents except Antarctica. They outnumber snakes of all other families in their continental distributions except for Australia, where members of the family Elapidae, to which coral snakes, cobras, and kraits belong, are more numerous. The structure of colubrids varies greatly in relation to their highly diverse habits, which include terrestrial, burrowing, arboreal, and aquatic modes of life. The family is therefore difficult to characterize and probably does not represent a natural group. Head plates are usually large and symmetrical, and teeth may be solid or grooved toward back of jaw. No hollow fangs. Some species, the rear-fanged snakes, are venomous, but none in our area is dangerous to humans. About three-quarters of the snakes in the West belong to this family. About 700 species worldwide.

RING-NECKED SNAKE *Diadophis punctatus*   Pl. 46, Map 133

IDENTIFICATION: 8–34 in. (20.3–87 cm). Typically a slender olive, brownish, blue-gray, or nearly black snake with a dark head and *usually a conspicuous yellow, orange, or cream neck band.* Neck band is absent in some populations in s. N.M., Utah, and elsewhere or sometimes occurs as a partial collar. Yellow-orange to red below, the red intensifying on underside of tail. Belly usually spotted with black. Rarely, melanistic individuals are found that lack both neck band and orange ventral color, and have dark crossbars on belly. In the West and cen. U.S., *when alarmed, this snake coils its tail and turns up the underside, revealing the bright red color.* Ringnecks in most of e. U.S. lack bright red ventral tail

Ring-necked Snake. When disturbed this species displays the bright ventral color of its tail and releases a foul-smelling secretion from its anal scent glands. The secretion is considered repugnant to some predators.

color and generally do not display the tail. Scales smooth, usually in 15 or 17 rows at midbody. Loreal scale present. **Young:** Often dark above, sometimes nearly black. **Male:** Tubercles on scales above the vent (sometimes also present, but less prominent, in female).

A snake of moist habitats—woodland, forest, grassland, chaparral, farms, and gardens. In arid parts of the West, is restricted to mountains, springs, and watercourses where it may descend, in desert areas, to around 2,400 ft. (730 m). In Utah, ranges into upland habitats of aspen, maple, and fir. Seldom seen in the open. Usually found on the ground under bark, beneath and inside rotting logs, and under stones and boards. One, perhaps 2 clutches of 2–10 eggs, laid June–July, often in communal nest. Eats Slender and other salamanders, small frogs, tadpoles, lizards (including *Anniella*), small snakes, insects, slugs, and earthworms. May be venomous to small animal prey and perhaps some snake predators. Rear upper-jaw teeth enlarged but not grooved. **SIMILAR SPECIES:** (1) Black-headed Snakes (*Tantilla* species, pp. 397–404) usually have whitish or beige neckband, and lack black spots on belly; reddish color on belly is bordered on each side by pale gray, and there is no loreal scale. (2) See also Sharp-tailed Snake. **RANGE:** S. Wash. and Idaho to n. Baja Calif. and San Luis Potosí, Mex. Atlantic to Pacific Coasts. Distribution spotty. Some localities in the Northwest are: Snake R. drainage of se. Wash. and sw. (including Hell's Canyon) and se. Idaho; reported from Granite Range, Washoe Co., Nev.; reported along Grande Ronde R. near Troy, Wallowa Co., Ore. Some isolated localities in the Southwest are Catalina I., Clark and Providence Mts., Calif.; Hiko Springs, Newberry Mts., and Spring Mts., Clark Co., Nev.; Virgin Mts. and Fall Canyon, Grand Canyon, Mohave Co., Ariz. Near sea level to around 7,200 ft. (2,200 m).

SHARP-TAILED SNAKE *Contia tenuis*   **Pl. 46, Map 134**

IDENTIFICATION: 12–18 in. (30–46 cm). Reddish brown or gray above, tending toward reddish on tail. Often indistinct yellowish or reddish line on each upper side. Distinctively marked with *regular, alternating crossbars of black and cream or light gray below*. Scales smooth. Single preocular. Tail with sharp spine at tip. **Young:** Reddish above, fine dark lines on sides.

Frequents woodland, grassland, broken chaparral, and forest usually near streams. Often found in pastures or open meadows on edge of coniferous forests or among oaks in lower foothills. Has been found in gravel deposits. Occasionally lives in groups. A secretive snake of moist environments; abroad when ground is damp but keeping out of sight under logs, bark of standing and fallen trees, rocks, and other objects. Most likely to be found fol-

A hatchling Sharp-tailed Snake displaying defensive behavior involving concealment of the head within tight body coils. Bear Creek, Skamania Co., Wash.

lowing rains; retreats underground when the surface dries. May be active at low surface temperatures (50° F). Clutch of 2–8 eggs, probably laid June–July. Communal laying may occur. Apparently feeds mostly on slugs, and their eggs, for which its long, curved teeth are especially suited. Captives have eaten Slender Salamanders (*Batrachoseps*). **SIMILAR SPECIES:** Melanistic Ring-necked Snakes (p. 345) resemble the Sharp-tail, sometimes including the dark and light crossbars on belly, but are much darker above and lack tail spine. **RANGE:** B.C. (Metchosin, s. Vancouver I. and s. Gulf Is.) to s. Sierra Nevada (to Tulare Co.) and cen. coast (Pine Mt. and base of Cuesta Grade, near San Luis Obispo, San Luis Obispo Co.), Calif.; in Wash. along Yakima Canyon from Cle Elum to south of Ellensburg, Kittitas Co. and Leavenworth, Chelan Co.; n. end Gravelly Lake and Chambers Creek, Pierce Co.; at 4.2 mi. (6.7 km) northeast of Carson, Skamania Co., and at Lyle, Klickitat Co.; in Ore. at Tygh Valley and Rock Creek Reservoir, Wasco Co. Record for McGillivray Lake area near Chase, B.C., requires confirmation. Distribution spotty. Near sea level to around 6,600 ft. (2,010 m).
REMARKS: Long-tailed variety of this snake associated with coniferous forests of coastal Calif. and sw. Oregon. Appears to be a new species, and seems to occupy cooler, more sheltered and humid habitats than Short-tailed form.

WESTERN HOG-NOSED SNAKE   Pl. 47, Map 129
Heterodon nasicus
IDENTIFICATION: 15–36 in. (38–92 cm). A heavy-bodied, blotched snake with broad neck and upturned snout. Dark blotches extend from back of head onto tail. *Rostral much enlarged, spadelike, and*

keeled above. Prefrontals separated by small scales. Dorsal scales keeled. Anal divided. Much black pigment on underside of body and tail with contrasting patches of orange, yellow, or white. Enlarged ungrooved teeth toward rear of upper jaw. Mildly venomous. Venom used to subdue struggling prey.

Primarily an inhabitant of the Great Plains, it frequents sandy or gravelly prairies, open brushland and woodland, farmlands, and floodplains of rivers. In extreme western part of range it occurs in semidesert habitats and occasionally in mountain canyon bottoms or on floodplains of streams where loose soil is suitable for burrowing. Stream course may be canopied by deciduous broadleaf trees. The Hog-nose uses its shovel-shaped snout in digging and its enlarged teeth in holding and apparently deflating toads, a staple food. Also eats frogs, salamanders, lizards, snakes, turtles, birds, small mammals, and bird and reptile eggs. Observed following scent trails to turtle nest sites and using its snout to uncover eggs. Clutch of 4–25 eggs, laid June–Aug.

When disturbed, often spreads its head and neck and strikes with open mouth, hissing but seldom biting. This behavior has earned it the names "puff adder" or "blow snake." It may "play possum," suddenly turning belly up, writhing violently for a few moments, then lying still with its mouth open and tongue lolling. The tail, in a tight coil suggesting a head, is often held near the head and foul-smelling excrement is discharged. **SIMILAR SPECIES:** (1) Hooked-nosed Snakes (*Gyalopion* species, p. 396) have smooth dorsal scales, and the rostral is concave rather than keeled above. (2) Leaf-nosed (*Phyllorhynchus* species, p. 349) and (3) Patch-nosed Snakes (*Salvadora* species, pp. 356–58) have tip of rostral turned back between internasals instead of extending forward and free. (4) Eastern Hog-nosed Snake (*H. platyrhinos*), expected in e. Colo., lacks black on underside of tail, and prefrontals meet. **RANGE:** S. Canada to San Luis Potosí, Mex.; se. Ariz. to cen. Ill. Confirmation is desired for reports of this species in nw. Colo. near Maybell, Moffat Co. Near sea level to around 8,000 ft. (2,440 m).

SUBSPECIES: PLAINS HOG-NOSED SNAKE, *H. n. nasicus.* Nine or more small scales (azygous scales) in the group on top of head directly behind rostral. MEXICAN HOG-NOSED SNAKE, *H. n. kennerlyi.* Two–6 azygous scales.

REMARKS: Bite can cause local swelling in humans. A specimen of the Eastern Hog-nosed Snake (*Heterodon platirhinos*) was collected in 1943, 9 mi. (14.5 km) west of Lamar, Bent Co., Colo. None found there since, so species not included here. Specimens from extreme w. Kans. suggest snake may extend up Arkansas R. valley into Colo. Differs from Western Hog-nosed Snake in having underside of tail lighter than belly, rather than with masses of black.

SPOTTED LEAF-NOSED SNAKE
Pl. 47, Map 136
Phyllorhynchus decurtatus

IDENTIFICATION: 12–20 in. (30–51 cm). A pale, blotched snake with a blunt snout formed by *much enlarged rostral scale with free edges.* Pink, tan, yellowish, or pale gray above, with more than 17 middorsal brown blotches between back of head and region above vent. Blotches also extend onto tail. White below, unmarked. Pupils vertical. Dorsal scales smooth, except occasionally in males. Suboculars present. Rostral completely separates internasals. Anal single.

Secretive, nocturnal snake of sandy or gravelly desert. Most of range in U.S. corresponds closely with distribution of creosote bush. Appears to be quite common in saguaro-mesquite-creosote bush association in s. Ariz. Found on open desert plains. Modified rostral used in burrowing. Clutch of 2–6 eggs, presumably laid June–July. Eats small lizards, including Banded Geckos, and their eggs. Search roads at night; otherwise rarely encountered. **SIMILAR SPECIES:** (1) Saddled Leaf-nosed Snake (below) has fewer than 17 blotches on back (excluding tail). (2) Patch-nosed Snakes (*Salvadora* species, pp. 356–58), have striped pattern and internasals usually only partly separated by rostral. (3) In Western Hog-nosed Snake (p. 347), front end of rostral extends forward and is free. **RANGE:** From Inyo Co., Calif., and s. Nev. to tip of Baja Calif. and s. Sonora, Mex.; s.-cen. and sw. Ariz. mostly to desert base of mountains in s. Calif. Below sea level (in desert sinks) to around 4,000 ft. (1,219 m).

REMARKS: Occasionally coexists in rocky, gravelly desert foothills with Saddled Leaf-nosed Snake (below).

SADDLED LEAF-NOSED SNAKE
Pl. 47, Map 135
Phyllorhynchus browni

IDENTIFICATION: 12–20 in. (30–51 cm). Resembles Spotted Leaf-nosed Snake (above) in form and scalation, including enlarged rostral scale, but differs greatly in color. *Fewer than 17 large,* brown, dark-edged blotches (saddles) on back, excluding tail. Light color on head and between blotches, pink or cream. White below, without markings.

In northern part of range, inhabits desert scrub grown to mesquite, saltbush, creosote bush, palo verde, and saguaro cactus. In southern areas, frequents thornscrub and lower edge of thornforest. A burrower in relatively coarse, loose, rocky soils as well as in sandy gravelly areas. Nocturnal. Usually found only by patrolling highways at night. Most active after summer rains begin, especially on humid nights. Clutch of 2–6 eggs, probably laid in summer. Apparently eats chiefly lizards and their eggs. **SIMILAR SPECIES:** See Spotted Leaf-nosed Snake (above). **RANGE:** Vicinity of

Tucson west to Organ Pipe Cactus Nat'l Monument, Ariz.; s. base of Ariz. plateau (Phoenix-Superior region) to s.-cen. Sinaloa, Mex. From about 1,000–3,000 ft. (300–910 m).

SMOOTH GREEN SNAKE *Opheodrys vernalis* Pl. 46, Map 142

IDENTIFICATION: 11–32 in. (28–81 cm). A slender snake, plain green above and white or yellowish below, often becoming bright yellow on underside of tail. Dorsal color changes to dull blue or gray upon death. *Dorsal scales smooth*, in 15 rows at midbody. Single anterior temporal scale. Each nostril centered in a single scale. Anal divided. **Young:** Dark olive gray above. Hatchlings slate gray to brown above.

Ranges from prairies to open damp grassy areas in forests. In the West it inhabits meadows, stream borders, and rocky habitats interspersed with grass, usually in upland areas. Secretive and chiefly ground-dwelling, but occasionally climbs bushes. Well-camouflaged in green plant growth. Several females may share a favorable nest site. Clutch of 2–12 (7) eggs, laid June–Sept., sometimes hatching within a few days after laying. Eats insects (including caterpillars and crickets) and spiders. **SIMILAR SPECIES:** (1) Greenish examples of Racers (p. 351) have 2 anterior temporals, lower preocular is wedged between upper labials, and each nostril is located between 2 scales. (2) Green Rat Snake (p. 359) has 25 or more rows of dorsal scales; middorsal rows are weakly keeled along middle of back. **RANGE:** Fairly continuous in the east but becomes increasingly fragmented in the west; many disjunct populations. Ranges from s. Canada to w.-cen. Va. and cen. Mo. and cen. Neb. to Atlantic Coast in e. part of range, and from sw. Sask. to Chihuahua, Mex., and ne. Utah to w. S.D. in the West. Isolated populations in se. Tex., probably introduced. Near sea level to around 9,500 ft. (2,900 m).

RACERS AND WHIPSNAKES:
GENERA *Coluber* AND *Masticophis*

Slender, fast-moving, diurnal snakes with broad head, large eyes, and slender neck. *Lower preocular wedged between upper labials* (Fig. 7, Pl. 7, p. 31). Adult racers (genus *Coluber*) are usually plain-colored above, and young are blotched. They range from s. Canada to Guatemala. Related species occur in Asia, Europe, and N. Africa. Whipsnakes (genus *Masticophis*) are striped or more or less crossbarred, and young generally resemble adults. Some 7 species occur in New World from Canada to n. S. America; 5 species occur in our area.

When hunting, these snakes commonly crawl with head held high and occasionally moving from side to side, perhaps to aid depth perception. Prey is seized with great speed, crushed with the jaws, or pinioned under loops of the body and engulfed without constriction. Can be aggressive, striking vigorously when cornered and biting when handled. When held by the neck with body dangling, may thrash with such force as to nearly jerk free. Most are good climbers and when pursued may escape by climbing shrubs or trees.

RACER *Coluber constrictor* Pl. 43, Map 141

IDENTIFICATION; 20–75 in. (51–190 cm); in our area usually under 36 in. (91 cm). A slim snake with large eyes and smooth scales, in 15–17 rows at midbody (15 rows just in front of vent). Lower preocular wedged between upper labials. Anal divided. In the West this snake is *plain brown, olive, or bluish above,* and unmarked whitish or pale yellow below. Bluish dorsal coloration predominates in region south of Great Lakes, black (including belly) in the East and Southeast, and light-colored speckling in e. Tex. and La. **Young:** Brown saddles on back, smaller blotches on sides, fading on tail. Faint blotching sometimes evident in our area in individuals 1 ½ ft. (45–60 cm) long.

In the West this snake favors open habitats—meadows, prairies, sagebrush flats, open chaparral, piñon-juniper woodland, and forest glades. Found in both semiarid and moist environments, but absent from extremely dry areas and usually from high mountains. Often found in grassy places near rocks, logs, and other basking sites sought by lizards, upon which it feeds, or in grass of streambanks. Chiefly ground-dwelling, but may climb shrubs and trees. Clutch of 2–31 eggs, laid June–Aug. (Western Yellow-bellied Racer, below, lays 3–11 eggs). Communal laying may occur. Eats small mammals, birds and their eggs, reptiles (snakes, lizards, hatchling turtles), frogs, and insects (crickets, grasshoppers, caterpillars). **SIMILAR SPECIES:** (1) Young resemble young of Gopher Snake (p. 361), but have smooth scales and wedged preocular (Fig. 7, Pl. 7, p. 31). (2) Night Snake (p. 403) has vertical pupils. (3) See also Smooth Green Snake (p. 350). **RANGE:** From s. B.C. (interior dry belt) and s. Sask. to Guatemala; Pacific to Atlantic Coasts. Distribution spotty in s. Calif. in w. Riverside, e. Orange, and s. San Diego Co.; where found, may be quite abundant. Old record for Santa Cruz I. off s. Calif. coast. Isolated populations in mountains and river valleys in arid Southwest—at St. George, Utah; Boulder Dam, Nev.; and Eagar, Apache Co., Ariz. Reported from 3.5 mi. (5.6 km) upstream from Gardiner, Mont., in Yellowstone Nat'l Park on Yellowstone R. Trail. Presence needs confirmation. Sea level to around 8,300 ft. (2,550 m).

SUBSPECIES: WESTERN YELLOW-BELLIED RACER, *C. c. mormon.* Usually 8 upper labials. Eighty-five or more caudals. Young have 70–85 dorsal blotches. EASTERN YELLOW-BELLIED RACER, *C. c. flaviventris.* Usually 7 upper labials. Usually fewer than 85 caudals. In some parts of range, belly is bright lemon yellow. Young have 65–80 dorsal blotches.

REMARKS: Western Yellow-bellied populations in w. Mont. appear to be separated from those in Idaho although there may be a connection (not yet found) along Clark Fork R. area.

COACHWHIP *Masticophis flagellum* Pl. 43, Map 138

IDENTIFICATION: 36–102 in. (91–260 cm). The *wedged lower preocular* (Fig. 7, Pl. 7, p. 31), *smooth scales in 17 rows at midbody* (13 or fewer just before vent), *and lack of well-defined lengthwise stripes* are diagnostic. Coloration highly variable (see Subspecies). Throughout most of our area, general tone above is tan, gray, cream, pink, or red, usually with black crossbars on neck. Occasional individuals are black. Slender body and tail, and scalation suggesting a braided whip, have earned common name. Usually 2 or 3 anterior temporals. Anal divided. **Young:** Blotched or crossbanded with dark brown or black on a light brown background. Black neck markings may be present or faint or absent.

Frequents a variety of habitats—desert, prairie, scrubland, juniper-grassland, woodland, thornforest, and farmland. Generally avoids dense vegetation. Ground surface may be flat or hilly, sandy or rocky. More tolerant than most snakes of dry, warm environments, hence abroad by day in hot weather even in deserts. Crawls with great speed, often taking refuge in a rodent burrow, among rocks, or in branches of a bush where it may defend itself with spirit, hissing and striking repeatedly, and sometimes approaching aggressively. When caught it usually attempts to bite; large individuals can severely lacerate the skin. Clutch of 4–20 eggs, laid June–July. Eats small mammals (sometimes including bats), birds and their eggs, lizards, snakes (including rattlers), frogs, young turtles, insects, and carrion. **Range:** S. half of U.S. from coast to coast. In our area from Sutter Buttes, Sutter Co., and near Arbuckle, Colusa Co., Calif. south, chiefly in inner coast range, and widely throughout s. Calif. and Baja Calif.; Winnemucca Lake Basin, Nev., south through cen. and s. Ariz. to nw. Sinaloa, Mex.; se. Colo. and N.M. except nw. part, south through Mex. to Queretaro. Record from near Felton, Santa Cruz Co., Calif., needs confirmation. Below sea level (in desert sinks) to around 8,250 ft. (2,515 m).

SUBSPECIES: Among the following subspecies, the Red Racer, Sonoran, and Baja California Coachwhips have a dark phase. Some localities where this phase has been found are shown with black squares within their ranges on Map 138. RED RACER, *M. f. piceus* (Pl. 43). Reddish or pinkish above, often grading to tan toward the tail. Wide black, dark brown, or pink crossbands on neck, sometimes more or less united, may be faint or absent. *Dark phase* (called Western Black Coachwhip): Black above. Pale below, or more or less blackened, becoming salmon pink to red toward tail. Found in s-cen. Ariz.; outnumbers red phase around Tucson. Young with dark crossbands about 3 scales wide. LINED COACHWHIP, *M. f. lineatulus.* Tan or light gray above, sometimes pinkish toward rear, each dorsal scale toward front of body with lengthwise streak. Salmon pink below, toward tail. Often yellowish to tan collar mark. Young with dark crossbands about 1 scale wide and a pale collar mark. Intergrades with Central Coachwhip (next subspecies) usually grayish or brown above, have fainter scale markings, and yellowish ventral color. WESTERN COACHWHIP (CENTRAL COACHWHIP), *M. f. testaceus.* Tan, brown, pinkish to red above with dark, narrow crossbands on neck (sometimes absent), may continue far toward rear. Some individuals are light-colored and lack pattern, others have a few broad (10–15 scales wide) crossbands. Cream below, with a double row of dark spots. Red phase most common in e. Colo., n. and e. N.M., and w. Tex. SAN JOAQUIN COACHWHIP, *M. f. ruddocki* (Pl. 43). Light yellow, olive brown, or occasionally reddish above with a few faint or no neck bands. May be light tan below. SONORAN COACHWHIP, *M. f. cingulum.* Coloration highly variable—wide dark red or reddish brown crossbands above, separated by narrower light pink interspaces (common color phase in our area); also plain pink, reddish brown, tan, or black; rarely only a pale collar band is present. Some individuals black above toward the front and reddish toward the rear. Dark individuals pink to salmon below, toward the rear. BAJA CALIFORNIA COACHWHIP, *M. f. fuliginosus.* Two color phases. *Dark phase:* Dark grayish brown above with light lines on sides, especially toward front. *Light phase:* Pale to dark yellow, tan, or light gray above with dark zigzag crossbands on body and wider dark bands on neck. Light phase common in cape region. Since so far there appears to be no clear indication that this coachwhip and the Red Racer intergrade at points of contact (see Map 138), they may have reached the species level of relationship.

CALIFORNIA WHIPSNAKE (STRIPED RACER)
Masticophis lateralis   **Pl. 43, Map 137**

IDENTIFICATION: 30–60 in. (76–152 cm). Plain black or dark brown above; lighter on tail. *Conspicuous pale yellow or whitish stripe on each side* (often orange in e. San Francisco Bay area), extending from back of head to or beyond vent. Whitish, cream, pale yellow, or orange below, becoming coral pink on underside of tail. Dorsal scales smooth, in 17 rows at midbody. Wedged lower preocular. Anal divided.

The "chaparral snake" of Calif. Favorite haunts are scrublands broken by scattered grassy patches, and rocky hillsides, gullies, canyons, or stream courses. Chiefly of the foothills, but in mountains into mixed deciduous and pine forests. Ranges onto open flatland desert in cen. Baja Calif. Active diurnal species that may be seen foraging with head held high. Sometimes climbs into vegetation or seeks shelter among rocks or in a burrow. Clutch of 6–11 eggs, laid May–July. Eats frogs, lizards, snakes (including rattlers), small mammals, birds, and insects. Lizards (particularly Spiny Lizards—*Sceloporus*) are especially important in diet. **SIMILAR SPECIES:** (1) Striped Whipsnake (below) has 15 scale rows at midbody and each light lateral stripe is bisected by a black line or series of dashes. (2) Sonoran Whipsnake (p. 355) has 2 or 3 light stripes on each side that fade out before reaching tail, and venter is pale yellow toward tail. **RANGE:** From n. Calif. (near Dunsmuir, Siskiyou Co.), west of Sierran crest and desert, to Cañon de Los Reyes in s. Baja Calif. Isolated locality at Misíon Santa Maria, Baja Calif. Norte. Apparently absent from floor of Great Valley except in northern part. In s. Calif. ranges to desert foothills. From near sea level to around 7,400 ft. (2,250 m).

SUBSPECIES: CHAPARRAL WHIPSNAKE, *M. l. lateralis* (Pl. 43). Stripes cream or yellow, 2 half-scale rows wide. ALAMEDA WHIPSNAKE, *M. l. euryxanthus* (Pl. 43). Stripes and anterior ventral surface orange. Stripes broad, 1 and 2 half-scale rows wide.

CAPE WHIPSNAKE
Masticophis aurigulus
Pl. 56, Maps 137, 202

Close relative of California Whipsnake confined to cape region of Baja Calif. (see p. 429).

STRIPED WHIPSNAKE *Masticophis taeniatus* Pl. 43, Map 139

IDENTIFICATION; 30–72 in. (76–183 cm). Close relative of California Whipsnake (above). In our area black, dark brown, or gray above,

Striped Whipsnake. This snake meets the California Whipsnake in extreme nw. Calif. Careful study of their relationship in this area may show them to be conspecific. Owyhee Co., Idaho.

often with olive or bluish cast. *Dark longitudinal stripe centered on each of first four pale dorsal scale rows (counted from ends of ventrals).* Cream to yellowish below, grading to white toward head and coral pink toward tail. Stripes may be yellow in northwestern part of range. Individuals from east of Wasatch Mts. in ne. Utah and nw. Colo. tend toward pale coloration and, toward s. and se. of range, color darkens (Edwards Plateau, Tex.), but again pales in the Chihuahuan Desert, Mex. Dorsal scales smooth, in *15 rows at midbody.* Lower preocular wedged between upper labial scales. Anal divided.

Frequents shrublands, grasslands, sagebrush flats, and canyons, piñon-juniper woodland, and open pine-oak forests. Often attracted to rocky stream courses, permanent and intermittent. Frequents both flatlands and mountains. Alert, fast-moving, diurnal; seeks shelter in rock outcrops, rodent burrows, and in trees and shrubs. Clutch of 3–12 eggs, laid June–July. Eats lizards, snakes (including rattlers), small mammals, young birds, frogs, and insects. **SIMILAR SPECIES:** See (1) Striped Racer (p. 353) and (2) Sonoran Whipsnake (below). **RANGE:** S.-cen. Wash. south in Great Basin between Cascade-Sierran crest and Continental Divide, thence southeast across Divide in N.M. into w. and cen. Tex.; south to se. Michoacan, Mex. Occurs west of Cascade Mts. in sw. Oregon in Rouge R. Valley and n. Calif. (to near Mugginsville and near junction of north and south forks of Salmon R., Siskiyou Co.). Sea level to 10,100 ft. (3,077 m), in White Mts., Inyo Co., Calif.

SUBSPECIES: DESERT STRIPED WHIPSNAKE, *M. t. taeniatus*, occurs in our area.

SONORAN WHIPSNAKE   Pl. 43, Map 140
Masticophis bilineatus

IDENTIFICATION: 24–67 in. (61–170 cm). Olive, greenish, bluish gray, or light gray-brown above; lighter on rear 2/3 of body. *Paired pale spots on anterior corners of dorsal scales. Usually 2 or 3 light-colored stripes on each side, fading rapidly toward tail.* Cream below, becoming pale yellow toward tail. Dorsal scales smooth, *usually in 17 rows at midbody.* Wedged lower preocular between upper part of upper labial scales. Anal divided.

Ranges from semiarid lower mountain slopes, with growth of grass, saguaro cactus, palo verde, and ocotillo through chaparral and juniper into pine-oak belt in mountains. Attracted to rocky stream courses. Both terrestrial and arboreal, climbing gracefully in bushes and trees. Clutch of 4–13 eggs, laid June–July. Eats birds, small mammals, lizards, snakes, and frogs. **SIMILAR SPECIES:** Striped Whipsnake (p. 354) is darker above, usually has 15 scale

Sonoran Whipsnake. This attractive snake reaches our area only in Ariz. and extreme sw. N.M. Like other whipsnakes, it has excellent binocular vision and usually catches its prey with a burst of speed.

rows at midbody, 4 conspicuous lengthwise dark lines on each side, and pink color on underside toward tail. **RANGE:** Cen. Ariz. and extreme sw. N.M., south through Colima, Mex. On Tiburón and San Esteban Is. in Gulf of Calif. From near sea level to around 7,500 ft. (2,290 m).

PATCH-NOSED SNAKES: GENUS *Salvadora*

Slim, fast, chiefly diurnal, with broad longitudinally striped patterns and generally smooth scales. Keels may appear on a few scales above the vent region in adult males and large females. Found chiefly in open arid to semiarid habitats. May strike spiritedly when threatened and vibrate tail. Named for enlarged rostral scale that may help them dig into loose soil in search of reptile eggs upon which they feed. Also eat lizards, snakes, and small mammals. Range from Calif. and n. Nev. to Tex. and south to Chiapas, Mex. Two species in our area.

WESTERN PATCH-NOSED SNAKE   Fig. 21, Pl. 47, Map 143
Salvadora hexalepis
IDENTIFICATION: 20–46 in. (51–117 cm). Slender, with a broad yellow, tan, or beige, dark-bordered middorsal stripe and a large, patchlike rostral. Middorsal stripe, except where it widens on neck, usually 3 scales wide (or nearly so); occasionally faint or obscured by crossbands. Dark stripe on side, to rear of neck region, usually on 3rd scale row. Plain white below, sometimes washed with dull orange, especially toward tail. *Two to 3 small scales between rear pair of chin shields. Nine upper labials, none or 1 or 2 of*

which sometimes reach eye. Dorsal scales smooth. Anal divided. **Male:** Keeled scales above vent and at base of tail. Keeling weak or absent in female.

Active diurnal resident of grasslands, chaparral, sagebrush plains, piñon-juniper woodland, and desert scrub. Found in both sandy and rocky areas on lower slopes of mountains and on low, dry mesquite, catsclaw, creosote bush plains, often in most extreme parts of desert. Crawls rapidly, like a whipsnake. Chiefly ground-dwelling, but occasionally climbs into vegetation. Clutch of 4–12 eggs, probably laid May–Aug. Eats small mammals, lizards, reptile eggs, and nestling birds. **SIMILAR SPECIES:** (1) Mountain Patch-nosed Snake (below) usually has 8 upper labials, and rear pair of chin shields either touch or are separated by a single small scale. (2) Rostral in Leaf-nosed Snakes (p. 349) more often completely separates internasals; back is blotched or crossbanded, rather than usually striped; and anal is single. **RANGE:** Nw. Nev. (Winnemucca Lake Basin and Black Rock Desert) and Honey Lake Basin, Lassen Co., Calif. se. through sw. Utah, Ariz., s. N.M. to Big Bend area of Tex. and to s. Sinaloa and Chihuahua, Mex. Farther west, ranges in coastal Calif. from n. end of Carrizo Plains to tip of Baja Calif. Isolated occurrence at Carlsbad Nat'l Park in se. New Mex. From below sea level (in desert sinks) to around 7,000 ft. (2,130 m).

SUBSPECIES: DESERT PATCH-NOSED SNAKE, *S. h. hexalepis.* One upper labial reaches eye. Loreal divided. Top of head gray. Median stripe 3 scale rows wide. COAST PATCH-NOSED SNAKE, *S. h. virgultea.* Like previous subspecies, but top of head brown, and dorsal stripe narrower—1 and 2 half-scale rows wide. Sides may be dark, including all but lowermost 1 or 2 scale rows. Usually 1 upper labial reaches eye. Loreal usually divided into 2–4 scales. MOJAVE PATCH-NOSED SNAKE, *S. h. mojavensis.* Upper labials usually fail to reach eye. Dorsal pattern of stripes sometimes vague or broken up and, around edges of range and especially in eastern part, crossbars obscure stripes. BAJA CALIFORNIA PATCH-NOSED SNAKE, *S. h. klauberi.* Two upper labials usually reach eye. Loreal often divided. Light middorsal stripe 3 scales wide; stripe extends onto top of head. Lower lateral stripe well defined, on 3rd and 4th scale rows. BIG BEND PATCH-NOSED SNAKE, *S. h. deserticola.* Two upper labials usually reach eye. Loreal usually single. Narrow dark stripe on 4th scale row (and sometimes including part of 3rd scale row) may shift to 3rd scale row toward front and rear.

MOUNTAIN PATCH-NOSED SNAKE   **Fig. 21, Pl. 47, Map 145**
Salvadora grahamiae
IDENTIFICATION: 22–47 in. (56–119 cm). White, gray, yellowish, or pale orange middorsal stripe that in our area is 3 (or nearly so)

scale rows wide; stripe lighter than sides and bordered on each side by a brown to nearly black stripe 2 or more scale rows wide. Some individuals may have faint narrow dark line on 3rd scale row. Plain white or yellowish below, sometimes with pinkish cast toward tail. *Rear pair of chin shields touch or are separated by 1 or 2 small scales. Eight upper labials.* Dorsal scales smooth. Anal divided.

A snake of rough terrain—rocky canyons, plateaus, and mountain slopes. In the West it lives chiefly in open woodland and forests in mountains (within general range of Big Bend Patch-nosed Snake, but usually at higher elevations, above 4,000 ft. [1,220 m]). In more humid eastern part of range, inhabits prairies, shrublands, and lowlands to sea level (s. Tex. and Mex.). Clutch of around 5–10 eggs, laid April–June. Eats lizards, small snakes, reptile eggs, nestling birds, and small mammals. **SIMILAR SPECIES:** (1) Big Bend Patch-nosed Snake, a subspecies of the Western Patch-nosed Snake that overlaps it in range, has 4 dark lines on dorsum, outermost ones on the 4th scale row throughout midbody, and posterior pair of chin shields in contact or separated by 1 or 2 small scales. (2) See also Western Patch-nosed Snake (p. 356). **RANGE:** Se. Ariz., n.-cen. N.M., and cen. Tex. to Hidalgo, Mex. Isolated population at Oak Creek Canyon, Ariz. Sea level to over 6,500 ft. (1,980 m) but in West seldom below 4,500 ft. (1,370 m). Distribution spotty.

SUBSPECIES: PLATEAU PATCH-NOSED SNAKE, *S. g. grahamiae,* occurs in our area.

RAT SNAKES: GENERA *Elaphe*, *Senticolis*, AND *Bogertophis*

Moderately slender snakes with flattened bellies, an adaptation for climbing. Although most spend much time on the ground, they readily ascend trees, cliffs, and other elevated surfaces; the flattened venter (most other snakes have a rounded belly), forming an angle at the sides, aids in grasping surface irregularities. Vary greatly in color, having both blotched and longitudinally striped patterns, depending upon species. Scales along back weakly keeled; elsewhere smooth. Anal plate divided. Often vibrates tail when annoyed. Kills prey by constriction. Five species in N. America, 3 in our area. Rat Snakes range south to Costa Rica. Also represented in the Old World.

CORN SNAKE *Elaphe guttata*   Pl. 45, Map 148
IDENTIFICATION: 18–72 in. (46–183 cm). Long, slender, usually light gray with dark-edged brown to olive-brown or dark gray blotches on back, and a pair of dark, lengthwise neck blotches that usually

unite to form a *spear point between the eyes.* Usually a distinct eye stripe. In the north, blotches are especially numerous and narrow. Belly with squarish black markings that usually merge to form stripes on underside of tail. In eastern part of range, blotches usually reddish with dark borders and ground color often reddish or orange. *Dorsal scales in 25–31 rows at midbody,* mostly smooth but weakly keeled on back. Ventral surface flat, forming an angle with the sides, which helps the snake climb. Anal divided.

Occurs in a variety of habitats — along stream courses and river bottoms, on rocky wooded hillsides, in canyons and arroyos, and in coniferous forests. May be found on farms. Climbs well, but is usually found on the ground. Secretive; spends much time in rodent burrows. Nocturnal during warm weather. Look beneath logs, rocks, and other objects, in caves, and on highways at night. When caught it often voids feces and the contents of its anal scent glands. Clutch of 3–37 (up to 16 more common) eggs, laid May–July. Eats small mammals (including rodents and bats), birds and their eggs, lizards, and frogs, which it usually kills by constriction. **SIMILAR SPECIES:** (1) Trans-Pecos Rat Snake (p. 360) has suboculars and H-shaped dorsal blotches. (2) Green Rat Snake (below) in our area is greenish above, with or without a faint pattern, and plain whitish below. Spotted young lack spear point on head. See also (3) Glossy Snake (p. 362), (4) Gopher Snake (p. 361), and (5) Common Water Snake (p. 372). **RANGE:** E. Utah and cen. N.M. to Atlantic and Gulf Coasts; s. Neb. to s. Coahuila and San Luis Potosí. In w. Colo. and e. Utah, found in major valleys of Colorado R., including Green R. near Colo. border, Uintah Co., Utah. Introduced in Bahamas. Sea level to around 7,218 ft. (2,200 m).
SUBSPECIES: GREAT PLAINS RAT SNAKE (*E. g. emoryi*) occurs in our area.
REMARKS: The western (*E. g. emoryi*) and eastern (*E. g. guttata*) populations of this snake, here treated as subspecies, may prove to be full species.

GREEN RAT SNAKE *Senticolis triaspis*   **Pl. 45, Map 149**
IDENTIFICATION: 24–50 in. (61–127 cm). In our area and over much of range, this is a *slim, plain green, greenish gray, or olive snake with unmarked, whitish or cream underparts* tinged with yellow. (Adults blotched on Yucatán Peninsula, Mex.). *Twenty-five or more dorsal scale rows,* weakly keeled along middle of back. Anal divided. **Young:** Hatchings tan above, with brown blotches.

In our area this species is primarily a mountain snake that frequents wooded, rocky canyon bottoms near streams. Occurs in woodland, thornscrub, and chaparral. Plants may include pine, oak, sycamore, walnut, cottonwood, wild grape, and willow.

Habits are little known; appears to spend much time during the day in trees or shrubs, but also evidently spends considerable time on the ground, retiring at night into rock crevices and other underground retreats. Its slender form and color help conceal it among plants. Clutches of 2–7 eggs. Eats rodents (woodrats), other small mammals, lizards, and birds. **SIMILAR SPECIES:** (1) Smooth Green Snake (p. 350) has smooth dorsal scales, in 15–17 rows at midbody. See also (2) Great Plains Rat Snake (above) and (3) Lyre Snake (p. 403). **RANGE:** Se. Ariz. and s. Tamaulipas, southward along slopes of Mexican highlands to Costa Rica. In Ariz. in Baboquivari, Pajarito, Santa Rita, Empire, Whetstone, and Chiricahua Mts.; in N.M. in Peloncillo Mts. Near sea level to around 7,000 ft. (2,130 m).

SUBSPECIES: NORTHERN GREEN RAT SNAKE, *S. t. intermedia,* occurs in our area.

REMARKS: Generic name refers to snakes' exceptionally large hemipenial spines.

BAJA CALIFORNIA RAT SNAKE Pl. 56, Map 202
Bogertophis rosaliae

Mostly endemic to Baja California (see p. 429).

TRANS-PECOS RAT SNAKE Pl. 45, Map 150
Bogertophis subocularis

IDENTIFICATION: 34–66 in. (86–168 cm). The "H-snake," named for its *dorsal pattern of black or dark brown H-shaped blotches,* with pale centers on a yellowish olive or yellowish tan background. Sides of H's may join to form lengthwise stripes down each side, especially toward head. Olive-buff below, becoming white on neck and throat. Dorsal scales in 31–35 rows at midbody, weakly keeled along middle of back. Head broad, body slender, eyes large. *A row of small scales (suboculars) below eye and preocular.* Anal divided.

Primarily nocturnal, of arid and semiarid habitats, found in the following plant associations—agave, creosote bush, acacia, and ocotillo; persimmon, shin oak, and cedar; yucca, mesquite, and cactus. Seems to prefer rocky areas with deep underground retreats. Chiefly an inhabitant of Chihuahuan Desert. Clutch of 3–7 eggs, laid June–Aug. Eats small mammals (rodents, including nestlings, bats), birds, and lizards; large prey killed by constriction. **SIMILAR SPECIES:** See (1) Corn Snake (p. 358), and (2) Lyre Snake (p. 403). **RANGE:** Southern N.M. to s. Coahuila. In w. Tex. in Apache, Guadalupe, Davis, and Chisos Mts. and sw. edge Edwards Plateau. From around 1,500–5,250 ft. (460–1,600 m).

IDENTIFICATION: 30–110 in. (76–279 cm). In our area, large, yellow or cream-colored, with black, brown, or reddish brown dorsal blotches, usually more widely spaced on tail than body. Some populations have tan or reddish orange in dorsal interspaces between blotches. Smaller secondary blotches on sides. *Usually a dark stripe across the head in front of eyes and from behind eye to the angle of jaw.* White to yellowish below, often spotted with black. Longitudinally striped-unblotched and striped-blotched individuals found occasionally, chiefly in cen. and w.-cen. Calif. *Middorsal scales keeled, in 27–37 rows* at midbody. *Usually 4 (2–6) prefrontals.* Anal single.

Lives in variety of habitats, from lowlands high into mountains. Frequents desert, prairie, brushland, woodland, open coniferous forest, and farmland. In the West, especially common in grassland and open brushland. Soil conditions vary — sand, loam, rock, or hardpan. A good climber and burrower, active chiefly by day except in hot weather. When aroused it hisses loudly and sometimes flattens and broadens its head and vibrates its tail. In dry leaves, vibrating tail may sound like a rattler. This behavior, along with its markings, sometimes diamond-shaped, causes these snakes to be mistaken for rattlesnakes and killed. One to 2 clutches of 2–24 eggs, laid June–August. Eats rodents, rabbits, moles, birds and their eggs and nestlings, and occasionally lizards and insects. Kills chiefly by constriction. **SIMILAR SPECIES:** (1) Blotched young of Racer (p. 351) resemble Gopher Snake, but they have smooth scales and large eyes. (2) Glossy Snake (p. 362) has smooth scales. (3) Corn Snake (p. 358) has a divided anal. See also (4) Western Lyre Snake (p. 403). **RANGE:** Pacific Coast east to Ind. and e.-cen. Tex. and from s. B.C., s. Alta., and sw. Sask., to n. mainland Mex. and tip of Baja Calif. On following islands: Channel Is. and Catalina I., off coast of s. Calif.; Coronado Is., San Martín, Cedros, Magdalena, and Santa Margarita Is. off w. coast Baja Calif., and San Jose and Tiburón Is. in Gulf of Calif. Formerly on Galiano I, B.C. (1800s). Below sea level (in desert sinks) to around 9,186 ft. (2,800 m).

SUBSPECIES: BULLSNAKE, *P. c. sayi.* Rostral narrow, much higher than wide, raised well above nearby scales. Snout somewhat pointed when viewed from above. 33–66 black, brown, or rusty body blotches, 9–19 black tail spots. Bases of light interblotch scales dark. Ground color pale to light yellow. Nape heavily spotted with black. 29–37 midbody scale rows. SONORAN GOPHER SNAKE, *P. c. affinis.* Rostral sharply rounded in front, raised only slightly, if at all, above nearby scales. 34–63 anteriorly unconnected, biconcave saddles, brown or rusty anteriorly (black in montane areas) and darkening toward rear. 9–21 tail blotches.

Bases of anterior interblotch scales dark. Nape tan or yellow with small black spots. 31 or 33 (29–35) midbody scale rows. Narrowly sympatric apparently without intergradation with San Diego Gopher Snake in s. Calif. However, in Paso de San Matias, Baja Cailf., apparent intergrades have been found. GREAT BASIN GOPHER SNAKE, *P. c. deserticola*. Snout blunt, rostral slightly rounded. 43–71 quadrangular body blotches, black anteriorly and dark to reddish brown toward rear, joined on neck, and to secondary blotches on sides of neck often forming a lateral dark band, leaving interspaces as pale dorsal blotches. 12–22 black tail spots. Dark keels on anterior interblotched spaces. Ground color cream to yellow. Nape pale in south, heavily mottled in north. Thirty-one (27–35) midbody scale rows. PACIFIC GOPHER SNAKE, *P. c. catenifer*. Rostral bluntly rounded. 47–90 square, brown, or black body blotches (lower counts occur inland), dorsolateral dark blotches reduced to streaks anteriorly. 14–31 black tail spots. Ground color tan or yellow. Suffusion of grayish dots on sides of body and on undersides of tail. Nape dark brown. Thirty-three (29–35) midbody scale rows. A striped morph occurs. SAN DIEGO GOPHER SNAKE, *P. c. annectens*. Rostral bluntly rounded. 65–106 rounded, black, or brown body blotches alternating with, and more or less joined to each other and the enlarged dorsolateral blotches on neck. 16–33 tail spots. Ground color tan or yellow with gray suffusion on sides. Nape often dull orange. Thirty-three (29–37) midbody scale rows. SANTA CRUZ ISLAND GOPHER SNAKE, *P. c. pumilus*. Snout short, somewhat flattened. Rostral rounded. 64–82 dark blotches, small and usually discrete, connected with dorsolateral blotches anteriorly. 17–28 black tail spots. Ground color olive. No black streaked scales toward front of body in light interspaces. Nape dark. 27–29 midbody scale rows. A dwarf subspecies. Santa Cruz, Santa Rosa, and perhaps (sight record) San Miguel Is. off s. Calif. coast. BAJA CALIFORNIA GOPHER SNAKE, *P. c. bimaris*. Ground color of sides not suffused with gray. Dorsal blotches on front of body usually black or, in immatures, composed of gray scales with black edges. Fewer than 50 blotches on body. Light dorsal interspaces toward front of body clear or faintly streaked. CAPE GOPHER SNAKE, *P. c. vertebralis*. Ground color as mentioned above. Dorsal blotches toward front of body red or burnt orange and united at sides; rear blotches black (at base of tail). Head may completely lack dark markings. Dark stripe usually present under tail.

REMARKS: Baja California and Cape Gopher Snake have been proposed as members of a new species, the Baja California Gopher Snake, *P. vertebralis*. Sympatry of former with San Diego Gopher Snake has been reported near El Rosario in n. Baja Calif.

GLOSSY SNAKE *Arizona elegans* Pl. 46, Map 147

IDENTIFICATION: 26–70 in. (66–178 cm). Moderately slender, well named because of its smooth shiny skin. Light brown, cream, pinkish, yellowish gray, or gray above, with tan, brown, or gray blotches edged with blackish. Sometimes called the "faded snake" because of its bleached appearance in more arid parts of range. White or pale buff below, with *no markings* (outer edges of ventrals sometimes have dark markings). *Dorsal scales smooth and glossy*, in 25–35 rows at midbody. Two prefrontals. *Lower jaw inset (countersunk)*. Pupils slightly vertical when contracted. *Anal single.*

Occurs in a variety of habitats — light shrubby to barren desert, sagebrush flats, grassland, chaparral-covered slopes, and woodland. Generally prefers open areas. Ground often sandy or loamy, but some rocks may be present. An excellent burrower. In the West it remains underground by day and is rarely encountered beneath objects on the surface. Active mostly at night except in eastern part of range, where it is often diurnal. Clutch of 3–23 (more often 5–12) eggs, laid June–July. Eats lizards (especially), snakes, small mammals (kangaroo rats, etc.), and occasionally birds. Prey may be killed by constriction, by pressing it against a firm surface, or by direct swallowing. **SIMILAR SPECIES:** (1) Gopher Snake (p. 361) has keeled scales. (2) Rat Snakes have keeled scales and divided anal. (3) Night Snake (p. 403) has flattened head, distinctly vertical pupils, and divided anal. (4) Corn Snake (p. 358) lacks inset lower jaw and has divided anal. (5) See also Western Lyre Snake (p. 403). **RANGE:** Sw. U.S. from sw. Neb. and e. Tex. to cen. Calif; s. Utah to s. Baja Calif., s. Sinaloa, and San Luis Potosí. Sand Hills region, Neb. Below sea level (in desert sinks) to around 7,218 ft. (2,200 m).

SUBSPECIES: *Long-tailed forms:* KANSAS GLOSSY SNAKE, *A. e. elegans.* Dark-blotched form. Body blotches avg. 53 (39–69). Ventrals in males usually avg. 206 (197–219), females avg. 216 (208–27). Dorsal scale rows at midbody 29–31. PAINTED DESERT GLOSSY SNAKE, *A. e. philipi.* Blotches more numerous than above — avg. 64 (53–80). Ventrals in males avg. 195 (183–202), females avg. 204 (192–211). Dorsal scale rows usually 27 or less (not over 29).

Short-tailed forms: CALIFORNIA GLOSSY SNAKE, *A. e. occidentalis.* Darkest western subspecies, ground color often quite dark, body blotches often chocolate-colored. Dark marks on edges of ventrals. Lower labials often spotted. Body blotches avg. 63 (51–75). ARIZONA GLOSSY SNAKE, *A. e. noctivaga.* No marks on ventrals or spots on labials except occasionally on last lower labial. Body blotches slightly wider, or equal to interspaces, 25–29 dorsal scale rows. DESERT GLOSSY SNAKE, *A. e. eburnata.* A pale subspecies avg. 68 (53–85) small narrow blotches, narrower than interspaces and rarely more than 7 scale rows wide at midline. Usually 1 preocular. Ventrals — males avg. 219 (208–38), females avg. 231 (220–41). Dorsal scale rows 27 or fewer. MOJAVE GLOSSY SNAKE, *A. e. candida.* A pale subspecies avg. 63 (53–73) narrow body blotches, narrower than interspaces and about 9 scale rows wide at midline. Usually 2 preoculars. Ventrals—males avg. 214 (203–20), females avg. 223 (220–32). Twenty-seven or fewer dorsal scale rows at midbody. PENINSULAR GLOSSY SNAKE, *A. e. pacata*. Differs from other subspecies in having fewer body blotches—avg. 39 (36–41), and 27 scale rows at midbody.

REMARKS: Because of a break in range, mostly in Ariz. uplands, and some morphological differences (tail-length averaging shorter, etc. west of the break, see Map 147), some herpetologists recognize two species, the Western (*A. occidentalis*) and Eastern (*A. elegans*) Glossy Snakes. Furthermore, the Peninsular Glossy Snake, here treated as a subspecies, is recognized as a species.

KINGSNAKES AND MILK SNAKES: GENUS *Lampropeltis*

The generic name means "shiny skin." Medium-sized snakes with smooth scales and a single anal. Head usually little wider than neck. Dorsal pattern highly variable, ranging from gaudy blotches and crossbands of red and orange of Milk Snakes and Mountain Kingsnakes to dark blotches and bands and salt-and-pepper speckling of Common Kingsnake.

Found in a variety of habitats—woodland, coniferous forests, grassland, cultivated fields, tropical scrub, and desert, from se. Canada to Ecuador. Although some species are excitable when first encountered, and vibrate the tail, hiss, and strike, many Kingsnakes quickly become tame and make good pets. Because of their snake-eating habits, which includes venomous species such as rattlers and coral snakes, they should not be caged with other snakes. Prey killed by constriction.

Six species north of Mexico, 5 in our area.

COMMON KINGSNAKE *Lampropeltis getula*   **Pl. 44, Map 153**
IDENTIFICATION: 30–85 in. (76–216 cm). Over most of range in the West, pattern consists of alternating *bands of plain black or brown to dark brown* and white or pale yellow, pale bands broadening on belly. Pattern alone will distinguish most individuals. In se. Ariz. and N.M., however, light bands give way to varying amounts of *light speckling on a dark background,* and some individuals are entirely speckled (Fig. 20, Pl. 44, p. 122). Other pattern types are found farther east. A black form without bands occurs in s. Ariz., and a striped phase with more or less continuous pale yellow or whitish middorsal stripe occurs at scattered localities chiefly in s. Calif. and Baja Calif. (See Map 153). Individuals with a banded

pattern but dusky above and dark below occur in coastal Los Angeles Co., Calif. Black-bellied individuals with pale crossbands that broaden on lower sides to form a lateral stripe are found in northern part of San Joaquin Valley, Calif.; also a report of such patterning from Palos Verdes Peninsula in s. Calif. (see Map 153). Scales smooth and glossy, in 19–25 rows at midbody. *Caudals divided.* Anal single. **Young:** Usually patterned like adult, but in s. Ariz. blotched at first, becoming spotted with age.

Frequents a great variety of habitats—coniferous forest, woodland, swampland, coastal marshes, river bottoms, farmland, prairie, chaparral, and desert. Often found near rock outcrops and clumps of vegetation and under rotting logs, old lumber, and rocks. Chiefly terrestrial but sometimes climbs. Active mostly in morning and late afternoon, but in hot weather abroad at night. Usually gentle but occasionally strikes, hisses, and vibrates tail. Sometimes rolls into a ball with its head often at center and everts lining of its vent. Clutch of 2–24 (6–12) eggs, laid May–Aug. Eats snakes (including rattlers), lizards, small turtles, reptile eggs, frogs, birds and their eggs, and small mammals. **SIMILAR SPECIES:** (1) In Sierra Nevada the California Mountain Kingsnake (p. 366) sometimes lacks red markings and resembles the Common Kingsnake, but white rings usually not broadened on lowermost rows of dorsal scales. (2) In Long-nosed Snake (p. 370) some or all caudals are undivided. **RANGE:** Coast to coast, from s. N.J. to Fla. in the East, Neb. to the Gulf in cen. U.S., and sw. Ore. (vicinity of Elkton, Douglas Co.) to tip of Baja Calif. in the West. On Mexican mainland to n. Sinaloa, San Luis Potosí, and n. Tamaulipas. Northernmost localities in Nev. are Gerlach and Dixie Valley/ Pleasant Valley area, Pershing Co., and vicinity of Battle Mt., Lander Co. Unconfirmed sighting near Elko, Elko Co. Other outlying localities are Hovenweep Nat'l Monument area, San Juan Co., Utah, and McElmo Canyon area, Montezuma Co., and near La Junta, Otero Co., Colo. Sea level to around 7,000 ft. (2,130 m). **SUBSPECIES:** CALIFORNIA KINGSNAKE, *L. g. californiae.* Two pattern types—(1) banded and (2) striped, with intermediate forms. (1) Dark brown or black above with 21–44 white to yellowish dorsal crossbands that extend to or onto belly. In desert habitats contrasting black-and-white banding may prevail. In some areas brown or dusky pigment may be present on bases of scales of the light crossbands—especially in s. Calif., sw. Ariz., and s. Baja Calif. (2) Dark brown or black above, with a whitish to cream middorsal stripe (often variously broken) and lateral stripes formed by a series of light-centered scales on rows 1–3 or 1–6 (lowermost scales may be almost completely light-colored). Usually uniformly dark or light below. Striped pattern especially common in San Diego Co., Calif. (seen in about one-third of snakes encountered). See Map 153 for some localities where this phase has been found. Intermediate forms between (1) and (2) are variously striped or crossbanded. In occasional individuals in cen. and s. coastal Calif., light crossbands do not extend to belly but stop on 1st scale row, leaving belly uniformly black. Other individuals may have crossbands connected along 1st scale row to form light lateral stripes, and belly is usually black. Sometimes a complete or partial middorsal stripe is present. This phase has been found in cen. Calif. at Gadwall, Firebaugh, Mendota, Los Banos, Friant, and Clovis and reported in s. Calif. at Palos Verdes. **WESTERN BLACK KINGSNAKE,** *L. g. nigrita.* Uniformly dark brown or slaty black above, usually without traces of crossbands or stripes. Sometimes small light centers on lateral scales. Usually solid black below, except for light-colored anal scale. **DESERT KINGSNAKE,** *L. g. splendida.* Brown or black above, usually with 42–97 narrow (1–2 scales wide) whitish to yellowish crossbands formed by light-centered scales. Light crossbands sometimes absent. Occasionally scales between light bands have light centers, producing an entirely light-spotted dorsum (see Fig. 20, Pl. 44, p. 122). Lateral scales with light centers, from rows 1–10. Usually dark below (except for light-colored anal scale) or sometimes blotched (in eastern part of range).

CALIFORNIA MOUNTAIN KINGSNAKE   Pl. 44, Map 151
Lampropeltis zonata

IDENTIFICATION: 20–48¼ in. (51–123 cm). A beautiful serpent with glistening scales and black, white, and red crossbands, the red bordered on each side with black. A harmless snake, sometimes called the Coral Kingsnake because of its resemblance to venomous coral snakes. Red bands may be interrupted on back, appearing as a wedge on each side within a broad black band; may be wider than either the black or white bands; and, on Todos Santos I. off Baja Calif. and occasionally in cen. Sierra Nevada, red bands may be completely absent or reddish color may be enclosed by black. The combination of red and black markings (a black band more or less split by red) is called a triad. Head black in front of 1st white band on back of head. *Snout generally black,* with or without red markings. *Usually white bands do not broaden conspicuously on lower scale rows.* Pattern on back imperfectly but variously carried onto belly. Scales smooth, in 21 or 23 rows at midbody. Anal single.

Inhabitant of coniferous forest, oak-pine and riparian woodland, chaparral, manzanita, and coastal sage scrub, ranging from sea level high into mountains. Frequents well-lit wooded areas where there are rotting logs and/or talus and rock outcrops. Chiefly diurnal, but nocturnal, especially in warm weather. May climb into bushes, perhaps in search of bird nests. Clutch of 3–9 eggs, laid June–July. Eats lizards, snakes, bird eggs and nestlings,

and small mammals. **SIMILAR SPECIES:** (1) In Sonoran Mountain Kingsnake (below), black bands become narrow or disappear on sides, and snout is white or pale yellow. (2) In Milk Snake (p. 368), white bands usually become wider on the lowermost scale rows. (3) Long-nosed Snake (p. 370) has single caudals. (4) In Sonoran Coral Snake (p. 405), red markings are bordered with white or yellow rather than black. **RANGE:** S. Wash. to n. Baja Calif.; mountains of coastal and interior Calif. except deserts. Populations in s. Calif. in San Gabriel, San Bernardino, San Jacinto, Santa Monica, Santa Ana, Santa Rosa, Corta Madera, Cuyamaca, Hot Springs, Palomar, and Laguna Mts., and in Baja Calif. on S. Todos Santos I. (treated as a full species, *Lampropeltis herrerae,* by some herpetologists) and in Sierra de Juarez and Sierra San Pedro Martir; along Columbia Gorge in Klickitat and Skamania Cos. and reported in Ellensburg and Sunnyside areas in Yakima R. drainage, Wash. In Ore. reported near The Dalles, in the Maupin-Tygh Valley area (sight records) and in Blue Mts. All these Ore. localities need verification. Near sea level to around 9,000 ft. (2,750 m).
SUBSPECIES: SIERRA MOUNTAIN KINGSNAKE, *L. z. multicincta.* Rear edge of 1st white band on head located behind corner of mouth. 23–48 (avg. 35) body triads, usually fewer than 60 percent of triads split by red (red sometimes absent). ST. HELENA MOUNTAIN KINGSNAKE, *L. z. zonata.* First white band as above but 24–30 (avg. 27) body triads, usually 60 percent or more completely split by red. Snout dark. Black pigment, bordering the red on sides, usually more than 1 scale wide. COAST MOUNTAIN KINGSNAKE, *L. z. multifasciata.* Rear edge of 1st white band on head located behind or in front of corner of mouth. 26–45 (avg. 35) body triads, 60 percent or more completely split by red. Snout with red markings. SAN BERNARDINO MOUNTAIN KINGSNAKE, *L. z. parvirubra.* Rear edge of 1st white band located on or in front of last upper labial. 35–56 (avg. 41) body triads, usually fewer than 60 percent split by red. Snout dark. SAN DIEGO MOUNTAIN KINGSNAKE, *L. z. pulchra.* First white band as in San Bernardino Mountain Kingsnake. 26–39 (avg. 33) body triads, usually 60 percent or more split by red. Snout dark. BAJA CALIFORNIA MOUNTAIN KINGSNAKE, *L. z. agalma.* High triad count—over 40 on body. Considerable red on body and red on snout.
REMARKS: Illegal collecting of this beautiful snake and associated destruction of its log and rock refuges is believed to have significant local impacts on its survival.

SONORAN MOUNTAIN KINGSNAKE   Pl. 44, Map 154
Lampropeltis pyromelana

IDENTIFICATION: 18–42 in. (46–107 cm). A red-, black-, and white-banded Kingsnake, with a rather wide, flat head. Amount of red in black bands varies greatly, forming a wedge on each side or completely splitting the black bands. In some individuals, red forms broad bands narrowly bordered by black. *Black bands often become narrow or disappear on sides.* Pattern on back imperfectly but variously carried onto belly. *Snout white, pale yellow, or sometimes black flecked with white.* Scales smooth, in 23 or 25 rows at midbody. Anal single.

Mountain-dweller, ranging from oak-juniper and piñon-juniper woodland and chaparral to woodlands of pine and oak and pine and fir, but may descend to lowland areas in moist canyons. Attracted to streams and springs. Usually found in places with rocks, logs, and dense clumps of vegetation—under objects or occasionally exposed. Clutch of 2–9 eggs, laid June–July. Eats lizards, snakes, small mammals (including nestlings) and frogs. **SIMILAR SPECIES:** (1) Snout of California Mountain Kingsnake (p. 366) is solid black or black with red markings, and black bands usually do not become narrow on sides of body. (2) Milk Snake (below) in the West has fewer than 210 ventrals (usually fewer than 200 in areas of overlap with Sonoran Mountain Kingsnake), has less white on nose and less sharply set off from black of head, and pale bands become wider on lower sides. Neck is thicker and head less short and less flattened. (3) Long-nosed Snake has mostly single caudals. (4) Venomous Sonoran Coral Snake (p. 405) has broad red bands bordered with white or yellow rather than black. **RANGE:** Distribution spotty: Cen. Utah and e. Nev. south in mountains of Ariz. and sw. N.M. into Sierra Madre Occidental to s. Chihuahua, Mex. Isolated populations in Egan (Water and Sawmill Canyons), Snake, and Shell Creek Ranges, Nev., the Wah Wah Mts., Utah, and in Black Rock, Poverty, Mt. Trumbull, and Hualapai Mts., Ariz. Other scattered mountain populations farther south. From 2,800–9,100 ft. (850–2,800 m).

MILK SNAKE *Lampropeltis triangulum* **Pl. 44, Map 152**
IDENTIFICATION: 14–54 in. (35–137 cm). In our area marked with bands or saddles (the latter extending far down on sides of dorsum), of red or orange, bordered by black and separated by narrower white or yellowish interspaces. Black borders may encroach upon red ones on midline of back, sometimes splitting them. Snout black, sometimes flecked or mottled with white or red. *White or cream-colored interspaces tend to widen low on sides.* Red bands very wide in se. and s. U.S. within range of venomous Eastern Coral Snake (which also has wide red bands), a condition regarded as mimicry which may help protect the Milk Snake from predators. Dorsal pattern usually imperfectly but variously carried onto belly. Some individuals, however, may have partially or completely white, light-colored interspaces extending onto sides of

venter, and some may have much dark banding. Scales smooth, in 19 or 21 rows at midbody. Caudals mostly divided (arranged in 2 rows). Anal single.

In our area much of range is short-grass prairie. Other habitats include sagebrush covered grasslands, piñon-juniper and broadleaf woodland, canyons grown to oak and maple, and upland pine forests. Frequents canyons, river bottoms, rocky hillsides, sand dunes, farmland, and suburban areas. Secretive — found inside rotten logs and stumps and under rocks, logs, bark, and boards. Occasionally encountered in the open. Often nocturnal, especially in warm weather. Clutch of 2–24 eggs (4–6 more common in our area), laid May–July in U.S. Eats snakes, lizards, reptile eggs, small mammals, birds and their eggs, and occasionally insects and earthworms. Often found in barnyards where they hunt mice, therefore erroneously accused of milking cows, hence the common name. **SIMILAR SPECIES:** See (1) California Mountain (p. 366) and (2) Sonoran Mountain Kingsnakes (p. 367). (3) Long-nosed Snake (p. 370) has single caudals. (4) Sonoran Coral Snake (p. 405) has red bands bordered with white or pale yellow instead of black. **RANGE:** One of the most widely distributed of all snake species, ranging from se. Canada to Ecuador, Atlantic Coast to n. Mont. and cen. Utah. Old records for Ft. Benton, Chouteau Co., Mont., and Ft. (Camp) Apache, Navajo Co., Ariz. In Ariz., known from drainage of Little Colorado R. at Wupatki Nat'l Monument, from near Holbrook, Navajo Co. and near St. Johns, Apache Co.; reported from Petrified Forest Nat'l Park. A far northern locality in the West is near Sun Prairie, Phillips Co., Mont. Near sea level to around 9,000 ft. (2,740 m).
REMARKS: Population in Stansbury Mts., Tooele Co., Utah, highly variable in color. Many have dorsal markings similar to those of Sonoran Mountain Kingsnake. Subspecies relationships of this snake are uncertain.

GRAY-BANDED KINGSNAKE   Pl. 44, Map 151
Lampropeltis alterna

IDENTIFICATION: 20–57 in. (51–145 cm). Ground color above is light to dark gray (very dark in dark-color phase). *Widely spaced crossbands of black on gray background* often narrowly to widely split (sometimes wider than intervening gray areas) with orange or reddish. Crossbands edged with whitish. Below gray with black blotches and spots. The narrow-banded, light-gray phase in our area and elsewhere bears striking resemblance to Rock Rattlesnake and may perhaps derive some protection thereby from snake-eating predators. Rather broad head may reinforce the resemblance. Eyes slightly protuberant. Scales smooth and glossy. Anal single.

Inhabitant of arid and semiarid regions from desert flats into mountains. Appears to be primarily a rock-crevice snake. Often found in rocky habitats of fissured canyon outcrops, escarpments, and road cuts. Vegetation characteristic of Chihuahuan Desert, such as cactus, mesquite, ocotillo, and creosote bush. Nocturnal and secretive. Clutch of 5–9 eggs laid June–July. Eats lizards and rodents (including nestlings); single record of a Canyon Treefrog. **SIMILAR SPECIES:** (1) Rock Rattlesnake has rattle and keeled scales. (2) Lyre Snake has vertical pupils. **RANGE:** In our area, at present, verified for only two localities: Walnut Canyon near Whites City, Carlsbad Caverns Nat'l Park, and near El Paso Gap, both in Eddy Co., N.M., thence south to ne. Durango and extreme w. Nuevo León, Mex. Trans-Pecos region east to Edwards Co., Tex.

LONG-NOSED SNAKE *Rhinocheilus lecontei*   **Pl. 44, Map 155**
IDENTIFICATION: 20–60 in. (51–152 cm). Typically slim and speckled, with black saddles flecked with whitish on sides. Spaces between saddles cream, yellow, pink, or red, except for whitish border next to saddles. Spaces between saddles usually marked with dark flecks on sides. Belly whitish or yellow, with a few dark spots toward sides. Snout long and pointed, and head only slightly wider than neck. Lower jaw countersunk (inset). Most *scales under tail in a single row.* Scales smooth, in 23 rows. Anal single. **Young:** Speckling on sides faint or absent.

Inhabits deserts, prairies, shrubland, and tropical habitats (in Mex.) In the Southwest it is crepuscular and nocturnal, likely to be found on roadways at night. In the Northwest, at least, it is cold-tolerant. When alarmed may vibrate tail, writhe hind part of body, and evert vent lining, releasing blood and feces. A good burrower. One, perhaps 2, clutches of 4–11 eggs, laid June–Aug. Eats lizards and their eggs, small snakes, small mammals, and occasionally birds and insects. Lizards, especially Whiptails (*Cnemidophorus*), appear to be favored. Large prey is killed by constriction. **SIMILAR SPECIES:** (1) Differs from Kingsnakes (pp. 364–370) in having most caudal scales in a single rather than double row. (2) See also Thornscrub Hook-nosed Snake (p. 396). **RANGE:** Sw. Idaho (Snake R. Valley area) and se. Colo. to cen. Baja Calif. (Misión San Borja), San Luis Potosí and s. Tamaulipas; cen. Tex. to cen. and s. coastal Calif. Ranges north in Calif. to Sutter Buttes in Sacramento Valley. Old record for Mt. Sanhedrin, Mendocino Co., Calif. Populations apparently isolated in Snake R. Valley, Idaho, and Dragerton area, Carbon Co., Utah. On Cerralvo I., Gulf of Calif. Below sea level (in desert sinks) to around 6,233 ft. (1,900 m).
SUBSPECIES: TEXAS LONG-NOSED SNAKE, *R. l. tessellatus.* Snout sharp; rostral raised above nearby scales, giving snout an upward tilt. WESTERN

LONG-NOSED SNAKE, *R. l. lecontei.* Snout blunter than in Texas Long-nosed Snake; rostral only slightly raised and snout without upward tilt. In more arid parts of range a contrastingly banded color phase occurs (formerly regarded as a distinct species, *R. clarus*) that usually lacks red in interspaces and has scant black spotting on sides. Black saddles are longer and fewer than in the typical form.

NORTH AMERICAN WATER SNAKES: GENUS *Nerodia*

Large, heavy-bodied snakes, plain-colored above or variously crossbanded or blotched and with colorful underparts — yellow or red and often patterned. Heavily keeled dorsal scales. Anal scale usually divided. Semiaquatic. Often forage in or near water for frogs, salamanders, fish, etc. Nine species. E. and cen. U.S. and Mex.; 1 species along n. coast of Cuba. Two species barely reach our area. Some taxonomists place these snakes with the Garter Snakes (*Thamnophis*).

PLAIN-BELLIED WATER SNAKE   Pl. 48, Map 156
Nerodia erythrogaster
IDENTIFICATION: 30–62 in. (76–157 cm). In our area known only from extreme se. N.M. Moderately heavy bodied; plain-colored or blotched; *strongly keeled scales with apical pits* (see glossary). Olive, gray, brown, or reddish brown above, often with dark brown blotches edged with black down back. In our western subspecies, adults tend to retain juvenile blotching. Smaller blotches on sides often alternate with dorsal ones. Sometimes dorsal pattern is represented only by pale crossbars edged with black. *Belly plain yellow* (in our area), orange, or red, but occasionally with dark color on edges of ventrals. In our subspecies, underside of tail usually plain orange or reddish. In central and eastern part of range, adults usually plain-colored above, belly red or orange-red, hence the names "redbelly" and "copperbelly." Anal usually divided. **Young:** Prominently marked with alternating dorsal and lateral blotches. **Male:** Knobs on scale keels above anal region.

Highly aquatic, usually found in or near water, but may move away from it in wet weather. Frequents river bottoms, springs, swamps, wooded borders of streams, rivers, lakes, and ponds. In the West it follows river courses into arid country, seeking permanent or semipermanent water of streams, ditches, and cattle tanks. When first caught, often bites and discharges foul-smelling musk from anal scent glands. Live-bearing. One, perhaps 2, litters of 2–32 young, born Aug.–Oct. Eats crayfish, fish, frogs, tadpoles, and salamander larvae. **SIMILAR SPECIES:** (1) Garter Snakes (*Thamnophis* species, pp. 373–90) lack apical pits on dorsal

scales and have a single anal. (2) Rat snakes (pp. 358–60) have weakly keeled scales, confined to upper part of back. (3) See also Common Water Snake (below). **RANGE:** S. Mich. to Gulf Coast and cen. Nuevo León with isolated populations in e.-cen. Durango and Zacatecas, Mex.; Atlantic Coast to extreme w. Okla. and se. N.M. (Lower Pecos R. drainage including Black and Delaware Rs. and Rocky Arroyo). Sea level to around 6,700 ft. (2,040 m, in Mexico).
SUBSPECIES: BLOTCHED WATER SNAKE, *N. e. transversa*, occurs in our area.

COMMON WATER SNAKE   **Pl. 48, Map 157**
(NORTHERN WATER SNAKE) *Nerodia sipedon*
IDENTIFICATION: 22–53 in. (56–135 cm). In our area, known only from e. Colo. Moderately heavy-bodied, with prominently keeled scales that have apical pits (see p. 508). Pits are sometimes represented by oval discolored spots not actually indented. Dark crossbands on front part of body give way near midbody to large dorsal blotches that continue onto tail and alternate with smaller blotches on sides. Ground color varies from pale gray to dark brown or black, and markings from bright reddish brown to black. Some individuals and populations have little or no dorsal pattern. Old individuals may be black. *Black or reddish half moons on belly, in regular or irregular arrangement;* or sometimes absent. Anal divided. **Young:** More contrastingly marked than adult. Pattern black or dark brown on pale gray or light brown background. **Male:** Knobbed keels on dorsal scales in anal region.

Found in or near swamps, marshes, ponds, streams, rivers, lakes, reservoirs, and coastal areas of brackish water or saltwater. May be seen basking on shore, or on logs or piles of rotting vegetation in the water. When alarmed, may swim to bottom or to cover of emergent vegetation. Highly aquatic; seldom ventures far from water. When caught it often bites and may expel a foul-smelling secretion from anal glands. Live-bearing, 8–46 (rarely to around 100) young, born Aug.–Oct. Eats crayfish, insects, fish, salamanders, frogs, toads, tadpoles, young turtles, and small mammals. **SIMILAR SPECIES:** (1) Plain-bellied Water Snake (p. 371) usually has unmarked belly, and crossbands are largely confined to neck. (2) Garter Snakes (*Thamnophis* species, pp. 373–90) lack apical pits on dorsal scales and have single anal. (3) Corn Snake (p. 358) has smooth scales on sides and spear-shaped mark on head. Range: E. Colo. to Atlantic Coast; se. Canada to Gulf Coast from e. La. to w. Fla. In Colo. frequents S. Platte, Arikaree, and Arkansas drainages. Sea level to around 5,500 ft. (1,680 m).
SUBSPECIES: NORTHERN WATER SNAKE, *N. s. sipedon*, occurs in our area.

Storeria occipitomaculata

IDENTIFICATION: 8–16 in. (20.3–41 cm). Typically red-bellied with dorsal stripes and usually 3 *light-colored blotches at back of head.* Top of head blackish. Blotches may be small or absent in Black Hills population in our area (see below). *Usually 4 narrow, dark dorsal stripes* or a broad, light-colored middorsal stripe, or both. Commonly 2 color morphs are present in populations — plain brown or gray above. However, occasionally black individuals are found. The belly, usually bright red, varies through orange to pale yellow, or may be dark in generally darkened individuals. Dorsal scales keeled, in 15 rows. Anal divided. **Young:** Resemble adult but darker, sometimes blackish.

Over much of range, primarily lives in wooded hilly and mountainous regions. Occurs under stones, logs, and boards, and inside rotten stumps, often at edges of clearings and in or near sphagnum bogs. Found near houses and other buildings. Livebearing; 1–21 young, born June–Sept. Eats slugs, snails, earthworms, and soft-bodied insects. **RANGE:** Widespread over e. U.S. but distribution spotty. Extreme s. Canada to Gulf Coast. Atlantic Coast to e. N.D. in north, and e. Tex. in south. Populations near the Platte R., s.-cen. Neb. In our area an isolated population in Black Hills of sw. S.D. and ne. Wyo. Sea level to around 5,600 ft. (1,710 m).

SUBSPECIES: BLACK HILLS RED-BELLIED SNAKE, *S. o. pahasapae,* occurs in our area. Two color phases — (1) gray and (2) reddish brown with a pair of black dorsolateral stripes bordering a paler brown middorsal stripe. Also reported to lack (or rarely have) nape and neck blotches or light upper-lip spot.

REMARKS: A Brown Snake (*Storeria dekayi*) reported collected in Las Animas Co., Colo. in 1883. Since snake occurs in sw. Kans., should continue to be sought in Colo. Differs from Red-bellied Snake in having 17 dorsal scale rows and in lacking a red belly.

GARTER SNAKES: GENUS *Thamnophis*

Moderately slender with head slightly wider than neck. Dorsal scales keeled and without apical pits. Anal scale single except in Mexican Garter Snake. Scales of Water Snakes (genus *Nerodia*) have apical pits (see p. 508) and anal is divided. Dorsal scale counts are important in identification. A count of 17, 17, 15 means 17 rows at neck, 17 at midbody, and 15 in front of vent. Most species have conspicuous pale yellow or orange middorsal stripe and pale stripe low on each side. The fancied resemblance of this pattern to an old-fashioned garter has earned these snakes their common name. Position of side stripe varies; it may be on scale rows 2 and 3, 3 and 4, or confined to row 3. Count upward from ends of ventrals about ¼ body length behind the head. Some species are unstriped or have only ventral stripes and a spotted or checkered pattern. Most species of Garter Snakes have a red or orange tongue with black tips. Conspicuous flickering tongue is thought sometimes to act as a lure, attracting fish and other prey to near the mouth of the snake.

Garter Snakes have long been the bane of many taxonomists and further changes in their classification can be expected (note the many changes since publication of my 1985 Field Guide!). Many are notoriously difficult to identify. Rely heavily on geographic location.

Garter Snakes occupy a great variety of habitats from sea level to high in mountains. Many are aquatic or semiaquatic but some are almost completely terrestrial. Like the Water Snakes (*Nerodia*), when caught they often void feces and expel musk from their anal glands. Live-bearing. Thirty species occur in region from Canada to Costa Rica and Pacific to Atlantic Coast, 14 in our area. Common Garter Snake ranges farther north than any other reptile in the Western Hemisphere (see Map 162).

NARROW-HEADED GARTER SNAKE Pl. 48, Map 163
Thamnophis rufipunctatus

IDENTIFICATION: 18–44 in. (46–112 cm). Olive, tan, gray-brown, or brown above, marked with *conspicuous dark brown, blackish or reddish spots* that fade on tail. No well-developed stripes or pale crescent behind corner of mouth as in some species of Garter Snakes. Dark bars on labial scales. Traces of dorsal and side stripes sometimes present on neck. Brownish gray below, paling on throat. Often a row of black wedge-shaped marks on each side of belly. Tongue black. Head long and narrow. Eyes high on head. *Eight or 9 upper labials.* Scales keeled, usually 21 rows at midbody. Anal usually single. **Young:** Throat often cream-colored and belly dull yellowish.

Ranges from piñon-juniper and oak-pine belts into forests of ponderosa pine along rocky lakeshores and clear permanent or semipermanent rocky streams, where it seems to prefer quieter, well-lit sections. Highly aquatic, remaining close to water. When frightened, usually dives to bottom for refuge, often hiding under a stone or within a rock crevice. Live-bearing; 8–18 young born July–Aug. Eats fish, frogs, toads, tadpoles, and larval Tiger Salamanders. **SIMILAR SPECIES:** Distinctive color, head shape, and elevated eyes of this species combined with its highly aquatic habits separate this snake from our other species. **RANGE:** Upland drainages of cen. and e. Ariz. and sw. N.M. N. Chihuahua to cen.

Durango. In Ariz. originally ranged north to Fort Valley Creek, Coconino Co. From around 2,300 to 7,972 ft. (700 to 2,430 m).

REMARKS: In our area this snake has suffered a severe decline because of human disturbances, including introduction of predatory fish and bullfrogs.

COMMON GARTER SNAKE
Thamnophis sirtalis

Pl. 48, Map 162

IDENTIFICATION: 18–55 in. (46–140 cm). Coloration highly variable, but dorsal and side stripes usually well defined. Dorsal stripe may be gray, tan, green, blue, yellow, orange, or white. Frequently red spots or blotches and a double row of alternating black spots on sides between stripes, or dark blotches may join vertically to form dark bars or horizontally to form dark stripes (San Francisco Garter Snake). Some populations in the Northwest have nearly solid dark coloration between stripes. Light-colored side stripe usually on 2nd and 3rd scale rows. Top of head brown, olive, gray, red, or black. Upper labials often with black wedges. Frequently bluish gray, or blue-green below, sometimes becoming dusky or black especially toward tail, or venter may be pale and unmarked. Throat pale. Eyes relatively large. *Usually 7 upper labials.* Rear pair of chin shields usually longer than front pair. Dorsal scales keeled, in up to 19 rows at midbody. Anal single. **Male:** Knobbed keels on scales above vent.

Found in many environments—grassland, woodland, scrub, chaparral, and forest. Lives in or near ponds, marshes, prairie swales, roadside ditches, streams, sloughs, damp meadows, woods, farms, and city lots. Tends to stay near water, entering it freely and retreating to it when alarmed. Excellent swimmer. When emerging from overwintering sites, especially in cooler parts of range, may be present in great numbers. Spirited; often defends itself energetically when cornered. When caught it often bites and smears its captor with excrement and odorous contents of anal glands. Live-bearing; 3–85 (often 12–18) young, born May–Nov., the earlier months in southern part of range. Appears to be capable of activity at lower body temperature than any other Garter Snake. Eats fish, toads, frogs, tadpoles, salamanders and their larvae, birds and their eggs, small mammals, reptiles, earthworms, slugs, and leeches. One of the few predators that can eat adult Pacific Newts (*Taricha* species, pp. 164–67) without suffering lethal poisoning. **SIMILAR SPECIES:** Usual presence of red markings between stripes, often dark wedges on upper labials, the 7 (occasionally 8) upper labials, and relatively large eyes (see Pl. 48) generally distinguish this species from other Garter Snakes within its western range. See also (1) Northwestern (p. 386), (2)

Western Terrestrial (p. 377), and (3) Sierra Garter Snakes (p. 381). **RANGE:** Pacific to Atlantic Coasts; se. Alaska (Stikine R. area) and s. Canada to Gulf Coast and nw. Chihuahua. In coastal s. Calif. extends south to just north of San Diego but populations greatly fragmented and localized as a result of human impacts south of Santa Clara R. in Ventura and Los Angeles Cos. Widespread along Rio Grande and recorded from Bitter Lakes, Chaves Co., and near Artesia, Eddy Co., in Pecos R. drainage, N.M. Absent from most of arid Southwest. All isolated populations shown in Montana need verification. Sea level to around 8,000 ft. (2,438 m).

SUBSPECIES: RED-SPOTTED GARTER SNAKE, *T. s. concinnus* (see Pl. 48). Ground color of back and sides black, extending onto belly. Broad, pale dorsal stripe well defined. Sides with large red or orange-red blotches or vertical bars. Side stripes sometimes hidden by black pigment. Top and sides of head usually reddish or orange. Occasional individuals in nw. Ore. and w. Wash. have white or bluish white dorsal stripe, side blotches, and head. PUGET SOUND GARTER SNAKE, *T. s. pickeringii* (see Pl. 48). Dark-colored, including top of head; dorsal stripe largely confined to middorsal scale row. VALLEY GARTER SNAKE, *T. s. fitchi* (see Pl. 48). Ground color slaty, black, or brownish. Dorsal stripe broad, with regular, well-defined borders. Top of head black, brown, or dark gray. Single series of red spots along lower margin of dorsolateral area. Black on belly usually confined to tips of ventrals. Slate gray individuals that match their rock background occur within the caldera of Crater Lake, Ore. (along the lakeshore and on Wizard I.). SAN FRANCISCO GARTER SNAKE, *T. s. tetrataenia* (Pl. 48). One of the most beautiful serpents in N. America. Wide dorsal stripe greenish yellow edged with black, bordered on each side by broad red stripe, bordered below by a black one. Belly greenish

Two basking male Common Garter Snakes (Valley subspecies) await females to exit a den site in spring. Klickitat Co., Wash.

blue. Top of head red. Most typical form found in western part of San Francisco Peninsula from about San Francisco Co. line south along crest of hills at least to Crystal Lake and along coast to Point Año Nuevo, San Mateo Co., Calif. RED-SIDED GARTER SNAKE, *T. s. parietalis*. Ground color dark olive to nearly black. Dark spots on back. Usually red or orange spots on bars on sides varying in size and intensity. Top of head olive, gray, brown, or black. Dorsal stripe may be yellow, orange, greenish, or bluish. If top of head dark, then usually black spots are present on ends of ventrals. Melanistic individuals in populations in cen. Mont. lack red side markings. CALIFORNIA RED-SIDED GARTER SNAKE, *T. s. infernalis*, (Pl. 48). Resembles Red-sided Garter Snake, but ground color generally darker. Dark spots less distinct. Stripes usually narrower and bright greenish yellow, those on sides often merging with ground color on belly. S. Calif. populations from Santa Clara R. area, Ventura Co. south may prove to be a new species. However, they have already disappeared from approximately 75 percent of historic localities. NEW MEXICO GARTER SNAKE, *T. s. dorsalis*. Resembles Red-sided Garter Snake but looks duller —dusky or muddy with more diffuse pattern, or generally greenish with prominent white or yellowish white stripes. Olive on upper sides, with red flecks and alternating rows of black spots. Upper black blotches tend to fuse with each other along their upper edges to form a black border along dorsal stripe. Young occasionally rust-colored. Isolated populations along Rio Casas Grandes, Chihuahua.

WESTERN TERRESTRIAL GARTER SNAKE
Thamnophis elegans   Fig. 26, Pl. 49, Map 166
IDENTIFICATION: 18–43 in. (46–109 cm). Usually a well-defined, often yellowish or white middorsal stripe extends length of body, and a pale stripe on each side, on 2nd and 3rd scale rows. Dorsal

Common Garter Snake (California Red-sided Garter Snake ssp.). A colorful subspecies that is declining in some areas of its southern range.

stripe at some localities may be dull with irregular borders. Ground color between stripes may be brown, olive, gray, reddish, or black with scattered whitish flecks (Fig. 26). Gray, brown, or bluish below, flecked or blotched with black, reddish, or salmon. Some individuals have broad central area of black. *Internasals usually broader than long and not pointed in front.* Usually 8 upper labials (occasionally 7). Usually 10 lower labials. *Both pairs of chin shields about equal in length.* Dorsal scales keeled, in 19 or 21 rows at midbody. Anal single.

Occurs in a great variety of habitats—grassland, brushland, woodland, and open forest, from sea level to high in mountains. Often occurs near streamsides, springs, and lakes. *Habits chiefly terrestrial.* When frightened, often seeks shelter in dense plant growth or other cover on land rather than seeking shelter in water. May be semiaquatic, however, in arid Great Basin and Rocky Mt. regions where associated with streams and ponds. Live-bearing; 4–27 young, born July–Sept. Eats slugs, snails, leeches, earthworms, fish, salamanders, frogs, toads, tadpoles, lizards, snakes, small mammals, and occasionally birds (including eggs and nestlings), and carrion. In Northwest, reported to feed on intertidal fish and crustaceans. SIMILAR SPECIES: (1) Distinct dorsal stripe will usually distinguish members of this group in areas of overlap with Oregon and Sierra Garter Snakes. East of crest of Calif. Sierra Nevada, however, some difficulty may be encountered in distinguishing Wandering Garter Snake (see Subspecies, below) from Sierra Garter Snake (p. 381). The latter has a narrow, dull dorsal stripe, ordinarily confined to front third of body, and a checkered pattern of large squarish spots. Wandering Garter Snake usually has a wider stripe extending full length of body, and a pattern of more rounded, well-separated spots. Along Calif. coast where striped members of Aquatic Garter Snake (p. 382) overlap in range the Coast Garter Snake (p. 379), the former differs in lacking red markings and in usually having an orange (rather than yellow) dorsal stripe. Generally golden to orange suffusion or blotches occur on ventrals. (2) Northwestern Garter Snake (p. 386) usually has 17, 17, 15 scale rows; 7 upper labials; 8 or 9 lower labials; and a bright yellow, red, or orange dorsal stripe; whereas in area of overlap with Western Terrestrial Garter Snake the latter has 19, 19, 17 or more scale rows; usually 8 upper labials; 10 lower labials; and usually a dull yellow, brown, or gray dorsal stripe. (3) Common Garter Snake (p. 375) has relatively larger eyes, generally 7 upper labials, and usually a plain bluish gray belly. Where it coexists with Coast Garter Snake, it usually has a greenish yellow dorsal stripe. RANGE: B.C. (coastal drainage, the Bella Coola, Skeena, and Nass, and, in the east, the

Peace R. district) to n. Baja Calif.; w. S.D. and extreme w. Okla. to Pacific Coast. Isolated populations in nw. Ore.; Amargosa R. and San Bernardino Mts., s. Calif.; San Pedro Martir Mts., Baja Calif.; Ash Meadows, Nye Co., Nev.; Capitan-Sacramento Mts. area, N.M.; and elsewhere. Sea level to 13,100 ft. (3,990 m) in San Miguel Co., Colo.

SUBSPECIES: MOUNTAIN GARTER SNAKE, *T. e. elegans* (Pl. 49, Fig. 26). Well-defined stripes on sides and back separated by velvety black to dark gray-brown (San Bernardino Mts.) ground color. Dorsal stripe yellow, orange-yellow, or whitish, and in occasional dark individuals reduced to trace on neck. No red markings. Belly pale, with no markings except light dusky spots or some black down middle of belly. Ranges into Willamette Valley along foothills of Cascade Mts. as far north as Molalla, Ore. Isolated populations occur on northwestern side of valley along foothills of Coast Range from west of Yamhill west to vicinity of Scappoose. Individuals from N. Fork of Yamhill R. have conspicuous white irregular dorsal stripes and bluish gray venters. Terrestrial. COAST GARTER SNAKE, *T. e. terrestris* (Pl. 49, Fig. 26). Dorsal stripe typically bright yellow. Bright red or orange flecks or blotches usually present on belly and sides, including side stripes. Usually seeks shelter on land. Considerable color variation occurs in the s. Bay area and to the south. On San Francisco peninsula 3 yellowish stripes evident, and a checkerboard of dark spots occurs between the stripes on a reddish ground color. The dark spots give way to alternating dark and reddish bars on sides in areas along outer coast from cen. San Mateo Co. to near Moss Landing, Monterey Co. This color type also occurs in East Bay Hills. Increase in dark color, with almost solid dark fields between the dorsal and side stripes, occurs in Santa Cruz Mts. and Monterey area, south to southern end of range near Lake Casitas, Ventura Co. Middorsal stripe is pale yellow and side stripes are yellowish. However, salmon or reddish side stripes are found in Santa Cruz Mts. and elsewhere at some localities in San Francisco Bay area. WANDERING GARTER SNAKE, *T. e. vagrans* (Pl. 49, Fig. 26). Mostly brown, greenish, or gray, with a dull yellow, yellowish orange, or brown dorsal stripe, fading on tail and edged with dark markings that make its borders irregular and which may break the stripe into dots and dashes.

Dark spots on body usually small and well separated, but sometimes absent or variously enlarged, occasionally forming a completely black area between the stripes. Venter with scattered, or medially concentrated, black markings or uniformly black except for ends of ventrals and throat. Melanistic individuals (Fig. 26) occur in w. Wash. (Puget Sound region) and e. Ore. Aquatic and terrestrial. SAN PEDRO MARTIR GARTER SNAKE, *T. e. hueyi.* Dark olive or grayish brown above with usually faint dark spots that are sometimes distinct. Stripes well defined, dorsal one yellow. Little or no spotting below. Often has 7 upper labials.

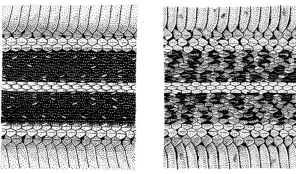

1. Mountain *(elegans)*   2. Coast *(terrestris)*

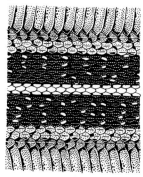

Intergrade 1 × 2

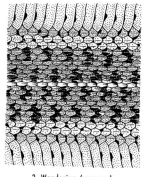

3. Wandering *(vagrans)*

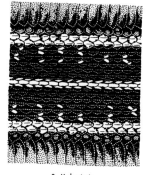

3. Melanistic
(Puget Sound region)

Fig. 26. Pattern variation in Western Terrestrial Garter Snake

SIERRA GARTER SNAKE
Thamnophis couchii

IDENTIFICATION: 18–38 in. (46–96 cm). Dark blotches on olive brown, dark brown, or blackish ground color. Blotches are obscure in dark snakes as in a population at Plum Creek, Tehama Co., Calif., which are melanistic as adults. Dorsal stripe indistinct or absent, except on neck. Side stripe, when present, located on 2nd and 3rd scale rows. Northern populations may have extensive black mottling on labials, throat, and venter—with reduction and finally loss of these markings progressively to the south. Internasals tend to be longer than wide and pointed at front end. *Usually 8 upper labials, 6th longer than 7th. Ordinarily not higher than wide.* Dorsal scales keeled, usually in 19 or 21 rows at midbody. Anal single.

Primarily a snake of rivers and streams, but occurs in a great variety of aquatic environments, from foothill streams and seasonal creeks to rapidly flowing high mountain rivers, meadow ponds, and lakes. Associated vegetation ranges from foothill oak woodland and chaparral to montane coniferous forests. East of montane crest, is found in pine, juniper, and sagebrush habitats. Usually retreats to water when frightened. Primarily diurnal. Live-bearing; 5–38 young, born July–Sept., time depending chiefly on elevation. Eats fish, frogs, toads, tadpoles, and salamanders and their larvae. **SIMILAR SPECIES:** (1) Mountain Garter Snake (p. 379) has solid black areas between stripes and stripes usually well-defined. Terrestrial. (2) Valley Garter Snake (p. 376) usually has well-developed dorsal stripe, red markings between stripes, and 7 upper labials. Terrestrial. (3) Oregon Garter Snake (p. 384), where its range contacts Sierra Garter Snake's (Pit R. drainage) and where it contacts Sacramento R., cannot be reliably distinguished from Sierra Garter Snake. (4) Common Garter Snake (p. 375) usually has 7 upper labials, larger eyes, a well-defined dorsal stripe, and distinct red blotches on sides. **RANGE:** N. cen. Calif. from Pit and Sacramento Rs. south through Sierra Nevada to western end Tehachapi Mts. Population at California City, Kern Co., appears to be of this species. East of Sierra in Owens Valley. Truckee, Carson, and Walker R. drainages in Nev. From around 300 ft. (91 m) on floor of Sacramento Valley to around 8,000 ft. (2,440 m) in Sierra. Hybridizes with Oregon Aquatic Garter Snake in Pit R. drainage and with Two-striped Garter Snake at western end Tehachapi Mts., Calif. Oregon Aquatic Garter Snake (*T. a. hydrophilus*) and Sierra Garter Snake (*T. couchii*) occur along Pit R., Shasta Co., Calif., where a few intergrades or hybrids have been found. In Pit R. area, Sierra Garter Snake has much black pigment on both head (especially upper labials) and venter.

GIANT GARTER SNAKE *Thamnophis gigas* **Pl. 49, Map 167**

IDENTIFICATION: 37–65 in. (94–165 cm). Above brown or olive *with two alternating rows of well-separated small dark spots between stripes on each side*. Dorsal stripe, when evident, yellowish, often with irregular edges. Side stripe, when present, confined to 2nd and 3rd scale rows. Venter light brown or light gray. *Upper labials 8 (the 6th usually shorter than the 7th).* Dorsal scales keeled, usually in maximum of 23 or 21 rows. Anal single. In upper Sacramento Valley this snake tends to be dark brown with distinct dorsal and lateral stripes, whereas farther south, stripes may be indistinct or absent and dorsal pattern of dark spots may or may not be distinct.

Frequents marshes, sloughs, mud-bottom canals of rice farming areas, and occasionally slow streams. Tules and cattails usually present, used for basking and cover. Extremely aquatic, rarely found far from water. Native Americans referred to it as the "water snake." Live-bearing; 8–40 young born July–Sept. Eats fish, frogs, toads, their larvae, and sometimes bush and ground nesting birds and their young. **SIMILAR SPECIES:** (1) Sierra Garter Snake averages much smaller. Sixth upper labial is usually longer than 7th (front suture to rear) whereas in Giant Garter Snake, 6th is usually shorter than 7th. (2) Common Garter Snake usually has 7 upper labials and red blotches on sides. **RANGE:** Formerly widespread throughout bottomland drainages and tule lakes of Great Valley of Calif. (except for a midway historic gap) from Butte Co. in Sacramento Valley, originally to Kern R. and Buena Vista Lake, Kern Co., in San Joaquin Valley. Current range extends from near Orland, Glenn Co., and Delevan Nat'l Wildlife Refuge, Colusa Co., to Los Banos Creek and Mud Slough, San Joaquin Valley. Now apparently absent or extremely rare in San Joaquin Valley south of n. Fresno. Sea level to 400 ft. (122 m).

REMARKS: Damming of Kern R. at Lake Isabella and San Joaquin R. at Friant, other flood control and water diversion projects, and major wetlands and habitat lost due to agriculture have severely impacted this species. It is now gone from an estimated 98 percent of former range in San Joaquin Valley. Protection of waterfowl habitats in Delta and Sacramento Valley appear to be its best chance for survival.

AQUATIC GARTER SNAKE **Pl. 49, Map 167**
Thamnophis atratus

IDENTIFICATION: 18–40 in. (46–102 cm). Dorsal coloration highly variable — pale gray with alternating rows of dark blotches on each side, dark brownish with less distinct blotches, or nearly black. Dorsal stripe usually dull yellow, distinct, indistinct, confined to neck or occasionally absent. Lateral stripe, when present,

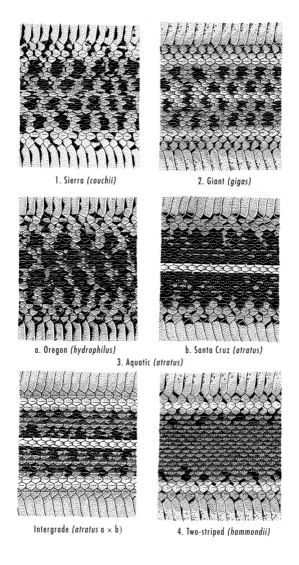

1. Sierra *(couchii)*

2. Giant *(gigas)*

a. Oregon *(hydrophilus)*

b. Santa Cruz *(atratus)*

3. Aquatic *(atratus)*

Intergrade *(atratus a × b)*

4. Two-striped *(hammondii)*

Fig. 27. *Pattern differences in garter snake species (1–4) and subspecies of Aquatic Garter Snake (a.–b.).*

on 2nd and 3rd scale rows. Throat whitish to lemon yellow. In Santa Cruz Mts. (e. slope drainages), Santa Cruz Co., Calif., some lack or have faint lateral stripes, strong orange to orange-yellow dorsal stripes, yellow throat and dark bellies. Dorsal scales keeled in up to 19 or 21 rows (the latter mostly in northern populations). *Upper labials usually 8, 7th longer than 6th. Internasals elongate and pointed in front.*

Frequents woodland, brushland, forest, and grassland-woodland edges in vicinity of ponds, small lakes, streams, and rocky creeks. Highly aquatic over much of range. When threatened, often seeks refuge in water and hides beneath rocks on the bottom. Live-bearing; 3–12 young (5 litters, San Francisco Bay area), born late Aug. to mid-Oct. Eats fish, amphibians and their larvae.

SIMILAR SPECIES: (1) South of Monterey Bay, Santa Cruz Aquatic Garter Snake (*T. a. atratus*) and Coast Garter Snake (*T. e. terrestris*) (p. 379) are somewhat similar in color, but the former has a deeper yellow stripe broader in neck region, and venter is marked with large and essentially continuous orangish blotches, whereas the latter usually has irregular sprinkling of orange or red flecks. (2) Common Garter Snake (p. 375) usually has 7 upper labials and, in areas of overlap with this species, usually red or orange bars between dorsal and side stripes. (3) Mountain Garter Snake (p. 379) has well-defined stripes and uniformly dark interstripe areas. (4) See also Two-striped Garter Snake (p. 385) and (5) Northwestern Garter Snake (p. 386). **RANGE:** Coastal regions from Umpqua R. valley in sw. Ore. to Sierra Madre Mts., Santa Barbara Co., Calif. Ranges inland in n. Calif. to lower reaches of Pit R. Sea level to around 6,300 ft. (1,920 m).

SUBSPECIES: SANTA CRUZ AQUATIC GARTER SNAKE, *T. a. atratus* (Pl. 49). Color between dorsal and lateral stripes may be dark brown with two alternating rows of dark spots, or nearly black. Dorsal stripe may be yellow or orange and distinct, indistinct, or nearly absent. Lateral stripe may also be distinct, vague, or absent. Throat whitish to lemon yellow. Iris nearly black. In Santa Clara, Santa Cruz, San Mateo, and San Francisco Cos., dark pigment obscures side stripes and middorsal stripe is yellowish. OREGON AQUATIC GARTER SNAKE, *T. a. hydrophilus* (Pl. 49). Color between dorsal and lateral stripes may be gray or olive-gray with two alternating rows of dark spots, brown with spots less distinct, or nearly black; spots may be variously joined. Dorsal stripe may be yellow or orange and distinct or indistinct. Lateral stripe may be distinct, dull, or lacking. Below light-colored and unmarked, with flesh-colored or purplish tinge toward tail. Throat may be lemon yellow. Usually 10 lower labials. Permanent streams with rocky beds and swift clear water.

REMARKS: The "Aquatic Garter Snake" (*Thamnophis couchii aquaticus*) of my 1985 Field Guide is now considered to represent "intergrade" popula-

Aquatic Garter Snake (Oregon subspecies). A snake of permanent streams with rocky beds and swift clear water. Josephine Co., Ore.

tions between the above 2 subspecies. In this zone the striped form is often intermixed with the spotted form in the same population. Intergrades may have a yellow to orange dorsal stripe, dark olive to dusky area between dorsal and lateral stripes, often a lemon yellow throat, and venter may be blotched with yellowish or pale salmon on a light blue to greenish ground color; iris gray. Santa Cruz Aquatic Garter Snake coexists, and apparently hybridizes with, the Two-striped Garter Snake (below). Oregon Aquatic Garter Snake (above) and Sierra Garter Snake (*T. couchii*) occur along Pit R., Shasta Co., Calif. where some apparent hybrids have been found. In overlap zone with Two-striped Garter Snake (below) few hybrids have been found. Most populations are either one species or the other.

TWO-STRIPED GARTER SNAKE   Fig. 27, Pl. 49, Map 167
Thamnophis hammondii

IDENTIFICATION: 24–40 in. (61–102 cm). A two-striped garter snake —*middorsal stripe absent or represented by a trace (nuchal spot) on the neck.* Lateral stripe (sometimes absent) on 2nd and 3rd scale rows. Olive, brown, or brownish gray above, often with 4 lengthwise rows of small, well-separated dark spots over dorsum between lateral stripes (sometimes absent), or dark spots confined to lower sides above lateral stripes, or absent. Nonstriped/spotted and striped/nonspotted morphs are thus recognized, depending upon locality. No red flecks on sides. Dull yellowish to orange-red or salmon below, either unmarked or slightly marked with dusky. Throat may be whitish. Black individuals, sometimes with obscure or without lateral stripes, or even spots, found along outer coast from Oceano to Montana de Oro State Park, San Luis Obispo Co., and are to be expected from Monterey Bay to Gaviota

State Beach, Santa Barbara Co., Calif. Along Piru R. in ne. Ventura Co., two color morphs occur—dark greenish and dull reddish. Dorsal scales keeled in a maximum of 21 rows. Upper labials usually 8. Eyes relatively large.

Found in or near permanent or intermittent freshwater, often along streams with rocky beds bordered by willows or other streamside growth. In Baja Calif. in riparian habitats and oases. Frequents oak woodland, brushlands, and sparse coniferous forests. Highly aquatic. Often active at dusk or at night but also found in daytime. Live-bearing, 4–36 young born in summer. Eats tadpoles, California Newt larvae, toads, frogs, fish, fish eggs, and earthworms. SIMILAR SPECIES: Garter Snakes that overlap in range with Two-striped Garter Snake and have middorsal stripe: (1) Common (p. 375), (2) Western Terrestrial (p. 377), and (3) Aquatic (p. 382) (stripe sometimes vague or absent). RANGE: Coastal Calif. from vicinity of Salinas, Monterey Co., to nw. Baja Calif., in more or less continuous range to somewhat south of El Rosario; scattered localities in Baja Calif. Sur—San Ignacio, Muelge, Cadeje, Comondu, San Pedro la Presa, and elsewhere. Status of a small melanistic Catalina I. population off s. Calif. coast needs close attention. Sea level to around 8,000 ft. (2,450 m).

REMARKS: Along cen. Calif. coast south of Monterey, Two-striped Garter Snake coexists with Common, Western Terrestrial, and Aquatic Garter Snakes. Occurs adjacent to (and seems to overlap) range of Sierra Garter Snake (*T. couchii*) in Mt. Pinos–Frazer Mt. area. Housing, urban development and other human impacts have reduced historic range of Two-striped Garter Snake in Calif. by an estimated 40 percent.

NORTHWESTERN GARTER SNAKE   Pl. 50, Map 169
Thamnophis ordinoides

IDENTIFICATION: 13–38 in. (33–96 cm). A beautiful serpent with coloration that varies greatly: Usually a well-defined dorsal stripe of yellow, orange, red, blue, or white, but stripe may be faint, a trace on neck, or absent. Side stripes distinct, faint, or absent, located on 2nd or 3rd scale rows. Dorsal ground color varies—black, various shades of brown, olive, greenish, gray, or bluish; usually spotted or speckled with black and/or reddish. Belly yellowish, olive, brown, bluish, slaty, or black; *often with reddish blotches or tinge and sometimes marked extensively with black,* especially in northern part of range. Dorsal scales keeled, usually in up to 17 rows at midbody, rarely 19 rows. *Usually 7 upper labials.* Anal single. Some populations in coastal Ore. have individuals with 1, 2, or 3 stripes that vary from brown, black, or bluish to almost all red. Occasional melanistic individuals may be all black above with faint dorsal stripe on the neck. Young: Often profusely dark-spotted.

Chiefly terrestrial, usually frequenting meadows and clearings in forested areas where there is abundant low vegetation. Active on warm sunny days. When frightened, usually seeks dense vegetation rather than water, but has been reported swimming in open waters. It appears that striped individuals tend to crawl rapidly away from predators, the stripe apparently delaying recognition of direction and speed, whereas blotched or plain-colored individuals tend to move abruptly and then hold still, their coloration apparently working best when immobile. Live-bearing; 3–20 young born June–Aug. Eats slugs, snails, earthworms, small amphibians, and perhaps fish. **SIMILAR SPECIES:** (1) Western Terrestrial Garter Snake (p. 377) usually has 8 upper labials and up to 19 or 21 dorsal scale rows at midbody. (2) Oregon Garter Snake, subspecies of Aquatic Garter Snake (p. 382), with which it overlaps in range, usually has 8 upper labials and 19 or 20 dorsal scale rows. Striped, plain-colored, and blotched pattern types occur. (3) Common Garter Snake (p. 375) lacks red markings on belly; has longer, more triangular head; larger eyes; and usually 19 scale rows at midbody. **RANGE:** From Bella Coola area to lower Fraser R. drainage, Vancouver I. and some adjacent islands in sw. B.C. to extreme nw. Calif.; chiefly west of crest of Cascade Mts., but extends east of crest in Wash. over Snoqualmie and White Passes and n. Ore. through Columbia R. Gorge to vicinity of The Dalles. Sea level to around 5,500 ft. (1,676 m).

BLACK-NECKED GARTER SNAKE Pl. 50, Map 161
Thamnophis cyrtopsis

IDENTIFICATION: 16–46 in. (41–117 cm). In our area a whitish or pale yellow middorsal stripe usually separates 2 *large black blotches at back of head.* Stripe may be orange and wavy in neck region. White crescent between each blotch and corner of mouth. Top of head gray. Pale *side stripe on 2nd and 3rd scale rows,* sometimes wavy because of intrusion of bordering black spots. Olive-brown or olive-gray above, 2 alternating rows of black or uniformly dark spots between stripes. Spots may fade out at about midbody. Upper labial sutures black-barred. Belly light greenish white, bluish white, or brownish. Dorsal scales keeled, *usually in 19 rows at midbody.* Seven or 8 upper labials. Anal single.

Chiefly a stream snake of foothills, high plateaus, and mountains. Habitats vary—desert, grassland, mesquite flats, chaparral-covered hillsides, oak woodland, and forests of pine and fir. Extends into tropical habitats in southern part of range. Frequents permanent and intermittent streams, spring seepages, and irrigation canals, but in wet weather may wander far from water. Live-bearing; about 7–25 young, born June–Aug. Eats frogs, toads, tadpoles, fish, occasionally salamanders, lizards, earthworms, and crustaceans (*Triops*). **SIMILAR SPECIES:** (1) Checkered Garter Snake (p. 389) usually has 21 scale rows at midbody and side stripe on front of body is confined to 3rd scale row. Checkered pattern extends well out onto tail. (2) Mexican Garter Snake (below) has 19 or 21 scale rows at midbody and side stripe anteriorly is on 3rd and 4th scale rows. (3) Common Garter Snake (p. 375) lacks or has less well defined dark neck blotches and usually has red or orange markings on sides. **RANGE:** Se. Utah and se. Colo. to w.-cen. Guatemala; cen. Tex. to cen. and s. Ariz. Isolated populations in Cane and San Juan R. drainages in extreme northern part of range and in Hualapai Mts., Burro Creek area, and Ajo Mts. in w. Ariz. Distribution spotty. Sea level to around 8,700 ft. (2,700 m). **SUBSPECIES:** WESTERN BLACK-NECKED GARTER SNAKE, *T. c. cyrtopsis,* occurs in our area.

MEXICAN GARTER SNAKE   Pl. 50, Map 160
Thamnophis eques

IDENTIFICATION: 18–49 in. (46–124 cm). In our area, may have whitish to greenish crescent behind each corner of mouth, *paired black blotches at back of head,* a yellow to cream middorsal stripe, and *side stripe on 3rd and 4th scale rows at front of body.* Sides checkered with dark spots on an olive or brown ground color. In some parts of range, dark ground color may obscure black spots. Dorsal scales keeled, in 19 or 21 rows at midbody. 8–9 upper labials with interlabial sutures marked with black. Anal single.

Primarily a highland canyon snake of pine-oak forest and piñon-juniper woodland, but also enters mesquite grassland and desert, especially along valleys and stream courses. Strongly attracted to permanent water sources with associated vegetation. In se. Ariz. occurs in lowland areas such as San Pedro Valley and near Douglas. Formerly at Rillito Wash near Tucson. Eats fish, larval and transformed amphibians, and sometimes lizards, small mammals, and invertebrates (earthworms, leeches). Live-bearing, 7–26 young born June–Aug. **SIMILAR SPECIES:** (1) In Checkered Garter Snake (p. 389), side stripe usually confined to the 3rd scale row on front of body, with more prominent paired dark blotches at back of head. See also (2) Black-necked (p. 387) and (3) Plains Garter Snakes (p. 389). **RANGE:** Cen. Ariz. and sw. N.M. (Gila R. drainage), south in highlands of w. and s. Mex., to Veracruz with an apparently isolated population in cen. Oaxaca. Now nearly gone from lowland habitats in Ariz. and nearby Sonora. Two N.M. localities are 5 mi. (8 km) east of Virden, Hidalgo Co. and Mule Creek, Grant Co. Old record (1911) from Clark Co., Nev., opposite Ft. Mohave, Ariz. From around 2,000–8,500 ft. (610–2,590 m).

CHECKERED GARTER SNAKE   Pl. 50, Map 159
Thamnophis marcianus

IDENTIFICATION: 1 2¾–42¼ in. (32–107 cm). In our area, rather pale with a checkered pattern of large *black blotches on a brownish yellow, brown, or olive ground color.* Cream or white middorsal stripe becomes yellowish toward head. Paired black blotches at back of head. Whitish or yellowish crescent between dark blotches and corner of mouth. *Distinctive black-bordered area of head color extends downward covering the 7th and 8th upper labials.* Side stripe *usually confined to 3rd scale row on front of body* (may include 4th row in lower Colorado R. area) and on 2nd and 3rd scale rows on rear of body. Top of head usually olive. White below, sometimes with a tinge of yellowish, greenish, or clouding of slaty gray. Dorsal scales keeled, usually in 21 rows at midbody. Usually 8 upper labials. Anal single.

Chiefly a lowland river system snake that frequents ponds, springs, streams, rivers, and irrigation ditches in arid and semiarid regions. Also ranges sparingly into pine-oak belt in mountains. A grassland species, able to exist along streams in the desert; has entered irrigated areas in some parts of desert. Live-bearing, 3–35 young, born May–Oct. Eats fish, toads, frogs, tadpoles, salamanders, lizards, snakes, mice, and invertebrates such as slugs and earthworms. In warmer, more arid parts of range, feeds chiefly at night. **SIMILAR SPECIES:** (1) Black-necked Garter Snake (p. 387) usually has 19 scale rows at midbody and side stripe on 2nd and 3rd scale rows on front of body. (2) In Plains (below) and (3) Mexican Garter Snakes (p. 388), side stripe is on 3rd and 4th scale rows. (4) Wandering Garter Snake (p. 379) has side stripe on 2nd and 3rd scale rows and usually lacks well-defined dark neck blotches. **RANGE:** Sw. Kans. and s. Ariz. south through Mex. to Costa Rica. Se. Calif. to e.-cen. Tex. Reported from 3 mi. (4.8 km) south of Show Low, Navajo Co., Ariz., but substantiation needed. Sea level to around 7,218 ft. (2200 m). Apparently hybridizes with Plains Garter Snake (below) in sw. Kans. **REMARKS:** In decline on major river systems of s. Ariz., N.M., and adjacent Mex.

PLAINS GARTER SNAKE *Thamnophis radix*   Pl. 50, Map 165
IDENTIFICATION: 14¼–42¼ in. (37–107 cm). Well-defined dorsal stripe, orange or yellow on front of body, becoming paler toward rear. *Side stripe on 3rd and 4th scale rows toward front.* Double

row of dark blotches, often in a checkered arrangement, between stripes on a greenish gray, olive, reddish, or brownish ground color. Occasional dark individuals with obscure blotches. Prominent black bars on whitish or yellow upper labials. Whitish, yellow, bluish green, or gray below, with a row of dark, sometimes vague spots down each side of belly and sometimes varying amounts of black pigment medially. *Usually 7 upper labials. Dorsal scales keeled, usually in 21 rows at midbody.* Anal single.

Often inhabits wet prairies and farmland, but ranges into piñon-juniper belt and pine-fir and aspen forests. Found near ponds, sloughs, marshes, lakes, streams, and rivers, but may stray far from water into dry grasslands and other arid environments. Live-bearing, 5–62 (occasionally 90 or more) young, born July–Sept. Eats salamanders, frogs, toads, tadpoles, fish, small mammals, earthworms, leeches, slugs, and carrion. **SIMILAR SPECIES:** (1) In Common (p. 375), (2) Western Terrestrial (p. 377), and (3) Black-necked (p. 387) Garter Snakes, side stripe is on 2nd and 3rd scale rows on front part of body. (4) Checkered Garter Snake (p. 389) usually has side stripe on 3rd scale row only. (5) Mexican Garter Snake (p. 388) has 8–9 upper labials. (6) See also Western Ribbon Snake (below). **RANGE:** S. Canada through Great Plains to ne. N.M., n. Tex., and sw. Ill.; n. and e. Mont. to nw. Indiana. An isolated population in cen. Ohio. From around 400–7,500 ft. (120–2,290 m).

WESTERN RIBBON SNAKE   Pl. 50, Map 164
Thamnophis proximus
IDENTIFICATION: 18–48½ in. (46–123 cm). Slender, with *pale, unmarked upper labials that contrast with darker color on top of head.* Dorsal stripe usually orange or tan in our area but yellow, orange, reddish, brown, or greenish elsewhere. *Lateral stripe on 3rd and 4th scale rows* sometimes bordered below by a narrow, dark stripe. Ground color between stripes olive-brown, brown, gray, or black. Light-colored parietal spots conspicuous and usually touching each other. Belly unmarked. *A very long tail, ¼–⅓ total length of snake.* Eight (rarely 7) upper labials. Dorsal scales keeled, in maximum of 19 rows. Anal single.

Highly adaptable species; occurs in a great variety of habitats from temperate woodland and grassland to tropics. Agile and alert, frequents vegetation bordering streams, lakes, ponds, sloughs, and marshes. When frightened, often retreats to water and swims with speed and grace, usually staying among emergent plant growth near shore. An efficient climber; may first be seen as it drops from a basking site in overhanging vegetation into the water. Live-bearing; 4–36 young, born June–Oct. Eats frogs, toads, tadpoles, salamanders, fish, and lizards. Sometimes scavenges.

SIMILAR SPECIES: (1) Plains Garter Snake (p. 389) has black-barred upper labials. (2) Common, (3) Western Terrestrial, (4) Checkered, and (5) Black-necked Garter Snakes have lateral stripe on scale rows 2 and 3. Long tail and contrasting, pale, unmarked upper labials also help distinguish this snake from coexisting species. **RANGE:** S. Wisc. to Gulf Coast, and through ne. Mex. to Costa Rica; e. N.M. to Miss. Valley. In N.M. occurs along lower Pecos R. drainage and in northeast along Canadian R. In Colo. known only from Furnace Canyon, sw. Baca Co. Sea level to around 8,000 ft. (2,440 m in Sierra Madre Oriental, Mex.). **SUBSPECIES:** ARID LAND RIBBON SNAKE, *T. p. diabolicus*, occurs in our area.

CAPE GARTER SNAKE *Thamnophis validus* **Pl. 56, Map 203**
Baja California Sur (see p. 430).

LINED SNAKE *Tropidoclonion lineatum* **Pl. 50, Map 168**
IDENTIFICATION: 7½–22½ in. (19–57 cm). Close relative of Garter Snakes. Middorsal and side stripes well-defined and bordered by dark spots set in a dark or light olive-gray or light brown ground color. Middorsal stripe whitish, pale gray, yellow, or orange. Side stripe on 2nd and 3rd scale rows. Belly whitish to yellow, marked with 2 *rows of black spots along midline.* Head about same width as neck. *Five or 6 upper labials.* Scales keeled, in 19 rows at midbody. Anal single.

A locally abundant but secretive snake of prairies, open woods, floodplains, city dumps, grassy vacant lots, and parks. Excellent burrower in loose moist soil. Hides under objects in daytime, venturing forth at dusk and at night in search of earthworms upon which it feeds. Activity stimulated by wet weather. When first caught, often voids the contents of anal glands. Live-bearing; 2–17 young, born in Aug.–Sept. **RANGE:** Se. S.D. to s. Tex.; cen. and ne. N.M. and e. Colo. (Boulder-Denver region and southeastern part) to cen. Ill. Notable populations near Sandia Park, Bernalillo Co. and in Capitan Mts., Lincoln Co., N.M. Near sea level to around 6,562 ft. (2,000 m). **SUBSPECIES:** NORTHERN LINED SNAKE, *T. l. lineatum*, occurs in our area.

WESTERN GROUND SNAKE **Pl. 45, Map 170**
Sonora semiannulata
IDENTIFICATION: 8–18 in. (20.3–46 cm). Small crossbanded, striped, or plain-colored, with a head only slightly wider than neck. Brown, olive, reddish, orange or gray above, lighter on sides. Dorsal pattern varies greatly—(1) dark crossbands may encircle body,

form saddles on back, or be reduced to a single neckband; (2) dark crossbands may be entirely absent; (3) some populations (along lower Colorado R.) have a broad beige, red, or orange middorsal stripe and greenish gray or bluish gray sides. Orange-striped individual and a black-and-white crossbanded one found, along with the usual orange and black crossbanded form, in Owyhee R. drainage in se. Ore. Plain, crossbanded, and striped individuals sometimes all occur at same locality. In Colo. some are found with only an orange dorsal stripe. Baja Calif. populations are generally plain-colored. *Usually all types of coloration have a dark blotch or bar (sometimes faint) at the front of each scale, particularly evident on sides.* Whitish or yellowish below, unmarked or with dark crossbands. Scales smooth and glossy, usually in 15 rows toward front. Anal divided.

Secretive nocturnal snake of arid and semiarid regions, where soil may be rocky, gravelly, or sandy and has some subsurface moisture. In Colo. often occurs on hillsides with many scattered rocks partially imbedded. Frequents riverbottoms, desert flats, sand hummocks, and rocky hillsides where there are pockets of loose soil. Vegetation may be scant, as on sagebrush plains of Great Basin and in creosote bush desert, but along the lower Colorado R. this snake occurs among thickets of mesquite, arrow weed, and willows. Ranges from prairies through desert plant communities, thornscrub, piñon-juniper to oak-pine zone. Clutch of 3–6 eggs, laid June–Aug. Eats spiders, scorpions, centipedes, crickets, solpugids, grasshoppers, and insect larvae including ant brood. Shallow grooves on outer sides of rear teeth suggest snakes may be venomous, but they are not dangerous to humans. SIMILAR

Western Ground Snake. A widely ranging species that displays a remarkable array of color patterns, sometimes all color types at one locality— crossbanded, single neck band, longitudinally striped. Owyhee Co., Idaho.

SPECIES: (1) Shovel-nosed Snakes (*Chionactis* species, below) and (2) Variable Sandsnake (p. 395) have flatter snouts and deeply inset lower jaws. (3) Black-headed Snakes (*Tantilla* species, pp. 397–402) have black heads, no loreal, and lack crossbands on body. (4) Long-nosed Snake has mostly a single, undivided row of scales on underside of tail. **RANGE:** Snake R. region of sw. Idaho south to tip of Baja Calif., cen. Durango, and n. Tamaulipas, Mex.; se. Calif. to sw. Mo. and e.-cen. Tex. Ne. Utah records are Vernal, Uintah Co., and Jump Creek, Carbon Co. Northernmost records in Nev. are near Denio, Humboldt Co., and an unverified observation near Battle Mt., Lander Co. Recently reported at Wupatki Nat'l Monument, Ariz. In Baja Calif. ranges from cape north to vicinity of Valle de Trinidad and San Telmo. Sea level to around 6,000 ft. (1,830 m).

WESTERN SHOVEL-NOSED SNAKE

Pl. 45, Map 172

Chionactis occipitalis

IDENTIFICATION: 10–17 in. (25.4–43 cm). *A dark- and light-banded snake* with a shovel-shaped snout, flatter than in most other snakes; *lower jaw deeply inset (countersunk)* and nasal valves well developed. Belly concaved. Head slightly wider than neck. *Dark brown or black crossbands, usually 21 or more, on body,* are saddlelike or encircle body. Ground color is whitish or yellow. Orange or red saddles sometimes present between black ones. *Dorsal scales smooth, usually in 15 rows at midbody.* Internasals not separated by rostral. Anal divided.

Restricted to desert, occurring even in driest parts. Frequents washes, dunes, sandy flats, loose soil, and rocky hillsides with sandy gullies or pockets of sand among rocks. Vegetation usually scant—creosote bush, desert grasses, cactus, or mesquite. A burrowing nocturnal species that can move rapidly through loose sand. Smooth scales, inset lower jaw, nasal valves, and angular abdomen are adaptations for "sand swimming"—wriggling through sand rather than tunneling in it. Angular, concaved abdomen is also thought to reduce slippage when crawling on surfaces. Usually stays underground in daytime but roams surface at night, especially after rainfall, leaving smoothly undulating tracks on bare sand between bushes. When hunting these snakes on foot, move quickly from bush to bush with light in hand in order to catch them on the surface before they have time to submerge or climb into lower branches of bushes. Clutch of 2–5 (perhaps as many as 9) eggs, laid late spring and summer. Eats insects (including larval stages), spiders, scorpions, centipedes, and buried chrysalids (pupae) of moths. **SIMILAR SPECIES:** (1) Variable Sandsnake (p. 395) has 13 scale rows at midbody, and rostral separates internasals. (2) Western Ground Snake (p. 391) has dark pigment at base of most dorsal scales and less extreme flattening of snout. (3) See also Sonoran Shovel-nosed Snake (below). **RANGE:** Sw. Nev. to upper end of Gulf of California in Baja Calif. to vicinity of Bahía Santa Maria; s. Ariz. to desert base of mountains of s. Calif. Below sea level to around 4,700 ft. (1,430 m).

SUBSPECIES: MOJAVE SHOVEL-NOSED SNAKE, *C. o. occipitalis.* Bands brown, no black or brown secondary bands between primary ones. Usually 45 or more bands on body plus unmarked front band positions on lower surface (indicated by ends of dorsal bands). Narrow red crossbands faint or absent. COLORADO DESERT SHOVEL-NOSED SNAKE, *C. o. annulata.* Bands usually black. Usually fewer than 45 bands on body plus unmarked front band positions on lower surface. Narrow red crossbands present. TUCSON SHOVEL-NOSED SNAKE, *C. o. klauberi.* Black or brown secondary bands between primary bands. Usually fewer than 152 ventrals in males and fewer than 160 in females. NEVADA SHOVEL-NOSED SNAKE, *C. o. talpina.* A pale race. Dark scales in interspaces between broad bands may form secondary bands. Some red may be present in light areas. Usually 152 or more ventrals in males and 160 or more in females.

SONORAN SHOVEL-NOSED SNAKE   Pl. 45, Map 171
Chionactis palarostris

IDENTIFICATION: 10–17 in. (25.4–43 cm). Resembles Sonoran Coral Snake but is harmless. Crossbanded with black, yellow (or whitish), and red, most of the black bands encircling body. Red saddles vary in width: in s. Ariz. about same width as the black bands, but in Sonora may be 2 or nearly 3 times wider. Usually fewer than 21 black bands on body, bordered in front and back by a narrow or wide (Sonora) yellow band. Snout yellow, slightly convex in profile; back of head black. Lower jaw countersunk. Belly concaved. Nasal valves well developed. Scales smooth, usually in 15 rows. Anal divided.

A snake of arid lands. Vegetation includes saguaro, ocotillo, creosote bush, and mesquite. In Ariz. occurs in upland desert in palo verde–saguaro association. Ground surface may be rocky or sandy, but generally is coarser (rockier) and more irregular than that occupied by Western Shovel-nosed Snake. Eats insects, centipedes, spiders, and other invertebrates. Four eggs found in female of Organ Pipe subspecies (see below). **SIMILAR SPECIES:** (1) Western Shovel-nosed Snake (p. 393) lacks broad red saddles, usually has more than 21 body bands, and has flatter, more pointed snout. (2) Sonoran Coral Snake (p. 405) has black snout, broader black bands, and the red bands encircle the body. **RANGE:** In our area, known only from extreme s. Ariz., mainly in Organ Pipe Cactus Nat'l Monument, and along Sonoyta (Mex.)–Ajo road to about 25 mi. (40 km) north of Mex. line; in nw. Sonora to south of Hermosillo. Sea level to around 2,500 ft. (760 m).

SUBSPECIES: ORGAN PIPE SHOVEL-NOSED SNAKE, *C. p. organica*, occurs in our area.

VARIABLE SANDSNAKE
Pl. 45, Map 173
Chilomeniscus cinctus

IDENTIFICATION: 7–11 in. (17.8–28 cm). A highly efficient "sandswimmer." Adaptations for burrowing life even more extreme than those of the Shovel-nosed Snakes (p. 393). Head no wider than neck, lower jaw deeply inset, snout flat, nasal valves present, eyes small and upturned, and belly concaved, angular on each side. The skin appears varnished. Two color morphs — plain-colored (unbanded) and banded, the former predominating in the cape region of Baja Calif. In banded morph, total number of black or brown dorsal crossbands varies from 19 to 49; bands on tail usually completely encircle it. Ground color whitish, pale yellow, yellowish cinnamon, or reddish orange, sometimes with orange saddles or a continuous area of orange on back, between black bands. One further variable feature of patterning: (1) in cape region of Baja Calif., dorsal scales are brownish, especially toward their bases, and *a small dark brown dot* is usually present *near tip of each dorsal scale,* except those of 1st and sometimes 2nd rows; (2) north of cape, dark dots absent and scale bases dark brown; (3) in Sonora, dark dots absent on dorsal scales, and scale bases not notably darkened. Belly whitish to dull yellow. *Rostral separates internasals. Scales smooth, in 13 rows at midbody.* Anal divided.

An arid lands species that lives in fine to coarse sand or loamy soil, in which it "swims." Seldom emerges on surface except at night. Frequents both open desert (mesquite–creosote bush association), sandy-gravelly washes and arroyos in rocky uplands (palo verde–saguaro association), and thornscrub habitats in Mex. In cape region of Baja Calif., most commonly found in deposits of fine, chiefly wind-sorted sand of coastal and inland dunes, flats, hummocks, and wash borders. Search under dead cardons and other surface debris in washes and sandy areas in thornscrub and desert-edge habitats. Excellent burrower. Observed at dusk with just its head exposed, the pale cap blending with the sandy background. When sandsnakes burrow near surface, soil collapses behind them to form serpentine furrows usually found in sandy areas among bushes. Use a stick, hoe, or rake to uncover buried individuals. Two captives laid 2 and 4 eggs in June. A female from cen. Baja Calif. contained 3 large eggs (ova) in late July. Eats centipedes, sand-burrowing cockroaches, grasshoppers, and probably ant pupae and other insects. **SIMILAR SPECIES:** See Western Shovel-nosed Snake (p. 393). **RANGE:** Cen. and sw. Ariz. from about 12 mi. (20 km) e.-ne. of Wickenburg to s. Sonora; throughout Baja Calif. except northern and northeastern part. On Pacific Coast of Baja Calif., ranges north to vicinity of Santo Tomás. Found on Tiburón I., Gulf of Calif. Sea level to 3,000 ft. (910 m).

Taxon throughout most of Baja Calif. is treated as a distinct species, *C. stramineus,* by some herpetologists.

CHIHUAHUAN HOOK-NOSED SNAKE Pl. 47, Map 174
Gyalopion canum

IDENTIFICATION: 7–15 in. (17.8–38 cm). A smooth-scaled, cross-banded snake with a rather stout, cylindrical body and upturned snout. *Rostral scale is flat or concave above and widely separates internasals.* Thirty or more brown or yellowish brown, dark-edged crossbands on body, 8–12 on tail; bands on head may be particularly prominent. Ground color above grayish brown, tan, or yellowish gray. Whitish or pale gray below, sometimes with salmon down middle of belly. Usually 17 scale rows at midbody. Anal divided.

Often difficult to find, perhaps because of its burrowing and nocturnal habits. Most found roaming the surface on nights following rains. Primarily of Chihuahuan Desert. In U.S. inhabits semiarid environments of grass, creosote bush, and piñon-juniper woodland. Found in rocky areas, deposits of loose soil, and on desert flats. When first disturbed, often writhes and contorts its body, swings its tail forward, and everts lining of its vent with a bubbling, popping sound. May strike with mouth closed when molested. An individual laid 4 eggs on June 10, another single egg on July 1. A road-killed female in early June contained 2 eggs. Eats spiders (especially), centipedes, scorpions, and small snakes. **SIMILAR SPECIES:** (1) Western Hog-nosed Snake (p. 347) has keeled scales, and rostral has a ridge down the middle. (2) See also Thornscrub Hook-nosed Snake (below). **RANGE:** Se. Ariz., cen. and s. N.M. to cen. Tex., south to ne. Sonora, Nayarit, Zacatecas, San Luis Potosí, and Michoacan, Mex. From around 1,000–6,890 ft. (330–2,100 m).

THORNSCRUB HOOK-NOSED SNAKE Pl. 47, Map 175
Gyalopion quadrangulare

IDENTIFICATION: 6–12 in. (15.2–30 cm). The *upturned* snout and, in our area, *black saddles on the back* distinguish this snake, rarely found in U.S. A *red or rust-colored band,* broken by black saddles, runs length of body on each side. Ground color between saddles and red bands is ash white, and from above forms pale rectangular patches along middle of back. Belly pale greenish yellow without pattern. Scales smooth, usually in 17 scale rows at midbody.

Anal usually single. **Young:** Red bands usually darker than adult.

Secretive burrower, found in loose soil of canyon bottoms and outwash plains on western slope Sierra Madre Occidental of Mex. and southern headwaters of Gila R. drainage in Ariz. In Ariz. occurs in rolling foothills of mesquite grassland, including partly cultivated sections. Ranges from Sonoran Desert creosote bush habitats and tropical thorn woodland into dry tropical and subtropical forest in w. Mex. Evidently strictly nocturnal and crepuscular, seen abroad on surface chiefly during and after rains in summer and fall. Eats spiders, centipedes, and scorpions. **SIMILAR SPECIES:** (1) Chihuahuan Hook-nosed Snake has brown crossbands on a light brown or grayish dorsum rather than broad black saddles and usually a divided anal. (2) Long-nosed Snake (p. 370) lacks upturned snout. (3) See also Western Hog-nosed Snake (p. 347). **RANGE:** Extreme s. Ariz. in Patagonia-Pajarito Mts. area, Santa Cruz Co., south to Nayarit, Mex. One reported crossing a paved road in the evening near Salome, La Paz Co., Ariz., on July 12, 1993. This record requires verification. From near sea level to around 4,400 ft. (1,340 m). Overlaps range of Chihuahuan Hook-nosed Snake in se. Ariz.

BLACK-HEADED SNAKES: GENUS *Tantilla*

Small, slender, smooth-scaled, flat-headed snakes. Top of head black or dark brown; back plain (unpatterned) brown. Most species have a white collar, usually followed by a black band or row of black dots. Belly salmon or coral red (Pl. 46), without dark spotting, the color not extending to ends of ventrals. Slightly enlarged and grooved teeth at rear of upper jaw are thought to aid in injection of venom (not considered dangerous to humans) into prey. Scales in 15 rows. No loreal. Anal divided. Absence of loreal scale and lack of reddish color on ends of ventrals distinguish these snakes from Ring-necked Snakes (p. 345). Differences in copulatory organs (hemipenes) are sometimes useful in species recognition, so, although ordinarily not possible to examine in the field, they are mentioned in the accounts (see Fig. 28).

Secretive and ground-dwelling; spends much time underground, hence locality information is often scant.

Search by turning over flat rocks and other surface objects, and watch for them on road surfaces when driving *slowly* at night on dark-paved, little traveled roads. Food includes millipedes, centipedes, spiders, and insects. About 50 species. Eleven species in U.S., 5 in our area. S.-cen. and s. U.S. to n. Argentina.

Most of these snakes are so similar in appearance that they are difficult to distinguish. General appearance is illustrated in Pl. 46, the California Black-headed Snake. See Fig. 29 for a sum-

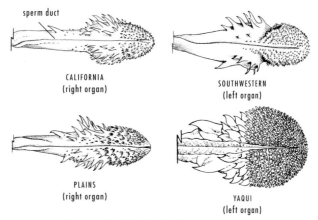

Fig. 28. Hemipenes of black-headed snakes

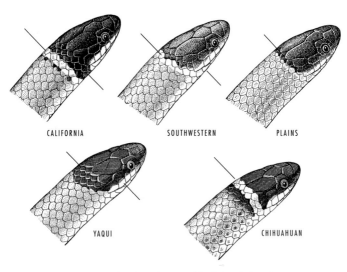

Fig. 29. Variation in head markings of black-headed snakes (See p. 399–402)

mary of species differences. Rely heavily on geographic location to identify species.

CALIFORNIA BLACK-HEADED SNAKE
(WESTERN BLACK-HEADED SNAKE)

Tantilla planiceps **Figs. 28, 29, Pl. 46, Map 177**

IDENTIFICATION: 5–15 1/2 in. (12.7–39 cm). The blackish cap usually extends 2–3 scale lengths beyond posterior (hindmost) end of furrow between parietal scales, and downward 1/2–2 scales below corner of mouth. Rear border of cap convex or straight, followed by a narrow white or cream collar, 1/2–1 scale wide, which may or may not be bordered by dark dots. Plain brown to olive-gray above, sometimes faintly *marked with a narrow dark middorsal stripe.* Broad orange or reddish stripe down middle of belly, not extending to tips of ventrals; rest of belly whitish, unmarked. *Hemipenes nearly cylindrical, without enlarged globular tip, lacking small spines near enlarged basal spine* (Fig. 28). Scales smooth, in 15 rows. Anal divided.

In more arid parts of range (desert side of mountains in s. Calif.), upper surface is pale brown and dark cap usually does not extend below corner of mouth. White collar may be faint or absent and seldom has a dark border,

Little known about habits of this snake. Found in grassland, chaparral, oak and oak-pine woodland, desert-edge and thorn-scrub habitats, under stones on both level ground and hillsides. In arid lands, occurs along rocky edges of washes, arroyos, and streams and on rocky hillsides. Apparently spends most of its time underground in crevices and in burrows of other animals. Seldom encountered on surface except on warm nights, when it may be found on roadways. Look under flat rocks, logs, boards, dead agaves, yuccas, and other plant debris. Clutch of 1–3 eggs, laid May–June. Eats insects (especially beetle larvae) and centipedes.

SIMILAR SPECIES: (1) In Southwestern Black-headed Snake (p. 400), black cap usually does not extend below corner of mouth, and no dark spots border pale collar. Hemipenes have enlarged globular tip and 2 enlarged spines at base. (2) Plains Black-headed Snake (p. 400) usually larger, and black cap usually somewhat pointed toward rear and extends 3–5 scales behind furrow separating parietal scales; no light collar. **RANGE:** Coastal mountains of Calif. from vicinity of San Francisco Bay (south of San Jose and southeast of Livermore) to tip of Baja Calif. In s. Calif. ranges to desert side of mountains as at White Water Canyon, Riverside Co. Near sea level to around 4,000 ft. (1,220 m).

REMARKS: Distribution of this species and Southwestern Black-headed Snake in cen. Calif needs further study. Structure of hemipenes has been chief basis for species recognition in determining present ranges.

SOUTHWESTERN BLACK-HEADED SNAKE (SMITH'S BLACK-HEADED SNAKE)
Tantilla hobartsmithi   **Figs. 28, 29, Map 177**

IDENTIFICATION: 5 1/5–15 in. (13.2–38 cm). Similar to California Black-headed Snake. Head cap dark brown or black, extending 1/2–3 scales beyond posterior end of furrow between parietal scales, but usually *not below corner of mouth*. Rear border of cap usually convex or straight, followed by a white to cream collar 1/2–2 scales wide. *Usually no dark band or dark spots bordering rear edge of collar.* Plain brown or beige above. Broad coral red or rufous stripe below, not extending to outer edges of ventrals. *Hemipenes club-shaped with enlarged globular tip and 2 medium to large spines at base* (Fig. 28, p. 398). Mental scale usually touches front pair of chin shields. Scales smooth, in 15 rows at midbody. Anal divided.

Frequents habitats of brushland, grassland, sagebrush-greasewood, mesquite-yucca and creosote bush, open chaparral, thornscrub, piñon-juniper woodland, and open coniferous forests. In eastern part of range enters persimmon–shin oak, mesquite–creosote bush, and cedar-savanna habitats. Attracted to canyon bottoms and stream courses. Found beneath rocks, logs, boards, dead yuccas, agave, sotols, and other plant debris. Clutch of 1–3 eggs, laid June–July or perhaps Aug. Eats centipedes, millipedes, and insects (beetle larvae, caterpillars, etc.). **SIMILAR SPECIES:** (1) Plains Black-headed Snake usually has black cap extending 3–5 scales beyond furrow between parietal scales rather than 1–3. Rear margin of cap more convex or pointed than in Southwestern Black-headed Snake. (2) Yaqui Black-headed Snake has more distinct white neck ring bordered along rear edge with cap color. (3) See also California Black-headed Snake (p. 399). **RANGE:** Distribution very spotty. From s. San Joaquin Valley, s. Sierran foothills and Great Basin Desert, Calif., east through s. Nev. and s. and e. Utah to w.-cen. Colo. Farther south it ranges from se. Calif. through Ariz. across s. N.M. to w. Tex.; south in Mex. to cen. coast of Sonora, se. Chihuahua, and n. Coahuila. Some localities in s. Calif. are Tulare Lake area, s. side Tehachapi Pass (desert portion) and Jawbone and Hogback Canyons to the north (Jawbone now severely impacted by off-road vehicles). Sight record, Stansbury Mts., Tooele Co., Utah, needs confirmation. Near sea level to around 6,500 ft. (1,981 m).

PLAINS BLACK-HEADED SNAKE   **Figs. 28, 29, Map 178**
Tantilla nigriceps

IDENTIFICATION: 7–15 in. (17.8–38 cm). *Black or gray-brown cap, convex or pointed behind, extending 2–5 scale lengths behind posterior end of furrow separating parietals.* Usually *no white collar.*

Back brown with yellowish or grayish cast. Whitish below with pink or orange stripe on belly. Mental scale usually separated from chin shields by 1st lower labials. Hemipenes lack globular tip; 1 large spine at base near sperm groove and a moderate-sized one on opposite side (Fig. 28, p. 398). Scales smooth, in 15 rows. Anal divided. **Young:** Hatchlings grayish silver with black head cap and salmon midventral stripe.

Secretive snake of plains and desert grassland, shrubland, and woodland; found under rocks, boards, and other objects by day and occasionally in the open at night. Look under flat rocks on hillsides, especially when soil is damp. Clutches of 1–3 eggs, laid spring and summer. Eats centipedes, millipedes, spiders, and insect larvae, pupae, and adults. **SIMILAR SPECIES:** See Southwestern Black-headed Snake (p. 400). **RANGE:** Along Platte R. in se. Wyo. and sw. Neb. south into Mex.; se. Ariz. to cen. Tex. Near sea level to around 7,000 ft. (2,130 m).

CHIHUAHUAN BLACK-HEADED SNAKE
Tantilla wilcoxi   **Fig. 28, Map 176**

IDENTIFICATION: 7–14 in. (17.8–35 cm). Black cap bordered by a contrasting *broad white collar that crosses tips of parietals*. Collar bordered with black. Cap extends on side of head to corner of mouth. Brown above, with dark spots on sides. Scales smooth, in 15 rows. Anal divided.

Found under rocks, logs, and dead plants (agave, yucca, and sotol) in shaded rocky canyons and on relatively open, sunny, rocky slopes in desert-grassland and evergreen woodland. Extremely rare in our area. **SIMILAR SPECIES:** The broad white collar crossing the tips of the parietals will distinguish this species from all our other Black-headed Snakes. **RANGE:** Huachuca (Ramsey Canyon), Santa Rita, and Patagonia Mts., north to Ft. McDowell, Maricopa Co., Ariz.; south at scattered localities to San Luis Potosí, Mex. Approx. 3,000 to 8,000 ft. (910–2,440 m).

YAQUI BLACK–HEADED SNAKE
Tantilla yaquia   **Figs. 28, 29, Map 179**

IDENTIFICATION: 7–12¾ in. (17.8–32 cm). Dark brown or black cap, usually strikingly darker than light brown or beige back. Cap extends 2–4 scales beyond posterior end of furrow that separates parietals, and downward ½–3 scales below corner of mouth. Rear border of cap usually straight, followed by a white or cream collar ½–1½, scales wide, which may be bordered by several distinct brown to black spots. *White or cream-colored area on side of head contrasts strongly with dark cap.* Ventral color pinkish-orange. Hemipenes with somewhat globular tip and 2 very large spines at base (Fig. 28, p. 398). Mental scale usually separated from anterior (front) pair of chin shields by anterior lower labials. Scales smooth, in 15 rows. Anal divided.

Chiefly inhabits deciduous short-tree forests (thorn forests) of Sierra Madre Occidental of Mex., but reaches coastal plain to the south where it occurs in tropical and semiarid woodland. Found in evergreen and streamside woodlands in se. Arizona, where it generally occurs above 3,300 ft. (1,010 m). In N.M. found in riparian habitats with sycamore, oak, walnut, and mesquite. Southwestern Black-headed Snake tends to occur at lower elevations, chiefly in desert grassland and scrub. Clutch of 1–4 eggs, probably laid late spring and summer. Apparently eats mainly soft-bodied invertebrates. **SIMILAR SPECIES:** Whitish temporal scale area on side of head will distinguish this species from our other Black-headed Snakes (Fig. 29, p. 398). **RANGE:** Se. Ariz. in Pajarito, Mule, and Chiricahua Mts., south through Sonora and Sinaloa to Rio Santiago Valley in Nayarit, Mex. In N.M. occurs on lower slopes of Guadalupe and Peloncillo Mts. Near sea level to around 5,500 ft. (1,680 m).

REMARKS: Is sympatric with Southwestern and Plains Black-headed Snakes in Hidalgo Co., N.M.

BROWN VINE SNAKE *Oxybelis aeneus*   Pl. 47, Map 144

IDENTIFICATION: 36–60 in. (91–152 cm). Extremely slender, *vinelike in shape and color*. Head long, snout elongate and pointed. In our area, ash gray to grayish brown above, grading to bronze, tan, or yellowish brown on front of body. Gray below, grading through whitish to yellow on underside of head. Lips cream to yellowish, unmarked. A dark eye stripe. Scales smooth, in 17 rows. Anal divided.

Rare in our area. Lives chiefly on brush-covered hillsides and stream bottoms grown to sycamore, oak, walnut, and wild grape. To the south in both arid and moist tropical forest. Primarily a predator on arboreal lizards for which its slender form, coloration, and behavior are superbly adapted. In approaching prey, it tends to move at intervals when air currents stir the vegetation and, at the same time, sways its foreparts, thereby further obscuring its advance. When at striking range, it lures its prey by extending and wriggling the tip of its wormlike tongue. Prey is subdued by injecting venom with its enlarged grooved teeth toward back of upper jaw. A person bitten on the hand experienced numbness for about 12 hours. Look closely at vinelike objects in brush tangles and treetops. Hunt for this snake in the morning or late afternoon when lizards are basking, or at night when it may be found sleeping in a loose coil on top of low bushes. Clutch of 3–6 (perhaps to 8) eggs, laid spring and summer. **RANGE:** Pajarito and Patagonia

Mts. of extreme s. Ariz. south through w. and e. Mex. to se. Brazil and Peru. Sea level to around 8,200 ft. (2,500m).

WESTERN LYRE SNAKE
Trimorphodon biscutatus

IDENTIFICATION: 18–47¾ in. (46–121 cm). A "cat-eyed" snake; *pupils vertical.* Head broad; neck slender. *Named for the lyre- or V-shaped mark on top of head.* Light brown to pale gray above, with brown blotches on back; each blotch roughly hexagonal in shape and split by a pale crossbar. Cream, gray, or pale yellow below, often with brown dots scattered on belly. Dark individuals that tend to have a middorsal stripe of light brown have been found at the Pisgah lava flow in the Mojave Desert, Calif. Scales smooth, in 21–27 rows. Lorilabial scale present. Anal single or divided.

In our area chiefly a rock-dwelling snake of lowlands, mesas, and lower mountain slopes but may occur in rockless areas. Often frequents massive rocks, hiding by day in deep crevices and emerging at night. Found in desert grassland, creosote bush desert scrub, chaparral, piñon-juniper and oak woodland, open coniferous forest, thornscrub, and thorn forest. A good climber. The larger southern forms in Mex. and to the south often forage arboreally. Eats lizards, especially crevice dwellers, snakes, birds, and small mammals, including bats, which are caught at their roosts and immobilized with venom injected by enlarged grooved teeth toward back of upper jaw. Prey may be constricted. Persons bitten report mild swelling. Handle with care. To find this snake, search roads in rocky areas at night. Clutches of 7, 12, and 20 eggs have been reported. **SIMILAR SPECIES:** (1) Gopher Snake (p. 361) and (2) Glossy Snake (p. 362) have round pupils and a broad neck. (3) See also Night Snake (below). **RANGE:** S. Calif., sw. Utah, sw. N.M., south to tip of Baja Calif. and Costa Rica; s. Calif. coast to w. Tex. Some localities in the Calif. desert are near Barstow, Bristol Mts., and Pisgah lava flow area, San Bernardino Co., and the Panamint, Argus, and Amargosa Mts., Inyo Co. On Cerralvo, San Marcos, and Tiburón Is. in Gulf of Calif. Sea level to around 7,874 ft. (2,400 m).
REMARKS: Information on distribution is fragmentary due to secretive habits and apparent spotty occurrence.

NIGHT SNAKE *Hypsiglena torquata*

IDENTIFICATION: 12–26 in. (30–66 cm). A pale gray, light brown, or beige snake with dark gray or brown blotches on back and sides, and usually a pair of large dark brown blotches on neck. Neck markings vary considerably. Blotches may be connected, sometimes in a group of 3, or occasionally absent. A black or dark brown bar behind the eye contrasts with whitish upper labials. Belly yellowish or white. Head rather flat. *Pupils vertical.* Scales smooth, in 19–21 rows at midbody. Anal divided.

Frequents a variety of habitats—grassland, chaparral, sagebrush flats, deserts, woodland, moist mountain meadows, and in Mex. thornscrub, and thorn forest. Occurs in both rocky and sandy areas. A secretive, nocturnal and crepuscular prowler that eats lizards, including their eggs (Side-blotched Lizards seem especially favored), small snakes (blind snakes, rattlers, and others), frogs, and salamanders, which it subdues by injecting venom with enlarged teeth toward back of upper jaw. Look in crevices and under rocks, boards, dead branches of Joshua trees, mesquite, saguaro, and other surface litter. Sometimes found on highways at night. Clutch of 2–9 eggs, laid April–Sept. **SIMILAR SPECIES:** (1) Western Lyre Snake (p. 403) has pale crossbars within hexagonal blotches on body and usually a V- or lyre-shaped mark on head. (2) Young Racers (p. 351), which are blotched, have round pupils and wedged lower preocular. (3) Young Gopher Snakes (p. 361) have round pupils and usually 4 prefrontals. (4) Young rattlers (pp. 407–18) have a horny button or rattle on tail. **RANGE:** N. Calif., s. B.C. (s. Okanagan and Similkameen Valleys), n. Utah, sw. Kans. south to tip of Baja Calif. and through mainland Mex. to Guerrero; coastal mountains of Calif. east to e. Tex. Populations in n. Calif., perhaps isolated, occur southwest of Tulelake, at Lava Beds Nat'l Monument, and south of Hornbrook, Siskiyou Co., evidently having penetrated west from Cascade Mts. along Klamath R. canyon. Old record for Santa Cruz I. off s. Calif. coast. Sea level to around 8,700 ft. (2,650 m).
REMARKS: Many insular subspecies are recognized off Baja Calif.

Night Snake. A nocturnal prowler that subdues its prey by injecting venom with enlarged teeth at the back of its jaws. The dark neck markings are usually distinctive. Mariposa Co., Calif.

Venomous serpents with immovable, hollow fangs in front of mouth. Around 300 species. Old World representatives of the family occur in Africa, Asia, Malay archipelago, and Australia and include the cobras, kraits, mambas, and most of the snakes of Australia, notably the deadly Taipan and Tiger Snakes. New World representatives, the Coral Snakes, are usually gaudily ringed with red, black, and yellow, and are particularly abundant in Central and S. America. Only 2 coral snakes reach the U.S. Although they seldom bite, their venom is highly dangerous, and they should not be handled. Among our harmless snakes the Red-banded Kingsnakes, Shovel-nosed Snakes, and Variable Sandsnake have a color pattern resembling that of the Coral Snakes. Differences between these snakes and the Western Coral Snake are pointed out in the accounts of these species.

SONORAN CORAL SNAKE   Pl. 44, Map 181
Micruroides euryxanthus

IDENTIFICATION: 11–24½ in. (28–62 cm). A strikingly colored snake with broad, *alternating rings of red and black separated by narrower rings of white or yellow.* Markings encircle body, becoming paler on the belly. Head black to behind the eyes. A broad white or yellow band at back of head extends across tips of parietals. Snout blunt; head and body somewhat flattened. Scales smooth and glossy, in 15 rows at midbody. No loreal. Anal divided.

An inhabitant of arid and semiarid regions in a variety of habitats, including thornscrub, brushland, woodland, grassland, and farmland. Occurs both on the plains and lower mountain slopes, often among rocks. In Ariz., most abundant in rocky upland desert, especially along arroyos and river bottoms. A secretive species, abroad chiefly at night but sometimes encountered in daytime on overcast days or after rains. Spends much time underground. The flattened shape suggests crevice-dwelling habits. When disturbed the head may be hidden under coils, the tail elevated and waved with the tip in a tight coil, and the vent lining everted with a popping sound. Clutch of 2–3 eggs laid July–Aug. (to Sept. in Sonora, Mex.). Eats lizards (skinks etc.) and snakes, especially blind and ground snakes but also Black-headed, Night, and Ring-necked Snakes. **SIMILAR SPECIES:** (1) In Red-banded Kingsnakes (*Lampropeltis* species, pp. 364–69) the red bands are bordered by black. (2) Shovel-nosed (pp. 393–94) and (3) Variable Sandsnake (p. 395) have pale snouts. **RANGE:** Cen. Ariz. and sw. N.M. to Mazatlán in s. Sinaloa. Chocolate Mts., La Paz Co., Ariz. Tiburón Is., Gulf of Calif., Mex. Sea level to 5,800 ft. (1,770 m).

SUBSPECIES: ARIZONA CORAL SNAKE, *M. e. euryxanthus,* occurs in our area.

REMARKS: Venom neurotoxic (affects the central nervous system) and highly dangerous.

SEA SNAKES: FAMILY HYDROPHIIDAE

Sea-dwelling snakes that primarily eat fish. All sea snakes are venomous and have a fang structure like that of their close relatives, the Coral Snakes (previous family, Elapidae). Fangs located in front of mouth—erect, immovable, and hollow. Most species reach 3 or 4 ft. (1–1 ½ m) in length, but some grow to around 9 ft. (2 ¾ m). Highly adapted for marine life, these snakes can swim and dive gracefully, propelled by side-to-side undulations of the body and tail. Tail is a flattened sculling organ in many species. Most sea snakes, including the single species that reaches our area, bear live young born at sea or in rocky tidal areas near shore. Other sea snakes, however, come on shore to lay eggs. Sea snakes are widespread in tropical and subtropical seas, but absent from the Atlantic Ocean. Some 160 species in the family.

YELLOW-BELLIED SEA SNAKE   **Pl. 56**
Pelamis platurus
    IDENTIFICATION: 20–45 in. (51–114 cm). An ocean-dwelling snake, highly adapted for marine life. In our area, and over much of its range, it is dark brown or black above and bright yellow or cream below, the two colors meeting in a sharp line along the sides. Tail contrastingly marked with black spots or bars on a bright yellow or whitish background. Dark spotting or barring may extend forward on body in some individuals. Head elongate, narrow, and flattened. *Body, and especially tail, flattened from side to side,* which facilitates the snake's eel-like swimming. *Tail oarlike* and used as a scull. Valvular nostrils set high on head. *No straplike scutes across belly,* as in most other snakes. Short fangs in front of upper jaw. **Male:** Usually smaller than female, with a slightly longer tail.
    The bright colors and contrasting pattern are considered to be warning coloration. This snake appears to have few predators.
    Completely aquatic. Attracted to offshore waters of continental and insular coasts, but also found far out in the open sea. Eats small fish, including eels, which it immobilizes with its quick-acting venom. Forages, often in large numbers, along slicks (where sea currents converge) and where flotsam of seaweed, wood, and other debris accumulates. The small fishes that comprise the diet are attracted to such floating material. The Yellow-bellied Sea Snake is an excellent diver and swimmer, but completely helpless

when stranded on land. Bears 1–8 young, perhaps throughout the year. Venom potent, but few human fatalities. Generally not aggressive and are reluctant to strike except at the small fish upon which they feed. When humans are bitten, venom appears to be seldom injected. **RANGE:** The most widely distributed snake. Indian and Pacific Oceans from the coasts of Africa, Asia, and Australia to s. Siberia and the Pacific Coast, including Central America and Mex., where it ranges north to n. Gulf of Calif. and along west coast Baja Calif. Occasionally reaches San Diego area of s. Calif. and has been reported off the coast as far north as San Clemente, Orange Co.

VIPERS: FAMILY VIPERIDAE

PIT VIPERS: SUBFAMILY CROTALINAE

Rattlesnakes, cottonmouths, and the Copperhead—all venomous serpents—are members of this subfamily, but only the rattlesnakes reach our area. The family has the most highly developed venom-injection mechanism among snakes. Large, hollow, movable fangs are located at the front of the upper jaw. In biting, the fangs are swung forward from their folded position of rest and the victim is stabbed and poisoned in a rapid thrust. Pit vipers have a distinctive loreal pit—a temperature-sensitive structure on each side of the face between the eye and nostril, which helps them locate their prey.

Pit vipers range from s. Canada to Argentina and in the Old World in e. Europe and Asia. Closely related to the Old World "true vipers" (subfamily Viperinae), they probably were derived from them; hence their inclusion in the same family. True vipers occur in Europe, Asia, and Africa. About 230 species in the family (Viperidae); about 157 species in the subfamily (Crotalinae).

RATTLESNAKES: GENERA *Sistrurus* AND *Crotalus*

Thirty-four species from s. Canada to n. Argentina, the greatest number in sw. U.S. and n. Mexico. Thirteen species in our area, one of which is a Pygmy or Ground Rattlesnake (*Sistrurus*), readily distinguished by its enlarged head scales. Rattlesnakes frequent a great variety of habitats from sea level to around 11,000 ft. (3,350 m).

These are heavy-bodied, dangerously venomous snakes with a slender neck, broad triangular head, elliptical pupils, keeled scales, and usually single caudals, especially toward base of tail. The rattle, a series of loosely interlocking horny segments at the end of the tail, is found in no other serpents. A segment is added at the base each time the snake sheds. A young snake may add 3 or 4 segments a year, but an old one will add only 1 or none. Recently born young have a blunt horny button at the tip of the tail that persists until broken off. All other western snakes except the boas have a slender tapered tail. Boas have no button and the neck is often nearly as broad as the head. The rattle is not included in measurements of rattlesnakes.

Rattlers are often heard before they are seen. When alarmed, make a sound resembling a sudden burst of steam, but when only slightly disturbed may merely click the rattle. Volume and quality of the sound vary with age, size, and species. The rattling of the little Twin-spotted Rattler (p. 417) resembles the sound made by some kinds of cicadas. Occasionally a harmless snake such as a Gopher Snake vibrates its tail among dry leaves, making a sound resembling that of a rattler, and may broaden its head, hiss, and strike in a threatening manner. If you hear a rattlesnake, stand still until you have located it; avoid jumping and running blindly. Treat a dead rattler with care. People have been bitten by reflex action of the jaws, even of badly mangled specimens.

Small mammals and birds are the chief foods, but lizards, frogs and other prey are also eaten. Live-bearing. Some very young rattlers (see species accounts) may engage in "caudal luring," lying coiled and immobile as they elevate and wriggle their tails, which attracts prey within striking distance. In some species the tail is yellow, adding to its conspicuousness.

MASSASAUGA *Sistrurus catenatus*   Pl. 52, Map 183

IDENTIFICATION: 16–40½ in. (41–103 cm). A row of large rounded dark brown, gray, or black blotches down middle of back; 3 rows of smaller, usually fainter, alternating spots on the sides. *Elongate dark brown markings on the head extend onto the neck,* sometimes forming a lyre-shaped mark. Broad dark eye stripe. Ground color of back gray or grayish brown. Belly pale, largely unmarked in the West. Some individuals nearly or completely black, especially in northeast part of range. *Large plates on top of head.* Dorsal scales keeled, in 23–25 rows. **Young:** Ground color paler and pattern more conspicuous than in adult. Tail yellowish white.

The "swamp rattler" of e. U.S. It frequents river bottoms, wet prairies, swamps, and bogs, but also enters dry plains grassland and dry woodland. In the West it occurs in desert grassland, particularly in low areas of rank growth—in Rio Grande Valley in low plains of mesquite, juniper, and grassland, especially where soils are sandy, and in se. Ariz. in yucca grassland. Also found in cactus-agave habitats. Live-bearing; 2–19 young, born July–Sept.

Eats lizards, snakes, small mammals (woodrats, pocket mice, etc.), frogs, and invertebrates including centipedes. Report of feeding on eggs of Bobwhite Quail. Very young individuals may wiggle the tail to lure insect-eating prey. **SIMILAR SPECIES:** Enlarged head scales and elongate head markings of this snake will distinguish it from our other rattlers. **RANGE:** Cen. N.Y. and s. Ont. diagonally across U.S. to extreme se. Ariz. and Gulf Coast of Tex. Population in se. Colo. apparently now isolated and intermediate in characteristics between the Desert Massasauga and the subspecies to the east (the Western Massasauga). Sea level to around 6,890 ft. (2,100 m).

SUBSPECIES: DESERT MASSASAUGA, *S. c. edwardsii*, occurs in our area.

REMARKS: Although the Massasauga is widely ranging, it has narrow habitat requirements. Its primary habitat is grassland, which is often converted to agricultural uses incompatible with the snake's existence.

WESTERN DIAMOND-BACKED RATTLESNAKE
Crotalus atrox   Pl. 51, Map 190

IDENTIFICATION: 30–90 in. (76–229 cm). The largest western rattlesnake. Gray, brown, pink, or yellowish above, with light brown to blackish, light-edged, diamond-shaped or hexagonal blotches on back and fainter smaller blotches on sides. Melanistic populations on dark lava flows in cen. N.M. *Markings often indefinite and peppered with small dark spots,* giving the snake a speckled or dusty appearance overall. *Tail with broad black-and-white or light gray rings,* about equal in width; thus sometimes called the "coontail" rattler. A light diagonal stripe behind each eye intersects the upper lip well in front of the corner of the mouth. Dorsal scales keeled, in 25–27 rows. **Young:** Markings more distinct than in adult.

Western Diamond-backed Rattlesnake. Perhaps our most dangerous rattlesnake because of its size and boldness, possibly matched only by the Mojave Rattler with its neurotoxic venom. Christmas Tree Pass, Clark Co., Nev.

Frequents a variety of habitats in arid and semiarid regions from plains to mountains—desert, grassland, shrubland, woodland, open pine forests, and rank growth of river bottoms. Ranges from sandy flats to rocky upland areas. Crepuscular and nocturnal, but also abroad in daytime. Perhaps the most dangerous N. American serpent, often holding its ground and boldly defending itself when disturbed. Live-bearing; 4–25 young, born in summer and fall. Eats mammals (rabbits, squirrels, mice, rats), lizards, birds and their nestlings, and occasionally frogs and toads. Young individuals may eat insects (cicadas, locusts, etc.). **SIMILAR SPECIES:** (1) Red Diamond Rattlesnake (below) is pink to reddish brown, lacks conspicuous dark dots in body blotches, and the first pair of lower labials is usually divided transversely. (2) Mojave Rattlesnake (p. 416) has enlarged scales between the supraoculars (Fig. 22, Pl. 51, p. 136), narrow black tail rings, and white stripe behind eye extends behind corner of mouth. (3) Speckled Rattlesnake (p. 412) usually has salt-and-pepper markings; the prenasals are usually separated from the rostral by small scales; or the supraoculars are pitted, deeply furrowed, or appear to have broken outer edges. **RANGE:** Se. Calif. to Ark. and e. Tex.; Ariz., N.M., and Okla. south to n. Sinaloa and San Luis Potosí. Isolated populations in s. Mex. Sea level to around 8,200 ft. (2,500 m).

RED DIAMOND RATTLESNAKE   Pl. 51, Map 192
Crotalus ruber

IDENTIFICATION: 30–65 in. (76–165 cm). A tan, pink, reddish or reddish brown relative of the Western Diamond-backed Rattlesnake (p. 409). Diamonds on back usually light-edged, sometimes indistinct; diamonds usually have only faint pepper marks, if any. A con- spicuous "coontail"—broad black-and-white rings contrast with the rest of body color. *First pair of lower labials usually divided transversely.* Scales keeled, in 29 rows. **Young:** Dark gray at first, but in northern part of range changing to reddish brown.

Frequents desert scrub, thornscrub, coastal sage, chaparral, and woodland; occasionally also found in grassland and cultivated areas. On desert slope in s. Calif. it often occurs in areas of mesquite and cactus on rocky alluvial fans near bases of mountains, but it also ranges well out onto the desert floor. A retiring, secretive, often docile species, usually far less aggressive than the Western Diamondback—less prone to stand its ground. Live-bearing; 3–20 young, born July–Sept. Eats ground squirrels (whitetailed antelope and California ground squirrels), rabbits (desert cottontails and brush rabbits), birds, lizards, and carrion. **SIMILAR SPECIES:** See Western Diamond-backed Rattlesnake (p. 409). **RANGE:** Sw. Calif. from near Pioneertown and Morongo Valley, San

Bernardino Co., Desert Hot Springs, Riverside Co. (northeast of San Gorgonio Pass), and w. Riverside and Orange Cos. to the west; southward through Baja Calif. to the cape. Found on both sides of the Peninsular Ranges in s. Calif., but mostly below 4,000 ft. (1,200 m). Sea level to 5,000 ft. (1,520 m).

SUBSPECIES: NORTHERN RED RATTLESNAKE, *C. r. ruber.* Brick red to pinkish tan diamonds, usually uniformly colored, with no light areas. Ground color light pinkish gray or tan. Little or no pattern on head. CAPE RED RATTLESNAKE, *C. r. lucansensis.* Brown diamonds usually contain light areas. Ground color light yellowish brown. Top of head with dark spots. Baja Calif. Sur from Loreto south to cape.

ROCK RATTLESNAKE *Crotalus lepidus* Pl. 52, Map 187

IDENTIFICATION: 15—33 in. (38—84 cm). In our area, with the exception of snakes from the Guadalupe Mts., N.M. (see Mottled Rock Rattlesnake below), *back marked with widely and regularly spaced, narrow, black, dark brown, or gray crossbands,* which sometimes become faint toward front of body. Bands are bordered with light color and irregular in outline. General tone of the back varies greatly and usually matches background colors—pale gray, bluish gray, greenish gray, tan, or pinkish, sometimes heavily speckled with dusky. Tail yellowish brown or salmon, with narrow, dark, often widely spaced rings. Upper preocular split vertically. Scales keeled, in 23 rows. **Young:** Tail tip bright yellow or orange.

Chiefly a mountain rock-dweller that frequents rocky ridges, hillsides, streambeds, and gorges in arid and semiarid habitats, but may occur in lowlands. Ranges from desert grassland through brushland to lower edge of ponderosa pine forest. Often found near permanent or intermittent streams. Basks among rocks on rather barren ridges or in open areas in woods. Livebearing; 2—9 young, born July–Aug. Eats lizards, snakes, frogs, and small rodents. Young individuals may eat crickets, locusts, and centipedes. **RANGE:** Se. Ariz., s. N.M., and w. Tex., south to Jalisco, Mex. From around 1,000 ft. (outside our area) to 9,600 ft. (300–2,930 m).

SUBSPECIES: MOTTLED ROCK RATTLESNAKE, *C. l. lepidus.* Dusky overall, but sometimes quite pale in color, with fading of blotches, especially anteriorly (Stockton and Edwards Plateaus, Tex.). Considerable dark spotting between the dark body bands, sometimes forming additional bands between the primary ones. Dark stripe extends from eye to corner of mouth. In our area known only from Guadalupe Mts. of se. N.M. BANDED ROCK RATTLESNAKE, *C. l. klauberi.* Dark body bands distinct and widely spaced, contrasting with bluish green or greenish (males), or bluish gray (females) ground color. Spaces between bands moderately dark-spotted or unspotted. No dark stripe from eye to corner of mouth.

Mts. of sw. N.M. (Black Range, Magdalena, and Big Hatchet Mts.) and se. Ariz. (Santa Rita, Dragoon, Huachuca, and Chiricahua Mts.).

REMARKS: See account of Gray-banded Kingsnake (p. 369) for comments on possible mimicry of this snake.

SPECKLED RATTLESNAKE   Pl. 51, Map 193
Crotalus mitchellii

IDENTIFICATION: 23–52 in. (58–132 cm). Color of dorsum varies greatly—cream, gray, yellowish, tan, pink, brown, or black—and usually harmonizes with background. Dark individuals on Pisgah lava flow, San Bernardino Co., Calif. The rough scales and salt-and-pepper speckling, in specimens from some areas, suggest decomposed granite. The markings, sometimes vague, usually consist of bands, but may be hexagonal, hourglass- or diamond-shaped. Dark rings on tail. *Prenasals usually separated from rostral by small scales; or supraoculars pitted, creased, or with rough outer edges* (Fig. 22, Pl. 51, p. 136). Scales keeled, in 23–27 rows.

Over much of range, this rattler is a rock-dweller but it also occurs occasionally on loose soil or in sandy areas. Found in sagebrush, creosote bush, and succulent desert, thornscrub, chaparral, and piñon-juniper woodland. Usually an alert, nervous snake that often holds its ground when cornered. Live-bearing; 2–12 young, born July–Aug. Eats small mammals (mice, kangaroo rats, ground squirrels), lizards, and birds. **SIMILAR SPECIES:** (1) Western Diamond-backed Rattlesnake (p. 409) has "coontail" markings, lacks pitted and creased supraoculars and small scales between the prenasals and rostral. (2) Mojave Rattlesnake (p. 416) has enlarged scales between supraoculars and usually a better-defined dorsal pattern. (3) See also Tiger Rattlesnake (p. 414). **RANGE:** S. Nev. to tip of Baja Calif.; s. Calif. to nw. and w.-cen. Ariz. Sea level to around 8,000 ft. (2,440 m).
SUBSPECIES: SOUTHWESTERN SPECKLED RATTLESNAKE, *C. m. pyrrhus.* (Fig. 22, p. 136). Small scales usually separate prenasals from rostral. Supraoculars unmodified (see below). Ground color highly variable—white to dark gray or varying shades of pink or orange. Dark bands on back, often split by a lighter color. PANAMINT RATTLESNAKE, *C. m. stephensi* (Fig. 22). No small scales between prenasals and rostral. Supraoculars often pitted, furrowed, or outer edges irregular. Tan or gray, with light brown blotches or bands more regular in outline and more distinctly edged with light color than in previous subspecies. SAN LUCAN SPECKLED RATTLESNAKE, *C. m. mitchellii.* Ground color yellowish gray. Blotches heavily speckled with dark spots. Head small. Rattle large.
REMARKS: Recent study indicates that where the Southwestern and San Lucan Rattlesnakes meet in Central Baja Calif., they cannot be differentiated. The subspecific taxonomy of this species will require reevaluation.

SIDEWINDER *Crotalus cerastes*

IDENTIFICATION: 17–33 in. (43–84 cm). The sidewise locomotion, with the body moving in an S-shaped curve, is characteristic. Back generally pale, harmonizing with background—cream, tan, pink, or gray, patterned with grayish, yellowish brown, or tan blotches down back. A dark eye stripe. *Supraoculars hornlike, pointed, and upturned*—this snake is sometimes called the "horned rattler." Scales keeled, usually in 21 rows at midbody.

A desert species, usually found in areas of fine windblown sand near rodent burrows (kangaroo rats, etc.). Most common where there are sand hummocks topped with creosote bushes, mesquite, or other desert plants, but may also occur on windswept flats, barren dunes, hardpan, and rocky hillsides. Sidewinding is a rapid form of locomotion and appears to be best suited to open terrain where the broadside movements of sidewinding are unobstructed by rocks and vegetation. Sidewinding also minimizes slippage on loose soil and heat uptake from hot surfaces because of the greatly reduced contact between the snake's body and the ground. Sidewinders are most easily found by tracking or night driving along roads in sandy areas. The track often shows impressions of the belly scutes and consists of a series of parallel J-shaped marks with the hook of the J pointing in the direction of travel. Chiefly nocturnal, usually hiding by day in animal burrows or coiled, camouflaged, in a shallow self-made pit at the base of a shrub. Eats pocket mice, kangaroo rats, gophers, lizards, and occasionally birds and their nestlings. The horns may fold down over the eyes when the snake crawls in burrows. Live-bearing; 2–18 young, born July–Sept. Young engage in caudal luring. **RANGE:** S. Nev. and extreme sw. Utah into ne. Baja Calif. (to Llano de San Pedro) and nw. Sonora; desert base of mountains of s. Calif. to s.-cen. Ariz. Below sea level (in desert sinks) to around 6,000 ft. (1,830 m).

SUBSPECIES: MOJAVE DESERT SIDEWINDER, *C. c. cerastes.* Basal segment of rattle brown in adult. Usually 21 dorsal scale rows at midbody. SONORAN SIDEWINDER, *C. c. cercobombus.* Basal segment of rattle black in adult. Dorsal scales usually in 21 rows. COLORADO DESERT SIDEWINDER, *C. c. laterorepens.* Basal segment of rattle black in adult. Usually 23 dorsal scale rows.

BLACK-TAILED RATTLESNAKE
Crotalus molossus

IDENTIFICATION: 28–54 in. (71–137 cm). *Tail and sometimes snout black,* contrasting with rest of body. Tail sometimes gray with vague rings. Back with black or brown blotches or crossbands of irregular outline, each edged with whitish and having a single or double patch of light scales at center. Dark markings toward front and middle of back sometimes diamond-shaped. Scales in pattern areas usually one color, not partly dark and light. Ground color cream, yellow, grayish, olive, greenish, or dark rust. Dark individuals occur on dark lava flows. Enlarged scales on the upper surface of snout. Scales keeled, in 27 rows. **Young:** Dark rings visible on tail.

Over much of range, this is a mountain snake that inhabits rockslides, outcrops, areas near cliffs, and stream courses. Avoids barren desert. Ranges from arid tropical scrub and palo verde-cactus-thornbush association through chaparral, into the pine-oak belt. Abroad both day and night; especially active after warm rains. Usually nonaggressive. Live-bearing; 3–16 young, born July–Aug. Female defends brood until after their first molt. Eats small mammals (woodrats, mice, kangaroo rats, rabbits, gophers), birds, and lizards. A moderate-sized Gila Monster was found in the stomach of a Black-tail from Castle Dome Mts., Ariz. **RANGE:** N. Ariz. to southern edge Mexican plateau; w. Ariz. to Edwards Plateau of cen. Tex. In w. Ariz. in Ajo, Kofa, Castle Dome, and Hualapai Mts. On Tiburón I. in Gulf of Calif. Sea level to around 9,600 ft. (2,930 m).
SUBSPECIES: NORTHERN BLACK-TAILED RATTLESNAKE, *C. m. molossus,* occurs in our area.

TIGER RATTLESNAKE *Crotalus tigris*   Pl. 52, Map 186
IDENTIFICATION: 18–36 in. (46–91 cm). Back with irregular cross-bands ("tiger" markings) of gray or brown; composed of dark dots and often with vague borders. Generally *more extensively cross-banded* than other western rattlesnakes. *Head small,* rattle large. Ground color gray, bluish gray, pink, lavender, or buff, becoming pale orange or cream on sides. Tail rings usually indistinct because of darkened light rings. Scales keeled, in 23 rows.

Largely restricted to rocky canyons and foothills of desert mountain ranges, where it occurs in arid environments of cactus, mesquite, creosote bush, ocotillo, saguaro, and palo verde on the lower slopes up into the oak belt. Active both day and night; often abroad after warm rains. Live-bearing. Clutch of 1–6 young. Eats lizards and small mammals (kangaroo rats, pocket mice, deer mice, and often woodrats). **SIMILAR SPECIES:** (1) Speckled Rattlesnake (p. 412) has small scales between rostral and prenasals. (2) Western Rattlesnake (below) has dark dorsal blotches on front part of body rather than crossbands. **RANGE:** Cen. and s. Ariz. to s. Sonora. Peloncillo Mts., Cochise Co., Ariz. On Tiburon I. in Gulf of Calif. Sea level to around 4,800 ft. (1,460 m).

WESTERN RATTLESNAKE *Crotalus viridis*   Pl. 51, Map 189
IDENTIFICATION: 15–65 in. (38–165 cm). A blotched rattlesnake, usually with a light stripe extending from behind the eye to corner of

mouth. Blotches various shades of brown to black, usually edged with darker color and often with light-colored borders. Blotches often give way at rear to crossbands. Ground color of this snake varies greatly over its wide range, often harmonizing with soil color—may be cream, yellowish, gray, pink, greenish, brown, or black. Tail with dark and light rings but usually not sharply contrasting with body color. Our only rattlesnake that *usually has more than 2 internasals touching the rostral* (Fig. 22, Pl. 51, p. 136). Scales keeled, in 25–27 rows.

Frequents a great variety of habitats, from shrub-covered coastal sand dunes to timberline and from prairies and desert-edge habitats of mesquite scrublands to piñon-juniper woodland and montane forests. Rocky outcrops, talus slopes, rocky stream courses, and ledges are favorite haunts; in cooler areas (more northerly parts of range and at high elevations) it may den in mammal burrows, rock crevices, or caves, sometimes in large numbers. Live-bearing; 1–25 (often 4–12) young, born Aug.–Oct. Eats mammals (mice, rats, ground squirrels, prairie dogs, rabbits), birds, including their eggs and nestlings, lizards, snakes, amphibians, and insects. **SIMILAR SPECIES:** The presence of more than 2 internasals touching the rostral generally will distinguish this rattler from all other species. **RANGE:** Extreme sw. Canada to cen. Baja Calif. and n. Coahuila; Pacific Coast to w. Iowa and cen. Kans. Absent from lowland desert. On Santa Cruz, Santa Catalina, and s. Coronado Is. Sea level to around 11,000 ft. (3,350 m).

SUBSPECIES: PRAIRIE RATTLESNAKE, *C. v. viridis.* Usually has a greenish cast above, may also be brown or grayish. Blotches brown, usually well defined and edged with light color. Typically 27 or 25 dorsal scale rows at midbody. Commonly exceeds over 33 in. (84 cm) total length. GRAND CANYON RATTLESNAKE, *C. v. abyssus.* Red or salmon above. Body blotches slightly darker, fading with age; oval-shaped on back. Found in Grand Canyon, Ariz. ARIZONA BLACK RATTLESNAKE, *C. v. cerberus.* Dark gray, olive, brown, or black above, with large dark brown or black blotches often separated by light lines. Blotches on sides conspicuous except in dark individuals. Some individuals nearly solid black but at night may pale to brown or gray with dark blotches. Usually 2 loreal scales on each side. Mts. of Ariz. and extreme w. N.M. MIDGET FADED RATTLESNAKE, *C. v. concolor.* Cream, yellowish, tan, or, rarely, pinkish, above. In adults, blotches are oval and slightly darker than ground color (often faint or absent). Twenty-three or 25 dorsal scale rows at midbody. Seldom more than 24 in. (61 cm) in total length. A 36 in. (91 cm) individual reported from Moab, Utah! Venom potent. SOUTHERN PACIFIC RATTLESNAKE, *C. v. helleri.* Resembles Arizona Black Rattler but ground color usually lighter; a single loreal scale. Blotches dark, angular, and light-edged. Terminal dark tail ring poorly defined and about twice as wide as the others. Young with bright yellow tail. Ranges s. in Baja Calif.

Western Rattlesnake (Northern Pacific ssp.) basking at its hibernation site. Snake hibernation sites are special underground locations that provide escape from winter cold. Some have no doubt been used for millennia. Catherine Creek, Klickitat Co., Wash.

to vicinity of Guerrero Negro. Hybridizes with Mojave Rattlesnake in w. Antelope Valley, Calif. NORTHERN PACIFIC RATTLESNAKE, *C. v. oreganus.* Resembles Southern Pacific Rattler, but dark tail rings well defined and of quite uniform width. Young with bright yellow tail. GREAT BASIN RATTLESNAKE, *C. v. lutosus.* Usually buff, pale yellowish, light gray, or tan above, with contrasting brown to blackish blotches about as wide as spaces between them. HOPI RATTLESNAKE, *C. v. nuntius.* Pink, red, or reddish brown above, with well-defined reddish brown blotches that have light edges. Similar in scalation and body size to Midget Faded Rattlesnake. Rarely over 24 in. (61 cm). The rattler commonly used in the Hopi Indian snake dance. CORONADO ISLAND RATTLESNAKE, *C. v. caliginis.* Small size, up to 28 in. (71 cm). Ground color often gray. Endemic to South Coronado I., off nw. Baja Calif.

REMARKS: Western Rattlesnakes may occasionally exhibit unusual coloration—dorsal blotches may be fused in varying degree, longitudinal striping may occur, and dorsal pattern may be vague or absent.

MOJAVE RATTLESNAKE *Crotalus scutulatus*   Pl. 51, Map 194

IDENTIFICATION: 24–51 in. (61–129 cm). Well-defined, light-edged dark gray to brown diamonds, ovals, or hexagons down middle of back; light scales of pattern usually entirely light-colored. (Dorsal blotches usually lack light borders at extreme southern end of range.) Ground color greenish gray, olive green, brownish, or yellowish. A white to yellowish stripe extends from behind the eye to a point behind the corner of the mouth (except at extreme southern end of range). Tail with contrasting light and dark rings; dark rings narrower than light rings. Enlarged scales on snout and usually between the supraoculars (Fig. 22, Pl. 51, p. 136). Scales keeled, in 25 rows.

Chiefly inhabits upland desert and lower mountain slopes, but ranges to about sea level near mouth of Colorado R. and to high elevations in Sierra Madre Occidental, Mex. Habitats vary—barren desert, grassland, open juniper woodland, and scrubland. Seems to be most common in areas of scattered scrubby growth such as creosote bush and mesquite. Not common in broken rocky terrain where vegetation is dense. Live-bearing; 2–17 young, born July–Sept. Eats small mammals (kangaroo rats, mice, ground squirrels, rabbits, hares), lizards, snakes, birds and their eggs. An extremely dangerous snake—often excitable and with potent venom that contains both neurotoxic and haemotoxic properties. **SIMILAR SPECIES:** See (1) Western Diamond-backed Rattlesnake (p. 409), (2) Western Rattlesnake (p. 414), and (3) Speckled Rattlesnake (p. 412). **RANGE:** S. Nev. to Puebla, near s. edge of Mexican plateau; w. edge of Mojave Desert, Calif., to extreme w. Tex. From near sea level to around 8,300 ft. (2,530 m). May hybridize with Western Rattlesnake.
SUBSPECIES: MOJAVE GREEN RATTLESNAKE, *C. s. scutulatus,* occurs in our area.

TWIN-SPOTTED RATTLESNAKE
Crotalus pricei

Pl. 52, Map 184

IDENTIFICATION: 12–27 in. (30–67 cm). A small, slender, light brown to bluish gray rattlesnake with 2 *rows of brown or blackish spots on its back;* spots alternate or are arranged in pairs and sometimes joined across the back to form transverse blotches. Smaller spots on sides. Fine brown speckling over upper surfaces. Dark stripe behind the eye with light border. Tail often with distinct brown bands. Throat sometimes salmon pink. Scales keeled, in 21 rows. **Young:** Dark, often with obscure spotting.

A mountain rock-dweller of pine-oak woodland, grassy and brushy areas, and open coniferous forest. Activity is restricted by cool night temperatures and thundershowers, but may be abroad during warm rains. Search well-lit rocky slopes on sunny mornings when snakes are basking or hunting. Well camouflaged. Hidden individuals can sometimes be made to rattle by tossing rocks into talus. The sound is weak, resembling a locust or beetle buzzing among leaves. Usually a mild-tempered snake. Live-bearing; 3–9 young, born July–Aug. Eats small rodents, lizards, especially Mountain Spiny Lizards, and nestling birds (Yellow-eyed Junco). **RANGE:** Se. Ariz. (Pinaleno, Graham, Dos Cabezas, Santa Rita, Huachuca, and Chiricahua Mts.) south in Sierra Madre Occidental to s. Durango and possibly Aguascalientes. Isolated populations in ne. Mexico. From around 4,000–10,500 ft. (1,220–3,200 m). **SUBSPECIES:** WESTERN TWIN-SPOTTED RATTLESNAKE, *C. p. pricei,* occurs in our area.

RIDGE-NOSED RATTLESNAKE
Pl. 52, Map 188
Crotalus willardi

IDENTIFICATION: 15–25½ in. (38–65 cm). Reddish brown or gray above, with *whitish crossbars edged with dark brown or black; crossbars merge with color on sides.* A ridge contours the snout, which may have a single vertical white line at its tip. Often with contrasting light and dark stripes on each side of face. Tail rings usually confined to anterior part of tail, near base. Scales keeled, 25–27 rows at midbody. **Young:** Sometimes with bright yellow tail.

A mountain snake chiefly found in the pine-oak and pine-fir belts, but ranges into foothill canyons in piñon-juniper habitat. May be found basking on sunny rocky slopes in moist woodland and forest, or crawling over the forest floor. Frequents canyon bottoms grown to alder, box elder, maple, oak, and other broadleaf deciduous trees. Live-bearing; 2–9 young, born July.–Sept. Young engage in caudal luring. Eats small mammals, birds, lizards, scorpions, centipedes, and insects. **RANGE:** Se. Ariz. and extreme sw. N.M. south in Sierra Madre Occidental to Zacatecas. From around 5,000–9,000 ft. (1,520–2,750 m). An apparent hybrid between this species and the Rock Rattlesnake reported from Peloncillo Mts., N.M.

SUBSPECIES: ARIZONA RIDGE-NOSED RATTLESNAKE, *C. w. willardi.* A white vertical line on the rostral and mental scales. Back brown. Little dark spotting on head. Found in Huachuca (Ramsey and Carr Canyons), Patagonia, Whetstone, and Santa Rita Mts., and perhaps the Empire Mts., Ariz. NEW MEXICO (ANIMAS) RIDGE-NOSED RATTLE-SNAKE, *C. w. obscurus.* No vertical white line on rostral or mental scales; white markings on sides of face often obscure. Back gray or brown above, with abundant dark spotting on head. In U.S. known only from Peloncillo and Animas Mts., N.M., in pine, oak, and juniper forest.

REMARKS: This beautiful snake may be threatened by illegal, irresponsible collecting and some habitat destruction.

BAJA CALIFORNIA RATTLESNAKE
Pl. 56, Map 201
Crotalus enyo
Endemic to Baja Calif. (see p. 431).

BAJA CALIFORNIA "ENDEMICS"

See Maps 89, 124, 195–204. Ninety-six species of reptiles and amphibians covered in the present Field Guide occur in Baja California. However, since 18 of these species are endemic to Baja California they are of special interest and are here described. Two introduced geckos are included. Several other species come close to being endemic. Examples are Cope's Leopard Lizard, the Black-tailed Brush Lizard, and the Baja California Rat Snake. All range widely in Baja California. I decided to include the Rat Snake here, because it has no nearby relatives. Accounts of the others are to be found among their relatives elsewhere. Baja California is thus a treasure-trove of opportunities for the enjoyment and study of reptiles and amphibians, aided now by the publication of professor Lee Grismer's superb book (see Bibliography), which also includes information on island occurrences. Unfortunately, because of space limitations in this guide, it has not been possible to list or even always show in species maps all islands occupied.

Poor road access made it difficult to study the plants and animals of Baja California until 1974, when Mexican Highway 1 (which runs the length of the peninsula) was paved, and other roads were improved. Intensive exploration and study of the peninsula's reptiles and amphibians is now underway and much new distributional information is being obtained.

The following accounts are deficient in a number of ways— size ranges of adults may be unknown, information on food habits and reproduction is frequently scanty, and details of elevational and geographic ranges in some cases are poorly known. These gaps should be a challenge to field observers to improve our knowledge of Baja California reptiles and amphibians.

LIZARDS

SAN LUCAN GECKO *Phyllodactylus unctus*   Pl. 55, Map 195

IDENTIFICATION: 1 ½–2 ⅛ in. (3.8–5.4 cm). Similar to Leaf-toed Gecko (Pl. 24). Purplish sooty to yellowish above, blotched with yellowish to dark brown. Yellowish brown eye stripe may extend onto neck. Tail with dark brown crossbars. Pale pinkish purple to whitish below, sometimes slightly tinged with brown. Underside of toe pads white. In pale phase becomes pale gray or creamy white. Minute *rounded dorsal scales not interspersed with larger tubercles.* No enlarged tubercles on tail. *Each toe has 2 large plates at tip.*

Nocturnal. By day found in rock crevices and beneath bark, rocks, and other objects on the ground. Abroad on rock and bark surfaces at night. **SIMILAR SPECIES:** Leaf-toed Gecko (p. 266) has numerous projecting keeled tubercles on its back and, in the cape region of Baja Calif., where it is sympatric with San Lucan Gecko, it averages about twice the size of the latter. **RANGE:** Known only from cape region of Baja Calif. and Partida and Ballena Is. (off western side of Espiritu Santo I.) in the gulf. Ranges to vicinity of La Paz. Appears to be absent from northwestern part of the cape region. Coexists with the Leaf-toed Gecko (p. 266) in some areas.

COMMON HOUSE GECKO   not shown, Map 195
Hemidactylus frenatus

IDENTIFICATION: 1 ¾–4 ¼ in. (4.4–10.7 cm). Structurally similar to Mediterranean Gecko (see p. 266), including broad toepads of transverse plates, but lacks prominent tubercles on dorsum. Tail moderately long, somewhat flattened, a lateral fringe along each side with numerous small tubercles or spines (when not regenerated). Light gray to dark brown above with diffuse mottling. Below whitish.

An urbanized gecko, especially active at night and attracted to outdoor and indoor lights where it feeds on insects. Typically lays 2 brittle-shelled eggs. **VOICE:** A quite loud *cluck-cluck-cluck.* **SIMILAR SPECIES:** Leaf-toed and San Lucan Geckos, both present in Baja Calif. cape region, have two flaring pads at tips of toes (see Fig. 6, No. 1, p. 29), whereas the Common House Gecko has transverse plates. **RANGE:** Cape region of Baja Calif. Introduced and established at La Paz. Now occurs at several other sites in the cape and at Laredo. Widespread in s. Asia and on Pacific Is.

STUMP-TOED GECKO *Gehyra mutilata*   not shown, Map 195

IDENTIFICATION: 1 ¾–2 ¼ in. (4.4–5.7 cm.) Broad spatulate toe pads, nearly circular and with V-shaped transverse plates. *Tail flattened, broad at base, and constricted at juncture with body.* Wide median row of enlarged ventral tail scales. Can vary its body color to blend with almost any brown, gray, or pale background. Dorsum with fine dusky speckling and *widely spaced paired pale spots on back and tail*. Tail with narrow well-spaced crossbands. Venter pale, without markings. **Young:** Darker than adults; crossbanded with dark lines and often with dark spotting.

Frequents human habitations as well as uninhabited areas where it may be found under rocks, inside rock piles, and on roots, trunk, and under bark of trees. Nocturnal. May be found around lighted areas at night. **SIMILAR SPECIES:** (1) Mediterranean Gecko has knobby tubercles on dorsal surfaces and lacks constricted tail base. (2) Common House Gecko has numerous small spines or tubercles along sides of tail. (3) San Lucan Gecko and (4) Leaf-toed Gecko have toes with 2 large plates at tips. **RANGE:** La Paz and vicinity where introduced. Also introduced in w. Mex. and Hawaiian Is. Widely ranging elsewhere in Madagascar, Sri Lanka, India, se. Asia, Okinawa, Philippines, Indo-Australian archipelago, New Guinea, and Oceana.

BAJA CALIFORNIA SPINY-TAILED IGUANA
Ctenosaura hemilopha   **Pl. 55, Map 196**

IDENTIFICATION: 8–10 in. (20.3–25 cm). The largest lizard in Baja Calif. Adults are easily recognized by their *large size and spiny tails*. Back and sides covered with small smooth scales. Grayish or olive gray above, mottled with black. Dark crossbands across upper back. Ground color varies from pale gray or yellowish gray to dark slaty brown. May undergo marked color change from pale gray to sooty. Limbs dark, spotted and mottled with gray. Throat, chest, and sometimes front part of belly dusky or black. Belly pale dull yellowish. **Male:** Spiny crest on neck and shoulders well developed. Throat, chest, and sometimes upper abdomen black. **Female:** Crest absent or reduced; less dark color on throat and chest. **Young:** Middorsal row of slightly enlarged keeled scales from neck to midback. Dark crossbands or saddles extend length of back. Ground color may be greenish.

Found on rocks, in trees, cardon cacti, especially those with woodpecker holes that afford retreats from predators, mesquites and other plants providing well-elevated perches; seldom descends to the ground. Seeks shelter in crevices where, like the Chuckwalla, it may resist extraction by puffing up its body and lashing out with its tail. Handle with care—large individuals can inflict a severe bite. Feeds chiefly on plants, but occasionally eats reptiles and invertebrates, including crabs in coastal areas. **RANGE:** S. Baja Calif. from just south of Loreto through Sierra de la Giganta to the cape. On Cerralvo I. Sea level to 4,000 ft. (1,220 m).
REMARKS: Evidently introduced from Mexican mainland, but may also have been present naturally. Baja form now considered distinct species.

Crotaphytus grismeri

IDENTIFICATION: To 3 9/10 in. (9.9 cm). *General dorsal coloration brown, spotted and occasionally dashed with white.* Fore and aft collar markings present, the front collar complete ventrally in males. *Green color often present in white area separating black collars.* Limbs tan to yellowish. Inside throat pale. Tail flattened side-to-side with dorsal light stripe. **Male:** Dorsal stripe on tail well defined. Gular area dark blue-gray with black central patch. Large inguinal black patches present. **Female:** Colors generally duller than in males. Tail stripe faint or absent, anterior collar incomplete, and black inguinal and throat patches lacking. When gravid, orange or red lateral bars present. Subadults have burnt orange tails.

Like other collared lizards, this species is a rock-dweller. At the type locality, seen basking on rocks of various sizes from rock rubble at bases of hills to their tops. Active at least from early March to early Nov. Several gravid females observed in early to mid-May and one in early Sept. **SIMILAR SPECIES:** (1) Eastern Collared Lizard adult males lack dark inguinal patches, and both sexes have rounded tails and black throat lining. (2) Great Basin Collared Lizard has more extensively patterned forelimbs, lacks greenish color in whitish collar and dark throat lining. (3) Baja California Collared Lizard usually has a wide dorsal gap in the posterior black collar. (4) Sonoran Collared Lizard has rounded tail and black lining of throat cavity. **RANGE:** Known only from s. Sierra de los Cucapás (Cañon David), a low pass connecting this mountain range from contiguous Sierra El Mayor to the south where it has been seen at Casa de La Palma, Baja Calif. This mountain system lies isolated between the Colorado R. drainage into Gulf of Calif. and bordering ephemeral Playa Laguna Salada to the west (see Map 200).

CAPE SPINY LIZARD *Sceloporus licki* **Pl. 54, Map 199**

IDENTIFICATION: 2 1/2–3 1/8 in. (6.3–7.9 cm). Olive brown or gray-brown above, with a *light dorsolateral stripe* on upper side; stripe pale beige or yellowish on front of body, fading at midbody or near hind limbs. Top of head light brown to coppery brown. Dusky or black blotch toward lower side of neck, with or without a white or iridescent blue spot at center or lower edge. *Throat pale with diagonal gray streaks, the 2 streaks at center often parallel.* **Male:** Broad blue to metallic purple dorsal stripe extends from area above forelimbs to tail base. Blue-green patches on belly become dull, light brownish yellow toward sides. Central part of belly, underside and front of thighs, and groin blackish. Sometimes a blue throat patch. Tail with dusky-edged, light yellowish green or greenish scales that become yellowish tan toward tip. Scales on neck and sides edged with brown, with light areas of scales yellowish or with a pinkish copper cast. **Female:** Lacks blue or purple dorsal stripe, has duller markings on belly and lower sides, lacks black color on thighs and groin, and tail lacks greenish markings. Dusky flecks on body and limbs.

Generally found on large rocky outcrops like those occupied by the Hunsaker's Spiny Lizard (below), but also in trees. Particularly common in more sheltered gullies and canyon bottoms, and often found on rocks in mottled light and shade of strangler figs. Seems to be less wary than Hunsaker's Spiny Lizard. **SIMILAR SPECIES:** Hunsaker's Spiny Lizard (below) lacks dorsolateral stripe on neck and shoulders. **RANGE:** Found at intermediate to high elevations in cape region of Baja Calif.

HUNSAKER'S SPINY LIZARD
Pl. 54, Maps 89, 199
Sceloporus hunsakeri

IDENTIFICATION: 2 ½–3 ½ in. (6.3–8.9 cm). Closely resembles the Granite Spiny Lizard (Pl. 31). Blue throat in male mostly or entirely suffused with black. Blue belly patches usually fused with throat patches. Sides with steeply diagonal crossbars. **Male:** Blue belly and throat markings brighter than in female; markings sometimes quite faint in female.

Chiefly a rock-dweller, frequenting arid tropical scrub and forest. Eats insects. **SIMILAR SPECIES:** (1) The Granite Spiny Lizard (p. 287) is usually larger and has lower combined dorsal scale–total femoral pore count (59 or fewer, not 61 or more). Count dorsal scales along midline, from interparietal scale to rear of thighs. (2) See also Cape Spiny Lizard (p. 422). **RANGE:** Cape region of Baja Calif., and on Ballena, Espiritu Santo, Gallo, and Partida Sur Is. in the gulf. **REMARKS:** Coexists with Cape Spiny Lizard.

BAJA CALIFORNIA BRUSH LIZARD
Pl. 55, Map 198
Urosaurus lahtelai

IDENTIFICATION: 1 ½–2 ⅛ in. (3.8–5.4 cm). Resembles the Long-tailed Brush Lizard (Pl. 32). Sooty to pale gray above, depending on color phase, with crossbars on sides. Broad gray area down center of back, sometimes with scalloped borders. *Tail long and of same general color as body, not notably darkened.* Ground color dusky to dull white below, variously streaked and flecked with gray. *Strip of enlarged keeled scales down middle of back.* Granular scales on sides. Scales on tail and large scales on limbs keeled, those on tail also mucronate. A *single frontal scale.* **Male:** Buff speckling on body and limbs. Orange-yellow or orange throat. Blue-green belly patches. Enlarged postanal scales. **Female:** Lacks buffy spotting, has yellowish to orange throat patch, no belly patches, and postanal scales not enlarged.

Frequents an area of rounded granite boulders in an upland region of s.-cen. Baja California Norte. Tends to occur on smaller boulders about larger outcrops, often where rocks are shaded by shrubs. Rock surfaces and decomposing granite soil are beige with rust tints. Plants in the area include cardons, boojum, creosote bush, mesquite, agave, saltbush, ocotillo, goatnut, cholla, buckwheat, encelia, and mulefat along seeps. SIMILAR SPECIES: (1) Spiny Lizards (*Sceloporus* species, pp. 283–94), have an incomplete gular fold and lack strip of enlarged scales down middle of back. (2) Side-blotched Lizard (p. 295) has a dark blotch on each side behind forelimb, back scales of nearly uniform size, and lacks distinct bluish belly patches. (3) Black-tailed Brush Lizard (p. 297) has a shorter and dark tail, fewer enlarged dorsal-scale rows, and a less distinct dorsal pattern. (4) Long-tailed Brush Lizard (p. 295) has a divided frontal scale and more supraoculars (5–7, not 3–5). RANGE: Baja Calif. from near Cataviña to about 10 mi. (16 km) north. Restricted to a unique granitic area near Cataviña and Las Palmas. This species is surrounded by its sister species, the Black-tailed Brush Lizard, yet the two have, at this writing, not been found sympatric.

BLACK-TAILED BRUSH LIZARD   Pls. 32, 55
Urosaurus nigricaudus
Almost completely endemic to Baja Calif. (see p. 297).

SAN LUCAN ROCK LIZARD   Pl. 54, Map 197
Petrosaurus thalassinus
IDENTIFICATION: 3 ½–7 in. (8.9–17.5 cm). *Body somewhat flattened.* Scales on back smooth and granular; those on tail may be weakly keeled. *Three or 4 dark crossbars on upper back, each edged at rear and sometimes at front with orange.* Head bluish with red or orange in eye region. Blue spots and streaks on neck. Lower back dull yellowish to salmon, with broad crossbands of yellowish brown, slaty, to bluish. Numerous dusky vermiculations (wormlike markings) often present on back. Rump rust to tan. Tail with bluish crossbands separated by narrower paler bands. Throat yellowish to orange with diffuse sooty to black patch at center. Chest yellow to orange with sooty to brownish blotches; rest of underparts dull whitish to pale beige with dusky blotches. Back of head and base of tail often tan. Young: Stripes on rear part of back more pronounced than in adult. Male: Usually considerably larger than female. Crossbands on upper back edged at rear with yellow. Enlarged postanal scales. Femoral pores larger than in female. Female: In breeding season, black crossbands on upper back are edged at rear with bright orange or red. Sides of neck suffused with red or

orange. Orange or red on throat and chest; color sometimes extends to midbelly. No enlarged postanal scales. Femoral pores minute. Although these lizards are readily seen at close range, beyond about 30 yds. (27 m) they usually blend well with rock surfaces.

Primarily a rock-dweller, found especially in areas of massive outcrops, but occasionally found on the ground when foraging and when traveling between rocky areas. Excellent climber that moves over rocks with legs spraddled and leaps nimbly from rock to rock. Eats leaves, blossoms, berries, and probably insects. **SIMILAR SPECIES:** The Short-nosed Rock Lizard (below) is usually less vividly colored, has a thin postorbital stripe, and usually 1 row of scales between suboculars and labials. **RANGE:** Cape region of Baja Calif. and on Espiritu Santo and Partida Sur Is. in gulf. Near sea level to around 5,709 ft. (1,740 m).

SHORT-NOSED ROCK LIZARD   not shown, Map 197
Petrosaurus repens

IDENTIFICATION: Similar to San Lucan Rock Lizard. Usually 1 row of scales between subocular and labials. Snout shorter and blunter. Hind limbs shorter. Head brown sometimes with bright blue spots; body grayish olive. Some individuals may be predominantly sulphur yellow. A thin dark postocular stripe. Four dark crossbands toward front of body. Tail with bluish or dark crossbands. Throat brownish, becoming blackish toward center.

A rock-dwelling species with habits similar to San Lucan Rock Lizard. **SIMILAR SPECIES:** (1) See San Lucan Rock Lizard (p. 424). (2) Banded Rock Lizard (p. 298) has a single black collar mark. **RANGE:** Baja Calif. from vicinity of Cerro Motomi toward s. end of San Petro Martir Mts. to isthmus in cape region. On Danzante I. in gulf.

REMARKS: There is about an 80 mi. (130 km) range overlap of this subspecies with that of the Banded Rock Lizard (*Petrosaurus mearnsi*).

BAJA CALIFORNIA WHIPTAIL   Pl. 53, Map 199
Cnemidophorus labialis

IDENTIFICATION: 2–2 ⅓ in. (5.1–5.9 cm). A striped whiptail that has no light spots in dark fields. Dark fields on sides tan or *reddish brown* to black. *At least 6, usually 7, and sometimes 8 pale stripes;* a total of 8 results when middorsal stripe is divided. Upper stripes beige to yellowish; lowermost stripes whitish. Top of head greenish olive to gray-brown. Tall grades from greenish blue through blue to purplish blue at tip, with a *black stripe on each side, almost to tip.* Whitish below. **Male:** Bluish wash on sides of face, limbs, and belly. **Female:** Lacks or has reduced blue color.

Frequents areas of fine sand and scattered low shrubs and grass along the coast, mostly within about ½ mi. (1 km) from high-tide mark. Search for it after coastal fog has lifted, which may be near midday. SIMILAR SPECIES: Orange-throated Whiptail (p. 317) has an undivided frontoparietal and, at midbody, has 5 light dorsal stripes where it coexists with Baja California Whiptail. Its middorsal stripe, however, is sometimes partly forked at both ends. RANGE: W. coast Baja Calif. Norte from Rio San Rafael at Colonet to Guerrero Negro and west to Punta Eugenia in n. Baja Calif. Sur.

SAN LUCAN ALLIGATOR LIZARD   Pl. 53, Map 198
Elgaria paucicarinata

IDENTIFICATION: 3–5 in. (7.6–12.7 cm). In general appearance, resembles Southern Alligator Lizard (Pl. 41), but dark crossbars on back are usually narrower and often more numerous; also usually has conspicuous *alternating black and white marks on upper labials.* Usually a distinct dark postocular stripe. Sometimes a broad dorsal stripe of olive, brown, orange, reddish, or grayish olive. Pale gray to dusky on sides. Some 11–14 irregular, narrow dark brown or black crossbands on body (not counting tail). Similar but sometimes less clearly defined markings on tail. Some adults have a broad, bronze-colored stripe above, with faint or indefinite crossbars. Soft skin of lateral fold (see p. 140) cream-colored, pale beige, or yellowish orange, crossed by dusky to black bands and/or a network that often sets off pale spots of ground color. Yellowish or grayish white below, with dark line or series of dots along middle of each lengthwise scale row. Temporal scales smooth. Usually 14 or 16 transverse dorsal scale rows; *each scale moderately keeled on back but only faintly so on sides.* **Young:** A broad, bronze-colored or brownish dorsal stripe.

At higher elevations, frequents grassy meadows in mixed forests of pine, oaks, madrone, and shrubs. At lower elevations it ranges into habitats with agaves, cactus, mesquite, and acacias, often near springs or in other cool, moist localities. Usually found under dead yuccas, logs, and other plant debris or crawling among grass and leaves. Eats insects and other invertebrates. SIMILAR SPECIES: (1) Southern Alligator Lizard (p. 331) lacks black and white markings on labials and has greater keeling of dorsal scales. (2) Central Peninsular Alligator Lizard usually has numerous pale crossbands and has more prominent keeling of dorsum. (3) Cedros Island Alligator Lizard has dark irregular markings on head and black markings in lateral fold less developed. White markings in fold more circular and well defined. RANGE: Confined to cape region of Baja Calif.

CENTRAL PENINSULAR ALLIGATOR LIZARD
Elgaria velazquezi **Pl. 53, Map 198**

IDENTIFICATION: To around 3⅗ in. (9.1 cm). Dorsal pattern of *numerous pale crossbands on neck, body, and anterior portion of tail.* Markings fade with age. Some individuals may lack banding. Black and white markings on labial scales. Postorbital stripe usually evident. Rather evenly spaced, dark, circular markings usually present on head. Bar-shaped transverse dark markings in lateral fold. *Strongly keeled dorsal scales.* Transverse dorsal scale rows 14. **Young:** Dorsum strongly crossbanded with pale-colored stripes. Adult tends to retain juvenile banded pattern.

Found in rocky habitats, takes refuge in rock crevices, beneath boulders, and under surface debris. Inhabits andesitic lava flows or granitic outcroppings in arid Magdalena region of cen. deserts of Baja Calif. Individuals found abroad from March through Nov. Observed during nighttime hours from 9:00 PM to 1:00 AM and on overcast days during Sept. prior to or following rainstorms. **SIMILAR SPECIES:** (1) Cedros Island and (2) San Lucan Alligator Lizards lack juvenile pattern of pale, numerous crossbands. They also lack strongly keeled dorsal scales. **RANGE:** Extends from at least 26 mi. (41.5 km) west of Santa Rosalia, southward through the Sierra de la Giganta to at least Misión de Delores, Baja Calif. Probably ranges at least another 19 mi. (30 km) or so north into Sierra de San Francisco in continuous volcanic habitat. Found to around 5,900 ft. (1,800 m).

CEDROS ISLAND ALLIGATOR LIZARD   not shown, Map 198
Elgaria cedrosensis

IDENTIFICATION: Dorsum usually with faintly to well-developed zigzag dark bands edged with white on sides but often not dorsally. Individuals from Cedros I. tend especially to lack dorsal segment of bands. Postorbital stripe usually distinct. Dark spotting on top of head varies. Island individuals tend to have head-spotting reduced or absent. Only largest individuals have a few scattered spots of irregular shape. Coastally, some, regardless of size, have larger irregular dark blotches. Many, however, have same condition as insular population. A distinct postorbital stripe is usually present in coastal populations, but distinctiveness varies in insular populations. Dark markings in lateral fold area reduced and form a reticulated pattern around whitish markings that may be circular and well defined in coastal populations. Fourteen transverse scale rows. **SIMILAR SPECIES:** See Central Peninsular Alligator Lizard. **RANGE:** Cedros I. and coastal Vizcaino region, extending at least 137 mi. (220 km) along Pacific Coast from near Puerto Santa Catarina southward to at least Laguna Manuela, Baja Calif.

BAJA CALIFORNIA LEGLESS LIZARD   Pl. 55, Map 200
Anniella geronimensis

IDENTIFICATION: 4–6 in. (10.1–16.5 cm). Resembles California Legless Lizard (Pl. 40), but snout flatter in profile, less pointed from above. Movable eyelids. Silvery to light beige above, with a dark, narrow middorsal line. Dull white stripes on sides between *numerous narrow lengthwise blackish lines.* Blackish below. Tail more pointed than in California Legless Lizard.

Frequents coastal dunes and sand flats in areas stabilized by low-growing bushes and mats of ice plants (*Mesembryanthemum*), and sand verbenas. Can be found by raking surface layers of sand beneath bushes where invertebrates are abundant and sand just below the surface is damp. Seems to prefer southern, sunny side of bushes and hummocks in cool weather. One to 2 young born in summer. Eats small arthropods. **SIMILAR SPECIES:** In California Legless Lizard (p. 336), snout is more pointed from above but more rounded in profile; body has fewer thin, lengthwise dark lines. Orange-yellow below. **RANGE:** Narrow zone along w. coast Baja Calif. Norte, from Rio Santo Domingo at Colonia Guerrero south to El Rosario. San Geronimo I.

REMARKS: Coexists with California Legless Lizard in northern part of range (see p. 337).

MOLE LIZARD (*Ajolote*) *Bipes biporus*   Pl. 55, Map 200

IDENTIFICATION: 7–9½ in. (17.4–23.8 cm). A subterranean, burrowing, earthwormlike reptile with a short, broad, *molelike pair of sharply clawed forelimbs and no hind limbs.* A member of the family Amphisbaenidae, it is not a true lizard. Tail short and blunt, not regenerated when lost. Head short, snout rounded, no neck constriction. Eyes vestigial. Body and tail ringed with numerous, regularly spaced, closely set furrows. Usually pinkish to pinkish white above; occasionally whitish with bluish cast. Deeper pink below, especially beneath forelimbs. **Young:** Generally more pinkish than adults.

This animal burrows in fine, loose alluvial soils of Baja Calif. lowlands. Search by digging around bases of shrubs, trees, and termite-infested stumps and abandoned fence posts until you find a network of tunnels, each about ¼–⅜ in. (6–9 cm) in diameter. Best results are usually obtained where damp soil is available within a spade-depth or so of the surface. Look for patches of shade and a leaf-litter mat that slows the loss of soil moisture, provides warm and cool areas near the surface, and attracts small arthropods, upon which this animal feeds. Mole lizards rarely expose themselves on the surface, but when surface moisture is suitable they may emerge to forage just beneath the leaf litter.

They dig by ramming their blunt, solidly constructed head into the soil and moving it from side to side as they scrape away soil with one forelimb, then the other.

When this animal crawls on the surface, the walking movements of the forelimbs are aided by a "caterpillar" action of the body, resembling that of some snakes. The short, forked tongue is frequently protruded. Clutch of 1–4 eggs, laid in July. Eats insects and other arthropods. **RANGE:** Slopes and plains of w. side of Baja Calif. peninsula, from Bahía de Sebastian Viscaino and near Guerrero Negro to the cape. Includes Viscaino Desert and Magdalena Plain.

SNAKES

CAPE WHIPSNAKE *Masticophis aurigulus* Pl. 56, Map 202

IDENTIFICATION: 30–62 in. (75–158 cm). Similar to California Whipsnake (Pl. 43), and a close relative. Head long, with flattened top and a narrow, rounded snout. Body very slender. Dark brown above, becoming black toward the head. Head light brown to black, sometimes spotted with yellowish brown. Narrow yellowish or light orange stripe from eye to snout. Yellowish stripe on side broken toward the front. *A dark stripe along lower edge of light side stripe covers 2nd and 3rd scale rows, and is interrupted by light-colored areas.* Labials, chin, and anterior part of belly yellow or orange, unspotted. Belly dull yellowish grading to coral pink on underside of tail. Scales smooth, in 17 rows. Anal divided.

Found near springs and stream courses. At San Bartolo, has been found along a wash bottom in sandy soil bordered by bush lupines, clumps of willow, and palms, with strangler figs on nearby rocky slopes. Eats small mammals, birds, snakes, and lizards. **SIMILAR SPECIES:** In California Whipsnake (p. 353), dark side stripe is solid, not interrupted by a series of lighter areas. **RANGE:** Cape region of Baja Calif. Restricted to upper slopes of Sierra de Laguna south of La Paz.

BAJA CALIFORNIA RAT SNAKE Pl. 56, Map 202
Bogertophis rosaliae

IDENTIFICATION: 34–60 in. (85–152 cm). Head moderately long, distinct from neck. Body rather slender. *Uniform olive, yellowish, or reddish brown above,* usually with no dark markings other than dusky edging of scales that becomes especially notable at midbody and beyond to tip of tail. Dorsal coloration lightens on lower sides. Below unpatterned. Throat, underside of neck, and lower jaw, especially toward rear, whitish. Venter grades from dull light yellow to pale rust or tan toward rear. Iris gray to yellow green.

Tongue pink. Scales smooth, each with 2 *apical pits* (see rear end-papers); in 33 or 34 rows. Anal divided. **Young:** Paler than adult and with cream or light yellow streaks across back.

Frequents hill slopes and arroyos, especially near springs, seeps, and streams, but also occurs in dry areas. Has been taken in native fan palms, date palms, mesquite, palo verde, and creosote bush associations. An excellent climber. When crawling often sways head from side to side. Primarily nocturnal. Presumed to feed mainly on rats and other small mammals. Clutch of 2–10 eggs. **RANGE:** Ranges from about 2⅖ mi. (3.8 km) east of Mt. Spring, Imperial Co., Calif., south, on e. slope Baja Calif. peninsula, through Sierra de la Giganta to the cape.

CAPE GARTER SNAKE *Thamnophis validus* **Pl. 56, Map 203**
IDENTIFICATION: 23–38 in. (58–94 cm). Head distinct from neck. *Eyes set high on head. Uniformly light grayish, olive gray, brownish, or black above;* with more or less distinct *blackish markings on sides,* in alternating rows. Pale grayish yellow to sooty below; tips of ventrals tinged with back color. (Melanistic individuals are grayish black above and below.) A beige-colored lateral stripe, set low on the side, extends from neck to tail, often becoming indistinct toward rear. Lateral stripe, when present, confined to 1st and 2nd, or all 3 lowermost scale rows. Some individuals have a number of alternating light and dark stripes. Scales keeled, usually in 21 rows. Upper labials usually 8. Anal divided.

Highly aquatic. Found in and near oases, ponds, seeps, volcanic lakes, rocky arroyos with pools, and intermittent streams that flow from mountains to the sea. Live-bearing. Eats frogs, toads, tadpoles, and fish. **RANGE:** Cape region of Baja Calif. and chiefly coastal plain of mainland Mex. from s. Sonora to Guerrero. From sea level to around 3,900 ft. (1,200 m).
SUBSPECIES: CAPE LOWLANDS GARTER SNAKE, *T. v. celaeno,* occurs in our area.

BAJA CALIFORNIA NIGHT SNAKE **Pl. 56, Map 204**
Eridiphas slevini
IDENTIFICATION: 12–22½ in. (30–56 cm). Resembles the Night Snake (Pl. 46), but *parietal scale usually touches lower postocular scale.* A slender, dark-blotched snake with a somewhat elongate, rather flattened head only slightly wider than its neck. Eyes large, tipped somewhat upward, *pupils vertical.* Rear maxillary teeth enlarged but not grooved. Numerous dark brown or gray-brown blotches on back and tail, largest along back where some may join to form irregular, sometimes dumbbell-shaped crossbars. Scales

in areas of ground color have light-colored edges. Occasionally dark spots on neck form large blotches similar to Night Snake. Unmarked yellow-gray color may be present along ventral midline. Dorsal scales smooth, in 21–23 rows at midbody. Anal divided. Venomous, but not considered dangerous to humans; however, handle large ones with care.

Frequents rocky areas chiefly on warm, humid eastern slope of Baja Calif. Chiefly nocturnal. Found on roadways after dark and along rock-strewn washes and arroyos. One specimen was taken from a small crack at the base of a boulder and another from moist wood inside the decaying trunk of a palm tree. A captive laid 2 elongate, kidney-shaped eggs found in a terrarium on Oct. 9. Captives have eaten lizards, snakes, frogs, toads, and salamanders. Sometimes holds its prey toward the back of its mouth for several minutes before swallowing it, perhaps to give the venom time to be absorbed. **SIMILAR SPECIES:** In the Night Snake (p. 403), parietal scale does not touch lower postocular scale; usually has large nuchal blotches on neck, not just spots. **RANGE:** Distribution spotty; from near Bahía de los Angeles to the cape. Nearly all localities north of cape are from east of crest of Sierra de la Giganta and other mountain ranges that border eastern side of peninsula. The snake is expected to occur farther north, probably to eastern side of San Pedro Martir Mts. On Cerralvo, Danzante, and San Marcos Is. in Gulf of Calif.

BAJA CALIFORNIA RATTLESNAKE Pl. 56, Map 201
Crotalus enyo

IDENTIFICATION: 20–35 ½ in. (50–89 cm). Head relatively narrow for a rattler. Eyes large; supraoculars slant notably upward. Ground color brown to silvery gray above, with reddish or yellowish brown, dark-edged blotches down the back. *Each blotch often has a black or dusky spot close to or attached to its lower border on each side,* especially in blotches from midbody toward the tail. Blotches tend to fade and become more like bands toward rear part of body and on tail. Tail lacks contrasting light and dark rings. A light stripe extends across head over eyes. Two internasal scales. General coloration darkens in northern part of range from El Rosario northward. Dorsal scales keeled, in 25–27 rows. Anal single.

Frequents arid thornscrub, mainly in rocky canyons and mesas. Eats small rodents, lizards, and centipedes. Large centipedes *(Scolopendra)* are eaten by adults. Live-bearing; 2–9 young, presumably born in summer and fall. **SIMILAR SPECIES:** (1) Western Rattlesnake (p. 414) has more than 2 internasals and, in Baja Calif., usually blackish to dark brown dorsal blotches with contrasting light edges. (2) Red Diamond Rattlesnake (p. 410) has contrasting black-and-white bands on tail and dark speckling in diffusely bordered blotches on back. (3) Speckled Rattlesnake (p. 412) has contrasting black-and-white marks on tail. **RANGE:** Throughout most of Baja Calif., from vicinity of San Telmo to the cape.

Amphibian Eggs and Larvae

The eggs and larvae of most western amphibians are illustrated here in Figs. 30–39. Species omitted are mostly those not described or poorly known. Descriptions of some species are brief and not fully diagnostic because of inadequate information. Refer to information on distribution (see maps), habitat, and breeding sites under the species accounts. See p. 25 for help in using the keys, which differ only in minor details from those in Chapter 4.

Counts of eggs laid are obviously subject to change as more information becomes available. In some cases clutch size is inferred from counts of enlarged ova in ovaries or eggs in oviducts of gravid females.

In making identifications, examine the mouthparts of tadpoles and gelatinous envelopes of eggs under magnification. Tooth rows are expressed as a fraction—2/3, 3/4, etc. The numerator is the number of rows in the upper lip; the denominator, the number of rows in the lower lip. Hyphenated numbers (2–3/3–4) indicate variation in the number of rows. To examine specimens, immerse them in shallow water to eliminate distracting highlights. Color patterns may also be enhanced in this way. A dissecting microscope will usually be needed to study egg capsules; view eggs with transmitted light. To count gill rakers in salamander larvae (Fig. 33, p. 447), enlarge the gill openings of preserved specimens by snipping the tissues between the gill arches. All measurements of salamander larvae and tadpoles are of total length. The keys to eggs and larvae apply only to western species.

CAUTION: Amphibian eggs and larvae may quickly succumb if overheated. Keep them cool if to be studied fresh; otherwise, preserve in 1 part commercial Formalin to 14 parts of water.

REFERENCES:

McDiarmid, R. W., and R. Altig. 1999. *Tadpoles: The Biology of Anuran Larvae.* University of Chicago Press.

Corkran, C. C., and C. Thoms. 1996. *Amphibians of Oregon, Washington, and British Columbia*. Lone Pine Publishing, Vancouver, B.C. Has excellent keys and comparisons for egg and tadpole identification.

KEY TO AMPHIBIAN EGGS

See Fig. 30 for explanation of terms, and Figs. 31 and 32 (pp. 436 and 442) for illustrations of eggs.

1 A.   Ovum uniformly white or cream, unpigmented **see 2**
1 B.   Upper surface or entire ovum pigmented olive, brown, or black **see 5**

2 A.   Eggs arranged like a string of beads, connected by slender strands of jelly; found in cold streams [Tailed Frog]
2 B.   Eggs not connected like a string of beads, or, if so, found on land **see 3**

3 A.   Each egg suspended by a single slender strand of jelly (Figs. 31, 13–15) or in a rosary-like string (Figs. 31, 12); eggs may become separated and bear a slender jelly strand at one or both ends (Fig. 31, 12) **see 4**
3 B.   Eggs attached by very short jelly strands, or broadly clinging to each other or attachment surface (Fig. 31, 7–11) [Olympic, Pacific Giant, Woodland Salamanders, and Ensatina]

4 A.   Eggs suspended by their jelly strands; strands elongated, often intertwined (Fig. 31, 13–15) [Climbing Salamanders]
4 B.   Eggs more or less connected by their strands, arranged like a string of beads (Fig. 31, 12) [Slender Salamanders]

5 A.   Gelatinous envelope firm, rubberlike; ovum (when fertilized) moves freely in large capsular chamber (Fig. 31, 1–4); eggs usually in globular clusters (laid singly in Rough-skinned Newt) [Newts and Northwestern Salamander]
5 B.   Jelly less firm; ovum not in large capsular chamber (Fig. 32); eggs in rounded clumps, strings, floating rafts, or single **see 6**

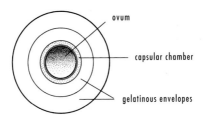

ovum

capsular chamber

gelatinous envelopes

Fig. 30. Amphibian egg

6A. Eggs in cylindrical strings (Fig. 32; 7, 8, 10–12) or more or less connected like string of beads (Fig. 32; 9, 13, 14) [True Toads]

6B. Eggs not in strings but in grapelike cluster or single   **see 7**

7A. Gelatinous envelope flattened on 1 side (Fig. 32; 3) [Great Plains Narrow-mouthed Toad]

7B. Gelatinous envelope not flattened   **see 8**

8A. Eggs in floating raft, 1 to few eggs thick (Fig. 32) [Bullfrog and Green Frog]

8B. Eggs single, or in globular or irregular clusters [Tiger and Long-toed Salamanders, Frogs and Hylids]

EGGS OF SALAMANDERS

See Fig. 31, p. 436 (× 1¾). In Fig. 31, eggs shown in black have pigment on the upper surface of the ovum and are usually exposed to daylight. Those shown in white are unpigmented and laid in concealed locations under stones or in crevices in logs or the ground. Numbers in parentheses are averages.

Eggs Pigmented

Rough-skinned Newt, *Taricha granulosa.* In this and other newts, eggs are in firm 2- or 3-layered gelatinous capsules. Fertilized egg moves freely in large capsular chamber. Usually laid singly, attached to vegetation and other objects in quiet or slowly flowing water.   **Map 8**

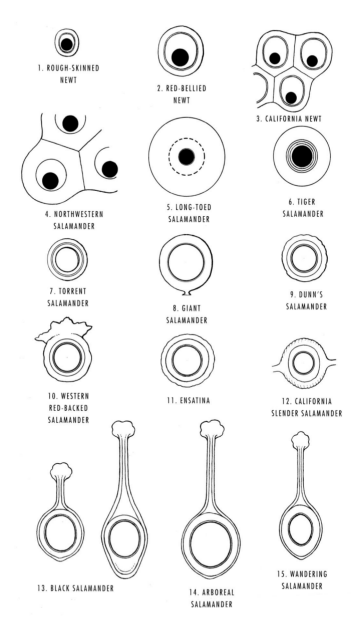

1. ROUGH-SKINNED NEWT

2. RED-BELLIED NEWT

3. CALIFORNIA NEWT

4. NORTHWESTERN SALAMANDER

5. LONG-TOED SALAMANDER

6. TIGER SALAMANDER

7. TORRENT SALAMANDER

8. GIANT SALAMANDER

9. DUNN'S SALAMANDER

10. WESTERN RED-BACKED SALAMANDER

11. ENSATINA

12. CALIFORNIA SLENDER SALAMANDER

13. BLACK SALAMANDER

14. ARBOREAL SALAMANDER

15. WANDERING SALAMANDER

Fig. 31. Eggs of salamanders

California Newt, *Taricha torosa.* Laid in rounded, firm clusters of 7–39 (often 16–23) eggs. Clusters about ½–1 in. (1.2–2.5 cm) in diameter, attached to sticks, undersides of stones, and vegetation or lying free on bottom in quiet or flowing water. Estimates of overall clutch size based on mature ova in the Coast Range subsp. ranged from 130–160. The Sierra Newt, which often frequents rivers and streams, tends to attach its eggs to undersides of stones where they are less likely to be washed away. **Map 11**

Red-bellied Newt, *Taricha rivularis.* Laid in flattened, firm clusters of 5–16 (10) eggs. Clusters about 1 in. (2.5 cm) in greatest diameter, often only 1 egg thick, and usually attached to undersides of stones in streams. As many as 70 egg masses have been found attached to underside of a single stone. ⁻ **Map 10**

Northwestern Salamander, *Ambystoma gracile.* Laid in rounded to elongate, usually, firm clusters of 30–270 (often 60–140) eggs. Clusters 2–6 in. in diameter; attached to submerged branches and other firm supports in ponds, lakes, and slowly flowing streams. Individual eggs in large capsular chambers. Recently fertilized ova surrounded by 2 jelly coats. **Map 2**

Long-toed Salamander, *Ambystoma macrodactylum.* Laid singly or in a clump of 5–100 eggs. Clumps may be rounded or elongate, moderately firm and smooth-surfaced. Ova within elongate clumps sometimes arranged in rows. Eggs attached to vegetation, sticks, rocks, or free on bottom of shallow pools, ponds, lakes, and quiet parts of streams. A single female may contain from around 85 to over 400 eggs. **Map 3**

Tiger Salamander, *Ambystoma tigrinum.* In our area, usually laid singly or in small rows or clusters ranging in size from a few to around 120 eggs; attached to twigs, weeds, and other objects in ponds, lakes, and quiet parts of streams. Large adult gilled morphs may lay over 7,000 eggs and transformed adults over 8,000 eggs (w. Texas). **Map 7**

California Tiger Salamander, *Ambystoma californiense.* Eggs laid singly or in small clusters attached to grass, dead weeds, or other objects, often in temporary pools. **Map 6**

Eggs Unpigmented

Torrent Salamanders, *Rhyacotriton.* Laid singly, apparently without special organs of attachment, clustered or scattered in springs and seepages, and deposited beneath stones and in crevices in streams or other concealed sites. Clutch size estimate of 2–16

(8–10) eggs, based on mature ovarian eggs, but larger clusters may be expected because of probable communal laying. Two egg clusters of Columbia Torrent Salamander found in a spring in Ore. in cracks in sandstone. Each contained 16 eggs laid unattached. **Map 4**

California Giant Salamander, *Dicamptodon ensatus*. Laid singly, close together, attached by short peduncles to rocks and other objects, usually on roof of nest chamber. In concealed locations in springs and streams. A clutch of about 70 eggs was found on the underside of a large submerged timber in a creek. **Map 1**

Pacific Giant Salamander, *Dicamptodon tenebrosus* (not shown). Eggs attached singly by short pedicels to undersides of logs, rocks, and other submerged, concealed locations in streams. Clutches rarely found. Clutches of 146 and 83 eggs found in Ore. and 129 eggs in Wash. **Map 1**

Cope's Giant Salamander, *Dicamptodon copei* (not shown). Laid in hidden nest sites (under stones, logs, cut banks) in streams, clustered together, each egg attached by a short pedicel. Clutches of 25–115 (50) eggs. Brooding females vigorously guard their nests. **Map 1**

Dunn's Salamander, *Plethodon dunni*. Laid in grapelike clusters attached by a slender stalk in damp hollows in rotting logs, in crevices, or other underground sites. Clutches of 4–18 (9) eggs. Drawing based on eggs laid in the laboratory. **Map 14**

Western Red-backed Salamander, *Plethodon vehiculum*. Laid in clusters, the individual eggs attached by broad flaring bases to sides and roofs of moist cavities in logs or underside of rocks or bark; also laid in talus or deep crevices. Clutch size (based on enlarged ova and eggs laid) 4–19 (10). **Map 13**

Del Norte Salamander, *Plethodon elongatus* (not shown). Laid in a grapelike cluster suspended by a common strand in a damp, concealed location. Females with 2–18 (7–9) enlarged ova. A clutch of 10 eggs found. **Map 15**

Jemez Mountains Salamander, *Plethodon neomexicanus* (not shown). Eggs on stalks, 5–12 (8) per clutch, laid in concealed sites, probably usually underground (count based on enlarged ova). **Map 17**

Larch Mountain Salamander, *Plethodon larselli* (not shown). Presumably laid in damp talus, concealed locations, in clutches of 2–12 (7) eggs (counts based on enlarged ova). **Map 16**

Van Dyke's Salamander, *Plethodon vandykei* (not shown). Information scant. A cluster of eggs in a grapelike arrangement was found attached by 1 or more slender strands of jelly inside a moss-covered large coniferous log in an old-growth forest near a stream. Two gravid females from Wash. contained 11 and 14 mature ova. **Map 18**

Coeur d'Alene Salamander, *Plethodon idahoensis* (not shown). Counts of large ovarian eggs in individuals from n. Idaho, 4–12 (7); clutch size 1–13 (6). Eggs found under flat rock in waterfall spray zone. **Map 18**

Ensatina, *Ensatina eschscholtzii.* Laid in grapelike clusters; outer envelopes may be more or less adherent. Deposited in mammal burrows, ground crevices, beneath bark and in hollows or beneath decayed logs. Clutches of 3–25 (13) eggs, including counts of enlarged ova. **Map 12**

Sacramento Mountains Salamander, *Aneides hardii* (not shown). Laid in grapelike clusters suspended by intertwined strands usually united at a common base; attached to chambers in decomposing logs, and probably elsewhere in concealed sites. Clutches of 3–10 eggs based on nests in the field and on enlarged ova. **Map 23**

Black Salamander, *Aneides flavipunctatus.* Clusters as in Sacramento Mountain Salamander. 5–25 (12), eggs based on counts of enlarged ova. Laid in cavities in soil, under rocks, and in other concealed locations. **Map 21**

Clouded and Wandering Salamanders, *Aneides ferrus* and *vagrans.* Attached separately, but close together, on stalks twisted around one another and attached at a common point to roof or wall of a cavity, often in a log. An egg site found at a height of over 100 ft. (30 m) in a large coast redwood. Clutches of 6–9 eggs in Calif. and 8–17 in Ore. 14–26 (avg. 18) ova in females from Vancouver I., B.C. **Map 20**

Arboreal Salamander, *Aneides lugubris.* Eggs resemble those of Wandering Salamander, deposited in tree hollows (chiefly live oaks), decaying logs, or in cavities in the ground. Clusters of 12–24 eggs, but as many as 26 expected based on counts of mature ovarian eggs. **Map 22**

Oregon Slender Salamander, *Batrachoseps wrighti* (not shown). In clusters or scattered; eggs joined by a single strand, like a string of beads, but strands may break; probably commonly laid in hollows under bark and in rotten logs. Clutches of 2–11 (5–7) eggs. Communal laying not thought to occur. **Map 19**

Kern Plateau Salamander, *Batrachoseps robustus.* Presumed to have small clutches (perhaps 4–6) of relatively large eggs laid under cover near springs and seeps. **Map 19**

California Slender Salamander, *Batrachoseps attenuatus.* Laid in clusters; individual eggs connected by slender jelly strand like a string of beads, but strands may break and eggs become separated. Under logs, rocks, and other objects on the surface and in hollows in logs or the ground. Clutches of 2–12 (commonly 4–7) eggs, but far higher counts at communal laying sites. **Map 24**

Black-bellied Slender Salamander, *Batrachoseps nigriventris* (not shown). Cluster and egg-laying sites presumed to resemble those of California Slender Salamander. Three females from Santa Monica Mts. in s. Calif. contained 4, 6, and 9 large ovarian eggs. **Map 24**

Gregarius Slender Salamander, *Batrachoseps gregarius* (not shown). Laid in clusters, connected by a slender strand that may break; under rocks, bark, and logs in spring and fall, depending on locality. **Map 24**

Garden Slender Salamander, *Batrachoseps major* (not shown). Clusters and egg-laying sites as in California Slender Salamander. Information fragmentary. 15–20 enlarged ova in females and a group of 18 eggs found. Communal laying probably occurs. **Map 24**

Mount Lyell Salamander, *Hydromantes platycephalus* (not shown). Information fragmentary; presumably lays in damp crevices and soil cavities. Counts of enlarged ova, 6–14. **Map 9**

Shasta Salamander, *Hydromantes shastae* (not shown). Most eggs have a slender stalk at each end, the stalks intertwined at center of the cluster. Clutches of 9–12 eggs, laid in recesses of limestone caves. **Map 9**

Limestone Salamander, *Hydromantes brunus* (not shown). Seven large ova recorded in the type specimen. **Map 9**

See Fig. 32, p. 442 (× 1 4/5). In Fig. 32, eggs shown in black have pigment on the upper surface and are usually exposed to daylight. Those shown in white are unpigmented and laid in concealed locations. Broken lines indicate indistinct boundaries between gelatinous envelopes. Numbers in parentheses are averages. Maximum counts of eggs laid are approximate.

Eggs Pigmented

Western Spadefoot, *Spea hammondii.* In irregular cylindrical clusters of about 10–42 (24) eggs, attached to plant stems and other objects in temporary or permanent ponds and quiet parts of streams. **Map 27**

Mexican Spadefoot, *Spea multiplicata* (not shown). Clusters of 10–42 eggs, attached in cylindrical masses to plants or other objects. A single female may lay 300–500 eggs. Adult females in cen. and s. N.M. estimated to contain an average of 1,070 eggs. **Map 27**

Plains Spadefoot, *Spea bombifrons* (not shown). In loose cylindrical or elliptical masses, usually less than 1 in. (2.5 cm) in diameter, of about 10–250 eggs; attached to vegetation or other support in permanent and temporary waters. Adult females in cen. and s. N.M. estimated to contain an average of 1,600 eggs, those in w. Iowa 2,626 eggs. **Map 26**

Great Basin Spadefoot, *Spea intermontana* (not shown). In small irregular packets of jelly, 3/5–4/5 in. (1.5–2 cm) in diameter, of around 10–40 eggs; attached to vegetation, pebbles, or lying on the bottom of pools. Female's total complement may be 300–500 or even approach 800 eggs. **Map 25**

Couch's Spadefoot, *Scaphiopus couchii.* Eggs resemble Western Spadefoot's, but smaller. Laid in cylindrical masses of 6–145 eggs. A single female may lay 350–500 eggs. Females from cen. and s. N.M. estimated to contain an average of approximately 3,310 up to 4,025 eggs. **Map 28**

Great Plains Narrow-mouthed Toad, *Gastrophryne olivacea.* Laid singly, but often close together in groups as a surface film in shallow temporary pools or quiet parts of streams. Capsules flattened on one side. One envelope. A single female may lay around 500 to over 2,000 eggs. **Map 31**

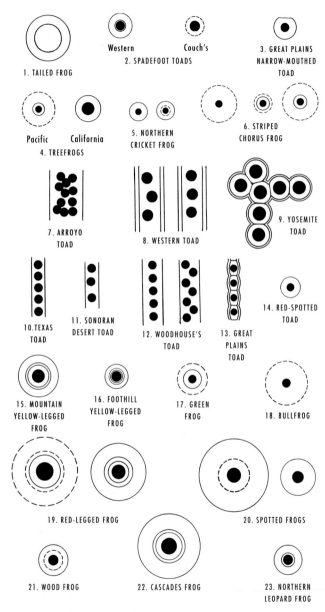

Fig. 32. Eggs of frogs and toads

Pacific Treefrog, *Hyla regilla*. Laid in loose, irregular clusters of 9–80 (often 20–25) eggs; attached to plant stems, sticks, or other objects in shallow, quiet water of ponds, lake borders, and streams. 2 envelopes. A single female may lay over 700 eggs. **Map 44**

Mountain Treefrog, *Hyla eximia* (not shown). Laid in loose masses, about the size of a teacup; loosely attached to grass or weed stems just below the surface. **Map 46**

California Treefrog, *Hyla cadaverina*. Laid singly; attached to leaves, sticks, rocks, or free on the bottom in quiet water of rocky, clear streams. One envelope. **Map 47**

Northern Cricket Frog, *Acris crepitans*. Laid singly or in small clusters; attached to leaves, twigs, grass stems, or on the bottom in shallow, quiet water of springs, ponds, and streams. Two envelopes. A single female may lay around 150–400 eggs. **Map 45**

Western Chorus Frog, *Pseudacris triseriata*. In small, soft, loose, irregular or elongate clusters—diameter often less than 1 in. (2.5 cm)—of around 7–300 (often 30–75) eggs; attached to vegetation in clear, quiet water of ponds, lakes, and marshy fields. One indistinct envelope. A single female may contain up to 1,500 eggs. Colo. females laid 137–793 (450) eggs. Egg masses in Ont., Canada, contain 18–140 (63) eggs. **Map 42**

Arroyo Toad, *Bufo californicus*. Laid in tangled strings of up to 4,000 eggs. Eggs in 1–3 irregular rows, usually deposited on the bottom in quiet parts of clear streams. One envelope. **Map 34**

Western Toad, *Bufo boreas*. Laid in tangled strings of up to 16,500 (often around 12,000) eggs, in 1–3 rows within strings; often greatly entwined in vegetation along edges of ponds, reservoirs, and streams. Two envelopes. Eggs often in a zigzag double row. **Map 32**

Black Toad, *Bufo exsul* (not shown). Eggs resemble Western Toad's, but less often in a zigzag double row; single row common. Up to about 26,000 eggs. **Map 32**

Yosemite Toad, *Bufo canorus*. Eggs in beadlike string of single or double strands, or in radiating clusters of 4 or 5 eggs deep, often covered with silt, in shallows of meadow pools. Two envelopes. Individual females estimated to lay around 1,000 to 1,500 eggs. **Map 33**

Texas Toad, *Bufo speciosus*. In strings coiled about in rain pools, irrigation and cattle tanks, and other quiet water. One envelope, sometimes slightly scalloped. **Map 38**

Sonoran Desert Toad, *Bufo alvarius*. Laid in long strings of 7,500–8,000 eggs, in temporary pools or shallow streams. Look for them after the first heavy summer showers. One envelope. **Map 40**

Woodhouse's Toad, *Bufo woodhousii*. Laid in strings of over 28,000 eggs, in 1 or 2 rows within strings; intertwined about vegetation or debris in almost any type of pool or stream. One envelope. **Map 35**

Canadian Toad, *Bufo hemiophrys* (not shown). Laid in long strings, like closely strung beads; entwined among vegetation or not. One envelope. **Map 36**

Great Plains Toad, *Bufo cognatus*. Laid in strings of from over 1,000 to over 45,000 eggs; attached to vegetation and debris on the bottom of temporary pools, reservoirs, springs, and small streams. Two envelopes, decidedly scalloped. **Map 37**

Red-spotted Toad, *Bufo punctatus*. Laid singly, in short strings, or as a loose flat cluster, on the bottom of small, shallow, often rocky pools. One envelope. **Map 41**

Green Toad, *Bufo debilis* (not shown). Laid in small clumps or strings, or perhaps occasionally laid singly; attached to grass and weed stems. Ova faintly pigmented. Two envelopes. **Map 39**

Sonoran Green Toad, *Bufo retiformis* (not shown). Eggs resemble those of the Green Toad. **Map 39**

Mountain Yellow-legged Frog, *Rana muscosa*. Laid in globular but often somewhat flattened clumps, around 1–2 in. (2.5–5.1 cm) across, ranging from around 15 to 350 eggs per clump; attached to stems of sedge or other vegetation, rocks, gravel, under banks, or to the bank itself in ponds, lakes, and streams mostly above 5,000 ft. (1,500 m) in Sierra Nevada, and in streams at lower elevations in mountains of s. Calif. Egg clumps often aggregated. Eggs may be unattached to supports in quiet water. **Map 54**

Foothill Yellow-legged Frog, *Rana boylii*. Laid in a compact, grapelike cluster—2–4 in. (5–10 cm) in diameter—of around 100 to over 1,000 eggs; in shallow water near edges of clear streams and attached to gravel or larger stones (often on downstream side). May become coated with silt. Three thin, firm envelopes. **Map 51**

Green Frog, *Rana clamitans.* In a floating cluster usually 1 egg thick and less than 1 sq. ft. (30 sq. cm) in area, of around 1,000–7,000 eggs. Attached to vegetation or free, usually deposited near the edges of permanent quiet water. Two envelopes. **Map 51**

Bullfrog, *Rana catesbeiana.* Eggs resemble Green Frog's, but clusters large, 1–5 ft. (0.3–1.5 m) across and containing up to over 47,000 eggs. When first laid, egg raft floats but later sinks. One envelope. **Map 49**

California Red-legged Frog, *Rana aurora draytonii.* In loose to compact, round to oval clusters—3–12 in. (7.5–30 cm) in diameter—of around 1,000–6,000 (often 500–1,000) eggs. Jelly loose and viscid. Eggs usually attached to emergent vegetation at the surface of lake margins and permanent pools. Three envelopes. **Map 50**

Northern Red-legged Frog, *Rana aurora aurora.* May oviposit at depths of 1 to over 16 ft. (30–500 cm) and eggs may be attached to stalks or twigs about 2 ft. (60 cm) or more apart (north of Sisters, Jefferson Co., Ore.). **Map 50**

Oregon Spotted Frog, *Rana pretiosa.* Laid in globular clusters—3–8 in. (7.5–20 cm) in diameter—of around 150–2,000 (often 500–600) eggs; in shallow water, often unattached among grasses at edges of ponds, the top layer of eggs exposed at surface. One or 2 envelopes. A single female may contain about 3,000 eggs. **Map 52**

Columbia Spotted Frog, *Rana luteiventris.* Eggs resemble Oregon Spotted Frog's but are smaller and lack inner envelope. Laid in communal masses, around 700–1,500 in a clutch. **Map 52**

Wood Frog, *Rana sylvatica.* Laid in firm spherical masses—2 1/2 to sometimes 6 in. (6.2–15 cm) in diameter—of around 100–3,000 eggs (42–1,570, avg. about 780, in an Alaskan study; 700–1,250, avg. about 900 [Colorado]; 350–709 eggs per mass, 618–966 in ovaries [Alabama]; and 510–1,433 eggs per mass, 645–1,331 in ovaries [Arkansas]). Often many clusters in a small area, in contact and on top of one another. Usually in shallow ponds, lakes, and streams near the surface, occasionally to depths of 2 or 3 ft. (60–90 cm) attached to vegetation or floating free. Two envelopes. Jelly layers thin. **Map 48**

Cascades Frog, *Rana cascadae.* Eggs resemble Red-legged Frog's but clusters usually smaller—300 to around 600 eggs, deposited in shallow water of pools and lake margins. Egg clusters may be aggregated, unattached to plant supports, and often laid on top of each other. **Map 53**

Northern Leopard Frog, *Rana pipiens.* In firm globular clusters (2–6 in. [5–15 cm] in diameter) of up to around 6,500 eggs; usually attached to vegetation in quiet water of ponds, lake margins, reservoirs, canals, and streams. Two or 3 envelopes. **Map 56**

Plains Leopard Frog, *Rana blairi* (not shown). Eggs resemble Northern Leopard Frog's but clusters smaller, containing around 200–600 eggs; deposited in temporary or permanent pools, usually attached to plants in shallow water. **Map 58**

Rio Grande Leopard Frog, *Rana berlandieri* (not shown). Eggs resemble Northern Leopard Frog's. Clutches of around 500–1,200 eggs. **Map 57**

African Clawed Frog, *Xenopus laevis* (not shown). Attached singly or sometimes in pairs to grass, reeds, and submerged stems. Three envelopes. Eggs of a single female number in the thousands. **Map 60**

Eggs Unpigmented

Tailed Frog, *Ascaphus truei.* In rosary-like strings of around 33–98 (44–75) eggs, arranged in globular clumps and attached to undersides of stones in cold running water. **Map 29**

Barking Frog, *Eleutherodactylus augusti* (not shown). Laid on land in rain-soaked hollows, seepage areas, or damp places under rocks or in caves. Clutches of 50–76 eggs (based on enlarged ova) reported. **Map 30**

KEY TO SALAMANDER LARVAE

See Fig. 33, p. 447, for explanation of terms, and Fig. 34, p. 449, for illustrations of larvae. Both front and hind limbs present; external gills.

1 A.	Pond type, usually found in ponds, lakes, or quiet parts of streams	**see 3**
1 B.	Stream type, usually found in streams or trickles	**see 2**
2 A.	Usually prominent light and dark mottling on tail fin; gills short but bushy and well developed; eyes small; to over 11 in. (27.5 cm) [Giant Salamanders]	
2 B.	Tail fin not colored as in 2A; gills reduced to nubbins; eyes large; under 3 in. (7.5 cm) [Torrent Salamanders]	

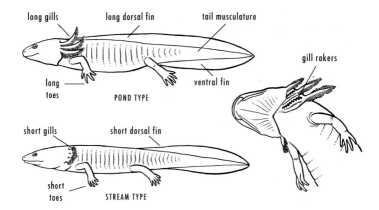

Fig. 33. *Salamander larvae*

3A. Head broad and rather flat; eyes set well in from
outline of head as seen from above; 9–22 gill
rakers on front side of 3rd gill arch   **see 6**

3B. Head narrower and less flattened; eyes on or
near outline of head as seen from above; 5–7 gill
rakers on front side of 3rd gill arch   **see 4**

4A. Dorsal fin does not reach shoulders; dark color
rather evenly distributed over back and sides;
streams of Sonoma, Medocino, and s. Humboldt Counties, Calif.; usually under 2½ in. (6.2
cm) [Red-bellied Newt]

4B. Dorsal fin usually reaches shoulders; dark color
not evenly distributed; usually under 2½ in.
(6.2 cm)   **see 5**

5A. Two irregular black stripes on back, 1 on each
side of dorsal fin [California Newt]

5B. No black stripes; light spots on sides often arranged in lengthwise rows that may join to form
light stripes [Rough-skinned Newt]

6A. Rough strip of skin (formed by openings of poison glands) along upper side of tail musculature,
near base of upper fin; similar rough patch behind eyes on each side of head; glandular

patches in preserved specimens often with adherent whitish secretion; to approximately 6 in. (15 cm) [Northwestern Salamander]

6B.   No roughened glandular areas   **see 7**

7A.   9–13 gill rakers on front side of 3rd gill arch; usually under 3 in. (7.5 cm) [Long-toed Salamander]

7B.   15–24 gill rakers on front side of 3rd gill arch; to 10 in. (25 cm) [Tiger Salamander]

SALAMANDER LARVAE

See Fig. 34, p. 449; relative size not shown. Measurements are approximate total length near time of transformation.

California Newt, *Taricha torosa.* Pond type. Dark dorsolateral stripes, irregular in Sierran populations. Transformation at usually under 2 ½ in. (6.2 cm).   **Map 11**

Rough-skinned Newt, *Taricha granulosa.* Pond type. Trunk, and sometimes tail musculature with a lengthwise row of light spots, which may sometimes more or less unite to form a single light stripe on each side. Belly may be orange or pink in more advanced larvae. Sometimes reaches 3 in. (7.5 cm) at transformation, but may metamorphose at less than 1 in. (2.5 cm) SV length. Gilled adults are found at some localities.   **Map 8**

Red-bellied Newt, *Taricha rivularis.* Tends toward stream type (Fig. 34); dorsal fin usually fails to reach shoulders. Back and sides of nearly uniform pigmentation. Transformation at around 2 in. (5 cm).   **Map 10**

Torrent Salamanders, *Rhyacotriton* sp. Stream type. Gills and gill rakers (0–3 per gill arch) reduced to nubbins. Olive or brown above, speckled with black. Large dorsally positioned eyes. Venter yellow or orange, especially in older larvae. May transform at nearly adult size, around 2 ½ in. (6.2 cm).   **Map 4**

California Giant Salamander, *Dicamptodon ensatus.* Stream type. Often brown above with smoky dark and light mottling on back and fins; light stripe behind eye. Upper surfaces dark and pattern obscure in streams with dark-colored rocks. Short, bushy, dark red gills. Toes of adpressed limbs usually overlap 1–4 costal folds. Transformation usually at 6–8 in. (15–20 cm), but as gilled adult may reach 11 in. (27.5 cm).   **Map 1**

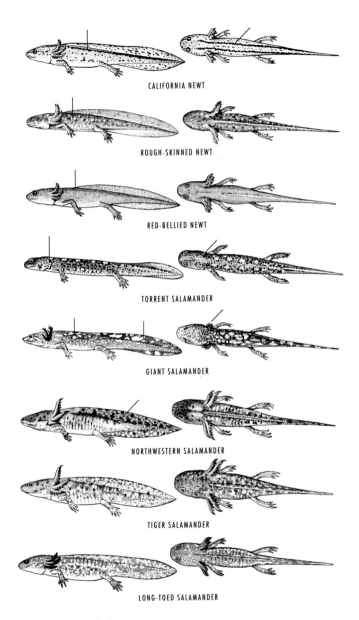

CALIFORNIA NEWT

ROUGH-SKINNED NEWT

RED-BELLIED NEWT

TORRENT SALAMANDER

GIANT SALAMANDER

NORTHWESTERN SALAMANDER

TIGER SALAMANDER

LONG-TOED SALAMANDER

Fig. 34. Salamander larvae

Pacific Giant Salamander, *Dicamptodon tenebrosus* (see Pl. 3).
Stream type. May be light to dark brown above with plain white
venter. Tail tip may be black and upper tail fin mottled with dark
and light more so than *D. ensatus.* Usually a light stripe behind eye.
Markings usually become less conspicuous with age. Larval coloring highly variable. Largest gilled adults on record, 14 in. (35.1
cm).
Map 1

Idaho Giant Salamander, *Dicamptodon aterrimus* (not shown).
Stream type. Darker than larvae of Pacific Giant Salamander.
Larger larvae may have faint stripe behind eye, a purplish brown
dorsum with few or no markings, and a bluish gray venter. Gilled
adults occur in some populations. Larvae common in small
streams above 3,200 ft. (975 m).
Map 1

Cope's Giant Salamander, *Dicamptodon copei.* Stream type. Resembles Pacific Giant Salamander larva, but slimmer and does
not grow as large. Costal folds between toes of adpressed limbs
2½ to none. Belly much darker at sizes above 2 in. (5 cm) in SV
length. Rarely transforms. (See Pl. 3 and p. 160 for further description.)
Map 1

Northwestern Salamander, *Ambystoma gracile.* Pond type (Fig.
33). Deep brown, olive green, or light yellow above, blotched with
sooty and spotted with yellow on sides. Poison glands become evident in parotoid areas and along base of dorsal fin in more advanced larvae. Chunky build. 7–10 gill rakers on front border of
3rd arch. Transformation at 3–6 in. (7.5–15 cm). Neotenics
(gilled adults) may reach 10 in. (26 cm).
Map 2

Tiger Salamander, *Ambystoma tigrinum.* Pond type. Usually dull
yellow, brown, olive or greenish above, mottled with dark brown
or black. Head large, gill stalks long and wide, the largest longer
than head length. 17–22 gill rakers on front border of 3rd arch.
Transformation often at 3–5 in. (7.5–12.5 cm), but as axolotl may
reach over 15 in. (38 cm).
Map 7

California Tiger Salamander, *Ambystoma californiense* (not
shown). Pond type. Similar to Tiger Salamander. Yellowish gray
above. Head broad and flat. Gills large and feathery. Transforms
prior to reaching sexual maturity.
Map 6

Long-toed Salamander, *Ambystoma macrodactylum.* Pond type.
Light olive gray, brownish gray, or tan above, mottled with brown-
ish and black. 9–13 gill rakers on 3rd arch. Rather slender build.
Transformation at 2½–4 in. (6.2–10 cm).
Map 3

KEY TO TADPOLES

See Fig. 35 for explanation of terms, and Figs. 36–39, pp. 453–59, for illustrations of tadpoles.

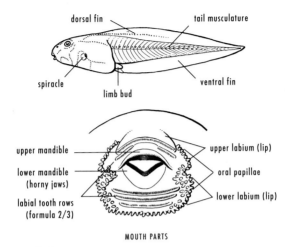

Fig. 35. Tadpole

| 1A. | No horny jaws or rows of labial teeth | **see 2** |
| 1B. | Horny jaws and labial teeth present | **see 3** |

2A. Tentacle at each side of mouth (see Pl. 19, Fig. 12) [African Clawed Frog]

2B. Tentacles absent [Great Plains Narrow-mouthed Toad]

3A. Large, round, suckerlike mouth occupying ⅓ to ½ underside of body [Tailed Frog]

3B. Mouth not greatly enlarged   **see 4**

4A. Oral papillae encircle mouth or are interrupted by a very small gap in middle of upper labium (lip) [Spadefoot Toads]

4B. Upper labium (lip) without oral papillae except at sides; middle part of lower labium with or without papillae   **see 5**

5A. Oral papillae on lower labium confined to sides
[True Toads]

5B. Oral papillae present along entire edge of lower
labium   **see 6**

6A. Lip margin indented at sides [True Frogs]
6B. Lip margin not indented [Treefrogs and Relatives]

TADPOLES

See Fig. 35, p. 451 (× ⁵⁄₆). Most tadpoles are dark-colored when young.
Descriptions of color here and in subsequent accounts are of
older tadpoles. Measurements are of approximate total length at
time of transformation. Large dark areas on bodies of Tailed
Frogs, Spadefoot Toads, Treefrogs, and Chorus Frog tadpoles
(shown in Figs. 36, 38) result from loss of overlaying pigment in
preserved specimens.

Tailed Frog and Narrow-mouthed Toad

Tailed Frog, *Ascaphus truei.* Large round mouth occupying
nearly ½ lower surface of body. Labial tooth rows 2–3/7–10. Tip
of tail often white or rose-colored, set off by dark band. To 2 ⅓ in.
(5.8 cm). Cold streams.   **Map 29**

Great Plains Narrow-mouthed Toad, *Gastrophryne olivacea.*
Feeds on both surface and suspended organic material. Distinctive mouth parts—upper lip fleshy, notched at midline, overlying
beaklike lower lip. No horny jaws or labial teeth. Eyes widely separated, on outer edges of head as viewed from above. Under 1 ½
in. (3.7 cm). Often hangs suspended below surface film. Extreme
s. Ariz. and sw. N.M.   **Map 31**

Spadefoot Toads (Spea *and* Scaphiopus)

Oral papillae encircle mouth (occasionally a small gap in middle
of upper labium). Labial tooth rows usually 4–5/4–5. Eyes set
close together and situated well inside outline of head as viewed
from above. Some populations of Plains, Western, Great Basin,
and Southern Spadefoot Toads tend to develop predaceous and
cannibalistic tadpoles that have a beak on upper jaw, a notch in
lower jaw, and enlarged jaw muscles.

Plains Spadefoot, *Spea bombifrons.* Body broadest just behind
eyes, giving a "muttonchop" contour. Light to medium gray or
brown above. In predaceous and cannibalistic tadpoles, upper
mandible beaked, lower mandible notched. Labial tooth rows often 4/4, but there may be considerable variation in some areas. To
2 ¾ in. (6.8 cm). Often in muddy temporary pools.   **Map 26**

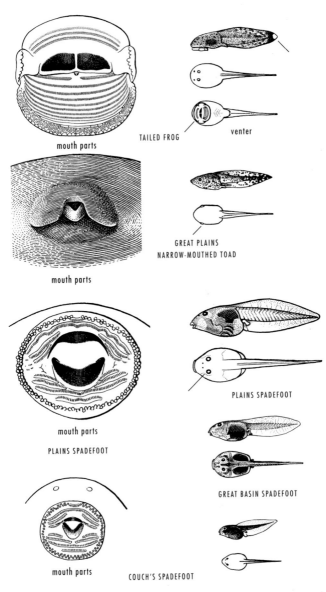

mouth parts

TAILED FROG   venter

mouth parts

GREAT PLAINS
NARROW-MOUTHED TOAD

mouth parts

PLAINS SPADEFOOT

PLAINS SPADEFOOT

GREAT BASIN SPADEFOOT

mouth parts   COUCH'S SPADEFOOT

Fig. 36. *Tailed Frog, Great Plains Narrow-mouthed Toad,*
and Spadefoot Toads

Western Spadefoot, *Spea hammondii.* Resembles Plains Spade-foot tadpole, but jaws of predaceous and cannibalistic tadpoles have a less-developed beak and notch. Labial tooth rows usually 5/5. To around 2⅘ in. (7 cm). **Map. 27**

Great Basin Spadefoot, *Spea intermontana* (not shown). Resembles Western Spadefoot. Dark gray-brown, brown to blackish above often with gold or brassy flecks and patches. Golden high-lights may be present on abdomen. To around 2⅘ in. (7 cm). Predaceaus tadpoles may be present. **Map 25**

Couch's Spadefoot, *Scaphiopus couchii.* Smaller and darker than Great Basin Spadefoot larva—dark gray, bronze, to nearly black above. To 1 ¼ in. (3.1 cm). **Map 28**

True Toads (Bufo)

See Fig. 37, p. 455 (× ⅚). Tadpoles often small and dark. Oral papillae confined to sides of mouth and indented. Labial tooth rows usually 2/3. Anus usually on ventral midline.

Western Toad, *Bufo boreas.* Body uniformly black, charcoal, dark brown, or dark gray, including tail musculature. Dorsal fin may be heavily speckled with gray or black. To around 2 in. (5 cm) but of-ten much smaller. **Map 32**

Black Toad, *Bufo exsul* (not shown). Resembles Western Toad tadpole, but tip of tail more rounded. Labial tooth rows some-times 1/3. Body nearly solid black above. **Map 32**

Yosemite Toad, *Bufo canorus.* Resembles Western Toad tadpole, but body and tail musculature darker, snout blunter, and tip of tail more rounded. To around 1 ½ in. (3.7 cm). Sierra Nevada, Calif., usually above 6,500 ft. (1,980 m). **Map 33**

Sonoran Desert Toad, *Bufo alvarius* (not shown). Body some-what flattened, gray to light golden brown. Tail tip rounded. Throat and chest with a few or no dark specks. To around 2 ¼ in. (5.6 cm). **Map 40**

Red-spotted Toad, *Bufo punctatus.* Black or deep brown above. Rather coarse spotting on dorsal fin. Upper labium (lip) and its tooth rows extend downward on each side of mouth. To around 1 ⅖ in. (3.5 cm). **Map 41**

Green Toad, *Bufo debilis* (not shown). Patches of gold on back. Belly black laterally with golden flecks. In late stages of develop-

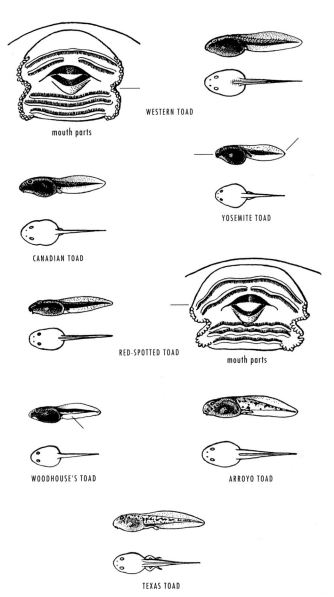

WESTERN TOAD

mouth parts

YOSEMITE TOAD

CANADIAN TOAD

RED-SPOTTED TOAD

mouth parts

WOODHOUSE'S TOAD

ARROYO TOAD

TEXAS TOAD

Fig. 37. True toads

ment, tadpole may be relatively transparent and lightly stippled with melanophores. Labial tooth rows usually 2/2. Anus on right side of ventral midline. **Map 39**

Sonoran Green Toad, *Bufo retiformis* (not shown). Resembles Green Toad tadpole. Tail musculature tends to be bicolored, and larger individuals lack melanophores (black spots) in ventral fin. **Map 39**

Canadian Toad, *Bufo hemiophrys.* Black or nearly so above, slightly lighter below. Clear area on throat and chest. Tail musculature dark except for narrow light ventral area. **Map 36**

Woodhouse's Toad, *Bufo woodhousii.* Dark brown, gray to slate above, commonly with light mottlings. Lower part of tail musculature may lack or have little melanic (dark) pigment. Dorsal fin may have few markings. To around 1 in. (2.5 cm). **Map 35**

Arroyo Toad, *Bufo californicus.* Olive, gray, or tan above, commonly spotted or mottled with blackish to brown. Tail musculature colored like body. White below. Cryptically colored, blending closely with background; however, very young tadpoles are black. To around 1 ½ in. (3.7 cm). **Map 34**

Texas Toad, *Bufo speciosus.* Drab or grayish olive above. Tail musculature with irregular, dark-colored lateral stripe, or blotches tending to form a stripe. Light tan to pinkish below. Extreme se. N.M. **Map 38**

Great Plains Toad, *Bufo cognatus* (not shown). Mottled brown and gray, dark gray, or blackish above, but becomes paler and may develop adult pattern at around 1 in. (2.5 cm). Light greenish below with yellow and reddish iridescence. Dorsal fin highly arched. To around 1 in. (2.5 cm). **Map 37**

Treefrogs and Relatives
See Fig. 38, p. 457 (× ⅚). Mouth round, not indented at the sides. Middle part of upper lip lacks oral papillae. Labial tooth rows usually 2/3. Large dark areas on bodies of treefrog and chorus frog tadpoles shown in Fig. 38 result from loss of overlying pigment in preserved specimens.

Pacific Treefrog, *Hyla regilla.* Eyes on outline of head as viewed from above. Blackish, dark brown, to olive brown above, often heavily spotted with blackish. Whitish below with bronze or coppery sheen. Intestines not visible. To around 1 ¾ in. (4.4 cm). **Map 44**

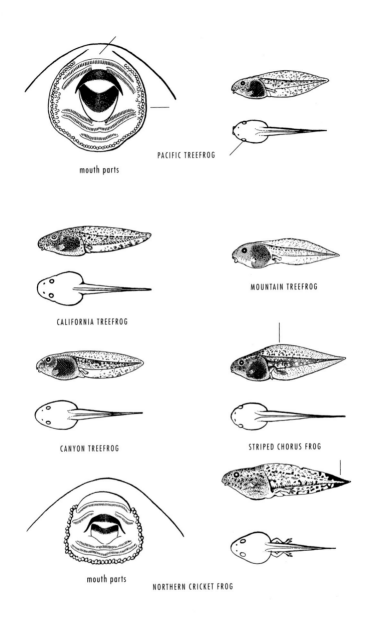

mouth parts

PACIFIC TREEFROG

CALIFORNIA TREEFROG

MOUNTAIN TREEFROG

CANYON TREEFROG

STRIPED CHORUS FROG

mouth parts

NORTHERN CRICKET FROG

Fig. 38. Treefrogs and relatives

Mountain Treefrog, *Hyla eximia.* Eyes as in Pacific Treefrog. Brown above with minute silvery gold flecks. Dark below with overlying tinge of pale gold. **Map 46**

California Treefrog, *Hyla cadaverina.* Eyes set inside outline of head, as viewed from above. Light to dark brown above. Dorsal surface of tail musculature marked with alternating dark cross-bars. Intestines visible. Third lower row of labial teeth about ½ length of 2nd row. To 1 ¾ in. (4.4 cm). **Map 47**

Canyon Treefrog, *Hyla arenicolor.* Eyes as in California Treefrog. Dark brown above changing to golden brown as tadpole matures. No dark bars on tail musculature. Third lower row of labial teeth usually shorter than 2nd. To around 1 ¼ in. (3.1 cm). **Map 47**

Western Chorus Frog, *Pseudacris triseriata.* Black, gray, to olive above. Silver with a coppery sheen below. Dorsal fin highly arched. Eyes positioned as in Pacific Treefrog. To around 1 ½ in. (3.7 cm). **Map 42**

Northern Cricket Frog, *Acris crepitans.* Fins with bold dark markings. Tip of tail usually black but in a Kans. study tadpoles in lakes and creeks were mostly plain-tailed whereas many of those in ponds had black tail tips. Labial tooth rows 2/2 or 2/3. To around 1¾ in. (4.4 cm). **Map 45**

Northern Casque-headed Frog, *Pternohyla fodiens* (not shown). Body globular, tail little longer than body. Dull tan with olive brown mottling above. A whitish stripe behind eye. Whitish below. To around 1 ¾ in. (4.2 cm). **Map 43**

True Frogs (Rana)

See Fig. 39, p. 459, (× ⅚). Oral papillae absent from middle part of upper lip. Mouth indented at sides. Eyes situated well inside outline of head as viewed from above.

Red-legged Frog, *Rana aurora.* Dark brown or yellowish above; pinkish iridescence below. Dorsolateral rows of minute whitish spots (glands of dorsolateral folds) may be evident, extending from between the eyes posteriorly. Labial tooth rows 2/3 or 3/4. To around 3 in. (7.5 cm). Ponds, lakes, or slowly flowing streams. **Map 50**

Oregon Spotted Frog, *Rana pretiosa* (not shown). Uniformly dark above, brown or gray flecked with gold; iridescent bronze be-

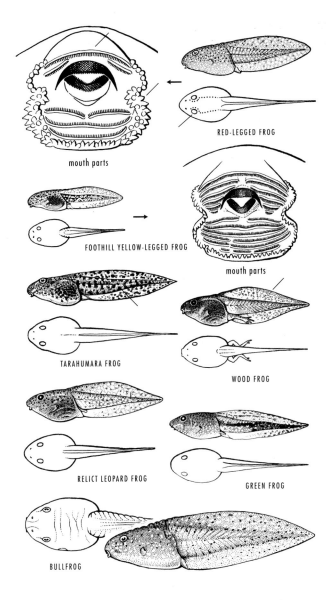

RED-LEGGED FROG

mouth parts

FOOTHILL YELLOW-LEGGED FROG

mouth parts

TARAHUMARA FROG

WOOD FROG

RELICT LEOPARD FROG

GREEN FROG

BULLFROG

Fig. 39. True frogs

low. Labial tooth rows usually 2/3 but also 1–3/3. To around 3 in. (7.5 cm), occasionally to 4 in. (10 cm). **Map 52**

Cascades Frog, *Rana cascadae* (not shown). Dark brown, charcoal, or black or occasionally greenish above. Silvery to brassy below. Tail long. Labial tooth rows 3/4. To around 2 in. (5 cm). **Map 53**

Foothill Yellow-legged Frog, *Rana boylii.* Body and tail musculature olive gray with rather coarse brown mottling, usually matching stream bottom. Body more flattened, tail musculature better developed, and more labial tooth rows than in other ranid frog tadpoles in our area, characteristics apparently related to stream-dwelling habits. May cling by suction to rocks. Labial tooth rows often 6–7/6. To around 2 in. (5 cm). Rivers and streams. **Map 51**

Mountain Yellow-legged Frog, *Rana muscosa* (not shown). Brown with golden tint above. Faintly yellow below, intestines vaguely evident. Dark spots often present on massive tail musculature and fins. Labial tooth rows usually 2–4/4. To over 2 in. (5 cm). **Map 54**

Tarahumara Frog, *Rana tarahumarae.* Greenish gray to dark brown above. Body and tail with numerous dark spots. Labial tooth rows usually 4–5/3. To around 4 in. (10 cm). Streams. In our area known only from extreme s. Ariz. Now presumed extinct in U.S. **Map 55**

Wood Frog, *Rana sylvatica.* Above dusky, brownish, or black with gold flecks that sometimes impart a greenish sheen. Cream or golden below, with pinkish iridescence. Cream or golden line along edge of mouth that may radiate, suggesting whiskers. Belly may be dark with silvery sheen. Tail fins high. Labial tooth rows usually 2–4/3–4. To around 2 in. (5 cm). **Map 48**

Northern Leopard Frog, *Rana pipiens.* Dark brown or olive to gray above, often with fine gold spots. Cream to whitish below, often weakly pigmented, intestines showing through. Labial tooth rows usually 2/3. To around 3 ½ in. (8.7 cm). **Map 56**

Plains Leopard Frog, *Rana blairi* (not shown). Resembles Northern Leopard Frog tadpole, but body more cylindrical — less full-bodied toward rear, and snout more rounded from above. Mouth set further back from tip of snout. In N.M., the palest of the Leopard Frog tadpoles. **Map 58**

Rio Grande Leopard Frog, *Rana berlandieri* (not shown). Olive with a yellowish cast on dorsum and sides. Tail may average longer than in Northern and Plains Leopard Frogs; tail musculature well developed, fins relatively low and mottled or blotched.   **Map 57**

Relict Leopard Frog, *Rana onca* (not shown). Greenish olive above. Tail pale greenish yellow with heavily mottled fins. Intestines visible. To around 3¼ in. (8.1 cm). (Based on animals from Vegas Valley, Nev., now apparently extinct.)   **Map 61**

Green Frog, *Rana clamitans.* Olive green to brown above, with numerous distinct dark spots. Cream below, with a coppery sheen. Tail spotted. Labial tooth rows usually 2/3 or 1/3. To around 4 in. (10 cm). Introduced in our area (see Species Account for localities).   **Map 51**

Bullfrog, *Rana catesbeiana.* Resembles Red-legged Frog tadpole, but snout more rounded from above and eyes more widely separated. Olive green above. Dorsum and fins speckled with small dark spots. Whitish to pale yellow below, without pinkish iridescence. No dorsolateral fold glands as in Red-legged Frog tadpole. Labial tooth rows usually 2/3 or 3/3. To around 6½ in. (16.2 cm).   **Map 49**

Clawed Frogs (Xenopus)
African Clawed Frog, *Xenopus laevis* (see Fig. 12, Pl. 19). Body transparent, internal organs evident. Tentacle on each side of mouth. Mouth parts soft, no labial teeth. A filter feeder that strains minute food particles from the water. To 1½ in. (3.7 cm). Introduced in s. Calif., nw. Baja Calif., and Ariz.   **Map 60**

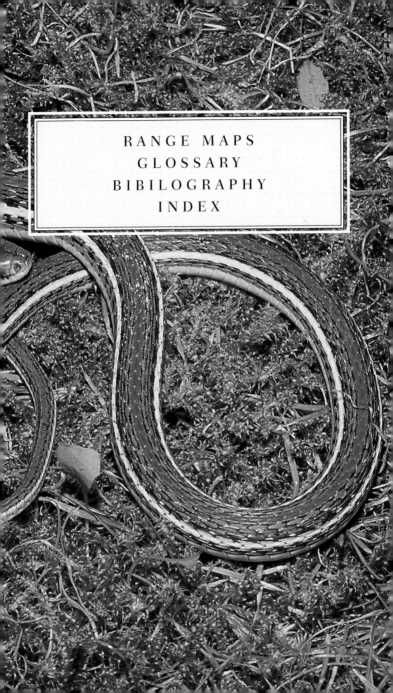

RANGE MAPS
GLOSSARY
BIBILOGRAPHY
INDEX

RANGE MAPS

There are 204 maps showing the ranges of all the species covered in this Field Guide. They are preceded by 3 maps depicting the distribution of native vegetation in the western United States and Baja California. The distribution of vegetation also reflects topography and climate. These maps may help understanding of species ranges. (See text, p. 10.)

KEY TO MAP SYMBOLS

DOT. Isolated population. Usually shown in the same color as the taxon it represents. However, where related taxa (species or subspecies) join or closely approach one another, the taxonomic relationship of some of their nearby isolated populations is sometimes uncertain. Such populations are shown as black dots. Examples: Maps 65, 101, 146. Whether all isolated populations are viable or not is often unknown.

QUESTON MARK (?). Record questionable or information inadequate.

PALE GRAY. Zone of intergradation.

BLACK. Zone of sympatry or hybridization (see text for which applies).

PALE BLUE WITH CROSS (†). Symbol for severe species or subspecies decline. Areas in pale blue within their ranges indicate regions of significant loss. See Remarks sections of species accounts for comments on causes and levels of endangerment.

BOX WITH DIVISON. Symbol used to identify two taxa (species or subspecies) overlaps. Each taxon involved is identified by a box that contains two colors—the upper one representing its range outside the area of overlap and the lower one that is shared with its overlap partner. A bicolored box is also used for taxa that have suffered serious declines in range. The lower part of the box is shown in pale blue, as are areas of loss on the map. The upper part bears the taxon color.

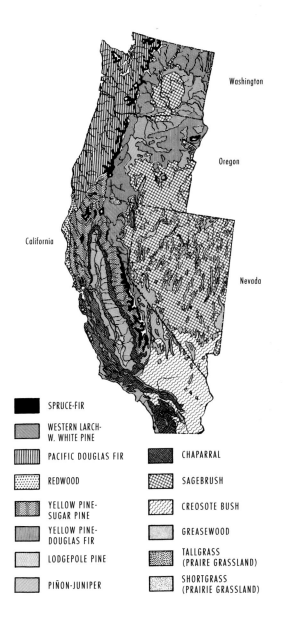

Washington

Oregon

California

Nevada

SPRUCE-FIR

WESTERN LARCH-
W. WHITE PINE

PACIFIC DOUGLAS FIR

REDWOOD

YELLOW PINE-
SUGAR PINE

YELLOW PINE-
DOUGLAS FIR

LODGEPOLE PINE

PIÑON-JUNIPER

CHAPARRAL

SAGEBRUSH

CREOSOTE BUSH

GREASEWOOD

TALLGRASS
(PRAIRIE GRASSLAND)

SHORTGRASS
(PRAIRIE GRASSLAND)

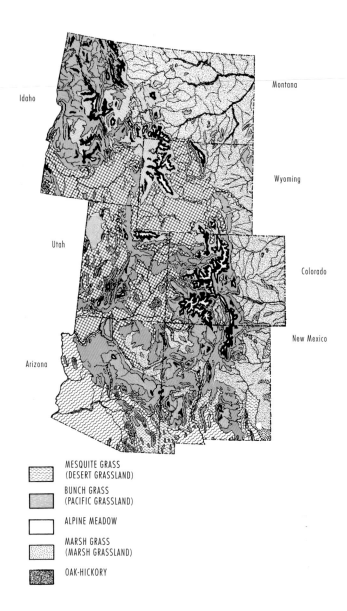

Montana

Idaho

Wyoming

Utah

Colorado

New Mexico

Arizona

MESQUITE GRASS
(DESERT GRASSLAND)

BUNCH GRASS
(PACIFIC GRASSLAND)

ALPINE MEADOW

MARSH GRASS
(MARSH GRASSLAND)

OAK-HICKORY

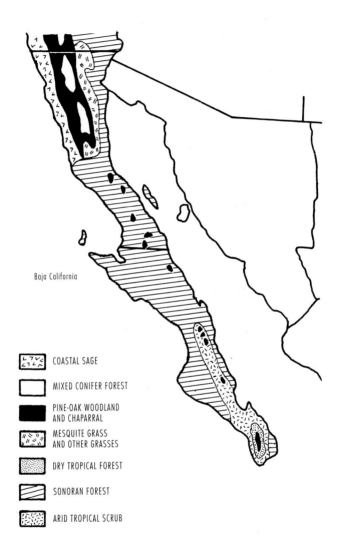

Baja California

COASTAL SAGE

MIXED CONIFER FOREST

PINE-OAK WOODLAND AND CHAPARRAL

MESQUITE GRASS AND OTHER GRASSES

DRY TROPICAL FOREST

SONORAN FOREST

ARID TROPICAL SCRUB

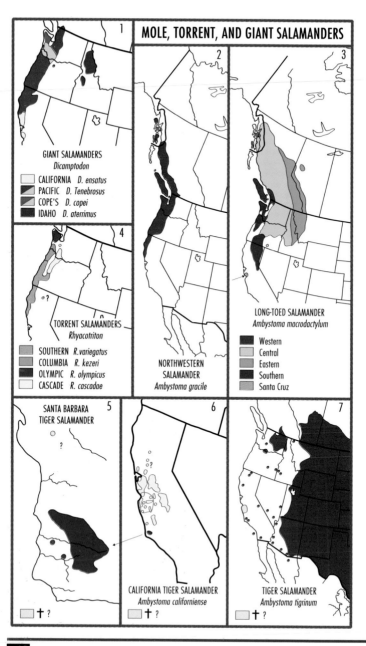

MOLE, TORRENT, AND GIANT SALAMANDERS

1

GIANT SALAMANDERS
Dicamptodon

- CALIFORNIA *D. ensatus*
- PACIFIC *D. Tenebrosus*
- COPE'S *D. copei*
- IDAHO *D. aterrimus*

4

TORRENT SALAMANDERS
Rhyacotriton

- SOUTHERN *R.variegatus*
- COLUMBIA *R. kezeri*
- OLYMPIC *R. olympicus*
- CASCADE *R. cascadae*

2

NORTHWESTERN SALAMANDER
Ambystoma gracile

3

LONG-TOED SALAMANDER
Ambystoma macrodactylum

- Western
- Central
- Eastern
- Southern
- Santa Cruz

5

SANTA BARBARA TIGER SALAMANDER

† ?

6

CALIFORNIA TIGER SALAMANDER
Ambystoma californiense

† ?

7

TIGER SALAMANDER
Ambystoma tigrinum

† ?

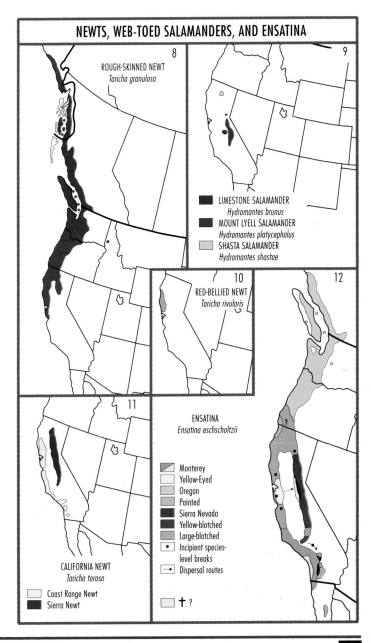

NEWTS, WEB-TOED SALAMANDERS, AND ENSATINA

8

ROUGH-SKINNED NEWT
Taricha granulosa

9

■ LIMESTONE SALAMANDER
Hydromantes brunus
■ MOUNT LYELL SALAMANDER
Hydromantes platycephalus
□ SHASTA SALAMANDER
Hydromantes shastae

10

RED-BELLIED NEWT
Taricha rivularis

12

ENSATINA
Ensatina eschscholtzii

Monterey
Yellow-Eyed
Oregon
Painted
Sierra Nevada
Yellow-blotched
Large-blotched
• Incipient species-level breaks
→ Dispersal routes

11

CALIFORNIA NEWT
Taricha torosa

□ Coast Range Newt
■ Sierra Newt

□ † ?

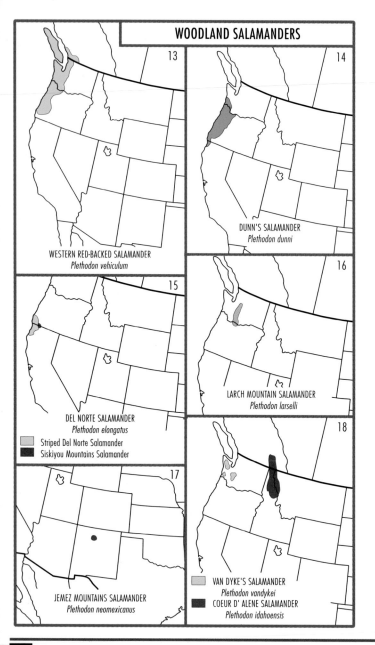

WOODLAND SALAMANDERS

13

WESTERN RED-BACKED SALAMANDER
Plethodon vehiculum

14

DUNN'S SALAMANDER
Plethodon dunni

15

DEL NORTE SALAMANDER
Plethodon elongatus

☐ Striped Del Norte Salamander
■ Siskiyou Mountains Salamander

16

LARCH MOUNTAIN SALAMANDER
Plethodon larselli

17

JEMEZ MOUNTAINS SALAMANDER
Plethodon neomexicanus

18

☐ VAN DYKE'S SALAMANDER
Plethodon vandykei
■ COEUR D' ALENE SALAMANDER
Plethodon idahoensis

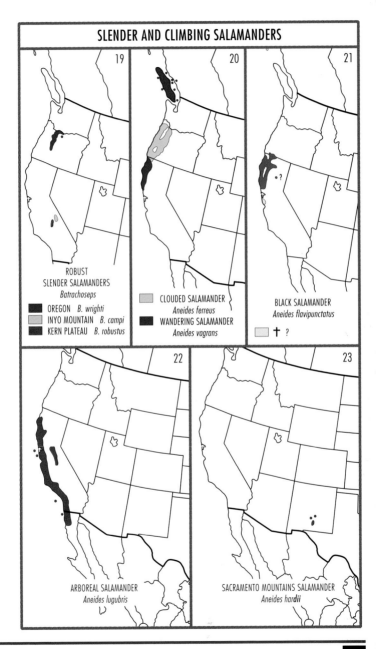

SLENDER AND CLIMBING SALAMANDERS

19

ROBUST
SLENDER SALAMANDERS
Batrachoseps

- ■ OREGON *B. wrighti*
- ▨ INYO MOUNTAIN *B. campi*
- ■ KERN PLATEAU *B. robustus*

20

▨ CLOUDED SALAMANDER
Aneides ferreus

■ WANDERING SALAMANDER
Aneides vagrans

21

BLACK SALAMANDER
Aneides flavipunctatus

▨ † ?

22

ARBOREAL SALAMANDER
Aneides lugubris

23

SACRAMENTO MOUNTAINS SALAMANDER
Aneides hardii

SLENDER SALAMANDERS

	distribution overlaps	See page 11 for explanation of numbers.	
■		distribution overlaps	
	1,2	CALIFORNIA	*Batrachoseps attenuatus*
	12	SANTA LUCIA MTS.	*Batrachoseps luciae*
	2,3,12	GABILAN MTS.	*Batrachoseps gavilanensis*
	4	SAN SIMEON	*Batrachoseps incognitus*
	5	LESSER	*Batrachoseps minor*
	3 to 9	BLACK-BELLIED	*Batrachoseps nigriventris*
		GARDEN	*Batrachoseps major*
	9	GARDEN	*Batrachoseps m. major*
		DESERT	*Batrachoseps m. aridus*
	8	CHANNEL ISLANDS	*Batrachoseps pacificus*
	7	SAN GABRIEL MTS.	*Batrachoseps gabrieli*
	6	TEHACHAPI	*Batrachoseps stebbinsi*
		OREGON	*Batrachoseps wrighti*
	1	HELL HOLLOW	*Batrachoseps diabolicus*
		GREGARIUS	*Batrachoseps gregarius*

ENLARGED VIEW

		KERN PLATEAU	*Batrachoseps robustus*
	11	KERN CANYON	*Batrachoseps simatus*
		RELICTUAL	*Batrachoseps relictus*
	10	SEQUOIA	*Batrachoseps kawia*
		GREGARIUS	*Batrachoseps gregarius*
		KINGS RIVER	*Batrachoseps regius*
		INYO MTS.	*Batrachoseps campi*

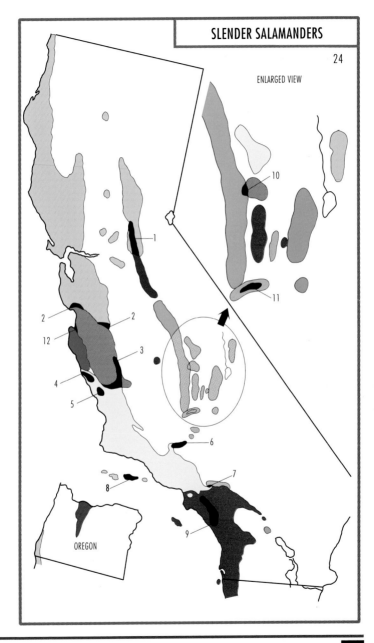

ENLARGED VIEW

10

11

1

2

2

12

3

4

5

6

7

8

9

OREGON

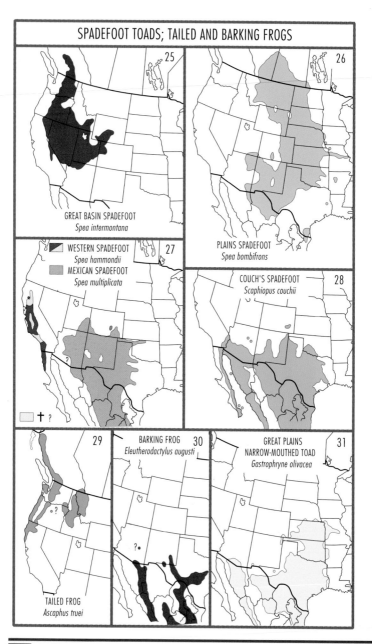

SPADEFOOT TOADS; TAILED AND BARKING FROGS

25

GREAT BASIN SPADEFOOT
Spea intermontana

26

PLAINS SPADEFOOT
Spea bombifrons

27

WESTERN SPADEFOOT
Spea hammondii
MEXICAN SPADEFOOT
Spea multiplicata

28

COUCH'S SPADEFOOT
Scaphiopus couchii

† ?

29

TAILED FROG
Ascaphus truei

30

BARKING FROG
Eleutherodactylus augusti

31

GREAT PLAINS
NARROW-MOUTHED TOAD
Gastrophryne olivacea

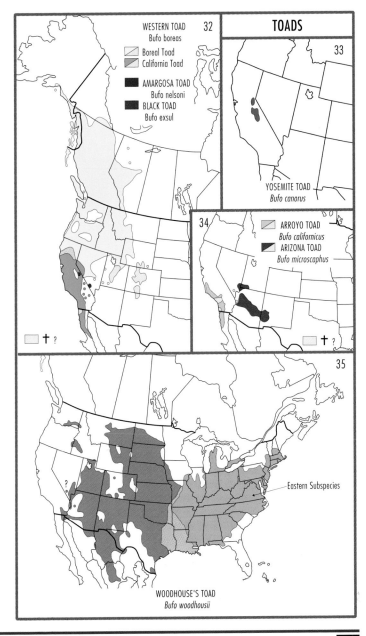

TOADS

WESTERN TOAD 32
Bufo boreas

Boreal Toad
California Toad

AMARGOSA TOAD
Bufo nelsoni
BLACK TOAD
Bufo exsul

33

YOSEMITE TOAD
Bufo canorus

34

ARROYO TOAD
Bufo californicus
ARIZONA TOAD
Bufo microscaphus

☐ † ?

☐ † ?

35

Eastern Subspecies

?

WOODHOUSE'S TOAD
Bufo woodhousii

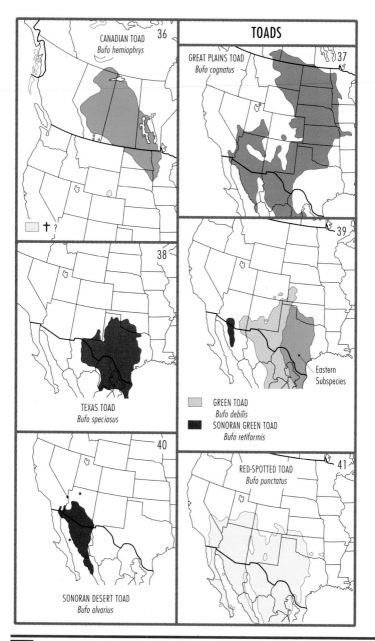

TOADS

CANADIAN TOAD
Bufo hemiophrys
36

GREAT PLAINS TOAD
Bufo cognatus
37

TEXAS TOAD
Bufo speciosus
38

39

Eastern
Subspecies

GREEN TOAD
Bufo debilis
SONORAN GREEN TOAD
Bufo retiformis

SONORAN DESERT TOAD
Bufo alvarius
40

RED-SPOTTED TOAD
Bufo punctatus
41

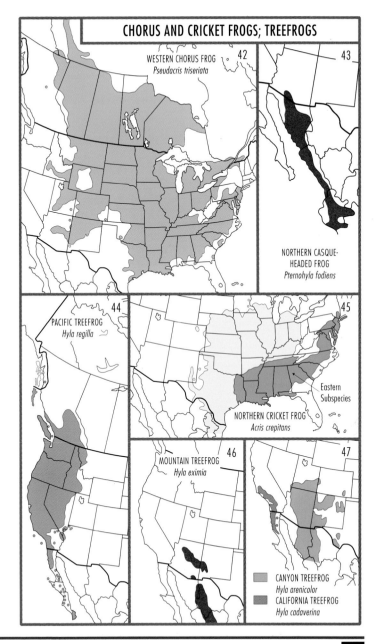

CHORUS AND CRICKET FROGS; TREEFROGS

42 WESTERN CHORUS FROG
Pseudacris triseriata

43 NORTHERN CASQUE-HEADED FROG
Pternohyla fodiens

44 PACIFIC TREEFROG
Hyla regilla

45 NORTHERN CRICKET FROG
Acris crepitans

Eastern Subspecies

46 MOUNTAIN TREEFROG
Hyla eximia

47

CANYON TREEFROG
Hyla arenicolor

CALIFORNIA TREEFROG
Hyla cadaverina

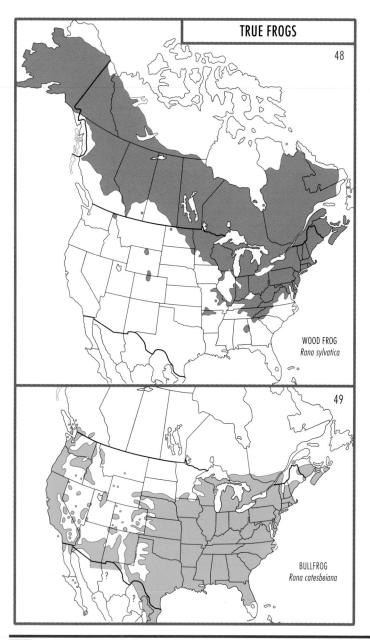

TRUE FROGS

48

WOOD FROG
Rana sylvatica

49

BULLFROG
Rana catesbeiana

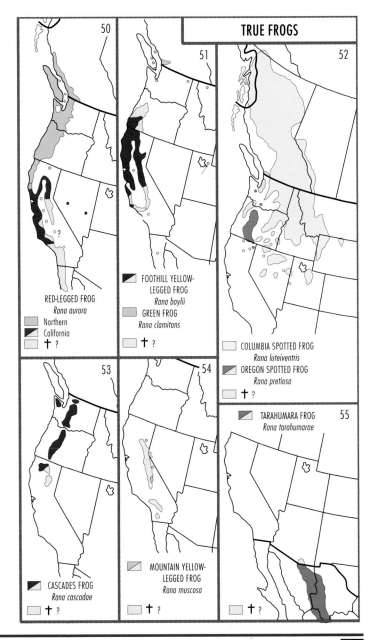

TRUE FROGS

50

51

52

RED-LEGGED FROG
Rana aurora
- Northern
- California
- ✝ ?

FOOTHILL YELLOW-
LEGGED FROG
Rana boylii
GREEN FROG
Rana clamitans
- ✝ ?

COLUMBIA SPOTTED FROG
Rana luteiventris
OREGON SPOTTED FROG
Rana pretiosa
- ✝ ?

53

CASCADES FROG
Rana cascadae
- ✝ ?

54

MOUNTAIN YELLOW-
LEGGED FROG
Rana muscosa
- ✝ ?

55

TARAHUMARA FROG
Rana tarahumarae
- ✝ ?

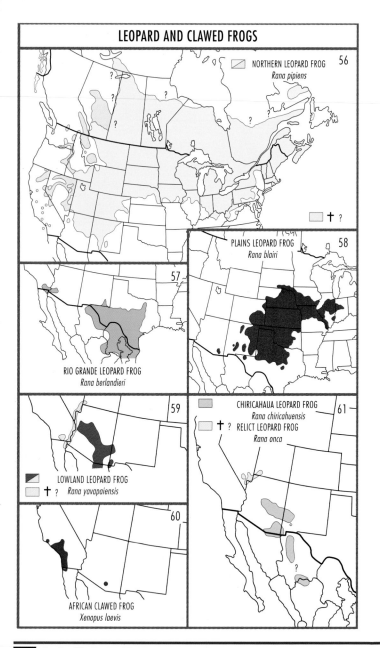

LEOPARD AND CLAWED FROGS

NORTHERN LEOPARD FROG
Rana pipiens
56

† ?

PLAINS LEOPARD FROG
Rana blairi
58

RIO GRANDE LEOPARD FROG
Rana berlandieri
57

LOWLAND LEOPARD FROG
† ? *Rana yavapaiensis*
59

CHIRICAHAUA LEOPARD FROG
Rana chiricahuensis
† ? RELICT LEOPARD FROG
Rana onca
61

AFRICAN CLAWED FROG
Xenopus laevis
60

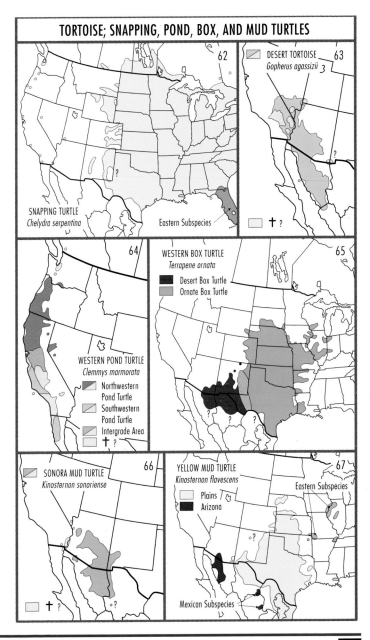

TORTOISE; SNAPPING, POND, BOX, AND MUD TURTLES

SNAPPING TURTLE
Chelydra serpentina

Eastern Subspecies

DESERT TORTOISE
Gopherus agassizii

WESTERN POND TURTLE
Clemmys marmorata

Northwestern Pond Turtle
Southwestern Pond Turtle
Intergrade Area

WESTERN BOX TURTLE
Terrapene ornata

Desert Box Turtle
Ornate Box Turtle

SONORA MUD TURTLE
Kinosternon sonoriense

YELLOW MUD TURTLE
Kinosternon flavescens

Plains
Arizona

Eastern Subspecies

Mexican Subspecies

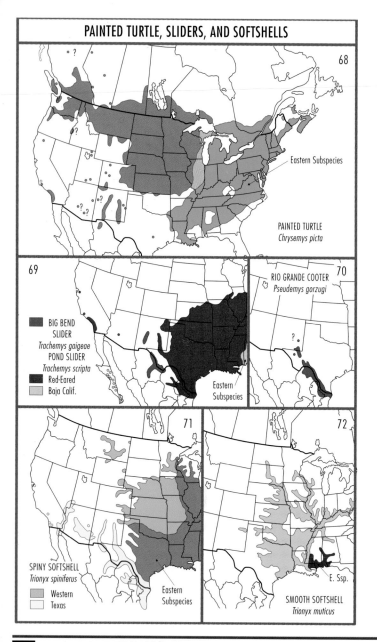

PAINTED TURTLE, SLIDERS, AND SOFTSHELLS

68

Eastern Subspecies

PAINTED TURTLE
Chrysemys picta

69

BIG BEND
SLIDER
Trachemys gaigeae
POND SLIDER
Trachemys scripta
Red-Eared
Baja Calif.

Eastern
Subspecies

70 RIO GRANDE COOTER
Pseudemys gorzugi

71

SPINY SOFTSHELL
Trionyx spiniferus
Western
Texas

Eastern
Subspecies

72

E. Ssp.

SMOOTH SOFTSHELL
Trionyx muticus

GECKOS, IGUANA, CHUCKWALLA, AND NIGHT LIZARDS

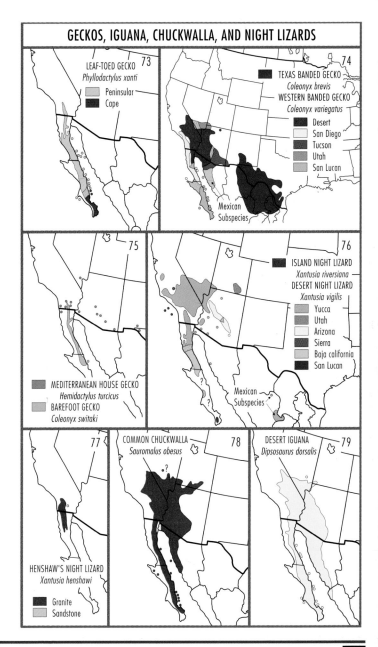

LEAF-TOED GECKO 73
Phyllodactylus xanti
- Peninsular
- Cape

TEXAS BANDED GECKO 74
Coleonyx brevis
WESTERN BANDED GECKO
Coleonyx variegatus
- Desert
- San Diego
- Tucson
- Utah
- San Lucan
Mexican Subspecies

MEDITERRANEAN HOUSE GECKO 75
Hemidactylus turcicus
BAREFOOT GECKO
Coleonyx switaki

ISLAND NIGHT LIZARD 76
Xantusia riversiana
DESERT NIGHT LIZARD
Xantusia vigilis
- Yucca
- Utah
- Arizona
- Sierra
- Baja california
- San Lucan
Mexican Subspecies

HENSHAW'S NIGHT LIZARD 77
Xantusia henshawi
- Granite
- Sandstone

COMMON CHUCKWALLA 78
Sauromalus obesus

DESERT IGUANA 79
Dipsosaurus dorsalis

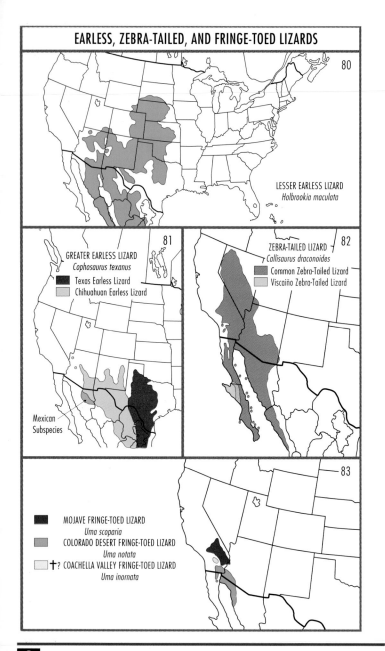

EARLESS, ZEBRA-TAILED, AND FRINGE-TOED LIZARDS

80

LESSER EARLESS LIZARD
Holbrookia maculata

81

GREATER EARLESS LIZARD
Cophosaurus texanus
■ Texas Earless Lizard
■ Chihuahuan Earless Lizard

Mexican
Subspecies

82

ZEBRA-TAILED LIZARD
Callisaurus draconoides
■ Common Zebra-Tailed Lizard
■ Viscaíno Zebra-Tailed Lizard

83

■ MOJAVE FRINGE-TOED LIZARD
Uma scoparia
■ COLORADO DESERT FRINGE-TOED LIZARD
Uma notata
□ †? COACHELLA VALLEY FRINGE-TOED LIZARD
Uma inornata

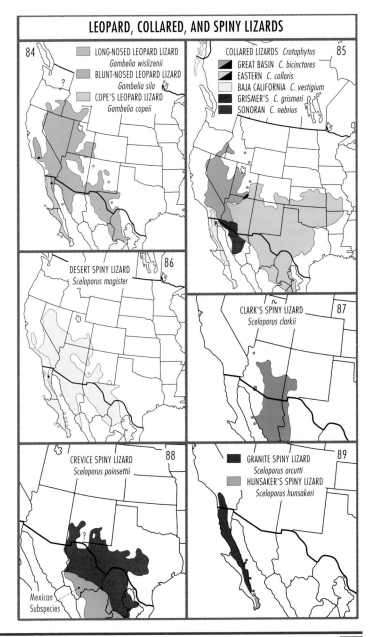

LEOPARD, COLLARED, AND SPINY LIZARDS

84

LONG-NOSED LEOPARD LIZARD
Gambelia wislizenii
BLUNT-NOSED LEOPARD LIZARD
Gambelia sila
COPE'S LEOPARD LIZARD
Gambelia copeii

85

COLLARED LIZARDS *Crotaphytus*
GREAT BASIN *C. bicinctores*
EASTERN *C. collaris*
BAJA CALIFORNIA *C. vestigium*
GRISMER'S *C. grismeri*
SONORAN *C. nebrius*

86

DESERT SPINY LIZARD
Sceloporus magister

87

CLARK'S SPINY LIZARD
Sceloporus clarkii

88

CREVICE SPINY LIZARD
Sceloporus poinsettii

Mexican
Subspecies

89

GRANITE SPINY LIZARD
Sceloporus orcutti
HUNSAKER'S SPINY LIZARD
Sceloporus hunsakeri

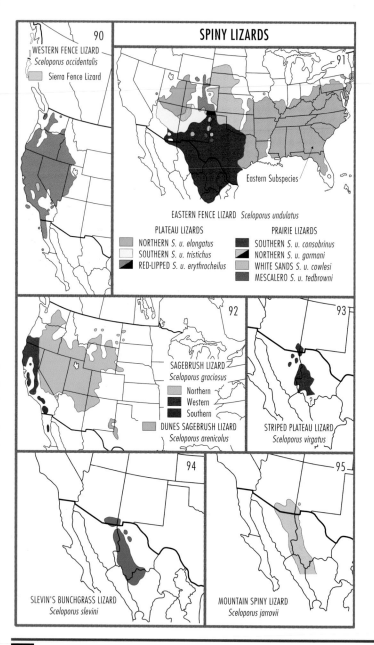

SPINY LIZARDS

90
WESTERN FENCE LIZARD
Sceloporus occidentalis
  Sierra Fence Lizard

91
EASTERN FENCE LIZARD *Sceloporus undulatus*
Eastern Subspecies

PLATEAU LIZARDS
  NORTHERN *S. u. elongatus*
  SOUTHERN *S. u. tristichus*
  RED-LIPPED *S. u. erythrocheilus*

PRAIRIE LIZARDS
  SOUTHERN *S. u. consobrinus*
  NORTHERN *S. u. garmani*
  WHITE SANDS *S. u. cowlesi*
  MESCALERO *S. u. tedbrowni*

92
SAGEBRUSH LIZARD
Sceloporus graciosus
  Northern
  Western
  Southern
DUNES SAGEBRUSH LIZARD
Sceloporus arenicolus

93
STRIPED PLATEAU LIZARD
Sceloporus virgatus

94
SLEVIN'S BUNCHGRASS LIZARD
Sceloporus slevini

95
MOUNTAIN SPINY LIZARD
Sceloporus jarrovii

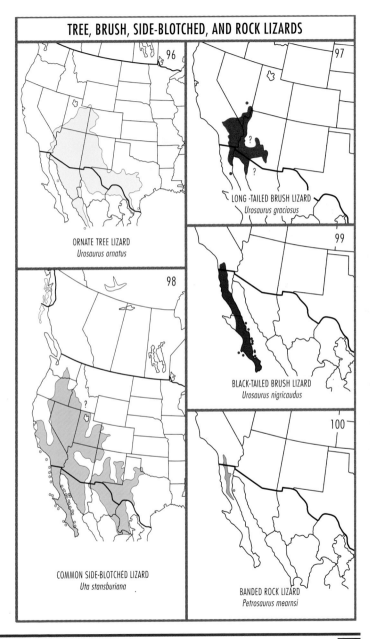

TREE, BRUSH, SIDE-BLOTCHED, AND ROCK LIZARDS

96

ORNATE TREE LIZARD
Urosaurus ornatus

97

LONG-TAILED BRUSH LIZARD
Urosaurus graciosus

98

COMMON SIDE-BLOTCHED LIZARD
Uta stansburiana

99

BLACK-TAILED BRUSH LIZARD
Urosaurus nigricaudus

100

BANDED ROCK LIZARD
Petrosaurus mearnsi

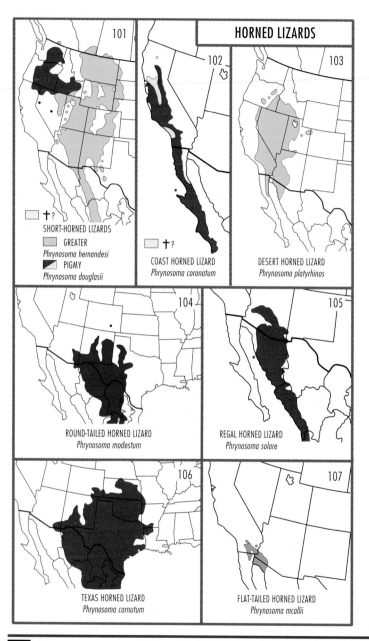

HORNED LIZARDS

101
† ?
GREATER
SHORT-HORNED LIZARDS
GREATER
Phrynosoma hernandesi
PIGMY
Phrynosoma douglasii

102
□ † ?
COAST HORNED LIZARD
Phrynosoma coronatum

103
DESERT HORNED LIZARD
Phrynosoma platyrhinos

104
ROUND-TAILED HORNED LIZARD
Phrynosoma modestum

105
REGAL HORNED LIZARD
Phrynosoma solare

106
TEXAS HORNED LIZARD
Phrynosoma cornutum

107
FLAT-TAILED HORNED LIZARD
Phrynosoma mcallii

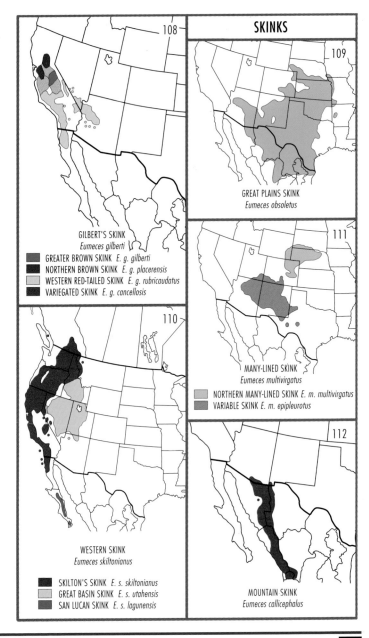

SKINKS

108

109

GILBERT'S SKINK
Eumeces gilberti
GREATER BROWN SKINK *E. g. gilberti*
NORTHERN BROWN SKINK *E. g. placerensis*
WESTERN RED-TAILED SKINK *E. g. rubricaudatus*
VARIEGATED SKINK *E. g. cancellosis*

GREAT PLAINS SKINK
Eumeces obsoletus

111

110

MANY-LINED SKINK
Eumeces multivirgatus
NORTHERN MANY-LINED SKINK *E. m. multivirgatus*
VARIABLE SKINK *E. m. epipleurotus*

112

WESTERN SKINK
Eumeces skiltonianus

SKILTON'S SKINK *E. s. skiltonianus*
GREAT BASIN SKINK *E. s. utahensis*
SAN LUCAN SKINK *E. s. lagunensis*

MOUNTAIN SKINK
Eumeces callicephalus

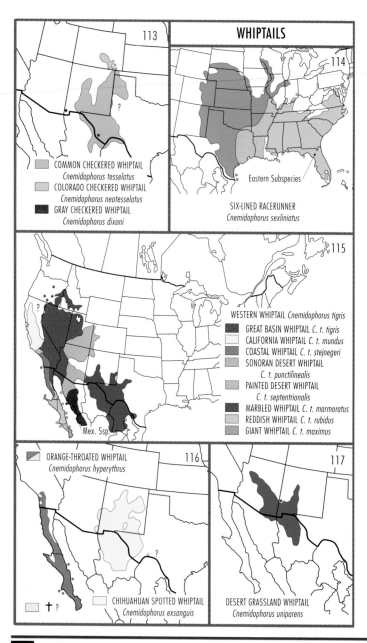

WHIPTAILS

113

COMMON CHECKERED WHIPTAIL
Cnemidophorus tesselatus
COLORADO CHECKERED WHIPTAIL
Cnemidophorus neotesselatus
GRAY CHECKERED WHIPTAIL
Cnemidophorus dixoni

114

Eastern Subspecies

SIX-LINED RACERUNNER
Cnemidophorus sexlineatus

115

WESTERN WHIPTAIL *Cnemidophorus tigris*
GREAT BASIN WHIPTAIL *C. t. tigris*
CALIFORNIA WHIPTAIL *C. t. mundus*
COASTAL WHIPTAIL *C. t. stejnegeri*
SONORAN DESERT WHIPTAIL
C. t. punctilinealis
PAINTED DESERT WHIPTAIL
C. t. septentrionalis
MARBLED WHIPTAIL *C. t. marmoratus*
REDDISH WHIPTAIL *C. t. rubidus*
GIANT WHIPTAIL *C. t. maximus*

Mex. Ssp.

ORANGE-THROATED WHIPTAIL
Cnemidophorus hyperythrus

116

117

† ?

CHIHUAHUAN SPOTTED WHIPTAIL
Cnemidophorus exsanguis

DESERT GRASSLAND WHIPTAIL
Cnemidophorus uniparens

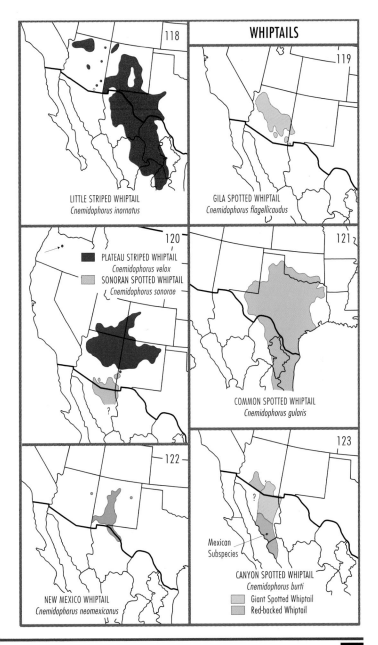

WHITETAILS

LITTLE STRIPED WHIPTAIL
Cnemidophorus inornatus

GILA SPOTTED WHIPTAIL
Cnemidophorus flagellicaudus

PLATEAU STRIPED WHIPTAIL
Cnemidophorus velox
SONORAN SPOTTED WHIPTAIL
Cnemidophorus sonorae

COMMON SPOTTED WHIPTAIL
Cnemidophorus gularis

NEW MEXICO WHIPTAIL
Cnemidophorus neomexicanus

Mexican
Subspecies

CANYON SPOTTED WHIPTAIL
Cnemidophorus burti
  Giant Spotted Whiptail
  Red-backed Whiptail

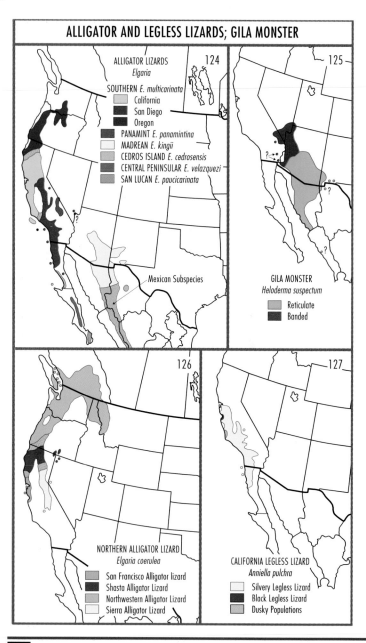

ALLIGATOR AND LEGLESS LIZARDS; GILA MONSTER

ALLIGATOR LIZARDS
Elgaria

SOUTHERN *E. multicarinata*
California
San Diego
Oregon
PANAMINT *E. panamintina*
MADREAN *E. kingii*
CEDROS ISLAND *E. cedrosensis*
CENTRAL PENINSULAR *E. velazquezi*
SAN LUCAN *E. paucicarinata*

124

Mexican Subspecies

125

GILA MONSTER
Heloderma suspectum
Reticulate
Banded

126

NORTHERN ALLIGATOR LIZARD
Elgaria coerulea
San Francisco Alligator lizard
Shasta Alligator Lizard
Northwestern Alligator Lizard
Sierra Alligator Lizard

127

CALIFORNIA LEGLESS LIZARD
Anniella pulchra
Silvery Legless Lizard
Black Legless Lizard
Dusky Populations

BLIND AND HOG-NOSED SNAKES; BOAS

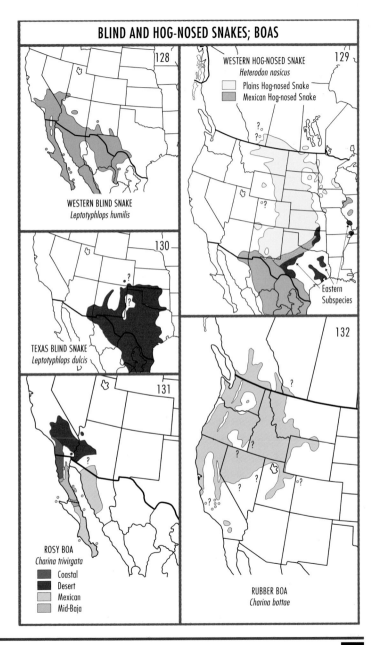

128

WESTERN BLIND SNAKE
Leptotyphlops humilis

129

WESTERN HOG-NOSED SNAKE
Heterodon nasicus

Plains Hog-nosed Snake
Mexican Hog-nosed Snake

Eastern
Subspecies

130

TEXAS BLIND SNAKE
Leptotyphlops dulcis

131

ROSY BOA
Charina trivirgata

Coastal
Desert
Mexican
Mid-Baja

132

RUBBER BOA
Charina bottae

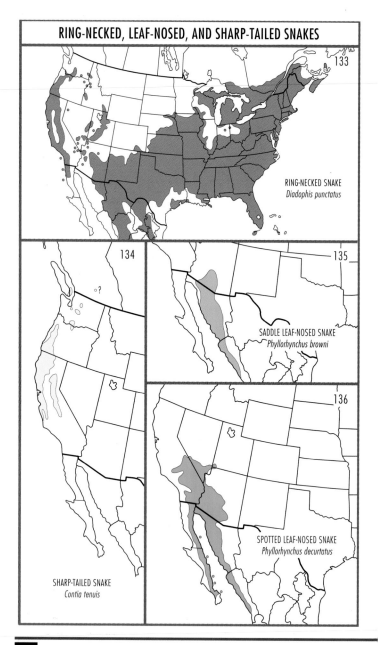

RING-NECKED, LEAF-NOSED, AND SHARP-TAILED SNAKES

133

RING-NECKED SNAKE
Diadophis punctatus

134

135

SADDLE LEAF-NOSED SNAKE
Phyllorhynchus browni

136

SHARP-TAILED SNAKE
Contia tenuis

SPOTTED LEAF-NOSED SNAKE
Phyllorhynchus decurtatus

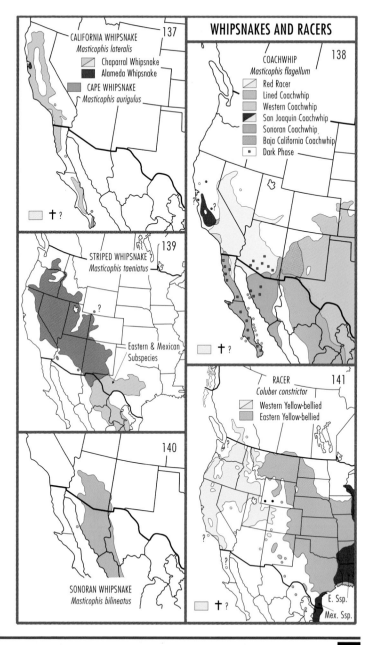

WHIPSNAKES AND RACERS

CALIFORNIA WHIPSNAKE
Masticophis lateralis
- Chaparral Whipsnake
- Alameda Whipsnake

CAPE WHIPSNAKE
Masticophis aurigulus

137

□ † ?

COACHWHIP
Masticophis flagellum
- Red Racer
- Lined Coachwhip
- Western Coachwhip
- San Joaquin Coachwhip
- Sonoran Coachwhip
- Baja California Coachwhip
- ▪ Dark Phase

138

□ † ?

STRIPED WHIPSNAKE
Masticophis taeniatus

139

Eastern & Mexican Subspecies

SONORAN WHIPSNAKE
Masticophis bilineatus

140

RACER
Coluber constrictor
- Western Yellow-bellied
- Eastern Yellow-bellied

141

E. Ssp.

Mex. Ssp.

□ † ?

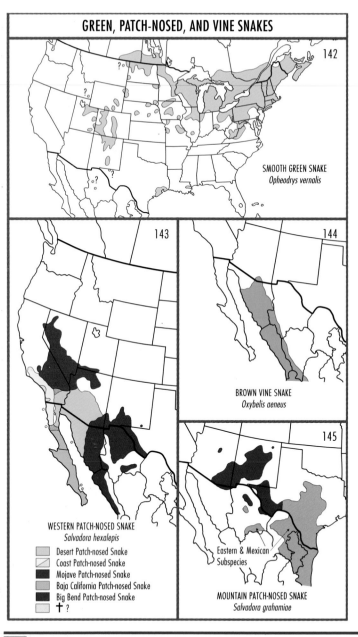

GREEN, PATCH-NOSED, AND VINE SNAKES

142

SMOOTH GREEN SNAKE
Opheodrys vernalis

143

144

BROWN VINE SNAKE
Oxybelis aeneus

145

WESTERN PATCH-NOSED SNAKE
Salvadora hexalepis

Desert Patch-nosed Snake
Coast Patch-nosed Snake
Mojave Patch-nosed Snake
Baja California Patch-nosed Snake
Big Bend Patch-nosed Snake
✝ ?

Eastern & Mexican
Subspecies

MOUNTAIN PATCH-NOSED SNAKE
Salvadora grahamiae

GOPHER, GLOSSY, CORN, AND RAT SNAKES

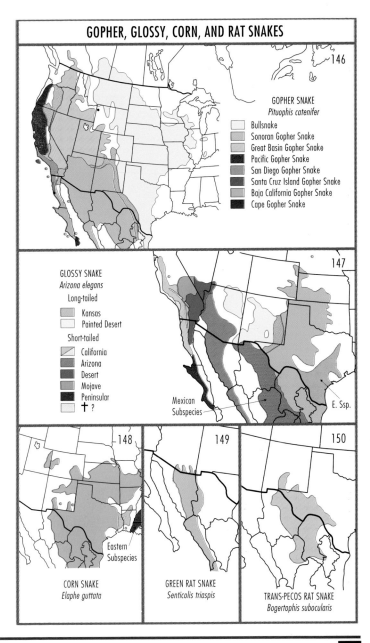

146

GOPHER SNAKE
Pituophis catenifer

- [ ] Bullsnake
- [ ] Sonoran Gopher Snake
- [ ] Great Basin Gopher Snake
- [ ] Pacific Gopher Snake
- [ ] San Diego Gopher Snake
- [ ] Santa Cruz Island Gopher Snake
- [ ] Baja California Gopher Snake
- [ ] Cape Gopher Snake

147

GLOSSY SNAKE
Arizona elegans

Long-tailed
- [ ] Kansas
- [ ] Painted Desert

Short-tailed
- [ ] California
- [ ] Arizona
- [ ] Desert
- [ ] Mojave
- [ ] Peninsular
- [ ] † ?

Mexican Subspecies

E. Ssp.

148

CORN SNAKE
Elaphe guttata

Eastern Subspecies

149

GREEN RAT SNAKE
Senticolis triaspis

150

TRANS-PECOS RAT SNAKE
Bogertophis subocularis

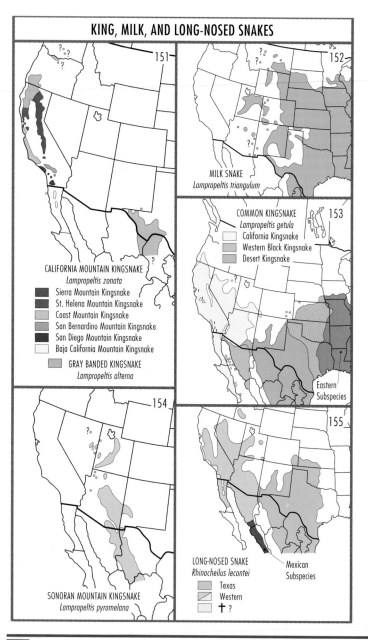

KING, MILK, AND LONG-NOSED SNAKES

151

152

MILK SNAKE
Lampropeltis triangulum

COMMON KINGSNAKE 153
Lampropeltis getula
- California Kingsnake
- Western Black Kingsnake
- Desert Kingsnake

CALIFORNIA MOUNTAIN KINGSNAKE
Lampropeltis zonata
- Sierra Mountain Kingsnake
- St. Helena Mountain Kingsnake
- Coast Mountain Kingsnake
- San Bernardino Mountain Kingsnake
- San Diego Mountain Kingsnake
- Baja California Mountain Kingsnake

GRAY BANDED KINGSNAKE
Lampropeltis alterna

Eastern
Subspecies

154

155

SONORAN MOUNTAIN KINGSNAKE
Lampropeltis pyromelana

LONG-NOSED SNAKE
Rhinocheilus lecontei
- Texas
- Western
- † ?

Mexican
Subspecies

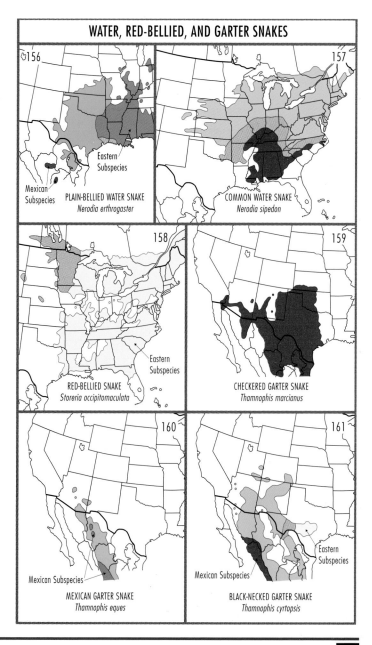

WATER, RED-BELLIED, AND GARTER SNAKES

156 PLAIN-BELLIED WATER SNAKE
Nerodia erthrogaster
Eastern Subspecies
Mexican Subspecies

157 COMMON WATER SNAKE
Nerodia sipedon

158 RED-BELLIED SNAKE
Storeria occipitomaculata
Eastern Subspecies

159 CHECKERED GARTER SNAKE
Thamnophis marcianus

160 MEXICAN GARTER SNAKE
Thamnophis eques
Mexican Subspecies

161 BLACK-NECKED GARTER SNAKE
Thamnophis cyrtopsis
Mexican Subspecies
Eastern Subspecies

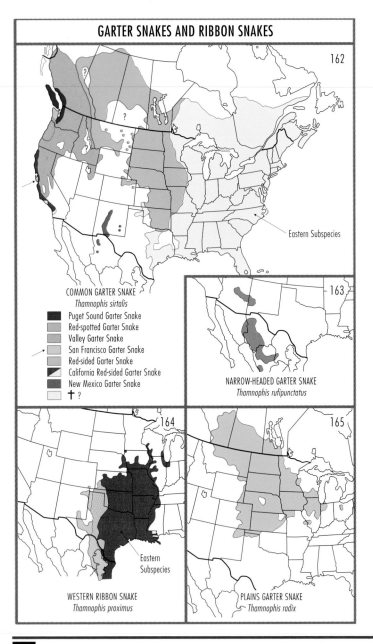

GARTER SNAKES AND RIBBON SNAKES

162

Eastern Subspecies

COMMON GARTER SNAKE
Thamnophis sirtalis

Puget Sound Garter Snake
Red-spotted Garter Snake
Valley Garter Snake
San Francisco Garter Snake
Red-sided Garter Snake
California Red-sided Garter Snake
New Mexico Garter Snake
† ?

163

NARROW-HEADED GARTER SNAKE
Thamnophis rufipunctatus

164

Eastern Subspecies

WESTERN RIBBON SNAKE
Thamnophis proximus

165

PLAINS GARTER SNAKE
Thamnophis radix

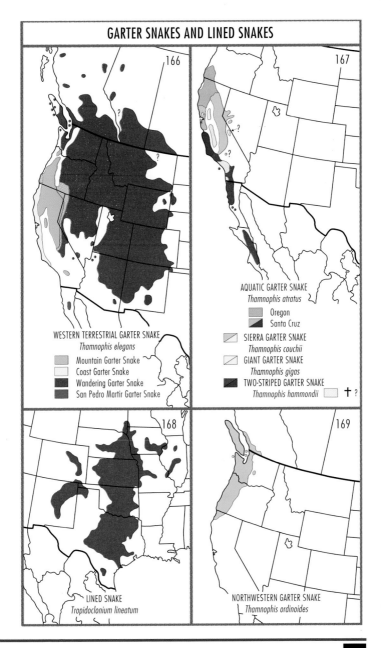

GARTER SNAKES AND LINED SNAKES

166

167

WESTERN TERRESTRIAL GARTER SNAKE
Thamnophis elegans

- Mountain Garter Snake
- Coast Garter Snake
- Wandering Garter Snake
- San Pedro Martir Garter Snake

AQUATIC GARTER SNAKE
Thamnophis atratus

- Oregon
- Santa Cruz

SIERRA GARTER SNAKE
Thamnophis couchii

GIANT GARTER SNAKE
Thamnophis gigas

TWO-STRIPED GARTER SNAKE
Thamnophis hammondii † ?

168

LINED SNAKE
Tropidoclonium lineatum

169

NORTHWESTERN GARTER SNAKE
Thamnophis ordinoides

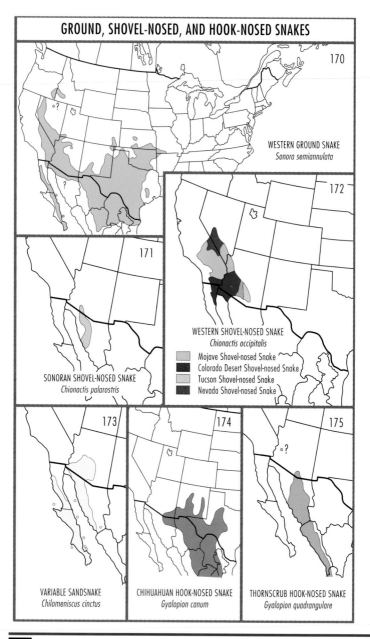

GROUND, SHOVEL-NOSED, AND HOOK-NOSED SNAKES

170

WESTERN GROUND SNAKE
Sonora semiannulata

172

171

WESTERN SHOVEL-NOSED SNAKE
Chionactis occipitalis

  Mojave Shovel-nosed Snake
  Colorado Desert Shovel-nosed Snake
  Tucson Shovel-nosed Snake
  Nevada Shovel-nosed Snake

SONORAN SHOVEL-NOSED SNAKE
Chionactis palarostris

173

VARIABLE SANDSNAKE
Chilomeniscus cinctus

174

CHIHUAHUAN HOOK-NOSED SNAKE
Gyalopion canum

175

THORNSCRUB HOOK-NOSED SNAKE
Gyalopion quadrangulare

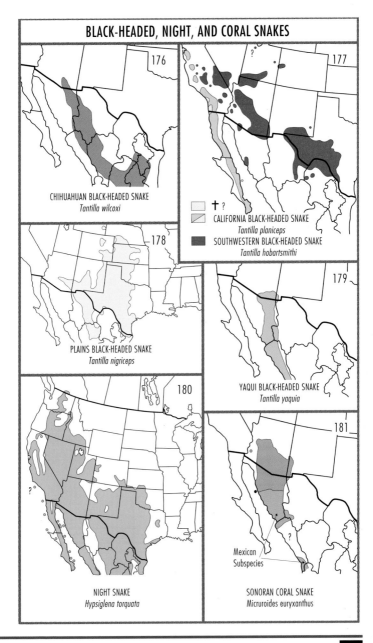

BLACK-HEADED, NIGHT, AND CORAL SNAKES

176

CHIHUAHUAN BLACK-HEADED SNAKE
Tantilla wilcoxi

177

† ?
CALIFORNIA BLACK-HEADED SNAKE
Tantilla planiceps
SOUTHWESTERN BLACK-HEADED SNAKE
Tantilla hobartsmithi

178

PLAINS BLACK-HEADED SNAKE
Tantilla nigriceps

179

YAQUI BLACK-HEADED SNAKE
Tantilla yaquia

180

NIGHT SNAKE
Hypsiglena torquata

181

Mexican
Subspecies
SONORAN CORAL SNAKE
Micruroides euryxanthus

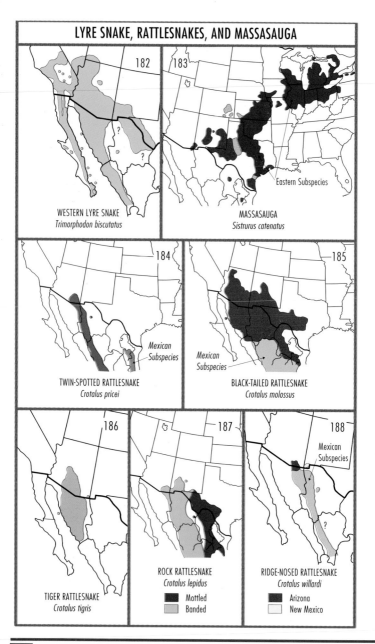

LYRE SNAKE, RATTLESNAKES, AND MASSASAUGA

182

WESTERN LYRE SNAKE
Trimorphodon biscutatus

183

Eastern Subspecies

MASSASAUGA
Sistrurus catenatus

184

Mexican Subspecies

TWIN-SPOTTED RATTLESNAKE
Crotalus pricei

185

Mexican Subspecies

BLACK-TAILED RATTLESNAKE
Crotalus molossus

186

TIGER RATTLESNAKE
Crotalus tigris

187

ROCK RATTLESNAKE
Crotalus lepidus

- Mottled
- Banded

188

Mexican Subspecies

?

RIDGE-NOSED RATTLESNAKE
Crotalus willardi

- Arizona
- New Mexico

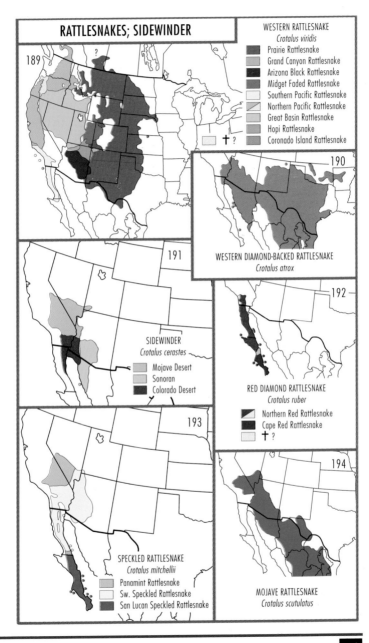

RATTLESNAKES; SIDEWINDER

189

WESTERN RATTLESNAKE
Crotalus viridis
- Prairie Rattlesnake
- Grand Canyon Rattlesnake
- Arizona Black Rattlesnake
- Midget Faded Rattlesnake
- Southern Pacific Rattlesnake
- Northern Pacific Rattlesnake
- Great Basin Rattlesnake
- Hopi Rattlesnake
- Coronado Island Rattlesnake

190

WESTERN DIAMOND-BACKED RATTLESNAKE
Crotalus atrox

191

SIDEWINDER
Crotalus cerastes
- Mojave Desert
- Sonoran
- Colorado Desert

192

RED DIAMOND RATTLESNAKE
Crotalus ruber
- Northern Red Rattlesnake
- Cape Red Rattlesnake
- † ?

193

SPECKLED RATTLESNAKE
Crotalus mitchellii
- Panamint Rattlesnake
- Sw. Speckled Rattlesnake
- San Lucan Speckled Rattlesnake

194

MOJAVE RATTLESNAKE
Crotalus scutulatus

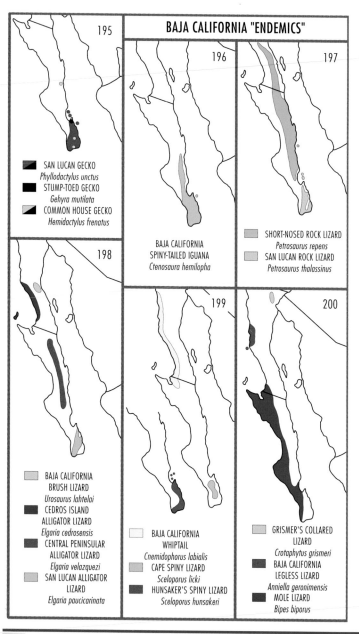

BAJA CALIFORNIA "ENDEMICS"

195

SAN LUCAN GECKO
Phyllodactylus unctus
STUMP-TOED GECKO
Gehyra mutilata
COMMON HOUSE GECKO
Hemidactylus frenatus

196

BAJA CALIFORNIA
SPINY-TAILED IGUANA
Ctenosaura hemilopha

197

SHORT-NOSED ROCK LIZARD
Petrosaurus repens
SAN LUCAN ROCK LIZARD
Petrosaurus thalassinus

198

BAJA CALIFORNIA
BRUSH LIZARD
Urosaurus lahtelai
CEDROS ISLAND
ALLIGATOR LIZARD
Elgaria cedrosensis
CENTRAL PENINSULAR
ALLIGATOR LIZARD
Elgaria velazquezi
SAN LUCAN ALLIGATOR
LIZARD
Elgaria paucicarinata

199

BAJA CALIFORNIA
WHIPTAIL
Cnemidophorus labialis
CAPE SPINY LIZARD
Sceloporus licki
HUNSAKER'S SPINY LIZARD
Sceloporus hunsakeri

200

GRISMER'S COLLARED
LIZARD
Crotaphytus grismeri
BAJA CALIFORNIA
LEGLESS LIZARD
Anniella geronimensis
MOLE LIZARD
Bipes biporus

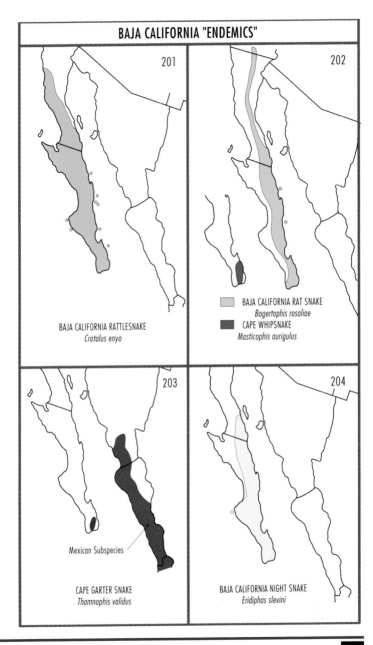

BAJA CALIFORNIA "ENDEMICS"

201

BAJA CALIFORNIA RATTLESNAKE
Crotalus enyo

202

BAJA CALIFORNIA RAT SNAKE
Bogertophis rosaliae
CAPE WHIPSNAKE
Masticophis aurigulus

203

Mexican Subspecies

CAPE GARTER SNAKE
Thamnophis validus

204

BAJA CALIFORNIA NIGHT SNAKE
Eridiphas slevini

Glossary

ADPRESS. To press close to or against; to lay flat against. As a measure of relative limb length in salamanders, the fore and hind limbs on one side are laid straight along the side of the body and the amount of overlap of the extended toes, or the distance separating them (measured in number of folds), is noted. (See front end papers.) In frogs the hind limb is extended forward, while the body is held straight, and the position of the heel in relation to the nostril is noted. Species accounts refer to condition in adults only.

ALLOPATRIC POPULATIONS. Two or more distinct populations (species or subspecies) that do not overlap and replace each other geographically, their boundaries sometimes adjacent to each other.

ALLUVIAL FAN. The alluvial deposit (silt, etc.) of a stream where it issues from a gorge onto an open plain.

AMPLEXUS. An embrace; the sexual embrace of a male amphibian. *Pectoral amplexus:* position of amplexus in which the forelimbs of the male clasp the female from behind in the chest or axillary region. *Pelvic or inguinal amplexus:* position of amplexus in which the male clasps the female from behind about her waist.

ANAL SCENT GLANDS. Scent glands that open on each side of the vent in certain snakes and lizards.

ANAL SPUR. A horny, pointed, sometimes hooked, spur (a hind limb vestige), one on each side, just in front of vent in boid snakes (boas and pythons).

ANTERIOR. Before, or toward the front.

ANURAN. A tailless amphibian. A member of the group of frogs and toads.

APICAL PITS. *See* Scale pits.

ARBOREAL. Dwelling in shrubs or trees.

AURICULAR SCALES. Enlarged scales along the anterior border of the ear opening.

AXILLA. The "armpit."

AXOLOTL. Any of several larval salamanders of the genus *Ambystoma*. Such larvae may live and breed in the larval condition but are capable of absorbing their gills and fins, while beginning to breathe air at the surface, and of eventually being able to live on land as terrestrial adults.

BARBEL. Nipplelike projection.

BOSS. A protuberance or rounded swelling between the eyes in some Spadefoot Toads and True Toads. May be glandular or bony.

CAPSULAR CAVITY. In amphibians, the chamber occupied by the egg and enclosed by the jelly envelope(s). Typically filled with a viscous jelly in which the egg moves freely, after fertilization.

CARAPACE. In turtles, the upper part of the shell, including its bony plates and horny shields.

CASQUE-HEADED. Having an armored head; an area of thickened skin and/or bone on the heads of certain amphibians.

CLONE. Any group of individuals produced asexually from a single ancestor.

COAST RANGES. Mountains along the coast of California. South of San Francisco Bay, these consist of the inner (toward the Great Valley) and outer (toward the coast) Coast Ranges.

CONSPECIFIC. Of the same species.

COSTAL FOLDS. In salamanders, the vertical folds of skin on the sides of the body set off by the costal grooves.

COSTAL GROOVES. In salamanders, the vertical furrows on the sides of the body that set off the costal folds.

COUNTERSUNK. Sunk beneath the margins of—as in the jaws of some burrowing snakes, in which the lower jaw fits snugly within the margins of the upper jaw.

CRANIAL CRESTS. Ridges that frame the inner rim of upper eyelids in toads.

CUSP. A toothlike projection, as on the jaw of a turtle.

CYCLOID SCALES. Scales that have smoothly rounded free rear borders.

DIPLOID. Having double the number of chromosomes characteristic of the germ cells of a species.

DIURNAL. Active in daytime.

DORSAL. Pertaining to the upper surface of the body.

DORSAL SCALE COUNT (LIZARDS). Number of scales along the dorsal midline between rear of parietal scale and an imaginary line across the tail base connecting the rear surfaces of the thighs.

DORSOLATERAL. Pertaining to the upper sides of the body.

DORSOLATERAL FOLD. A lengthwise glandular ridge between the side of the body and the middle of the back in certain frogs.

DORSUM. The upper, or dorsal, surface of the body.

EGG CAPSULE. In amphibians, the covering of the egg, consisting of the jelly envelope(s).

EGG ENVELOPE. In amphibians, a jellylike membrane that surrounds the egg. May be 1–3 or more envelopes, depending on the species.

FEMORAL PORES. Pores containing a waxlike material, found on the underside of the thighs in certain lizards.

FEMUR. Part of the leg between the knee and hip.

FONTANELLE. Small opening, as in the roof of the skull in some Spadefoot Toads.

GILL ARCH. One of the bony or cartilaginous arches or curved bars located one behind the other on each side of the pharynx, supporting the gills of fishes and amphibians.

GILL RAKER. One of the bony or cartilaginous filaments on the inside of the gill arches of fishes and certain amphibians (larvae, etc.), which help prevent solid substances from being carried out through the gill slits.

GRAVID. Laden with eggs; pregnant.

GULAR FOLD. Fold of skin across rear or lower part of the throat; well developed in salamanders and some lizards.

HEMIPENIS (PL., HEMIPENES). One of the paired copulatory organs of lizards and snakes.

HYBRID. Offspring of the union of a male of one race, variety, species, genus, etc., with the female of another; a crossbred animal or plant.

INGUINAL PLATE. In turtles, a shield or scute at rear of shell bridge in the region of the groin.

INSET LOWER JAW. *See* Countersunk.

INTERGRADE. With reference to subspecies, to gradually merge one subspecies with another through a series of forms that are intermediate in color and/or structure.

INTERORBITAL. Region between the eyes. In reptiles, interorbital scales may occupy the area between the supraoculars (see rear endpapers).

INTERSPACE. Patch of color or area between two markings (such as bands or blotches) on the back of lizards and snakes.

JUVENILE. Young or immature individual, often displaying proportions and coloration differing from that of the adult.

KEEL. A lengthwise ridge on the scales of certain lizards and snakes, or down the carapace or plastron of a turtle.

KERATINIZED. Rendered horny.

LABIAL TEETH. Small horny teeth arranged like teeth of a comb and attached in crosswise rows to the lips (labia) of tadpoles. The number of rows in the upper and lower lips is expressed by a fraction. The upper digit indicates the number of rows (a row divided at the midline is counted as one) on the upper lip, while the lower digit is the number of rows on the lower lip. A common formula is 2/3.

LABIUM (PL., LABIA). Lip.

LAMELLAE. Transverse plates or straplike scales that extend across undersides of toes in lizards.

LARVA (PL., LARVAE). Early form of an animal that, while immature, is unlike its parent and must pass through more or less of a metamorphosis before assuming adult characteristics. The tadpole of a frog is an example among amphibians.

LATERAL STRIPE. Lengthwise stripe on the side of the body.

LINEAGE. Descent in a direct line from an ancestor.

LORILABIAL SCALE. Scale between the loreal and the labial found in Lyre Snakes (*Trimorphodon*).

MELANISTIC. The condition in which black pigment is accentuated, sometimes to the point of obscuring all other color.

MELANOPHORE. Pigment cell containing black or brown pigment (melanin).

MENTAL GLAND. Gland on the chin of certain male salamanders. Its secretion appears to make the female receptive to mating.

MESOPTYCHIAL SCALES. Scales immediately anterior to gular fold.

MORPH. Differing in form.

MORPHOTYPE. As used in this book, a morphologically recognizable set of populations with a geographic range that may be out of synchrony with taxonomic findings based on molecular evidence. Many "subspecies" have now fallen into this category, thus making, in such cases, the term inappropriate as an expression of taxonomic relationships. In this definition the term morphology (form) is used in its broadest sense to include not only structure (including color) but sometimes also aspects of behavior and physiology.

NASOLABIAL GROOVE. A hairline groove extending from the nostril to the edge of the upper lip in all salamanders of the family Plethodontidae. A hand lens may be needed to see it.

NEOTENIC (NEOTENY). Having the period of immaturity indefinitely prolonged. Some salamanders may remain in the larval condition well beyond the usual time of metamorphosis, and may even breed as "larvae."

NUPTIAL PAD. In amphibians, a patch of roughened, usually darkly pigmented skin that appears in males during the breeding period. Such pads generally develop on certain of the digits and help the male hold the female during amplexus.

OCELLUS (PL., OCELLI). A small eyelike spot.

OCULAR SCALE. In blind snakes, the enlarged scale overlying the vestigial eyes. In boas, small scales encircling the eyes. *See also* Subocular scales.

ORAL PAPILLAE. In tadpoles, the small nipplelike projections that commonly form a fringe encircling the mouth. They are sensory in function, perhaps picking up tastes and scents as well as sensing surface textures.

OVIPAROUS. Producing eggs that hatch after laying.

OVOVIVIPAROUS. Producing eggs that have a well-developed shell or membranous covering, but which hatch before or at the time of laying, as in certain reptiles.

OVUM (PL., OVA). A female germ cell; an egg cell or egg apart from any enclosing membrane or shell.

PARAVERTEBRAL STRIPE. A stripe (usually one of a pair) located to one side and parallel to the dorsal midline.

PAROTOID GLAND. One of a pair of large, wartlike glands at the back of the head in toads, and rarely in some salamanders.

PARTHENOGENESIS. Reproduction by development of an unfertilized egg.

PECTORAL. Pertaining to the chest.

PEDICEL. A small stalk.

PENINSULAR RANGES. Mountains of s. Calif. and n. Baja Calif., extending from Mt. San Jacinto to the San Pedro Martir.

PLASTRON. Underside of the shell of a turtle, consisting typically of 9 symmetrically placed bones overlaid by horny shields.

PLAYA. Flat-floored bottom of an undrained desert basin, which may lack water much of the time.

PLETHODONS. Lungless salamanders of the genus *Plethodon*.

POSTANAL SCALE. A scale situated behind the vent or anus. In the males of most iguanid lizards, 2 or more of these scales are enlarged.

POSTANTEBRACHIALS. Scales on the back of the forearm of lizards.

POSTERIOR. Behind or to the rear; at or toward the hind end of the body.

POSTOCULAR STRIPE. Stripe behind the eye.

POSTROSTRAL SCALES. Scales between the rostral and internasals, as in certain rattlesnakes.

PREANAL SCALE. A scale situated in the pelvic region, in front of the vent or anus. In certain lizards, several of these scales may have pores that secrete a waxlike substance.

PREHENSILE. Adapted for seizing or grasping, especially by wrapping around; in this guide, used in reference to tails.

PREMAXILLARY TEETH. Teeth attached to the premaxillary bones, located at the front of the upper jaw.

PRENASAL. In rattlesnakes, the scale located immediately in front of the nostril.

RELICT. A survivor, especially of a vanishing race, type, or species; belonging to a nearly extinct class.

SCALE PITS. Small paired pits or oval-shaped modifications near the free (apical) end of the scales of certain snakes.

SCUTE. Alternative term for shield.

SHIELD. In turtles, any one of the horny plates that cover the shell.

SUBOCULAR SCALES (ALSO CALLED INFRAOCULARS). In boas, small scales between the eye that contact the upper labial scales.

SUBSPECIES. A subdivision of a species; a variety or race; a category (usually the lowest category recognized in classification) ranking next below a species. The differences separating subspecies are usually slight and commonly bridged in zones of intergradation (intermixture of characters). Some researchers insist that intergradation should be the criterion in deciding whether 2 adjacent, slightly different animal populations should be considered as subspecies or species; if intergradation does not exist, they are regarded as distinct species.

SUPRAORBITAL RIDGES. Ridges above the eyes.

SYMPATRIC POPULATIONS. Two or more distinct populations (species or subspecies) that overlap geographically, yet maintain their distinctness.

TAXON. Refers to a taxonomic or classification unit without reference to rank.

TEMPORAL HORNS. In horned lizards, the horns toward the sides of the crown.

TIBIA. The part of the leg between the knee and heel.

TRANSFORMATION. A marked and more or less abrupt change in form and structure (and usually also in habits, food, etc.) of an animal during postembryonic development, as when the larva of an insect becomes a pupa, or a tadpole changes to a frog.

TRANSVERSE MOUNTAIN SYSTEM. The mountains of s. Calif., extending west to east from the Sierra Madre to, and including, the San Bernardino Mts.

TRIPLOID. Having 3 times the number of chromosomes characteristic of the germ cells of a species.

TUBERCLE. Any of various small, knoblike projections or bumps; generally considered to be smaller than a wart.

VENT. The opening on the surface of the body of the cloaca, which in reptiles and amphibians is the common chamber into which the intestinal, urinary, and reproductive canals discharge.

VENTER. The underside of an animal, including the tail when present.

VENT LOBES. Fleshy lobes located on each side and usually to the rear of the vent. Found in certain male salamanders.

VENTRAL. Pertaining to the underside, or lower surface, of the body.

VENTRAL SCALE COUNT (LIZARDS). Number of scales along ventral midline between postmental scale(s) and anterior edge of vent.

VERTICAL PUPIL. An elliptical pupil with its long axis vertical.

VOCAL SAC. A sac of loose skin on the throat of frogs and toads that becomes distended and acts as a resonating chamber when they vocalize.

BIBLIOGRAPHY

Listed below are journals and selected general references that provide further information on species covered by this book and general information on the biology of reptiles and amphibians. Many additional references are cited in the bibliographies of most of these publications. Some of the older works are out of print but available in libraries.

GENERAL REFERENCES

Bellairs, A. 1970. *The Life of Reptiles.* New York: Universe Books. 2 vols.

Brown, P. R. 1997. *A Field Guide to Snakes of California.* Houston, Tex.: Gulf Publishing Co.

Cochran, D. M. 1961. *Living Amphibians of the World.* Garden City, N.Y.: Doubleday.

Conant, R., and J. T. Collins. 1998. *A Field Guide to Reptiles and Amphibians of Eastern and Central North America.* 3rd ed. extended. Boston: Houghton Mifflin Co.

Crother, Brian I., chair. 2000. *Scientific and Standard English Names of Amphibians and Reptiles of North America North of Mexico, with Comments Regarding Confidence in Our Understanding.* Committee on Standard English and Scientific Names, Society for the Study of Amphibians and Reptiles.

Duellman, W. E., and L. Trueb. 1986–1994. *Biology of Amphibians.* New York: McGraw-Hill.

Ernst, C. H., J. E. Lovich, and R. W. Barbour. 1994. *Turtles of the United States and Canada.* Washington, D.C.: The Smithsonian Institution Press.

Fitch, H. S. 1970. *Reproductive Cycles in Lizards and Snakes.* University of Kansas Museum of Natural History, Misc. Publication no. 52.

Greene, H. W. 1997. *Snakes: The Evolution of Mystery in Nature.* Berkeley and Los Angeles: University of California Press.

Klauber, L. M. 1972. *Rattlesnakes: Their Habits, Life Histories, and Influence on Mankind.* 2nd ed. Berkeley and Los Angeles: University of California Press. 2 vols. Reissued 1997 with a foreword by Harry W. Greene.

Leviton, A. E. 1972. *Reptiles and Amphibians of North America.* New York: Doubleday.

Noble, G. 1931. *The Biology of the Amphibia.* New York: McGraw-Hill. Reprinted by Dover Publications 1955.

Petranka, J. W. 1998. *Salamanders of the United States and Canada.* Washington, D.C.: The Smithsonian Institution Press.

Pough, H. F., et al. 2001. *Herpetology.* 2nd ed. Upper Saddle River, N.J.: Prentice Hall.

Rossman, D. A., et al. 1996. *The Garter Snakes: Evolution and Ecology.* Norman, Okla., and London: University of Oklahoma Press.

Schmidt, K. P., and R. F. Inger. 1957–1966. *Living Reptiles of the World.* Garden City, N.Y.: Hanover House.

Shaw, C. E., and S. Campbell. 1974. *Snakes of the American West.* New York: Alfred A. Knopf.

Smith, H. M. 1946–1995. *Handbook of Lizards.* Ithaca, N.Y.: Comstock Publishing Co.

Stebbins, R. C., and N. W. Cohen. 1995. *A Natural History of Amphibians.* Princeton, N.J.: Princeton University Press.

Wright, A. H., and A. A. Wright. 1949. *Handbook of Frogs and Toads of the United States and Canada.* Ithaca, N.Y.: Comstock.

———. 1957–1989. *Handbook of Snakes of the United States and Canada.* 2 vols. Ithaca, N.Y.: Cornell University Press.

REGIONAL REFERENCES

NORTH AMERICA — WESTERN REGION

Bartlett, R. D., and A. Tennant. 2000. *Snakes of North America: Western Region.* Houston: Gulf Publishing.

St. John, Alan D. 2002. *Reptiles of the Northwest.* Edmonton, Alta.: Lone Pine Publishing.

PACIFIC NORTHWEST

Campbell, R. W., M. G. Shepard, B. M. Van Der Raay, and P. T. Gregory. 1982. *A Bibliography of Pacific Northwest Herpetology.* Victoria, B.C.: British Columbia Provincial Museum, Heritage Record no. 14.

Corkran, C. C., and C. Thoms. 1996. *Amphibians of Oregon, Washington and British Columbia: A Field Identification Guide.* Vancouver, B.C.: Lone Pine Publishing.

Fournier, M. 1998. *Amphibians and Reptiles in the Northwest Territories.* Ecology North, c/o Mink Fournier, 5093 Finlayson Drive, Yellowknife, N.T.: Artisan Press Ltd.

Leonard, W. P., H. A. Brown, L. L. C. Jones, K. R. McAllister, and R. M. Storm. 1993. *Amphibians of Washington and Oregon.* Seattle: Seattle Audubon Society.

Nussbaum, R. A., E. D. Brodie, Jr., and R. M. Storm. 1983. *Amphibians and Reptiles of the Pacific Northwest.* Moscow, Idaho: The University Press of Idaho.

Slough, B. G. 1997. *Frogs, Toads, and Salamanders: Amphibians of the Yukon and Northern British Columbia.* Whitehorse, Yukon: Canadian Wildlife Service.

Storm, R. M., and W. P. Leonard. 1995. *Reptiles of Washington and Oregon.* Seattle: Seattle Audubon Society. The Trailside Series.

UNITED STATES
Alaska

Hodge, R. P. 1976. *Amphibians and Reptiles of Alaska, the Yukon and Northwest Territories.* Anchorage: Alaska Northwest Publishing Co.

Arizona

Lowe, C. H. Jr. 1964. *The Vertebrates of Arizona: Annotated Check Lists of the Vertebrates of the State: The Species and Where They Live.* Tucson: University of Arizona Press.

California

Fisher, R. N., and T. J. Case. 1997. *A Field Guide to the Reptiles and Amphibians of Coastal Southern California.* Sponsored by Biology Resources Div., U.S.G.S. Lazer Touch, San Mateo, Calif.

Colorado

Hammerson, G. A. 1999. *Amphibians and Reptiles in Colorado.* 2nd ed. Boulder, Colo.: University Press of Colorado and Colorado Division of Wildlife.

Idaho

Groves, C. 1994. *Idaho's Amphibians and Reptiles.* 2nd ed. Idaho Dept. of Fish and Game, Nongame Wildlife Leaflet No. 7.

Linder, A. D., and E. Fichter. 1977. *The Amphibians and Reptiles of Idaho.* Pocatello: Idaho State University Press.

Idaho Fish and Game. 1989. *Idaho's Amphibians and Reptiles. Description, Habitat, and Ecology.* Nongame Wildlife Leaflet 7.

Montana

Black, J. H. 1970. *Amphibians of Montana.* Montana Wildlife, Montana Fish and Game Commission. Animals of Montana Series.

Maxell, B. A., J. K. Werner, D. P. Hendricks, and D. Flath. Submitted for publication. *Herpetology in Montana: a history, status summary, checklist, dichotomous keys, high-elevation records, dot distribution maps, and indexed bibliography.* Northwest Fauna No. 5. Olympia, Wash.: Society for Northwestern Vertebrate Biology.

Werner, J. Kerwin, B. A. Maxell, D. P. Hendricks, and D. Flath. *Field Guide to the Amphibians and Reptiles of Montana.* Submitted for review.

Nevada

Banta, B. H. 1965. "An Annotated Chronological Bibliography of the Herpetology of Nevada." *Wasmann Journal of Biology* 23, nos. 1 and 2.

Lindsdale, J. M. 1940. "Amphibians and Reptiles in Nevada." *Proceedings of the American Academy of Arts and Sciences* 73, no. 8.

New Mexico

Degenhardt, W. G., C. W. Painter, and A. H. Price. 1996. *Amphibians and Reptiles of New Mexico.* Albuquerque: University of New Mexico Press.

Oregon

St. John, A. D. 1980. *Knowing Oregon Reptiles.* Salem, Ore.: Salem Audubon Society.

Utah

Cox, D. C., and W. W. Tanner. 1995. *Snakes of Utah.* Provo, Utah: Brigham Young University.

Tanner, W. W. 1975. "Checklist of Utah Amphibians and Reptiles." *Proceedings of the Utah Academy of Sciences, Arts and Letters* 52, part 1.

Washington

Johnson, M. L. 1954. "Reptiles of the State of Washington." *Northwest Fauna* 3: 5–80.

McAllister, K. R. 1995. "Distribution of Amphibians and Reptiles in Washington State." *Northwest Fauna* 3: 81–112.

Wyoming

Baxter, G. T., and M. D. Stone. 1985. *Amphibians and Reptiles of Wyoming.* 2nd ed. Wyoming Game and Fish Department, Bulletin no. 16.

Koch, E. D., and C. R. Peterson. 1995. *Amphibians and Reptiles of Yellowstone and Grand Teton National Parks.* Salt Lake City, Utah: University of Utah Press.

BAJA CALIFORNIA

Grismer, L. 2002. *Amphibians and Reptiles of Baja California, Including Its Pacific Islands and the Islands in the Sea of Cortés.* Berkeley, Calif.: University of California Press.

McPeak, R. H. 2000. *Amphibians and Reptiles of Baja Calif.* Monterey, Calif.: Sea Challengers.

Murphy, R. W. 1983. "Paleobiogeography and Genetic Differentiation of the Baja California Herpetofauna." *Occasional Papers of the California Academy of Science,* no. 137.

CANADA

Cook, F. R. 1984. *Introduction to Canadian Amphibians and Reptiles.* Ottawa: National Museum of Natural Sciences. National Museums of Canada.

Alberta

Russell, A. P., and A. M. Bauer. 2000. *The Amphibians and Reptiles of Alberta: A Field Guide and Primer of Boreal Herpetology.* 2nd ed. Calgary and Edmonton, Alta.: University of Calgary Press and University of Alberta Press.

British Columbia

Gregory, P. T., and R. W. Campbell. 1984. *The Reptiles of British Columbia.* Victoria, B.C.: British Columbia Provincial Museum, Handbook no. 44.

Matsuda, B. M., D. M. Green, P. T. Gregory, and R. W. Campbell. *The Amphibians and Reptiles of British Columbia, Royal British Columbia Museum Handbook.* Vancouver, B.C.: Royal B.C. Museum and University of B.C. Press, in prep. The British Columbia database for this handbook has been developed by WBT Wild Bird Trust of British Columbia and is housed in their Wildlife Resources Center in Victoria, B.C.

Saskatchewan

Cook, F. R. 1966. *A Guide to the Amphibians and Reptiles of Saskatchewan.* Regina: Saskatchewan Museum of Natural History, Popular Series, no. 13.

Fung, K., ed. 1999. "Reptiles and Amphibians of Saskatchewan." *Atlas of Saskatchewan,* 2nd ed. Saskatoon: University of Saskatchewan.

JOURNALS

Copeia. Published quarterly by the American Society of Ichthyologists and Herpetologists, 810 East 10th Street, PO Box 1897, Lawrence, KS 66044.

Herpetologica. Published quarterly by the Herpetologists League, Inc., Divison of Biological Sciences, Emporia State University, Emporia, KS 66801.

Journal of Herpetology. Published quarterly by the Society for the Study of Amphibians and Reptiles, St. Louis University, 3507 Laclede, St. Louis, MO 63103. The society also publishes the Catalogue of American Amphibians and Reptiles, a series of loose-leaf accounts of species, each prepared by a specialist, and *Herpetological Review,* which often includes a comprehensive list of current herpetological titles.

INDEX

Numbers in *italics* refer to illustrations within the text; numbers in **boldface** type refer to the color plates at the beginning of the book; numbers in ***boldface italics*** refer to range maps.

THE PETERSON SERIES®
PETERSON FIELD GUIDES®

BIRDS

ADVANCED BIRDING North America 97500-x
BIRDS OF BRITAIN AND EUROPE 0-618-16675-0
BIRDS OF TEXAS Texas and adjacent states 92138-4
BIRDS OF THE WEST INDIES 0-618-00210-3
EASTERN BIRDS Eastern and central North America
74046-0
EASTERN BIRDS' NESTS U.S. east of Mississippi River 93609-8
HAWKS North America 67067-5
HUMMINGBIRDS North America 0-618-02496-4
WESTERN BIRDS North America west of 100th meridian
and north of Mexico 91173-7
WESTERN BIRDS' NESTS U.S. west of Mississippi
River 0-618-16437-5
MEXICAN BIRDS Mexico, Guatemala, Belize,
El Salvador 97514-x
WARBLERS North America 78321-6

FISH

PACIFIC COAST FISHES Gulf of Alaska to Baja California 0-618-00212-x
ATLANTIC COAST FISHES North American Atlantic coast 97515-8
FRESHWATER FISHES North America north of Mexico 91091-9

INSECTS

INSECTS North America north of Mexico 91170-2
BEETLES North America 91089-7
EASTERN BUTTERFLIES Eastern and central North America 90453-6
WESTERN BUTTERFLIES U.S. and Canada west of 100th
meridian, part of northern Mexico 79151-0

MAMMALS

MAMMALS North America north of Mexico 91098-6
ANIMAL TRACKS North America 91094-3

ECOLOGY

EASTERN FORESTS Eastern North America 92895-8
CALIFORNIA AND PACIFIC NORTHWEST FORESTS 92896-6
ROCKY MOUNTAIN AND SOUTHWEST FORESTS 92897-4
VENOMOUS ANIMALS AND POISONOUS PLANTS) North America north of
Mexico 93608-x

AUDIO AND VIDEO

EASTERN BIRDING BY EAR
cassettes 0-618-22591-9
CD 0-618-22590-0

WESTERN BIRDING BY EAR
cassettes 97526-3
CD 97525-5

EASTERN BIRD SONGS, Revised
CD 0-618-22594-3

WESTERN BIRD SONGS, Revised
cassettes 51746-x
CD 97519-0

BACKYARD BIRDSONG
cassettes 0-618-22593-5
CD 0-618-22592-7

EASTERN MORE BIRDING BY EAR
cassettes 97529-8
CD 97530-1

WATCHING BIRDS
Beta 34418-2
VHS 34417-4

PETERSON'S MULTIMEDIA GUIDES: NORTH AMERICAN BIRDS
(CD-ROM for Windows) 73056-2

PETERSON FLASHGUIDES™

ATLANTIC COASTAL BIRDS 79286-x
PACIFIC COASTAL BIRDS 79287-8
EASTERN TRAILSIDE BIRDS 79288-6
WESTERN TRAILSIDE BIRDS 79289-4
HAWKS 79291-6
BACKYARD BIRDS 79290-8
TREES 82998-4
MUSHROOMS 82999-2
ANIMAL TRACKS 82997-6
BUTTERFLIES 82996-8
ROADSIDE WILDFLOWERS 82995-x
BIRDS OF THE MIDWEST 86733-9
WATERFOWL 86734-7
FRESHWATER FISHES 86713-4

PETERSON FIELD GUIDES can be purchased at your local
bookstore or by calling our toll-free number, (800) 225-3362.

When referring to title by corresponding ISBN number,
preface with 0-395, unless title is listed with 0-618.

LIZARDS

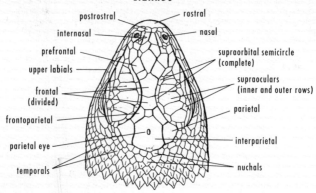

- postrostral
- rostral
- internasal
- nasal
- prefrontal
- supraorbital semicircle (complete)
- upper labials
- supraoculars (inner and outer rows)
- frontal (divided)
- parietal
- frontoparietal
- parietal eye
- interparietal
- temporals
- nuchals

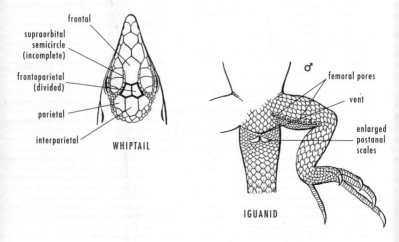

- frontal
- supraorbital semicircle (incomplete)
- frontoparietal (divided)
- parietal
- interparietal

WHIPTAIL

- ♂
- femoral pores
- vent
- enlarged postanal scales

IGUANID

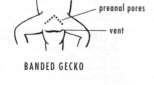

- preanal pores
- vent

BANDED GECKO

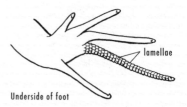

- lamellae

Underside of foot

Scales with apical pits
(*Nerodia*)

Cycloid

Keeled mucronate

Granular

SCALE TYPES
(Lizards and Snakes)

SNAKES

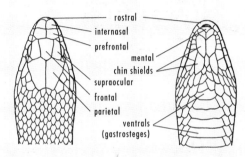

rostral
internasal
prefrontal
mental
chin shields
supraocular
frontal
parietal
ventrals
(gastrosteges)

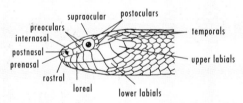

supraocular
preoculars
internasal
postnasal
prenasal
rostral
loreal
postoculars
temporals
upper labials
lower labials

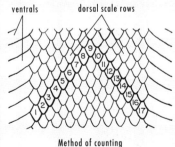

ventrals
dorsal scale rows

Method of counting
dorsal scale rows

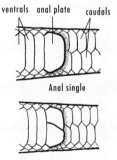

ventrals
anal plate
caudals

Anal single

Anal divided